T0339470

THE ROUTLEDGE HANDBOOK OF THE POLITICAL ECONOMY OF SCIENCE

The political economy of research and innovation (R&I) is one of the central issues of the early twenty-first century. 'Science' and 'innovation' are increasingly tasked with driving and reshaping a troubled global economy while also tackling multiple, overlapping global challenges, such as climate change or food security, global pandemics or energy security. But responding to these demands is made more complicated because R&I themselves are changing. Today, new global patterns of R&I are transforming the very structures, institutions and processes of science and innovation, and with it their claims about desirable futures. Our understanding of R&I needs to change accordingly.

Responding to this new urgency and uncertainty, this handbook presents a pioneering selection of the growing body of literature that has emerged in recent years at the intersection of science and technology studies and political economy. The central task for this research has been to expose important but consequential misconceptions about the political economy of R&I and to build more insightful approaches. This volume therefore explores the complex interrelations between R&I (both in general and in specific fields) and political economies across a number of key dimensions from health to environment, and universities to the military.

The Routledge Handbook of the Political Economy of Science offers a unique collection of texts across a range of issues in this burgeoning and important field from a global selection of top scholars. The handbook is essential reading for students interested in the political economy of science, technology and innovation. It also presents succinct and insightful summaries of the state of the art for more advanced scholars.

David Tyfield is a Reader in Environmental Innovation and Sociology at the Lancaster Environment Centre, Lancaster University, UK, and Research Professor at the Chinese Academy of Sciences Guangzhou Institute of Geochemistry (GIGCAS).

Rebecca Lave is an Associate Professor in Geography at Indiana University, USA.

Samuel Randalls is a Lecturer in Geography at University College London, UK.

Charles Thorpe is an Associate Professor in the Department of Sociology and a member of the Science Studies Program at the University of California, San Diego, USA.

THE ROUTLEDGE HANDBOOK OF THE POLITICAL ECONOMY OF SCIENCE

*Edited by David Tyfield, Rebecca Lave,
Samuel Randalls and Charles Thorpe*

LONDON AND NEW YORK

First published 2017
by Routledge
2 Park Square, Milton Park, Abingdon, Oxon OX14 4RN

and by Routledge
52 Vanderbilt Avenue, New York, NY 10017

First issued in paperback 2020

Routledge is an imprint of the Taylor & Francis Group, an informa business

British Library Cataloguing in Publication Data
A catalogue record for this book is available from the British Library

Library of Congress Cataloging in Publication Data
Names: Tyfield, David, editor.
Title: The Routledge handbook of the political economy of science / edited
by David Tyfield, Rebecca Lave, Samuel Randalls and Charles Thorpe.
Description: Abingdon, Oxon ; New York, NY : Routledge, 2017. |
Includes index.
Identifiers: LCCN 2016050527| ISBN 9781138922983 (hardback) |
ISBN 9781315685397 (ebook)
Subjects: LCSH: Science--Economic aspects.
Classification: LCC Q175.5 .R684 2017 | DDC 303.48/3--dc23
LC record available at https://lccn.loc.gov/2016050527

ISBN 13: 978-0-367-58127-5 (pbk)
ISBN 13: 978-1-138-92298-3 (hbk)

Typeset in Bembo
by Saxon Graphics Ltd, Derby

CONTENTS

FIGURES

TABLES

CONTRIBUTORS

Eric Best is a postdoctoral researcher at the Center for Applied Demography and Survey Research in the School of Public Policy and Administration at the University of Delaware. He is a co-author of *The Student Loan Mess: How Good Intentions Created a Trillion-Dollar Problem*, a book about the history and relationship between generations of student loan policies in the United States.

Kean Birch is an associate professor in the Business and Society program and member of the Science and Technology Studies Graduate Program at York University, Canada. His recent books include: *We Have Never Been Neoliberal* (2015); *The Handbook of Neoliberalism* (2016, Routledge, co-edited with Simon Springer and Julie MacLeavy); *Innovation, Regional Development and the Life Sciences: Beyond Clusters* (2016, Routledge); and *Business and Society: A Critical Introduction* (forthcoming, co-authored with Mark Peacock, Richard Wellen, Caroline Shenaz Hossein, Sonya Scott, and Alberto Salazar). He is currently working on a book called *A Research Agenda for Neoliberalism*.

Alessandro Delfanti is assistant professor of Culture and New Media at the University of Toronto, where he holds a joint appointment at the Institute of Communication, Culture, Information and Technology, and at the Faculty of Information (iSchool). He is the author of *Biohackers: The Politics of Open Science* (2013). His work on open science, hacking, and digital participation has been published by journals such as *Media, Culture & Society*, *Social Studies of Science*, *Journal of Science Communication*, and *New Genetics and Society*.

Pierre Delvenne holds a PhD in Political and Social Sciences. He is currently research associate at the Fund for Scientific Research (FNRS) and the associate director of the SPIRAL Research Centre at the University of Liège, Belgium, where he coordinates the research unit in science, technology, and society.

David Edgerton was educated at St John's College, Oxford and Imperial College London. After teaching the economics of science and technology and the history of science and technology at the University of Manchester, he became the founding director of the Centre for the History of Science, Technology and Medicine at Imperial College London, and Hans Rausing Professor of History of Science and Technology. In 2013, he led the move of the Centre for the History of Science, Technology and Medicine to the Department of History at King's College London. He has published, among other works, *Warfare State: Britain 1920–1970* (2005) and *The Shock of the Old: Technology and Global History since 1900* (2006).

Manuela Fernández Pinto is an assistant professor in the Department of Philosophy and the Center of Applied Ethics at Universidad de los Andes in Bogotá, Colombia. She is also an affiliated researcher in the Academy of Finland Centre of Excellence in the Philosophy of the Social Sciences at the University of Helsinki. After receiving her PhD in History and Philosophy of Science from the University of Notre Dame (2014), she obtained a postdoctoral fellowship at the University of Helsinki to examine the interdisciplinary relation between economics and social epistemology, particularly the use of economic models for addressing philosophical questions on the social organization of science. Her current research, also related to the social organization of science, examines the epistemic and ethical consequences of the recent move toward commercially driven scientific research. Other research interests include social epistemology, the history and philosophy of economics and feminist philosophy.

Rebecca Harrison is a doctoral student in Science and Technology Studies. Her work considers how agricultural biotechnologists are deliberate, ethical actors navigating both a complex political economy and increasing public concern about genetic engineering. Harrison earned a bachelor's degree in animal science from Cornell University. She began her training as a graduate student in STS at Rensselaer Polytechnic Institute and has since returned to Cornell for her PhD. She has professional experience in agriculture, science and technology policy, and science communication.

Maki Hatanaka is associate professor in the Department of Sociology at Sam Houston State University. Her research focuses on food governance, in particular issues related to standards, certification, and accreditation. Her recent projects examine ways to promote democratic food governance and enhance justice and sustainability in food and agriculture. Her work has been published in numerous journals and edited books, including *Science, Food Policy, Agriculture and Human Values, World Development, Journal of Rural Studies, Sociologia Ruralis, The Local Environment: The International Journal of Justice* and *Sustainability,* and *Sustainability.*

David J. Hess is professor of Sociology, associate director of the Vanderbilt Institute for Energy and Environment, Director of the Program in Environmental and Sustainability Studies, and James Thornton Fant Chair in Sustainability Studies at Vanderbilt University. He is the recipient of various prizes and awards in science and technology studies, including the Robert Merton Prize and the Diana Forsythe Prize. He currently works on the politics of sustainability transitions and on social movements, science, and technology. His most recent book is *Undone Science: Social Movements, Mobilized Publics, and Industrial Transitions.*

Matt Hopkins, Ken Jacobson, Mustafa Erdem Sakinç, and **Öner Tulum** are researchers at theAIRnet. Jacobson is also theAIRnet communications director. Sakinç has just completed a PhD in Economics at the University of Bordeaux. Tulum is a PhD student at the University of Ljubljana.

Sheila Jasanoff is Pforzheimer Professor of Science and Technology Studies and Director of the Program on Science, Technology and Society at Harvard University's John F. Kennedy

School of Government. Her research centers on the engagements of science and technology with law, politics and policy in modern democratic societies, with a particular focus on the role of science in cultures of public reason. Her books include *The Fifth Branch* (1990), *Science at the Bar* (1995), *Designs on Nature* (2005), and *The Ethics of Invention* (2016).

Leigh Johnson is assistant professor in the Department of Geography at the University of Oregon, where she teaches on environment, development, and economic geography. Her research engages with markets in climate risk transfer, ranging from reinsurance, catastrophe bonds, and weather derivatives in the Global North, to index-based microinsurance for farmers and pastoralists in the Global South. This work interrogates the changing forms of accumulation, knowledge production, environmental vulnerability, and solidarity accompanying the growth of formal risk transfer markets.

Abby Kinchy (PhD, Sociology, University of Wisconsin-Madison) is an associate professor in the Science and Technology Studies Department at Rensselaer Polytechnic Institute, where she currently serves as director of the STS graduate program. She is the author of *Seeds, Science, and Struggle: The Global Politics of Transgenic Crops* (2012) and numerous articles on science, technology, the environment, and social protest. Her current research, the Watershed Knowledge Mapping Project, looks at civil society organizations that are attempting to monitor the impacts of shale gas development on surface water quality, and how these efforts are transforming what is known and unknown about this controversial new form of energy production.

Jason Konefal is an associate professor of sociology at Sam Houston State University. His research examines private forms of governance in agriculture, particularly with regards to sustainability, and the financialization of agriculture. His research has been widely published, including in the journals *Agriculture and Human Values*, *Journal of Rural Studies*, and *Organization and the Environment*.

Pablo Kreimer is a sociologist and PhD at Science, Technology & Society (STS Center, Paris). He is a principal researcher at CONICET (Argentinian National Research Council) and Director of the Science, Technology & Society Center, Maimonides University, Buenos Aires, Argentina.

Chris Langley has worked for more than thirty years in practical and research aspects of science policy and governance and the communication of science, technology and medicine. He has contributed to book chapters and peer-reviewed journals on military science and technology. He is a graduate of University College London and received a doctorate from the University of Cambridge. He was Director of the Media Resource Service in London and presently runs ScienceSources, an independent consultancy which facilitates public accountability in and access to, science, technology and medicine. Chris was principal researcher for Scientists for Global Responsibility, where he wrote and co-authored *Soldiers in the laboratory: Military involvement in science and technology – and some alternatives*; *Scientists or soldiers? Career choice, ethics and the military*; *More soldiers in the laboratory: The militarisation of science and technology*; and *Behind closed doors*. He also critiqued nuclear research for the Nuclear Information Service.

Rebecca Lave is an associate professor in Geography at Indiana University. Her research takes a critical physical geography approach, combining political economy, STS, and fluvial geomorphology to focus on the construction of scientific expertise, the privatization of science, and market-based environmental management. She is the author of *Fields and Streams: Stream Restoration, Neoliberalism, and the Future of Environmental Science* (2012) and has published in journals ranging from *Science* to *Social Studies of Science*. She is a co-editor of the *Handbook of Political Economy of Science* and three forthcoming collections: the *Handbook of Critical Physical Geography* and a pair of volumes devoted to the work of Doreen Massey, all expected in 2017. She is also a series editor for the 'Critical Environments: Nature, Science and Politics' book series at University of California Press, and for the 'Economic Transformations' book series at Agenda Publishing.

William Lazonick is professor of economics, University of Massachusetts Lowell; visiting professor, University of Ljubljana; professeur associé, Institut Mines-Télécom; and president, The Academic-Industry Research Network (theAIRnet).

Allison Loconto is a research fellow at the National Institute for Agricultural Research (INRA), based in the Interdisciplinary Laboratory for Science, Innovation and Society (LISIS). She is currently a visiting scientist on Standards and Institutions for Sustainable Agriculture at the Food and Agriculture Organization of the United Nations (FAO). Dr Loconto holds a PhD in Sociology from Michigan State University and an MA in International Affairs and Development from American University in Washington, DC. She is currently the president of the Research Committee on the Sociology of Agriculture and Food (RC40) of the International Sociological Association (ISA). Dr Loconto's fields of research include governance by standards, innovations in certification systems, regulatory intermediaries, social innovation and governance of transitions to sustainable agriculture. Her most recent book entitled *Innovative markets for sustainable agriculture: How innovations in market institutions encourage sustainable agriculture in developing countries* is published by FAO.

Larry Lohmann works with The Corner House, an advocacy and research organization based in the UK (www.thecornerhouse.org.uk). He spent the 1980s teaching and working in environmental movements in Thailand, is a founding member of the Durban Group for Climate Justice, and chairs the advisory board of the World Rainforest Movement. He has contributed to scholarly journals in sociology, politics, development, science studies, law, social policy, environment, accounting and Asian studies, as well as to many popular publications. His books include *Energy, Work and Finance* (with Nicholas Hildyard) (2014); *Mercados de Carbono: La Neoliberalizacion del Clima* (2012) and *Pulping the South: Industrial Tree Plantations and the Global Paper Economy* (with Ricardo Carrere) (1996).

Rachel G. McKane is a PhD student in the Department of Sociology at Vanderbilt University. She received her BA in Global Studies from the University of Tennessee, Knoxville, in 2012 and her MA in Sociology from Vanderbilt University in 2016. Her research interests include environmental justice, environmental sociology, stratification and health, and quantitative methods. Her recent research focuses on applying theories of intersectionality to environmental justice studies and examining the intersections of environmental inequity and health disparities.

Philip Mirowski is Carl Koch Chair of Economics and the History and Philosophy of Science, and Fellow of the Reilly Center, University of Notre Dame. He is author of, among others, *Machine Dreams* (2002), *The Effortless Economy of Science?* (2004), *More Heat than Light* (1989), *Never Let a Serious Crisis Go to Waste* (2013), and *ScienceMart: Privatizing American Science* (2011). He is editor of *Agreement on Demand* (2006) and *The Road from Mont Pèlerin: The Making of the Neoliberal Thought Collective* (2009), among other works. His next book, with co-author Edward Nik-Khah, will be *The Knowledge we have Lost in Information: A History of the Economics of Information*, which will be accompanied by a video lecture series from INET.

Chris Muellerleile is a lecturer of economic and urban geography at Swansea University in the UK. He researches the social construction and political economy of markets, especially in the context of urban space. He recently finished a study of the emergence of financial derivatives markets in Chicago during the 1970s and 1980s. He is now researching the political economy of academic knowledge production as well as the growing influence of the financial industry in the emergent higher education sectors in the US and UK. His work on financial markets and financialization has been published in venues such as the *Journal of Economic Geography* and *Environment and Planning A*.

Edward Nik-Khah is an associate professor of Economics at Roanoke College (USA). He has completed research on interactions between the Chicago School of Economics, the pharmaceutical industry, and pharmaceutical science; the neoliberal origins of economics imperialism; the distinctive role of George Stigler as architect of the Chicago School; and the tensions emerging from economists' assumption of a professional identity as designers of markets. His forthcoming book on the history of knowledge and information in economics (with Philip Mirowski) is entitled *The Knowledge We Have Lost in Information*.

Gwen Ottinger is an associate professor in the Department of Politics and the Center for Science, Technology, and Society at Drexel University. Her research focuses on the politics of science, technology, and expertise in environmental justice issues, and her current project examines the history of citizen science and do-it-yourself monitoring in community-based environmental activism. Ottinger is a recipient of a CAREER grant from the National Science Foundation and the author *of Refining Expertise: How Responsible Engineers Subvert Environmental Justice Challenges*, which was awarded the 2015 Rachel Carson Prize by the Society for Social Studies of Science.

Ugo Pagano is professor of Economics and the director of the PhD program in Economics of the University of Siena. He also teaches at the Central European University, Budapest. He got his PhD at the University of Cambridge where he was university lecturer and a fellow of Pembroke College. He is the author of the monograph *Work and Welfare in Economic Theory* and of numerous articles focusing on law and economics, the economics of organization, bio-economics, nationalism and globalization, intellectual property rights and the current economic crisis.

Stuart Parkinson is executive director of Scientists for Global Responsibility (SGR), a UK-based organisation of about 750 natural scientists, social scientists, engineers and others concerned about the use and misuse of science, design and technology. Parkinson has degrees in physics, engineering and environmental science. He has worked in academia and industry and for campaign groups, including a period as an expert reviewer for the Intergovernmental Panel on Climate Change. He has been SGR's Director since 2003, co-ordinating research and advocacy work on range of issues, including military and corporate influence on science and technology. He is lead author of *Offensive Insecurity: The Role of Science and Technology in UK Security Strategies*, and has written widely on these issues for both lay and specialist audiences.

Luigi Pellizzoni is professor of Environmental Sociology at the University of Pisa. His theoretical and empirical interests are located at the intersection of the following themes: risk, uncertainty, environmental change and sustainability; the impacts of scientific advancement and technological innovation; and conflict, participation, and new forms of governance. On these topics he has a long experience of research (e.g. European Commission's IV, V, VI, VII and

Interreg programs) and has published in leading journals. He has recently authored *Ontological Politics in a Disposable World: The New Mastery of Nature* (2015) and co-edited *Neoliberalism and Technoscience: Critical Assessments* (2012).

Claude Peloquin has taught geography at Macalester College and at the University of Arizona. His work examines the place and role of nature–society entanglements in the political geographies of development, science, and colonialism.

Sebastian Pfotenhauer is Assistant Professor of Innovation Research at the Munich Center for Technology in Society (MCTS) and the TUM School of Management, both Technical University of Munich, where he heads the Innovation, Society and Public Policy group. His research interests include regional innovation cultures, the global circulation of innovation models, institutional and national innovation strategies, and complex (international) partnerships for capacity-building in science, technology, and innovation. Before joining TU Munich, he was a research scientist and lecturer with the MIT Technology & Policy Program and the MIT Sociotechnical Systems Research Center, as well as a research fellow at the Harvard Program on Science, Technology and Society. His work has appeared, among other outlets, in *Social Studies of Science, Research Policy, Nature*, and *Issues in Science and Technology*. He holds an S.M. in MIT and a PhD from the University of Jena, Germany.

Laura Rabinow (MS, Science and Technology Studies, Rensselaer Polytechnic Institute) is a doctoral student in Science and Technology Studies Department at Rensselaer Polytechnic Institute. She has previously worked in agricultural microfinance and was a 2015–16 graduate fellow at the New York State Senate. Her current research looks at the ways knowledge production, epistemic authority and governance are contested in the context of water contamination.

Costanza Rampini received her PhD from the Environmental Studies Department at the University of California, Santa Cruz. Her research focuses on the interlinked issues of hydropower development, floods, climate change impacts and sustainable development in the Brahmaputra river basin. Her objective is to understand how the combined impacts of climate change and dam building efforts on water resources will transform the riparian landscapes of Northeast India and the livelihoods of local riparian communities.

Samuel Randalls is a lecturer in Geography at University College London. His research primarily focuses on the relationship between commerce, environment and science, particularly in the context of weather and climate. Publications explore topics such as weather futures trading, histories of climate change economics, the politics of resilience, and underwater logging. In the last few years, he has co-edited a Routledge set on *Future Climate Change* and a special issue of *Geoforum* on 'The Politics of Expectations' and has published in journals such as *Dialogues in Human Geography, Osiris*, and *Social Studies of Science*. He is currently researching Victorian weather insurance, particularly insurance companies' practices in pricing weather and climate risks.

Elizabeth P. Ransom is an associate professor of sociology in the Department of Sociology and Anthropology at the University of Richmond. Her research focuses on international development and globalization, the sociology of agriculture and food, and social studies of science and technology. Specifically, she concentrates on the intersection of science and technology policy within agriculture and food systems, with particular emphasis on analyzing the ways in which policy changes impact producers and production practices in both the

United States and sub-Saharan Africa. Her published research is oriented towards both academic and policy audiences including, most recently, a co-edited book *Rural America in a Globalizing World: Problems and Prospects for the 2010s*. Ransom received her PhD in Sociology from Michigan State University.

Daniel Rich is director of University Community Engagement and university professor of Public Policy in the School of Public Policy and Administration at the University of Delaware. He also serves as senior policy fellow in the Institute for Public Administration. From 2001–9 he served as university provost. From 1996–2001, he served as founding dean of the College of Human Services, Education and Public Policy, and from 1991–6, as dean of the College of Urban Affairs and Public Policy at the University of Delaware. His research has focused on education policy, urban policy, energy policy, and science and technology policy. His publications include 13 books and edited volumes, and more than 100 articles, monographs and professional papers. His public and professional service contributions include a variety of appointments in support of preK-12 education and higher education.

Morgan Robertson is an associate professor of Geography at the University of Wisconsin-Madison. He received his PhD from the University of Wisconsin-Madison in 2004, and conducted postdoctoral research at the US Environmental Protection Agency developing regulations governing wetland credit markets. He taught and conducted research at the University of Kentucky from 2007 to 2012. His research focuses on the interface of science and economics in ecosystem service markets.

Mark Robinson is an assistant professor at the Center for Health Policy and Ethics at Creighton University School of Medicine. His current interests include the social study of science and technology-based innovations in health, with a view towards their ethical and social implications and dimensions. Robinson's work is especially attentive to the roles of global finance, psycho-pharmaceuticalization and technological transformation in the shaping of agendas and outcomes in health. Robinson's current project explores the global emergence and expansion of Translational Science and Medicine and its impact upon biomedical innovation. Robinson's work has received recognition from Princeton University's Center for Health and Wellbeing, the Wenner-Gren Foundation, and Italy's Gianinno Bassetti Foundation.

Jairus Rossi is a research scientist for the Community and Economic Development Initiative of Kentucky in the University of Kentucky's College of Agriculture, Food, and Environment. He is broadly interested in understanding how diverse environmental, economic, and social technologies shape the production of landscapes. His dissertation research examined how scientists and citizen scientists use genetic technologies and concepts to restore ecosystems. His current research centres on delineating the political economies involved in the development of direct-to-consumer alternative food networks. His research generally draws from political ecology, science and technology studies, and cultural landscape geography. He received his PhD in Geography at the University of Kentucky in 2013.

Maria Alessandra Rossi is Associate Professor of Economic Policy at the Department of Economics and Statistics of the University of Siena. Her research interests cover the law and economics analysis of innovation, telecommunications and media economics and digital economics, as well as competition and regulation policy. She was visiting researcher at the University of Oxford, the Council of Europe, the Department of Economics at UC Berkeley, the Santa Fe Institute of Technology, the University of Paris X and the Florence School of Regulation. She carried out research and reports for OECD, the Italian Telecommunications NRA (AGCOM), the Italian Ministry of Finance and the Independent Regulatory Group (IRG). She has written numerous essays on national and international journals. Maria Alessandra holds a PhD in Law and Economics from the University of Siena.

Dan Schiller is Professor Emeritus of Library & Information Science and of Communication at the University of Illinois at Urbana-Champaign. He is a historian of information and communications in the context of the five hundred-year development of the capitalist political economy. Earlier in his career, he was a professor at UCSD, UCLA and Temple Universities. He is the author of several books, including, most recently, *Digital Depression: Information Technology and Economic Crisis* (2014), and he is now completing archival research for a long-standing project on the history of US telecommunications. With ShinJoung Yeo, Schiller administers the Information Observatory website (www.informationobservatory.info).

Sergio Sismondo teaches in the departments of Philosophy and Sociology at Queen's University, Canada. His current research examines relationships between medical research and pharmaceutical marketing in areas from clinical trials through medical education. He is the author of *An Introduction to Science and Technology Studies* (2nd ed. 2010) and a number of other general and philosophical works in STS, and is editor of the journal *Social Studies of Science*. He has recently co-edited, with Jeremy Greene, *The Pharmaceutical Studies Reader* (2015).

Richard P. Suttmeier is a Professor of Political Science, Emeritus, at the University of Oregon. He has served as a Senior Analyst at the Congressional Office of Technology Assessment, as a consultant to the World Bank and the UNDP, and as the Director of the Beijing Office of the Committee for Scholarly Communication with China. From November, 2010 to January, 2011, he was a visiting senior scholar at the Institute of Policy and Management of the Chinese Academy of Sciences. Suttmeier has written widely on science and technology development issues in China. He received his A.B. degree from Dartmouth College and his PhD from Indiana University. Copies of recent papers are available at http://china-us.uoregon.edu/papers.php.

Charles Thorpe is associate professor in Sociology, and a member of the Science Studies Program, at the University of California, San Diego. He is the author of *Oppenheimer: The Tragic Intellect* (2006), a sociological biography of the physicist J. Robert Oppenheimer, and *Necroculture* (2016), a study of the culture of alienation in late capitalism. He has published in *Anarchist Studies*, *The British Journal of Sociology*, *Modern Intellectual History*, *Science as Culture*, *Science Fiction Studies*, *Social Studies of Science*, *Sociological Theory*, and *Theory, Culture, and Society*.

David Tyfield is a Reader in Environmental Innovation & Sociology at the Lancaster Environment Centre, Lancaster University, and research professor at the Chinese Academy of Sciences Guangzhou Institute of Geochemistry (GIGCAS). He is Director of the International Research and Innovation Centre for the Environment (I-RICE), Guangzhou (a joint initiative between Lancaster and GIGCAS) and co-director of the Centre for Mobilities Research (CeMoRe), Lancaster University. His research focuses on the interaction of political economy, social change, and developments in science, technology and innovation, with a particular focus on issues of low-carbon transition in China, especially urban e-mobility. Recent publications include articles in *Sustainable Development*, *Mobilities*, *Journal of Responsible*

Innovation, Theory, Culture & Society, and *Minerva*. He is author of *The Economics of Science* (Routledge, 2012, in two volumes).

Hebe Vessuri is currently visiting professor at the Centro de Investigaciones en Geografía Ambiental (CIGA) and Level 3 researcher at the National Research System in Mexico, emeritus researcher at the Venezuelan Institute of Scientific Research (IVIC), and main researcher at CONICET-CENPAT in Argentina. She has contributed to the emergence and consolidation of the social studies of science and technology in Latin America. Her current research examines relations between researchers outside the world science-hubs and the peculiar dynamics of international academic prestige, connectivity and power in contexts from Mexico through Patagonia.

Honggang Xu is a professor at the School of Tourism Management, Sun Yat-sen University. She has published extensively in international journals. Her research interests include regional tourism development, tourism planning, system dynamics, tourism geographies and mobility.

Tian Ye is an MPhil candidate at the School of Tourism Management, Sun Yat-sen University. She has personal experience of changes in Chinese higher education as a female student from a rural area. Her research interests include destination image, tourist experience, intimate relationships, and gender issues and she has published in international journals on these issues.

ShinJoung Yeo is a lecturer at Loughborough University London in the Institute for Media and Creative Industries. Her current research focuses on the political economy of the search engine industry encompassing labour, geopolitics of information, and material infrastructures. She is currently working on a book based on her dissertation *Behind the Search Box: The Political Economy of a Global Internet Industry*.

INTRODUCTION

Beyond crisis in the knowledge economy

David Tyfield, Rebecca Lave, Samuel Randalls and Charles Thorpe

In July 2016, an article in the *Wall Street Journal* declared "Election 2016 is propelled by the American economy's failed promises" (Hilsenrath and Davis, 2016; see also Beams, 2016). The article effectively acknowledges that the political economic orthodoxy of the day – for which the *Journal* has long been a primary proponent – is in tatters and that anger at economic dislocation is creating seismic shifts in Americans' political outlook. Among the failed promises that the article lists is that of technology in the 'knowledge economy', namely that "Technology would lead to rising incomes and broadly shared prosperity." The reality is that "Productivity and output growth have slowed and technology has been polarizing the workforce."

Technological unemployment, a notion treated as heretical, if not absurd, in the 1990s, is now increasingly taken seriously as a key factor holding down job creation, wages, living standards, and economic growth. The article further notes that in the past "those with bachelors' degrees in science seemed safe from automation-prompted layoffs—their knowledge was tough for computers to duplicate." But this is no longer the case, with a whole swathe of middle-class employment now being downgraded or eliminated: "Between 2000 and 2012… the hollowing-out of work spread to professions including librarians and engineers." These trends have contributed to the widening of income inequality. In the UK, the surprise vote for 'Brexit', with the UK quitting the EU, has been explained in similar terms of mass political and economic disenfranchisement and anger (Harris, 2016; Elliott, 2016).

It is salutary to contrast the reality of today's low growth, low productivity, and low employment economy with the rhetoric of the 'knowledge economy' not so very long ago. This was supposed to be a 'new economy' for which the old rules of boom and bust did not apply. The new economy would almost overcome economics itself, escaping materiality, since scarcity could be banished in the realm of information (Kelly, 1997; see also Thorpe, 2016, 105–6). Buying and selling knowledge meant "living on thin air" as British knowledge economy pundit Charles Leadbeater (1999) declared. The ethereal knowledge economy would be more ecologically sensitive, less demanding of resources. High-tech was also green. It also would allow for a change in the character of work itself, liberating us from the routinized, standardized world of Fordist mass production and mass consumption (cf. Clark, Foster and York, 2009; York and Rosa, 2003).

This also translated into new bold high-technology promises about research and innovation (R&I). Genetic engineering would solve world hunger, with a reduced ecological footprint, and/or cure persistent diseases, while also thereby developing whole new industries for profitable investment and rewarding, knowledge-intensive work. New digital and information communication technologies would revolutionize our capacity to understand and skilfully manage complex problems, such as those of the environment, while also unlocking unprecedented innovation and generation of new knowledge through a new fluid, global interconnectivity. And this would seed further breakthroughs in science and technology, unleashing undreamt-of progress in the human mastery of matter (e.g. nanotechnology), living systems (e.g. biotechnology) and consciousness (e.g. artificial intelligence) (cf. Birch, et al., 2010; Cooper, 2008; Thorpe, 2013; Tyfield, 2012a: 43–62; Walker, 2016).

Just as the political turmoil of 2016 lays bare the broken shells of those economic promises, so too we find the promises regarding R&I equally battered. Indeed, the greater political and economic importance of R&I has clearly proven a double-edged sword. For instance, consider the case of genetically modified agriculture. Expectations for genetic engineering of plants have been frequently founded on ideals of public benefits, whether in terms of agricultural crop disease resistance, ability to withstand environmental changes or economic development prospects for local communities. Yet agricultural engineering has also offered one of the most consistent arenas for contestation over the past three decades, whether about the potential for increased corporate power or fears of 'playing God' (Delborne, 2008; Delborne and Kinchy, 2008; Kinchy, 2012; Kleinman, 2003; Kloppenburg, 1988).

In recent years, therefore, ag-biotech has been forced to outline its public-spiritedness to ward off persistent and powerful critique. As Harrison et al. (this volume) show, however, contemporary political economic policies and practices towards R&I restrict the possibilities of change, thereby, in turn, entrenching opposition. Water-efficient maize and the American chestnut are differently constituted in political-economic terms. But while both offer some pushback on commercialization imperatives, they both also re-instantiate the norms of the contemporary political economy of science through forms of regulation, economic ideals, intellectual property frameworks and profitability – even if dressed up in humanitarian terms.

It seems, therefore, that if the ardent pursuit of the 'knowledge economy' has produced anything in recent decades, it is not the world that was promised but the ascendancy of the political economy of science – or more appropriately, the political economy of R&I – into a key issue of contestation for contemporary society, and amongst the public at large, not just the relatively small groups directly employed in these fields.

Putting the production of knowledge in question…

In a sense, it is obvious that the subject of a political economy of R&I (PERI) is the production – and inseparably, the distribution and consumption – of knowledge, and how this shapes and is shaped by (distinct) political economies. From the point of view of mainstream economics of science/knowledge, we are here studying two things – knowledge (incorporating both science and innovation) and economy – and how these fit together: knowledge, once produced, is commercialized, leading to economic development and further knowledge production. Yet profound assumptions are built into this picture; assumptions that not only have significant causal effects in the actual trajectories of contemporary socio-technical change, but also, in fact, are highly problematic.

Two of these assumptions regarding 'knowledge' emerge as particularly important: first, that 'knowledge' is a familiar beast, namely the (growing) body of factual, normatively neutral truths that enables people to serve their needs and desires; and, secondly, that it is therefore obvious and axiomatic that, when it comes to the question of the *production* of knowledge, more knowledge always leads to economic growth and societal benefit. In short, more knowledge is always better. Let us call these joint presumptions the 'knowledge economy credo'.

The unquestioned presumption that the goal at hand is to maximize the production of straightforward, unproblematic knowledge (research, innovation and education) is highly consequential in the *actual* political economy of R&I today, since it underpins policies and practices. Mainstream economics of science adopts this goal as both achievable and self-evidently good, and proceeds to focus on how best to maximize (quantitatively) this output, 'knowledge'. The actual interaction of knowledge production and an expressly *political* economy, however, quickly dissolves this neat picture. The example of agbiotech above demonstrates the necessity of the political legitimation of new forms of knowledge and technology in a contested public sphere and political economy, and therefore the mutual co-constitution or co-construction of knowledge, economy, culture, and politics.

While both knowledge and political economy have been the object of significant bodies of insightful work, they are not generally conceptualized together. In recent decades, Science & Technology Studies (STS) has thoroughly transformed the empirical study of knowledge production by taking science not as an obvious and unproblematic production of empirical truth, but as a complex social and cultural practice requiring sociological/anthropological study. STS thus brings together a broad range of approaches from the social sciences and humanities. But political economy is conspicuous by its relative absence. This is, in part, because of the field's dominant micro-scale focus on the particularities of scientific practice, in particular (academic) labs and field sites. It is also due to its foundation in heated debates about constructivist, anti-realist philosophy of science that elicited a deep-seated empiricist disposition towards anti-structural, including non-Marxist, approaches, approaches that have unquestionably proven extremely illuminating and conceptually productive. Yet the vast majority of STS work, but by no means all of it, shows little interest in, and sometimes even scant toleration of, issues of political economy (Tyfield, 2012b, 8–51; Lynch and Fuhrman, 1991, 1992; Winner, 1993; Klein and Kleinman, 2002; Mirowski, this volume).

For its part, mainstream economics of R&I shows little interest in issues of knowledge production as irreducibly cultural-political processes (Tyfield, 2012a, 13–25), while knowledge production is not generally a primary concern from political economy approaches. PERI, as pursued in this volume, therefore, seeks to draw on and continue the attention that STS scholars have given to the culturally constructed aspects of science and technology, but also to show how science is a force of production, embedded in the broader economic, political, and social institutions and relations of modern capitalism (cf. Bernal, 1939; Rose and Rose eds, 1976; Levidow and Young, 1981).

From this perspective, the 'knowledge economy' must not be understood as entirely novel and distinct from the production and distribution of material (and immaterial) goods. Instead, the marketization of scientific and technical knowledge must be understood within the overall framework of industrial capitalism, while the novelties of political economies increasingly dominated by production of knowledge(s) must also be attended to. This is the mode of understanding that has taken shape over the last 10–15 years under the rubric of PERI.

The growing PERI literature has repeatedly shown, in abstract and in concrete, how exploring the dynamic interrelations between 'knowledge' and an irreducibly political 'economy' necessarily problematizes both pillars of the knowledge economy credo, viz. the common-sense definition of knowledge and the axiomatic presumption that economic prosperity and socio-environmental well-being necessarily follow from the increase in knowledge and technology. Instead, 'knowledge' is revealed to be a key arena and instrument of political contestation. Meanwhile, the 'economy' conditioning and conditioned by this production of knowledge is itself shown to be an inherently contradictory and always deeply political sphere of human social life, characterized by specific political projects and the broad underlying systemic imperatives of continued accumulation of capital.

The mainstream approach thus attempts to explore the interaction of what it treats as two fundamentally different phenomena – namely factual knowledge (and its embodiment in new 'technologies') and a material economy of (possibly 'optimal') production and distribution. In contrast, PERI treats 'knowledge' and 'economy' as different and analytically distinguishable aspects of one and the same thing, namely systems of power/knowledge-mediated relations. PERI investigates empirical instances of how specific political economic regimes and specific practices of R&I are co-produced in self-sustaining and contested feedback loops. In the process, PERI unravels the ontological assumptions underpinning the knowledge economy credo, clearing the way toward a richer co-productionist perspective in which solutions to problems of knowledge are solutions to problems *not only* of local social orders *but also* macro-scale political-economic order (Shapin and Schaffer, 1985; Jasanoff, 2004). In this way, PERI exposes the deep fallacy that the 'immaterial' and 'neutral' thing called knowledge somehow escapes the deeper contradictions and constraints of the political and economic relations of capitalism.

... in neoliberal times

The need for this both dynamically historical and structural political-economic perspective is particularly acute given the period within which PERI has arisen and which it has immediately sought to analyse, namely the broadly neoliberal era of the past few decades. PERI work has often involved a profound engagement with analysis of the nature and trajectory of neoliberalism itself alongside the specific issue of the transformation of knowledge production that has happened in tandem (Birch and Mykhnenko, 2010; Lave et al., 2010, Tyfield, 2012c; Mirowski, 2011 and 2014).

While often unfortunately reduced to a politically progressive swear word, incorporating a contradictory multitude of positions and presumptions, 'neoliberalism' remains a useful – and, we would argue, essential – term for contemporary PERI work insofar as it is given a sufficiently substantive and rigorous definition (see e.g. Springer et al., 2016). For our purposes, following the discussion above about systems of power/knowledge-mediated relations, we take neoliberalism as an example or regime of such a system that has, contingently, dominated the evolution of global capitalism since the late 1970s/early 1980s (e.g. Harvey, 2005; Peck and Tickell, 2002). This regime has several key characteristics, all of which are best conceptualized as iterative processes and political projects that have proven, to date, extremely productive (in terms of creative destruction) and resilient regarding their own self-propagation. This has included: a model and political dogma of global economic liberalization and domestic privatization, unleashing and/or introducing markets to replace state provision and protection; the financialization of the economy in terms of growing economic and political heft of the financial sector, debt and new financial products; growing corporate power, on a global scale; and the takeover and use of state power to drive forward and clear obstacles to privatisation, marketisation, and financialization.

Thus, neoliberalism is a *dynamic* project that has evolved through different phases and in different ways in different places (Ong, 2006; Peck and Tickell, 2002) and draws on multiple sources of intellectual inspiration (Mirowski and Plehwe, 2009; Peck, 2010; Stedman Jones, 2014). But it is unified by a radical commitment to the 'market' as panacea and supreme decision-maker. Indeed, a clear finding from seminal PERI work in the history of economics is the deeply epistemic nature of neoliberalism (Mirowski and Plehwe, 2009; Nik-Khah, this volume), with significant implications for its interaction with and dependence upon a specifically neoliberal(ized) model of R&I (Tyfield, 2016).

As Mirowski (2009) has shown, the political radicalism – and extraordinary strategic efficacy – of neoliberalism lies in large part in its synthetic rethinking of the 'market' and 'knowledge'. For this political project, the fundamental – and, indeed, fundamental*ist* – truth is that the market always 'knows best', and certainly knows better than any limited individual or collective intelligence (see Nik-Khah, this volume). Neoliberalism, therefore, promotes the maximization of the production (and consumption) of knowledge, but where this is understood to mean the maximized subjection of human social life to markets, as the ultimate and superhuman decision-maker (Mirowski, 2009; Peck, 2010; Brown, 2015). Where optimal government of society hinges on optimal decisions about the trajectory of societal development, for neoliberals it is the market that can best achieve this. Developing in parallel with and through the much-hyped emergence of the 'knowledge economy', therefore, neoliberalism has sponsored the knowledge economy credo and given it a particular political form as a highly dynamic, destructively creative and evangelical political patron.

This strong epistemic aspect of neoliberalism has significant repercussions for science. Neoliberals present science as best organized as a literal 'marketplace of ideas', for example in the increasing subjection of academic, 'public good' research and higher education to market forces. This reorganization of knowledge production assumes a pivotal role in the broader neoliberal project, as the talisman and/or cornerstone of the larger edifice of an optimal (since market-organized) society. As such, the strategic strength of neoliberalism has rested to a great extent upon its relatively unchallenged popular *appeal*. For it is founded in an argument about optimal socio-political order based in the optimal *organization of the production of knowledge*.

However, the definition of 'knowledge' that neoliberalism actually deploys is a radical and oft-overlooked departure.[1] Indeed, neoliberalism's ambiguous use of the knowledge economy credo – as seemingly anodyne common sense that conceals the profound radicalism of its interpretation, in a 'double truth' regime (Mirowski, 2012) – is an essential aspect both of the resilience and slipperiness of neoliberalism itself to date, and of how the knowledge economy credo has become so deeply entrenched, empowered and thence (self-)destructive in recent years.

So one key contribution to date of a PERI approach is to illuminate the mutually supporting, but also destructive (see below), relations between the neoliberal project and the knowledge economy credo, and the specific and problematic assumptions on which both rest. As such, insights that assist the rejection of the latter are also *de facto* political interventions against the former. Indeed, the existing mainstream discourse of the 'economics of science' must itself be understood as both the product of and, reciprocally, a key element in the construction of neoliberalism's profound changes in the institutions of science and its role in society (Mirowski, 2009). The continuing dominance of this political economic orthodoxy is thus not just an epistemic obstacle to a more productive analysis, but *itself* a key causal aspect of any comprehensive explanation of the current crises of (the political economy of) science *and* of the persistent misfiring of policy regarding research and innovation. PERI is thus directly tackling all of these issues.

In these circumstances, the *political* economy of 'science' also emerges as a key issue and lens for two major reasons. On the one hand, the dominant political economic regime of the day is highly epistemic in its abstract legitimation and this translates into its intense concrete dependence on forms of knowledge production and their transformation through marketization. As a result, an interest in neoliberalism implies a focus on R&I. For instance, recent work has explored how the pharmaceutical industry has instantiated the model of a neoliberal R&I as envisaged by key neoliberal intellectuals (Nik-Khah, 2014). On the other, the multiple problematic *effects* of the current regime of knowledge production are often what initially stimulate critical and engaged scholarship in STS, driving such research towards an interest in neoliberalism and political economy more broadly. Notably, concerns about contemporary environmental or social issues, and the production and contestation of knowledge claims regarding these, have propelled many scholars to research how neoliberal organizations construct their cases and shape broader public understanding (Thorpe and Gregory, 2010; Thorpe, 2010; Welsh and Wynne, 2013; Marris, 2015).

Whether born out of enquiry seeking to understand these problematic effects of the specific regime of neoliberalism or neoliberalism's manifestation in R&I, however, PERI offers one further, and crucial, contribution that is not limited to, and promises to lead beyond, this particular context. This is as a key source of ongoing insight (abstract and concrete) to dislodge the publicly sedimented misunderstanding about 'knowledge' – as in the knowledge economy credo – as well as, thereby, a stimulus for and moment in the practical and strategic engagement in an *alternative* knowledge politics. In short, the primary purpose of the political economy of R&I, as a growing body of work, is arguably to repudiate these misleading presumptions and replace them with something that promises to mediate the emergence of better socio-technical – and political economic – futures.

As the selection of PERI work in this Handbook demonstrates, however, these better futures are desperately needed today, while the globalizing 'knowledge' societies and economies being built on the neoliberal-sponsored knowledge economy credo are causing ever-deeper social, political and environmental problems. In the rest of this Introduction, rather than summarize the content of all the subsequent chapters – an impossible task and one better served by the chapter abstracts in any case – we draw on some of their insights to discuss four ways in which these profound challenges to the neoliberal knowledge economy are in evidence. These are:

1 immanent crises of the production of knowledge (innovation, research, HE) itself;
2 extrinsic crises of R&I that is failing to serve the public purposes of dealing with grievous global risks, and possibly even compounding them, even as R&I is increasingly cast by policy as panacea to all these challenges;
3 changing political/social relations to the use or consumption of knowledge; and
4 changing geographies of knowledge production and political epistemologies.

Crises and changes in production of knowledge

Surveying knowledge production around the world today we find four fundamental beliefs (or dogmas), all elaborations of the knowledge economy credo, that are both widely accepted and manifest in R&I policy and strategy, but also increasingly threadbare when confronted with the empirical record of deepening problems with the production of research and innovation. These are that:

Dogma 1: Science (R&I) contributes substantially to economic growth, and that funding of R&I is best legitimated in such terms; hence

Dogma 2: R&I may be best explained and arranged in terms of a 'marketplace of ideas'; hence

Dogma 3: Domination by corporate and speculative entrepreneurial investment ensures a unique dynamism and productivity in R&I, presumptively to the maximized benefit of all (especially as consumers and investors); and

Dogma 4: Such R&I can be expected, given time and investment, to resolve (or at least optimally to tackle) all social challenges with which it is tasked.

We turn to the last of these four in the next section. As regards the first three, though, it is increasingly clear that none of them stands up to scrutiny, while acting as if they are true serves only to compound the evidence to the contrary and the stagnation of socio-economically productive innovation thus organized.

First, as regards dogma 1, current literature shows, at best, significant ignorance still regarding any relationship between R&I (let alone 'science', and especially academic or 'basic' science as the term is often understood) and economic growth and, at worst, arguably an inverse relationship (see Edgerton, this volume). But what are the effects of this dogma and of basing legitimation of (public) funding of R&I upon it?

As Pagano & Rossi (this volume) show, the specific regime of R&I funding today, which supports R&I primarily to the extent it promises swift translation into profitable commercial impact, is conditioning a generalized stagnation of innovation and private-sector R&I investment, which has historically been the dominant site of R&I (Edgerton, this volume). This has involved the propagation of an overly proprietary model of innovation that locks up knowledge-intensive products of innovation and research into an increasingly impenetrable thicket of mutually exclusive claims of ownership. This has produced not only an 'anti-commons' (Heller and Eisenberg, 1998), in which the shared commons of 'ideas', upon which the generation of further ideas are premised, are increasingly inaccessible. But it also has generated a deepening 'investment strike' (Pagano and Rossi, 2009), in which private ownership of knowledge ironically disincentivizes investment in its generation in the first place, even as strong intellectual property rights are advocated for precisely the opposite reason. Meanwhile, such innovation as does occur is increasingly the parasitic mobilization of existing assets, perhaps via online platforms, by a new class of rentiers (Birch, this volume).

This, in turn, substantially underlies the crisis of productivity and stagnation of the broader political economy that culminated in the Great Financial Crash of 2007/8. Nor does this account seem merely historical despite being nearly a decade down the road, with an ongoing and deepening crisis in productivity growth across the global economy for similar reasons of stalled business investment. For not only has little changed in the Global North where these dynamics were strongest and most efficacious, but they now seem to be reaching similar crisis-inducing proportions in the Global South as well, which has been the effective engine of global economic growth since the beginning of the century.

This discussion, however, immediately leads to dogma 2, regarding knowledge production as a marketplace of ideas (MoI). For it is precisely the untrammelled expansion of markets of contending *private* ownership of knowledge and the systematic shrinking of a legitimate discourse and institutional capacity of *public* knowledge production (notwithstanding a 'stealth industrial policy' in the US throughout the neoliberal period (Block, 2008)) that has sown this cannibalistic trajectory. This self-defeating logic is arguably intrinsic, there from the outset, to the entire conception and project of the 'marketplace of ideas', even as this has indeed become the dominant public framing for thinking about R&I. For instance, as Nik-Khah (this volume) shows, the successful political propagation of this concept was built upon a radical commitment to academic freedom, in an open marketplace not an arena of scholarly debate, together with an equally foundational determination that the course of knowledge production should be guided by a specific elite committed to the superiority of the market. While apparently contradictory, these twin commitments have afforded the productive 'double truth' regime discussed above. This has then driven a deepening acceptance and empowerment of a knowledge production regime that, in both these commitments, is essentially committed to the destruction of any space for public reasoning (i.e. reasoning *about* matters of public interest and *in* the public sphere with *a view to* shaping the public good) by its subsumption in an ever-growing, all-knowing market. And in practice, this 'market' is actually powerful corporations and wealthy individuals (Crouch, 2011).

This concrete manifestation of the MoI is captured in dogma 3. Again, though, far from yielding unprecedented productivity and advances in R&I, Lazonick et al. (this volume) set out the multiple negative effects that are increasingly apparent from organizing innovation as a financialized market, based on a model of maximizing shareholder value (MSV). They illustrate this focusing on the pivotal case of the pharmaceutical biotech industry.

Both Lazonick et al. and Pagano and Rossi (both this volume) thus explain a political economic model of R&I that generates 'profits without prosperity' (Lazonick, 2014), and hence that demonstrably contravenes this key dogma of neoliberal political economy. Indeed, the combination of dominant neoliberal models of innovation and financialization even subverts the key figure of the entrepreneur. Instead of the creator of new markets and commodities, s/he becomes its antithesis, the rentier, developing new technoscientific interventions that aim to exploit the (positive externalities associated with) monopolization of *existing* stocks of assets (Birch, this volume; Zeller, 2008).

But this model is also culpably constraining production of the various forms of 'knowledge' seemingly most dependent on this model of innovation. This is the case whether in terms of (possibly hi-tech) innovation within industries dependent upon regular, proprietary breakthroughs (with pharmaceuticals again archetypal (see chapters by Sismondo, Lazonick et al.)) or even of the production of 'basic' knowledge and 'knowledgeable' people through the institutions of academic research and higher education (Tyfield, 2013; see also Muellerleile, this volume).

For instance, a massive shift in the global political economy of higher education is afoot (chapters by Best and Rich; Xu and Ye). Dependence on ballooning and largely national-based student debt is clashing with increasingly global market 'competition' between universities for students and research funding, now reconfigured as 'services' and 'consumers' respectively. Not only is this drawing a deepening split into top and lower tier 'providers'. It is also shaping a system of higher education that is financially unstable (if not unsustainable) and for *all* parties – increasingly part-time staff and heavily indebted students *and* universities themselves, building new attractive campuses – even as there are arguably diminishing (financial) returns regarding the 'product' of (even a high-quality, if not globally elite) higher education.

Crucially, this is not just a phenomenon of the 'core' of the Global North, as Xu and Ye (this volume) show, regarding the key example of China, as possible global 'leader' or hegemon in the coming century. For here, the compound effect of exposure to global competition and rankings and of determination by the central government to create a handful of globally leading institutions is creating a particularly steep hierarchy of HE institutions. This is thereby transforming HE – and *with* significant state support and oversight – into a key mediation of cycles not of socioeconomic mobility and knowledge-based meritocracy but of deepening inequality and political economic dysfunction regarding the national goal of building a broad-based 'moderately well-off' (*xiaokang*) knowledge economy in China.

Here, then, we have analyses that challenge not just the claim of a unique dynamism from this model of R&I but also its seeding *qualitatively* optimal trajectories. In similar vein, Schiller and Yeo (this volume) show how instrumental state funding has continued to be in what dynamism *is* evident – albeit wedded to a specifically neoliberal imaginary – but also how the combined effect of the conditioning by (US) state and capital is producing a qualitatively specific and problematic trajectory of innovation in information communication technologies.

Moreover, once we are prepared to explore the cycles of co-production of knowledges as specific political technologies and equally specific political economic regimes, the forms of knowledge relevant to the concerns of a PERI are not just those of the R&I but also those enabling, constraining and framing that process. This includes, in particular, policy knowledges, not least of 'science' or 'innovation' policy. And, indeed, these forms of knowledge have also been profoundly exposed to neoliberal conditioning and marketization in recent decades, with profound impact on the political economy of R&I.

Neoliberal R&I policies frequently lead to a crisis in the production of knowledge and its corollary, a deepening crisis of policy legitimacy. For instance, the reformulation of public data provision or modelling creates conflicting economic priorities that do not necessarily translate into better policy, let alone more competitive, efficient knowledge production (see chapters by Johnson and Rampini; Randalls; Ransom et al.; Suttmeier). Policies to enable a wider diversity of actors to engage in knowledge production equally open up spaces in which think-tanks and lobbyists can play central roles in both claiming expertise and simultaneously powerfully disclaiming expertise (as we show later; Fernández Pinto, this volume). There is thus a crisis of legitimacy that, perhaps ironically, further substantiates a claimed need for more and deeper neoliberalisation of science and science policy as the 'depoliticized' solution currently to hand.

In short, then, at the level of *policy* and political knowledges, a political economy of R&I perspective reveals a similar crisis of production of knowledge as is visible in R&I itself. Treading the boundary of power/knowledge, therefore, this crisis of *production* of knowledge verges into a crisis of the *productivity* or *usefulness* of what knowledge *is* produced: the present neoliberal conjunction of unprecedented global challenges and R&I as supposed panacea that is dogma 4, to which we now turn.

Crises and changes in the productivity of knowledge

The funding of science, whether by public/state or private/market sources, inevitably calls upon arguments for legitimation of spending money in that way and not on some other priority. Fundamental to the arguments discussed above, therefore, is the final dogma of this progress narrative of 'knowledge' and its economics: that science, or R&I, should be funded (to *this* extent and in *these* ways) so that it can grow and thereby provide (profitable) solutions to the world's many ills. Indeed, discourses of how research and innovation promise to tackle and eliminate the multiple problems of the present – e.g. squaring 'green' and 'growth', or Big Pharma profits and global public health – have arguably reached new heights in recent years, manifesting almost a fetishism of innovation (and preferably of the high-technology, privately owned and research-intensive kind) (Godin, 2006; Tyfield, 2012c).

It is thus a deepening problem for this perspective that current R&I seems unable to deal with, let alone resolve, what appear to be deepening systemic problems and new global risks; while, conversely, R&I is intimately implicated in the emergence of these very problems, as key enablers of both clear and present dangers and new, threatening socio-technical (and socio-natural) futures. Far from delivering on the promise of greater human capacities, mastery and spontaneous order, therefore, 'more knowledge' seems to be delivering precisely the opposite. This thus presents a fundamental challenge to the productivity and usefulness of knowledge that underpin the knowledge economy credo. And, again, this is increasingly evident in multiple forms.

First, consider R&I that deals with contemporary challenges in relation to health and well-being, environments, resources and consumption around the world. To those concerned with 'planetary boundaries' (Rockström et al., 2009), these global problems require a significant investment in R&I. Yet surveying the current landscape of such innovation seems to reveal a depressing vista of politically locked-in systems of planetary destruction and stalled transitions (e.g. Hess and McKane, this volume), not to mention the limitations to transitions imposed by neoliberalism-framed international trade agreements, already in force and/or under negotiation.

This also plays out in terms of the contemporary fortunes of disciplines and fields of research enquiry relevant to these global challenges (see chapters by Harrison et al.; Johnson and Rampini; Lave and Robertson; Lohmann; Robinson). Attuned to profit as much as public benefits, scholars have demonstrated that current political economic drivers play an important role in shaping the kinds of science produced and the ends to which it is produced (e.g. chapters by Harrison et al.; Johnson and Rampini; Lohmann). The stagnation of precisely the R&I that is urgently needed is inseparable from the specific political economic model that currently dominates these processes.

Conversely, currently powerful imaginaries about future advances in many spheres of R&I themselves elicit profound, even ontological, anxiety for many, just as they seem irresistibly enticing and enabling to others; or, indeed, can produce both reactions, as Fisher (2017) shows regarding leading scientists in nanotechnology. Examples of these essentially contested – if also currently stuttering – horizons of hi-tech innovation abound, including synthetic biology, new biotech and GM agriculture (chapters by Rossi; Delfanti; and Harrison et al. respectively), information capitalism (Schiller and Yeo, this volume), smart mobility and smart cities (Tyfield, this volume), geoengineering and the Anthropocene, Artificial Intelligence and nanotechnology. But it is the specific dominant *form* of each of these fields of innovation as sponsored by neoliberalism that is arguably the greatest source of this unease and controversy.

More generally, and returning to the issue of *policy* knowledges, these heightened concerns about R&I's trajectories and their broader effects have underpinned new calls for a 'responsible' R&I (RRI) (Stilgoe et al., 2013). Yet a major lacuna in the current dominant policy framing of RRI is attention to different *political economies* of R&I as a key aspect of its 'responsiveness' to the demands and concerns of a specific relevant public. This is a significant gap since RRI at its best promises to move beyond experiments with 'upstream public engagement' in R&I, which were often desultory exercises in seeking legitimation of policies already settled upon, towards a more concerted involvement of publics in the very constitution of R&I politics (Irwin, 2006). Here, then, PERI not only problematizes current policies and practices of R&I, sponsoring calls for RRI in the first place, but could also assist in its realization.

Yet significant challenges remain for RRI. For instance, confronted with enterprises and institutions of R&I that are increasingly remote from and unaccountable to public scrutiny, this raises difficult questions about what such a politics – as a *democratic* politics – could look like. At the very least, we are once again confronted with the problematic presumption of a central and essentially benign role of *knowledge*: here in terms of the supposedly pivotal role (at least in principle) of reasoned debate, in the public sphere, in a functioning democratic politics as against a pragmatic and power/knowledge relational contestation of actual technoscientific developments. Here, then, we see deepening challenges, increasingly apparent even to 'common sense', to the key ideas that knowledge is always enlightening, and hence the more knowledge is produced and consumed, the better. And this leads to the next issue.

Crises and changes in the consumption, and definition, of knowledge

As 'knowledge' and its production and consumption have become increasingly central to contemporary political economic life, the roles it plays and our relations to it have also demonstrably and noticeably changed. This is progressively changing even the lay public understanding of 'knowledge' – what it is, what it does, its capacities, limits and limitations – in ways that are disintegrating the knowledge economy credo from within, just as the preceding two sections have discussed its assault from without. There are multiple tendencies at work here, and these range across a spectrum of the extent to which they are conceptually challenging to the identification of (more and better) knowledge with a social and personal progressive Enlightenment.

At the least challenging end of this spectrum is the simple dawning realization of the reality of the problems of information overload and the concomitant challenge of superficial skimming and diminishing intervals of concentration and 'deep' thought. Here knowledge – produced in a marketplace of ideas that, via the echo-chamber of social media, privileges self-projection over reflection, speaking and shouting not listening – is increasingly reduced to readily consumable information, or even infotainment, rather than the deepening strategic wisdom arguably necessary to tackle the unprecedented global challenges just discussed. The bountiful quantity of 'knowledge' thus often appears to be directly in inverse proportion to quality: of the knowledge itself, of its material manifestation (in 'innovation'), or of the lives it shapes and (supposedly) enriches (cf. Schiller and Yeo, this volume, on information capitalism).

But such reflections quickly lead on to the growing acknowledgement of the extent to which dominant trajectories of R&I and socio-technical change are shaped – and have been historically, with profound effects on the contours and texture of everyday lives (and around the world) – by forces that are not only isolated from public accountability, but also very difficult even to analyse and trace. Take, for instance, the utter domination of medicines by a small number of highly proprietary transnational corporations. Not only do these companies claim exclusive rights (what Drahos and Braithwaite (2002) call 'intellectual monopoly privileges', not 'intellectual property rights') over key medicines – often developed with significant public investment. But they also assert commercial confidentiality over their data, including the data establishing the efficacy and safety of the drugs. As Sismondo (this volume) documents, the 'science' of clinical trials and medical journal articles are entirely ghost-managed by the pharmaceutical industry.

Similarly, and more high-profile still, is the shaping of ICT and Web 2.0 technologies by deliberately clandestine interventions from corporate and state surveillance, and in the US as much as in a clearly authoritarian regime such as China's (Schiller and Yeo, this volume). Yet this points to an even bigger arena of R&I that is all but impossible to hold up to public scrutiny, even as it is – and has long been (chapters by Thorpe; and Edgerton) – pivotal in the broader co-evolution of techno-science and political systems: the military. New, specifically neoliberal, combinations of these two forces of state (military) and corporate initiatives, however, seem to make these innovation processes even *more* in need of oversight, as in the growing possibility of lethal (micro)drones, cyber-attacks or bio-warfare being first developed and then slipping out of government hands (Langley and Parkinson, this volume). 'Knowledge economies' were not supposed to be so dark.

Yet the current confounding of the given concept of knowledge goes way beyond this too. In particular, sponsored by the 'double truth' regime of neoliberalism and its active cultivation of 'truthiness', a new regime of knowledge production has emerged: agnotology (Oreskes and Conway, 2011; Fernández Pinto, this volume). Here 'knowledge' is deliberately treated as, first and foremost, a tool in political or commercial strategic projects; a device, moreover, whose effectiveness is parasitic upon the 'scientific' status and epistemic (and hence *political*, not least amidst widespread acceptance of the knowledge economy credo) authority of such claims in winning high-stakes contests in the public sphere.

A key element of this process is the production of *ignorance*, and of three kinds:

- as obstacles to (conventional) 'science' that is politically disadvantageous to specific and (R&I-) empowered interests (e.g. quintessentially regarding tobacco, nutrition or climate change);
- its converse of 'science-as-PR', not science-as-truth, where the primary goal of the knowledge work is to secure some credibility for a particular strategic project, not to establish actual knowledge (e.g. as described above regarding medicines); and
- ignorance regarding a systematically unaccountable scientific process (e.g. again, pharmaceuticals).

Indeed, the last of these is crucial and arguably the most self-destructive of the three. For the epistemic authority of science actually reposes upon a foundation of broad-based and generally unquestioned public trust in the (supposedly) open, sceptical and unaligned *process* of its production. We suppose we *can* hold 'science' to account, even if we personally do not do so in every (or perhaps, any) particular instance. A dawning cynicism, if not rejection, regarding that trust thus threatens this key pillar of the elevated political status of knowledge – and killing the host, would destroy the agnotology parasite with it.

A key element of this process is the politicization of science, where this is the unintended consequence of the neoliberal attempt – true to its epistemic and anti-political fundamentalism – to depoliticise *politics* with science. This 'scientification' of politics involves the attempt to minimize the inevitable political challenges to growing governance by the market by transferring the forum of their legitimate contestation: from a restive and unruly public sphere, to 'sound' scientific expertise... which is, in turn, increasingly subject to market discipline (Levidow et al. 2007; see also chapters by Delfanti; Harrison et al.; Johnson and Rampini; Lohmann; Ottinger; Ransom et al.; Rossi). The actual effect of this process, however, has been precisely the opposite, as political controversy has leached in the other direction, ever-deeper into the science itself, as regarding GM agriculture or climate change. To the extent this penetrates to issues that remain essentially undecided and uncertain as being towards the forefront of scientific advance, this also can then pollute and frustrate the whole enterprise since, caught up in political suspicion and recrimination, reasoned argument becomes practically impossible.

Moreover, this process is also observable again regarding policy knowledges. For instance, judgement over such growing public concerns about R&I is increasingly handed to 'expert' ethics committees. As Pellizzoni (this volume) describes, this is in many respects a subversion of a *politics* of knowledge production through 'ethicization' of the research process. This calls on governance by a form of knowledge (i.e. ethics) that may also largely be ignored when confronted with powerful political considerations, perhaps precisely because, agnotologically, it can be dismissed as a suspicious 'expert' judgement. Here, in other words, neoliberalism constructs an imposing castle front, guarding innovation under the banner of 'ethics', while the backdoor is systematically open to precisely those interests currently most empowered and most in need of policing. This process also tragically pits a politics and an ethics of R&I against each other, to the strategic weakness of them both.

Overall, then, in these concerns we see how neoliberalism's extraordinary success regarding the apotheosis of knowledge – where 'knowledge' is specifically conceived, at its weakest, as a commodity and, at its strongest, as itself a market – achieves the exact opposite: a progressive evisceration of the very concept of 'knowledge' as an essential tool and source of human insight and capacity for normatively appealing action and change. Beset by disintegration from within and uncontrollable overspill from without, then, the political economy of R&I – and the twin pillars of the knowledge economy credo – are currently subject to rapid and profound change. But we can no more do without or transcend 'knowledge' than we can voluntaristically repudiate or move beyond 'knowledge societies'.

So where next? Perhaps a key pointer for future directions is to take this question quite literally and look at *where* (globally significant) knowledge production is happening and how this is changing. And changing it undoubtedly is.

Crises and changes in the geography of knowledge

The preceding sections have all revealed conditions of the incumbent regime of knowledge production (and its knowledge economy credo) that it has also systematically denied and destroyed: a vibrant public realm of knowledge production *not* produced in search of immediate profit; R&I directed to significant contemporary social challenges, not just the (re-) fashioning of consumer desires; and a scientific process that is at least *trusted* to be publicly accountable and actively cultivates that trust. What all these have in common is that they highlight and illustrate the irreducibly concrete and located nature of the production of (perhaps, presumptively universal) R&I, just as STS has been showing for some time. A PERI, however, also brings out the key and co-produced political economic aspects of these conditions that STS often neglects.

A key aspect of this locatedness that has received far too little attention to date, however, is the (political, economic) geographies of knowledge. There are obvious reasons that this gap has persisted for so long. These include the evident dominance of R&I – and of *study* of it, in STS – in the Euro-American Global North. For this allows even comparative work across these contexts to take for granted the overwhelming similarity of their political economies, if not their political cultures or 'civic epistemologies' (Jasanoff 2005), as all wealthy, highly techno-economically developed and capitalist. But looking to the future of the political economy of R&I, as both a reality and the work that studies it, it is clear that the geographical aspects will become increasingly central.

There are two primary, and interacting, reasons for this growing importance. On the one hand, that 'evident dominance' just described is progressively eroding, and in two ways. First, with the surge of economic growth, including in R&I, in the Global South (and especially its most massive and populous countries, such as China, India, Brazil, Indonesia etc.) since 2000 (Mason 2015: 94–104), the geographical global centre of R&I and the sites of greatest global influence are shifting demonstrably away from the transatlantic (plus north-east Asian) axis of the 20th century.

Secondly, though, is the ongoing emergence of a qualitatively unprecedented novelty in the continuing construction of a 'global' geography of knowledge, via globalized and globalizing networks (Ernst and Kim, 2002). This plays out through (also currently changing, if specific) forms and processes of globalization and cosmopolitization (Beck et al., 2013; Zhang, 2012) that problematize the crude conception of a 'shift' from 'West' to 'East', 'North' to 'South'. Instead, we see qualitative changes, mediated by compression and distanciation through novel connections, in which, for instance, leading global mega-cities and their R&I clusters and campuses are more closely connected to each other than with the rural or peri-urban and co-national cities in their hinterland. The ongoing emergence of 'global' R&I, therefore, raises *new questions* about the *specific* substantive form it will take, (newly) benefitting and burdening whom, from where and how (e.g. chapters by Pfotenhauer and Jasanoff; Delvenne and Kreimer).

But, on the other hand, the combined effect of the 'Rise of the Rest' (Amsden, 2001) and global integration brings into stark relief the specific political and economic geography presupposed, to date at least, by the success of the neoliberal project over the past few decades. Certainly, there seems little doubt that neoliberalism is an overwhelmingly (Euro-)American project, even as it has (and/or has conditioned) powerful variants around the world. But whether regarding the history of the intellectual-political project behind its formulation (see Nik-Khah, this volume), or its most graphic implementation (e.g. Harvey, 2005), or the political-cultural milieu to which it most directly speaks (as in Jasanoff's (2005) apt characterization of the US as a *Wissenschaftstaat*, a 'science state', the acme product of the 18th-century Enlightenment), or its presupposed power base (of briefly unrivalled global dominance with the 'End of History' in the 1990s) for global roll-out (e.g. Sell, 2003; Harvey, 2005)… all of these are clearly and uniquely American.

Faced with the combined fast-changing geography of knowledge just described, however, we confront a fascinating and unstable conjunction. For, notwithstanding the profound influence of a neoliberal globalization on *domestic* politics across the Global South, including even in 'Communist' China (Harvey, 2005; Nonini, 2008) or neo-Bolivarian Latin America (Burchardt and Dietz, 2014), there remain significant and enduring differences in cultural, political and socio-economic processes, practices and tacit knowledges that underpin and enable political regimes and their co-production with R&I across the world. Again, therefore, this is to raise new and globally significant questions about how these processes will interact: of a changing and emerging *global* geography of knowledge and an incumbent global regime heavily dependent on a *geographically specific* understanding of 'knowledge'.

These questions call for attention across the issues and changes discussed. Hence, on the one hand, greater understanding of the actual trajectories of R&I in China, say – away from the headlines of fear or triumph about China 'ruling' the world or not – is obviously crucial (chapters by Suttmeier; Tyfield; Xu and Ye). But China no more exhausts the emerging global world than the Global North does the passing one. Research is also needed, therefore, on the diverse political economics of R&I elsewhere across the world and their emerging positionality in the global networks of capital, ideas, stuff and people (whether as 'global talent' or 'migrants').

Moreover, amidst deepening global risks, such as climate change, which appear most immediately threatening to hot, 'developing' countries, the extent to which R&I is (or is not) addressing these challenges calls for significant attention to the less spectacular stories than China's in the majority of geographical locations (countries, regions) that have no imminent prospect of global hegemony (chapters by Delvenne and Kreimer; Peloquin; Vessuri). Together, then, a new focus on understanding the changing and unfamiliar role of knowledge in both ascendant (non-Euro-American) global powers and continuing 'subaltern' societies in the global system may furnish the kinds of critical, but also positive and promising, insights regarding the shape of both emergent futures *and* their strategic openings and limitations that are necessary for, and as part of, construction of alternatives.

Conclusion

Forging these positive alternatives is never just intellectual work. Insights, exemplars and new approaches are unquestionably needed, however, and *these* a PERI can, and must, help provide. But which (political economic) perspectives do we use to reach these insights? Responding to the diverse pressures on incumbent understandings about knowledge here discussed, this Handbook presents for the first time a broad collection of the growing body of literature that is constructing a compelling, wide-ranging and synthetic replacement for a mainstream 'economics of science' and an economically uninterested STS.

As the subsequent chapters demonstrate, this is work that not only rigorously and critically exposes misunderstanding and misconceptions about economies of knowledge and their negative societal effects, but also highlights more insightful approaches and more promising and credible initiatives. Indeed, this work is now of sufficient scope, depth, and breadth that it deserves – demands – the concerted attention of all scholars, policymakers and stakeholders concerned with the roles of research and innovation in future societies.

Yet this work is definitely *not* unified by a single approach. There *is* no single definitive way to conduct a political economy of R&I, just as there is, in reality and in principle, no single 'economics of science'. Instead, multiple approaches and perspectives are used, including diverse disciplinary and geographically located lenses, and even many conceptions of 'political economy' itself, in a varied and vital ecology of contending heterodoxy: Marxian, post-Keynesian, Schumpeterian, World Systems Theory, Foucauldian, Institutionalist, Evolutionary, etc. ...

The pioneering PERI work presented here thus draws upon a wide array of disciplines including: history of economic thought and economic philosophy; (international) political economy; economic sociology; science and technology studies; economic geography; innovation studies; economic history; (international) law; and social scientific studies of specific scientific-technological fields such as medicine, agriculture, environment, education, energy and mobility.

Across all these, however, is convergence on calls for a research agenda that seeks to broaden current understanding of the 'economics of science' in at least four directions, as an empirical project that:

1 on the one hand, demands attention to the concrete sociotechnical diversity of particular *knowledge practices* and in particular *places*, hence engendering analysis of a political and economic geography of R&I against the tendency to evoke a generic 'science' and a single 'economics of science';
2 while, on the other, embeds analysis of the quantitative and qualitative contributions of R&I within a (possibly global) analysis of socio-technical *systems* and their transformation.

And where such a systemic analysis must also include two dimensions usually overlooked by purely economistic analysis, namely:

3 attention to the irreducible *political* economic dimensions of funding scientific research and its relation to regimes of capital accumulation; and
4 incorporation of the *cultural and discursive* dimensions of such policies, including the power of (some) visions and future imaginaries to shape the trajectories of both science funding and research itself (as in a 'cultural' political economy (Jessop & Sum, 2006; Best and Paterson, 2008)).

These four demands shape the following chapters. And we hope they will also stimulate a new generation of PERI work making formative contributions towards articulating and instantiating positive visions of better 'knowledge economies'.

Note

1 What 'knowledge' is and what are its relevance and roles regarding good government are historical questions that change with changing social context. As Mirowski and Sent (2008) show, for instance, the neoliberal period with its 'globalized privatization regime' for R&I was preceded by a post-Second World War common sense in which knowledge was considered a public good best secured through generous state financing; and before that as an unownable body of truths best produced by disinterested private gentlemen.

References

Amsden, A. 2001. *The Rise of the Rest: Challenges to the West from Late-Industrializing Economies*. Oxford: Oxford University Press.
Beams, N. 2016. "A Dangerous Turn to Economic Nationalism", *World Socialist Web Site*, July 12, available at: www.wsws.org/en/articles/2016/07/12/pers-j12.html.
Beck, U., Blok, A., Tyfield, D. and Zhang, J.Y. 2013. "Cosmopolitan Communities of Climate Risk: Conceptual & Empirical Suggestions for a New Research Agenda". *Global Networks*, 13(1): 1–21.
Bernal, J. D. 1939. *The Social Function of Science*. London: Routledge.
Best, J. and Paterson, M. (eds) 2008. *Cultural Political Economy*, London: Routledge.

Birch, K. and Mykhnenko, V. (eds) 2010. *The Rise and Fall of Neoliberalism: The Collapse of an Economic Order?* London: Zed Books.

Birch, K., Levidow, L. and Papaioannou, T. 2010. "Sustainable Capital? The Neoliberalization of Nature and Knowledge in the European 'Knowledge-Based Bio-Economy'". *Sustainability*, 2: 2898–2918.

Block, F. 2008. "Swimming Against the Current: The Rise of a Hidden Developmental State in the United States" *Politics & Society*, 36(2): 169–206.

Bowring, F. 1999. "Job Scarcity: The Perverted Form of a Potential Blessing". *Sociology*, 33(1): 69–84.

Brown, W. 2015. *Undoing the Demos: Neoliberalism's Stealth Revolution*. Cambridge, MA: MIT Press.

Burchardt, H.-J. and Dietz, K. 2014. "(Neo-)extractivism – A New Challenge for Development Theory in Latin America". *Third World Quarterly*, 35(3): 468–486.

Clark, B., Foster, J.B. and York R. 2009. "Capitalism in Wonderland". *Monthly Review* 61(1) (May), available at: http://monthlyreview.org/2009/05/01/capitalism-in-wonderland/.

Cooper, M. 2008. *Life as Surplus: Biotechnology and Capitalism in the Neoliberal Era*. Seattle: University of Washington Press.

Crouch, C. 2011. *The Strange Non-Death of Neoliberalism*. Cambridge: Polity.

Delborne, J. 2008. "Transgenes and Transgressions: Scientific Dissent as Heterogeneous Practice". *Social Studies of Science*, 38(4): 509–541.

Delborne, J. and Kinchy, A.J. 2008. "Genetically Modified Organisms", in Restivo, S. and Denton, P.H. (eds). *Battleground Science and Technology*, Westport, CT: Greenwood Press: 182–195.

Drahos, P. and Braithwaite, J. 2002. *Information Feudalism: Who Owns the Knowledge Economy?* London: Earthscan.

Elliott, L. 2016. "Brexit is a Rejection of Globalisation". *The Guardian*, June 26, available at: www.theguardian.com/business/2016/jun/26/brexit-is-the-rejection-of-globalisation.

Ernst, D. and Kim, L. 2002. "Global Production Networks, Knowledge Diffusion, and Local Capability Formation". *Research Policy*, 31(8–9): 1417–1429.

Fisher, E. 2017. [forthcoming] *Sociology of the Sciences Yearbook*.

Godin, B. 2006. "The Knowledge-Based Economy: Conceptual Framework or Buzzword?" *Journal of Technology Transfer*, 31: 17–30.

Harris, J. 2016. "If You've Got Money, You Vote In... If You Haven't Got Money, You Vote Out", *The Guardian*, June 24, available at: www.theguardian.com/politics/commentisfree/ 2016/jun/24/divided-britain-brexit-money-class-inequality-westminster.

Harvey, D. 2005. *A Brief History of Neoliberalism*. Oxford: Oxford University Press.

Heller, M. and Eisenberg, R. 1998. "Can Patents Deter Innovation? The Anti-Commons in Biomedical Research". *Science*, 280: 698–701.

Hilsenrath, J. and Davis, B. 2016. "Election 2016 is Propelled by the American Economy's Failed Promises". *Wall Street Journal*, July 7, available at: www.wsj.com/articles/election-2016-is-propelled-by-the-american-economys-failed-promises-1467909580.

Irwin, A. 2006. "The Politics of Talk: Coming to Terms with the 'New' Scientific Governance". *Social Studies of Science*, 36(2): 299–320.

Jasanoff, S. ed., 2004. *States of Knowledge: The Co-Production of Science and the Social Order*. London: Routledge.

Jasanoff, S. 2005. *Designs on Nature*. Princeton: Princeton University Press.

Jessop, B. and Sum, N.L. 2006. *Beyond the Regulation Approach: Putting Capitalist Economies in their Place*. Cheltenham: Edward Elgar.

Kelly, K. 1997. "New Rules for the New Economy". *Wired*, January 9, available at www.wired.com/1997/09/newrules/.

Kinchy, Abby. 2012. *Seeds, Science, and Struggle: The Global Politics of Transgenic Crops*. Cambridge, MA: MIT Press.

Klein, H.K. and Kleinman, D.L. 2002. "The Social Construction of Technology: Structural Considerations". *Science, Technology, & Human Values*, 27(1): 28–52.

Kleinman, D.L. 2003. *Impure Cultures: University Biology and the World of Commerce*. Madison: University of Wisconsin Press.

Kloppenburg, J.R. 1988. *First the Seed: The Political Economy of Plant Biotechnology*. 2nd ed. Cambridge: Cambridge University Press.

Lave, R., Mirowski, P. and Randalls, S. 2010. "Introduction: STS and Neoliberal Science". *Social Studies of Science*, 40(5): 659–675.

Lazonick, W. 2014. "Profits without Prosperity". *Harvard Business Review*, 92(9), 46–55.

Leadbeater, C. 1999. *Living on Thin Air: The New Economy*. New York: Viking.

Levidow, L. and Young, R. 1981. *Science, Technology and the Labour Process: Marxist Studies*. London: Humanities Press.

Levidow, L., Murphy, J. and Carr, S. 2007. "Recasting 'Substantial Equivalence': Transatlantic Governance of GM Food". *Science, Technology & Human Values*, 32: 26–64.

Lynch, W.T. and Fuhrman, E. 1991. "Recovering and Expanding the Normative: Marx and the New Sociology of Scientific Knowledge". *Science, Technology, & Human Values* 16(2): 233–248.

Lynch, W.T. and Fuhrman, E. 1992. "Ethnomethodology as Technocratic Ideology: Policing Epistemic Boundaries". *Science, Technology, & Human Values*, 17(2): 234–36.

Marris, C. 2015. "The Construction of Imaginaries of the Public as a Threat to Synthetic Biology". *Science as Culture*, 24(1): 83–98.

Mason, P. 2015. *Post-Capitalism*. London: Allen Lane.

Mirowski, P. 2009. "Postface: Defining Neoliberalism", in Mirowski, P. and Plehwe, D., eds. *The Road from Mont Pelerin: The Making of the Neo-Liberal Thought Collective*. Cambridge, MA: Harvard University Press: 417–456.

Mirowski, P. 2011. *Science-Mart: Privatizing American Science*. Cambridge, MA: Harvard University Press.

Mirowski, P. 2012. "The Modern Commercialization of Science is a Passel of Ponzi Schemes". *Social Epistemology*, 26(3/4): 285–310.

Mirowski, P. 2014. *Never Let a Serious Crisis Go to Waste: How Neoliberalism Survived the Financial Meltdown*. London: Verso.

Mirowski, P. and Plehwe, D. eds. 2009. *The Road from Mont Pelerin: The Making of the Neo-Liberal Thought Collective*. Cambridge, MA: Harvard University Press.

Mirowski, P. and Sent, E.-M. 2008. "The Commercialization of Science and the Response of STS", in Hackett, E., Wacjman, J., Amsterdamska, O., and Lynch, M., eds. *The Handbook of Science and Technology Studies*. Cambridge, MA: MIT Press: 635–90.

Nik-Khah, E. 2014. "Neoliberal Pharmaceutical Science and the Chicago School of Economics". *Social Studies of Science*, 44(4): 489–517.

Nonini, D. M. 2008. "Is China becoming neoliberal?" *Critique of Anthropology*, 28(2), 145–176.

Ong, A. 2006. *Neoliberalism as Exception: Mutations in Citizenship and Sovereignty*. Durham, NC: Duke University Press.

Oreskes, N. and Conway, E. M. 2011. *Merchants of Doubt*. New York: Bloomsbury Publishing USA.

Pagano, U. and Rossi, M.A. 2009. "The Crash of the Knowledge Economy". *Cambridge Journal of Economics*, 33: 665–683.

Peck, J. 2010. *Constructions of Neoliberal Reason*. Oxford: Oxford University Press.

Peck, J. and Tickell. A. 2002. "Neoliberalizing Space". *Antipode*, 34(3): 380–404.

Rockström J. *et al.* 2009. "A Safe Operating Space for Humanity". *Nature*, 461(7263): 472–475.

Rose, H. and Rose, S. eds. 1976. *The Political Economy of Science: Ideology of/in the Natural Sciences*. London: Macmillan.

Sell, S. 2003. *Private Power, Public Law: The Globalization of Intellectual Property Rights*. Cambridge: Cambridge University Press.

Shapin, S. and Schaffer, S. 1985. *Leviathan and the Air Pump: Hobbes, Boyle, and the Experimental Life*. Princeton, NJ: Princeton University Press.

Springer, S., Birch, K. and MacLeavy, J. eds. 2016. *The Routledge Handbook of Neoliberalism*. London and New York: Routledge.

Stedman Jones, D. 2014. *Masters of the Universe: Hayek, Friedman, and the Birth of Neoliberal Politics*. Princeton University Press.

Stilgoe, J., Owen, R. and Macnaghten, P. 2013. "Developing a Framework of Responsible Innovation". *Research Policy*, 42(9): 1568–1580.

Thorpe, C. 2010. "Participation as Post-Fordist Politics: Demos, New Labour, and Science Policy". *Minerva*, 48(4): 389–411.

Thorpe, Charles. 2013. "Artificial Life on a Dead Planet", in Gates, K. ed., *The International Encyclopedia of Media Studies, Volume VI: Media Studies Futures*. Chichester, West Sussex: Wiley-Blackwell: 615–647.

Thorpe, C. 2016. *Necroculture*. London: Palgrave Macmillan.

Thorpe, C. and Gregory, J. 2010. "Producing the Post-Fordist Public: The Political Economy of Public Engagement with Science". *Science as Culture*, 19(3): 273–301.

Tyfield, D. 2012a. *The Economics of Science: A Critical Realist Overview. Volume 1: Illustrations and Philosophical Preliminaries*. Abingdon and New York: Routledge.

Tyfield, D. 2012b. *The Economics of Science: A Critical Realist Overview. Volume 2: Towards a Synthesis of Political Economy and Science and Technology Studies.* Abingdon and New York: Routledge.

Tyfield, D. 2012c. "A Cultural Political Economy of Research and Innovation in an Age of Crisis". *Minerva*, 50(2): 149–167.

Tyfield, D. 2013. "Transition to Science 2.0: 'Remoralizing' the Economy of Science". *Spontaneous Generations*, Special Issue on "The Economics of Science", September.

Tyfield, D. 2016. "Science, Innovation and Neoliberalism", in Springer, S., Birch, K. and MacLeavy, J. eds., *The Handbook of Neoliberalism.* London: Routledge.

Walker, J. 2016. "The Creation to Come: Pre-Empting the Evolution of the Bioeconomy", in Marshall, J.P. and Connor, L.H. eds., *Environmental Change and the World's Future: Ecologies, Ontologies and Mythologies.* Abingdon: Routledge: 264–281.

Welsh, I. and Wynne, B. 2013. "Science, Scientism and Imaginaries of Publics in the UK: Passive Objects, Incipient Threats". *Science as Culture*, 22(4): 540–566.

Winner, L. 1993. "Upon Opening the Black Box and Finding It Empty: Social Constructivism and the Philosophy of Technology". *Science, Technology, & Human Values*, 18(3): 362–378.

York, R. and Rosa, E.A. 2003. "Key Challenges to Ecological Modernization Theory: Institutional Efficacy, Case Study Evidence, Units of Analysis, and the Pace of Eco-Efficiency". *Organization & Environment*, 16(3): 273–280.

Zeller, C. 2008. "From the gene to the globe: Extracting rents based on intellectual property monopolies". *Review of International Political Economy*, 15(1): 86–115.

Zhang, J. 2012. *The Cosmopolitanization of Science: Stem Cell Governance in China.* Basingstoke: Palgrave Macmillan.

PART I

From the 'economics of science' to the 'political economy of research and innovation'

1

THE POLITICAL ECONOMY OF SCIENCE

Prospects and retrospects

David Edgerton[1]

The most common higher discourse around science has been a philosophical and moral one. Science and Technology Studies (STS) has measured itself against this, and more generally against what it takes as public and elite misunderstanding of science, including particular sorts of claims for the economic centrality of science. While its evaluative and normative framework has been very different from those it criticises, there is a shared understanding of what counts. STS, for all its critical positioning, can and does amplify, rather than displace, all sort of claims for the centrality of this or that form of knowledge, or this or that account of the various industrial and scientific revolutions; it can and does incorporate many unhelpful assumptions about science, and about the economy. For example, much of STS, while dismissive of a strange construct called the 'linear model of innovation' in fact relies on what appear to be key assumptions of this supposedly discredited concept (Edgerton 2004). As Thomas (2015) has rightly insisted, STS and history of science need to abandon the entrenched notion of the backwardness of scientists' and lay understandings of science and society, which has become so central to its identity, and adopt a less triumphalist view of its own understanding of these complex matters. It is in this light that a political economic approach based on empirical understanding of actually existing science, I believe, has the *potential* to remap radically what we understand as scientific knowledge, research and innovation, offering a profound challenge not merely to the conventional discourses but to STS itself (Edgerton 2004, 2010, 2012).

Actually existing political economy of science is far from ready and waiting to transform our understanding. Since the 1980s, as Philip Mirowski notes with appropriate acidity, an economics of knowledge has made its appearance, but it simply did not work (Mirowski 2007). He held that 'the postwar triad of linear model/public good/growth theory is a badly flawed and expendable set of concepts to structure inquiry into the economics of science. No such simplistic macroeconomic statements concerning science and economic growth have been found to hold water, and they certainly do nothing to explicate contemporary shifts in the use of knowledge as leverage in a globalized economy.' (Miroski, 2007, p. 492). We need, he suggests, a critique of actually existing (political) economics of science. I very much agree. Yet I also think that critical new approaches to the political economy of science, including Mirowski's, in part rely on images of what 'science' is that are themselves inappropriate.

An older tradition of critical political economy of science got at the central issue, though with limited influence. For example, in 1976, Hilary and Steven Rose published an essay with the title 'The Incorporation of Science' in an edited collection called *The Political Economy of Science* (Rose and Rose, 1976).[2] Here 'political economy' stood for asking what 'science' was for. They argued that, since more than 75 per cent of R&D (research and development) expenditures were directed towards production and social control, science was 'industrialised'. Taking science to be something 'such as molecular biology or, possibly, high-energy physics' resulted, they argued, in seriously misunderstanding the 'nature of the production of scientific knowledge' (Rose and Rose, 1976: 14–15). They complained that the history and philosophy of science and sociology of science studied only academic elites, that the outputs of science policy studies were useless, that the 'fundamental character of science and technology in their social functions was lost to sight' (Rose and Rose, 1976: 21). Their critique is still valid today, with these same particular parts still standing for a misunderstood whole in both STS and political economy of science. A realistic political economy of all research, in its many guises, will require not only a transformation in STS (Mirowski, this volume) but also of most existing political economies of science.

Past political economies

STS has a pre-history in writings on science which reflect particular political economic positions. Political economy is a standard form of analysis of the world, of great ideological and material import. The political economic form of analysis was also applied to knowledge, and knowledge creation, and to science. These analyses often presented themselves as if they were the products of 'science' rather than political economy, and they have been interpreted as such. But to understand the work of J. D. Bernal, for example, it is crucial to understand that it is not primarily scientist or technocratic (though it is powerfully so), but Marxist. It takes very particular positions on monopoly capital, war and imperialism, which are central to its analysis, and it also wishes to challenge – and this is central – an idealist philosophy stressing the purity of scientific knowledge. It thus pioneered mapping where the money for research was going, making clear just how much was going to the military (though he severely underestimated the role of British capitalist industry). At an intellectual level, post-war 'history and philosophy of science' was significantly a counter to this emergent quasi-discipline of 'history and political economy of science', quickly dooming it to the reduced status of a mere 'externalism' (Shapin 1992; Werskey 2007). But what made it of intellectual interest, and drove much of the criticism, was not its externalism, or its scientism, but its Marxism.

Marxism was not the only political economy of science in play in the 1930s or 1940s. In contention was the emergent Austrian *critique* of Marxism and planning, and thus holism and scientism, closely linked, through ideas and persons, to the philosophy of science of Michael Polanyi, and a set of ideas around innovation promoted by the economist John Jewkes (Edgerton and Hughes 1989; Reinisch 2000; Thorpe 2009). This has proved to be a rather hidden set of influences on STS. While Polanyi's ideas of tacit knowledge were of great importance in STS from the 1980s, Austrian economics was not. The rich critical commentary of Jewkes on invention is, for example, not part of the received wisdom of STS (Giffard 2016).

Much more significant than either Marxist or Austrian accounts, however, were those accounts of science which reproduced the most banal and ideological versions of liberal political economy. Thus it was, for instance, that various wonders of science like the aeroplane and the radio supposedly shrunk the world and brought about world peace (Zaidi 2011a, 2011b), as indeed the internet continues to do so to this day. In the field of science policy studies, and broader reflections on the place of science in national life, another sort of political economy held sway. Nationalist political economy, with no famous name associated with it since the nineteenth-century German Friedrich List, has been profoundly influential in discussions of science though this is barely recognised within STS. In assuming the centrality of national-level interconnections between science and the economy, it has shaped most analyses of science and economic growth. In the British case, national political economies of science have been central to declinism, the doctrine that the British economy has done relatively badly because of particular national failures. A central supposed failure has been in-state support for the right kind of research, due to the dominance of the wrong kind of elite (Edgerton 1996; Thomas 2015). Such writing dominated accounts of twentieth-century British science until recently.

There was a revival of Marxism in the late 1960s and 1970s which was much less political economic than 1930s Marxism, yet did lead to important studies of production from the labour process perspective and thinking of the labour process in research and knowledge creation more generally (Levidow 1981). This was also the era of rich work on scientific management, higher technical education and industrial research, and how they related to capitalism (Noble 1979). The new academic departments of Science Studies, Liberal Studies in Science, History and Sociology of Science, and Science and Technology Policy (thinking just about British cases) of the period had a powerful strand of political economy within them, though it has since been written out of standard readings of the history of STS. The study of technology in development and industrial research, technologies of political control, industrial hazards and the like were the bread and butter of analysis in that politicised era (Werksey 2007). But perhaps such studies also placed far too much emphasis on science and technology, especially in regard to the heavily hyped technologies of the day, as the means through which capitalism worked, ignoring many other obvious factors such as the liberalisation of markets and increased control of labour by other means.

In the more recent past, 'political economy of science' has been a label adopted by workers at the Science Policy Research Unit in Sussex to describe their own non-neoclassical economics of innovation (e.g. Clark 1985; Martin and Nightingale 2000), a rather odd technocratic variant of Schumpeter's distinctively Austrian approach. On the other hand, 'political economy of science' can mean the application of neo-classical economics to the issue of science policy (David 1990). As will become clear below, I am very critical of both these traditions, even more so than is Tyfield (2012b). There are thus a series of actually existing political economies of science, as well as economies of science, which need to be reckoned with, though most are not prominent in accounts of STS and its development.

Tools and names

The category 'research and development' emerged during and after the Second World War as a way of bringing together what had previously been discussed in somewhat separate realms, though had long been conjoined in practice: the development and design done in the design department, the testing station and the pilot plant, on the one hand and, on the other, research in industrial research laboratories, and government and academic research laboratories. Yet 'development' was still what was really expensive, so the category would have been more usefully called 'development and research'. That would have helped avoid the standard narrative focusing on 'research' and on the shift from individual inventor to 'research laboratory', and the tendency to see the pre-history of R&D only in research and not in the separate and larger realm of design and development (Edgerton 2007; Giffard 2016). Such accounts focused on the research laboratory are unable to deal with some of the most important innovations of the twentieth century as recent work shows, for example the jet engine: a new account is needed of the history and historiography of invention and innovation, as has been provided by Giffard (2016).

The collection of national statistics on R&D and patents on a standardised basis since the 1960s has made these an important focus of the policy discourse. There are poorly recognised dangers in using these figures. National expenditures are usually divided by GDP, to make them seem internationally comparative. But there is no good analytical reason for this procedure. What it reveals is a belief – and no more than that – that a greater share of GDP devoted to R&D is likely to lead to greater innovation. That is not so – absolute expenditures matter, and so of course does duplication, but it is not to be assumed that these issues are avoided either by using absolutes or dividing by GDP. Patents and patent counts are even more problematic, and should not be used (though often are) for turning (varying) legal tests of novelty into measures of technical worth. While treated as measures of success, it is more instructive to see patent records as archives of *failure*, since the overwhelming majority are never exploited.

There are also great systematic problems with the terms 'science' and 'technology'. The first is used in ways which vary from a system of knowledge, to very particular kinds of research activity (usually in the academy), but the latter often stands for the former. 'Science' is distinguished from 'technology' which itself ranges in meaning from 'all technique', to the more usual, latest digital gizmo (now often even abbreviated just to 'tech'). Generally, both are today associated with 'innovation', a term which means anything from a change, even an imitative one, to the application of a major invention. So serious are the category errors these terms facilitate that some of us have suggested avoiding using these terms altogether (Edgerton 2010), and sticking to terms like 'scientific knowledge' or, better, biology or chemistry or whatever applies, and to use 'research' or say 'chemical research' when that is what is meant. 'Technology' can be easily avoided altogether, as it effectively was before the 1940s in Britain (before then 'technology' was the name given to the higher study of certain kinds of things) (Schatzberg 2006) – we have many words for machines and techniques, and many words for novelties too. Category errors concerning 'science' and 'technology' have led to systematically misleading accounts of policy initiatives and principles, for example the belief that policy elites were beholden to the linear model, that the NSF was the key agency for funding research in the USA, or that invented principles like the 'Haldane principle' in the British case governed state research policy.

Why does this matter? Well, because STS has tended to take as its subject matter a very particular narrow definition of 'science', as if it were the whole. Thus it can tell stories of science coming under the sway of economic forces through neo-liberal science policies (cf chapters by e.g. Nik-Khah; Lazonick et al.; Tyfield; Lave and Robertson; Lohmann; Randalls; Fernández Pinto); or science being reduced to technology in policy terms (nanotechnology, biotechnology, information technology) in the recent past. Thus Mirowski subtitles his book *Privatizing American Science* (Mirowski 2011), and Tyfield asks 'How should we respond to the increasing privatisation of scientific knowledge production and the academy more generally?' (Tyfield 2012b, Preface). The literature is replete with condemnatory references to 'commodification', 'impurity', and so on. All this, compounded when reference is made to 'neo-liberalism', suggests that the once public science is now being turned private, commercial, impure. Yet taking a broader definition of research, one more appropriate indeed to a concern with innovation and impact, the base reality is that the great bulk of even research science has always been under industry and government working to order; science has long been private. In the twentieth century, most research in science has been quite unproblematically conducted in the search for profit, production, or military security (see chapters by Thorpe; Langley and Parkinson), except in the writings of intellectuals (Shapin 2008; Edgerton 2004, Edgerton 2012).

It is striking too how much STS-inspired policy work assumes that the appropriate site of intervention is the university research, the province of the NSF, or in Britain the 'science base', in other words, what comes under 'science policy'. 'Upstream' is where 'engagement' to pursue 'responsible innovation' should take place (Stilgoe and Macnaghten, this volume). There is no suggestion in this work of intervening in the board-level decisions of firms, or the procurement divisions of the armed services, where concepts like 'upstream', or 'public engagement', or 'science policy' make little sense. These concepts, like 'privatisation' of science, only make sense if the focus is something like public academic research and if one believes that academic research is the main determinant of what happens downstream, that is, if one assumes the 'linear model'. For example, Tyfield (2012a) tellingly sees science and (civilian) science policy of states as being very similar things, a standard view.

Of course, I have no objection to the study of the nature and impact of academic research, or even limited parts of that effort. But they must be labelled as such and properly contextualised with the history and sociology of the university, and their limited scope within a broader account noted. What is not appropriate is the systematic, long-standing conflation of science, meant broadly, with publicly funded academic research, usually in some fields only (as the Roses noted). Academic research is not a part which can stand for the whole. Recognising this has serious implications. It means abandoning notions like an implied singular 'science policy' or discussions of the character of relations of 'science and society' or 'science and the state'. Such concepts ignore or misrepresent most forms of knowledge and research we might want to call science, and all the relevant relations with state and society, for example, research in industry or government laboratories, the role of advisers and executives who are not academics and so on. We need to recognise, in short, that such terms as 'science policy' are far from neutral and profoundly limiting.

The linear model of innovation

The 'linear model of innovation' provides another example of a term of art in STS which needs critical examination. The linear model of innovation was a term, and concept, invented in 1969, as something to be attacked, and has remained this ever since, though it has been popular only since the 1980s (Edgerton 2004). It is taken to be a false, but hugely influential view, which dominated 'science policy' from the 1940s, the argument that policy was driven by scientists who believed that investing in pure research was the way to stimulate innovation. This view is seen by STS as involving a dangerously naive and misleading account of science. And so it is. But the problem is that 'the linear model' is not something which any serious analyst of innovation ever put forward positively as general model of innovation. This is not to say that arguments that look a bit like what is very loosely taken to be the linear model were not commonplace, for such arguments were after all a standard propagandist claim for 'science', used not just by academic scientists but many other commentators too. So common was it indeed that serious studies long ago made a point of noting that it was wrong to think of innovation coming only or mainly from 'science', that indeed the linear model is wrong. Indeed, this is how the term arose. The linear model is an invention of STS: it was something analysts of innovation convinced themselves their predecessors believed in, not the actual practice of innovation in the past, or ideas about innovation from the past.

Despite impassioned belief to the contrary 'the linear model' did not in fact dominate policy for innovation – that was driven above all by mission-oriented projects, the opposite of 'linear model' thinking. Examples might be the Manhattan Project (Thorpe, this volume) and most subsequent nuclear development, though much historical work turns the story into a linear model one, starting with theoretical physics, and dribbling down to the factories and the United States Army Air Forces (USAAF) at the end. Indeed the 'linear model' is not even to be found where it is supposed to have been enshrined, not least by historians, for example in Vannevar Bush's *The Endless Frontier*. Taking the full range of research programmes supported by both government and industry, looking seriously at the rationale and organisation of such projects, in itself makes a nonsense of any idea of the linear model as a universal policy for research or innovation. It is only by looking, naively, at only 'science policy', that is university research policy, that one might come to claim its centrality.

Something like the linear model did exist in the *practice* of history of science and STS (despite its protestations against the *ideology* of the linear model among historical actors). History of science and STS defined 'science policy' in a very narrow, academic way and assumed that was where the key decisions were made and then wrote histories structured on linear model lines, for example by focusing the history of the atomic bomb on theoretical physicists (Edgerton 2004). STS assumed that the naive propagandistic pronouncements of pure academic scientists were what mattered, and trickled down to the rest. In other words, it is STS which grants far too much power to academic pure research, to the ideology of the academics, and refuses, it seems, to look at where innovation is actually happening, how it is happening, and how it is thought about by actual practitioners. This is not very clear because, of course, STS says the linear model is wrong to the point of stupidity, yet it is itself trapped within it, endlessly criticising a figment of its own imagination.

Some analysts believe that there was a linear model in the thinking of economists (Godin 2006; Mirowski 2011: 52, 357). For example, Mirowski is right to point to growth accounting and public goods models in this context since these have made assumptions which look like the linear model, or are in what are taken to be linear models. But that is not the same as finding historical actors who have put forward, with evidence and reasoned argument, the belief that say R&D is the main source of economic growth. Mirowski also uses the term 'linear model' to imply a belief in the importance of 'pure' research, and a separate notion that this should be state funded (Mirowski 2011: 50–5). I agree with Mirowski that there is a serious lack of understanding of the realities of innovation among economists, for many different reasons, and agree with his critical comment that the new evolutionary economics of science is concerned to save the false assumptions of economists on these matters (Mirowski 2011, 78). But I don't believe calling some or all the linear model helps explain what is wrong with these assumptions. We need to understand these assumptions in detail, not because they are stupid (as in calling them the 'linear model', which we know from the get-go is the acme of ignorance) but because they are powerful and deeply embedded in the work of highly intelligent and respected STS practitioners. We need to move away from criticising invented composites of ignorance (the same applies to 'technological determinism' and 'Whig history') and instead examine specific arguments, which often turn out to be much richer than we allow, for example in the work of economists like Jacob Schmookler, Charles Carter, Bruce Williams, John Jewkes, and Christopher Freeman, to take only those active in the 1950s and 1960s.

Free riders, long-waves, GPTs and national systems of innovation

Economists of innovation and science, as Mirowski has observed, have got a lot wrong. In this section I set out some specific criticism of their approaches to particular important issues. Let us start with rationales for the state support of science. States have supported research, scientific education, and invention for a very long time. They did so without the benefit of an economic theory to support it. In fact, for the UK and USA, state funding of R&D as a percentage of

GDP started falling at the very moment economic theories appeared that purported to justify fractions of this expenditure. Arrow and Nelson developed an argument for the state support of research (Nelson 1959; Arrow 1962; Hounshell 1997, 2000). They argued that the state should support pure research, which was available to all, because this very quality meant that no one would support it. That is, there was a market failure, which would be overcome by state action. The free-rider argument was in fact far removed from any empirical reality even in its own terms. It assumed a one-state model; in a world of many states, states faced exactly the same free-rider problem. Still, it was to prove an influential formulation in the 1980s – a hard-nosed economically liberal rationale for state support. Indeed, later it perhaps helped delegitimise the state support of anything but pure science – hence, for example, the privatisation of, and more importantly, cuts in, much government 'near-market' research in Britain in the 1980s (Edgerton and Hughes 1989). But it was a theory which did not, could not, examine or explain the great bulk of state support of R&D.

One argument associated with economics of innovation since the 1970s (when it was reintroduced by the Marxist economist Ernest Mandel) has been that of innovative activity being concentrated in bursts every 50 or so years, leading to long waves of cycles of growth. Each wave was typically associated with around three new technologies. The evidence for both concentration of innovation and wave effects due to the diffusion of these particular innovations was in fact non-existent, yet the model was widely reproduced (for critiques see Rosenberg and Frischtak 1984; Edgerton 2006). A reduced version of the model became popular among economists in the form of the idea of 'General Purpose Technologies', of which there were essentially three: steam, electricity and ICT, each of which, it was argued, were associated with revolutionary, general transformations in productivity, though over long periods (David 1990). The general argument has been criticised (Field 2011; Edgerton 2006), and the evidence for steam and electricity, and indeed IT, being found to be non-existent or very weak (Crafts 2004; Ristuccia and Solomou 2014).

Long-waves and GPTs have also been associated with particular nation states as is clear in Freeman (1987). In each particular historical period, it was argued, the radical technologies were associated with nation states (e.g. Germany with the 'second Industrial Revolution'). Such ideas lay behind the notion of national systems of innovation, popular from the 1980s (for example, Lundvall 1992). Such an emphasis demonstrates that it is perhaps nationalist political economy that has been the most influential political economy of science. This may seem odd given the emphasis on the global and globalising nature of science and technology, and it is perhaps this very fact which keeps this deep nationalism from being noted. The scientific nationalism of the nineteenth-century German political economist Friedrich List has in practice been much more important as a political economic justification for state-funded research than the economics of Arrow or Nelson (Edgerton 2006, 2007b).

A thoroughgoing global approach to science would stress that national economic or indeed linguistic barriers have not impeded the movement of people, inventions or ideas. It would assert that, with rare exceptions, most nations would get most of their new ideas, practices, and techniques from abroad. That is, the stock of inventions and knowledge is essentially global. The rate of development of an economy would then be determined (making many assumptions) by the rate of accessing this global pool. It might well mean that those with most to learn will grow fastest, those who already use most of what is known the slowest.

This model accounts for the key stylised facts of economic development for rich countries: the convergence of economies as a result of some of the poorer nations growing faster than rich ones even as we may assume that rich nations invent more than poorer ones. Indeed, this points to a correlation well-attested by inspection of measures of invention and growth rates:

that the more a nation spends on R&D as a proportion of GDP (itself usually correlated with the level of socioeconomic development), the lower its rate of growth (Williams 1967; Edgerton 1996; Kealey 1996). The Williams–Edgerton–Kealey inverse correlation at national level should be the most elementary stylised fact in the political economy of science; instead it is at best an elementary dirty secret, certainly not one to be found in the standard handbooks (e.g. Fagerberg, Mowery and Nelson 2005; Hall and Rosenberg 2010). The relations of economic growth and R&D are treated as if the nation were the world in microcosm, a serious error (Edgerton 2007b). We find the assumption (some might want to call it a linear model) widespread in both historical, STS and policy literature, that the more a nation invents, all other things being equal, the faster it will grow; it is assumed to be a causal relationship, backed by evidence. Thus, analysts wondered why high R&D spending nations (for example, Steil, Victor and Nelson (2002)) – say, the USA or the UK in the 1960s and Japan in the 1990s – had low rates of growth! But they did not wonder, in this context, why poorer nations, with practically no R&D, grew very much faster (on the interesting case of China, see Suttmeier, this volume). Indeed, one needs to be sceptical of claims that even at the global level more R&D leads to more growth: that is not the experience of the last 40 years (Jones 1995a, 1995b). This does not of course mean that, especially for the richest countries, R&D does not cause growth at all, or that it is not necessary for growth, but it is to point out the fallacy of the orthodox nationalist belief in national R&D being the main cause of national growth.

Actual political economies of research

Studies of what the objects and context for research policy have been are few and far between but have been illuminating. For example, for the British case, historians looking at the era of liberal free trade have pointed to the use of research as a form of masterly inactivity by government – research was a cheap alternative to policies which would change things (Palladino 1990, 1996; Clarke 2010). Under autarchic regimes research was typically well-funded as a means of promoting national industries and agricultures (HSNS 2010; Camprubi 2015). We are also developing a sense of changes over time (Horrocks 2007). Research on firms is less well developed – what were the actual research policies of firms should not be assumed, as is clear from important work showing that patent-blocking research strategies were sometimes important (Reich 1977). What were the policies of plant breeders – in whose interests did they work (Harwood 2012)? The green revolution – the central case of science for the poor in the Cold War – was not mainly due, to the extent it happened at all, to new varieties but to new ways of obtaining and organising the supply of water (Subramanian 2015).

In recent years, the concept of neo-liberalism has become general as a term of abuse – in common usages it conflates all sorts of state action and economic doctrines together – from technocratic planning to Austrian economics. It has come into use in relation to science policy as well, and here seems to mean something like pressure to manage the university, to link it with industry, to generate spin-offs and intellectual property, all moves regarded in this literature in a negative light. In fact, what the rationales for policy actually are is a complex matter, involving different kinds of economic thinking, and, even in the recent past, a powerful dose of naive techno-nationalism (Edgerton and Hughes 1989). It should be remembered that states have, if anything, increased public funds for academic research in the last decades (contrary to the implications of accounts of privatisation), and that much attention is given in the associated rhetoric to the usual suspects of nanotechnology, biotechnology and information technology, from the United States to Argentina. In fact, given the lack of success in innovation of such strategies, with the exception of a few US universities, one needs to wonder what actually is going on (Edgerton 2015; Delvenne and Kreimer, this volume). The bigger point however, is that there are multiple worlds of research, many different forms of state policy for research, which generate and direct research. They cannot be reduced to old dichotomies like freedom versus planning in research, nor modern variants like neo-liberal versus social democratic (or whatever the opposite is supposed to be), where neo-liberalism represents something like inappropriate corporate planning or control of (academic) research (an implicit definition of neo-liberalism at odds with the dominant sense of free market entrepreneurial capitalism).

Conclusion

There is indeed much to be upset with in the way science and society is discussed, but we should first direct our criticisms at our invented derogatory caricatures of the ideas of others, like 'neo-liberalism' or 'linear models of innovation'. We should analyse and criticize actual positions held by actors, and not assume we know them, as Shapin (2008) has done for industrial research managers and Thomas (2015) has done for operational researchers and others. Equally we need to study serious work, not least that produced by academic specialists in STS and the political economy of science, to examine the assumptions made, which I have argued have been very particular ones which do not map well on to the actual nature of research. The expert literature begins to appear not merely as a special case (focused on the academic) but rather a product of multiple elisions, category errors and internal dialogues with strange constructed concepts. For example, a vast quantity of commentary takes policy to have been shaped by a 'linear model of innovation', which is, I have suggested, in fact implicit in STS itself, rather than in the real world of research. We need to understand that STS has a peculiar critical relationship to other forms of discourse on science, yet a deep dependence on such discourses. It is also very engaged with, and reflective of, very particular research funding agencies – it is not accidental that STS work is focused on those areas which academic research agencies believe are central to the future, like nano-, bio-, and geo-engineering, and much less concerned with, say, industrial and military research.

Political economy provides a means of remapping what we mean by science, and its effects, too. It also helps to decentre science and technology from the central role they have been ascribed in most accounts of modernity; they have not been the only way to change the world (by a long way). We need to appreciate that scientists interacted with the real world in complex ways, and sometimes recognised that complexity; analyses which assume at best naiveté on their part, and assume we as analysts know the great story will no longer do, as Thomas (2015), so graphically demonstrates. Political economic approaches have the capacity to break away from the agenda created by a narrow range of technical experts (academic scientists in certain fields), to open up the field as the study of many technical experts, and to decentre many central standard stories. Only then can we meet the challenges of our era (Bonneuil and Fressoz 2016). Physician, heal thyself!

Notes

1   I am most grateful to the editors, Thomas Kelsey and William Thomas, for their incisive comments and observations, many of which I will have to address in future.
2   Hilary Rose and Steven Rose (eds), *The Political Economy of Science: Ideology of/in the Natural Sciences* (London: Macmillan, 1976). It was paired with another volume by the same editors, *The Radicalisation of Science*, which shared the same sub-title.

References

Arrow, K. J. 1962. 'Economic Welfare and the Allocation of Resources for Invention'. *The Rate and Direction of Inventive Activity*. NBER, Princeton, Princeton University Press: 609–25.

Bonneuil, C. and Fressoz, J-B. 2016. *The Shock of the Anthropocene: The Earth, History and Us*. London: Verso Books.

Camprubí, L. 2014. *Engineers and the Making of the Francoist Regime*. Cambridge, MA: MIT Press.

Clark, Norman. 1985. *The Political Economy of Science and Technology*. Oxford: Blackwell.

Clarke, S. 2010. 'Pure science with a practical aim: The meanings of fundamental research in Britain, circa 1916–1950'. *Isis*, 101.2: 285–311.

Crafts, N.F.R. 2004. 'Steam as a general purpose technology: a growth accounting perspective'. *Economic Journal*. 114:338–51.

Dasgupta, P. and P. A. David. 1994. 'Toward a New Economics of Science'. *Research Policy* 9: 487–521.

David, P.A. 1990. 'The dynamo and the computer: an historical perspective on the modern productivity paradox'. *American Economic Review*, 80:355–61.

David, P.A. 2002. 'The political economy of public science', in Helen Lawton Smith, ed., *The Regulation of Science and Technology*, London: Macmillan Publishers.

Edgerton, D. 1996. *Science, Technology and the British Industrial 'Decline', 1870–1970*. Cambridge University Press.

Edgerton, D. 2004. 'The linear model did not exist: Reflections on the history and historiography of science and research in industry in the twentieth century'. In Grandin, Karl, Nina Wormbs, and Sven Widmalm (eds.) *The Science-Industry Nexus: History, Policy, Implications*. Massachusetts, USA: Science History Publications.

Edgerton, D. 2006. *The Shock of the Old: Technology and Global History since 1900*. London: Profile Books.

Edgerton, D. 2007. 'The contradictions of techno-nationalism and techno-globalism: A historical perspective'. *New Global Studies*, 1(1).

Edgerton, D. 2010. Innovation, technology, or history: What is the historiography of technology about?. *Technology and Culture*, 51.3: 680–97.

Edgerton, D. 2012. 'Time, money, and history'. *Isis*, 103.2: 316–27.

Edgerton, D. 2015. 'L'Etat entrepreneur de science'. In B. Christoph, and D. Pestre (eds.), *Histoire de Science Moderne Volume 3: A century of science and techno-industry, 1914–2014*. Paris: Le Seuil.

Edgerton, D. and Hughes, K. 1989. 'The poverty of science: a critical analysis of scientific and industrial policy under Mrs Thatcher'. *Public Administration*, 67.4: 419–33.

Fagerberg, J., Mowery, D.C. and Nelson, R.R. 2005. *The Oxford Handbook of Innovation*. Oxford: Oxford University Press.

Field, A.J. 2011. *A Great Leap Forward: 1930s Depression and U.S. Economic Growth*. New Haven & London: Yale University Press.

Freeman, Christopher. 1987. *Technology Policy and Economic Performance: Lessons from Japan*. Brighton: Pinter.

Giffard, Hermione. 2016. *Making Jet Engines in World War II: Britain, Germany and the United States*. Chicago: Chicago University Press.

Godin, B. 2006. 'The linear model of innovation: The historical construction of an analytical framework'. *Science, Technology & Human Values*, 31.6: 639–67.

Godin, B. 2009. 'National Innovation System: The System Approach in Historical Perspective'. *Science, Technology, & Human Values*, 34.4: 476–501.

Hall, Bronwyn A. and Rosenberg, N. (eds). 2010. *Economics of Innovation*. Amsterdam: North Holland.

Harwood, J. 2012. *Europe's Green Revolution and its Successors: The Rise and Fall of Peasant-friendly Plant Breeding*. London: Routledge.

Historical Studies in the Natural Sciences Vol. 40, No. 4 (Fall 2010), pp. 499–531 (special issue).

Horrocks, S.M. 2007. 'Industrial chemistry and its changing patrons at the University of Liverpool, 1926–1951'. *Technology and Culture*, 48.1: 43–66.

Hounshell, David. 1997. 'The Cold War, RAND, and the generation of knowledge, 1946–1962'. *Historical Studies in the Physical and Biological Sciences* 27.2: 237–67.

Hounshell, David. 2000. 'The medium is the message, or how context matters: the RAND Corporation builds an economics of innovation, 1946–1962'. In Hughes, A. C., Hughes T. P. *Systems, experts, and computers: the systems approach in management and engineering. World War II and after*. Cambridge, Massachusetts: MIT Press. 255–310.

Jones, Charles. 1995a. 'R&D Based Models of Economic Growth', *Journal of Political Economy*, 103.4: 759–84.

Jones, Charles. 1995b. 'Time Series Tests of Endogenous Growth Models', *Quarterly Journal of Economics*, 100.2: 1127–70.

Kealey, Terence. 1996. *The Economic Laws of Scientific Research*. London: Macmillan.

Levidow, Les, ed. 1981. *Science, Technology, and the Labour Process: Marxist Studies*. London: CSE Books.

Lundvall, B.A. 1992. *National Systems of Innovation: An Analytical Framework*. London: Pinter.

Martin, B.R. and Nightingale, P. eds. 2000. *The Political Economy of Science, Technology and Innovation*. Cheltenham: Edward Elgar Publishing.

Mirowski, P. and Sent, E. M. 2002. *Science Bought and Sold: Essays in the Economics of Science*. University of Chicago Press.

Mirowski, P. 2007. 'Review essay: Did the (returns to) scales fall from their eyes?' *Journal of the History of Economic Thought*, 29.4: 481–94.

Mirowski, P. 2011. *Science-mart: Privatizing American Science*. Cambridge, MA: Harvard University Press.

Nelson, R. R. 1959. 'The simple economics of basic scientific-research'. *Journal of Political Economy*. 67.3: 297–306.

Noble, D. F. 1979. *America by Design: Science, Technology, and the Rise of Corporate Capitalism*. New York: Oxford University Press, USA.

Palladino, P. 1990. 'The political economy of applied research: Plant breeding in Great Britain, 1910–1940'. *Minerva*, 28.4: 446–68.

Palladino, P. 1996. 'Science, technology, and the economy: plant breeding in Great Britain, 1920–1970'. *The Economic History Review*, 49.1: 116–36.

Reich, L.S. 1977. 'Research, patents, and the struggle to control radio: a study of big business and the uses of industrial research'. *Business History Review*, 51.2: 208–35.

Reinisch, Jessica. 2000. 'The society for freedom in science, 1940–1963'. MSc diss., University of London, London.

Ristuccia, Cristiano Andrea and Solomou, Solomos. 2014. 'Can general purpose technology theory explain economic growth? Electrical power as a case study'. *European Review of Economic History* 18.3: 227–47.

Rose, Hilary and Rose, Steven (eds). 1976. *The Political Economy of Science: Ideology of/in the Natural Sciences*. London: Macmillan.

Rosenberg, Nathan and Frischtak, Claudio R. 1984. 'Technological innovation and long waves'. *Cambridge Journal of Economics* 8.1: 7–24.

Schatzberg, E. 2006. 'Technik comes to America: Changing meanings of technology before 1930'. *Technology and Culture*, 47.3: 486–512.

Shapin, S. 1992. 'Discipline and bounding: The history and sociology of science as seen through the externalism-internalism debate'. *History of Science*, 30.4: 333–69.

Shapin, S. 2008. *The Scientific Life: A Moral History of a Late Modern Vocation*. Chicago: Chicago University Press.

Steil, Benn, Victor, D.G. and Nelson, R.R. 2002. *Technological Innovation and Economic Performance*. Princeton: Princeton University Press.

Subramanian, K. 2015. 'Revisiting the Green Revolution: Irrigation and Food Production in 20th-Century India'. PhD diss., Dept. of History, Kings College London.

Thomas, William. 2015. *Rational Action: The Sciences of Policy in Britain and America, 1940–1960*. Cambridge: MIT Press.

Thorpe, C. 2009. 'Community and the market in Michael Polanyi's philosophy of science'. *Modern Intellectual History*, 6.1: 59.

Tyfield, David. 2012a. 'A cultural political economy of research and innovation in an age of crisis'. *Minerva* 50: 149–167.

Tyfield, David. 2012b. *The Economics of Science: A Critical Realist Overview*: Vol. 2 *Towards a synthesis of political economy and science and technology studies*. London: Routledge.

Wersky, Gary. 2007. 'The Marxist critique of capitalist science: A history in three movements?' *Science as Culture* 16.4: 397–461.

Williams, B. R. 1967. *Technology, Investment and Growth*. London: Chapman and Hall.

Zaidi, W.H. 2011a. 'Aviation will either destroy or save our civilization: Proposals for the international control of aviation, 1920–45'. *Journal of Contemporary History*, 46.1: 150–78.

Zaidi, W. 2011b. 'Liberal internationalist approaches to science and technology in interwar Britain and the United States'. In Laqua, Daniel ed. *Internationalism Reconfigured: Transnational Ideas and Movements Between the World Wars*. London: IB Tauris.

2

THE "MARKETPLACE OF IDEAS" AND THE CENTRALITY OF SCIENCE TO NEOLIBERALISM

Edward Nik-Khah

> The marketplace of ideas is a metaphoric
> kudzu vine whose resources have shaped
> English-language reflection on public space for
> the past five decades for good and ill.
>
> *(Peters, 2004)*

Introduction

The concept of the "marketplace of ideas" often structures discussions about the institutions promoting and the laws governing political and intellectual life. To the novice, submitting views to a competition within the marketplace of ideas seems to convey a sense of judicious pragmatism, an even intellectual playing field, a respect for diverse voices, a defense of unpopular speech, even the foundation for a mature democratic order. For the scientist, it serves as a stand-in for the ideal of subjecting scientific theories to rigorous competitive trials.

But on closer glance, the "marketplace of ideas" looks very different. In recent years, it has taken on an increasingly economic construction, opening the door for *economists* to assume increased responsibility for the development and circulation of this concept. Significantly, science studies scholars have begun to note the increasing influence of economists in the management of science, a circumstance closely related to the reconceptualization of intellectual life as a kind of market.[1]

From a certain viewpoint, it might seem surprising if this were not the case: who has been more strident in claiming to possess a singular expertise in operation of markets—any markets—than economists? Yet the history was not that straightforward. John Stuart Mill famously linked intellectual life to markets in *On Liberty*, but the link was tenuous, certainly unsuggestive of any specific analytical method of studying the creation and dissemination of knowledge. Such links between economic doctrine and intellectual life would have to wait nearly a century longer for the emergence of a (relatively) new breed of economists—the *neoliberal* economists. For members of the Mont Pèlerin Society (MPS), the historical epicenter of the transnational and transdisciplinary politico-intellectual movement that served to incubate neoliberal ideas and to put them into practice, the existence of such a market would serve as something approaching a foundational principle.[2]

Having been shaped by the neoliberal project over the course of the past six decades, the "marketplace of ideas" no longer resembles its earlier (common-sense) understanding. What began as a critique of state reason transmogrified into a thoroughgoing and generalizable critique of academic science: the government could never know enough to plan a complex economy, and the scientist had no privileged access to truth outside of the market.

This chapter examines how the "marketplace of ideas" as a concept fared at the hands of these neoliberal economists. To maintain focus, I will attend most closely to the views of the neoliberal who most doggedly pursued the implications of this concept for the neoliberal project, the Chicago School economist, George Stigler.[3]

Sovereignty in the intellectual marketplace

The concept of the "marketplace of ideas" is of relatively recent origin, i.e. in popular interpretations of the US Supreme Court jurist Oliver Wendell Holmes's famous dissenting opinion in *Abrams v. United States* in 1919 (Peters, 2004).[4] In the decades that followed, appeals to the marketplace of ideas were used in protecting unpopular speech and fostering robust democratic discussion. At this time, economists steered clear of such market-talk: knowledge was held to be beyond their purview. However, immediately following the close of World War II, two momentous events changed this. First was the rise of "information" as a primary ontological principle across the sciences (Gleick, 2011). Economists would increasingly study not the allocational, but the *informational* properties of markets (Mirowski and Nik-Khah, 2017). Second, some liberals became alarmed that the intellectual tide had moved against them, prompting them to re-examine the features of intellectual life, leading them to espouse conclusions quite at odds with their liberal predecessors.

Both events contributed to the development of the MPS. The MPS was an association of pro-market intellectuals founded in 1947 to countervail "collectivism", by which they meant not only socialism, but also social welfare liberalism. Famously, Friedrich Hayek intervened in the socialist calculation controversy by reconceptualizing the economy from a system of allocation to a system of *communications*, and arguing for the superiority of the price mechanism on the grounds of its unsurpassed ability to make use of knowledge.[5]

It is not surprising then that the question of the role knowledge plays in a modern society now came within the purview of these *neoliberal* economists, and some questioned the kind of knowledge that was being produced. They began to scrutinize the metaphor of the marketplace of ideas and to explore different ways of operationalizing it.

One finds exactly this sort of exploration in a 1957 MPS session entitled "Egalitarianism and 'Democratisation' in Education." Within it, the economist Benjamin Rogge (at that time dean of Wabash College, a US liberal arts college) delivered a paper on the financing of higher education.[6] Rogge argued that the appropriate way to respect a pro-market creed in the organization of colleges and universities would be to finance all their operations out of student tuition fees. Rogge decried subsidized funding of student education—what he called "below-cost pricing"—on the grounds that it served as an unnecessary and unwarranted intervention in the education market. He found it especially objectionable that people routinely denied the principle of consumers' sovereignty in this market on the grounds that those seeking education were uneducated.

To subsidize students' education, colleges and universities needed funds from the government, alumni, the wealthy, and corporations. But relying on these groups for funding gave them undue sway over the curriculum, stifling intellectual diversity. Rogge noted, "he who pays the piper will call the tune" (Rogge, [1957] 1979, p. 255). He did not begrudge funders for seeking to "call the tune," but he sought to diffuse such power among many more, and dispersed rather than organized, tune-callers (the students themselves). A full cost pricing method would achieve this because the consumers of education—the students—were, in his view, many and diverse. Consequently, full cost pricing would also promote *intellectual* diversity. Specifically, by eliminating the state's funding of professors' activities, full cost pricing would help to combat "collectivism."

The person assigned to discuss Rogge's paper was the economist and founding MPS member, George Stigler. Stigler would come to occupy an unusual position within the intellectual and political crosscurrents of the Cold War economics profession—we might even characterize his position as unique. He was able to combine an interest in formal models of information, orthodox economics, pro-market politics, and the role of the intellectual in capitalism into something approaching a coherent set of views and practices that he and his students then deployed both inside and outside economics—indeed, inside and outside the academy—all the while claiming to uphold the best traditions of science, and gaining a reputation among even intellectual antagonists for doing just this.

Stigler rejected Rogge's argument. First, he denied that full cost pricing would necessarily attract a variety of funders, promoting intellectual diversity: although research funding already utilized full cost pricing, the US federal government and the Ford Foundation exerted tremendous authority in setting research priorities. Second, Stigler objected to Rogge's proposal to promote student sovereignty over higher education. He argued students lacked the qualification to judge either the quality of courses or the quality of research.

Stigler then attacked the metaphor of democratic diffusion of power that underpinned Rogge's consumer sovereignty argument:

In general in intell[ectual] affairs democracy is not a proper system of organizing. The best econ[omics] in the US is not the one the public would elect; a science must impose the standards of an elite upon a profession.

Affairs of science, and intellectual life generally, are not to be conducted on democratic procedures. One cannot establish a mathem[atical] theorem by a vote, even a vote of mathematicians. An elite must emerge and instill higher standards than the public or the profession instinctively desire.[7]

The preferences of the patrons of science might indeed triumph, but their sovereignty over the knowledge produced was nothing necessarily to celebrate. Unless, that is, they were the right kind of patrons.

Stigler elaborated on his views in his 1963 publication *The Intellectual and the Market Place*. Here, Stigler wanted to persuade intellectuals to reexamine their attitudes towards markets:

If one asks where, in the Western university world, the freedom of inquiry of professors has been most staunchly defended and energetically promoted, my answer is this: not in the politically controlled universities…and not in the self-perpetuating faculties…. No, inquiry has been most free in the college whose trustees are a group of top-quality leaders of the marketplace, men who, experience shows, are remarkably tolerant of almost anything except a mediocre and complacent faculty.

(Stigler, 1963, p. 87)

Those who cherish freedom of inquiry, Stigler argued, should show greater appreciation for those who make their living in the marketplace, not only because their actions have provided for the material progress necessary to support a class of intellectuals, but also because by their oversight of elite private universities they have *personally* safeguarded freedom of inquiry.

If bringing the good deeds of businesspersons to the attention of intellectuals was insufficient to convince them to re-examine their attitudes, then perhaps closer scrutiny of the deep similarities between the marketplace and the intellectual world would do the trick:

> The organizing principles of [the marketplace and intellectual world] are the same… Just as real markets have some fraud and monopoly, which impair the claims for the market place, so the intellectual world has its instances of coercion and deception, with the coercion exercised by claques and fashion. But again these deviants are outside the logic of the system.
>
> *(Stigler, 1963, pp. 87–8)*

The rationality of science and the effectiveness of the market for goods were due to the same organizational principles, Stigler argued. Hence, intellectuals should regard the marketplace favorably.

But if the organizing principles were the same, and if markets generally worked, then how could one reasonably hold—as Stigler did—that intellectual life persisted in producing the wrong kind of knowledge? Stigler's answer is worthy of close scrutiny. Markets *did* give people what they wanted. But this was nothing to celebrate, because most people are instinctually predisposed to hold the wrong views about markets. Markets produce the wrong kind of knowledge *because* they give people what they want. After all, there was something to be said for coercion: an elite could potentially countervail such views. But larger political forces hampered its ability to do so. Stigler complained that the demand expressed by government for science as channeled through the system of publicly funded universities and grant programs had become intertwined with a set of egalitarian concerns. This encouraged "diffusion" of talent, leading ultimately to a decrease in the quality of research, entrenching professional consensus. Estate taxes eliminated the possibility of a future Rockefeller, and therefore the establishment of another University of Chicago was out of the question; states had diverted resources to the system of public universities that otherwise would have gone to a Harvard or, better yet, a Chicago.

At this moment, in the early 1960s, Stigler was skeptical of the prospects for US higher education. But he held out limited hope that a small set of institutions might yet help to impose the higher standards that Stigler so desired.

Intellectual failure and market failure

Neoliberals expressed a commitment to promote "freedom of inquiry." But what this freedom would look like, who should get to exercise it, how best to promote it, and how such promotion related to existing structures of knowledge creation remained contested. Such contestation involved distinctive views about how markets generate knowledge.

In 1964, Fritz Machlup (a founding MPS member) delivered a defense of academic freedom, and in particular, its tenure protection. At that time, he was serving as president of the American Association of University Professors. In his talk, Machlup focused specifically on how tenure helped "to secure the great benefit of academic freedom and of the fruit it bears."

Machlup viewed the professor as playing a crucial role in the advancement of knowledge. He cited the example of pressure exerted by a pharmaceutical company on a junior researcher studying the toxicity of one of its drugs. In order for them to play this important role, professors would need protection. But to obtain this protection, they would have to personally sacrifice:

> [T]he free competitive market for higher learning would not guarantee all the academic freedom which society ought to provide in the interest of progress; without

the interference through the universal tenure system the degree of academic freedom would be only that which professors would be willing to pay for, and this would be much less than what is socially desirable.

(Machlup, 1964, pp. 119–20)

Machlup portrayed the intellectual marketplace as beset by "externalities," a form of "market failure." For Machlup, professors produced the fruits of academic freedom. The problem was that they did not reap the full benefits of such freedom, while at the same time they solely bore the costs of it. According to the argument, a competitive market would produce too little academic freedom, for the same reason markets may fail to sufficiently protect against pollution. In forging a binding commitment amongst professors, trustees, and administrators, tenure operated as a corrective for this "market failure," guaranteeing the correct amount of academic freedom.

Machlup's position would have been intolerable to Chicago neoliberals for a variety of reasons. This was the time of the advent of the "Coase theorem" (a term Stigler himself claims to have "christened"), which effectively denied that externalities posed any significant problem for economies.[8] But Stigler had an additional reason for rejecting Machlup's argument:

> The censorship of professors is more severe than that of either trustees or the market. Could you conceive of Princeton appointing an economist who actively professed racist views? Indeed I am impressed that Allen Wallis has yet to receive his first L.L.D. – I would welcome an explanation other than his association with Nixon in 1959-1960. Professors are highly conformist and make very poor custodians of intellectual freedom when it conflicts with the academy's beliefs.[9]

The faculty had gained control of the university—even the elite private university—and the freedom to espouse views unpopular within the academy had suffered. What had happened?

The intervening years between *The Intellectual and the Market Place* and Stigler's correspondence with Machlup had been a turbulent time in US higher education. Chicago was not spared. In 1967 the Chicago campus was roiled by a series of disruptive student protests. Students demanded greater say in administering the university. This disturbed Stigler. But the decisions of some faculty to support them in their demands had shaken him. And by now his experience tempered his admiration of the trustees, to say the least: "[T]he trustees have been as craven and irresponsible as the faculties."[10] The numbers to be found in the university whom Stigler trusted to carry forth its proper mission were now vanishingly small. Stigler concluded that matters had become dire. In a 1969 letter, Stigler admitted, "I am becoming increasingly more critical of present-day higher education."[11]

Hence, by the time of his 1969 correspondence, Stigler would have rejected Machlup's argument that an agreement between trustees, regents, administrators, scholars, and teachers would foster intellectual freedom. He would have been skeptical that any one of those groups could be trusted to do so. Instead, Stigler began to contemplate a radical reorganization of knowledge. Recall, he believed in a science advanced by imposing the standards of an elite on a profession and, ultimately, a society. The elite class was very small; it was outnumbered, and its freedom of inquiry needed to be protected from coercion by students, the state, and the *faculty*. Moreover, inquiry would have to be structured such that the elite would prevail. He posed the question: "Is the university a sensible base of operations for the research scholars?"[12]

The division of intellectual labor is limited by the extent of the market

On October 20 and 21, 1972, a conference was held at the University of Virginia in honor of Milton Friedman's sixtieth birthday. It coincided with the tenth anniversary of the publication of *Capitalism and Freedom*. The conference was framed as an exploration of the issues raised by that book—of its "Problems and Prospects." George Stigler took the occasion to express his concern about one troubling feature of the work of his old friend and close colleague:

> As I mentally review Milton's work, I recall no important occasion on which he has told businessmen how to behave… Yet Milton has shown no comparable reticence in advising Congress and public on monetary policy, tariffs, schooling, minimum wages, the tax benefits of establishing a ménage without benefit of clergy, and several other subjects… Why should businessmen—and customers and lenders and other economic agents—know and foster their own interests, but voters and political coalitions be so much in need of his and our lucid and enlightened instruction?
>
> *(Stigler, 1975, p. 312)*

Stigler took exception with what he believed to be the confused image of the marketplace of ideas that was implicit in *Capitalism and Freedom*. If Friedman's popularization of Chicago neoclassical economics in his advice to the public was effective, this would imply that the public "underinvests" in knowledge, a market failure. But if agents maximize in collecting information (since his 1961 paper "The Economics of Information," Stigler argued that they did), they will already have gathered all the information that is appropriate for them to have. Friedman's efforts at popularization would be of no use to them.

Stigler posed a provocative question: If markets generally work, then why should this not be the case for the marketplace of ideas? And if the marketplace of ideas works, then why should the public need a Milton Friedman? Or, for that matter, a George Stigler? It was a threatening question for an economist, and Stigler knew it: he had entitled one journal article "Do Economists Matter?"

Within that article, Stigler answered his question affirmatively by adopting something akin to the commonsense view of science as rational and reflecting nature (or, in this case, society), and expressing it in the language of commodity exchange. Science was a very special kind of commodity, differing from other information-commodities in its *effects*. Science is rational, and so is society (albeit in a different way), and therefore a rational society must make use of science. Society *did* need Friedman's work—not his popularizations, but the economic science itself, that is his work aimed at fellow economists. It needed his *Monetary History of the United States*, but not his *Capitalism and Freedom*.

But "society" doesn't purchase knowledge: people do, for specific purposes. Students decide from which college or university to purchase knowledge. Patrons of research do much the same, Stigler observed: "[the] huge area of antitrust & I[ndustrial] O[rganization economics] in [the] US [was] generated by both public policy and business defenses against it."[13] Stigler was in an excellent position to make such an observation: he played an important role in developing a distinctive Chicago approach to industrial organization, and had consulted for and testified on behalf of firms facing antitrust action. Economists develop ideas in response to consumer demand for them; in Stigler's words, the economist—the scientist—was a "customer's man."[14]

The argument led Stigler to state what he *himself* called a "paradoxical" conclusion: economists were truly influential only when they work on technical matters for an audience of technical economists and not when they speak directly to society. Only in the former case would economists achieve the fundamental effect of changing the platform upon which policy debates take place, a change due to the special reception given by the public and polity to science.

Stigler believed the university was beset by serious problems. He set out to construct an institution exempt from them. He would concentrate scholars in a setting freed from teaching obligations (and the influence of students), removed from the inconvenient protection of tenure, and placed under the watchful supervision of an "authoritarian" master. In this way, Stigler hoped to impose the standards of an elite upon his profession.

To do so it would be necessary to find a set of patrons who were uncontaminated by the egalitarian views of the government and the public at large. Stigler found them in corporations and pro-market foundations. Such patrons had funded the rise of University of Chicago Law and Economics and the development of a University of Chicago neoliberal version of Industrial Organization.

Stigler heeded his own advice; so did those in his orbit. The topics Stigler settled on, studies of the economy and the state, had the virtue of appealing to a paying clientele. Stigler believed that economists and political scientists held unrealistically optimistic views about the ability of democracy to address social problems, and that these views tainted their studies of democracy and regulation. Stigler held that studies of the "capacities of democracy" could counteract prevailing beliefs about the way the political system functions.

Stigler was keen to persuade his newfound patrons that science's effects truly were special. In an unpublished 1971 memo proposing a privately funded research institute, he insisted, "The relevance of this work to public policy will be both indirect and decisive… The work will often shatter the fond hopes of the scholarly professions."[15] Stigler argued that using science was the best—indeed the *only*—way to achieve the influence that patrons might desire. He proposed using two types of studies to deliver this "decisive influence." The first would study the effects of past economics policies to develop techniques for auditing and guiding, and thereby controlling, administrative bodies. The second would study and test hypotheses on the nature of the political process, for the purpose of counteracting the attitudes of political scientists and economists within those academic disciplines. Together, they would impose the standards of an economic elite on the social sciences. Stigler's memo was a brief for the private funding of economics imperialism and neoliberal governmentality; they have, indeed, decisively shaped the academy and science in the four decades since.

Chicago and neoliberal science

Viewed as practical strategy in the political mobilization of science, the measures laid out by Stigler in his memo made one crucial omission that sympathizers to the neoliberal project would have clearly and immediately perceived.[16] Consumer protection regulation often enjoyed the support not only of the public, economists, and political scientists, but also scientists with expertise specific to the fields covered by such regulation. For example, clinical scientists overwhelmingly tended to favor the measures taken by a newly empowered US Food and Drug Administration (FDA). Because neoliberals (particularly of the Chicago variant) often advanced their arguments *in the name of science*, the support of scientists for regulation (and their opposition to Chicago-style neoliberal arguments, which many were quite willing to voice publicly) was surely an obstacle to achieving neoliberal aims.

Neoliberals developed an ingenious response: they forged relationships with a select set of scientists, resulting in a variety of interlinked and coordinated research institutes spanning economics, politics, and even the biomedical sciences. These efforts were significant enough to draw the attention of Michel Foucault who, in his *Birth of Biopolitics*, not only mentions Stigler's research by name, but also singles out the work of the American Enterprise Institute's Center for Health Policy Research as an exemplary instance of the "permanent criticism of governmental policy" so characteristic of neoliberalism (Foucault, 2008, pp. 246–7). This center was also an outgrowth of Stigler's efforts.

Such efforts took aim not only at the FDA, but also at academic (clinical) science. Neoliberals, especially those housed at the Center for the Study of Drug Development, advanced a novel claim: academics were predisposed to be too skeptical of industry claims. Regulation informed by an academic consensus amounted to a kind of "Lysenkoism": the state ignored industry claims, sought instead a (biased) academic consensus and forced the medical community (and, hence, consumers) to heed it. Neoliberals argued in favor of inviting pharmaceutical companies to counteract the "nihilism" of academic scientists. Academics and industry would present their preferred scientific interpretations, and the marketplace of ideas would sort it all out.

It was a lesson that scientists themselves would internalize. To wit:

> It is common for critics of the use of the marketplace as a criterion of efficacy to point to the misplaced confidences of the past – in bleeding, leeches, puking, and purging. But such practices long ago fell into disrepute, not because of the double-blind, controlled trials, but because obviously better treatments came along.
>
> *(Lasagna, 1978, p. 872)*

In sum, academic science was no match for the marketplace.[17] Machlup's position on academic freedom—both in general, and in the specific case of drugs—had been thoroughly repudiated.

Conclusion

At the beginning of the 1970s, the moment that the emerging critique of academic science first began to take shape, Stigler articulated to fellow neoliberals the task that lay before them: "The great majority of Americans would not dream of abandoning the important regulatory policies … [but] what is not commonly realized is that there are several ways to skin even a reforming cat" (Stigler, 1973, pp. 10–12). The debates between neoliberals over how to operationalize the marketplace of ideas gave rise to alternative strategies for "skinning the cat." A first involved popularizing Chicago neoliberal analysis, to help gain popular acceptance for eliminating regulatory agencies. A second involved keeping regulatory agencies in place, forcing them to follow cost–benefit procedures, and then identifying the relevant set of costs and benefits. Importantly, these approaches were structurally related: they were coordinated by interlocking directorates and shared memberships, and often funded by the same clients.

A third strategy, also structurally related to the first two, involved subjecting science used by regulatory bodies to the judgments of the marketplace.[18] A market-governed science would utilize contract research and be conducted outside the structure of academic departments, under close supervision of one empowered to deliver on promises made to patrons. The purpose was not merely to produce "more" science, and certainly not to ensure the freedom of the individual scientist to pursue independent inquiry. Instead, it would satisfy the demands of patrons by producing the "right" kind of knowledge.

But there was nothing whatsoever dictating that the knowledge demanded would necessarily produce enlightenment. Neoliberal think tanks would repeatedly participate in activities to manufacture ignorance about the effects of using consumer products, playing instrumental roles in forestalling negative regulatory judgments (see Pinto, this volume). This has won them the generous sponsorship of industries threatened by regulation and legislation—as well as some opprobrium in those instances where such activities have come to light (e.g., Oreskes and Conway, 2010). Yet, such activities have been far more widespread than the well-known cases of tobacco cancer and anthropogenic global warming denial. In pharmaceutical science, too, one finds traces of the "echo chamber" effect, often involving the very same institutions (Nik-Khah, 2014, 2016, Sismondo, this volume). Moreover, neoliberal arguments were used to justify the privatization and globalization of science, enabling specific practices implicated in the production of ignorance (Nik-Khah, 2014; Pinto, this volume).[19] Consequently, there is a clear connection between neoliberalism and "agnotology," between subscribing to the market's unsurpassed epistemic virtues and ignorance for the masses.[20]

Acknowledgements

This paper is a revised version of the working paper "What is 'Freedom' in the Marketplace of Ideas," published in no. 2 of the Whitlam Institute Human Rights and Public Life Series. I wish to thank Stephen Stigler for his permission to access the George J. Stigler Papers and Anna Yeatman for helpful comments in improving a previous draft. Archival materials from the George J. Stigler Papers (Special Collections Research Center, Regenstein Library, University of Chicago) are quoted with permission.

Notes

1 On the appeal to economics in setting communications policy, see Napoli (1999). On the role of economists in the management of science, see Mirowski (2011) and Berman (2012).
2 For histories of the MPS, see Plehwe et al. (2006) and Mirowski and Plehwe (2009).
3 Moreover, over time, rival views of the marketplace of ideas gave way to Stigler's. This was surely the case at one of the most influential academic centers of neoliberal thought, the University of Chicago. By the 1980s, those at Chicago had acknowledged that Stigler's views had prevailed over those of his more famous colleague Milton Friedman (Reder, 1982). I will forgo explaining the circumstances leading Stigler's views to assume significance there, and instead direct the reader to Nik-Khah (2011).
4 (250 U.S. 616) (1919). The case concerned the imprisonment of Jacob Abrams, along with four co-defendants, who were tried, found guilty, and sentenced under the Sedition Act of 1918 for criticizing the US government's deployment of troops to Russia and for advocating for a labor strike in munitions factories aiding in this effort. They appealed their convictions to the US Supreme Court under the free speech clause of the First Amendment of the US Constitution; the Supreme Court upheld the convictions by a 7–2 margin. In dissent, Holmes (joined by Louis Brandeis) argued, "the best test of truth is the power of the thought to get itself accepted in the competition of the market"—a phrase that continues to attract scholarly scrutiny to this day.
5 Hayek's argument resists quick summary; his views on where economic information was supposedly located and how it would be accessed changed considerably over the course of his career. See Mirowski and Nik-Khah (2017).
6 The paper, "Financing Higher Education in the United States," would later be published as a chapter in Rogge's (1979) book *Can Capitalism Survive?*
7 "Comments on Rogge's 'Financing Higher Education in the United States'," GSRL Box 26, File: Mont Pèlerin Society 10th Anniversary Meeting.
8 The argument was, in a nutshell, that if commodities were conceived as bundles of rights, then it would immediately become apparent that it was possible to unbundle them and allow the market to efficiently assign each one. The initial assignment of these legal rights would have no effect on the utilization of economic resources—subject to conditions that Ronald Coase called "zero transactions costs." Hence, economic problems caused by externalities would simply dissolve.
9 Letter of Stigler to Fritz Machlup, dated April 14, 1969. GSRL Box 10, File: Machlup. Allen Wallis was an MPS member, and as dean of Chicago's Graduate School of Business the person most responsible for hiring George Stigler to the University of Chicago.
10 GSRL Box 22, File: "Do Trustees Have a Place in Education?"

11 Letter of Stigler to Robert Leach, dated May 23, 1969, GSRL Box 22, File: 1969 Student Aid.

12 GSRL Box 22, File: "Are There Any Professors Left?"

13 GSRL Box 20, File: "To What Tune Does Science Dance?" The economic field of industrial organization had traditionally concerned itself with assessing the competitiveness of market structures; work in this field was often used in adjudicating antitrust cases in the US, and economists often served as expert witnesses.

14 At times Stigler did portray the scientific community as, if not exactly autonomous, then as bringing a handful of distinct values to the table—for example, in its disengagement from issues of immediate concern and esteeming generalizability (Stigler, [1972] 1982). This view was clearly at tension with portrayal of the scientist as "customer's man." Stigler later attempted to reconcile these two distinct accounts of the forces driving science by appealing to the passage of time—scientists' judgments would dominate in the short run, but in the long run, market judgments would prevail (Stigler, 1988, pp. 85–6)—or by assigning to the scientist the role of discovering the latent desires of patrons (Hazlett, 1984, p. 48). What is noteworthy is that he reserves the role of making the final judgment on scientific knowledge not for the community of scientists but for the *market*.

15 GSRL Box 21, File: A Research Institute in Economics.

16 This section summarizes a history covered comprehensively in Nik-Khah, 2014.

17 On the current state of commercialized pharmaceutical science, see Sismondo, this volume.

18 Moreover, we can associate each approach with a personage. Milton Friedman adopted the first strategy; Stigler (in his published work) adopted the second. The third emerged only after the efforts to forge relationships with scientists bore fruit.

19 For discussions of such practices, see Michaels, 2008a, 2008b; Mirowski, 2011; Sismondo, this volume.

20 On agnotology, see Proctor, 2008; Pinto, this volume.

References

Berman, E. P. 2012. *Creating the Market University: How Academic Science Became an Economic Engine.* Princeton, NJ: Princeton University Press.

Foucault, M. 2008. *The Birth of Biopolitics.* New York: Palgrave Macmillan.

Gleick, J. 2011. *The Information.* London: Fourth Estate.

Hazlett, T. 1984. "Interview of George Stigler." *Reason* (January): 44–8.

Machlup, F. 1964. "In Defense of Academic Tenure." *AAUP Bulletin*, 50.2: 112–24.

Lasagna, L. 1978. "The Development and Regulation of New Medicines." *Science*, 200.4344: 871–3.

Michaels, D. 2008a. *Doubt is Their Product: How Industry's Assault on Science Threatens Your Health.* New York: Oxford University Press.

Michaels, D. 2008b. "Manufactured Uncertainty: Contested Science and the Protection of the Public's Health and Environment," in Proctor, R. and Schiebinger, L., eds. *Agnotology: The Making and Unmaking of Ignorance.* Stanford, CA: Stanford University Press: 90–107.

Mirowski, P. 2011. *ScienceMart: Privatizing American Science.* Cambridge, MA: Harvard University Press.

Mirowski, P. and Nik-Khah, E. 2017. *The Knowledge We Have Lost in Information.* Oxford University Press.

Mirowski, P. and Plehwe, D. 2009. *The Road from Mont Pèlerin: The Making of the Neoliberal Thought Collective.* Cambridge, MA: Harvard University Press.

Napoli, P. 1999. "The Marketplace of Ideas Metaphor in Communications Regulation." *Journal of Communications*, 49.4: 151–69.

Nik-Khah, E. 2016. "Smoke and Thalidomide." *Perspectives*, 14. Whitlam Institute within Western Sydney University.

Nik-Khah, E. 2014. "Neoliberal Pharmaceutical Science and the Chicago School of Economics." *Social Studies of Science*, 44.4: 489–517.

Nik-Khah, E. 2011. "George Stigler, the Graduate School of Business, and the Pillars of the Chicago School," in Van Horn, R., Mirowski, P., and Stapleford, T., (eds.) *Building Chicago Economics: New Perspectives on the History of America's Most Powerful Economics Program.* New York: Cambridge University Press: 116–47.

Nik-Khah, E. and Van Horn, R. 2012. "Inland Empire: Economics Imperialism as an Imperative of Chicago Neoliberalism." *Journal of Economic Methodology*, 19.3: 259–82.

Oreskes, N. and Conway, E. 2010. *Merchants of Doubt.* New York: Bloomsbury.

Peters, J. D. 2004. "The 'Marketplace of Ideas': A History of the Concept," in Calabrese, A. and Sparks, C., eds. *Toward a Political Economy of Culture.* Lanham, MD: Rowman and Littlefield: 65–82.

Plehwe, D., Walpen, B. and Neuhnöffer, G., eds. 2006. *Neoliberal Hegemony: A Global Critique.* New York: Routledge.

Proctor, R. 2008. "Agnotology: A Missing Term to Describe the Cultural Production of Ignorance (and its study)," in: Proctor, R. and Schiebinger, L., eds. *Agnotology: The Making and Unmaking of Ignorance.* Stanford, CA: Stanford University Press: 1–33.

Reder, M. 1982. "Chicago Economics: Permanence and Change." *Journal of Economic Literature*, 20.1: 1–38.

Rogge, B. [1957] 1979. "Financing Higher Education in the United States," in Rogge, B. *Can Capitalism Survive?* Indianapolis, IN: Liberty Fund.

Stigler, G. 1988. *Memoirs of an Unregulated Economist.* New York: Basic Books.

Stigler, G. [1972] 1982. "The Adoption of the Marginal Utility Theory," in Stigler, G., ed. *The Economist as Preacher and Other Essays.* Chicago: University of Chicago Press.

Stigler, G. 1975. "The Intellectual and His Society," in Selden, R., ed. *Capitalism and Freedom: Problems and Prospects.* Charlottesville, VA: University Press of Virginia: 311–21.

Stigler, G. 1973. "The Confusion of Means and Ends," in: Landau, R., ed. *Regulating New Drugs.* Chicago, IL: University of Chicago Center for Policy Studies: 10–19.

Stigler, G. 1963. *The Intellectual and the Market Place.* New York: Free Press of Glencoe.

3

THE POLITICAL ECONOMY OF THE MANHATTAN PROJECT

Charles Thorpe

Introduction

On September 15, 1945, exactly one month after the surrender of Japan, and less than two weeks after the ceremony on the USS *Missouri* ended the Second World War, Major General Lauris Norstad of the Army Air Force sent a memorandum to Manhattan Project chief General Leslie Groves. It concerned how many atomic bombs the US should aim to stock in its arsenal for "M-day," or the start of mobilization for a new war. Its estimate of a minimum requirement of 123 and an optimum of 466 bombs was accompanied by a map showing Russia's "population and industrial concentrations," with figures for the number of bombs required to destroy each location. Norstad stated, "It is obvious that the immediate destruction of the complete list of 66 cities would have a … devastating effect on Russia. Therefore, an optimum requirement for atomic bomb stocks would be the number necessary to obliterate all of these cities."

The memorandum encapsulated the logic of total war: since countries' whole industrial capacity had been swept up in the mobilization for modern warfare, "crippling the ability of the enemy to wage war" meant the destruction of that industrial capacity, workforce, and population.[1] Atomic bombs were weapons against modern industrial society. But these weapons were also the products of industrial processes and organizations, in particular the vast industrial facilities built at Oak Ridge, Tennessee and Hanford, Washington, for separating and refining Uranium-235 and for producing plutonium (Sanger, 1995; Gerber, 1992: 35–6; Thayer, 1996; cf. Herman, 2012). Producing the quantities of weapons that Norstad's memorandum mandated meant the intensified industrialization of nuclear weapons production.

The work at Los Alamos Laboratory of designing and assembling the Hiroshima and Nagasaki bombs involved teams of elite scientific specialists. Scientists were required even for the final assembly of bomb components on the island of Tinian. Norstad wanted to routinize all of this, so that the bomb would no longer be a gift of esoteric science but could be integrated into the Army Air Force arsenal as just another weapon.

Norstad's original wish-list of under 500 fission bombs was dwarfed by the expansion of the American stockpile, which reached a peak of 32,040 fission and hydrogen bombs in 1966 (the Soviet stockpile peaked at 45,000 in 1986) (Natural Resources Defense Council, 2006; Norris, Kosiak and Schwartz, 1998, 184–9). As Anthony Giddens observed in *The Nation-State and*

Violence, "Once they had first been constructed, nuclear weapons soon came to be made in batch-production, like other industrial products" (Giddens, 1985: 241).

The atomic bomb project established an organizational template for not only the direction of scientific research toward military goals, but also the integration of science with large-scale industrial production within a complex technological system (Martinez and Byrne, 1996). According to historian Thomas Hughes, "The Manhattan Project, with its systematic linking of military funding, management, contract letting, industrial, university, and governmental research laboratories, and numerous manufacturers, became the model" for such "massive technological systems" as Trident, ABM, Minuteman, and the Strategic Defense Initiative ("Starwars") (Hughes, 1989: 442; see also Kurtz, 1988: 92–6). The Manhattan Project ushered in what Philip Mirowski calls the "Cold War regime" in science, a designation that appropriately emphasizes the domination of science funding and research agendas by the military (Mirowski, 2011: 105–14).

The Cold War regime was also, this chapter will suggest, a Fordist regime in which science was tightly coupled with mass production. Fordism was a technological and economic system, combining mass production with mass consumption, and also a set of stabilizing social relations or a mode of regulation (Aglietta, 1987; Jessop, 2002). Of particular importance was the integration of bureaucratic unions as means for managing and controlling labor. On the Manhattan Project, the disciplining of labor was achieved by securing the cooperation of unions but also through the coercive power of the military and the ideological appeal to patriotism.

This instantiates how the so-called "consensus capitalism" of the post-war period was achieved in the context of the militarization of the culture, the coercive power of the national-security state, and domestic anti-Communism (Renshaw, 1991: 125–7, 185–6). The system of ideological and social control legitimated by the Cold War was central to the social regulation of the period of "Fordist growth" and the Manhattan Project may be seen as a laboratory for militarized industrial production and social control. The crisis in 1960s and 1970s of the militarized forms of control underpinning the Fordist-Cold War regime spurred the reassertion of market discipline in the neoliberal university.

The atomic bomb was co-constructed with a social order in which Fordist economic relations were interwoven with militarized social control. If the nuclear bomb was the central technology and symbol of the Cold War, the social relations in which nuclear weapons production was embedded also emblematized the postwar American Fordist growth, suburban affluence, and patriotic consensus that are now, for some, the object of nostalgia (Freeman, 2015). This chapter shows how this was a coerced consensus, solidified in war and legitimized by the external "threat" of the Soviet Union (Nathanson, 1988). The chapter also argues that the crisis of the economic conditions and forms of social control underlying this consensus led to the emergence of the neoliberal economic and institutional forms in which science is embedded today. A deeper understanding of the social relations of science in this period requires further research into the intersections between science and the broader economic and political regime of Fordism-Keynesianism, and the political-economic foundations of military-Keynesianism (cf chapters by Edgerton; Langley and Parkinson; Schiller and Yeo). This would contribute to our understanding of the longer-term evolution of relations between political and Research & Innovation, add to our understanding of the crucial period of transition from the Fordist-Cold War regime to the neoliberal "globalized privatization regime" in the political economy of science, and illuminate the social and economic contradictions that produced this shift (see also Mirowski, 2011: 87–138).

The Manhattan Project, labor, and the social relations of Fordism

Thomas Hughes presents the Manhattan Project both as the model for later technological system-building developments and as a "continuation of the growth of large production systems" since the late nineteenth century (Hughes, 1989: 383). One precedent in the sheer scale of technology and organization was Henry Ford's Rouge River automobile plant (Hughes, 1989: 385). Another key precedent was the Tennessee Valley Authority (TVA), an iconic site of New Deal public works, which provided electrical power to the Manhattan Project's Oak Ridge facilities for the separation of uranium isotope (Hughes, 1989: 382–5). The Manhattan Project combined large-scale production facilities and processes, dwarfing even Rouge River, in a government-run project that, like the TVA, transformed regions and built new settlements. The relationship and contrast between the TVA and the Manhattan Project exemplify how the newly economic interventionist stance of the New Deal state was redirected for military ends, and subsumed by military organization, in the Second World War (Hooks, 1991).

Military planning of the Manhattan Project operated in a close relationship with corporate monopoly or oligopoly capital. The manufacture of plutonium at Hanford, Washington, was carried out by the Du Pont corporation, which took over the process from the Metallurgical Laboratory scientists (Gerber, 1992, 25–6; Hughes, 2002, 59–60; Hounshell and Smith 1988: 338–46; Sanger, 1995: 29–65; Hales, 1999: 41). Tennessee Eastman, Kellex (a subsidiary of Kellogg), General Electric, Union Carbide and Carbon, and Monsanto operated key processes involved in the separation and refinement of uranium (Hales, 1999: 35). These firms were employed in a web of contracts by the Army Corps of Engineers. Peter Bacon Hales describes the structure of General Groves' Manhattan Engineer District (MED) as "an elaborate web of interconnected corporations, contracts, projects, and subprojects, all presided over by a military bureaucracy" (Hales, 1999: 35).

The sprawling project had an insatiable demand for labor. The US Army official history puts the total number employed by the project at a peak of 129,000 in June 1944 (Jones, 1985: 344; Thorpe, 2006: 1). The project had to find ways to sate its intense demand for labor within the context of the national wartime labor shortage. It not only had to compete with other industries, it also had to attract workers to secret sites, keep them there once they arrived, and keep them working. The way in which this was done, through a combination of compromise and coercion, modeled how national security culture would be a means for controlling labor within America's Cold War "consensus capitalism" (Renshaw, 1991, 106–51).

The balance of coercion and cooptation also reflected broader features of Fordism as a regime of accumulation. At the level of the production process, Fordism meant Taylorist methods of exerting managerial control over the labor process, combined with mechanization as represented by Ford's mobile assembly line (Braverman, 1974; Beynon, 1984). As he implemented these changes to his factory system, Ford obliterated the older form of craft control of labor, and was faced with the problem of how to exert discipline over the labor force. The broader social regime that the Regulation School and others describe as "Fordism" is associated in particular with Ford's "five-dollar day," a doubling of worker's pay rate introduced in 1914, and the high wage as the basis for mass consumption. Crucially, the "five-dollar day" was linked to the surveillance and regulation of the non-working life of labor by the Ford Company's "Sociological Department" (Meyer, 1980; Hooker, 1997).

According to Massimo de Angelis, the Sociological Department prefigured the broader Keynesian forms of the social regulation of Fordism in wartime and postwar America (De Angelis, 2000: 49). But the five-dollar day did not solve Ford's problems of controlling and retaining labor. Huw Beynon notes that "The paternalism of the Sociological Department was soon to give way to the brutality of the Service Department" (Beynon, 1984: 39). Workers in the River Rouge site were in a Panopticon prison-like regime in which fraternizing was banned and these rules were enforced by an army of Service Department spies (Beynon, 1984: 42–7). It was only when River Rouge was finally unionized by the United Auto Workers (UAW) as a result of a strike in 1941 that there emerged the kind of accommodation between management and bureaucratic unions that has come to be seen as characteristic of "Fordism" (Beynon, 1984: 49–50).

The Fordist "factory-society," in which "the disciplinary capitalist regimes are extended across the entire social terrain" (Hardt and Negri, 2000: 243), was reflected in attempts to create planned communities on Manhattan Project sites, as well as in attention to the nonworking lives and desires of workers, both as a necessary corollary of creating communities from scratch and as an attempt to combat turnover and absenteeism. Unions were also incorporated to some extent as means for controlling labor on the project, as well as in facilitating recruitment.

There are also clear parallels between Ford's Service Department and the militarized security regime that was used to stymie union organizing and intimidate labor at Oak Ridge and Hanford. Anti-Communism, patriotism, and national security were ideological forms that facilitated the disciplining and incorporation of labor on the Manhattan Project, prefiguring the forms of ideological control that coercively enforced "consensus capitalism" in the Cold War.

Attracting workers to secret and remote sites under conditions of a national labor shortage was a continual problem for the MED (Goldberg, 1998: 56–7). The project's high wages (at least in comparison with pre-war levels) and lucrative overtime attracted migrant labor from the mid-West (Olwell, 2004: 13; Hales, 1999: 172). Over time, Groves was able to win greater powers from the War Manpower Commission (WMC) for the District, ensuring the project's priority for labor recruitment. Eventually, the WMC "simply wouldn't allow workers needed by the District to take non-MED work anywhere in the nation where there was spare labor" (Hales, 1999: 167).

Coercive methods of recruiting combined with draconian methods for controlling and retaining labor (Olwell, 2004: 34). According to Hales, "Spies and 'informants' riddled every part of the District's culture, and labor was not immune" since informants would report on attempts at union organizing (Hales, 1999: 180). "Public information officers" would plant stories that the District would have dissidents fired and immediately drafted and sent to the war front. When the pipefitters union sought to organize in the summer of 1944, the District began employing soldiers as replacement workers (Hales, 1999: 178). During a spontaneous work stoppage and protest march at Oak Ridge "the men found that the guards had set up machine guns and had tear gas so the workers caused little disturbance" (Manhattan District files, quoted in Hales, 1999: 180).

Labor policies on the Manhattan Project were developed in the context of the growing strength of unions in the Second World War. The 1930s saw the development of national industrial unionism in the Congress of Industrial Organizations (CIO). The Wagner Act, upheld by the Supreme Court in 1937, secured the rights of unions to organize, and engage in collective bargaining on behalf of the workforce. The creation of the National Labor Relations Board (NLRB) represented the bureaucratic institutionalization of this recognition of unions as bargaining agents, a key component of the development of the broader social-institutional regime of Fordism and "Keynesian" modes of regulation. During the war, relations between labor and capital were mediated by bureaucratic agencies such as the NLRB and the WMC (Renshaw, 1991: 53–7; Levine, 1988: 133–6; Hales, 1999: 164–5). An aspect of this regime was that the right to strike, cemented in the New Deal, was undercut by the wartime "no strike pledge" between the federal government and national unions (Renshaw, 1991: 57–9, 64–7).

Groves reluctantly allowed American Federation of Labor (AFL) construction unions on the project, but he managed to get special dispensation from the NLRB to prevent unions from organizing the project's production or "operator" workforce (Olwell, 2004: 29). John M. Findlay and Bruce Hevly write that at Hanford "The army and Du Pont regarded organized labor as a threat to both efficiency and secrecy" (Findlay and Hevly, 2011: 29).

The Army's history of the Manhattan Project praises the "effectiveness of the project's labor policies" as indicated by the "almost complete absence of work stoppages from late 1944 until the end of the war" (Jones, 1985: 375; Olwell, 2004: 35). Russell Olwell notes that the walkouts that did occur were wildcat strikes "in defiance of the army, their managers, and their unions" (Olwell, 2004: 34). Manhattan District officials found the large national unions to be a useful conduit for labor recruitment. This meant, Hales writes, that "With the war as justification, and with patriotism as the goad, the District was effectively asking that the national offices of the largest unions became managerial entities – labor recruiters and suppliers, smoothly expediting labor flow" (Hales, 1999: 168; see also Jones, 1985: 370). Hales contextualizes this move within the broader shift in relations between labor, capital, and the state: the District's relationship to organized labor "continued to replicate the New Deal vision, whereby government agencies (the WMC, the Labor Relations Board) intervened between the hostile forces of labor and management" (Hales, 1999: 169). But in the context of wartime, the Manhattan District's incorporation of the unions was also "part of a larger attempt to expand military culture beyond the sites and into the institutions of civil life" (Hales, 1999: 171; see also Mackaman, 2014).

Secrecy and "Patriotic Consensus"

On the Manhattan Project, the industrial-capitalist control of the labor process was achieved by the military-security regime of compartmentalization. This meant that communication was channeled up the hierarchical line of supervision and horizontal communication between workers was strictly limited. The scientists at Los Alamos had sufficient clout that they were able to insist on the weakening of compartmentalization within that laboratory (Thorpe, 2006: 99–108, 131). But most Manhattan Project workers had little or no idea what went on outside the plant, or even room, in which they worked (Olwell, 2004: 42–3; Hales, 1999: 117–19, 131–50).

Hales describes how compartmentalization meant that most Manhattan Project workers had no understanding of what they were making, nor the reasons for it: "Theirs was truly labor alienated from its product" (Hales, 1999: 163; see also Olwell, 2004: 45). The Y-12 electromagnetic separation plant at Oak Ridge used calutrons, cyclotrons modified for separating out uranium isotope. The dials had false readings and the female operators had no idea what the machines were or what was their product (Olwell, 2004: 46; see also Kiernan 2013). Compartmentalization exacerbated danger to workers. Pipefitters, for example, would be charged with fixing leaks in pipes containing toxic or radioactive material about which they were kept ignorant (Olwell, 2004: 48; Hales, 1999: 132).

The Manhattan Project was highly dependent on skilled labor, such as pipefitters, welders, and electricians who were in short supply (Sanger, 1995: 73). It was also highly dependent on scientific workers who were in many cases "indispensable." In terms of their level of skill and knowledge, these workers were not Fordist "abstract labor." But compartmentalization provided a way of imposing control on this kind of highly skilled and educated labor force. They would be carrying out skilled and complex work, but in a fragmented way, isolated (to a varying degree depending on the type of worker) from other workers and from knowledge of the system as a whole.

Groves acknowledged that compartmentalization had functions other than just security. In his biography, he recalled that compartmentalization was a way of making the scientists "stick to their knitting" (quoted in Thorpe, 2006: 100). This system of secrecy also hindered union organizing. Compartmentalization limited social interaction, and therefore solidarity, between different plants of the project and made it hard for labor organizers to get information on conditions in different parts of the project.

According to Olwell, "limits on unions' access to information and right to strike at Oak Ridge facilities would weaken union power from the beginning" (Olwell, 2004: 81). Despite such restrictions, 1946 saw both the AFL and the CIO begin organizing production workers at Oak Ridge, and unions organized two of the three production facilities at the site (Olwell, 2004: 84–5). Still, security continued to provide the corporations ammunition against the unions. For example, Union Carbide and Carbon told the CIO's United Gas Coke and Chemical Workers (CIO-UGCCW) that it would only agree to a contract with a clause making any "stoppage or slowdown" cause for immediate dismissal (Olwell, 2004: 105). When, in 1947, the Manhattan District was taken over by the new Atomic Energy Commission (AEC), unions found that the AEC put pressure on its contractors to take a hard line in their labor negotiations (Olwell, 2004: 106, 108). The development of the Cold War saw the tightening of security restrictions at the atomic sites and workers fired under security rules for minor infractions. Olwell describes how, when UGCCW of Oak Ridge held a strike vote in March 1947, the *New York Times* headline was "Strike vote perils U.S. atomic output." Olwell writes, "The rhetoric of impending crisis … made workers appear selfish and unpatriotic for exercising their right to strike" (Olwell, 2004: 109; see also 109–12, 118, 120).

In his history of the post-war American labor movement Patrick Renshaw emphasizes how the Cold War ideology of anti-Communist patriotism was used to police the postwar accommodation between capital and organized labor (Renshaw, 1991: 99–100, 105–6, 114). So even as union membership reached a high-point, the establishment of patriotic hegemony was a means of controlling working-class demands through the culture and organization of the union. The Second World War involved, as Vaclav Smil puts it, "the deployment of just about every employable worker" (Smil 2013: 79; see also Freeman et al., 1992: 445–6). In this full-employment context in which workers were potentially in a very strong position to demand improvements in wages and conditions, national security and patriotic consensus provided significant means for disciplining workers and unions and attacking radicalism in the labor movement (De Angelis, 2000: 4; Midnight Notes Collective, 1984: 20–1). The legal and ideological resources of the national security state were similarly deployed to undermine the new social and political authority that scientists gained from their indispensable wartime role.

The mass scientist

According to Thomas Hughes, "The Manhattan Project set a precedent" for future technological system building in "the extensive employment and the influence of highly trained physicists and chemists, who interacted creatively with industrially experienced engineers, metallurgists, and skilled machinists" (Hughes, 1989: 385). However, as the Manhattan Project melded science with large-scale industrial production, it also changed the character of scientific work so as to integrate it with the organizational patterns of large-scale industry.

Even though the Los Alamos scientists, under the leadership of J. Robert Oppenheimer, tried to insist on academic practices against military norms, as fissionable material began to arrive from the industrial sites, and pressure built to "freeze" the design of the bomb, work patterns at Los Alamos began to be more industrialized. This was felt most intensely in the pressure to meet schedules. These schedules tied activity at Los Alamos to the pace of production of fissionable material coming from the production sites, since the pressure was for Los Alamos to be ready with a bomb mechanism as soon as there was sufficient fissionable material available (Thorpe, 2004; Thorpe, 2006: 128–59; Norris, 2002: 211–12, 361–72; Goldberg, 1998: 61–5).

A new model of the scientist was being developed in the Manhattan Project. It was a scientific role that contrasted greatly with the elite autonomy and self-image as independent scholar that was held to, especially by European émigrés such as Leo Szilard and Eugene Wigner, who worked at the Chicago Metallurgical Laboratory (Hughes, 1989: 394–6; see also Sanger, 1995: 42; Goldberg, 1998: 48–9). The kind of scientific role that was being worked out in the Manhattan Project was encapsulated in the title of a memo circulated by General Eisenhower in 1946: "Scientific and technological resources as military assets" (Hughes, 2002: 100).

The view that scientists themselves were resources of the state was symbolically institutionalized by the Oppenheimer loyalty-security hearing in 1954. If Oppenheimer's opposition to the development of the hydrogen bomb was illegitimate, this suggested that scientists working on government projects should be in service to whatever goals were set by agencies like the AEC (Thorpe, 2002; Thorpe, 2006: 200–42; McGrath, 2002: 158–95; Cassidy, 2005: 328–34).

It is revealing to look at the membership of the panels tasked with making the Oppenheimer judgment. Apart from the scientists, chemistry professor Ward Evans on the Personnel Security Board, and Henry Smyth on the AEC, these were business, financial, and bureaucratic-administrative figures, often with ties to the military (Stern, 1969: 259–62). This suggests that the hearing can be seen as the scientific elite being subject to discipline by other more powerful elite groups – business, financial, military and governmental-bureaucratic (Thorpe, 2002; Thorpe, 2006: 214; see also McGrath, 2002: 129–93).

Even before the Oppenheimer hearing, the security system imposed a narrow hegemonic middle-class Americanism on the scientific community. Obtaining clearance, a vital rite of passage for physicists whose employment opportunities were dominated by military-related research, meant foregoing any behavior, friendships, or political interests that might put one on the wrong side of the opaque and Kafkaesque clearance system (Wang, 1999; Kaiser, 2005; Mullett, 2008).

The normalizing effects of the security system reinforced the way in which physics was becoming routinized as a path to secure employment within the military-industrial complex. David Kaiser has documented the massive growth of the physics profession after the Second World War as returning veterans drove an expansion of higher education, and as the expansion of the military-industrial complex created demand for physicists. He describes the "suburbanization of physics" as the subject became a route to a middle-class affluence and stability (Kaiser, 2004; see also Freeman, 2015; Brown, 2013; Markusen, 1991).

Los Alamos was a model for the post-war suburban communities of scientists and engineers working in the military-industrial complex (Hunner 2004: 108; Markusen, 2001) The suburbanized physicist described by Kaiser was also the scientist as "organization man," in what C. Wright Mills called "Brains Inc." (Kaiser, 2004: 851–3, 856; Mills, 2002: 142). Physics departments were producing PhDs, specializing in fields with military-industrial applications, who "moved easily between industry and the academy" (Kaiser, 2004: 879).

As physics became a mass profession involving large sums of money and large-scale equipment (Hughes, 2002: 100–121), how to promote and manage growth was a problem for science policy, just as it was for macro-economic policy under Keynesianism. The early post-war period saw consistent growth in federal science budgets. Elizabeth Berman notes that "Between 1953 and 1967, federal support for academic R&D increased an average of 15.8% per year in real terms" (Berman, 2012: 35). Derek de Solla Price's influential *Little Science, Big Science*, published in 1963, was devoted to tracking the growth of "scientific manpower" and scientific production, in numbers of journals, abstracts, machines, and energy used (e.g. "the rate of increase of operating energy in particle accelerators") as well as the share of science (e.g. citations) between different countries (Price, 1963: 12, 18, 28). Price's development of indicators for science, establishing the field of scientometrics, mirrored the development of new economic indicators, such as Gross National Product, that facilitated economic planning in the New Deal and the Second World War (Furner, 2003; Hart, 1998: 23).

The new suburbanized physicist, or physicist as "manpower," was a corollary of the growth of the military-industrial complex. But the expansion of the ranks of scientists, and the integration of science into government and industry as a form of white-collar labor, can also be seen as a feature of deeper and longer-term structural shifts in the capitalist economy. The *mass scientist* was the corollary and accompaniment of the Fordist mass worker. The expansion of higher education and the ranks of the scientifically trained was part of the general expansion of bureaucratic, managerial and accounting work that accompanied the routinization, control, and mechanization of labor (Clawson, 1980; Noble, 1977). An increasingly technologized production process was also increasingly energy-dependent, again giving weight to the expertise of physicists, holding the promise of nuclear energy as "energy too cheap to meter" (Welsh 2000: 42; Keefer, 2010; Sovacool and Brossmann, 2013: 208–10). The expansion of the scientific workforce meshed with the needs of corporate capital and the emerging economy of mass production and mass consumption.

Scientists in the military-Keynesian state

Even though the promises of "energy too cheap to meter" failed to materialize, the prestige of science was crucially important in the ideological framework of the period. As working-class aspirations were co-opted through economic growth, the idea of progress, driven by science and technology, was a key feature of the culture of the post-war period: science would bring about the better tomorrows for which sacrifices were made during the war (Boyer, 1994: 109–21; Welsh, 2000). If the future was the atomic age or the space age, and better lives would be delivered by the technocrats and experts, this was not something to be won through political struggle.

A key issue in the relationship between science and the state in the post-war decades was whether scientists were to be "on top or on tap," visionary shapers of policy or neutral technicians (Shapin, 2001; Shapin, 1999; Shapin 2008: 70–1; King and Szelenyi, 2004: 194–5). The New Deal brought an influx of economic advisors into government and, as Brian Balogh argues, the war forged a more permanent link between expertise and the state: "The federal government bankrolled the production of record numbers of experts... Agencies courted experts: they were now an essential political resource" (Balogh, 1991: 12–13). The New Deal had seemed to open up a more powerful new role for experts within the polity, with the potential to realize the vision, put forward by Thorstein Veblen and the technocracy movement, of the carriers of knowledge as a "new class" able to challenge the power of the owners of capital (Hooks, 1991: 219; Segal, 2005; Brick, 2006; King and Szelenyi, 2004). The activist role of experts and bureaucrats in reshaping society and economy in the New Deal may be seen as part of the background and inspiration for the new politicization of scientists in the 1930s in groups such as the American Association of Scientific Workers and for the emergence of the scientists' movement after the end of the Second World War, with its vision of the international control of atomic energy (Kuznick, 1987; Smith, 1970; Thorpe, 2006: 165–88).

In his account of the American proposals for international control of atomic energy, Gregoire Mallard has emphasized the role of what he calls "New Deal lawyers" such as David Lilienthal and Dean Acheson (Mallard, 2009: 90–1). Plans for international control of atomic energy could be seen as an example of what Hardt and Negri have called "A New Deal for the World": the generalization of the New Deal as a model for governance. They write, "In the aftermath of the war, many viewed the New Deal model as the only path to global recovery (under the pacific powers of U.S. hegemony)" (Hardt and Negri, 2000: 241–4, quoting 244). But, contrary to the expectations of liberal scientists, the reality was that the US had no intention of giving up its "winning weapon" and the atomic bomb did not end, but became part of, imperialist power politics (Herken, 1988; Alperowitz, 1995; Gerson, 2007; Saccarelli and Varadarajan, 2015: 119–64).

The continuity and ultimate break with the New Deal can be seen in Lilienthal's trajectory from head of the TVA to his role as Chairman of the AEC. Initially, Lilienthal presented the AEC as having the potential to be a nuclear TVA, harnessing nuclear energy for social good. But these hopes were dashed and this broad vision abandoned with the beginnings of the Cold War and the emphasis on nuclear armament at the expense of civilian nuclear power (Neuse, 1997; Hughes, 1989: 426). Oppenheimer understood the defeat of the internationalist hopes of the Acheson–Lilienthal report as meaning also the defeat of the domestic legacy of the New Deal: "this will fit perfectly into the planning of that growing number who want to put the country on a war footing, first psychologically, then actually. The Army directing the country's research; Red-baiting; treating all labor unions, CIO first, as Communist and therefore traitorous, etc." (quoted in Thorpe, 2006: 182).

The failure of internationalism also led Oppenheimer to embrace, or at least accede to, a more narrowly instrumental and technical role for the scientist (Thorpe, 2006: 188–99). When Truman gave the go-ahead for the development of the hydrogen bomb, Lilienthal said that the AEC was now "nothing more than a major contractor to the Department of Defense" (quoted in Thorpe, 2006: 195). As the AEC was more and more geared toward military purposes, the broader role for experts that arose in the New Deal, and that internationalist scientists and allied New Deal liberals like Lilienthal hoped to carry over into the atomic age, gave way to a circumscribed instrumental-professional role. The trajectory of the AEC reflects the broader fate of the New Deal apparatus of government planning and public projects, which was increasingly taken over and absorbed by military planning during the Second World War (Hooks, 1991: 163).

The absorption of planning by the Pentagon was mirrored in the fate of science. As Philip Mirowski puts it, the military was given a "free hand … in orchestrating and subsidizing science in the immediate postwar period" (Mirowski, 2011: 60). To the extent that Cold War science operated under a Keynesian regime of public funding, it was decidedly *military* Keynesianism (Melman, 1970; Baran and Sweezy, 1968: 178–214; Block, 1977: 10, 103–9, 122; Prins, 1983: 133–68; Harman, 2009: 165–68). Science funding instantiates Hooks's point that the apparatus of planning built up in the New Deal had been absorbed into war planning in the Second World War and carried on in the defense sector after the war as military planning (Hooks, 1991; Mirowski, 2001: 110; see also Berman, 2012: 22).

Crisis of the Fordist-Cold War regime

In the 1960s, the disciplinary structures of the Cold War began to break down. One marker of this might be the strike called in January 1969 by 48 MIT faculty members who signed the March 4 manifesto against the militarization of American science (Leslie, 1993: 233). While the Cold War funding regime assumed the cooperation of universities with the military goals of the federal government, in the 1960s that ceased to be taken for granted:

> the anti-Vietnam protests erupting on college campuses were creating a backlash among policymakers who, like most of the public, continued to support the war. This led to a variety of proposals to punish universities who let the unrest go too far, like a 1969 bill that would have cut off all federal funds to universities that did not maintain discipline on campus.
>
> *(Berman, 2012: 36; see also Walshok and Shragge, 2014: 99–101;*
> *Moore, 1999; Moore, 2013)*

The mass production of scientific experts through expanded higher education was undermining the controlled, hierarchical and insulated world built up in organizations like the AEC. Balogh writes that "Longstanding safety questions within the nuclear community ... were now played out in crowded and politically charged arenas" (Balogh, 1991: 288). The environmental movement brought attention to the environmental degradation that was a hitherto unacknowledged corollary of Fordist growth and challenged the technocratic ideology and unaccountability of Cold War government agencies (Egan, 2007).

The social and institutional crisis of American universities in the 1960s and early 1970s was an aspect of the wider corrosion of the linked disciplinary structures of the Cold War and Fordism in the face of new political demands and aspirations of youth (Renshaw, 1991: 152–70; Downs, 1999; Caffentzis, 1975). The notion that the universities were the breeding ground for radicalism was a central plank of the New Right's response to the sixties' movements and counter-culture (see also Nik-Khah chapter), and motivated Ronald Reagan's attacks on the University of California (Juutilainen, 2006). The "Powell memorandum" of August 1971, written by Virginia corporate lawyer Lewis F. Powell for the US Chamber of Commerce, was particularly important, a pivotal moment, in setting out a view of the university as a politically dangerous center for what Powell called the "attack" on the "American Free Enterprise System" (Newfield 2008: 52–3). What the memorandum marked was an emerging shift in the mode of control over scientists and intellectuals: from the disciplinary structures of the national-security state to the market itself as a disciplinary structure which imposes constraints in a more impersonal and pervasive way (Hollinger, 2000: 161).

In the 1970s, the American economy was stagnating in the face of increasing international economic competition. As Chris Harman puts it, "The dynamic of market competition was relentlessly undercutting the dynamic of military competition" (Harman, 2009: 200). This changed political-economic context spurred the emergence of the neoliberal "globalized privatization regime" in which research would be geared to the service of private industry and the university legitimized primarily as an "economic engine" (Mirowski, 2011: 114–38; Berman, 2012; Shapin, 2008: 213–14; cf Edgerton, this volume). The mass scientist produced by the Manhattan Project was to be transformed into the entrepreneur, or the flexibilized knowledge-worker, of the post-Fordist "knowledge economy," whose problems are now, in turn, increasingly evident (Kleinman and Vallas, 2001; Barley and Kunda, 2011; see also the Introduction to this volume and chapters by Pagano and Rossi; Schiller and Yeo; Lazonick et al.; Tyfield).

Note

1   Major General Lauris Norstad to General Leslie R. Groves, 'Subject: Atomic Bomb Production,' September 15, 1945, Manhattan Engineering District Correspondence: Top Secret 1942–1946, Reel 1, File 3, Stockpile, Storage, and Military Characteristics, Subseries I – Top Secret Manhattan Project Files, National Archives Microfilm Publications.

Bibliography

Aglietta, Michael, 1987. *A Theory of Capitalist Regulation: The US Experience*. London: Verso.
Alperovitz, Gar, 1995. *The Decision to Use the Atomic Bomb*. New York: Vintage Books.
Balogh, Brian, 1991. *Chain Reaction: Expert Debate and Public Participation in American Commercial Nuclear Power, 1945–1975*. Cambridge: Cambridge University Press.
Baran, Paul A. and Paul M. Sweezy, 1968. *Monopoly Capital: An Essay on the American Economic and Social Order*. Harmondsworth, UK: Penguin.
Barley, Stephen R. and Gideon Kunda, 2011. *Gurus, Hired Guns, and Warm Bodies: Itinerant Experts in a Knowledge Economy*. Princeton: Princeton University Press.

Berman, Elizabeth, 2012. *Creating the Market University: How Academic Science Became an Economic Engine*. Princeton: Princeton University Press.

Beynon, Huw, 1984. *Working for Ford*. Harmondsworth, UK: Penguin.

Block, Fred L., 1977. *The Origins of International Economic Disorder: A Study of United States International Monetary Policy from World War II to the Present*. Berkeley: University of California Press.

Bowring, Finn, 2004. "From the Mass Worker to the Multitude: A Theoretical Contextualisation of Hardt and Negri's *Empire*," *Capital & Class* 28 (2) (Summer 2004): 101–32.

Boyer, Paul, 1994. *By the Bomb's Early Light: Thought and Culture at the Dawn of the Nuclear Age*. Chapel Hill: University of North Carolina Press.

Braverman, Harry. 1974. *Labor and Monopoly Capital: The Degradation of Work in the Twentieth-Century*. New York: Monthly Review Press.

Brick, Howard, 2006. *Transcending Capitalism: Visions of a New Society in American Social Thought*. Cornell: Cornell University Press.

Brown, Kate, 2013. *Plutopia: Nuclear Families, Atomic Cities, and the Great Soviet and American Plutonium Disasters*. Oxford: Oxford University Press.

Caffentzis, George, 1975. "Throwing Away the Ladder: The Universities in the Crisis," *Zerowork* 1: 128–42.

Cassidy, David C., 2005. *Oppenheimer and the American Century*. New York: Pi Press.

Clawson, Dan, 1980. *Bureaucracy and the Labor Process: The Transformation of U.S. Industry, 1860–1920*. New York: Monthly Review Press.

De Angelis, Massimo, 2000. *Keynesianism, Social Conflict and Political Economy*. Houndsmill, Basingstoke: MacMillan.

Downs, Donald, 1999. *Cornell '69: Liberalism and the Crisis of the American University*. Ithaca, NY: Cornell University Press.

Egan, Michael, 2007. *Barry Commoner and the Science of Survival: The Remaking of American Environmentalism*. Cambridge, MA: MIT Press.

Findlay, John M. and Bruce Hevly, 2011. *Atomic Frontier Days: Hanford and the American West*. Seattle: Center for the Study of the Pacific Northwest/University of Washington Press.

Freeman, Joshua, Nelson Lichtenstein, Stephen Brier, David Bensman, Susan Porter Bensman, David Brundage, Bret Eynon, Bruce Levine, and Bryan Palmer, 1992. *Who Built America? Working People and the Nation's Economy, Politics, Culture, and Society, Volume 2: From the Gilded Age to the Present*. New York: Pantheon Books,

Freeman, Lindsey S., 2015. *Longing for the Bomb: Oak Ridge and Atomic Nostalgia*. Chapel Hill: University of North Carolina Press.

Furner, Jonathan, 2003. "Little Book, Big Book: Before and After Little science, big science: A Review Article, Part 1," *Journal of Librarianship and Information Science* 35 (2): 115–25.

Gerber, Michelle Stenehjem, 1992. *On the Home Front: The Cold War Legacy of the Hanford Nuclear Site*. Lincoln: University of Nebraska Press.

Gerson, Joseph, 2007. *Empire and the Bomb: How the U.S. Uses Nuclear Weapons to Dominate the World*. London: Pluto Press.

Giddens, Anthony, 1985. *The Nation-State and Violence. Volume Two of A Contemporary Critique of Historical Materialism*. Cambridge: Polity Press.

Goldberg, Stanley, 1998. "General Groves and the Atomic West: The Making and Meaning of Hanford," in Bruce Hevly and John Findlay eds, *The Atomic West*. Seattle: University of Washington Press, pp. 39–89.

Hales, Peter Bacon, 1999. *Atomic Spaces: Living on the Manhattan Project*. University of Illinois Press.

Hardt, Michael and Antonio Negri, 2000. *Empire*. Cambridge, MA: Harvard University Press.

Harman, Chris, 2009. *Zombie Capitalism: Global Crisis and the Relevance of Marx*. Chicago: Haymarket Books.

Hart, David, 1998. *Forged Consensus: Science, Technology, and Economic Policy in the United States, 1921–1953*. Princeton, NJ: Princeton University Press.

Herken, Gregg, 1988. *The Winning Weapon: The Atomic Bomb in the Cold War, 1945–1950*. Princeton, NJ: Princeton University Press.

Herman, Arthur, 2012. *Freedom's Forge: How American Business Produced Victory in World War II*. New York: Random House.

Hollinger, David A., 1983. "The Defense of Democracy and Robert K. Merton's Formulation of the Scientific Ethos," *Knowledge and Society* (4): 1–15.

Hollinger, David A., 2000. "Money and Academic Freedom a Half-Century after McCarthyism: Universities amid the Force Fields of Capital," in Peggie J. Hollingsworth ed., *Unfettered Expression: Freedom in American Intellectual Life*. Ann Arbor: University of Michigan Press.

Hooker, Clarence, 1997. "Ford's Sociology Department and the Americanization Campaign and the Manufacture of Popular Culture among Line Assembly Workers c.1910–1917," *Journal of American Culture* 20 (1) (Spring 1997), 47–53.

Hooks, Gregory, 1991. *Forging the Military-Industrial Complex: World War II's Battle of the Potomac*. Urbana: University of Illinois Press.

Hounshell, David A. and John Kenly Smith, Jr., 1988. *Science and Corporate Strategy: Du Pont R&D, 1902–1980*. Cambridge: Cambridge University Press.

Hughes, Jeff, 2002. *The Manhattan Project: Big Science and the Atomic Bomb*. New York: Columbia University Press.

Hughes, Thomas, 1989. *American Genesis: A Century of Invention and Technological Enthusiasm*. New York: Penguin Books.

Hunner, Joseph, 2004. *Inventing Los Alamos: The Growth of an Atomic Community*. Norman: University of Oklahoma Press.

Jessop, Bob, 2002. *The Future of the Capitalist State*. Cambridge: Polity Press.

Jones, Vincent C., 1985. *Manhattan: The Army and the Atomic Bomb*. Washington, DC: United States Army Center of Military History.

Juutilainen, Paul Alexander, 2006. *Herbert's Hippopotamus: Marcuse in Paradise*. [Video-recording] New York: Cinema Guild.

Kaiser, David, 2004. "The Postwar Suburbanization of American Physics," *American Quarterly* 56(4) (December): 851–88.

Kaiser, David, 2005. "The Atomic Secret in Red Hands: American Suspicions of Theoretical Physicists During the Cold War," *Representations* 90 (1) (Spring 2005): 28–60.

Keefer, Tom, 2010. "Machinery and Motive Power: Energy as a Substitute for and Enhancer of Human Labor," in Kolya Abramsky ed., *Sparking a Worldwide Energy Revolution: Social Struggles in the Transition to a Post-Petrol World*. Edinburgh: AK Press, pp. 81–90.

Kiernan, Denise, 2013. *The Girls of Atomic City: The Untold Story of the Women Who Helped Win World War II*. New York: Touchstone.

King, Lawrence and Ivan Szelenyi, 2004. *Theories of the New Class: Intellectuals and Power*. Minneapolis: University of Minnesota Press.

Kleinman, Dan and Steve Vallas, 2001. "Science, Capitalism, and the Rise of the 'Knowledge Worker': The Changing Structure of Knowledge Production in the United States," *Theory and Society* 30 (4) (August): 451–92.

Kurtz, Lester R., 1988. *The Nuclear Cage: A Sociology of the Arms Race*. Englewood Cliffs, NJ: Prentice-Hall.

Kuznick, Peter J., 1987. *Beyond the Laboratory: Scientists as Political Activists in 1930s America*. Chicago: University of Chicago Press.

Leslie, Stuart, 1993. *The Cold War and American Science: The Military-Industrial-Academic Complex at MIT and Stanford*. New York: Columbia University Press.

Levine, Rhonda, 1988. *Class Struggle and the New Deal: Industrial Labor, Industrial Capital, and the State*. Lawrence: University of Kansas Press.

Mackaman, Tom, 2014. "100 Years Since Ford's Five Dollar Day," *World Socialist Web Site*, March 5, www.wsws.org/en/articles/2014/03/05/ford-m05.html.

Mallard, Gregoire, 2009. "Who Shall Keep Humanity's 'Sacred Trust'? International Liberals, Cosmopolitans, and the Problem of Nuclear Proliferation," in Gregoire Mallard, Catherine Paradeise and Ashveen Peerbaye, *Global Science and National Sovereignty: Studies in Historical Sociology of Science*. New York: Routledge, pp. 82–119.

Markusen, Ann R., 1991. *The Rise of the Gun Belt: The Military Remapping of Industrial America*. Oxford: Oxford University Press.

Markusen, Ann R., 2001. "Cold War Workers, Cold War Communities," in Peter Kuznick and James Gilbert (eds,) *Rethinking Cold War Culture*. Washington, DC: Smithsonian, pp. 36–60.

Martinez, Cecilia and John Byrne, 1996. "Science, Society and the State: The Nuclear Project and the Transformation of the American Political Economy," in John Byrne and Steven M. Hoffman eds, *Governing the Atom: The Politics of Risk*. New Brunswick, NJ: Transaction Publishers, pp. 67–102.

McGrath, Patrick J., 2002. *Scientists, Business, and the State, 1890–1960*. Chapel Hill: University of North Carolina Press.

Melman, Seymour, 1970. *Pentagon Capitalism: The Political Economy of War*. New York: McGraw Hill.

Meyer, Stephen, 1980, "Adapting the Immigrant to the Line: Americanization in the Ford Factory, 1914–1921," *Journal of Social History* 14 (1): 67–82.

Midnight Notes Collective, "'Exterminism' or Class Struggle?" in Radical Science Collective ed., *No Clear Reason: Nuclear Power Politics, Radical Science* (14) (1984): 9–27.

Mills, C. Wright, 2002 [orig.1951] *White Collar: The American Middle Classes.* Oxford: Oxford University Press.

Mirowski, Philip, 2011. *Science-Mart: Privatizing American Science.* Cambridge, MA: Harvard University Press.

Moore, Kelly, 1999. "Political Protest and Institutional Change: The Anti-Vietnam War Movement and American Science," in Marco Giugni, Doug McAdam, and Charles Tilly, (eds.) *How Social Movements Matter.* Minneapolis: University of Minnesota Press, pp. 97–118.

Moore, Kelly, 2013. *Disrupting Science: Social Movements, American Scientists, and the Politics of the Military, 1945–1975.* Princeton: Princeton University Press.

Mullett, Shawn Khristian, 2008. *Little Man: Four Junior Physicists and the Red Scare Experience.* Doctoral Dissertation, Harvard University.

Nathanson, Charles E., 1988. "The Social Construction of the Soviet Threat: A Study in the Politics of Representation," *Alternatives* 13: 443–83.

Natural Resources Defense Council, "Global Nuclear Stockpiles, 1945–2006," Bulletin of the Atomic Scientists, July/August 2006.

Neuse, Steven M., 1997. *David E. Lilienthal: The Journey of an American Liberal.* Knoxville: University of Tennessee Press.

Newfield, Christopher, 2008. *Unmaking the Public University: The Forty-Year Assault on the Middle Class.* Cambridge, MA: Harvard University Press.

Noble, David, 1977. *America by Design: Science, Technology, and the Rise of Corporate Capitalism.* New York: Alfred A. Knopf.

Norris, Robert S., 2002. *Racing for the Bomb: General Leslie R. Groves, the Manhattan Project's Indispensable Man.* South Royalton, Vermont: Steerforth Press.

Norris, Robert S., Steven M. Kosiak and Stephen I. Schwartz, 1998. "Deploying the Bomb," in Stephen I. Schwartz ed., *Atomic Audit: The Costs and Consequences of U.S. Nuclear Weapons Since 1940.* Washington, DC: Brookings Institute.

Olwell, Russell, 2004. *At Work in the Atomic City: A Labor and Social History of Oak Ridge, Tennessee.* Knoxville: The University of Tennessee Press.

Price, Derek J. de Solla, 1963. *Big Science, Little Science.* New York: Columbia University Press.

Prins, Gwyn ed., 1983. *Defended to Death: A Study of the Nuclear Arms Race from the Cambridge University Disarmament Seminar.* Harmondsworth, UK: Penguin.

Renshaw, Patrick, 1991. *American Labor and Consensus Capitalism, 1935–1990.* Jackson: University Press of Mississippi.

Saccarelli, Emanuele and Latha Varadarajan, 2015. *Imperialism Past and Present.* Oxford: Oxford University Press.

Sanger, S. L., 1995. *Working on the Bomb: An Oral History of WWII Hanford.* Portland, OR: Continuing Education Press, Portland State University.

Saunders, Frances Stonor, 1999. *Who Paid the Piper? The CIA and the Cultural Cold War.* London: Granta Books.

Segal, Howard P., 2005. *Technological Utopianism in American Culture.* Syracuse, NY: Syracuse University Press.

Shapin, Steven, 1999. "Foreward to the 1999 Edition," in Daniel S. Greenberg, *The Politics of Pure Science.* Chicago: University of Chicago Press.

Shapin, Steven, 2001. "Guests in the President's House," *London Review of Books* 23 (20) (18 October): 3–7.

Shapin, Steven, 2008. *The Scientific Life: A Moral History of a Late Modern Vocation.* Chicago: University of Chicago Press.

Smil, Vaclav, 2013. *Made in the USA: The Rise and Retreat of American Manufacturing.* Cambridge, MA: MIT Press.

Smith, Alice Kimball, 1970. *A Peril and a Hope: The Scientists' Movement in America, 1945–1947.* Cambridge, MA: MIT Press.

Sovacool, Benjamin K. and Brent Brossmann, 2013. "Fantastic Futures and Three American Energy Transitions," *Science as Culture* 22 (2): 204–12.

Stern, Philip M. with Harold P. Green, 1969. *The Oppenheimer Case: Security on Trial.* New York: Harper and Row.

Thayer, Harry, 1996. *Management of the Hanford Engineer Works in World War II: How the Corps, DuPont and the Metallurgical Laboratory Fast Tracked the Original Plutonium Works.* New York: ASCE Press.

Thorpe, Charles, 2002. "Disciplining Experts: Scientific Authority and Liberal Democracy in the Oppenheimer Case," *Social Studies of Science* 32 (4): 525–62.

Thorpe, Charles, 2004. "Against Time: Scheduling, Momentum, and Moral Order at Wartime Los Alamos," *Journal of Historical Sociology* 17 (1) (March 2004): 31–55.

Thorpe, Charles, 2006. *Oppenheimer: The Tragic Intellect.* Chicago: University of Chicago Press.

Walshok, Mary and Shragge, Abraham J., 2014. *Invention and Reinvention: The Evolution of San Diego's Innovation Economy.* Stanford: Stanford University Press.

Wang, Jessica, 1999. *American Science in an Age of Anxiety: Scientists, Anti-Communism, and the Cold War.* Chapel Hill: University of North Carolina Press.

Welsh, Ian, 2000. *Mobilising Modernity: The Nuclear Moment.* London: Routledge.

4

THE KNOWLEDGE ECONOMY, THE CRASH AND THE DEPRESSION

Ugo Pagano and Maria Alessandra Rossi

1 Introduction

The knowledge economy is generally invoked as the key to progress, development and prosperity. Since the work of Schumpeter (1934; 1942), knowledge production and innovation have been identified as distinctive features of market economies, crucial to overcome societal inertia and, as later recognized by Abramovitz's (1959) and Solow's (1960) seminal contributions, more relevant than capital accumulation to explain growth. A recent strand of research has, however, emphasized that the present institutions of the knowledge economy, far from being infallible engines of economic growth, embody features that may lead to their own demise, resulting in stagnant growth.

The key to understanding why the endgame of the knowledge economy may be crash and depression is the analysis of the dynamics leading to a reduction of investment opportunities as a consequence of the escalation of knowledge enclosures associated to the strengthening of the intellectual property (IP) system and the weakening of the traditional institutions of 'Open Science' (Dasgupta and David, 1994). The progressive monopolization of intellectual resources gives rise to both virtuous and vicious feedback effects between the distribution of intellectual assets and incentives to learn and develop new knowledge. Even where virtuous cycles are at play, however, the more the share of non-privatized knowledge shrinks in favour of intellectual monopolies, the less global investment opportunities tend to be available, and therefore the less the knowledge economy is able to keep its growth promises.

The ongoing reduction of the share of publicly available knowledge resources is compounded by the political economy of IP protection and public funding of Open Science. At the national level, large firms' rent-seeking activities and corresponding decision makers' capture may explain many aspects of the evolution of national IP systems and innovation policies. However, this is not the end of the story. At the international level, many forces are at play that combine to increase the extent of knowledge enclosures.

Contemporary international IP treaties such as the Agreement on Trade-Related Aspects of Intellectual Property Rights (henceforth, also TRIPs Agreement) involve reciprocity rules such as that of 'national treatment': to obtain IP protection for their nationals in signatories to the Agreement, countries are obliged to grant foreign inventors the same treatment that they grant to domestic inventors. Once rules of this type are in place in the international IP domain, countries' incentives to (upwardly) harmonize their IP rules are magnified and an excessive degree of IP protection tends to result, not just for the majority (of nations) but arguably for all.

More generally, the global commons nature of knowledge resources creates scope for free-riding phenomena whereby each country has an incentive to use the public knowledge of other countries and to over-privatize the knowledge that is produced, leading to a one-way ratchet of increasing IP protection. Both at the national and at the international level, the problem is reinforced by ubiquitous feedback effects: once IP institutions are in place, firms (countries) find themselves in a prisoner's dilemma situation whereby patenting (strengthening patent protection and reducing the scope of publicly available knowledge) is a dominant strategy for all, even if choosing a strategy of greater openness would be consistent with joint welfare maximization.

In this paper, we propose that the existence of these forces endogenous to the knowledge economy and with self-reinforcing features should be conceived of as a new rationale and foundation for science policy, and particularly for a *global* science policy. Since there is no spontaneous antidote to the progressive drift towards excessive knowledge privatization, public policies expressly recognizing the risks inherent in over-privatization of intellectual resources are sorely needed. Moreover, these policies require efforts at international coordination, so as to avoid the inevitable distortion of incentives to invest in public research resulting from uncompensated cross-border externalities.

Our perspective suggests not only that neoliberal prejudices against direct public investments in research should be abandoned, but also that the issue of whether to fund public research should not be considered separately from the question of the appropriate form of diffusion of publicly funded research results. Without explicit policies aimed at redressing the balance between private and publicly available knowledge, the knowledge economy will hardly be able to meet its growth-enhancing promises.

The paper is organized as follows. Section 2 illustrates the reasons put forward to explain why the endgame of the knowledge economy may be crash and depression. Section 3 engages with the issue of the political economy of knowledge enclosures. Section 4 articulates the rationale for a new (global) science policy. Section 5 concludes by summarizing the main questions for future research.

2 Why may the endgame of the knowledge economy be crash and depression?

The widespread faith in the growth-enhancing features of the knowledge economy and of the underlying pillars of scientific and technological research and innovation has gone, in the past few decades, hand in hand with a similarly widespread belief that private property-like institutions may deliver in the realm of intangibles exactly the same sort of benefits they deliver in the tangible domain. This intellectual position has coalesced with the more mundane interests of large corporations of the developed world (most of which are highly IP-intensive), leading to an unprecedented strengthening of intellectual property protection at the global level (on which more will be said in Section 3).

The pervasiveness of the propertization of intellectual resources has also been sustained by extraordinary technological developments that, on one hand, underline the extension of patentable subject matter and, on the other hand, increase the scope for global copy and imitation of inventions and intellectual creations, both of which then lead to further tightening of IP laws. Advancements in information and communication technologies as well as the growing complexity of interactions across different scientific disciplines (e.g., in the realm of nanomaterials, bioinformatics etc.) are increasingly blurring the once much clearer distinctions between basic and applied science, leading to a significant expansion of so-called 'Pasteur's quadrant' (Stokes, 1997), i.e. of the scope of scientific research that is simultaneously basic and applied.

Products, production processes and entire industries are characterized by ever greater complexity and draw on inherently intertwined and cumulative innovations that are typically related both to numerous prior basic and applied research results and to parallel technological developments. With the blurring of lines between the realm of technology and the realm of pure science and the definite dismissal of the linear model of innovation (see chapter by Edgerton, this volume), the *scope* of patentable subject matter has thus increased considerably. At the same time, the pervasive global diffusion of ICT technologies has broadened the *global reach* or *scale* of technical knowledge and innovations, simultaneously expanding the scope for their misappropriation.

These scientific and technological developments also hint at some of the reasons why the analogy between property and intellectual property that underpins many policy discourses (in the domain of trade policy, industrial policy as well as science policy) is misleading and dangerous for the knowledge economy itself. Unlike tangible property, intellectual property involves a much greater scope for overlap of 'exclusive' rights. This makes it difficult to securely identify the owner of a given intellectual resource, gives rise to costly and unproductive conflicts in enforcement and, most importantly, may hamper its productive exploitation.

The root cause of this is the inherent (quasi) 'public good' (see below) features of knowledge. This gives rise to a mismatch between the legal relations defined by private property and the intrinsically unbounded nature of knowledge and information as productive resources (Arrow, 1996, 651). Non-rivalry of knowledge – meaning many people can use this 'good' at the same time without incurring additional marginal costs – entails a situation in which the artificial exclusion of third parties associated to intellectual property comes at the cost of an inefficiency. This inefficiency is usually accepted as a necessary evil in exchange for greater incentives to produce the underlying knowledge. However, non-rivalry also leads to the size and potential extent of the exclusion associated to intellectual property being of an order of magnitude that is incomparable to that of private property. As argued by one of us elsewhere: 'the full-blown private ownership of knowledge means a global monopoly that limits the liberty of many individuals in multiple locations' (Pagano, 2014, 1413).

Contributions from many intellectual backgrounds and with different research agendas have started to recognize these tensions and to highlight reasons why the undeniable trend of propertization of knowledge resources may be excessive from the social standpoint and may end up undermining the functioning of the very engines of knowledge production.

A first strand of the literature focuses on the drawbacks of the current intellectual property institutions, with special regard to the patent system. Contributions belonging to this category typically delve into the link between patents and innovation and highlight the existence of effects standing in contrast with the claim that greater patenting necessarily entails greater innovation. Sceptical views have been expressed by many legal scholars, especially by those that have been most directly exposed to the real-world mechanics of the intellectual property regime (e.g., Lemley, 2005; Benkler, 2002; Samuelson, 2006). However, there is by now also a consistent body of economics literature (well represented, for instance, by the books by Bessen and Meurer, 2008, Boldrin and Levine, 2008 and Jaffe and Lerner, 2004) advancing the view that patents may actually have, in many instances, a detrimental effect on innovation. This view has, especially after the inception of the 2008 crisis, been taken up in the broader policy discourse even by mainstream voices such as *The Economist*.

A number of contributions has long shown theoretically that, when research is sequential and builds upon previous innovations, stronger patents may discourage follow-on inventions (Merges and Nelson, 1990; Scotchmer, 1991) and that overlapping patent rights may give rise to the so-called "anticommons tragedy", an instance of under-exploitation of intellectual resources due to the excessive proliferation of veto rights over their use (Heller and Eisenberg, 1998).

Similarly, from the empirical standpoint, it has long been known (at least since the 1980s) that in most sectors patents are at best of limited usefulness and that firms often deem formal protection mechanisms less effective than the alternatives (Mansfield, 1986; Levin et al., 1987; Cohen et al., 2000; various editions of the Community Innovation Survey), yet their propensity to patent remains high. A number of studies has pointed out that firms may be patenting *because other firms are patenting* rather than for the intrinsic usefulness of patents. A 'patent paradox' may be at play: the patent system may be creating incentives to patent rather than to invest in R&D (Hall and Ziedonis, 2001), especially as firms refine their use of patents as a strategic tool to pre-empt competitors' innovative investments, to improve bargaining positions in licensing and/or to defend themselves from patent litigation (see, e.g., Arundel et al., 1995; Duguet and Kabla, 1998; Reitzig et al., 2010).

Other research has uncovered the distortionary effects patents may have on innovation, by inducing costly duplications of research efforts (inventing around), by distorting firms' technological trajectories, being forced away from areas with greater risks of third-party IP infringements and by discouraging altogether the undertaking of those innovative projects that are most likely to incur problems due to patent overlaps. These problems are compounded in areas where products are technologically complex and firms' patent portfolios can reach a substantial scale – an instance often referred to as the problem of 'patent thickets'.[1]

Lerner (1995) finds early evidence that new and small biotechnology firms that have high litigation costs refrain from patenting in areas where they are more likely to infringe on existing patents, particularly where ownership belongs to (large) firms with low litigation costs. Cockburn et al. (2010) provide evidence of the fact that the need to licence-in patents reduces firms' innovative performance, by undertaking a survey of German innovating firms. Noel and Schankerman (2013), in a study focused on the patenting in the computer software industry between 1980 and 1999, found that companies facing a high concentration of patent portfolios from their main rivals refrain from investing in R&D in those areas where rivals' patent portfolios are stronger.

A contiguous domain of research is that considering academic patenting. The 1980 U.S. Bayh-Dole Act has allowed the patentability of federally funded research results, opening the way to a trend of increasing propertization of publicly funded science that has rapidly expanded into many OECD countries (and increasingly beyond – e.g. see the chapter by Suttmeier, this volume, on China). The purported rationale for this shift in science policy is many-fold: to ease commercialization, to counteract the effect of shrinking public funding for science and, more generally, to re-orient academic and Public Research Organizations' (PROs) research towards directions suitable to better contribute to the growth-enhancing promises of the knowledge economy. In this regard, research has mainly focused on a double link: between patenting and speed of scientific advancement; and between academic patenting (particularly of research tools) and diffusion of research results (for a concise survey, see Franzoni and Shellato, 2010).

Three main results of this literature are relevant for the purposes of the present paper. The first is that universities and Public Research Organizations appear not to be very good at the patenting game, both if one looks at the share of their patents over total patenting (about 5 per cent of active patents in the US, according to Thursby and Thursby, 2007, and a similar share in Europe, according to Lissoni et al., 2008), and at the amount of revenues they are able to raise (Geuna and Nesta, 2006).

In addition to raising doubts about the effectiveness of academic patenting in promoting commercialization, this should be sufficient to raise the question whether, from the PROs' standpoint, the prospective benefits of patents outweigh the certain restriction to the freedom of research involved by the inevitable curtailment of the research exemption.[2] Indeed, while universities have traditionally enjoyed a relatively wide exemption from infringement of patent protection for the purpose of scientific experimentation, as academic patenting and overlaps between public and private research increase, it remains to be seen whether PROs' activities will continue to be considered entirely part of scientific experimentation and thus shielded from liability.

Second, evidence exists that academic patenting hampers diffusion of research results. One particularly interesting paper considers the 'natural experiment' given by the release into the public domain of patents related to a genetically engineered mouse (Murray et al., 2009). The authors find that the extent of research in the area significantly increased and became more diversified, with the opening of new research trajectories that were not pursued when patents were in place. With a different methodology, Franzoni and Scellato (2010) find significant delays in publication in scientific journals when results are patented. Finally, Campbell et al. (2002) and Walsh et al. (2007) found evidence of the withholding of information, data and materials on which research is based.

Third, not much can be said on the effect of patenting on the speed of scientific advancement. While simple trade-offs between publishing and patenting do not seem to be at play if one looks at the productivity of single researchers (e.g., Azoulay et al., 2009), there currently is no research addressing the key issue, from a broader systems perspective of the productivity of science more generally, of whether substantial negative externalities for other researchers in the same field are associated with patents (Franzoni and Scellato, 2011).

While the contributions so far mentioned have focused on direct causal links between patenting and innovation or patenting and scientific advancement, the authors of the present chapter have, in previous works, proposed the view that the links between IPRs and innovative investments have a self-reinforcing nature, which is at the root of both patterns of unequal distribution of intellectual resources and chances for growth, and of a global progressive reduction in investment opportunities. This, in turn, points to the existence of a mechanism endogenous to the knowledge economy that may be part of the explanation of its crisis.

The starting point for the recognition of the self-reinforcing relationships existing in the intellectual property domain is the mentioned difference between the property of tangibles and intellectual property. The key efficiency argument underlying the existence of private property institutions is linked to the incentive effect property is able to generate. Owners have incentives to maintain, improve and productively use their tangible property. Most importantly, they have incentives to invest in specific and value-increasing human capital, as recognized by proponents of the new property rights approach (e.g., Hart, 1995). Pagano and Rossi (2004) have highlighted that this incentive effect is much stronger for intellectual than for physical property because IP owners enjoy a right not just to use but to *exclude* that has a much broader scope, as it entails a restriction of the liberty of third parties to replicate similar means of production. This, in turn, is at the origin of important feedback effects: while owners have heightened incentives to invest in IP-specific learning and human capital and to further acquire intellectual assets, non-owners are disincentivized from investing in the acquisition of intellectual capital. Both virtuous circles of accumulation and vicious circles of exclusion from intellectual capital ensue, with evident self-reinforcing properties.

This perspective makes a step further from the mentioned analyses focusing on the effects of firm and patent portfolio size on R&D investment and patenting patterns by highlighting the self-reinforcing nature that these effects may have at both firms' and countries' level. At the firm level, ever-increasing knowledge propertization has the effect of preventing the development of more democratic forms of organization of production. This is paradoxical, considering that the higher knowledge content of contemporary production would appear *prima facie* to enable greater democratization of production (Pagano and Rossi, 2011; Pagano, 2014). When monopoly rights are in place and much knowledge relevant to production may be codified, disembodied and legally protected, capitalist firms enjoy a cost advantage with respect to worker-owned firms because their size and the artificial excludability induced by IP feed into a dramatic form of (firm-level artificially restricted) increasing returns.

The self-reinforcing effects of intellectual ownership are even more profound at the country level. IPR endowments tend to be at the origin of new forms of comparative advantage in the 'knowledge economy' (Belloc and Pagano, 2012): given pervasive and global IPRs, countries find obstacles in specializing in those productions that depend heavily on IP-protected knowledge held by other countries. This gives rise to patterns of forced specialization that feed into global trade, constituting a novel cause for increased international exchange, along with the classical explanations provided by trade theory. What is most relevant is that these patterns of forced specialization tend to perpetuate in time, giving rise to trajectories of development *and underdevelopment* associated to the unequal initial distribution of IP endowments into IP-, and hence rent-, rich and poor worlds.

Pagano and Rossi (2009) and Pagano (2014) have argued that these sorts of feedback effects impact not only on the relative gains and losses of asymmetrically endowed countries, but also on the overall availability of investment opportunities, and thus on growth at the global system level. The overall effect of the global strengthening of IP protection may, indeed, have been a global contraction of the chances for productive investment, which may be considered to underlie the recent crisis. The lack of good investment opportunities, together with abundant capital and lax financial regulations, may explain why capital was redirected away from productive uses, thus giving rise to the housing bubble and the ensuing subprime crisis (Pagano and Rossi, 2009; on financialization, see also chapters by Lazonick et al. and Birch, this volume). Moreover, knowledge propertization contributes to the financialization of the economy, as it turns intellectual resources into securely owned and tradable assets that, having no value defined in a competitive market, are easily exposed to the vagaries of speculative expectations (Pagano, 2014).

The evolution of global investment appears coherent with the view that global IPRs are progressively curtailing investment opportunities. As can be seen from Figure 4.1, after the major event triggering the global strengthening of IPRs (the 1994 Agreement on Trade-Related Aspects of Intellectual Property Rights - TRIPs) (e.g., May and Sell, 2006), global investment rose for about five years and then started a continuous decline. Our contention is that this global decline is to be attributed to the progressive erosion of the availability of non-privatized knowledge.

Thus, the uneven distribution of knowledge is an important cause of overall economic inequality and a brake to global growth. In a much-acclaimed book, Picketty (2014) has emphasized how a rate of profit greater than the rate of growth must necessarily lead to a growing relative impoverishment of the majority of the population. Picketty attributes the origin of the phenomenon to over-accumulation of capital. However, a careful reading of the evidence suggests that a more convincing explanation must be found in the under-investment of real capital goods (Rowthorn 2014), which has characterized the recent decades. This under-investment is consistent with the increase in wealth of firms because the latter has been often due to an increase in their monopoly rents (and also of the overall profit rate earned on their capital). As argued by Stiglitz (2015, 24): '[i]f monopoly power of firms increases, it will show up as an increase in the income of capital, and the present discounted value of that will show up as an increase in wealth (since claims on the rents associated with that market power can be bought and sold.'

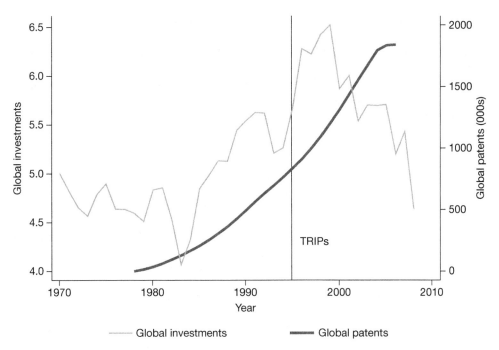

Figure 4.1 Global patents and global investments
Source: Belloc and Pagano (2012)

Knowledge propertization, although so far disregarded, may be an important part of the explanation for the puzzling simultaneous occurrence of under-investment, wealth accumulation, high profit and low growth. When much knowledge moves from the public to the private sphere, the increased monopolization is likely to increase profits and to decrease growth. And, moreover, almost by definition, subtracting from public knowledge resources increases inequality: everyone has equal rights of access to a public good. By contrast, the privatization of knowledge gives rise to only the monopolistic owner having full access to it. Thus increased rents (including also those that do not arise from the monopolization of knowledge) are likely to cause both declining growth and increasing inequality. The actual dismal economic record of recent years thoroughly corroborates these theoretical expectations.

3 The political economy of knowledge enclosures

As mentioned in the previous paragraph, the turning point in global IPR protection is given by the 1994 TRIPs agreement. This is the first international agreement on IP-related matters that, in addition to (upwardly) harmonizing an almost all-encompassing range of aspects of the legal protection of intellectual creations at the global level, explicitly foresees a mechanism of enforcement, under the oversight of the World Trade Organization (WTO). Since the TRIPs agreement, a number of less comprehensive but equally relevant agreements have contributed to further strengthening global IP protection. TRIPs-plus provisions (meaning those even stronger than TRIPs) have been introduced in countries such as Australia, Chile, Peru, countries of the Middle East and others as part of the negotiation of Preferential Trading Areas (PTAs) with the United States and the European Union. Horizontal agreements among developing countries (e.g., within members of ASEAN) have also raised their harmonized IP standards and procedures. IP-reinforcing provisions are also common in many bilateral investment treaties and international investment agreements (Maskus, 2014).

The rent-seeking activities of large (and IP-endowed) firms in developed countries have been an important trigger of these developments. This is particularly true for US firms which, at the onset of the Uruguay Round of negotiations, were perceived as falling behind their German and Japanese counterparts and were eager to increase the extent of monopoly and oligopoly rents they could appropriate in international markets. These private interests may have translated into industry capture of trade negotiators (Lanjouw and Cockburn, 2001).

However, countries' policy makers may have excessive incentives to strengthen global intellectual property protection even assuming away problems of politicians' capture. Scotchmer (2004) suggests that harmonization of IP protection leads to broader IP protection than would be chosen if choices were independent, and to stronger protection than would be optimal from a social standpoint. In addition, she also shows that, under the requirements of reciprocity (national treatment) embodied in the TRIPs agreement, countries have an incentive to tilt the policy mix in favour of IP and away from public sponsorship of research and innovation because the former, unlike the latter, allows to internalize cross-border knowledge externalities.

More generally, the fact that knowledge is a global commons and is therefore exposed to the usual free-rider problems that plague this sort of goods may help to explain why each country has an incentive to use the public knowledge of other countries and to over-privatize the knowledge that it is producing, even more so if globally harmonized protection is in place. Hence, each country is pushed towards a portfolio of instruments for intellectual property management that increases the weight of patenting well beyond what would happen in a closed economy and beyond the socially efficient level. This, in turn, amounts to a form of national free-riding on the global knowledge commons that can be seen as an instance of unfair competition. Seen from this angle, it is thus striking that this form of unfair competition goes unnoticed at the WTO level, while the forms of unfair competition associated to IP violations are severely sanctioned, even by allowing retaliation through trade restrictions (Pagano, 2014).

This free-riding-based incentive to favour privatized knowledge over Open Science has gone hand in hand with the substantial changes public research systems have been undergoing since the mid-nineties. The more knowledge has been recognized as a key ingredient of growth, the more universities and PROs have been oriented towards serving the training and research support needs of the economy. Reforms have been made to strengthen and intensify public-private collaborations, actively to promote patenting and patent-backed technology transfer with the institution of specialized technology transfer offices (TTOs), and to direct research efforts towards specific societal needs through the increased competitive allocation of funds (Geuna and Rossi, 2015). These developments are changing the overall attitude of publicly funded science institutions as well as of individual researchers and profoundly affecting the set of norms conventionally associated to Open Science.

This tends to extend to public research the sort of feedback effects that appear at play for firms and countries alike: once IP institutions are in place, producers of knowledge (be they researchers, firms or countries) find themselves in a prisoner's dilemma situation whereby patenting is a dominant but sub-optimal strategy even if choosing not to patent would be consistent with joint welfare maximization.

Thus, also if seen from the political economy angle, the present (international) institutions of the knowledge economy appear to embody an endogenous mechanism that tends to perpetuate their very existence as well as their negative implications for learning, growth and inequality. Most importantly, with the once Open Science-oriented public research institutions ever more active at the IP game, there currently seems to be a lack of endogenous antidotes to the ever-increasing enclosure of public knowledge. In the next section, we argue that the pressing need for such an antidote should be conceived of as a new rationale and foundation for science policy, and particularly for a *global* science policy. Without such an antidote, the knowledge economy will hardly be able to meet its growth-enhancing promises.

4 A new rationale for a global science policy

The economic literature has pointed to the existence of a multiplicity of rationales for science (and technology) policy. In the neo-classical approach (Arrow, 1962; Dasgupta and David, 1994) the main foundation of science policy is the existence of market failures linked to the public good nature of the knowledge that constitutes basic science. While technology can be privately appropriated through IPRs, fundamental research creates maximum spillover effects, which motivate public investment in their production to make up for lacking private incentives.

The literature on systems or networks of innovation (e.g., Freeman, 1995; Lundvall, 2007), by contrast, identifies the justification for public intervention in science and technology in the existence of innovation system failures. Since innovation depends on the complementarities and the links between multiple actors and resources, which may be subject to coordination and incentive alignment problems, there may be a role for public policy in helping to address these problems.

Evolutionary thinkers (e.g., Nelson and Winter, 1982; Dosi, 1988) highlight an additional role for science policy, residing in the need to promote knowledge diffusion and generation of diversity, so as to redress the consequences of path-dependent evolutionary trajectories.

Finally, proponents of the knowledge-based approach (e.g., Cohendet and Meyer-Krahmer, 2001) emphasize the collective nature of knowledge production, sharing and distribution and the importance of learning processes, finding in the existence of learning (cognitive) failures the justification for science and technology policy.

The perspective we propose in this paper (and in previous related work) offers a new rationale for (global) science policy. We have advanced so far two main contentions. The first is that excessive knowledge privatization should be considered responsible for the squeeze and distortion of investment opportunities and, ultimately, for hampering growth and increasing global inequality. The second is that the political economy underlying international global IP protection and investment in public research tends to magnify the effects of knowledge privatization, leaving 'intellectual monopoly capitalism' (Pagano, 2014) with no endogenous mechanism to redress the imbalances caused by knowledge propertization. From these two contentions we draw three main conclusions for science policy.

First, the (quasi-)public good nature of knowledge should not only be interpreted as a rationale underlying the need for public funding to substitute for private incentives, thus addressing a market failure. An even more pernicious failure of the system itself derives from the excessive reduction of the domain of non-propertized knowledge, due to the fact that knowledge ownership gives rise to the self-reinforcing positive and negative dynamics and to the overall squeeze in investment opportunities highlighted in the previous paragraphs. Open Science, intended as scientific knowledge that preserves its public good features, is thus key to unlock the growth-enhancing features of the knowledge economy.

Second, and relatedly, it is necessary to broaden the set of tools of science policy with more openness-preserving tools. Mazzucato (2013) has convincingly shown that substantial public investment in science underpins many of the most successful privately appropriated innovations of our time. This certainly backs the claim that public funding of research should be preserved and enhanced. However, given the present institutional framework skewed in favour of privatization of the results of basic research, increasing public research funding may not be enough. In other words, we propose that the question whether and how much public research should be funded should not be considered separately from the more fundamental question of whether privatization of public research results through IP should be encouraged. The efficiency-enhancing features of publicly funded research reside in the broad range of externalities it is able to propagate throughout the economy. Without these features, it is unclear why public research should be funded at all.

Third, the global dimension of knowledge production and its associated political economy dynamics should be explicitly taken into account as a foundation for science policy. Unlike the case of IP, in the domain of Open Science there are not (yet!) international institutions that ensure harmonization of public sponsorship policies so as to address the disincentive effects of cross-border externalities (Schotchmer, 2004; Pagano and Rossi, 2009). Undeniable difficulties notwithstanding, ways should be found to devise science policies with a global dimension. International coordination is sorely needed to ensure that the main engine of growth – knowledge production – does not run out of its indispensable fuel: freely accessible scientific knowledge.

A few possible tools have been already proposed in this connection. Stiglitz (1999) has suggested that it would be justified on both efficiency and equity grounds for the international community to 'claim the right to charge for the use of the global knowledge commons'. One way to achieve a similar outcome could be to foresee a minimum investment requirement in Open Science (e.g., 3 per cent of GNP) to all the countries that are members of the WTO organization (Pagano, 2014). Alternatively, funding of international knowledge institutions and internationally backed patent buyouts may be part of the set of tools (Pagano and Rossi, 2009). There is certainly a dearth of creative policy solutions in this important domain: the search for ways to overcome the negative consequences of excessive knowledge privatization should be a necessary part of the agenda of a political economy of science.

5 Conclusions and questions for future research

In this chapter, we have proposed the existence of a new foundation for a (global) science policy: the need to counteract the nefarious consequences of excessive knowledge privatization. The growth-enhancing promises of the knowledge economy may never be realized due to its endogenous tendency to drift towards excessive knowledge privatization. Excessive exclusion and blockage in the utilization of knowledge resources has already manifested its effects not only in the patterns of international production specialization and unequal growth, but also in the curtailment of the growth potential of the countries that enjoy the best endowments of privatized intellectual capital. In addition, the political economy of global intellectual property protection and of investments in public research suggests that this squeeze in investment and growth opportunities does not find easy antidotes.

This also suggests a range of new questions for a political economy of science. First, the mechanisms underlying the virtuous and vicious feedback effects existing between the distribution of intellectual assets and learning and knowledge investment should be further explored, with the purpose of identifying ways to break vicious circles and unlock the potential of the knowledge economy. Second, more research is needed to understand fully the global consequences of the changing attitudes and practices of publicly funded research that are progressively moving away from the norms of Open Science to embrace norms of 'closed science'. To what extent open access movements and policies promoted by some universities and research groups may be an appropriate solution? What alternatives are available (see chapters in this volume by Lazonick et al.; Tyfield; Muellerleile)? Third, a further crucial question concerns the identification of ways to overcome the ingrained resistance to devise global solutions for the production of Open Science and, more generally, of publicly available knowledge.

These questions by no means exhaust the range of issues relevant to the research agenda of a new, global, political economy of science policy. We believe, however, that they are a necessary starting point if further crash and depression of the knowledge economy are to be avoided.

Notes

1 Shapiro (2001) refers to 'patent thickets' as dense webs of overlapping patent rights, mostly belonging to multiple firms' large patent portfolios.
2 In the United States, the key judicial decision sanctioning the curbing of universities' research exemption is considered to be the Federal Circuit Court of Appeals' decision *Madey v. Duke University* (307 F.3d 1351, 1362 (Fed. Cir. 2002)). In this decision, the Court held that the exemption 'does not apply to activities conducted in the context of the normal "business" of a research institution, either for-profit or not-for-profit'. It is clear that the more PROs engage in patenting, the more their activities will be considered part of business, unworthy of a research exemption. In Europe, acts 'done privately and for purposes which are not commercial' and acts 'done for experimental purposes relating to the subject matter of the invention' have traditionally been shielded from liability.

References

Abramovitz, M. 1959. 'The welfare interpretation of secular trends in national income and product', in M. Abramovitz et al. (eds.) *The Allocation of Economic Resources: Essays in Honor of Bernard Francis Haley*, Stanford, California: Stanford University Press.

Arrow, K.J. 1962. 'Economic welfare and the allocation of resources for inventions'. In: Nelson, R.R. (ed.), *The Rate and Direction of Inventive Activity: Economic and Social Factors*. Princeton University Press, Princeton.

Arrow, K.J. 1996. 'Technical information and industrial structure', *Industrial and Corporate Change*, 5, 645–52.

Arundel, A., Van de Paal, G. and Soete, L., 1995. *Innovation Strategies of Europe's Largest Industrial Firms: Results of the PACE Survey for Information Sources, Public Research, Protection of Innovations and Government Programmes*. Final Report, MERIT, June 1995. DG XII of the European Commission.

Azoulay, P., Ding, W. and Stuart, T. 2009. 'The impact of academic patenting on the rate, quality and direction of (public) research output', *Journal of Industrial Economics*, 57, 637–76.

Belloc, F. and Pagano, U. 2012. 'Knowledge enclosures, forced specialization and investment crisis', *European Journal of Comparative Economics*, 9(3), 445–83.

Benkler, Y. 2002. 'Intellectual Property and the Organization of Information Production', *International Review of Law & Economics* 81.

Bessen, J.E. and Meurer, M.J. 2008. *Patent Failure: How Judges, Bureaucrats, and Lawyers Put Innovators at Risk*, Princeton, NJ: Princeton University Press.

Boldrin, M. and Levine, D. K., 2008. *Against intellectual Monopoly*, Cambridge: Cambridge University Press.

Campbell, E. G., Clarridge, B. R., Gokhale, M., Birenbaum, L., Hilgartner, S., Holtzman, N. A. and Blumenthal, D. 2002, 'Data withholding in academic genetics: Evidence from a national survey', *JAMA*, 287, 473–80.

Cockburn, Iain, Megan MacGarvie and Elisabeth Mueller 2010. 'Patent Thickets, Licensing and Innovative Performance', *Industrial and Corporate Change*, 19(3), 899–925.

Cohen, W., Nelson, R. and Walsh, J., 2000. 'Protecting their intellectual assets: appropriability conditions and why U.S. manufacturing firms patent (or Not)', NBER Working Paper 7552.

Cohendet, P. and F. Meyer-Krahmer 2001. 'The theoretical and policy implications of knowledge codification', *Research Policy* 30, 1563–91.

Dasgupta, P. and David, P.A. 1994. 'Toward a new economics of science', *Research Policy* 29, 487–521.

Dosi, G. 1988. 'Sources, Procedures and Microeconomic Effects of Innovation', *Journal of Economic Literature*, N. XXVI, 1120.

Duguet, E. and Kabla, I. 1998. 'Appropriation Strategy and the Motivations to Use the Patent System: An Econometric Analysis at the Firm Level in French Manufacturing', *Annales D'Economie et de Statistique* 49/50 pp. 289–327.

Franzoni, C. and Scellato, G. 2010. 'The grace period in international patent law and its effect on the timing of disclosure', *Research Policy*, 39, 200–13.

Franzoni, C. and G. Scellato 2011. 'Academic Patenting and the Consequences for Scientific Research', *The Australian Economic Review*, (44)1, 95–101.

Freeman, C. 1995. 'The "National System of Innovation" in historical perspective', *Cambridge Journal of Economics*, 19, 5–24.

Geuna, A. and F. Rossi 2015. *The University and the Economy: Pathways to Growth and Economic Development*, Edward Elgar.

Geuna, A. and Nesta, L. 2006. 'University patenting and its effects on academic research: The emerging European evidence', *Research Policy*, 35, 790–807.

Hall, B.H. and Ziedonis, R.H. 2001. 'The patent paradox revisited: an empirical study of patenting in the U.S. semiconductor industry 1979–1995', *RAND Journal of Economics*, 32, 101–28.

Hart, O. 1995. *Firms, Contracts and Financial Structure*, Oxford, Oxford University Press.

Heller, M. and Eisenberg, R. 1998. 'Can patents deter innovation? The anticommons in biomedical research', *Science*, 280, 698–701.

Jaffe, A. B. and Lerner, J. 2004. *Innovation and Its Discontents: How Our Broken Patent System is Endangering Innovation and Progress, and What to Do About It*, Princeton University Press.

Lanjouw, J.O. and I.M. Cockburn 2001. 'New Pills for Poor People? Evidence after GAT', *World Development*, 29, 265–49.

Lemley, Mark A. 2005. 'Property, Intellectual Property, and Free Riding'. *Texas Law Review*, 83: 1031.

Lerner, J. 1995. 'Patenting in the Shadow of Competitors', *Journal of Law and Economics*, 38, 463–90.

Levin, R., Klevorick, A., Nelson, R. and Winter, S. 1987. 'Appropriating the returns from industrial R&D', *Brookings Papers on Economic Activity*, n. 3.

Lissoni, F., Llerena, P., McKelvey, M. and Sanditov, B. 2008. 'Academic patenting in Europe: New evidence from the KEINS database', *Research Evaluation*, 17, 87–102.

Lundvall, Bengt-Åke 2007. 'National innovation systems – analytical concept and development tool', *Industry and Innovation*, 14(1), 95–119.

Mansfield, E. 1986. 'Patents and innovation: an empirical study', *Management Science*, n. 32.

Maskus, K. 2014. 'The new globalization of Intellectual Property Rights: what's new this time?', *Australian Economic History Review*, 54(3), 262–84.

May, C. and Sell, S.K. 2006. *Intellectual Property Rights: A Critical History*, Lynne Rienners Publishers: Boulder, USA.

Mazzucato, M. 2013. *The Entrepreneurial State: Debunking Public vs. Private Sector Myths*, Anthem Press: London, UK.

Merges, R. and Nelson R. 1990. 'On the Complex Economics of Patent Scope', *Columbia Law Review*, 90(4).

Murray, F., Aghion, P., Dewatripont, M., Kolev, J. and Stern, S. 2009. 'Of mice and academics: Examining the effect of openness on innovation', National Bureau of Economic Research Working Paper no. 14819, Cambridge, MA.

Nelson, R., S.G. Winter. 1982. *An Evolutionary Theory of Economic Change*. Belknap Press of Harvard University, London.

Noel, Michael and Schankerman, Mark 2013. 'Strategic patenting and software innovation', *Journal of Industrial Economics*, 61(3), 481–520.

Pagano, U. 2007. 'Cultural globalisation, institutional diversity and the unequal accumulation of intellectual capital', *Cambridge Journal of Economics*, 31(5), 649–67.

Pagano, U. 2014. 'The Crisis of Intellectual Monopoly Capitalism', *Cambridge Journal of Economics*, 38, 1409–29.

Pagano, U. and Rossi, M. A. 2004. 'Incomplete Contracts, Intellectual Property and Institutional Complementarities', *European Journal of Law and Economics*, 18(1), 55–76.

Pagano, U. and Rossi, M.A. 2009. 'The Crash of the Knowledge Economy', *Cambridge Journal of Economics*, 33(4), 665–83.

Pagano, U. and Rossi, M. A. 2011. 'Property Rights in the Knowledge Economy: An Explanation of the Crisis', in Brancaccio, E. and Fontana, G. (eds) *The Global Economic Crisis*, London, Routledge, pp. 284–97.

Partha, Dasgupta and David, Paul A. 1994. 'Toward a new economics of science', *Research Policy*, Elsevier, 23(5), 487–521, September. Arrow, 1962

Piketty, T. 2014. *Capital in the Twenty-First Century*, Harvard University Press, Cambridge.

Reitzig, M., Henkel, J. and Schneider, F. 2010. 'Collateral damage for R&D manufacturers: how patent sharks operate in markets for technology', *Industrial and Corporate Change*, 19, 947–67.

Rowthorn, R. 2014. 'A note on Piketty's Capital in the Twenty-First Century', *Cambridge Journal of Economics*, 38(5), 1275–84.

Samuelson, P. 2006. 'Enriching Discourse on Public Domains'. *Duke Law Journal*, 55: 783.

Schumpeter, J.A. 1912/1934/1983. *The Theory of Economic Development: An Inquiry into Profits, Capital, Credit, Interest, and the Business Cycle*, New Brunswick, NJ, Transaction Publishers.

Schumpeter, J.A. 1942. *Capitalism, Socialism, and Democracy*, New York: Harper Bros.

Scotchmer, S. 1991. 'Standing on the Shoulders of Giants: Cumulative Research and the Patent Law, Suzanne Scotchmer', *Journal of Economic Perspectives*, 5(1), Winter 1991, 29–41.

Scotchmer, Suzanne 2004. 'The Political Economy of Intellectual Property Treaties', *Journal of Law, Economics, and Organization*, October, 20(2), 415–37.

Shapiro, Carl 2001. 'Navigating the patent thicket: Cross licenses, patent pools, and standard setting', in *Innovation Policy and the Economy*, Volume 1. MIT Press. 119–50.

Solow, R.M. 1960. 'Investment and technical progress', in Arrow, K., Karlin, S. and Suppes, P. (eds.), *Mathematical Methods in the Social Sciences*, 1959. Stanford University Press: pp. 89–104.

Stiglitz, J. E. 1999. 'Knowledge as a Global Public Good', [online] available at http://p2pfoundation.net/Knowledge_as_a_Global_Public_Good.

Stiglitz, J. E. 2015. 'New Theoretical Perspectives on the Distribution of Income and Wealth among Individuals', NBER Working Paper 21189.

Stokes, D. 1997. *Pasteur's Quadrant: Basic Science and Technological Innovation*, Washington: Brookings Institution Press.

Thursby, J. and Thursby, M. 2007. 'University licensing', *Oxford Review of Economic Policy*, 23, 620–39.

Walsh, J. P., Cohen, W. M. and Cho, C. 2007. 'Where excludability matters: Material versus intellectual property in academic biomedical research', *Research Policy*, 36, 1184–203.

5

SCIENCE AND ENGINEERING IN DIGITAL CAPITALISM

Dan Schiller and ShinJoung Yeo

During recent decades, at a cost that is reckoned in the trillions of dollars, digital systems and applications have been introduced across the length and breadth of the business system.[1] This stupendous investment in ICTs, and the profit-strategies that it supports, constitute a basis for naming the contemporary political economy "digital capitalism." In much the same way that "industrial capitalism" extended beyond manufacturing to reorganize agricultural production and even information industries such as publishing, today digital capitalism has gripped every sector. Historically centered on the United States, yet transnational in scope, new network platforms continue to be innovated in order to extend and enlarge longstanding capitalist imperatives: exploitative wage relations; investment and product development decisions based on profit forecasts; ruthless pressures for cost-efficiency and growth (Schiller 1999, 2014; Wood 2003). This chapter foregrounds the place of science and engineering within this encompassing transition.

Science and capital: a changing historical matrix

Science has played a vital role in capitalist development historically. The economic historian Joel Mokyr (2002) credits a science-inflected "industrial enlightenment" with feeding the rise of industrial capitalism in eighteenth-century Europe. With the consolidation of this industrial capitalism, beginning late in the nineteenth century, capital tried to systematize its reliance on scientific invention. Around such industries as submarine and terrestrial telegraphy, electrical power networks, industrial dyeing, and modern munitions, distinctive and generally new institutional practices were forged (Braverman, 1974; Noble, 1977; Smith 1985; Hughes, 1983; Steckel, 1990).

The labor process of scientists working within the new corporate research laboratories shifted from individual and craft modes to systematized programs of collective research and testing (Noble, 1977; Reich, 1985; Israel, 1992). Between 1900 and 1940, U.S. industrial laboratories grew to over 2,000 (Shapiro, 1994, p. 41). Early science-based industries – chemical and electrical firms like General Electric (GE), DuPont and AT&T – established their research arms and employed large numbers of scientists. In 1906, GE's laboratory had 102 staff, but it then quickly expanded to 555 by 1929 (Drahos and Braithwaite, 2003, p. 41). By the early 1950s, Bell Telephone Laboratories – the largest U.S. corporate R&D facility – boasted a workforce of around 9,000, inclusive of PhDs, lab technicians, and clerical staff (Gertner, 2012, pp. 173–4).

Another feature was carried over: government support for the acquisition of economically valuable scientific knowledge. In the nineteenth-century U.S., this encompassed continental expeditions, often quasi-military in character, to survey land, climate, vegetation, and geology with an eye to farming, mining, and economic botany; by the early twentieth century, the government's role also extended to systematic research in agriculture and other fields (Dupree, 1957; Goetzmann, 1978; Kloppenburg, 2004). Newly established public, as well as privately endowed, research universities hosted ever more specialized inquiries – enabling corporations to keep an eye on the state of scientific advance and to cherry-pick from among those findings that were of interest – while educating cohorts of skilled scientific and technical labor: between 1880 and 1920 the number of U.S. engineers skyrocketed, from 7,000 to 136,000 (Lazonick, 2002, p. 199).

Another facet of the institutionalization of science and engineering as a foundation of high-tech industrial capitalism was the expansion and systematization of the patent system. In line with their specific profit-strategies, corporately held patents enabled units of capital to possess and exchange "rights" to the "intellectual property" that scientists and engineers invented.[2]

Today, the institutional matrix that was established a century ago around scientific and technical labor is being modified in light of ongoing mutations in the political economy. The essential changes have been to bind science more directly to capitalist imperatives and to foreground information and communications as analytical touchstones.

According to 2014 Science and Engineering Indicators, by 2011, corporations conducted roughly 70 percent of U.S. scientific R&D and employed a comparable fraction of scientists and engineers – a substantial contrast to a half-century before, when 67 percent of U.S. research was funded by the federal government (National Science Foundation, 2014a; Schiller, 2013, pp. 13–18; see also Edgerton, this volume). Yet this picture is somewhat deceptive. While corporate capital absolutely dominates "development," the government actually claims a larger role than before in funding "basic" research. Between 1976 and 2009, notably, federal money provided two-thirds of university funding for research in computer science and electrical engineering (Singer, 2014).

Notwithstanding this enormous public subsidy, academic science and engineering, which had chiefly been a supplier *for* capital, are gradually and incompletely – over decades – morphing *into* capital. Still nascent, this change signifies that university-based science and engineering themselves have partially internalized capitalist imperatives and merged more fully into the corporate sector.[3] Contributing to this complex result have been altered patent licensing laws, the promotion of academic start-ups, and proliferating public–private partnerships. Decades ago, the U.S. government began to precipitate this metamorphosis of university science, via the Bayh-Dole Act of 1980, the Stevenson-Wydler Technology Innovation Act of 1980 and the Federal Technology Transfer Act of 1986, to promote commercial spin-offs of federally funded research (see chapters by Pagano and Rossi; Lazonick et al., this volume).

The Obama administration carried forward under its "from lab to market" policy umbrella – which requires all federal executive agencies to set goals for speeding up R&D commercialization (Kalil and Choi, 2014). University administrators, legal staff, and professors now routinely collaborate to establish profit-making enterprises and to licence university research to corporations. By one account, since Bayh-Dole in 1980, U.S. universities have created 10,000 companies (4,000 of which continued to operate in 2013). Although the income that they derive from commercial patent licensing remains modest – $2.6 billion in 2013 (Allen, 2014) compared to over $140 billion federal R&D funding in the same year (Sargent Jr., 2013) – research universities' center of gravity has been substantially reconfigured around revenue-generation.

This sea change has simultaneously reset many science and engineering agendas, both so as to elevate conceptions of information and to assimilate information technology-based tools for sensing or probing, measuring, and processing scientific data. Though they must not be conflated, capital and the state have cooperated to enable and shape this development.

Government – and, especially, the military – has been the central axis of support for digitization since World War II (Flamm, 1988), and this remains true (see also chapters by Thorpe; Langley and Parkinson, this volume). Involved are government contracts for research and equipment, and the opening up of massive quantities of public data for capital to transform them into profit-making products and services (White House Office of the Press Secretary, 2013).

In 2015, the U.S. Department of Defense (DOD) accounted for almost 50 percent ($66.091 billion in current dollars) of all federal R&D spending (Hourihan and Parkes, 2016; Sargent Jr., 2015); meanwhile, DOD also spent more on IT than any other federal agency. According to the Office of Management and Budget (OMB), the 2016 budget requested a total of $86.4 billion in IT spending – consisting of $49.1 billion for civilian agency purposes and $37.3 billion (43 percent) for military and defense (Higgins, 2015). This does not include tens of billions of dollars in so-called "black budget" secret spending by intelligence agencies.

The U.S. government pivot toward information technology has reoriented the military toward "net-centric" systems for cyberwar, cyber command, cyber-security and signals intelligence capabilities. This changes the characteristics of military projects and generates torrents of R&D dollars for the tech industries. Such fields as advanced algorithms, data analytics, data fusion, artificial intelligence and data mining are heavily reliant on military funding (Lutton, 2015; Shalal, 2015). One important conduit is the Defense Advanced Research Projects Agency (DARPA), which increased its big data research funding by 69 percent over two years, from $97 million in 2014 to more than $164 million in 2016 (Lutton, 2015). DARPA also recently teamed up with a Silicon Valley consortium of 162 companies and universities including Boeing, General Motors, and Hewlett Packard, and funneled $75 million in R&D funding for wearable technologies (Worthington, 2015; Jacobsen, 2015).

The U.S. government role is, however, more encompassing. President Obama came into office and hired the federal government's first ever chief data scientist – a former PayPal and eBay executive, D.J. Patil. There followed an announcement that $200 million would be allotted for a "Big Data Research and Development Initiative" led by the White House Office of Science and Technology Policy (OSTP), in order to spur investments in several fields (Sottek, 2012). More recently, the president's FY 2016 budget allocated $9.8 billion in discretionary funding for the U.S. Commerce Department to promote the "data-driven economy" (US Department of Commerce, 2015). The White House also released its "New Strategy for American Innovation" and vowed to invest in R&D in the areas of advanced manufacturing, brain initiatives, precision medicine, self-driving cars and "smart cities" to ensure that "the United States remains an 'innovation superpower'" (White House Office of the Press Secretary, 2015).

The U.S. information industry has also become an influential patron of science: it is the largest sectoral R&D investor in the U.S., conducting almost one-third of the R&D total (Grueber and Studt, 2013). In 2014, notably, U.S. ICT companies were on track to generate 57 percent of the industry's global R&D expenditures (Grueber and Studt, 2013). Microsoft invested over $10 billion in R&D in 2014; closely following were Internet companies like Google and Amazon (Ausick, 2014). It is not coincidental that, boosted by an overall R&D outlay that exceeds many small nations' overall gross domestic product, the U.S. information industry remains the worldwide market leader.

Setting the U.S. agenda for science and engineering is a complex, multifaceted undertaking. One component of the institutional mechanism that performs this function is the President's Council of Advisors on Science and Technology (PCAST). Established by President George

H.W. Bush in 1991, PCAST makes "policy recommendations in the many areas where understanding of science, technology, and innovation is key to strengthening our economy and forming policy that works for the American people".[4] In the Obama administration, PCAST is flush with computer scientists, analytics specialists, biologists and aerospace engineers; and it includes both university scientists and corporate executives – notably Eric Schmidt (Google's Executive Chairman and erstwhile CEO) and Craig Mundie (who left Microsoft in 2014 after 22 years).[5] One PCAST member, Ed Penhoet, was a cofounder of Chiron, a pioneering biotech company, and serves both as an associate dean of biology at UC Berkeley and a director of Alta Partners, a life science venture capital firm.[6]

It needs to be stressed that, while ICT companies lead overall R&D investment to spearhead their product- and market-development, such companies constitute just one part of a more encompassing movement. The generation of commodities that wire social and cultural spaces to the Internet is multi-sectoral – economy-wide. Once-discrete industries, from automobiles (see also Tyfield chapter, this volume), manufacturing, finance, energy, and defense, to pharmaceuticals, agriculture, medicine, and education are aggressively investing in ICT R&D, blurring the lines between industries as they incorporate and apply digital technologies in new profit projects.

Science and engineering in corporate commodification projects

Worldwide IT spending, in one estimate, came in at over $3.5 trillion in 2015.[7] The banking and "security" industries topped the IT spending list with over $486 billion, closely followed by the manufacturing and natural resources industries with almost $477 billion.[8] The world's largest single non-IT-supplier spender on IT in 2014 was Walmart, with $10.16 billion in outlays (Gagliordi, 2015). One of Walmart's primary business strategies has long centered on digitizing business data. In 1998, Walmart founder Sam Walton stated, "People think we got big by putting big stores in small towns. Really, we got big by replacing inventory with information" (Roberts and Berg, 2012, p. 144). During the 1990s, the company dominated retail markets by digitizing product inventories and sales data, transforming its supply chain in light of ceaseless updates to its knowledge of consumer sales trends (Schiller, 2007, pp. 40, 211). Even so, over the last ten years, Walmart has lost ground to Amazon – whose modernized online selling model is both equally data-dependent and even more cost-effective.

Having cut tens of thousands of union jobs, curbed employees' rights, and received billions of dollars in federal bailout money at the height of the 2008–9 crisis, the U.S. automobile industry also has invested heavily in network systems and applications. Automakers are bidding to renew profit growth via digital commodification, shifting their profit strategies from hardware to software and network-enabled devices. Vehicles are, increasingly, mobile services arrays (Schiller, 2014, pp. 34–5). To restructure in this way, General Motors (GM) has built a $130 million dollar data center modeled after those of Google and Facebook (Rosenbush and Bennett, 2013), invested about $1 billion to expand its Warren Technical Center R&D facility (Fisher, 2015), and hired an army of 8,000 programmers to build custom software and internal infrastructure, seeking to hold off tech-industry interlopers such as Apple, Google, Oracle, Microsoft, and HP (Bennett, 2015). GM also has spent upwards of $3 billion a year on IT services outsourced to other firms (Rosenbush and Bennett, 2013). GM's European competitor Volkswagen employs 9,300 IT specialists and has poured about €3.8 billion ($4.15 billion) per year into information technology (Volkswagen, 2014). (Volkswagen's impressive IT capability can hardly have been irrelevant to its practice of installing software to cheat pollution-emissions tests.[9])

Rooted in still another sector, agri-business giant Monsanto likewise expanded its field of profit-making by leveraging IT investments. In 2013, Monsanto acquired the ability to perform big data analytics on a substantial scale, with an almost $1 billion pay-out for a hyper-local data analytics company, Climate Corporation (McDonnell, 2014), a San Francisco tech firm founded by former Google employees. Climate Corporation, backed by Founders Fund, Khosla, Google Ventures, NEA, Index Ventures and Atomico, employs over 200 scientists to analyze fifty terabytes of weather data, extracted from government satellites, weather simulations, and soil observations (Specter, 2013). These practices feed into Monsanto's program of generating and analyzing planting data to more closely control farming practices, throughout the entire cycle from planting to harvesting. Monsanto and farm equipment manufacturer John Deere have joined forces in this endeavor, as Deere tractors and other machinery are enhanced with software to collect micro-climate- and detailed soil data directly from farmers. The data then are fed into Monsanto's data analysis application *Climate Field View* – and sold back to farmers. Cargill Inc. and DuPont Pioneer have matched these initiatives, by investing in sensor technology, data analytics, and wireless transmitters. However unfamiliar they might appear, these agricultural companies are also increasingly information companies, rolling out data businesses around digital systems and services (Bunge and Tita, 2015).

In a bid to kick-start its own lagging profit-growth, meanwhile, IBM has set its scientists to building a Merger and Acquisition (M&A) tool that uses machine learning, to speed up the process by reducing human intervention; the company plans to sell this new tool as a service (Indap, 2016). To lower aircraft manufacturing costs, General Electric scientists are building backpack-sized jet engines by creating 3D models of parts as digital files and then transforming these files into objects via 3D printing (Knapp, 2015). Engineers at home automation company Nest Labs (acquired by Google) work to develop profitable digital services on the basis of data generated by "smart" thermostats, fire alarms, security cameras, baby monitors, and other appliances (Marr, 2015).

Scientific and technical labor anchors these digital commodities and cost-efficiency strategies. The result is to place a premium on specialized information-oriented disciplines such as bioinformatics, data analytics, robotics, and artificial intelligence (AI). Some of these specializations have become veritable industries in their own right as they fuel substantial profit projects. The global bioinformatics market, for example, is projected to reach $13.3 billion by 2020 (MarketsandMarkets, 2015). AI systems for enterprise applications are expected to reach $11.1 billion by 2024; the big data technology and services market is forecast to reach $46.8 billion by 2019 (IDC, 2015).

Within this sweeping reorientation toward a more networked-information-intensive political economy, however, the supply of prized scientific and engineering talent has become a significant issue.

Reconstructing the science and engineering labor supply chain

For some time, the tech industry has led a larger corporate campaign to address what it presents as a shortage of skilled labor, charging that this deficit threatens to damage U.S. "competitiveness." Capital's demand is to boost the available supply of specialized Science, Technology, Engineering, and Mathematics, or STEM labor, needed to devise and implement information-centric services and network applications.[10]

According to 2010 data from Science and Engineering Indicators 2014 (National Science Foundation, 2014a), computer and mathematical sciences and engineering are the largest category of occupations within the S&E field, with respectively 2.4 million and 1.6 million workers. Corporations are, by far, the largest employers of scientists and engineers, with a 70 percent share; education has 19 percent and government 11 percent (National Science

Foundation, 2014b). The U.S. science and engineering workforce is growing at a faster rate than the general labor force, especially in mathematics and computer-related occupations.[11]

Is the supply sufficient? Cisco predicts that approximately 220,000 new engineers will be needed globally every year for the next decade, simply to build what it hopes will be a trillion dollar business – the "Internet of Everything" (IoE) – based on machine-to-machine network connectivity, cloud computing, and network sensors (Krishnamurthi, 2014). The McKinsey consultancy forecasts that corporate demand for data scientists is likely to outrun supply for years, as between 140,000 and 190,000 data science positions in the U.S. go unfilled by 2018 (Orihuela and Bass, 2015). According to *Forbes*, in the year beginning June 2014, IBM alone advertised 2,307 positions requiring expertise related to big data (Columbus, 2015). Combing multiple labor markets, Amazon posted for more than 50 AI positions in the U.S. and Europe, searching for PhDs focused on machine learning, information science and statistics (Mizroch, 2015b). Microsoft and Google actually have acquired entire companies in order to gain access to their AI talent (Waters, 2016). Once again, the phenomenon is general: manufacturing, finance and insurance, and retail trade each draw in significant quantities of STEM labor (Columbus, 2015).

Resource-starved universities have responded by reorienting academic programs, to train students for coveted STEM specializations: as universities withdraw support for the humanities and languages, they promote new information-inflected specializations to students (American Academy of Arts & Sciences, 2014). For example, Ohio State University publicized "data scientist" as one of the top-ranked jobs in America (Ohio State University News, 2016). More than 40 universities – including Columbia, Cambridge, NYU, University of California Berkeley, and Michigan – have created data science programs (Vanni, 2015) and duly gained financial support from tech giants like Google, Amazon, and Microsoft. When the University of Washington wanted to bring prominent artificial intelligence experts from Carnegie Mellon to boost its computer science department, the e-commerce giant Amazon gave it a $2 million grant for the appointment of "Amazon professorships" (Miller, 2013). This process is not free of contradiction: companies simultaneously battle to poach experts from academic communities and demand that universities provide them with more appropriately skilled students (Mizroch, 2015a).

Beyond reshaping educational institutions to prioritize STEM education, corporations also have addressed scientific labor-market shortages by looking beyond borders. Transnational companies are uniquely placed to tap a global pool of talented scientists and engineers. At the same time, they want to deploy STEM labor wherever their profit strategies mandate – including in the center of the global information industry, the United States.

Led by, but not limited to ICT firms, a quarter-century-long political fight erupted in the mid-1990s to increase the U.S. H–1B visa quota – the permits that enable U.S. firms to hire temporary foreign workers. During the years after the H–1B visa program launched, as part of the 1990 Immigration Act, the quota for these visas has fluctuated. The number increased throughout the dot.com boom in the late 1990s, from an initial limit of 65,000 to a peak of 195,000 under President Bill Clinton's American Competitiveness in the 21st Century Act (Wilson, 2013). After the dot.com bubble burst, however, the number reverted back to 65,000, though the U.S. granted an additional 20,000 visas for those who had earned advanced degrees in U.S. universities – still insufficient, Bill Gates protested in 2008 (Wilson, 2013; Lee, 2008). More than one-third of H–1B visas are taken, significantly, by multinational IT outsourcing companies like Cognizant Technology Solution, Tata Consultancy Services, and Infosys, which use them to supply temporary IT workers to U.S. firms – at lower wages than they would otherwise have to pay (Hira, 2015). Google, Microsoft, Amazon, Intel and Facebook all avail themselves (Preston, 2015). By widening the pool of temporary workers and using these temps to perform "core" tasks (US Department of Labor Office of Foreign Labor Certification, 2014), the tech industry creates pressure to drive down the cost of its scientific and technical labor force.[12] Partly for this reason, the influx of foreign-born STEM workers raises political sensitivities (Cooper, 2015).

These churning changes, finally, also need to be situated within digital capitalism's dynamic global context.

Renewed inter-capitalist competition and inter-state geopolitics

Digital capitalism remains vulnerable to the violent shocks and downturns that have typified capitalist development throughout its history. As commodity production has been extruded and widened digitally, capitalism's crisis tendencies have reasserted themselves. The 2008 financial crisis ushered in the worst slump since the 1930s. In 2016, nearly nine years on, a new overhang of debt threatens global finance and what mainstream economists call "secular stagnation" (Vinik, 2013) has become chronic.

Digital capitalism has been built largely within a U.S.-centric control structure: it privileges U.S. capital and is presided over by the U.S. state. However, as we have seen, it is an economy-wide phenomenon and it has played out transnationally. Digital systems and applications constitute prized sources of growth in a political economy that is desperately short on it. As the "digital depression" has persisted, therefore, inter-capitalist rivalries over the science- and engineering-based information industries have intensified. U.S. attempts to renew its dominance over the digital realm have encountered mushrooming resistance. Struggles have broken out – chiefly in the sphere of economic diplomacy – to appropriate the coveted digital profit sources.

The EU had lagged behind the U.S. in ICTs since World War II.[13] Well before the slump, the EU commenced fresh attempts to carve out room for European capital within a U.S.-centric system. Facing a prospective new "American challenge" during the early Internet era, the Lisbon Summit – held in 2000 at a European Council meeting – declared that its goal was for Europe to be "the most competitive, knowledge-based economy in the world by 2010" (Padoan, 2009). In 2002, at the Barcelona Summit, EU member states pledged to invest 3 percent of their respective GDPs toward R&D (Padoan, 2009). The target had not been reached by 2016, partly because of the austerity measures put in place after the 2008 economic crisis. However, in 2010, the executive arm of the EU, the European Commission (EC), launched its Europe 2020 Strategy (European Commission, 2016). Its so-called "Digital Agenda" sought to boost Europe's digital economy and to emphasize "seven pillars" as sites of growth – including increased information infrastructure capacity, greater R&D investment in ICTs, and measures to promote ICT employment.

Yet the EU continues to struggle. Its injection of an R&D funding program to develop a European version of Google led by Germany and France has not been successful (Hern, 2015). Moving onto its back foot, the EU continues to try to push back. An antitrust case against Google is ongoing, the safe harbor agreement allowing the movement of data from the EU to the U.S. has been thrown out, a "Google Tax" has been imposed, and a competition inquiry has been launched into Amazon's dominance in the ebook market (Couturier, 2016; Bowers, 2015, 2016).

More impressive is the pushback from China, though this multifarious initiative needs to be carefully situated (see also chapters by Suttmeier and Xu). As of 2014, China's R&D outlay of $203.7 billion already exceeded Japan's and was about to pass that of the EU (gbtimes, 2015). According to the 2014 *Science, Technology and Industry Report* from the Organisation for Economic Co-operation and Development (OECD), Chinese universities produced over 27,000 doctorates in science and engineering in 2011, while the U.S. produced 24,792 doctorates. While the U.S. still accounts for the largest number of top-cited publications across all disciplines, China is the second-highest producer of top-cited academic articles in seven major disciplines – Materials Science, Chemistry, Engineering, Computer science, Chemical Engineering, Energy and

Mathematics (OECD, 2015). In 2013, moreover, China garnered 32.1 percent of the world's total patents – the U.S. had 22.3 percent and European Patent Office (EPO) shared 5.8 percent (World Intellectual Property Organization (WIPO), 2014). In 2014, China's Huawei, the world's largest telecommunications equipment manufacturer, filed the greatest number of international patents, beating out U.S. tech company Qualcomm (Jerin, 2015).

All this should not be seen as a function simply of China's "rise." China's growing prominence in science and technology actually possesses an ambiguous meaning. It testifies both to China's re-insertion into a U.S.-led trans-nationalized digital capitalism and to Chinese leaders' successes in reorganizing this system, better to foreground the expansionary needs of Chinese capital and Chinese military strategy.

China's effort to situate science-based digital systems and applications industries at the center of its overall economic development was initially based heavily on foreign direct investment (FDI). Through tax rebates, lower tariffs, and R&D subsidies, China encouraged foreign capital to invest in domestic high tech industries and, specifically, in R&D centers to seed the development of its domestic ICT industry.

Foreign companies invested considerably in China-based R&D, in particular in electronics, telecommunications, biotechnology, pharmaceuticals, chemicals and automobiles (Tselichtchev, 2011). Their goal was at once to tap into the Chinese market and to access an expanding pool of well-trained but less-highly paid scientists and engineers. Even before China's accession to the World Trade Organization (WTO), major transnational corporations (TNCs) were establishing R&D centers and joint-ventures with local firms, notwithstanding that China's party-state imposed requirements for technology transfer and training of local staff. China's foreign capital driven R&D policy was a key part of its economic strategy to develop its domestic information market and, ultimately, to help domestic units of capital to transnationalize. As of 2013, there were over 1,600 R&D centers in China, and among them at least 1,300 were affiliated with transnational corporations (Marro, 2015).

U.S. capital played an important role in China's R&D activities. Since 2007, over 40 percent of China's total FDI in R&D has come from the U.S., which is the largest R&D exporter to China (*China Daily*, 2015). China indeed attracts a greater amount of foreign direct investment in R&D projects than the U.S. itself: between January 2000 and December 2014, China drew 88 R&D laboratories (greenfield R&D) from foreign companies, involving $5.5 billion in capital investment, more than twice the amount of the U.S.'s 91 R&D projects (Fingar, 2015).

Targeted science and technology R&D has become a key aspect of the Chinese party-state's decision to prioritize information, culture and the Internet as "pillar industries" (Hong, in press and Shafaeddin, 2012, p. 252). This strategy has succeeded in aiding an impressive list of China-based companies in digital markets: China Mobile, Baidu, Alibaba, Tencent, Xiaomi, Huawei, Lenovo, and others. These companies either already exhibit, or else harbor, transnational aspirations and, akin to their U.S. counterparts, they cultivate ties with a much wider group of industrial and government users of networked systems and services.

Chinese companies correspondingly have established R&D activities in other countries, especially in the U.S. – San Jose, Detroit, and Dallas each host Chinese-funded R&D centers. China's tech firms Alibaba, Baidu, and ZTE Corp have built a U.S. presence; Huawei alone has erected six U.S. research centers. The U.S. government has imposed persistent pressure on Huawei, on grounds of "security concerns" about "cyber-espionage," to the point that the company announced a momentary withdrawal from the U.S. market (Tiezzi, 2013). However, for Huawei – which doubled its R&D to $6.6 billion in 2014, passing Apple (Truong, 2015) – the U.S. market is too important to neglect. The Internet equipment maker has reentered the U.S. with a new mobile handset, and has signaled a plan to compete with Apple, Samsung and Google.

Despite heavy participation by foreign capital, China's digitally inflected economic policies and its ready supply of science and engineering labor have helped it to develop into the world's second-largest national information and communication market. This concurrently enables China-based companies to project their interests internationally. This result constitutes a far-reaching structural change. Though it is still incomplete and there are many contingencies, China's build-up in high-tech systems and applications poses a destabilizing challenge to what has been a U.S.-structured digital capitalism.

U.S. leaders are keenly cognizant of this. Internationally, the U.S. state and U.S. capital seek to shore up their advantage. One contributing initiative is to push for greater control over scientific knowledge by expanding the existing, U.S.-centric, intellectual property regime (see also Pagano and Rossi chapter, this volume). The U.S. government has pressed to institute regional trade agreements that would allow it to shape rules for patents, copyrights and trademarks. In 2015, the U.S. reached agreement on the secretively negotiated Trans-Pacific Partnership (TPP) with 11 other Asia-Pacific countries,[14] one effect of which would be to exclude China from the rulemaking structure covering 40 percent of the world's economy. For the TPP, the U.S. pushed to adopt still more restrictive IP rules, to privilege already heavily advantaged U.S. capital while preempting its competitors. For instance, the U.S. Trade Representative campaigned to secure twelve years of exclusive protection for biologics data – on behalf of the U.S. pharmaceutical and biotechnology industry and to the detriment of people in less-developed countries and of poor people everywhere. Facing opposition from other countries, the U.S. was, however, compelled to acquiesce to a shorter five-year limit with an additional three years of "comparable" protection (Bradsher and Pollack, 2015).

It remains an open question whether China will, or could, mount a wide-ranging challenge to the existing U.S.-centric organization of digital capitalism. Also open, by contrast, is whether an oppositional movement may coalesce, and gain strength sufficient to push the international community to adopt a different and more just agenda. In the meantime, it is a near-certainty that digital capitalism will exhibit stepped-up inter-capitalist competition, as the U.S. struggles to preserve its advantageous position while China attempts to improve the terms on which it participates in transnational digital capitalism. Science in turn demarcates a contested field, on which capital and capitalist states contend amid a turbulent political economy.

Notes

1 2016 worldwide IT spending is set to reach a total of $3.54 trillion dollars. See www.gartner.com/newsroom/id/3186517.
2 For a scathing critique, see N.B. Danielian, *AT&T: Story of Industrial Conquest* (New York: Vanguard, 1939), 92–137.
3 For a perceptive early analysis, see Dickson, D. (1984) *The New Politics of Science*. New York: Pantheon. Schiller, D. (1999) *Digital capitalism: networking the global market system*. Cambridge, MA: MIT Press. pp. 143–202.
4 See About PCAST www.whitehouse.gov/administration/eop/ostp/pcast/about.
5 See PCAST members list https://m.whitehouse.gov/administration/eop/ostp/pcast/about/members.
6 Ibid.
7 See Worldwide Information Technology (IT) spending forecast from 2005 to 2016 www.statista.com/statistics/203935/overall-it-spending-worldwide/.
8 See IT spending worldwide by vertical industry in 2014 and 2015 www.statista.com/statistics/269400/global-it-spending-by-industry/. By a different tally, Banks alone spent about $188 billion on information and communications technology in 2014. See Arnold, M. and Braithwaite, T. (2015) "Banks Ageing IT Systems Buckle Under Strain," *Financial Times*, 18 June, www.ft.com/intl/cms/s/0/90360dbe-15cb-11e5-a58d-00144feabdc0.html#axzz3ddkVYDr7.

9 See Davenport, C. and Hakim, D. (2016) "US sues Volkswagen in diesel emissions scandal," *New York Time*, 4 January, www.nytimes.com/2016/01/05/business/vw-sued-justice-department-emissions-scandal.html?_r=0.

10 At the same time, it's worth noting, U.S. IT firms employing a large percentage of the scientific and technical workforce – such as Microsoft, Dell, and HP – slashed thousands of jobs in the face of a rapidly changing IT market. IBM is expected to cut no less than a quarter of its global workforce.

11 See What does the S&E job market look like for US graduates? www.nsf.gov/nsb/sei/edTool/data/workforce-03.html.

12 The minimum wage for H-1B workers can be as low as what the 17th-lowest wage earner out of 100 in a particular job category in a specific region would earn.

13 For an illuminating discussion, above all with regard to physics, see Krige, J. (2006) *American Hegemony and the Postwar Reconstruction of Science in Europe*. Cambridge: MIT Press.

14 See trans-pacific partnership: summary of US objectives https://ustr.gov/tpp/Summary-of-US-objectives.

References

Allen, J. (2014) "Does university patent licensing pay off?" *IPWatchdog*, 27 January, www.ipwatchdog.com/2014/01/27/does-university-patent-licensing-pay-off/id=47655/.

American Academy of Arts & Sciences (2014) "The State of the Humanities: Funding 2014", www.humanitiesindicators.org/binaries/pdf/HI_FundingReport2014.pdf.

Ausick, P. (2014) "Companies spending the most on R&D", *24/7 Wall Street*, 18 November, http://247wallst.com/consumer-products/2014/11/18/companies-spending-the-most-on-rd/.

Bennett, J. (2015) "Why GM hired 8,000 programmers", *Wall Street Journal*, 17 February, www.wsj.com/articles/gm-built-internal-skills-to-manage-internet-sales-push-1424200731.

Bowers, S. (2015) "European commission to investigate Amazon's ebook dominance", *Guardian*, 11 June, www.theguardian.com/technology/2015/jun/11/european-commission-investigate-amazon-ebook-dominance.

Bowers, S. (2016) "French finance minister blasts UK's £130m Google tax deal", *Guardian*, 2 February, www.theguardian.com/technology/2016/feb/02/french-finance-minister-blasts-mrcs-130m-tax-deal-with-google.

Bradsher, K. and Pollack, A. (2015) "What changes lie ahead from the trans-pacific partnership pact", *New York Times*, 5 October, www.nytimes.com/2015/10/06/business/international/what-changes-lie-ahead-from-the-trans-pacific-partnership-pact.html.

Braverman, H. (1974) *Labor and monopoly capital the degradation of work in the twentieth century*. New York: Monthly Review Press.

Bunge, J. and Tita, B. (2015) "Monsanto, Deere join forces over data services", *Wall Street Journal*, 5 November, www.wsj.com/articles/monsanto-deere-join-forces-over-data-services-1446580917.

China Daily (2015) *Top 10 R&D importing countries in the world*, 11 November, http://usa.chinadaily.com.cn/business/2015-11/11/content_22431133.htm.

Columbus, L. (2015) "Where big data jobs are in 2015 – midyear update", *Forbes*, 25 June, www.forbes.com/sites/louiscolumbus/2015/06/25/where-big-data-jobs-are-in-2015-midyear-update/.

Cooper, B. (2015) "With winter fast approaching the refugee crisis could become a medical disaster", *Open Democracy*, 2 December, www.opendemocracy.net/can-europe-make-it/benedict-cooper/with-winter-fast-approaching-refugee-crisis-could-become-medical-.

Couturier, K. (2016) "How Europe is going after Apple, Google and other U.S. tech giants", *New York Times*, 19 May, www.nytimes.com/interactive/2015/04/13/technology/How-Europe-Is-Going-After-U.S.-Tech-Giants.html?_r=0.

Dickson, D. (1984) *The New Politics of Science*. New York: Pantheon.

Drahos, P. and Braithwaite, J. (2003) *Information Feudalism: Who Owns the Knowledge Economy?* New Delhi: Oxford University Press.

Dupree, A. H. (1957) *Science in the Federal Government: A History of Policies and Activities to 1940*. Cambridge, Mass.: Belknap Press of Harvard University Press.

European Commission (2016) "Europe 2020 strategy: digital agenda for the Europe: Pillar VII: ICT-enabled benefits for EU society", 22 February, https://ec.europa.eu/digital-agenda/en/our-goals/pillar-vii-ict-enabled-benefits-eu-society.

Executive Office of the President (2014) "Big data: seizing opportunity preserving value", www. whitehouse.gov/sites/default/files/docs/big_data_privacy_report_may_1_2014.pdf.

Executive Office of the President President's Council of Advisors on Science and Technology (2015) "Report to the president and congress ensuring leadership in federally funded research and development in information technology", www.whitehouse.gov/sites/default/files/microsites/ostp/PCAST/nitrd_report_aug_2015.pdf.

Fingar, C. (2015) "China passes US in race for FDI in research and development", *Financial Times*, 22 July, www.ft.com/intl/cms/s/3/241d9366-3058-11e5-91ac-a5e17d9b4cff.html#axzz3sRhsbjUX.

Fisher, A. (2015) "Why General Motors is scrambling to find tech workers", *Fortune*, 26 May, http://fortune.com/2015/05/26/gm-tech-workers-hiring/.

Flamm, K. (1988) *Creating the Computer: Government, Industry, and High Technology*. Washington, D.C.: Brookings Institution.

Gagliordi, N. (2015) "Walmart tops IDC list of world's biggest IT spenders", *ZDnet*, 7 April, www.zdnet.com/article/walmart-tops-idc-list-of-worlds-biggest-it-spenders.

gbtimes (2015) "China's R&D spending up 10% in 2014", 23 November, http://gbtimes.com/china/chinas-rd-spending-10-2014.

Gertner, J. (2012) *The Idea Factory: Bells Labs and the Great Age of American Invention*. New York: Penguin Press.

Goetzmann, W. H. (1978) *Exploration and Empire: The Explorer and the Scientist in the Winning of the American West*. New York: W.W. Norton.

Grueber, M. and Studt, T. (2013) "Battelle-2014 global R&D funding forecast", *R&D Magazine*, www.battelle.org/docs/tpp/2014_global_rd_funding_forecast.pdf.

Hern, A. (2015) "In search of a European Google", *Guardian*, 6 December, www.theguardian.com/technology/2015/dec/06/europe-google-silicon-valley-digital-industry.

Higgins, J. (2015) "Proposed 2016 federal budget plumps IT spending by $2B", *Ecommerce Times*, 11 March, www.ecommercetimes.com/story/81805.html?rss=1.

Hira, R. (2015) "New data show how firms like Infosys and Tata abuse the H-1B program", *Economic Policy Institute*, 19 February, www.epi.org/blog/new-data-infosys-tata-abuse-h-1b-program/.

Hong, Y. (In Press) *Networking China: The Digital Transformation of the Chinese Economy*. University of Illinois Press.

Hourihan, M. and Parkes, D. (2016) "Federal R&D in the FY 2016 budget: an overview, American Association for the Advancement of Science", www.aaas.org/fy16budget/federal-rd-fy-2016-budget-overview.

Hughes, T. (1983) *Networks of Power: Electrification in Western Society*. Baltimore: Johns Hopkins.

IDC (2015) "New IDC forecast sees worldwide big data technology and services market growing to $48.6 billion in 2019, driven by wide adoption across industries", 9 November, www.idc.com/getdoc.jsp?containerId=prUS40560115.

Indap, S. (2016) "IBM bets on mergers and algorithms for growth", *Financial Times*, 12 January, www.ft.com/intl/cms/s/0/11010eea-ae5f-11e5-993b-c425a3d2b65a.html#axzz3xyvWvOQd.t.

Israel, P. (1992) *From Machine Shop to Industrial Laboratory: Telegraphy and the Changing Context of American Invention, 1830–1920*. Baltimore: Johns Hopkins University Press.

Jacobsen, A. (2015) *The Pentagon's Brain: An Uncensored History of DARPA, America's Top Secret Military Research Agency*. New York: Little, Brown.

Jerin, M. (2015) "China's Huawei top international patent filer ahead of Qualcomm and ZTE", *International Business Times*, 21 March 2015, www.ibtimes.co.uk/chinas-huawei-top-international-patent-filer-ahead-qualcomm-zte-1492947.

Kalil, T. and Charina Choi, C. (2014) "From lab to market: accelerating research breakthroughs and economic growth", *Office of the US President*, 14 March, www.whitehouse.gov/blog/2014/03/14/lab-market-accelerating-research-breakthroughs-and-economic-growth.

Kloppenburg, J. (2004) *First the Seed: The Political Economy of plant Biotechnology, 1492–2000*. Madison, Wis.: University of Wisconsin Press.

Knapp, A. (2015) "GE engineers 3D-printed a working, mini jet engine", *Forbes*, 11 May, www.forbes.com/sites/alexknapp/2015/05/11/ge-engineers-3d-printed-a-working-mini-jet-engine/#f5f1056246d5.

Krishnamurthi, S. (2014) "More education needed to realize the Internet of everything", *Network World*, 10 December, www.networkworld.com/article/2857890/internet-of-things/more-education-needed-to-realize-the-internet-of-everything.html.

Lazonick, W. (2002) *American Corporate Economy: Critical Perspectives on Business and Management*. London: Routledge.

Lee, T. (2008) "Gates to congress: Microsoft needs more H-1B visas", *Ars Technica*, 13 March, http://arstechnica.com/tech-policy/2008/03/gates-to-congress-microsoft-needs-more-h-1-b-visas/.

Leonard, R. (1985) *The Making of American Industrial Research: Science and Business at GE and Bell, 1876–1926*. Cambridge: Cambridge University Press.

Lutton, J. (2015) "DARPA is spending big on big data", *FCW*, 15 April, https://fcw.com/articles/2015/04/15/snapshot-data-programs.aspx.

MarketsandMarkets (2015) "Bioinformatics market worth $13.3 billion by 2020", 15 April www.marketsandmarkets.com/PressReleases/bioinformatics-market.asp.

Marr, B. (2015) "Google's nest: big data and the Internet of Things in the connected home", *Forbes*, 5 August, www.forbes.com/sites/bernardmarr/2015/08/05/googles-nest-big-data-and-the-internet-of-things-in-the-connected-home/#55a0525458a1.

Marro, N. (2015) "Foreign company R&D: in China, for China", *China Business Review*, 1 June, www.chinabusinessreview.com/foreign-company-rd-in-china-for-china/.

McDonnell, T. (2014) "Monsanto is using big data to take over the world", *Mother Jones*, 19 November, www.motherjones.com/environment/2014/11/monsanto-big-data-gmo-climate-change.

Miller, C. (2013) "Geek appeal: New York vs. Seattle", *New York Times*, 14 April, www.nytimes.com/2013/04/14/education/edlife/new-york-and-seattle-compete-for-data-science-crown.html?_r=0.

Mizroch, A. (2015a) "A talent war in artificial intelligence – tech firms, universities fund and poach experts, hoping to gain an edge in hot area of computing", *Wall Street Journal*, 4 May, B1.

Mizroch, A. (2015b) "Artificial-intelligence experts are in high demand", *Wall Street Journal*, 1 May, www.wsj.com/articles/artificial-intelligence-experts-are-in-high-demand-1430472782.

Mokyr, J. (2002) *The Gifts of Athena: Historical Origins of the Knowledge Economy*. Princeton, N.J.: Princeton University Press.

National Science Foundation (2014a) "Science and engineering indicators, research and development: national trends and international comparisons", Arlington, VA: National Science Board, www.nsf.gov/statistics/seind14/index.cfm/chapter-4/c4s1.htm.

National Science Foundation (2014b) "Science and engineering indicators, science and engineering labor force", Arlington, VA: National Science Board, www.nsf.gov/statistics/seind14/index.cfm/chapter-3/c3h.htm.

Noble, D. (1977) *America by Design: Science, Technology, and the Rise of Corporate Capitalism*. New York: Knopf.

Ohio State University (2016) "Data scientist is 'best job' in 2016", 20 January, https://data-analytics.osu.edu/news/data-scientist-best-job-2016.

Organisation for Economic Co-operation and Development (2014) "OECD science, technology, and industry outlook", www.oecd-ilibrary.org/science-and-technology/oecd-science-technology-and-industry-outlook-2014_sti_outlook-2014-en;jsessionid=6h0hml4q1fn6o.x-oecd-live-03.

Organisation for Economic Co-operation and Development (2015) "OECD science, technology and industry scoreboard 2015", www.oecd-ilibrary.org/docserver/download/9215031e.pdf?expires=1452367087&id=id&accname=guest&checksum=B527A14CB78EC4CAD0E265BF42BEA46F.

Orihuela, R. and Bass, D. (2015) "Help wanted: black belts in data", *Bloomberg Business*, 4 June, www.bloomberg.com/news/articles/2015-06-04/help-wanted-black-belts-in-data.

Padoan, P. (2009) "Revising the Lisbon strategy through the OECD innovation strategy", INCOM Workshop on Innovation and Growth Policy in the EU, Prague, 22–23 January, www.oecd.org/site/innovationstrategy/revisingthelisbonstrategythroughtheoecdinnovationstrategy.htm.

Preston, J. (2015) "Large companies game H-1B visa program, costing the US jobs", *New York Times*, 10 November, www.nytimes.com/2015/11/11/us/large-companies-game-h-1b-visa-program-leaving-smaller-ones-in-the-cold.html?_r=0.

Reich, L.S. (1985) *The Making of American Industrial Research: Science and Business at GE and Bell, 1876–1926*. Cambridge: Cambridge University Press.

Roberts, B.R. and Berg, N. (2012) *Walmart: Key Insights and Practical Lessons from the World's Largest Retailer*. London, Kogan Page.

Rosenbush, S. and Bennett, J. (2013) "GM opens new data center modeled on Google, Facebook", *Wall Street Journal*, 13 May, http://blogs.wsj.com/cio/2013/05/13/gm-opens-new-data-center-modeled-on-google-facebook/.

Sargent, J.F., Jr. (2013) "Federal research and development funding: FY2013", Congressional Research Service, 5 December, www.fas.org/sgp/crs/misc/R42410.pdf.

Sargent, J.F., Jr. (2015) "Federal research and development funding: FY2015", Congressional Research Service, 2 February, www.fas.org/sgp/crs/misc/R43580.pdf.

Schiller, D. (1999) *Digital Capitalism: Networking the Global Market System*. Cambridge, Mass.: MIT Press.

Schiller, D. (2007) *How to Think About Information*. Urbana: University of Illinois Press.

Schiller, D. (2013) "Pushing informationalized capitalism into science and information technology", *Media Development*, 50 (2), pp. 13–18.

Schiller, D. (2014) *Digital Depression: Information Technology and Economic Crisis.* Urbana: University of Illinois Press.

Shafaeddin, M. (2012) *Competitiveness and Development: Myth and Realities.* London: Anthem Press.

Shalal, A. (2015) "The Pentagon wants at least $12 billion to fund AI weapon technology in 2017", *Business Insider*, 14 December, http://uk.businessinsider.com/the-pentagon-wants-at-least-12-billion-to-fund-ai-weapon-technology-in-2017-2015-12?r=US&IR=T.

Shapiro, H. (1993) "The evolution of U.S. science policy", *Princeton Alumni Weekly*, 94, 41.

Singer, P. (2014) "Federally supported innovations: 22 examples of major technology advances that stem from federal research support", *Information Technology & Innovation Foundation*, www2.itif.org/2014-federally-supported-innovations.pdf.

Smith, M. (ed.) (1985) *Military Enterprise and Technological Change: The American Experience.* Baltimore: Johns Hopkins.

Sottek, T.C. (2012) "Obama administration announces $200 million 'big data' research and development initiative", *Verge*, 29 March, www.theverge.com/2012/3/29/2912137/obama-big-data-research-initiative.

Specter, M. (2013) "Why the climate corporation sold itself to Monsanto", *New Yorker*, 4 November, www.newyorker.com/tech/elements/why-the-climate-corporation-sold-itself-to-monsanto.

Steckel, F. (1990) "Cartelization of the German chemical industry, 1918–1925", *Journal of European Economic History*, 19(2), 329–51.

Thomson, I. (2015) "Safe harbor ripped and replaced with privacy shield in last-minute US-Europe deal", *Register*, 2 February, www.theregister.co.uk/2016/02/02/safe_harbor_replaced_with_privacy_shield.

Tiezzi, S. (2013) "Huawei officially gives up on the US market", *Diplomat*, 5 December, http://thediplomat.com/2013/12/huawei-officially-gives-up-on-the-us-market/.

Truong, A. (2015) "Huawei's R&D spend is massive even by the standards of American tech giants", *Quartz*, 31 March, http://qz.com/374039/huaweis-rd-spend-is-massive-even-by-the-standards-of-american-tech-giants/.

Tselichtchev, I. (2011) *China Versus the West the Global Power Shift of the 21st century*, Singapore: Wiley.

US Department of Commerce (2015) "2016 funding highlight", http://2010-2014.commerce.gov/sites/default/files/documents/2015/february/omb_fact_sheet--fy16_doc_budget_chapter--1_30_final.pdf.

US Department of Labor Office of Foreign Labor Certification (2014) "H-1B temporary specialty occupations labor condition program – selected statistics", www.foreignlaborcert.doleta.gov/pdf/H-1B_Selected_Statistics_FY2014_Q1.pdf.

Vanni, O. (2015) "Here are the schools with degrees in data science", *BostInno*, 15 October, http://bostinno.streetwise.co/2015/10/15/best-us-schools-for-data-science-colleges-degrees-in-data-science/.

Vinik, D. (2013) "Larry Summers gave an amazing speech on the biggest economic problem of our time", *Business Insider*, 17 November, http://uk.businessinsider.com/larry-summers-imf-speech-on-the-zero-lower-bound-2013-11?r=US&IR=T.

Volkswagen (2014) "Volkswagen Group expects new digitalization era in automobile industry", 9 March, www.volkswagenag.com/content/vwcorp/info_center/en/themes/2014/03/CeBIT.html.

Waters, R. (2016) "Swiftkey deal highlights gulf in artificial intelligence world", *Financial Times*, 5 February, www.ft.com/intl/cms/s/0/ab82bf82-cb5a-11e5-a8ef-ea66e967dd44.html#axzz3zJyNvA7x.

White House Office of the Press Secretary (2013) "Executive order – making open and machine readable the new default for government information", 9 May, www.whitehouse.gov/the-press-office/2013/05/09/executive-order-making-open-and-machine-readable-new-default-government-.

White House Office of the Press Secretary (2015) "FACT SHEET: The White House releases new strategy for American innovation, announces areas of opportunity from self-driving cars to smart cities", 21 October, www.whitehouse.gov/the-press-office/2015/10/21/fact-sheet-white-house-releases-new-strategy-american-innovation.

Wilson, J. (2013) "Immigration Facts: Temporary Foreign Workers", Brookings Institute, 18 June, www.brookings.edu/research/reports/2013/06/18-temporary-workers-wilson.

Wood, E. (2003) *Empire of Capita.* London: Verso.

World Intellectual Property Organization (2014) "Global intellectual property filings up in 2013, China drives patent application growth", 16 December, www.wipo.int/pressroom/en/articles/2014/article_0018.html.

Worthington, C. (2015) "Wearable tech goes to Washington", *Wall Street Daily*, 31 August, www.wallstreetdaily.com/2015/08/31/pentagon-wearable-tech-military/.

6

US PHARMA'S BUSINESS MODEL

Why it is broken, and how it can be fixed

William Lazonick, Matt Hopkins, Ken Jacobson,
Mustafa Erdem Sakinç and Öner Tulum

1 Drug-price gouging to "Maximize Shareholder Value"

The news in September 2015 that pharmaceutical company Turing, led by a 32-year-old hedge-fund manager, had raised the price of a 62-year-old drug from $13.50 to $750 focused public attention on price gouging in an industry in which the pursuit of wealth has trumped the improvement of health (Pollack 2015). The day after Democratic presidential candidate Hillary Clinton tweeted that this "price gouging" was "outrageous," the NASDAQ Biotechnology Index plunged by 4.7 percent, or $15 billion in market capitalization, in a few hours of trading. This reaction demonstrated the importance of the stock market to the fortunes that individuals can reap when pharmaceutical companies can keep drug prices high (Langreth and Armstrong 2015).

The industry trade group Pharmaceutical Researchers and Manufacturers of America (PhRMA) was quick to disown Turing, tweeting that its actions did not "represent the values of PhRMA member companies" (Cha 2015). Yet price gouging in the US pharmaceutical drug industry goes back more than three decades. In 1985 US Representative Henry Waxman, chair of the House Subcommittee on Health and the Environment, accused the pharmaceutical industry of "gouging the American public" with "outrageous" price increases, driven by "greed on a massive scale" (Horowitz 1985).

Despite many Congressional inquiries since the 1980s, including the case of Gilead Sciences' extortionate pricing of the Hepatitis-C drug Sovaldi since 2014 (United States Senate Committee on Finance 2015), the US government does not regulate drug prices. UK Prescription Price Regulation Scheme data for 1996–2008 show that, while drug prices in other advanced nations were close to the UK's regulated prices, those in the United States were between 74 percent and 152 percent higher (UK Department of Health 1996–2008, 2015; see also Kantarjian and Rajkumar 2015). Médecins Sans Frontières (MSF) has produced abundant evidence that US drug prices are by far the highest in the world (Médecins Sans Frontières 2015).

The US pharmaceutical industry's invariable response to demands for price regulation has been that it will kill innovation. US drug companies claim that they need higher prices than those that prevail elsewhere so that the extra profits can be used to augment R&D spending. The result, they contend, is more drug innovation that benefits the United States and indeed the whole world (see for example Kravitz 1985, Horowitz 1987, Pollack 1988, Rovner 1992, Leary 1995, Mossinghoff 1999, Levin 2001, Nordrum 2015).

It is a compelling argument, until one looks at how major US pharmaceutical companies actually use the profits that high drug prices generate. In the name of "maximizing shareholder value" (MSV), pharmaceutical companies allocate profits from high drug prices to massive repurchases, or buybacks, of their own corporate stock for the sole purpose of giving manipulative boosts to their stock prices. Incentivizing these buybacks is stock-based compensation that rewards senior executives for stock-price performance (Lazonick 2014b, Lazonick 2014c, Lazonick 2015b, Hopkins and Lazonick 2016).

Like no other sector, the pharmaceutical industry puts a spotlight on how the political economy of science is a matter of life and death. In this chapter, we invoke "the theory of innovative enterprise" to explain how and why high drug prices restrict access to medicines and undermine medical innovation. An innovative enterprise seeks to develop a high-quality product that it can sell to the largest possible market at the most affordable price (Lazonick 2015c). In sharp contrast, the MSV-obsessed companies that dominate the US drug industry have become monopolies that restrict output and raise price.

2 Buyback boosts to stock prices

US pharmaceutical companies claim that high drug prices fund investments in innovation. Yet the 19 drug companies in the S&P 500 Index in February 2015 and publicly listed from 2005–2014 distributed 97 percent of their profits to shareholders over the decade, 47 percent as buybacks and 50 percent as dividends (see Table 6.1). The total of $226 billion spent on buybacks was equivalent to 51 percent of their combined R&D expenditures. That $226 billion could have been returned to households in the form of lower drug prices without infringing on R&D spending, while providing ample dividends to shareholders. Or it could have been allocated to the development of drugs for high-priority access areas that are otherwise underfunded and underserved.

In the United States, massive distributions of cash to shareholders are not unique to pharmaceutical companies. From 2005–2014, 459 companies in the S&P 500 Index expended $3.8 trillion on buybacks, representing 53 percent of net income, on top of paying $2.6 trillion in dividends equaling 36 percent of net income. They held much of the remaining profits abroad, sheltered from US taxation (Rubin 2015). Many of America's largest corporations, Pfizer and Merck among them, routinely distribute more than 100 percent of profits to shareholders, generating the extra cash by reducing reserves, selling off assets, taking on debt, or laying off employees (Lazonick et al. 2015). Over the decade 2005–2014, Johnson & Johnson, Pfizer, and Merck, the three largest pharma companies, spent an annual average of $3.9 billion, $6.1 billion, and $2.6 billion, respectively, on buybacks, while Amgen, the largest independent biopharma company, spent $3.5 billion per year.

The profits that a company retains after distributions to shareholders are the financial foundation for investment in innovation. These retained earnings can fund investment in plant and equipment, research and development, and, of critical importance to innovation, training and retaining employees (Lazonick 2015b). Dividends are the traditional, and legitimate, way for a publicly listed corporation to provide income to shareholders. They receive dividends for *holding* shares. In contrast, by creating demand for the company's stock that boosts its price, buybacks reward existing shareholders for *selling* their shares.

The most prominent sharesellers are corporate executives, investment bankers, and hedge fund managers who can time their stock sales to take advantage of buyback activity done as open-market repurchases. Buybacks also automatically increase earnings per share (EPS) by decreasing the number of shares outstanding. Since EPS has become a major metric by which

Table 6.1 Stock buybacks and cash dividends, 2005–2014, at 19 US pharmaceutical companies in the S&P 500 Index

Company	REV, $b	NI, $b	BB, $b	DV, $b	R&D, $b	BB/ NI%	DV/ NI%	(BB+DV)/ NI%	R&D/ REV%	Employees 2014
Johnson & Johnson	629.8	120.9	38.8	56.7	78.2	32	47	79	12	126,500
Pfizer	541.2	91.1	60.8	66.6	84.0	67	73	140	16	78,300
Merck	347.7	63.3	26.5	41.3	66.5	42	65	107	19	70,000
Abbott Laboratories	283.6	40.5	9.0	24.1	30.4	22	59	82	11	26,000
Eli Lilly	203.9	30.5	3.7	20.3	43.3	12	67	79	21	39,135
Bristol-Myers Squibb	186.5	35.9	4.6	23.0	36.1	13	64	77	19	25,000
Amgen	157.8	41.5	34.7	4.9	34.5	84	12	95	22	17,900
Gilead Sciences	83.8	29.3	17.0	0.0	14.4	58	0	58	17	7,000
Allergan	53.7	6.5	4.1	0.6	8.6	62	9	71	16	21,600
Biogen Idec	48.7	11.2	10.0	0.0	12.6	89	0	89	26	7,550
Mylan	48.3	2.4	3.6	0.6	4.4	151	23	174	9	30,000
Actavis	47.2	-1.5	0.6	0.0	4.0	-42	0	-42	8	21,600
Hospira	36.9	2.1	0.6	0.0	2.6	29	0	29	7	19,000
Celgene	35.9	6.7	10.4	0.0	11.7	155	0	155	33	6,012
Perrigo	23.5	1.7	0.3	0.2	0.9	18	14	32	4	10,220
Endo International	18.5	-0.4	0.8	0.0	1.5	-187	0	-187	8	5,062
Regeneron	8.1	0.7	0.0	0.0	4.9	0	0	0	61	2,925
Alexion	7.0	1.4	0.4	0.0	1.7	27	0	27	24	2,273
Vertex	5.7	-3.9	0.0	0.0	6.1	0	0	0	107	1,830
Totals, 19 pharma companies, 2005–2014	**2,767.7**	**479.8**	**225.9**	**238.2**	**446.1**	**47**	**50**	**97**	**16**	**517,907**
Totals, 459 S&P 500 companies 2005–2014	86,893.9	7,120.7	3,751.6	2,539.8	1,736.9	53	36	88	2	24,580,511
19 pharma as % of 459 S&P 500=4.14%	3.19%	6.74%	6.02%	9.38%	25.69%					2.11%

Notes: REV=revenues; NI=Net Income; BB=stock buybacks (aka repurchases); DV=cash dividends; R&D=research and development expenditures.

a) The pharmaceutical business of Abbott Laboratories became AbbVie on January 1, 2013. b) In June 2015 Actavis, Plc, domiciled in Ireland, acquired Allergan, and changed the merged company's name to Allergan, Plc. c) In November 2012, US company Watson Pharmaceuticals acquired the Swiss company Actavis, taking its name. d) In October 2013, Actavis acquired the Irish company Warner Chilcott and changed the merged company's name to Actavis, Plc, headquartered in Ireland. e) In September 2015, Pfizer acquired Hospira. f) In February 2014, Endo acquired the Canadian firm Paladin Labs, established global headquarters in Ireland, and was renamed Endo International, Plc.

Source: S&P Compustat database.

stock-market traders evaluate a company's performance, buybacks tend to increase demand for a company's stock, thus creating opportunities for stock-market traders to sell their shares at a gain, even in the absence of increased corporate revenues or profits (Lazonick 2015a).

3 Pumping up executive pay

Why do companies buy back their own shares? In "Profits without prosperity: stock buybacks manipulate the market and leave most Americans worse off," Lazonick argues that the only logical explanation is that stock-based compensation gives senior executives personal incentives to do buybacks to boost stock prices (Lazonick 2014b). There are two main types of stock-based pay: stock options, for which the realized gains depend on the difference between the stock price on the date the option to buy the shares is exercised and the date the option was granted; and stock awards, for which the realized gains depend on the market price of the stock on the date that the award vests (Hopkins and Lazonick 2016).

By using stock buybacks to boost stock prices, executives can augment the gains that they realize from exercising options or the vesting of awards. As shown in Table 6.2, from 2006-2014, the average annual total compensation of the 500 highest-paid US executives (not including billion-dollar-plus outliers) ranged from $14.7 million in 2009 to $33.2 million in 2014, with realized gains from the combination of exercising options and vesting of awards constituting between 66 percent and 84 percent of the average annual total pay (Hopkins and Lazonick 2016).[1] Stock-based pay incentivizes executives to take actions that increase the company's stock price and rewards them for doing so. Buybacks serve these purposes.

Pharma executives are well represented among the 500 highest-paid executives at US corporations. In the most recent years, as their numbers among the top 500 have increased, the average total compensation of the drug executives has soared, with the proportion of their pay derived from exercising stock options substantially higher than the average for the top 500 as a whole in 2013 and 2014.

Table 6.2 500 highest-paid executives, US corporations, with the proportions of mean total direct compensation (TDC) from stock options and stock awards, and representation of pharmaceutical executives among the top 500, 2006–14

	500 highest-paid executives, all US corporations				Highest-paid executives, pharmaceutical corporations				
	TDC, $m	*SO/ TDC%*	*SA/ TDC%*	*(SO+SA)/ TDC%*	*TDC, $m*	*SO/ TDC%*	*SA/ TDC%*	*(SO+SA)/ TDC%*	*No. of pharma execs*
2006	26.8	60	15	75	26.5	68	12	81	14
2007	30.0	59	20	78	22.7	61	20	81	11
2008	20.2	50	26	76	23.5	67	14	81	16
2009	14.4	40	26	66	19.1	43	23	66	27
2010	18.5	40	28	68	17.8	46	28	74	17
2011	19.5	41	33	74	18.0	52	22	74	12
2012	30.3	42	40	82	31.5	64	27	91	23
2013	26.2	46	35	81	35.9	66	26	91	32
2014	29.7	47	36	82	46.2	67	22	89	30

Notes: TDC=total direct compensation; SO=realized gains from exercising stock options; SA=realized gains from vesting of stock awards.

Source: S&P's ExecuComp database.

Table 6.3 Biopharma and the explosion of executive pay, 2012–14

| Company (year founded) | Number of executives in top 500 and average total direct compensation | | | | | |
| | 2012 | | 2013 | | 2014 | |
	No. of executives	Average TDC, $m	No. of executives	Average TDC, $m	No. of executives	Average TDC, $m
Gilead Sciences (1987)	3	41.6	4	74.7	5	82.4
Regeneron (1988)	5	50.7	4	53.0	4	56.6
Alexion (1992)	4	21.6	4	20.8	2	111.4
Celgene (1986)	0		3	27.5	1	96.3
Vertex (1989)	0		1	30.9	0	
Executives, 5 pharma companies	**12**	**38.7**	**16**	**44.2**	**12**	**79.8**
Executives, 19 pharma companies	23	31.5	32	35.9	30	46.2
All executives on 500 highest-paid list	500	30.3	500	26.2	500	29.7

Source: S&P's ExecuComp database.

Table 6.3 shows that biopharma companies launched in the late 1980s and early 1990s account for the explosion in pharma executive pay. Table 6.4 identifies the six highest-paid pharma executives for each year from 2006-2014. Note the prominence, especially in 2012–2014, of executives from four of the companies in Table 6.3: Gilead Sciences (14 of the 54 cells), Celgene (7), Regeneron (7), and Alexion (3), and also note the extent to which their pay is stock based.[2] Gilead Sciences CEO John C. Martin appears on this top 6 list in all nine years, three times in first place, four times in second, and twice in third.

4 Gilead's greed

With 12-week treatments for hepatitis C virus (HCV) costing $84,000 for Sovaldi and $94,500 for Harvoni, Gilead Sciences exemplifies the price-gouging drug company. Prior to 2014, Gilead had two blockbuster drugs, with Truvada, launched in 2004, reaching $3.2 billion in sales in 2012, and Atripla, launched in 2006, generating a high of $3.6 billion in 2013. In their first full years on the market, Sovaldi had sales of $10.3 billion in 2014 and Harvoni $13.9 billion in 2015. As a result, Gilead's revenues and profits exploded in these two years (see Table 6.5).

Table 6.4 Six highest-compensated pharma executives, 2006–2014, with total compensation in millions of dollars (stock-based pay as % of total compensation)

	#1	#2	#3	#4	#5	#6
2006	John W. Jackson CELGENE $84.5m. (96%)	Sol J. Barer CELGENE $46.1m. (94%)	John C. Martin GILEAD SCIENCES $32.5m. (93%)	Robert A. Essner WYETH $29.6m. (84%)	Fred Hassan SCHERING-PLOUGH $25.4m. (41%)	N. W. Bischofberger GILEAD SCIENCES $24.7m. (95%)
2007	Miles D. White ABBOTT LABS $44.8m. (85%)	John C. Martin GILEAD SCIENCES $35.6m. (93%)	Richard A. Gonzalez ABBOTT LABS $29.4m. (91%)	Henri A. Termeer GENZYME $24.7m. (85%)	N. W. Bischofberger GILEAD SCIENCES $24.1m. (95%)	William C. Weldon J & J $18.7m. (7%)
2008	Robert. J. Hugin CELGENE $74.6m. (97%)	Sol J. Barer CELGENE $59.3m. (94%)	John C. Martin GILEAD SCIENCES $33.1m. (86%)	Miles D. White ABBOTT LABS $27.1m. (52%)	James C. Mullen BIOGEN $24.9m. (72%)	N. W. Bischofberger GILEAD SCIENCES $22.8m. (92%)
2009	Fred Hassan MERCK $89.8m. (63%)	John C. Martin GILEAD SCIENCES $59.2m. (96%)	Robert J. Bertolini MERCK $39.6m. (25%)	Carrie Smith Cox MERCK $36.1m. (51%)	Thomas P. Koestle MERCK $30.9m. (58%)	Sol J. Barer CELGENE $30.4m. (90%)
2010	John C. Martin GILEAD SCIENCES $42.7m. (91%)	David E. I. Pyott ALLERGAN $33.8m. (91%)	James C. Mullen BIOGEN $24.6m. (93%)	C. B. Begley HOSPIRA $23.1m. (90%)	William C. Weldon J & J $19.9m. (21%)	Frank Baldino, Jr. CEPHALON $18.2m. (81%)
2011	John C. Martin GILEAD SCIENCES $43.2m. (90%)	David E. I. Pyott ALLERGAN $33.8m. (91%)	William C. Weldon J & J $24.4m. (32%)	Miles D. White ABBOTT LABS $17.2m. (59%)	John C. Lechleiter ELI LILLY $15.6m. (73%)	Leonard Bell ALEXION $13.3m. (71%)
2012	G. D. Yancapoulos REGENERON $129.0m. (96%)	John C. Martin GILEAD SCIENCES $84.0m. (95%)	Leonard S. Schleifer REGENERON $51.5m. (92%)	Robert J. Coury MYLAN $51.3m. (93%)	Leonard Bell ALEXION $40.5m. (99%)	Neil Stahl REGENERON $39.7m. (99%)
2013	John C. Martin GILEAD SCIENCES $168.9m. (97%)	Paul M. Bisaro ALLERGAN $113.2m. (95%)	John F. Milligan GILEAD SCIENCES $79.7m. (97%)	G. D. Yancapoulos REGENERON $74.5m. (96%)	Leonard S. Schleifer REGENERON $73.5m. (96%)	Robert. J. Hugin CELGENE $46.4m. (81%)
2014	Leonard Bell ALEXION $195.8m. (98%)	John C. Martin GILEAD SCIENCES $192.8m. (97%)	Leonard S. Schleifer REGENERON $101.8m. (97%)	Robert. J. Hugin CELGENE $96.3m. (89%)	John F. Milligan GILEAD SCIENCES $89.5m. (97%)	G. D. Yancapoulos REGENERON $61.9m. (96%)

Source: S&P's ExecuComp database.

Table 6.5 Gilead Sciences, operating data, dividends, and buybacks, 2006–15

Fiscal year	REV $m	NI $m	BB $m	DV $m	R&D $m	NI/ REV %	BB/NI %	DV/NI %	BB/ R&D	R&D/ REV %	REV/ EMP $m	EMP
2006	3,026	−1,190	545	0	2,778	−39.3	−46	0	0.2	92	1.2	2,515
2007	4,230	1,615	488	0	591	38.2	30	0	0.8	14	1.4	2,979
2008	5,336	2,011	1,970	0	733	37.7	98	0	2.7	14	1.6	3,441
2009	7,011	2,636	998	0	940	37.6	38	0	1.1	13	1.8	3,852
2010	7,949	2,901	4,023	0	1,073	36.5	139	0	3.7	13	2.0	4,000
2011	8,385	2,804	2,383	0	1,229	33.4	85	0	1.9	15	1.9	4,500
2012	9,703	2,592	667	0	1,760	26.7	26	0	0.4	18	1.9	5,000
2013	11,202	3,075	582	0	2,120	27.4	19	0	0.3	19	1.8	6,100
2014	24,890	12,101	5,349	0	2,854	48.6	44	0	1.9	11	3.6	7,000
2015	32,639	18,108	10,000	1,900	2,845	55.5	55	10	3.5	9	4.4	7,500
2006–2015	**114,371**	**46,653**	**27,005**	**1,900**	**16,922**	**40.8**	**58**	**4**	**1.6**	**15**		

Notes: REV=revenues; NI=net income; BB=stock buybacks; DV=cash dividends; R&D=research and development expenditures; EMP=employees.

Source: S&P's Compustat database.

Once Gilead moved into sustained profitability in 2007, it had very high profit margins (NI/REV%), but these margins soared with its most recent blockbusters, as have sales per employee (REV/EMP$m). Pre-Sovaldi/Harvoni, Gilead was already doing substantial buybacks, but these reached massive levels in 2014 and 2015. The result, as the Sovaldi/Harvoni pricing strategy intended, was an exploding stock price from June 2012 (see Figure 6.1), about six months after its $11.2 billion acquisition of Pharmasset, which had substantially developed sofosbuvir (Sovaldi).

An eighteen-month Congressional inquiry by US Senators Ron Wyden (D-OR) and Charles Grassley (R-IA) probed the rationale for Gilead's Sovaldi pricing strategy, and, in a report issued on December 1, 2015, concluded that "a key consideration in Gilead's decision-making process to determine the ultimate price of Sovaldi was setting the price such that it would not only maximize revenue, but also prepare the market for Harvoni and its even higher price" (The Staffs of Senators 2015). But the Wyden-Grassley report made no attempt to probe the influence and impact of Gilead's pricing strategy on its stock price and executives' pay. In our view, the objective of Gilead's executives in setting high prices was not to maximize revenues but rather to "maximize shareholder value" so that soaring stock prices would translate into enormous executive pay packages.[3]

The greed of Gilead's top executives, sanctioned by MSV ideology, is preventing millions of people with HCV in the United States and abroad from accessing Sovaldi/Harvoni at an affordable cost.[4] What is needed is a business model that shares the gains from innovative medicines with households as taxpayers who fund the government agencies that provide intellectual and financial support to the drug companies; workers whose skills and efforts have

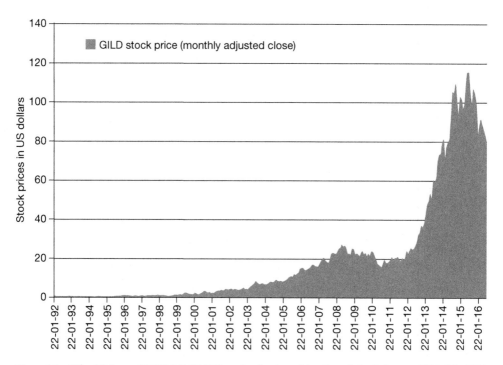

Figure 6.1　Gilead Sciences (GILD: NASDAQ) stock price (monthly adjusted close), January 1992–July 2016
Source: Yahoo Finance, monthly data.

developed the drugs; and consumers who have illnesses waiting to be cured or relieved. In contrast, the MSV business model concentrates the gains from innovative medicines in the hands of senior corporate executives who pad their paychecks by doing billions of dollars of stock buybacks to manipulate the company's stock price.

In the process, for millions who cannot afford access to innovative medicines, the life sciences become death sciences. In a hard-hitting article entitled "Gilead's greed that kills," economist Jeffrey Sachs (2015) makes this case:

> Gilead Sciences is an American pharmaceutical company driven by unquenchable greed. The company is causing hundreds of thousands of Americans with Hepatitis C to suffer unnecessarily and many of them to die as the result of its monopolistic practices, while public health programs face bankruptcy. Gilead CEO John C. Martin took home a reported $19 million last year in compensation – the spoils of untrammeled greed.

A glance at Table 6.4 reveals, however, that Martin's actual compensation in 2014 was $192.8 million. As Hopkins and Lazonick (2016) explain, the "reported $19 million" that Sachs cites is an estimated "fair value" accounting measure of executive compensation that, as can be seen, vastly understates actual compensation. For the decade 2005–2014, the "fair value" measure of Martin's pay totaled $141.5 million but his actual pay, reported to the US Internal Revenue Service, was $717.4 million, of which 95 percent was stock based.

In 2014 the actual pay packages of the other four Gilead executives named on the company's proxy statement were: John F. Milligan $89.5 million (97 percent stock based); Gregg H. Alton $52.6 million (97 percent); Norbert W. Bischofberger $50.7 million (96 percent); and Robin L. Washington $26.6 million (93 percent). In 2015 the compensation of Martin was $232.0 million (98 percent), Milligan $103.4 million (97 percent), Bischofberger $95.5 million (98 percent), Alton $33.6 million (94 percent), and Washington $22.0 million (91 percent). In the first six months of 2016, even with Gilead's stock price in decline, Martin, who stepped down as CEO in March but remains at the company as executive chairman, "earned" $55.1 million from stock-based compensation. In the first quarter of 2016 Gilead did $8.0 billion in buybacks, thus helping to "create value" for its senior executives as sharesellers. In the second quarter of 2016 Gilead scaled back its buybacks to $1 billion.[5]

In an interview in December 2013, Alton, Gilead vice-president of corporate and medical affairs, defended the price of Sovaldi by saying: "Really you need to look at the big picture. Those who are bold and go out and innovate like this and take that risk, there needs to be more of a reward on that. Otherwise it would be very difficult for people to make that investment" (The Staffs of Senators 2015, p. 108). But whose risks are being rewarded? Over its entire corporate history, Gilead has secured a total of $376 million from public share issues, all between 1991, when it did its Initial Public Offering (IPO), and 1996. Especially since Gilead only began paying dividends in 2015, it is probable that virtually all of those shareholders have long since sold their shares to secure capital gains. Current shareholders are just stock-market traders who have bought outstanding shares. So why are Gilead's senior executives so intent on "creating value" for shareholders who have contributed nothing to the development of Gilead's products? The executive pay numbers provide the answer.

Gilead is not an innovative company. Among the ten drugs that have generated 97 percent of Gilead's revenues since 1999, only two contain ingredients fully developed by Gilead researchers. Gilead gained control over the remaining ingredients, including sofosbuvir, the key component of Sovaldi and Harvoni, through acquisitions of companies that had brought the drugs to the later stages of development or had already put them on the market. And the history of the design and development of the drugs that Gilead sells reveals seminal research that was done with government funding from the National Institutes of Health (NIH).

Indeed, the NIH's 2016 budget of $32.3 billion is, in real terms, triple NIH's annual spending in the mid-1980s (National Institutes of Health 2016). Yet even three decades ago, before companies like Celgene, Gilead, Cephalon, Regeneron, Vertex, and Alexion had been founded, NIH funding was critical to drug innovation. At a meeting with French President François Mitterrand in Silicon Valley in 1984, documented in a *Washington Post* report (Henderson and Schrage 1984), venture capitalist Thomas Perkins, whose firm brought Genentech from startup in 1976 to IPO in 1980, "extolled the virtues of the risk-taking investors who finance the entrepreneurs." The *Post* article goes on to say:

> Perkins was cut off by Stanford University Professor Paul Berg, who won a Nobel Prize for work in genetic engineering. "Where were you guys in the '50s and '60s when all the funding had to be done in the basic science? Most of the discoveries that fueled [the industry] were created back then. ... I cannot imagine that if there had not been an NIH funding research, that there would have been a biotechnology industry," Berg said.

As these things go, Berg himself would be appointed to Gilead's board in 1998, and as a company director from 2004 to 2011 regularly exercised his stock options, netting an average of $2.9 million per year.[6]

But the acute problem of access to medicines goes far beyond the actions of individuals or even companies. The Gilead problem is an American problem, and given the centrality of US pharmaceutical research, the American problem is a global problem. The key cause of high drug prices, restricted access to medicines, and stifled innovation, we submit, is a social disease called "maximizing shareholder value." Armed with "the theory of innovative enterprise," policy-makers can take steps to eradicate the MSV disease (Lazonick 2014a).

5 The theory of innovative enterprise and the flaws in MSV

MSV is a *profit-driven* ideology that results in high drug prices, restricted access to existing medicines, and stifled pharmaceutical innovation. If widespread access to critical medicines at affordable prices is the goal, MSV needs to be replaced by a *product-driven* norm of corporate governance. Underpinning this product-driven norm is "the theory of innovative enterprise" (Lazonick 2012b; Lazonick 2016b).[7] The theory of innovative enterprise provides an analytical framework for understanding how a business enterprise can generate a product that is higher quality (in medicines, more effective and safer) and lower cost (more accessible and affordable) than products previously available.

The innovation process that can generate these outcomes is:

- **Uncertain:** When investments in transforming technologies and accessing markets are made, the product and financial outcomes cannot be known. Hence the need for *strategy*.
- **Collective:** To generate higher-quality, lower-cost products, the enterprise must integrate the skills and efforts of large numbers of people with different responsibilities and capabilities into the learning processes that are the essence of innovation. Hence the need for *organization*.
- **Cumulative:** Collective learning today enables collective learning tomorrow, and these organizational learning processes must be sustained over time until, through the sale of innovative products, financial returns can be generated. Hence the need for *finance*.

The theory of innovative enterprise identifies three social conditions – *strategic control*, *organizational integration*, and *financial commitment* – that can enable the firm to manage the uncertain, collective, and cumulative character of the innovation process.

- **Strategic control:** For innovation to occur in the face of technological, market, and competitive uncertainties, executives who control corporate resource allocation must have the abilities and incentives to make strategic investments in innovation. Their abilities depend on their knowledge of how strategic investments in new capabilities can enhance the enterprise's existing capabilities. Their incentives depend on alignment of their personal interests with the company's purpose of generating innovative products.
- **Organizational integration:** The implementation of an innovative strategy requires integration of people working in a complex division of labor into the collective and cumulative learning processes that are the essence of innovation. Work satisfaction, promotion, remuneration, and benefits are important instruments in a reward system that motivates and empowers employees to engage in collective learning over a sustained period of time.
- **Financial commitment:** For collective learning to cumulate over time, the sustained commitment of "patient capital" must keep the learning organization intact. For a startup company, venture capital can provide financial commitment. For a going concern, retained earnings (leveraged if need be by debt issues) are the foundation of financial commitment.

The theory of innovative enterprise explains how, in the United States during the twentieth century, a "retain-and-reinvest" allocation regime enabled a relatively small number of business enterprises in a wide range of industries to grow to employ tens, or even hundreds, of thousands and attain dominant product-market shares.[8] Companies retained corporate profits and reinvested them in productive capabilities, including first and foremost collective and cumulative learning. Companies integrated personnel into learning processes through career employment. Into the 1980s, and in some cases beyond, the norm of a career-with-one-company prevailed at major US corporations. A steady stream of dividend income and the prospect of higher future stock prices based on innovative products gave shareholders an interest in "retain-and-reinvest."

From the 1960s, however, a changing business environment encouraged executives of established US corporations to shift corporate resource allocation from "retain-and reinvest" to "downsize-and-distribute" (Lazonick 1992, Lazonick and O'Sullivan 2000, Lazonick 2009, Lazonick 2015b).[9] By the 1980s, even in good times, companies began to downsize their labor forces and distribute more profits to shareholders. Justifying this dramatic transformation in corporate resource allocation was a new ideology that taught that, for the sake of economic efficiency, companies should "maximize shareholder value" (Lazonick and O'Sullivan 2000, Lazonick 2014a).

The MSV argument is that, of all participants in the corporation, only shareholders make productive contributions *without a guaranteed return* (Jensen 1986). All other participants such as creditors, workers, suppliers, and distributors allegedly receive a market-determined price for the goods or services they render to the corporation, and hence take no risk of whether the company makes or loses money. On this assumption, only shareholders, as the sole risk-takers, have an economically justifiable claim to profits.

A fundamental flaw in MSV lies in the erroneous assumption that shareholders are the only corporate participants who bear risk. *Taxpayers* through government agencies and *workers* through the firms that employ them make risky investments in productive capabilities on a regular basis. Households, as taxpayers and workers, may have legitimate economic claims on the distribution of profits.

The National Institutes of Health (NIH), which from 1938-2015 spent $958 billion in 2015 dollars on life-sciences research, is a prime example of how taxpayers invest without a guaranteed return (National Institutes of Health 2016). Drug companies benefit from the knowledge that the NIH generates. As risk bearers, taxpayers fund investments in the knowledge base – as well as physical infrastructure such as roads – required by business, and hence have tax claims on corporate profits. But because profits may not be forthcoming and tax rates can be changed, the returns to taxpayers' investments are not guaranteed.

Through the application of skill and effort, workers regularly make productive contributions to the company's future products, and hence prospective profits. Their rewards take the forms of continued employment and career advancement, and hence workers invest in collective and cumulative learning without guaranteed returns. "Retain-and-reinvest" rewards innovative workers. But profits from innovation may not materialize, and even when they do, "downsize-and-distribute" may deny these workers shares of profits that, as risk bearers, they should have received.

As risk bearers, therefore, taxpayers whose money supports business enterprises and workers whose efforts generate productivity improvements have claims on corporate profits if and when they occur. MSV ignores the risk–reward relation for these two types of economic actors in the operation and performance of business corporations.

Another basic flaw in MSV is that the public shareholders whom it holds up as the only risk bearers typically do not invest in the value-creating capabilities of the company. Rather, as savers or speculators, they buy outstanding shares on the stock market for the sake of dividends and stock-price increases. Public shareholders generally make no productive contributions to the enterprise. Indeed, from 2006 through 2015, net equity issues in the United States were *over four trillion dollars in the negative*; US stock markets fund public shareholders rather than vice versa.[10]

The proponents of MSV (see Jensen 1986; Jensen and Murphy 1990) advocate that, through stock-based pay, senior executives should be incentivized to "disgorge" corporate earnings as buybacks and dividends to the corporate participants who matter least – just the opposite of the financial commitment needed for innovation. These distributions to shareholders generally come at the expense of the stable and remunerative career opportunities that integrate employees into processes of collective and cumulative learning. As for strategic control, a senior executive who sees MSV as the key to corporate success has lost not only the incentive but probably also the ability to allocate corporate resources to potentially innovative investments. In sum, MSV undermines investments in innovation that, if successful, can yield products that are higher quality and lower cost than previously available.

Major US pharmaceutical companies have the MSV disease, as evidenced by not only massive stock buybacks and exploding executive pay (Lazonick et al. 2014, Hopkins and Lazonick 2016) but also a "productivity crisis" in drug discovery (Pisano 2006, Cockburn 2007, Munos 2009, Lazonick and Tulum 2011, Pammolli et al. 2011, Khanna 2012, DeRuiter and Holston 2012). Companies such as Merck and Pfizer have spent the last two decades living off patented blockbuster drugs, with very little to replace them in the pipeline (Phillips 2014, McGrath 2014a, McGrath 2014b). In the name of MSV, they have been profit-driven. For a company to be an innovative enterprise, however, it needs to be product-driven.

Pfizer's focus on profits before products began before the 1980s. In the case of Merck, with Roy Vagelos as head of research from 1975 to 1985 and as CEO for the following decade, the company remained highly innovative through investments in organizational learning (Hawthorne 2003, Vagelos and Galambos 2004). In the decade that Vagelos headed Merck, the company generated both innovative products and high profits, with profit margins at over 20 percent for 1985–1994. The gains from innovation enabled Merck to provide its drug for river blindness for free to millions of poor people around the world (Vagelos and Galambos 2004, pp. 251–3).

But, as shown in Table 6.6, high profits also permitted the company to do substantial stock buybacks on top of dividends at a time when MSV was becoming the unchallenged ideology in corporate America. Once Vagelos stepped down as Merck CEO, innovation largely stopped at the company. According to a number of Merck insiders, his successor Raymond Gilmartin stifled research (Hawthorne 2006, p. 30), and, as suggested by the decadal figures on distributions to shareholders shown in Table 6.6, under CEOs Richard Clark (2005–2010) and Kenneth Frazier (from 2011), the financialization of Merck has only gotten worse. Since Frazier took over, Merck's revenues have fallen from $46.0 billion to $39.5 billion, and employment from 94,000 to 68,000. Yet buybacks have been 87 percent of net income and dividends another 99 percent, while Frazier's total compensation in 2014 was $17.6 million, of which 71 percent was stock-based.[11]

In November 2015 Pfizer commanded attention for its plan to acquire Allergan, and thus avoid US corporate taxation by establishing Ireland as its tax home. Pfizer CEO Ian Read moaned that Pfizer's US tax bill put the company at a "tremendous disadvantage" in global competition. "We're fighting," he said in the interview, "with one hand tied behind our back" (Rockoff et al. 2015). Yet from 2011 through September 2015, with Read as CEO, Pfizer's distributions to shareholders were 4.7 times its US tax payments. If Pfizer is cash-constrained, Read and his board should rethink why they did $45 billion in buybacks in 2011–2015. Perhaps it was the golden handcuffs of stock-based pay; in 2014 Read's total compensation was $22.6 million, of which 57 percent was from options and awards (Lazonick et al. 2015).

From 2010 to 2015, Pfizer's revenues fell from $67.8 billion to $48.9 billion, mainly because of expiration of patents on some of the company's blockbuster drugs, and employment was slashed from 110,600 to under 78,000. Pfizer has long since lost the capability to generate its own drug products. Since 2001 the company has launched only four internally developed products, the last one in 2005. Driven by profits rather than products, Pfizer has been, for even longer than Merck, the antithesis of an innovative enterprise.

Table 6.6 Stock buybacks and cash dividends, Merck and Pfizer, 1975–2015

	BB, $b	*DV, $b*	*BB/ NI%*	*DV/ NI%*	*(BB+DV)/ NI%*	*R&D/ REV%*
Merck						
1975–1984	0.4	1.6	9.7	44.8	**54.5**	9.4
1985–1994	4.8	7.3	30.3	46.1	**76.5**	10.8
1995–2004	26.4	25.8	46.4	45.5	**91.8**	7.9
2005–2014	26.5	42.2	42.3	67.3	**109.5**	19.1
2011–2015	22.7	25.7	68.5	77.5	**145.9**	17.2
Pfizer						
1975–1984	0.0	1.2	0.0	43.1	**43.1**	5.5
1985–1994	3.2	4.0	41.7	51.4	**93.1**	10.5
1995–2004	34.5	21.9	71.6	45.6	**117.2**	17.8
2005–2014	60.8	66.6	52.3	57.3	**109.5**	15.5
2011–2015	44.7	32.6	70.4	51.3	**121.7**	14.3

Notes: REV=revenues; NI=Net Income; BB=stock buybacks (aka repurchases); DV=cash dividends; R&D=research and development expenditures.

Sources: S&P Compustat database and company 10-K SEC filings.

6 How to fix a broken business model

In our view, a primary policy objective of all government agencies, civil society organizations, and business enterprises that seek innovative and affordable drugs should be the eradication of MSV as an ideology of corporate governance. MSV is a global problem, but the US pharmaceutical industry is where the ideology operates unconstrained. Here are, by necessity brief, steps that the US government can take to bring the MSV disease under control:

- Ban pharmaceutical companies from doing stock repurchases. Such a ban would go a long way to restoring stable and equitable growth to the US economy in general and a focus on access to medicines in the pharmaceutical industry in particular (Lazonick 2016a).[12]
- Require executive compensation that rewards the success of the pharmaceutical company in generating new medicines at affordable prices. Stock-based compensation rewards executives for draining earnings out of the company rather than mobilizing earnings to invest in innovation.
- Place stakeholders representing households as taxpayers, workers, and consumers on boards of directors of publicly listed pharmaceutical companies, along with shareholders who represent households as savers.
- Regulate the price of any drug that has benefitted from government funding, subsidies, and protection (however far upstream in the innovation process) with a view to making the drugs accessible to the largest numbers of people who need them at the most affordable prices (Trouiller et al. 2001).
- Increase the returns to households as taxpayers for their investments in life-sciences research. The Bayh-Dole Act of 1980, which facilitates commercialization of federally funded research, has given too much to business interests, including university scientists, who can make fortunes in the commercialization process. Within the university, the pursuit by "star scientists" of individual gain from publicly funded research has undermined the collective and cumulative learning that medical research requires (Wright 1986; Krimsky 2003).
- Use government funding, in collaboration with innovative businesses, to ensure the "collective and cumulative careers" of life-science researchers, who are the lowest-paid PhDs in the natural sciences (Lazonick et al. 2014, Hopkins and Lazonick 2014). There is evidence that the doubling of the NIH budget between 1998 and 2003 created large cohorts of life-science PhDs while contributing to an even more financialized biomedical industrial complex in which the prospects of collective and cumulative careers became more insecure (Teitelbaum 2008, Cyranoski et al. 2011, Stephan 2012, Teitelbaum 2014).

It is folly that the US government provides drug companies with NIH funding, patent protection, and, under the Orphan Drug Act, market exclusivity but does not regulate drug prices. In testimony to US Congress, Rohit Malpani (2015), MSF Director of Policy and Analysis, countered the drug companies' contention that higher prices generate profits that are reinvested in new drug development by arguing that "the sole reliance on high medicine prices, backed by monopolies, is a flawed paradigm for funding innovation" that

> leads to unaffordable prices while failing to stimulate innovation for diseases disproportionately affecting developing countries, where patients have limited purchasing power. Our current innovation model is also failing patients in developed countries, as with antibiotic resistance. In spite of the need for new antibiotics, pharmaceutical companies, including Pfizer, the world's largest, have abandoned

antibiotic drug development. Since antibiotics must be affordable and used sparingly, the industry response has been to withdraw.

We agree. Companies that are concerned with profits, not products, tend to be uninterested in allocating resources to the development of drugs that promise low profit margins. When the US government has sought to regulate drug prices, pharmaceutical companies have argued that they need high prices to fund investments in innovation. The fact is, however, that the largest drug companies allocate all of their profits and more to buybacks and dividends. Legitimized by MSV, "downsize-and-distribute" has enabled the senior pharma executives who make these resource-allocation decisions to secure enormous compensation for themselves.

The innovative drugs that are available are unaffordable while innovative drugs that hundreds of millions of people need are unavailable. Considering its terrible performance in the name of MSV, and its dependence on government for life-sciences research, market protection, and product demand, the US pharmaceutical sector is in need of a corporate governance revolution. Aided by government regulation and progressive social norms, US pharmaceutical companies need to reject MSV and begin the transformation to innovative enterprise.

Notes

1 We begin the series in 2006 because of changes in the availability of relevant executive pay data in that year. See Hopkins and Lazonick (2016).
2 Among executives from companies founded in the late 1980s or early 1990s, Table 6.4 also includes one executive from Cephalon, which was founded in 1987 in Pennsylvania and acquired by the Israeli company Teva in May 2011.
3 For an analysis of the relation between financialization and Gilead's drug pricing, see Roy and King (2016).
4 In March 2014, Gilead granted Egypt the price of $900 for a 12-week treatment of Sovaldi. See Fick and Hirschler (2014). One suspects that the pricing concession to Egypt was a condition of the deal that Pharmasset founder Raymond Schinazi, who was originally from Egypt, made with Gilead in the 2011 sale of Pharmasset. See Cookson (2014). Under Congressional scrutiny and with revenues rolling in, Gilead extended that price to other low-income nations. As of August 2015, Gilead had made a 12-week treatment of Sovaldi available in 101 countries for $900 (www.gilead.com/~/media/files/pdfs/other/hcv%20access%20fact%20sheet%20%20101615.pdf).
5 Note that the Securities and Exchange Commission does not require that companies reveal, at the time or after the fact, the precise days on which they do open-market repurchases. Monthly buybacks are reported in 10-Q filings with the Securities and Exchange Commission.
6 Insider trade data, filed on SEC Form 4, show that between 2004 and 2011, when he retired from Gilead's board, Berg's realized gains from exercising stock options were $23.1 million.
7 The "theory of innovative enterprise" builds upon a wide range of studies on the social conditions that support innovation at the national, industry, and company levels (see www.theAIRnet.org).
8 Over the last century, large corporations have dominated the US economy. In 2012, the 1,909 companies with 5,000 or more employees in the United States were only 0.03 percent of all firms, but, with an average employment of 20,366, employed 34 percent of the US business-sector labor force while covering 38 percent of all payroll expenditures and generating 44 percent of all revenues. See United States Census Bureau (2016).
9 These changes included the failure of the conglomerate movement of the 1960s, Japanese competition, the rise of Silicon Valley startups, and the transformation of Wall Street from investing in companies to trading in their securities. See Lazonick (1992), Lazonick and O'Sullivan (2000), Lazonick (2009), Lazonick (2012a), Lazonick (2014a). On the pharmaceutical industry, see Lazonick and Tulum (2011).
10 Board of Governors of the Federal Reserve System (2016). Net equity issues are all corporate stock issues minus those shares withdrawn from the market through stock repurchases and merger-and-acquisition activity.
11 We have recalculated Merck's reported net income in 2014 to exclude a gain $11.4 billion from the sale of a business that Merck recorded as an offset to expenses. Compensation data are from the company's DEF 14A (proxy statement) filings with the US Securities and Exchange Commission.

12 A number of prominent US politicians, including Senator Tammy Baldwin (D-WI), Vice-President Joseph Biden, and Senator Elizabeth Warren (D-MA), are outspoken critics of stock buybacks, and Senator Baldwin has been active in questioning the US Securities and Exchange Commission about why it permits them. See Lazonick (2016a). See also the website of the Academic-Industry Research Network: www.theAIRnet.org. Ken Jacobson and William Lazonick are writing a history of how the SEC adopted Rule 10b-18 in November 1982, giving US corporate executives license to do massive buybacks without fear of being charged with manipulating the company's stock price.

References

Board of Governors of the Federal Reserve System (2016), Federal Reserve Statistical Release Z.1, "Financial Accounts of the United States: Flow of Funds, Balance Sheets, and Integrated Macroeconomic Accounts," Table F-223: Corporate Equities, June 9, at www.federalreserve.gov/releases/z1/current/.

Cha, A. (2015), "Drug and biotech industry trade groups give Martin Shkreli the boot," *Washington Post*, September 24.

Cockburn, I. (2007), "Is the Pharmaceutical Industry in a Productivity Crisis?," in Josh Lerner and Scott Stern, eds., *Innovation Policy and the Economy*, Volume 7, MIT Press: 1–32.

Cookson, C. (2014), "Raymond Schinazi fled Nasser's Egypt to become a pioneer in antivirals," *Financial Times*, July 27.

Cyranoski, D., N. Gilbert, H. Ledford, A. Nayar and M. Yahia (2011), "Education: The PhD factory: The world is producing more PhDs than ever before. Is it time to stop?" *Nature*, 472: 276–9.

DeRuiter, J. and P. Holston (2012), "Drug Patent Expirations and the 'Patent Cliff'," *U.S. Pharmacist*, 37, 6: 12–20.

Fick, M. and B. Hirschler (2014), "Gilead offers Egypt new hepatitis C drug at 99 percent discount," *Reuters*, March 21, at www.reuters.com/article/us-hepatitis-egypt-gilead-sciences-idUSBREA2K1VF20140321.

Hawthorne, F. (2003), *The Merck Druggernaut: The Inside Story of a Pharmaceutical Giant*, John Wiley & Sons.

Hawthorne, F. (2006), "Merck's Fall from Grace," *The Scientist*, 20, 5.

Henderson, N. and M. Schrage (1984), "The roots of biotechnology: Government R&D spawns a new industry," *Washington Post*, December 16.

Hopkins, M. and W. Lazonick (2014), "Who Invests in the High-Tech Knowledge Base?" Institute for New Economic Thinking Working Group on the Political Economy of Distribution Working Paper No. 6, September 2014 (revised December 2014), at http://ineteconomics.org/ideas-papers/research-papers/who-invests-in-the-high-tech-knowledge-base.

Hopkins, M. and W. Lazonick (2016), "The Mismeasure of Mammon: The Uses and Abuses of the ExecuComp Database," Report on Executive Pay to the Institute of New Economic Thinking, August.

Horowitz, M. (1987), "Interview with Rep. Henry A. Waxman, Chairman, Subcommittee on Health and the Environment, U.S. House of Representatives," *Health Week*, September 28.

Horowitz, S. (1985), "Drug industry accused of gouging public," *Washington Post*, July 16.

Jensen, M. (1986), "Agency Costs of Free Cash Flow, Corporate Finance, and Takeovers," *American Economic Review*, 76, 2: 323–9.

Jensen, M. and K. Murphy (1990), "Performance Pay and Top Management Incentives," *Journal of Political Economy*, 98, 2, 1: 225–64.

Kantarjian, H. and S. Rajkumar (2015), "Why Are Cancer Drugs So Expensive in the United States, and What Are the Solutions?" *Mayo Clinic Proceedings*, April: 500–4.

Khanna, I. (2012), "Drug Discovery in Pharmaceutical Industry: Challenges and Trends," *Drug Discovery Today*, 17, 19, 20.

Kravitz, R. (1985), "Prescription drug industry accused of price gouging," *The Record*, July 16.

Krimsky, S. (2003), *Science in the Private Interest: Has the Lure of Profits Corrupted Biomedical Research?* Rowan and Littlefield.

Langreth, R. and D. Armstrong (2015), "Clinton's tweet on high drug prices sends biotech stocks down," *Bloomberg Business*, September 21.

Lazonick, W. (1992), "Controlling the Market for Corporate Control: The Historical Significance of Managerial Capitalism," *Industrial and Corporate Change*, 1, 3, 445–8.

Lazonick, W. (2009), *Sustainable Prosperity in the New Economy? Business Organization and High-Tech Employment in the United States*, Kalamazoo, MI, Upjohn Institute for Employment Research.

Lazonick, W. (2012a), "Alfred Chandler's Managerial Revolution," in W. Lazonick and D. Teece, eds., *Management Innovation: Essays in the Spirit of Alfred D. Chandler, Jr.*, Oxford University Press: 3–29.

Lazonick, W. (2012b), "The Theory of Innovative Enterprise: Methodology, Ideology, and Institutions," in J. Moudud, C. Bina and P. Mason, eds., *Alternative Theories of Competition: Challenges to the Orthodoxy*, Routledge, 2012: 127–59.

Lazonick, W. (2014a), "Innovative Enterprise and Shareholder Value," *Law and Financial Markets Review*, 8, 1: 52–64.

Lazonick, W. (2014b), "Profits Without Prosperity: Stock Buybacks Manipulate the Market and Leave Most Americans Worse Off," *Harvard Business Review*, September: 46–55.

Lazonick, W. (2014c), "Taking Stock: Why Executive Pay Results in an Unstable and Inequitable Economy," Roosevelt Institute White Paper, June 5, at http://rooseveltinstitute.org/taking-stock-why-executive-pay-results-unstable-and-inequitable-economy/.

Lazonick, W. (2015a), "Buybacks: From Basics to Politics," AIR Special Report, The Academic-Industry Research Network, August 1, at www.theairnet.org/v3/backbone/uploads/2015/08/Lazonick-Buybacks-Basics-to-Politics-20150819.pdf.

Lazonick, W. (2015b), "Stock Buybacks: From Retain-and-Reinvest to Downsize-and-Distribute," Center for Effective Public Management, Brookings Institution, April 17, at www.brookings.edu/research/papers/2015/04/17-stock-buybacks-lazonick.

Lazonick, W. (2015c), "The Theory of Innovative Enterprise: Foundation of Economic Analysis," AIR Working Paper, August, at www.theairnet.org/v3/backbone/uploads/2015/08/Lazonick.TIE-Foundations_AIR-WP13.0201.pdf.

Lazonick, W. (2016a), "How Stock Buybacks Make Americans Vulnerable to Globalization," paper presented to the Conference on Mega-Regionalism: New Challenges for Trade and Innovation, East-West Center, Honolulu, January 20.

Lazonick, W. (2016b), "Innovative Enterprise or Sweatshop Economics? In Search of Foundations of Economic Analysis," *Challenge*, 59, 2: 65–114.

Lazonick, W. and M. O'Sullivan (2000), "Maximizing Shareholder Value: A New Ideology for Corporate Governance," *Economy and Society*, 29, 1: 13–35.

Lazonick, W. and Ö. Tulum (2011), "US Biopharmaceutical Finance and the Sustainability of the Biotech Business Model," *Research Policy*, 40, 9: 1170–87.

Lazonick, W., M. Hopkins, and Ö. Tulum (2015), "Tax dodging just one part of Pfizer's corrupt business model," *Huffington Post*, December 4, at www.huffingtonpost.com/william-lazonick/tax-dodging-just-one-part_b_8721900.html.

Lazonick, W., P. Moss, H. Salzman, and Ö. Tulum (2014), "Skill Development and Sustainable Prosperity: Collective and Cumulative Careers versus Skill-Biased Technical Change," Institute for New Economic Thinking Working Group on the Political Economy of Distribution Working Paper No. 7, December 2014, at http://ineteconomics.org/ideas-papers/research-papers/skill-development-and-sustainable-prosperity-cumulative-and-collective-careers-versus-skill-biased-technical-change.

Leary, W. (1995), "U.S. gives up right to control drug prices," *New York Times*, April 12.

Levin, A. (2001), "Myth of the High Cost of Drug Research," Center for Medical Consumers, August 1, at https://medicalconsumers.org/2001/08/01/myth-of-the-high-cost-of-drug-research/.

Malpani, R. (2015), "MSF's Oral Testimony to the United States House of Representatives Committee on Ways and Means," Hearing on Access to Medicines, U.S. House of Representatives, December 8, at www.msfaccess.org/content/msfs-oral-testimony-united-states-house-representatives-committee-ways-and-means.

McGrath, M. (2014a), "Drug patent expirations continue to hit Pfizer revenue," *Forbes*, January 28.

McGrath, M. (2014b), "Merck sales slide on expiring drug patents but shares lifted by cancer-fighting collaboration," *Forbes*, February 5.

Médecins Sans Frontières (2015), "The Cost of Medicine: A Special Report," *Alert*, Fall, at www.doctorswithoutborders.org/article/alert-special-report-cost-medicine.

Mossinghoff, G. (1999), "Overview of the Hatch-Waxman Act and Its Impact on the Drug Development Process," *Food and Drug Law Journal*, 54: 187–94.

Munos, B. (2009), "Lessons from 60 years of pharmaceutical innovation," *Nature Reviews, Drug Discovery*, 8, 12, 959–68.

National Institutes of Health (2016), Budget, at www.nih.gov/about-nih/what-we-do/budget.

Nordrum, A. (2015), "Why are prescription drugs so expensive? Big Pharma points to the cost of research and development, Critics say that's no excuse," *International Business Times*, September 19.

Pammolli, F., L. Magazzini, and M. Riccaboni (2011), "The Productivity Crisis in Pharmaceutical R&D," *Nature Reviews, Drug Discovery*, 10, 6: 428–38.

Phillips, D. (2013), "Pfizer's pipeline story begins to unravel," *YCharts*, August 30, at http://finance.yahoo.com/news/pfizer-pipeline-story-begins-unravel-143509405.html.

Pisano, G. (2006), *Science Business: The Promise, the Future, and the Reality of Biotech*, Harvard Business School.

Pollack, A. (1988), "The troubling cost of drugs that offer hope," *New York Times*, February 9.

Pollack, A. (2015), "Drug goes from $13.50 a tablet to $750, overnight," *New York Times*, September 20.

Rockoff, J., D. Mattioli, and D. Cimilluca (2015), "Pfizer and Allergan begin merger talks," *Wall Street Journal*, October 29.

Rovner, J. (1992), "Should the government regulate prescription drug prices," *CQ Researcher*, July 17.

Roy, V. and L. King (2016), "Betting on Hepatitis C: How Financial Speculation in Drug Development Influences Access to Medicines," *BMJ*, 354: i3718, at www.bmj.com/content/354/bmj.i3718.

Rubin, R, (2015), "$2.1 trillion overseas to avoid taxes," *Bloomberg Business*, March 4.

Sachs, J. (2015), "Gilead's greed that kills," *Huffington Post*, July 27, at www.huffingtonpost.com/jeffrey-sachs/gileads-greed-that-kills_b_7878102.html.

Stephan, P. (2014), *How Economics Shapes Science*, Harvard University Press.

Teitelbaum, M. (2008), "Structural Disequilibria in Biomedical Research" *Science*, 321, 5889: 644–5.

Teitelbaum, M. (2014), *Falling Behind? Boom, Bust, and the Global Race for Scientific Talent*, Princeton University Press.

The Staffs of Senators Ron Wyden and Charles E. Grassley (2015), "The Price of Sovaldi and Its Impact in the U.S. Health Care System," Committee on Finance, United States Senate, December 1, 117, at www.finance.senate.gov/ranking-members-news/wyden-grassley-sovaldi-investigation-finds-revenue-driven-pricing-strategy-behind-84-000-hepatitis-drug.

Trouiller, P., E. Torreale, P. Olliaro, N. White, S. Foster, D. Wirth, and B. Pécoul (2001), "Drugs for neglected diseases: a failure of the market and a public health failure," *Tropical Medicine and International Health*, 6, 11: 945–51.

UK Department of Health (1996–2008), *The Pharmaceutical Price Regulation Scheme*, Report to Parliament, various years.

United States Census Bureau (2016), "Statistics of U.S. Businesses," Data on "U.S., NAICS sectors, larger employment sizes" at www.census.gov/econ/susb/.

United States Senate Committee on Finance (2015), "Wyden-Grassley Sovaldi investigation finds revenue-driven pricing strategy behind $84,000 hepatitis drug," Press release, December 1 at www.finance.senate.gov/ranking-members-news/wyden-grassley-sovaldi-investigation-finds-revenue-driven-pricing-strategy-behind-84-000-hepatitis-drug.

Vagelos, R. and L. Galambos (2004), *Medicine, Science, and Merck*, Cambridge University Press.

Wright, S. (1986), "Recombinant DNA Technology and Its Social Transformation, 1972–1982," *Osiris*, 2nd ser., 2: 303–60.

7

RESEARCH & INNOVATION (AND) AFTER NEOLIBERALISM

The case of Chinese smart e-mobility

David Tyfield

1 A cultural political economy of R&I as complex power/knowledge systems

Innovation matters in the twenty-first century. We need more and radical innovation to tackle unprecedented global challenges. But, conversely, many frontiers of innovation seem the very source of new existential insecurities. Meanwhile, innovation itself is a focus of intense political economic debate regarding its dwindling stagnation or its runaway acceleration, reflecting the prior two concerns respectively (Gordon, 2012; Brynjolfsson & McAfee, 2014). It seems, in short, that we cannot sidestep having to look anew at what 'innovation' really means as we explore where socio-technical change may lead next.

Here I introduce an approach that begins to do just that: a cultural political economy of research and innovation (R&I, altogether 'CPERI') that explores the co-production of R&I and socio-political regimes in terms of dynamic emergent systems of power/knowledge relations and technologies. This complex power/knowledge systems (CP/KS) perspective draws together cultural political economy (CPE) (Jessop & Sum, 2006), political ecology (Lawhon & Murphy, 2013), theories of socio-technical systems transition (Smith *et al.*, 2010) and Foucauldian analysis of government, regarding the 'conduct of conduct' of polities and selves (Dean, 2010; Lemke, 2011), with a specific focus on issues of research and innovation (Tyfield, 2012).

CPERI can be read or reached in many ways, including as insights into the current ecological predicament, what (e.g. low-carbon) 'system transition' is and how it may be expedited and shaped (Tyfield, Ely *et al.*, 2015). But it also leads to and emerges from exploration as to what 'neoliberalism' is and what its *crisis* is. Our primary interest here, though, is regarding how to think about R&I, and conversely how R&I is central to all of these prior issues and lenses, hence how all these are inter-related. Indeed, a CP/KS perspective not only helps us understand the present crisis but also offers insights into how we may get out of it… and the (political) questions, opportunities and limits this raises in turn.

Key to the CP/KS perspective is the reconceptualization of the process of system transition (and of innovation within it) through a CPE lens. This conception builds on Foucault's discussion of power to explore '"the total structure of actions brought to bear" by some on the actions of others' (Hindess, 2006, 116, quoting Foucault, 2001, 336). Against contemporary common-sense understandings, therefore, power is not conceived as a zero-sum and brute capacity held

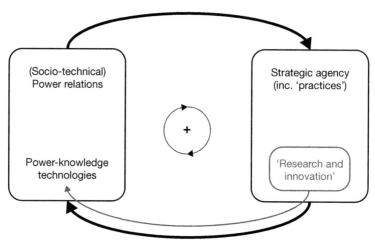

Socio-technical power system

Figure 7.1   Complex socio-technical power/knowledge systems

by the powerful over the powerless. Nor is power presumed to be normatively bad unless and until it is tamed by reasoned acceptance and legitimation. Instead, power – or power/knowledge – is dispersed, ubiquitous, strategic, relational, productive – of both larger 'systems' of government and of subjectivities – and normatively ambivalent. In particular, shifting from a structural account of power, as something possessed by some over others, to a relational and constitutive conception immediately loosens up and dynamizes concepts of system 'lock-in' and transition (Garvey *et al.*, 2015; cf Unruh, 2000; Geels, 2014). Instead of an analytical and practical paralysis, therefore, in which those structurally enabled today seem immoveable, openings are presented to explore (and perhaps assist) emergent alternative regimes.

In other words, reframed in CPE terms, transition becomes a process in which power/ knowledge relations mediate strategic agency that is, in turn, qualitatively shaping *new* power/ knowledge relations and technologies (and hence power systems) (see Figure 7.1). Furthermore, with innovation itself conceived as a process of socio-technical power – i.e. as *politics* – it also becomes a privileged window into this process, precisely as the key reflexive moment of *power/ knowledge acting on itself.*

The aim of this form of analysis – and especially in moments of system crisis, such as the present – is thus to draw on iteratively reinterpreted concrete evidence regarding contemporary processes of socio-technical innovation in order to trace possible emergent transitions in entire *systems* of power/knowledge relations. This involves searching for and testing embryonic glimmers of both: the dynamic, internally related and constitutive power 'logics' of such a system; and inseparably, the (power-saturated) process of *how it could emerge from where we are,* given the power–knowledge relations and technologies of the present, including, crucially, the specific dynamics of the 'crises' themselves.

This leads to three central claims that are taken in turn in the rest of this chapter.

- First, this approach reveals the aetiology of the present turbulence as the *crisis of the incumbent dominant power/knowledge system,* which I will call 'neoliberalism'. The key question that emerges, for CPERI and the world, is thus 'what comes after neoliberalism and how?'

- Second, we turn precisely to this question, showing how a CP/KS approach illuminates innovation trajectories that, in 2016, are beginning to seed embryonic power transition. This hinges on how the crises together act as an *urgence*, conditioning dynamics of contemporary innovation that engender essentially contested but dynamic emergence of something else: a new (if still unquestionably capitalist) regime 'after' neoliberalism, including of R&I.

- Finally, then, these dynamics are yielding futures that themselves threaten to be deeply troubling, but that also offer openings for strategic intervention, not least by a (critical) CPERI itself.

The key point throughout, then, is that innovation is not just needed to 'solve' these crises, as techno-economic problems 'out there', but as a crucial thread in the transformation of the broader *socio-political conditions* that prevent those problems being meaningfully addressed in the first place. And innovation is thus itself a key – still largely neglected – arena of twenty-first-century politics.

2 Neoliberalism, its crises, and R&I

What light can be shed on the present crisis conjuncture using this approach? The crisis is revealed to be one of a specific systemic regime of (liberal, capitalist) power/knowledge relations and technologies that may be called 'neoliberalism'. This includes a specifically *neoliberal* model of innovation. Following the schema above, 'neoliberal innovation' should strictly be understood in the broad sense of the recursive introduction of power/knowledge technologies that can promote and constantly renew the neoliberal project. This would thus include policy and cultural developments, new financial products and forms of organization etc. So as not to extend this discussion too far beyond our focus on research & innovation (R&I), however, we focus on these more familiar senses of 'innovation' – which have, in any case, a heightened significance for neoliberalism as a system.

'Neoliberalism' is here defined as a dynamic and voracious power/knowledge system built upon a political project and ideology of epistemic market fundamentalism (Mirowski, 2011; Mirowski & Plehwe, 2009). This means that it elevates the 'market' from optimal mechanism of *allocation*, as in neo-classical economics or 'classical liberal' thought à la Adam Smith, to optimal and supra-human *decision-maker*. The key elements of neoliberalism follow immediately, in terms of its intrinsic and insatiable limitlessness regarding: the potential revolutionizing of all social institutions by their marketization; and neoliberalism's particular thirst for rapid financialized economic growth and resource consumption, as these drive and are driven by growth of the 'market'. It also follows immediately that neoliberalism is a political radicalism. For there can in principle be no compelling argument *against* further marketization as this is precisely to claim an epistemic superiority over the market that is no longer available. Together, then, these more concrete manifestations drive a process of relentless and insatiable marketization via recursive feedback loops (see Figure 7.2).

Research and innovation is crucial to this process in several respects (Tyfield, 2016). First, consider how the neoliberal project is premised upon the redefinition of the market as a primarily epistemic device, a 'marketplace of ideas' (see Nik-Khah, this volume). As such, 'ideas' or power/*knowledges* become the privileged medium of politically reconstructing societies around markets, particularly in two key forms: the novel mediation of social relations by profit-seeking socio-technological innovations (e.g. technologies to time-discipline, or simply replace, the home-visiting care worker); and/or market-supporting government regulation and

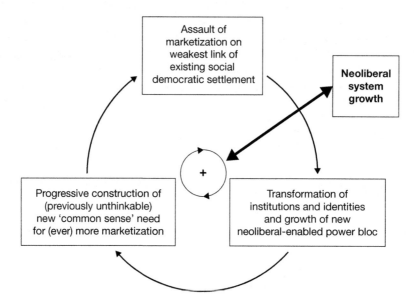

Figure 7.2 The system dynamics of neoliberalism

legitimation (quintessentially privatizations and introduction of quasi-markets through novel forms of measurement, e.g. of the research and teaching 'excellence' of universities, then linking this to calculations of public funding). Moreover, 'ideas' themselves become a key sphere of social life to be subjected to marketization.

The result is, respectively, the construction of ever-greater systemic demands for, and fetishization of, 'innovation' together with the tendential conflation of science with ('hi-tech') commercialized innovation. This, in turn, involves the state-sponsored corporate enclosure of existing knowledge commons as well as a specific model of innovation that privileges innovation that:

- promises high, short-term returns, especially as financial(izable) assets;
- focuses on products that service the market demands of corporate/individual consumers, as opposed to publics or states;
- supports projects of corporate enclosure of bodies of knowledge and so promises to maximize global corporate control of particular (technoscience-intensive) markets; and
- is constitutively dismissive of concerns about ontological limits and risks.

The quintessential example here of this broader neoliberal innovation model is GM agriculture (see Harrison *et al.*, this volume).

But R&I is also crucial to the *crisis* of neoliberalism. This follows directly, in fact, from the intrinsically voracious nature of neoliberalism and the key role R&I plays in this regard. First, the permanent social revolution of marketization necessarily elicits endless and proliferating systems challenges (Pellegrini, 2011; Klein, 2007). These are, however, not *crises* in the first instance but precisely the *opportunities* for further neoliberal innovation by the Promethean entrepreneur. Such innovation is thus a socio-economic safety valve of sorts to the extent new consumer goods with significant market demand can emerge from the increasingly system-wide context of instability. Innovation is thus crucial in neoliberal system maintenance because it is always and only the *next* round of neoliberal innovations that prevents the novel system challenges that neoliberal innovation *itself* produces from engendering broader system disintegration: an accelerating treadmill of innovation and novel risks (of growing scale and depth) that propels construction of a society and a dominant model of R&I of a *specific*, i.e. neoliberal, type.

Innovation is thus a key process in the 'normal' government of a neoliberal(izing) system always on the cusp of crisis but productively balanced as such. Yet, conversely, it follows that where this process has proceeded to the extent it is beginning to destroy (perhaps unacknowledged but nonetheless) essential conditions for such innovation, the accelerating feedback loop flies apart in a crisis of *crisis management*: the very definition of a system crisis (Jessop, 2013). As several other chapters in this volume amply demonstrate, there are strong arguments that this is exactly what is unfolding right now (see e.g. chapters by Schiller & Yeo; Pagano & Rossi; Lazonick *et al.*, this volume).

The key point for our purposes, however, is how a CPE understanding of the pivotal locus of innovation in the recursive dynamic cycles of power/knowledge system government illuminates both:

1   the specific – and apparently now self-destructive – dynamics of the neoliberal project, its transformation of social relations and selves, and the self-imposed constraints on its specific model of innovation as these together propel themselves into a deepening system crisis of crisis management, and, hence that;
2   the primary problem for R&I today is not stagnation nor acceleration of R&I *per se* but the looming limits of a *particular regime* of R&I (as political process). This thus also stimulates an empirical search for possible, existing alternatives.

3 After neoliberalism: 'liberty' and 'security' through innovation as political process

What can follow and emerge immanently out of neoliberalism, therefore, and how? Studying R&I within a CP/KS framework affords a key window into *this* question as well, but calling for a different tack. Our discussion in the last section could go directly to the abstract dynamics of the neoliberal system, since these are there for us to study and are clearly documented. But how can we trace the outlines of a new power/knowledge system, in which entirely different qualitative dynamics are forming, circulating and sedimenting?

In these circumstances, the existing tacit common senses regarding boundaries between different concepts and/or realities – *themselves* products of the incumbent constellation of power/knowledges – in which context the researcher is herself inextricably located no matter how critical her perspective, are likely a positive impediment. Yet grounds to differentiate one set of speculations about future trajectories from another are still needed. So we must start analysis of possible futures by working 'up' from the privileged window (described above) of existing concrete innovation cases and trajectories towards informed speculation about broader, if embryonic, social transformations.

One approach to such an analysis is first to acknowledge a meta-dynamic of the *specific* types of CP/KS that we are here thinking about, including neoliberalism, namely the broadly 'liberal' capitalist regimes that have ecologically dominated (Jessop, 2014) the modern period. Here, in keeping with the CP/KS perspective, 'liberal' connotes a *power/knowledge regime* characterized by government *through* maximal production and consumption of (individual negative) freedoms (Foucault, 2010, 63).

It is not, therefore, to be confused with 'liberalism' – vs. socialism or fascism, say – as a political philosophy and/or normative stance of individual human rights and equality before the law. Nor should it be misunderstood as synonym for (liberal) democracy. Liberal regimes do tend to deploy the former as a key hegemonic power/knowledge technology and have a contingent and contested correlation with the latter. But what is essential to such a regime of power/knowledge relations, however, is that it is constitutively dependent upon the continued exercise and expansion of new liberties. And 'liberties' in turn must be understood in CP/KS terms, connoting a strategic orientation and enablement of pursuit of the aspirations of concrete individuals and groups who are, in turn, themselves shaped and *constituted* by those liberties and their differential access to them.

Of course, a crucial medium and process for the expression and expansion of these liberties is innovation – including as innovation *of* liberties. Liberal regimes are thus dynamic constellations that generate cycles of innovation, asymmetrically empowering power/knowledge relations and (new) liberties, each of a specific concrete form that performs and manifests the particular system logic of that type of liberalism.

This form of power regime has proven exceptionally resilient and protean in the modern period, expanding over ever-increasing stretches of the Earth's surface through a turbulent and crisis-punctuated process that nonetheless has overcome rival regimes, including those it has itself engendered (e.g. Arrighi, 1994). Crucial to its dynamism, however, is the combination of the positive feedback loops of liberties as power/knowledges begetting and innovating further liberties.

But this process develops alongside an inextricable concomitant from a systems perspective: the dynamics of 'security' (Foucault, 2009) (see Figure 7.3). This denotes the emergence, shaping, (attempted) management and eventual overspill of existential 'security' threats to the integrity of that specific liberal system generated by the dynamics of its own particular model of (liberal) innovation. The comparatively unfettered proliferation of new liberties characteristic

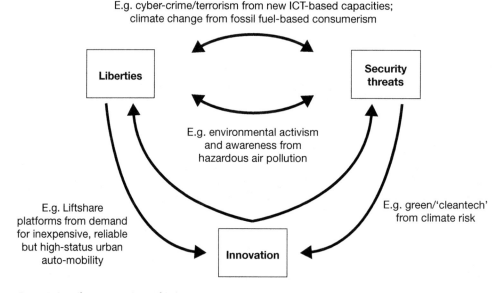

Figure 7.3 Liberty, security and innovation

of a specific liberal regime necessarily produces and incubates new security threats to the integrity of the system. These arise as a matter of course from the very unregulated nature of the innovation that is the liberalism's essential dynamic (Lemke, 2011; Dean, 2010). Indeed, the dynamic of neoliberal innovation and system growth/crisis management described above is evidently an instance of this dynamic.

Of course, liberties in turn beget further innovations, or counter-innovations, that attempt (more or less successfully) to domesticate and manage these innovation-generated security threats. Nonetheless, the parallel production of security threats with new liberties necessarily creates a specific dynamic and 'mood' to liberal regimes that adds a further aspect to the interaction of liberty and security. This concerns the inescapable construction of a deepening zeitgeist, and indeed reality, of multiple unsolved problems that are existentially challenging, both at system level and for individuals identified and shaped by that given system. Alongside the 'liberty' dynamics of innovation identified in essentially positive terms, therefore, there emerges a pervasive but largely unspeakable anxiety; a shadow-side that implacably compels ever greater innovation.

But this accelerating generation of liberties through innovation remains evermore deeply locked into the *existing system logic*. Hence, as unaddressed security risks accumulate with the very *success* of the specific model of liberal innovation (Biel, 2012) they increasingly *cannot* be addressed. For the existing and sedimenting common senses and institutions of that regime simply deepen the problems, while qualitatively novel problems also emerge that entirely exceed the capacities of existing power/knowledge technologies and their innovation. We see both of these factors at work today, not least in the barren conjunction of 'innovation' dominated by 'Tech' set against the unprecedented challenge of planetary ecocide. This eventually culminates in a definite overspill in which the security threats utterly overwhelm the existing liberal power regime: a system crisis (of crisis management), or in Foucauldian terms (1980, 195), an *urgence*.

Crucially, though, the emergence of an *urgence*, however, signals a renewed boost to the *very dynamics of liberty and security* not their collapse or transcendence. The *urgence* marks the incontrovertible emergence at system level of novel problems (including new ungovernable liberties) that are not amenable to the incumbent (liberal) CP/KS regime and its forms of innovation (out of problems). This thus stimulates systemic shifts in search of new orientations for actively pursued and liberalism-enabled strategic action.

This is a break with incumbent common-sense power/knowledges in terms of both: a newly earnest openness to both the 'new' itself and the potential for its *qualitative*, directional redefinition away from incumbent trajectories; *and*, conversely, a new openness and concern regarding the importance of 'security threats' that were previously blind spots. Together, these drive accelerated and pro-active adoption and development of innovations that both promise new 'liberties' and are newly 'security' conscious, drawing on what appears most 'promising' amongst the power/knowledge resources currently to hand.

In short, an *urgence* connotes a new public acceptance of both a new *problem field* for innovation (as political process) *and*, inseparably, demand for a new set of '*solutions*' from that innovation, generating the accelerated self-interested strategic *pursuit of* individualized 'liberty' in *flight from* the new threats to 'security' respectively. *These* innovations, however, are not just new 'hi-tech' gadgetry, but the new power/knowledge technologies that develop and then constitute a new regime of system government.

These dynamics not only illuminate the current global predicament in the abstract, regarding the present crises as the *urgence* marking the end of the neoliberal regime. They also do so in terms of supporting a more concrete and empirical investigation into the key question of 'what follows neoliberalism?' This involves exploration of contemporary and/or emergent dynamics of liberty/security that are profoundly transforming neoliberalism from *within*, through socio-political processes of innovation/counter-innovation.

Returning to the CP/KS schema above, therefore, specific arenas of socio-technical and techno-scientific innovation act as multiple empirical windows with privileged perspective concerning the necessary whole-system transformation immanent in the overflow and terminal crises of the incumbent power/knowledge system (of neoliberalism in this case). This analysis can also proceed in ways that, crucially, do not analytically need to take the existing dominant forms of any of the multiple system elements – institutions, agents and subjectivities, socio-cultural common senses, social 'structures' (cf Mirowski & Sent, 2008) – as 'given', even for heuristic purposes.

Instead, analysis of a given domain of innovation from a CP/KS perspective affords imaginative but empirically-informed speculation, as a genealogy of the emerging present. This approach studies how forms of innovation may specifically enable and disable particular socio-political constituencies, that in turn further pursue and promote those innovations, generating positive feedback loops of growing and self-sustaining 'power momentum' that can, over time, change what otherwise seem currently unshakeable and locked-in manifestations of institutional and structural logics (Tyfield, Ely *et al.*, 2015).

4 Chinese smart e-mobility beyond neoliberalism

Here, there is only space to illustrate briefly what such an investigation reveals, at least on one reading that focuses on a key locus of contemporary global system change. Two overwhelmingly important trends emergent from the crisis of neoliberalism, and now pushing beyond it, are the rise of China and the emergence of Web 2.0-based informationalization. Both are clearly amongst the most important developments over the last twenty years regarding global political economy, socio-technical change and the dependence of both on changing power/knowledge systems; and both are unquestionable products of neoliberalism while also deeply problematic to a neoliberal project built upon an unrivalled US global dominance and supremely proprietary models of R&I.

Together, though, these point to the particular importance of an example of contemporary innovation that draws these two major themes together, as well as the broader perspective of ecological crisis: namely low-carbon urban 'smart' mobility transition in China. Examining this case study from a CP/KS perspective reveals precisely the abstract dynamic above at work regarding innovation *within* and *beyond* the crises of neoliberalism. In particular, in this case complementary and mutually antagonistic, and hence self-propelling, dynamics of innovation (as political process) and essential contestation are indeed apparent regarding potent contemporary issues of the individualized pursuit of liberty and the flight from deepening security threats (see Figure 7.4) (Tyfield, Zuev *et al.*, 2015).

China in the 2010s presents a sociotechnical context of titanic and rapid change seemingly without precedent or contemporary rival. Moreover, at the core of these turbulent dynamics are precisely the twin issues of the progressive individualization of Chinese lives – i.e. liberties, albeit systematically constrained to the socio-economic not political realm by the party-state regime – together with intense exposure and lived concern regarding global risks (Ren, 2013; Yan, 2010) – i.e. security threats. Urban mobility innovation today in China presents a vivid example of this conjuncture in terms of anxious pursuit of the multiple, proliferating and uncertain prospects for personal development alongside profound concerns about socio-technical risk.

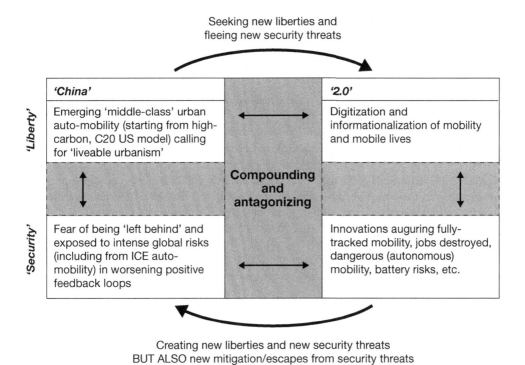

Figure 7.4 System dynamism in Chinese e-mobility innovation

We may start by noting how important autonomous mobility (including urban mobility or circulation) is, both to the market societies of liberal regimes (Foucault, 2009; Rajan, 2006) and to the contemporary (neoliberal-conditioned) globalizing world (Urry, 2007). This is all the more so in contemporary China, given the utter political imperative of uninterrupted economic growth as the central, load-bearing pillar of the party-state regime. Expanding and improving autonomous mobility is thus a key economic necessity of this marketizing and individualizing economy and, conversely, a key outlet for expression of growing personal appetite for autonomy, against the constraints in the civic/political sphere.

Indeed, and crucially, the societal dynamism of attempts to negotiate these twin imperatives is compounded (not diminished) by the fact that there is no clear model as to what substantively constitutes either 'liberties' (that will newly enable you individually or the society and country more broadly) or the 'security threats', only profound and dynamic disagreement. For instance, on the one hand, the incumbent and deeply locked-in global model of urban auto-mobility based on (aspiration for) personal ownership of a large, internal combustion engine (ICE) and glamorous (hence, in China, foreign) branded car exacts an irresistible attraction on the contemporary Chinese imagination. The obvious default definition of the expansion and consumption of liberty is thus growing (foreign) car ownership. Yet, of equal weight is the ubiquitous (and deepening) anxiety about the outcomes of this model of mobility: gridlocked congestion; commuter stress and isolation in massive new cities built and/or redesigned for cars; national industrial and innovation weakness in a 'pillar' industry; and hazardous air pollution and ballooning greenhouse gas emissions.

Is the incumbent ICE model thus 'liberty' or 'security threat'? The answer is that it is essentially contested. Seeking to seize this as an opportunity, the central government has thus pinned its hopes (and RMB10bn, £1bn) on leading the world in transition to the electric car (EV), 'overtaking around the corner' in the words of Science and Technology Minister and former Audi executive Wan Gang. But the various forms of electro-mobility vehicles systems that are springing up in competition are also essentially contested, and precisely in terms of liberty and security.

On the one hand, EVs as electric 'cars' have significantly struggled (for over a decade) to attract buyers, notwithstanding significant government perks including subsidized purchase and privileged access to hard-to-get licence plates and parking spaces. In short, set within a system (including infrastructures) of use and recharging that remains highly underdeveloped – and indeed a grid that would largely substitute tailpipe emissions with those of coal-generated electricity – the attractions of the new 'liberties' afforded by the EV do not in general trump the *dis*-incentives of exposing oneself to their unknown risks: of *im*mobility (as in a dead-battery breakdown in predictable heavy traffic), financial (given high upfront expense but low resale value) and health (e.g. a widespread fear of 'radiation' from the battery, as well as of high-profile cases of battery explosions and fires).

Moreover, there is a ubiquitous example of indigenous e-mobility *success* in China that also elicits intense political contestation in terms of the liberty/security dichotomy: the electric two-wheeler (E2W). Against the paltry (if growing) sales of electric cars, the E2W is everywhere, with over 200 million on China's roads, almost all of which are Chinese brands. And all of these have been bought with no government subsidy but on the basis that they have expanded the owner's liberty. The E2W is thus an essential form of demotic auto-mobility in China's marketizing society, and one that, unlike the EV, already has clear environmental advantages over the ICE car. It is thus potentially a key element of a new Chinese system of urban automobility, were its endogenous momentum harnessed. Yet for many in China, including the government, the E2W is also the epitome of contemporary security threats regarding urban mobility, as these nippy but silent – and often heavily overloaded – vehicles weave their unruly, wayward paths on and off pavements, against the traffic and ignoring all road signs and red lights.

Explicitly citing their 'security' dangers, therefore, the E2W has been officially banned in many major cities, including a recent clampdown across the country in April 2016 on sellers and owners. In short, whether regarding the incumbent (and still growing, in China) ICE car system, the government flagship but struggling EV or the budding mushrooms of the E2W, therefore, in this key social issue of socio-technical and low-carbon change we find an essentially contested landscape of recrimination and counter-accusation regarding the 'liberty' and 'security' aspects of each model.

How could this all play out? It is at this point that we must note two key dimensions of these processes and the formation of a new CP/KS to which they are contributing. First, at the heart of this contestation in all three cases is the key constituency and potential Gramscian historic bloc of the emergent Chinese urban 'middle-class'[es] (Arrighi, 2009; Goodman, 2014). For this still-forming class is not just best-resourced to consider car ownership or not, and to experiment with new socio-technical alternatives; but also the constituency most enabled to make their demands – and their socio-economic and/or environmental demands in particular – heard, given their increasingly pivotal role in supporting (or not) the incumbent party-state regime and its economic growth-based legitimacy (Goodman, 2014; Geall, 2013).

Moreover, similar dynamics also pertain to the second key issue of the emergence of the digitization and informationalization of mobility, a parallel but inseparable aspect of system innovation in urban mobility, not least given the manifest incompatibility of electric cars with incumbent models of personal ownership and use. By contrast, digitization of mobility is likely both essential for e-mobility (via the 'sharing economy') and itself uncertainly evolving on multiple fronts, including ride-sharing apps (of which China has its own in Kuaidi/Didi), car-sharing platforms, automated driving, real-time information about available parking and charging, etc.

On the one hand, this innovation is being embraced across China by start-ups, massive Chinese hi-tech companies (e.g. Alibaba, Tencent, Baidu) and even incumbent and powerful state-owned enterprises (SOEs) in electricity and telecoms, taking on the powerful automotive SOEs. In this respect, the comparative global weakness of Chinese car majors is arguably a strategic advantage regarding Chinese innovation of *new* urban mobility systems that shift the locus of primary industrial leverage from the mechanical vehicle to the ICT infrastructure. Moreover, while demand for an electric-powered 'car' is slight, demand for ICT-integrated gadgetry and networked individuality (Yu, 2014) amongst the urban middle class is both seemingly insatiable and, arguably already, technologically amongst the most advanced in the world. Yet, on the other, these novel forms of mobility are also generating contestation and counter-innovation, akin to the global controversial-ness of Uber, but where this must be understood to signal not innovation gridlock but its very opposite of significant systemic socio-technical and *political* dynamism.

This is generating new socio-technical innovations, but also, inseparably and no less importantly, new power/knowledge relations: hence institutions, common-senses, social groupings and self-policing subjectivities in a process that is essentially contested at every step. And it is driven by productive experiments of wrestling with the dynamic impulses of (networked) individualized (urban, 'middle class') Chinese striving both for new self-assertive autonomy, opportunity and aspiration and for security from both novel and familiar existential threats, including to these very freedoms.

5 Contesting the emergence of Liberalism 2.0

How, then, do these dynamics of liberty and security, innovation and counter-innovation, address neoliberalism's deepening system-dysfunctional twin dynamics of deceleration to stagnation and acceleration to collapse? What new regime of government emerges? The answer, of course, is far from settled – it is constitutively contested! Yet, generalizing from the case study of urban mobility transition in ways that are indeed also evident in other domains, such as agri-food or renewable energy, we can still find a core dynamic. This involves:

- the parallel formation of both new socio-technical systems and the substantive meaning and identity of the Chinese 'middle class' (as historic bloc), and *its* constitutive aspirations (i.e. liberties) and fears (viz. securities);
- by way of emergence and shaping of digitized, informationalized and inter-connected socio-technical systems that are constitutively shaped by contestations over the new forms of enablement (i.e. liberty) *and* the new forms of danger and risk they *themselves* give rise to (i.e. security);
- and the coming together and mutual shaping of these two processes, in terms of 2.0 systems (including of 'smart' mobility) that specifically service *this* class and its growth and, conversely, substantive meanings of the Chinese 'middle class' that specifically support development of *these* digital innovations, in positive feedback loops (see Figure 7.4).

Against the stagnation/runaway dynamic of neoliberal innovation, therefore, this signals the potential embryonic emergence of growing demand for, and achievement of, substantive socio-technical change (e.g. in urban mobility systems) in concert with the shift in (and/or constitution of new) *socio-political power relations* necessary for transition beyond neoliberalism. Moreover, foundationally shaped by profound contestation regarding the new security threats, this new CP/ KS regime and *its* model of innovation will be intrinsically attuned to tackling and mitigating the 'over-spilt' global system threats of neoliberalism, at least as regards the exposure of this newly dominant hegemonic political constituency (if certainly not humanity as a whole – see below).

This power momentum generates and is fed by a proliferation of new market entrants and productive businesses that are (genuinely! (see Breznitz & Murphree, 2011; Zeng & Williamson, 2007)) 'disruptive' corporate competition in new markets and newly defined hybrid industrial sectors; hence furnishing new opportunities for productive capital investment, including new B2B (not just consumer) services and infrastructures, potentially involving China's massive programmes of state funding. It also therefore feeds progressively into the formation and growth of new partnerships, forms of intellectual property, institutions and lobbies. Finally, as successful models take shape – an intrinsically uncertain and experimental process – and platforms open for further activity and innovation, a positive feedback loop emerges.

In this way, then, the key issue of *socio-political* change regarding the power/knowledge relations *conditioning* innovation such that it can, in turn, escape its current crises can begin to take place, and through a dynamic that is both immanent within the existing system and yet also intrinsically challenging to it. Indeed, from this central motor of system emergence progressive transformation of a whole host of other key systems dimensions can begin to be imagined. At the crucial global scale, for instance, this motor may drive the shifts in power/knowledge relations that lead to shifting geopolitics and global regulatory institutions and architectures, including of intellectual property, as well as a changing international division of labour of innovation and distribution its super-rent spoils.

In short, neoliberalism is actively replaced (its 'non-dead' zombie state (Crouch, 2011) *allowed* to die) because, in part, new self-sustaining, rather than self-destructive, models of (smart, low-carbon) urban mobility have emerged together with and through the emergence of the Chinese urban middle classes as the global historic bloc of the age – just as the motorcar, oil, inter-state highways, suburbs and out-of-town malls and the American consumerist middle and working classes were so central to the mid-twentieth century emergence of post-war Keynesianism from the ashes of nineteenth-century liberalism.

6 R&I politics as the key strategic arena of the twenty-first century

We must end any such analysis, however, by critically assessing the qualitative system dynamics of this emergent system in turn, including in comparison with neoliberalism. Certainly, the argument above offers no cause for complacency, as if all our problems are therefore solved. To the contrary, assessment of the tendential shape of the emergent system – as a 'liberalism 2.0' or 'complexity liberalism' – now becomes the key issue and responsibility, but also opportunity, for engaged scholarship of the political economy of R&I, a project taken up at length elsewhere (Tyfield, forthcoming).

Here, however, let us make just a few notes of outline. Let's start on a positive note, through comparison with neoliberalism. Constitutively focused on intense complex system security threats, this emergent system would surely repudiate – actively and directly – the core tenet of neoliberalism, namely its epistemic market fundamentalism and its consequent ontological agnosticism and Promethean limitlessness. Hence through dynamics of emerging successful low-carbon innovation alongside socio-political change, this new regime should likely be characterized by a quantum improvement in efforts to address climate change, since the very dynamism and socio-political hegemony of its new historic bloc will be founded precisely on that success (at least on some definition).

But this is hardly to augur some kind of new Golden Age (cf Perez, 2009). For, while marking a definitive step back from neoliberalism's politically neutralizing epistemic market fundamentalism, this remains a regime that is *still constituted*, politically, by the feedback loops of individualized liberties and security fears. And the outlines of this novel political spectrum can already be imagined, thereby revealing another way in which R&I will attain even greater political centrality. For the combination of digitization and a Chinese middle class suggests a socio-political order built not just on a revitalized rate of (2.0 informational-based) R&I, but also one in which these power/knowledge technologies are increasingly entrusted with 'normal' government, likely using complex systems that are not amenable to individual human cognition, oversight or accountability (cf Amoore, 2006). In these circumstances, therefore, recognizing that R&I is not only *central* to socio-political systems but also that it is *itself* thoroughly, if not primarily, political – *not* the neutral process of 'technological progress' that remains the orthodoxy in discussion of 'innovation' – is thus a key element of any prospect of a meaningful and contestable, and hence possibly 'democratic', politics in the twenty-first century.

Meanwhile, the mutually reinforcing and policing dynamics of liberty and security as strategic orientations of (networked) individual power/knowledge agency are necessarily enabling of *specific* groups and their liberties (in positive feedback loops), but in ways that thereby construct *this* view of the world as quasi-universal power/knowledges of growing legitimation and enablement. Conversely, this process also constructs the new and mutually constitutive common senses regarding the form, identity and best means of dealing with security threats to and states of exception from normal system of liberal autonomous (self-)government. Yet, as Foucault and other scholars of (nineteenth-century) liberalism have shown (Losurdo, 2011), this tends to active *construction* of groups subaltern to the newly enabled and ascendant groups of the historic bloc *as* themselves (new) security threats.

This is so even as the original growth and emergence of the new regime will likely in the first instance effect demonstrable progress in tackling the intense clear-and-present security threats of the *urgence* that catalyzed their very emergence. Indeed, such initial 'success' is a key dimension of that very dynamism, furnishing compelling if limited grounds for its claims to universal legitimacy. The more enabled, productive, self-confident and self-righteous the historic bloc becomes *by way of* specific power/knowledges, however, the more it also constructs parallel system-constitutive blindnesses, denials and aporia – the sources of considerable tensions that will likely, in turn, come to challenge *its* ecological dominance as a regime in time.

In short, while the Chinese urban middle classes and their global hegemony may be co-produced with a stunning and ecologically essential efflorescence of low-carbon and 'cleantech' innovation and systems transition, it is highly likely, in a country already so profoundly unequal and *formally* divided into two nations of urban and rural residents (Whyte, 2010) and with such poorly developed mechanisms for political protest, to take a specific form that greatly improves the livelihoods of the former (and their international cognates) while, at best, ignoring and, at worst, directly and significantly intensifying exploitation of the latter; and, at every step of its success, rendering the growing grievances of the latter increasingly 'illegitimate', 'unreasonable' and invisible. As I have detailed elsewhere, these embryonic dynamics are already visible regarding low-carbon mobility in China (Tyfield, Zuev *et al.*, 2015), regarding issues of personal quality (or *suzhi*) (Anagnost, 2004).

This leads us to the final key point about a CP/KS analysis: that this projected future is, of course, not a prediction, aiming to get the answer right and/or motivate a 'scientific' revolutionary movement. Instead it is an informed speculative meso-level extrapolation of existing system-productive power/knowledge dynamics, done primarily with a view to *strategic* illumination: of both relatively locked-in political trajectories and, equally, political openings and opportunities. Indeed, since (i) innovation is a political/knowledge process, amenable to shaping by diverse power/knowledge interventions and (ii) CPERI research is *itself* a power/knowledge process *within* that system change (and, importantly, amenable to self-conscious conceptualization of itself as such), together these spell the possibility and necessity for the latter to intervene directly in the former.

The tendential emergence of liberalism 2.0 should be interpreted in just this way. This points to a new direction and role for CPERI itself in socio-political life, as a key practice of situated, strategic and power-aware wisdom – a *phronesis* (Flyvbjerg *et al.*, 2013) – regarding the heightened and qualitatively novel importance of R&I *as political process* in the government of twenty-first-century global socio-technical systems. This would involve stimulating broad-based publics to engaged in strategic reflection and reflexivity regarding both specific emerging issues of R&I and sociotechnical change (again as political processes); *and*, crucially, meso-level tendencies of system dynamics as a whole, as in this chapter.

References

Amoore, L. (2006). 'Biometric borders: Governing mobilities in the war on terror'. *Political Geography*, 25(3), 336–51.

Anagnost, A. (2004). 'The corporeal politics of quality (*suzhi*)'. *Public Culture*, 16, 189–208.

Arrighi, G. (1994). *The Long Twentieth Century*. London: Verso.

Arrighi, G. (2009). *Adam Smith in Beijing*. London: Verso.

Biel, R. (2012). *The Entropy of Capitalism*. Boston and Leiden: Brill.

Breznitz, D. and Murphree, M. (2011). *Run of the Red Queen: Government, Innovation, Globalization, and Economic Growth in China*. New Haven, CT: Yale University Press.

Brynjolfsson, E. and McAfee, A. (2014). *The Second Machine Age*. New York: Norton.

Crouch, C. (2011). *The Strange Non-Death of Neoliberalism*. Cambridge: Polity.

Dean, M. (2010). *Governmentality: Power and Rule in Modern Society*. 2nd ed. London: Sage.

Flyvbjerg, B., Landmann, T. and Schramm, S. (eds). (2013). *Real Social Science*. Cambridge: Cambridge University Press.

Foucault, M. (1980). *Power/Knowledge: Selected Interviews and Other Writings 1972–1977*. Harlow: Longman.

Foucault, M. (2001). 'The subject and power'. In M. Foucault and J.D. Faubion (eds.), *Power: The Essential Works*, Vol. 3. (pp. 326–48). London: Allen Lane.

Foucault, M. (2009). *Security, Territory, Population: Lectures at the Collège de France 1977–1978*. Translated by Graham Burchell. Basingstoke: Palgrave Macmillan.

Foucault, M. (2010). *The Birth Of Biopolitics: Lectures at the Collège de France 1978–1979*. Translated by Graham Burchell. Basingstoke: Palgrave Macmillan.

Garvey B., Tyfield, D. and de Mello, L. F. (2015). '"Meet the new boss … same as the old boss?": technology, toil and tension in the agrofuel frontier'. *New Technology, Work & Employment*, 30(2), 79–94.

Geall, S. (ed.) (2013). *China and the Environment*. London: Zed.

Geels, F. (2014). 'Regime resistance against low-carbon transitions: Introducing politics and power into the multi-level perspective'. *Theory, Culture & Society*, 31(2), 21–40.

Goodman, D. (2014). *Class in Contemporary China*. Cambridge: Polity.

Gordon, R.J. (2012). 'Is U.S. economic growth over? Faltering innovation confronts the six headwinds'. National Bureau of Economic Research. doi:10.3386/w18315.

Hindess, B. (2006). 'Bringing states back in'. *Political Studies Review*, 4, 115–23.

Jessop, B. (2013). 'Revisiting the Regulation Approach: Critical reflections on the contradictions, dilemmas, fixes and crisis dynamics of growth regimes'. *Capital & Class*, 37(1), 5–24.

Jessop, B. (2014). 'Capitalist diversity and variety: Variegation, the world market, compossibility and ecological dominance'. *Capital & Class*, 38(1): 43–56.

Jessop, B. and Sum, N.-L. (2006). *Beyond the Regulation Approach*. Cheltenham: Edward Elgar.

Klein, N. (2007). *The Shock Doctrine*. London: Penguin.

Lawhon, M. and Murphy, J.T. (2013). 'Socio-technical regimes and sustainability transitions: Insights from political ecology'. *Progress in Human Geography*, 36(3), 354–78.

Lemke, T. (2011). *Foucault, Governmentality, and Critique*. Boulder, CO: Paradigm Publishers.

Losurdo, D. (2011). *Liberalism: A Counter-History*. London: Verso.

Mirowski, P. (2011). *ScienceMart: Privatizing American Science*. Cambridge, MA: Harvard University Press.

Mirowski, P. and Plehwe, D. (eds.) (2009). *The Road from Mont Pélérin*. Cambridge, MA: Harvard University Press.

Mirowski, P. and E.-M. Sent. (2008). 'The commercialization of science and the response of STS'. In E. Hackett, J. Wacjman, O. Amsterdamska and M. Lynch (eds.) *The Handbook of Science and Technology Studies*, (pp. 635–90), Cambridge, MA: MIT Press.

Pelligrini, L. (2011). 'Governing through disorder: Neoliberal environmental governance and social theory'. *Global Environmental Change*, 21, 795–803.

Perez, C. (2009) 'After crisis: Creative Construction', OpenDemocracy, March 5th. Retrieved from: www.opendemocracy.net/article/economics/email/how-to-make-economic-crisis-creative.

Rajan, S.C. (2006). 'Automobility and the liberal disposition'. *Sociological Review*, 54 (s1), 113–129.

Ren, H. (2013). *The Middle Class in Neoliberal China*. Abingdon & New York: Routledge.

Smith, A., Voß, J.P. and Grin, J. (2010). 'Innovation studies and sustainability transitions: the allure of the Multi-Level Perspective and its challenges'. *Research Policy*, 39(4), 435–48.

Tyfield, D. (2012). *The Economics of Science* (2 volumes), Abingdon & New York: Routledge.

Tyfield, D. (2016). 'Science, Innovation and Neoliberalism'. In S. Springer, K. Birch and J. MacLeavy (eds.), *The Routledge Handbook of Neoliberalism*, London: Routledge.

Tyfield, David. (forthcoming). *Liberalism 2.0 and the New Nineteenth Century: Innovation, China and the Crises of Neoliberalism*. London: Routledge.

Tyfield, D., Ely, A., Urban, F., Geall, S., Zuev, D. and Urry, J. (2015). 'Low-carbon innovation in China: prospects, politics and practices'. China Low Carbon Report 1 – STEPS Working Paper 69, STEPS Centre: Brighton.

Tyfield, D., Zuev, D., Li, P. and Urry, J. (2015). 'Low carbon innovation in Chinese urban mobility: Prospects, politics & practices'. China Low Carbon Report 3 – STEPS Working Paper 71. STEPS Centre: Brighton.

Unruh, G. (2000). 'Understanding carbon lock-in'. *Energy Policy*, 28, 817–30.

Urry, J. (2007). *Mobilities*. Cambridge: Polity Press.

Whyte, M.K. (2010). *One Country, Two Societies: Rural–Urban Inequality in Contemporary China*. Cambridge, MA: Harvard University Press.

Yan, Y. (2010). 'The Chinese path to individualization'. *British Journal of Sociology*, 61(3), 489–512.

Yu, L. (2014). *Consumption in China*. Cambridge: Polity.

Zeng, M. and Williamson, P. (2007). *Dragons at your Door*. Cambridge, MA: Harvard Business School Press.

PART II

Institutions of science and science funding

8

CONTROLLED FLOWS OF PHARMACEUTICAL KNOWLEDGE

Sergio Sismondo

The pharmaceutical industry, with more than US$1 trillion in sales annually and the highest level of profits of any major industry, is a nearly ubiquitous presence of the modern world. In this chapter I provide an overview of the industry's "ghost management" of medical science. This is when drug companies and their agents control or shape multiple steps in the research, analysis, writing, publication and dissemination of science, in ways that may not be entirely visible. Through constant and multiple interventions, drug companies have become the most influential of contributors to medical knowledge, and have normalized both their seen and unseen presence. We can see this as part of a political economy of medical knowledge, in which a small set of actors have established a certain measure of dominance over the economy as a whole.

1 The rise of expensive research

Changes in the importance of different kinds of medical research have been in the background of the pharmaceutical industry's gaining influence over medical knowledge (Edgerton, this volume). Pressures from both government regulators and internal medical reformers have led to the rise of the randomized controlled trial (RCT) as the most valued and important kind of medical research. This amounts to a change in style of scientific reasoning (Hacking, 1992), one that pharmaceutical companies have been well positioned to use to their advantage.

1.1 Medical pressures

Since the 1950s, medical reformers have made steady headway in promoting the idea that RCTs produce the most reliable medical knowledge. In the English-speaking world, credit for the first RCT in medicine is often given to Austin Bradford Hill, for his 1946 trial of the effect of streptomycin on tuberculosis, and for his advocacy of RCTs in medicine – although one can find a number of forerunners, such as Germany's Paul Martini, who advocated for and performed RCTs on drugs starting in the 1930s, and gained influence in the 1940s (Daemmrich, 2004). The RCT rose in importance over the following few decades to become the "gold standard" of clinical research by the 1990s, following extensive advocacy by statisticians and statistically-minded medical researchers (Marks, 1997).

For statisticians, random sampling in an experiment is the key requirement for making results amenable to statistical analysis. A well-designed and well-conducted RCT, by randomly assigning subjects from a population, produces results that have a defined probability of applying to the population. Perhaps more importantly for the rise of RCTs, random sampling, especially combined with double blinding, addresses some concerns about researcher bias that have long been widespread within medicine (Marks, 2000). Since the 1950s, appeals to RCTs as the center of scientific medicine have been rhetorically successful, and since the 1970s physicians have been repeatedly told that RCTs are the only kind of reliable information on which to base practice.

RCTs are not perfect tools, though. Some of the central concerns are about how the necessary artificialities of RCTs produce knowledge that does not map neatly onto the human world as we find it – the rigorously managed treatments of trials are rarely repeated in ordinary treatments, and populations studied are never exactly the same as populations to be treated (e.g. Worrall, 2007). Related to these problems, RCTs require and promote standardization of treatment that does not fit well the variability of the human world – the most effective standardized treatment may not be the most effective treatment for a particular patient in a particular context (Timmermans and Berg, 2003). In addition to these problems, as normally performed, RCTs are worse at identifying adverse events than they are at showing drug effectiveness (Healy, 2012). Evidence-based medicine's hierarchy of evidence does not take into account the possibility that unsound RCTs may be of less value than are sound versions of other kinds of studies (Bluhm, 2005; Grossman and MacKenzie, 2005). And illustrating that RCTs are less rigid than they appear is the fact that industry-sponsored studies produce more positive results than do independent ones (Lundh et al., 2012); the method does not eliminate bias.

The rise of what is known as "evidence-based medicine" has further promoted the idea that the practice of medicine should be based on RCTs – multiple RCTs, if possible. Evidence-based medicine's origins lie in the medical curriculum of McMaster University in Canada, based around practical clinical problem-solving. The clinical epidemiologist David Sackett led the way by developing courses on critical appraisal of the literature, which turned into a series of articles published in 1981 (Zimerman, 2013). A decade later, on an invitation and patronage by *Journal of the American Medical Association* editor Drummond Rennie, those articles were updated and republished as a manifesto. The approach rejected reliance on intuition – which had been attacked for many years (Marks, 1997) – and even physiological reasoning: "Evidence based medicine deemphasizes intuition, unsystematic clinical experience, and pathophysiologic rationale as sufficient grounds for clinical decision making and stresses the examination of evidence from clinical research" (quoted in Zimerman, 2013: 75).

1.2 Regulatory pressures

Medical reform was one of the reasons why RCTs moved toward the heart of medicine. A second reason was the fact that government regulatory bodies made RCTs central to the approval process for drugs.

Much of modern drug regulation descends from the US Kefauver-Harris Act of 1962. Interestingly, the Act did not address the two sets of problems to which its sponsors had responded, though it did have profound effects on the pharmaceutical industry and on medical research. In the years leading up to the Act, Senator Estes Kefauver had put his energies into challenging the pharmaceutical industry on terrain where the US consumer had the most visible complaints: monopolies stemming from patents, and consequent high prices. His efforts at reform were largely failures. Pharmaceutical companies and their industry association were able to deflect Kefauver's attacks on drug patents and prices (Tobbell, 2011). The 1962 Act was spurred more directly by the compelling story of how the US had narrowly avoided disaster by not being quick to approve thalidomide – an episode used by the Kennedy Administration to push the Act forward (Carpenter, 2010). Dr. Frances Kelsey of the Food and Drug Administration (FDA) had consistently expressed skepticism about the drug, and had delayed its approval. Meanwhile, in Europe, thousands of pregnancies and babies had been affected by the widespread use of thalidomide as an anti-nausea remedy and tranquillizer.

But while the Act was ostensibly to improve the safety of drugs, it added only a little to the existing regulation of safety. More importantly novel was a requirement that pharmaceutical companies show the efficacy of drugs before they could be approved. The Act specified that evidence of efficacy had to involve "adequate and well-controlled investigations" performed by qualified experts, "on the basis of which it can fairly and responsibly be concluded that the drug will have its claimed effect" (Carpenter, 2010: 272). The FDA structured its regulations around phased investigations that culminated in multiple similar clinical trials, which would ideally be RCTs. It was only on the basis of the evidence from these RCTs that a drug could be approved for sale in the US, and that any particular marketing claims for that drug could be made. Thus the key provisions of the Kefauver-Harris Act were about the appropriate and necessary scientific knowledge for the approval and marketing of drugs.

Over the following few decades, regulatory agencies around the world followed the FDA's lead, especially in using phased research culminating in substantial clinical trials as a model. For example, Canada's regulations followed swiftly, in 1963. The United Kingdom established new measures that same year, and followed them up with a framework similar to the FDA's in 1968. European Community Directives issued in 1965 required all members of the European Community to establish formal review processes, which they did over the following decade. Japan introduced its version of the regulations in 1967.

Especially since the expansion of drug regulation in the 1960s and 1970s, in-patent drugs are usually rhetorically constructed as more powerful than their older generic competitors: The drug patent has become a marker of quality. Meanwhile, the profitability of the industry is in part a result of layers of exclusivity established by drug patents and other regulations that establish marketing rights. This is even though versions of most of the competitors were once patented, and often recently so. There are, nonetheless, complex relations among in-patent, branded and generic drugs, with the generic often serving as a critique of the in-patent drug (Greene, 2014) and yet with brands of generics themselves being asserted as markers of quality (Hayden, 2015; Peterson, 2014).

In general, the pharmaceutical industry has opposed the introduction of new regulatory powers, which increase costs, hurdles, and sometimes uncertainties (e.g. Nik-Khah, 2014). It also has challenged aspects of regulators' authority in court. For example, in recent years, challenges to a core piece of the 1962 Act have been working their way through US courts: Drawing on the US's strong protection of freedom of speech, companies have been arguing successfully that the FDA does not have the authority to regulate off-label marketing (Sharfstein and Charo, 2015).

Pharmaceutical companies and industry associations are also continually lobbying regulators and legislators in more quiet ways, to shape regulation in their interests, in the US, Europe and around the globe (e.g. Davis and Abraham, 2013; Permanand, 2006). Industry interest in shaping regulation can be seen clearly in the International Conference on Harmonization of Technical Requirements for Registration of Pharmaceuticals for Human Use (ICH). It is strongly in pharmaceutical companies' interest to bring a new drug to market as quickly as possible, increasing the amount of time it can be sold while still under patent protection. Differences among the regulations for access to major markets slow the process by requiring that the companies engage in different research to meet those different demands. Thus, the International Federation of Pharmaceutical Manufacturers' Associations organized the creation of the ICH, bringing together the regulatory agencies of the European Union, Japan and the US (Abraham and Reed, 2002). In a series of meetings beginning in 1991, the ICH harmonized testing requirements, keeping the structure of phased investigations but ensuring that one set of investigations would suffice for these three major markets.

Estimates of the cost of bringing a new drug to market vary enormously, depending on whether those estimates are produced by the pharmaceutical industry or its critics, but few people would dispute that the costs are significant. Though the industry complains about these costs, and actively challenges the regulations that increase them, they have the unintended effect of preventing many non-industry researchers from contributing to the most valued kinds of medical knowledge, the RCTs of the kind that regulators require.

2 Integration of the industry into medical research

Novelty, patents and regulation are bound up with the intensification of scientific research. This has led to the accumulation and leveraging of what some scholars are calling "biocapital" (Sunder Rajan, 2006; Helmreich, 2008), which involves a circuit for the mutual cultivation of investment funds and biological products and knowledge (Birch, this volume). We can see this even in the development of public–private partnerships for drug development in the service of global health, with parties contributing so as to maintain claims on the circulating materials, knowledge and capital (see Vessuri; Harrison et al., this volume; Lezaun and Montgomery, 2015).

Because of the expense of RCTs, companies and researchers have had to develop novel formal structures to manage large clinical trials (e.g. Cambrosio et al., 2006; Helgesson, 2010). Because of the costs and organizational overhead, the emphasis on RCTs has significantly shifted the production of the most highly valued medical knowledge from independent medical researchers to pharmaceutical companies. The pharmaceutical industry has become integrated into the medical research community, both because it produces (generally through subcontractors) important medical knowledge itself and because it provides important funding for studies by more or less independent medical researchers.

Pharmaceutical companies sponsor most drug trials, and in so doing affect their results (e.g. Lundh et al., 2012; Sismondo, 2008). The companies fully control the majority of the research they fund, and they can choose what to disclose and how. Recent studies show that these companies do not (despite being mandated to do so) publicly register all of the trials they perform and do not publish all of the data even from the trials that they do register (Anderson et al., 2015). The articles they publish rarely display the full level of control that the companies have had over the production of data, its analysis or its presentation; for example, company statisticians are rarely acknowledged (Gøtzsche et al., 2007). This allows the companies to use RCT data selectively to quietly shape medical knowledge to support their marketing efforts. At the same time, their integration into medical research allows them to participate more overtly and broadly in the distribution of their preferred pieces of medical knowledge. The result is that pharmaceutical companies have considerable control over what physicians know about diseases, drugs and other treatment options (e.g. Applbaum, 2015). So while pharmaceutical companies have generally opposed new demands upon them, they also have benefitted enormously from those demands.

2.1 Contract research organizations

Pharmaceutical companies outsource almost all of their clinical research, some to academic organizations but the majority to for-profit contract research organizations (CROs), which perform 70–75 percent of industry-sponsored research on drugs (Fisher, 2009; Mirowski and Van Horn, 2005). CROs are involved at all stages of research and perform 95 percent of laboratory services related to trials. CRO-conducted trials are designed for either or both of the drug approval process and the further development of data to support the marketing of drugs. CROs, in turn, typically contract with clinics and physicians to do the hands-on work of clinical studies. They recruit patients in a variety of ways, through public advertisements, networks of specialists, or just through physicians' practices.

CROs tend to have access to large populations in multiple countries both within and outside North America and Western Europe, including poorer, "treatment naïve" countries where costs per patient are considerably lower (e.g. Cooper, 2008; Petryna, 2015). India, for example, is well positioned to provide subjects: India's *Economic Times* wrote in 2004: "The opportunities are huge, the multinationals are eager, and Indian companies are willing. We have the skills, we have the people" (Shah, 2006: 17). India has invested heavily to establish the material, social and regulatory infrastructure – for example, providing education in the running of trials and establishing ethical standards – to bring clinical trials to the country (Sunder Rajan, 2015).

North America and Western Europe still have more than 60 percent of the market share for industry trials. Why hasn't industry moved faster to lower-cost, lower-risk environments? Historical reasons are important. For example, before the ICH, the FDA insisted that the majority of trials used for a drug application be conducted in the US, resulting in the national development of material and social capital for running trials. In particular, Phase I trials (small safety trials on healthy subjects) are often in-patient exercises, which must be conducted in clinics with beds and other facilities, and that material infrastructure continues to be used. As there are in poorer countries (Sunder Rajan, 2015), there are even a number of established US and European populations of "professional guinea pigs" (Abadie, 2010). Also, pharmaceutical companies and CROs have established relationships with physicians who can provide patients and staff for Phase II (dosage and preliminary efficacy trials), III (safety and efficacy trials, typically large), and IV (post-marketing) trials, and perhaps those relationships continue to be useful. But for Phase II, III, and IV trials an important part of the reason for the continued dominance of North America and Western Europe is that contacts with physicians – who recruit subjects for trials – in large markets are important, and clinical trials create and maintain those contacts. Clinical trials can provide opportunities to sell drugs, and physician investigators can be enrolled to further help sell drugs once they are approved.

Although CROs need to perform research of high scientific quality if it is to support the approval and marketing of drugs, they also need to serve the particular goals of the pharmaceutical companies that hire them. CROs' orientation to their sponsors should lead them to make choices in the implementation and execution of the RCT protocol that are more likely to produce data favorable to those sponsors; they might, for example, skew the subject pool by systematically recruiting in certain populations, or they might close some sites for breaches of protocol, especially if results from those sites are throwing up red flags. Given the enormous complexity of protocols for large RCTs, it would be no surprise if these choices contributed to the relationship between sponsorship and favorable outcomes.

Unlike academics who are occasionally contracted to run clinical trials, CROs offer data to pharmaceutical companies with no strings attached. Data from CRO studies are wholly owned and controlled by the sponsoring companies, and CROs have no interest in publishing the results under their own names. The companies can therefore use the data to best advantage, as we will see below. Company scientists and statisticians, publication planners and medical writers use them to produce knowledge that supports the marketing of products.

2.2 *Planning and developing publications*

Some studies suggest that roughly 40 percent of medical journal articles on major new in-patent drugs are parts of *publication plans* (Healy and Cattell, 2003; Ross et al., 2008). Publication plans lay out the terms for constructing articles that establish consistent profiles for drugs, the scientific face of drugs that will be established in medical journals and conferences. The key organizational work is done by publication planners employed either within pharmaceutical companies or more often by the more than 50 agencies that advertise publication planning on the Internet. Some agencies claim to have hundreds of employees, and to handle many hundreds of manuscripts per year. Indicative of the scale of the activity, two competing international associations of publication planners – the International Society of Medical Planning Professionals and the International Publication Planning Association – organize meetings and seminars, and several for-profit agencies do the same.

At least some of the time, marketing is best done if it is invisible. The director of one agency portrays science and marketing as equal partners (Bohdanowicz, 2005). "Where shall we publish this study?" is paired with "Who are our customers?"; "What can we claim from the results?" is paired with "What are our customers' needs?" Science and marketing together thus determine what the research says and how the products can be sold. At a 2007 workshop for new planners, one presenter advised that the planning team should be assembled "before too much data has gone unpublished." Ideally, it would be in place for research design, especially when there is "need to create [a] market" or create an "understanding of unmet need."

In this and the following sections, unless a citation is provided, quotes stem from the author's fieldwork at pharmaceutical industry conferences, or from approximately fifteen open-ended interviews with people who work closely with the industry. In all cases, anonymity of speakers is preserved. For some more full accounts, see Sismondo (2015a, 2015b) and Sismondo and Chloubova (2016).

There are many reasons why planners aim to meet high scientific standards. First, and most centrally, the value of their work to pharmaceutical companies stems from its being taken as reputable science by medical researchers and practitioners. Second, scientific standards are considered a necessary part of ethical behavior, marking the distinction between doing publication planning and doing public relations. Third, publication planners can only publish to best advantage if their articles can successfully compete with independent articles. In this, they are apparently successful, because while top medical journals have rejection rates as high as 95 percent, planners claim to have high success rates; one agency claims "acceptance rate on first submission of 94% for abstracts and 78% for manuscripts" (GardinerCaldwell Group, 2007).

Academics, who will become the eventual nominal authors of those publications, provide the essential credibility for publications, but sponsoring companies do not trust academics to produce research and analysis that will serve their interests. Thus, as much as possible of the production of manuscripts is done by the company and the agencies it hires. This is suggested, for example, by an email from a publication planner to an author, accidentally forwarded to a journal editor in 2010; it insisted: "It will not be you personally who will have to write those articles but a ghost writer will do this for us/you and you kind of give your good name for this publication!" At a 2011 conference, an experienced planner waved an imaginary manuscript in the air and railed against its imaginary authors: "What is this? They're promoting the competitor!" Another planner said: "the approach of having an industry-authored [industry-written] first draft is a good one." Thus, in the sphere of publication planning, the concept of authorship does not necessarily involve substantial contributions to research, design, or writing.

Individual manuscripts are typically written by hired medical writers on the basis of statistical analyses provided by the company, one or more key messages that match the developing profile of the drug and fit the target journals and audiences, and a list of references. The manuscripts are often reviewed extensively within the company, and are then passed along to their prospective authors, most of them academics, for comments before submission to journals.

Planners sometimes suggest that academic authors are lazy and unreliable, typically offering few substantial contributions to the manuscripts and missing deadlines. The process creates the conditions for such deadbeat authors. According to one planner, 50 percent of companies show only the penultimate draft of a manuscript to authors, to solicit their input. Authors are unlikely to have much to add to a well-crafted and edited manuscript. That becomes especially likely if authors are given tight deadlines. According to one whistle-blowing medical researcher, part of the problem he faced was that he received abstracts only after they were submitted (and accepted) for meetings, and received manuscripts only days before the planners' deadlines for journal submission. The orderly and efficient rollout of presentations and papers means that the nominal authors are likely to contribute little.

Planners coordinate the work of multiple parties, such as company statisticians, company and agency researchers, medical writers and nominal authors. Their goal is to shape medical science to support drug companies' marketing efforts. The articles that are published are solid enough to meet the demands of medical journals and to influence readers, but at the same time present science done in the companies' interests.

3 Dominating the distribution of medical knowledge

3.1 Deploying sales representatives

Pharmaceutical sales representatives (generally known as "sales reps," but also "drug reps" and "detailers") use reprints of publications to distribute preferred knowledge directly to physicians. At a conference, a former sales rep giving a pep talk to publication planners said: "Folks, they're dying for your work, by the way. Field reps are dying every day for more of your work. You know that, right? Because that's what doctors are going to see." Distributing reprints creates opportunities to discuss not only the article, but also about how to use its information – setting up possible prescriptions and sales.

That sales reps transmit knowledge legitimizes their presence in physicians' offices, positioning them as contributors to the project of improving patient health. And although sales reps do much more than provide information (Oldani, 2004, Fugh-Berman and Ahari, 2015), medical knowledge is the tool that enables them to make pitches, offer their friendship, and convince physicians to prescribe specific drugs. The older terms "detailer" for sales reps, and "detailing" for what they do, highlight the idea that they bring useful information on drugs.

In the end, the goal is to increase the number of prescriptions or "scripts" for the sales representative's products, "changing physicians' prescribing behavior" in favor of those products. Sales reps do that by establishing relationships with doctors, using whatever common interests they can find; these generally include recent medical research. The relationships often have the appearance of being independent of sales reps' jobs, as this doctor claims: "A good number of my very close friends are sales representatives. … I like to think that those are real relationships just because they're relationships – and even when people have moved on to other companies or don't sell a product in my disease state."

Sales reps may also be involved in a further project in the dissemination of knowledge, identifying and then hiring key opinion leaders.

3.2 Managing key opinion leaders

The term "key opinion leader" stems from work by the sociologist Paul Lazarsfeld and his students, and entered the world of pharmaceutical companies beginning with research done for the company Pfizer by Lazarsfeld's group in the mid-1950s (Sismondo, 2015b). Pharmaceutical companies engage key opinion leaders (normally referred to as "KOLs") primarily as key mediators between them and physicians. A former sales rep says, "[t]here are a lot of physicians who don't believe what we as drug representatives say. If we have a KOL stand in front of them and say the same thing, they believe it" (Moynihan, 2008).

The most prestigious and highly paid KOLs are well-established researchers, typically academics with significant accomplishments. They might be asked to: serve as authors on medical journal articles stemming from company-led research, recruit patients for trials, consult on medical or marketing issues, be instructors for continuing medical education (CME) sessions, and in some cases, serve as conduits for information to government regulators (Fishman, 2015).

We can see the marketing and commercial goals in how KOL programs are presented. One speaker – a specialist in running KOL programs – at a 2012 meeting on KOLs, enthusing about a new approach to network analysis, said, "So it's really very, very interesting and starts to give us the tool and the power to be able to actually look at these network maps and start to think about the implication in terms of the things that we are doing commercially." A marketing firm writes in overview: "Interacting with qualified investigators, physicians experienced in regulatory reviews, well-known and respected speakers, and highly published authors will help to efficiently manage tasks within the critical path of the product and disseminate the message of the product to the end prescribing audience" (InsiteResearch, 2008). Since they usually do not simply present a company's script, high-level KOLs are nurtured through seminars, close contact, advisory boards and publications. Independent agencies identify KOLs who could serve the pharmaceutical companies' needs, and may design communication plans for companies to build relationships and knowledge with their prospective collaborators. Companies' ideal relationships with KOLs are part of general "KOL management" plans, with management implying "handling, direction and control" (InsiteResearch, 2008).

Equally valuable as the researcher KOLs, if less prestigious, are ordinary physicians who, as members of "speakers bureaus" for particular drugs, are paid to give talks to physicians, and occasionally to speak at community events. Explains one KOL, "the sales representatives, if they knew you, if they met you, if they thought that you would have the qualities of somebody that might be a good speaker, they would extend an offer to, to join the speakers bureau for that company." Then sales reps also organize KOL-led events, at which KOLs are simultaneously salespeople and educators. At a 2012 conference on KOLs, a marketer defined promotion in these terms: "you have a key opinion leader engagement with a group of doctors, and you measure sales before and after the engagement." Companies buy prescription data from health information services companies, which buy them from pharmacies (Moynihan, 2008), and thus they can track the effects of the KOLs' talks.

Either researcher or physician KOLs may be employed to sell drugs more indirectly, too. They might, for example, speak on diseases:

Another common objective … is to educate the marketplace and drive awareness of a particular disease state, mechanism of action, or existing treatment alternatives. A goal within this objective may be to successfully engage with key opinion leaders by completing a set number of advisory boards.

(CampbellAlliance, 2011)

KOLs are ideal conduits for the marketing process, a range of activities that coordinate products, distribution networks and demand (Applbaum, 2004). KOLs can create awareness of new opportunities and approaches, interest in and concern about particular conditions, and introduce fears about alternatives.

KnowledgePoint360, a company that supports KOL programs, treats KOL speaker-training just like sales employee-training: "Whether it is for external resources, such as speakers, or internal staff, including sales representatives and medical science liaisons, a robust training program is critical to the long-term success of any pharmaceutical, biotech, or medical device company" (KnowledgePoint360, 2010; also Carlat, 2007). Similarly, Wave Healthcare claims:

It's vital that advocates are able to communicate and influence colleagues with clarity and conviction. To ensure speakers are at the top of their game, we have developed a communication skills programme for clinicians.

(Wave Healthcare, 2011)

Like publication planning, KOL programs can be large. Speaking at a 2011 KOL management conference, one manager warned: "When you say 'I need 700 to 1000 speakers in this activity', the questions [that are] going to get pushed back to you in investigations are, 'Why do you need so many? How many is each speaker going to do? Why did you need a thousand?'" The manager was raising concerns that investigators might interpret speakers' fees as incentives to prescribe or to accept advertising messages – illegal marketing.

In the US, KOL speakers usually must follow pre-packaged PowerPoint slides, without deviating from their scripts. One highly paid psychiatrist said in an interview:

So if I am doing a promotional program for a company, I have to use the slide deck that they provide me – I am not allowed to alter it in any way and every word in that slide deck is basically reviewed by their own internal counsel ….

Answers to standard questions are also scripted, and speakers are trained to avoid providing answers that might be illegal or against companies' interests.

KOLs acknowledge that they are being used, but nonetheless find value in their role as educators. One interviewed endocrinologist bluntly explained: "The reason for giving the promotional talks is to help the company sell its drug – I mean that's basically – that's what a promotional talk is." A hospital-based hematologist said: "The honest answer is that promotional talks are not really for educating so – and I give plenty of promotional talks – … but some speakers are better than others at bending it into an educational talk." Every KOL interviewed said education was a reason to work for drug companies, often taking pride in their teaching. One said: "I am educating fellow physicians. I spend my day educating patients, I spend some of my evenings educating fellow physicians" (see Sismondo and Chloubova, 2016).

But, as already discussed, the data KOLs use to educate is produced by pharmaceutical companies, and shaped, arranged and presented to support those companies' interests. As authors, KOLs lend authority to that knowledge within the medical community. It makes some sense to say KOLs educate, but their pedagogy and knowledge have been shaped by and in the interests of the companies for which they are working.

KOL management, done correctly, facilitates distribution of knowledge. By spreading knowledge, changing opinions, and changing prescribing habits, KOL management generates a good return on investment for companies.

3.3 Orchestrating continuing medical education

CME courses, taken by physicians to maintain accreditation, are supposed to be independent of corporate interests. Directed at receptive audiences with motivation to learn, CME is, perhaps ironically, an ideal form of marketing for pharmaceutical companies.

Accredited CME providers are regulated, and a result of this is that sponsors such as pharmaceutical companies are prohibited from controlling the content of courses. However, in many jurisdictions pharmaceutical companies may provide funding for CME, recruit participants, find venues, pay for KOL speakers, help them prepare their talks, and provide entertainment for participants. Sometimes, independent organizations even ask companies to influence content. Soliciting funds for a CME conference, a Canadian medical organization said: "major sponsors will be given the opportunity to nominate participants to represent industry's interest and to participate actively in the conference" (Brody, 2007: 208).

It is not difficult for pharmaceutical companies to align with their own the interests of KOLs who deliver CMEs. If sponsors have chosen their speakers well, supported the research of these speakers, and given them templates and slides for their talks, the courses will convey preferred messages. As one medical education and communication company advertises: "Medical education is a powerful tool that can deliver your message to key audiences, and get those audiences to take action that benefits your product" (quoted in Angell, 2004: 139).

CME talks are parts of promotional campaigns, and the educational effects are aligned with the interests of the sponsoring companies. According to an industry education specialist, the ideal for CME is "control – leaving nothing to chance" (Bohdanowicz, 2009).

4 Conclusion: The ghost management of pharmaceutical knowledge

The past half-century has seen a dramatic change in political economies of medical knowledge. Between the 1962 amendments to the US Food, Drug and Cosmetic Act, and the rise of the evidence-based medicine movement, medicine has become increasingly focused on the randomized controlled trial as the best evidence to support science-based medical practice. However, this best evidence is very expensive to produce. As a result, the pharmaceutical randomized controlled trial is situated in a political economy of knowledge dominated by pharmaceutical companies.

The companies sponsor the majority of pharmaceutical trials and in so doing demonstrably affect their results. Contract research organizations handle most of the sponsored clinical trial research. Pharmaceutical company statisticians typically analyze the data produced. Publication planners and planning teams shepherd medical journal articles through to publication, hiring medical writers to write those articles and finding academic researchers to serve as authors on them. Sales representatives and industry-paid key opinion leaders give the science further life by presenting it to audiences of prescribing physicians. This process produces interested science, performed and distributed for marketing purposes.

Many aspects of the companies' activities are either unseen or are normalized. Thus, I call this whole chain the "ghost management" of pharmaceutical knowledge. Ghost management may often – perhaps almost always – produce and rest on good scientific knowledge, but the science in question is *partial* or *interested*, supporting the companies' interests. When pharmaceutical companies initiate and fund the design of trials, implement the research and do analysis of the results, they shape the knowledge around their products in terms of their preferences. When they write, choose authors for, and place medical journal articles, they select the messages that they prefer to circulate. When they go on to distribute their preferred knowledge and messages via sales representatives, key opinion leaders, and continuing medical education, they do so much more effectively than independent researchers ever could. Thus, pharmaceutical companies have established themselves as key parts of the political economy of medical knowledge, and are constantly shaping that terrain to support their own positions.

References

Abadie, R. 2010. *The Professional Guinea Pig: Big Pharma and the Risky World of Human Subjects*. Durham: Duke University Press.

Abraham, J. and Reed, T. 2002. "Progress, Innovation and Regulatory Science in Drug Development: The Politics of International Standard-Setting". *Social Studies of Science* 32.3: 337–369.

Anderson, M.L., Chiswell, K., Peterson, E.D., Tasneem, A., Topping, J. and Califf, R.M. 2015. "Compliance with Results Reporting at ClinicalTrials.gov". *New England Journal of Medicine* 372.11: 1031–1039.

Angell, M. 2004. *The Truth about the Drug Companies: How They Deceive Us and What to Do About It*. New York: Random House.

Applbaum, K. 2004. *The Marketing Era: From Professional Practice to Global Provisioning*. New York: Routledge.

Applbaum, K. 2015. "Getting to Yes: Corporate Power and the Creation of a Psychopharmaceutical Blockbuster", in Sismondo, S., and Greene, J., eds. *The Pharmaceutical Studies Reader*. Oxford: Wiley-Blackwell, 133–149.

Bluhm, R. 2005. "From Hierarchy to Network: A Richer View of Evidence for Evidence-Based Medicine". *Perspectives in Biology and Medicine* 48.4: 535–547.

Bohdanowicz, H. 2005. "A Guide to Strategic Communication Planning". *Pharmaceutical Executive Europe* Sept 21.

Bohdanowicz, H. 2009. "The Synergy of Public Relations and Medical Education". *Communiqué* 24: 14–16.

Brody, H. 2007. *Hooked: Ethics, the Medical Profession, and the Pharmaceutical Industry*. Lanham, MD: Rowman & Littlefield Publishers.

Cambrosio, A., Keating, P., Schlich, T. and Weisz, G. 2006. "Regulatory Objectivity and the Generation and Management of Evidence in Medicine". *Social Science & Medicine* 63.1: 189–199.

CampbellAlliance. 2011. "Communicating the Value of Medical Affairs". Brochure for a White paper.

Carlat, D. 2007. "Dr. Drug Rep". *New York Times*, November 25.

Carpenter, D. 2010. *Reputation and Power: Organizational Image and Pharmaceutical Regulation at the FDA*. Princeton: Princeton University Press.

Cooper, M. 2008. "Experimental Labour – Offshoring Clinical Trials to China". *East Asian Science, Technology and Society* 2: 73–92.

Daemmrich, A.A. 2004. *Pharmacopolitics: Drug Regulation in the United States and Germany*. Chapel Hill: University of North Carolina Press.

Davis, C. and Abraham, J. 2013. *Unhealthy Pharmaceutical Regulation: Innovation, Politics and Promissory Science*. Basingstoke: Palgrave Macmillan.

Fisher, J. 2009. *Medical Research for Hire: The Political Economy of Pharmaceutical Clinical Trials*. New Brunswick: Rutgers University Press.

Fishman, J. 2015. "Manufacturing Desire: The Commodification of Female Sexual Dysfunction", in Sismondo, S. and Greene, J., eds. *The Pharmaceutical Studies Reader*. Oxford: Wiley-Blackwell, 106–120.

Fugh-Berman, A. and Ahari, S. 2015. "Following the Script: How Drug Reps Make Friends and Influence Doctors", in Sismondo, S. and Greene, J., eds. *The Pharmaceutical Studies Reader*. Oxford: Wiley-Blackwell, 123–132.

Gardiner-Caldwell Group. 2007. www.thgc-group.com/ (accessed November 2007).

Gøtzsche, P.C., Hróbjartsson, A., Johansson, H.K., Haahr, M.T., Altman, D.G. and Chan A-W. 2007. "Ghost Authorship in Industry-Initiated Randomised Trials". *PLoS Medicine* 4(1): 47–52.

Greene, J. 2014 *Generic: The Unbranding of Modern Medicine*. Baltimore: Johns Hopkins University Press.

Grossman, J. and Mackenzie, F.J. 2005. "The Randomized Controlled Trial: Gold Standard, or Merely Standard?" *Perspectives in Biology and Medicine* 48.4: 516–534.

Hacking, I. 1992. "'Style' for Historians and Philosophers". *Studies in History and Philosophy of Science, Part A* 23.1: 1–20.

Hayden, C. 2015. "Generic Medicines and the Question of the Similar", in Sismondo, S. and Greene, J., eds. *The Pharmaceutical Studies Reader*. Oxford, Wiley-Blackwell, 261–267.

Healy, D. 2012. *Pharmageddon*. Berkeley: University of California Press.

Healy, D. and Cattell, D. 2003. "Interface Between Authorship, Industry and Science in the Domain of Therapeutics". *British Journal of Psychiatry* 183.1: 22–27.

Helgesson, C-F. 2010. "From Dirty Data to Credible Scientific Evidence: Some Practices Used to Clean Data in Large Randomised Clinical Trials", in Will, C. and Moreira, T., eds. *Medical Proofs, Social Experiments: Clinical Trials in Shifting Contexts*. Surrey: Ashgate, 49–66.

Helmreich, S. 2008. "Species of Biocapital". *Science as Culture* 17.4: 463–478.

InsiteResearch. 2008. "The Prescription for KOL Management". *Next Generation Pharmaceutical* 12. www.ngpharma.com/ (accessed 10 July 2013).

KnowledgePoint360. 2010. Promotional brochure.

Lezaun, J. and Montgomery, C.M. 2015. "The Pharmaceutical Commons: Sharing and Exclusion in Global Health Drug Development". *Science, Technology & Human Values* 40.1: 3–29.

Lundh, A., Sismondo, S., Lexchin, J., Busuioc, O.A. and Bero, L. 2012. "Industry Sponsorship and Research Outcome". *The Cochrane Library* 12: DOI: 10.1002/14651858.MR000033.pub2.

Marks, H.M. 1997. *The Progress of Experiment: Science and Therapeutic Reform in the United States, 1900–1990*. Cambridge: Cambridge University Press.

Marks, H.M. 2000. "Trust and Mistrust in the Marketplace: Statistics and Clinical Research, 1945–1960" *History of Science* 38: 343–355.

Mirowski, P. and Van Horn, R. 2005. "The Contract Research Organization and the Commercialization of Scientific Research". *Social Studies of Science* 35.4: 503–534.

Moynihan, R. 2008. "Key Opinion Leaders: Independent Experts or Drug Representatives in Disguise". *British Medical Journal* 336.7658: 1402–1403.

Nik-Khah, E. 2014. "Neoliberal Pharmaceutical Science and the Chicago School of Economics". *Social Studies of Science* 44.4: 489–517.

Oldani, M. 2004. "Thick Prescriptions: Toward an Interpretation of Pharmaceutical Sales Practices". *Medical Anthropology Quarterly* 18.3: 325–356.

Peterson, K. 2014. *Speculative Markets: Drug Circuits and Derivative Life in Nigeria*. Durham: Duke University Press.

Permanand, G. 2006. *EU Pharmaceutical Regulation: The Politics of Policy-Making*. Manchester: Manchester University Press.

Petryna, A. 2015. "Clinical Trials Offshored: On Private Sector Science and Public Health", in Sismondo, S. and Greene, J., eds. *The Pharmaceutical Studies Reader*. Oxford: Wiley-Blackwell, 208–221.

Ross, J.S., Hill, K.P., Egilman, D.S. and Krumholz, H.M. 2008. "Guest Authorship and Ghostwriting in Publications Related to Rofecoxib: A Case Study of Industry Documents from Rofecoxib Litigation". *Journal of the American Medical Association* 299.15: 1800–1812.

Shah, S. 2006. *The Body Hunters: Testing New Drugs on the World's Poorest Patients*. New York: New Press.

Sharfstein, J.M. and Charo, A. 2015. "The Promotion of Medical Products in the 21st Century: Off-Label Marketing and First Amendment Concerns". *JAMA* 314.17: 1795–1796.

Sismondo, S. 2008. "How Pharmaceutical Industry Funding Affects Trial Outcomes: Causal Structures and Responses". *Social Science & Medicine* 66.9: 1909–1914.

Sismondo, S. 2015a. "Pushing Knowledge in the Drug Industry: Ghost-Managed Science", in Sismondo, S. and Greene, J., eds. *The Pharmaceutical Studies Reader*. Oxford: Wiley-Blackwell, 150–164.

Sismondo, S. 2015b. "Key Opinion Leaders: Valuing Independence and Conflict of Interest in the Medical Sciences", in Dussauge, I., Helgesson, C-F. and Lee, F., eds., *Value Practices in the Life Sciences & Medicine*. Oxford: Oxford University Press, 31–48.

Sismondo, S. and Chloubova, Z. 2016. "'You're Not Just a Paid Monkey Reading Slides': How Key Opinion Leaders Explain and Justify Their Work". *BioSocieties* 11.2: 199–219.

Sunder Rajan, K. 2006. *Biocapital: The Constitution of Postgenomic Life*. Durham: Duke University Press.

Sunder Rajan, K. 2015. "The Experimental Machinery of Global Clinical Trials: Case Studies from India", in Sismondo, S. and Greene, J., eds. *The Pharmaceutical Studies Reader*. Oxford: Wiley-Blackwell, 222–234.

Timmermans, S. and Berg, M. 2003. *The Gold Standard: The Challenge of Evidence-Based Medicine and Standardization in Health Care*. Philadelphia: Temple University Press.

Tobbell, D. 2011. *Pills, Power, and Policy: The Struggle for Drug Reform in Cold War America and its Consequences*. Berkeley: University of California Press.

Wave Healthcare. 2011. "KOL Training". www.wavehealthcare.co.uk/en/1/koltraining.html (accessed 25 March 2011).

Worrall, J. 2007. "Evidence in Medicine and Evidence-Based Medicine". *Philosophy Compass* 2.6: 981–1002.

Zimerman, A.L. 2013. "Evidence-Based Medicine: A Short History of a Modern Medical Movement". *AMA Journal of Ethics* 15.1: 71–76.

9

OPEN ACCESS PANACEA

Scarcity, abundance, and enclosure in the new economy of academic knowledge production[1]

Chris Muellerleile

1 Introduction

Academic journal publishing is experiencing a revolution, much of it driven by a desire to "open" access to knowledge. For about a century up until 2000, the dominant model of publishing limited access to fee-paying subscribers of printed journals, the majority of which were university libraries. But, with the emergence of digital publishing and distribution tools, many now argue that this "closed" subscription model is out-dated, if not immoral. Advocates for open access argue that academic knowledge is a public good, and with digital technologies for-profit publishers no longer have legitimate claims to reap profits from a process to which they add little value. These advocates argue that, whatever the new funding model, readership should not be restricted to subscribers, but freely open to anyone with an internet connection. Yet, despite its drawbacks, the subscription model did more than limit *access*. It also checked the volume and quality of academic knowledge produced.

Among many researchers, librarians, and funding agencies over the last ten years, scepticism, if not the outright rejection of the subscription model has turned into vitriol towards for-profit publishers. But has the move to open access really hurt their business? Has it liberated researchers, universities, and the public from publishers' power to enclose the results of academic research? I will argue that at least for the large publishers it has not. Take for instance, the regularity of 30 per cent profit margins for the big publishers,[2] or consider a recent Wall Street analysis of Elsevier, the world's largest academic publisher, subtitled "The Fading Threat of Open Access". The report upgrades the company's investment rating, citing strong expectations for ongoing profitability (Bernstein Research 2014).

In this chapter I will focus on two particular aspects of the "opening" of academic knowledge production: the transition from a political economy of scarcity to one of abundance, and the business strategies of large for-profit publishers, who are responding to the growing demand for data and information *about* "open" knowledge. The large for-profit publishers, particularly but not exclusively Elsevier, are the vanguard of an information-based economy that captures and constructs vast quantities of data about seemingly everything related to academic research and researchers. I will argue that these publishers' products are becoming more, not less, necessary as a result of "openness". As such, publishers increasingly profit by assisting data-driven higher education governance and knowledge-based economic development strategies.

Through this, publishers are transforming their historical role from that of *making things public* towards making academic research—wherever it may be "published"—useful and meaningful to "the knowledge economy".

2 Background: from scarcity to abundance

The modern academic journal began in 1665 in France and England with *Le Journal des Scavans* and the *Philosophical Transactions of the Royal Society of London*. While the historical definition of a scholarly or scientific journal is contested, there were roughly 100 journals across the globe in 1700, 1,000 in 1800 and as many as 10,000 in 1900 (Tenopir and King 2009). A meta-analysis in 2010 estimated there were approximately 24,000 active and refereed journals across the globe (Larsen and Ins 2010). Until recently, journals were typically printed on paper and distributed to those who paid a subscription fee of one sort or another. The first systems designed to distribute scientific knowledge digitally emerged in the 1970s (see Gitelman 2014: 111–135), and formal open access (OA) journals first emerged in the 1990s. In recent years, OA journals have grown very quickly: from 20 in 1993 to 4,767 in 2009 (Laakso, *et al.* 2011). As this chapter is written in February of 2016, the Directory of Open Access Journals lists 11,336 OA journals, containing roughly 2.2 million articles.[3]

The open access "movement" was largely defined in the early 2000s by three manifestos: the Budapest Open Access Initiative, the Bethesda Statement on Open Access Publishing, and the Berlin Declaration on Open Access to Knowledge in the Sciences and Humanities. Peter Suber, one of the main authors of the Budapest initiative, refers to the commonalities in these declarations as the "BBB definition" or "libre" definition of OA (Suber 2012: 7–8), which he explains by quoting the Budapest statement:

> By "open access" to this literature, we mean its free availability on the public internet, permitting any users to read, download, copy, distribute, print, search, or link to the full texts of these articles, crawl them for indexing, pass them as data to software, or use them for any other lawful purpose, without financial, legal or technical barriers other than those inseparable from gaining access to the internet itself.

In the mid-2000s, governments and research funding institutions in the US and UK began protesting high subscription fees, and advocating for OA with three main arguments that continue to shape the discourse today (for an overview see OECD 2007). The first is that properly functioning democratic societies are dependent upon the free circulation of knowledge (Stiglitz 1999), an argument that is particularly persuasive when public resources fund research. The second and related argument is that academic research and knowledge are important drivers of innovation (Stiglitz 1999, Howels *et al.* 2012) and the results ought to be easily accessible to fuel economic competitiveness and growth. The third was a reaction to the "serials crisis" or the inability of university libraries to afford access to all the journals deemed necessary, coupled with what were widely considered unjustified profits accumulated by publishers[4] (Ciancanelli 2007). The familiar argument then and now is that once the first digital copy of an article is produced, the marginal cost of reproduction is almost zero (cf. Suber 2012: 21).

Furthermore, subscription based publishers are criticized for "double appropriating" the labor of academic researchers and academic institutions (Beverungen *et al.* 2012). First, they claim intellectual property (copy)rights over knowledge they have played almost no role in producing, and second, they sell this knowledge back to universities at inflated prices. Possibly the most resented tactic is the so called "big deal" where publishers package together large sets of journals for a single price. At the same time, they raise the prices of the most prominent, or flagship journals so high that universities might as well pay a little more for the additional journals. As such, universities supplement the costs of new and/or low-circulation journals because the costs are hidden in the aggregate price.

The big deal packages contribute to the monopoly-like character of large, for-profit publishers (Ciancanelli 2007). Because universities cannot easily replace (especially high-profile) journals with alternatives, there is little competition (or "inelastic demand"), and publishers can significantly raise their prices without losing customers. Similarly, the big deals foreclose a competitive market for journals—a market that might otherwise establish a price for any given journal, which makes it more difficult for universities to make cost-benefit decisions.

Despite the recent consolidation of publishers into larger firms (see Lariviere *et al.* 2015), there are many smaller and independent publishers, particularly in the humanities, which operate subscription journals on very thin margins. This includes the emergence in recent years of all sorts of small-scale independent journals managed by groups of academics—what we might call a "peer-to-peer" publishing model. But many OA advocates flatly reject *any* subscription fee, some going as far as arguing that publishing behind a paywall is immoral.[5]

Regardless of the size of a publisher or journal, the economy of subscription-based publishing is based on scarcity. Through copyright, access to paper copies, and now digital paywalls, publishers control access to codified academic knowledge. However perverse it may seem to restrict access, in the subscription model the incentives for publishers and editors—even authors—are aligned. Everyone's goal is to increase distribution by increasing subscriptions. Furthermore, it is in the publisher's interest to "filter" (see Bhaskar 2013) academic work to ensure a quality product, just as it is in the editor's interest to reproduce the "prestige" of the journal by only including the highest quality work (see Eve 2014).

However, as the digital reproduction and distribution of articles has become widespread, it has become more difficult for publishers to maintain scarcity of copyrighted materials. One example is the website and search engine "Sci-Hub" developed by a Russian neuroscientist and software developer. Upon request from a user, the website will almost instantly locate and digitally reproduce most academic papers for free. According to UK- and US-based publishers, this is illegal and they are working hard to shut the site down, but in the meantime Sci-Hub allows "black open access" (Bjork 2017) free access to huge numbers of articles normally protected behind paywalls.

On the other hand, the OA movement seeks a legal way around barriers to access by eliminating the subscription altogether and instead recouping the costs of digital publication from authors or other sources. Indeed, the OA model does remove all barriers to distribution, but it also changes the incentive structure of publishing from one based on scarcity to one based on abundance.

3 Emergent economy of openness

Yes costs matter. But high journal costs were a product of scholars needing a proxy for quality...OA has done nothing to help that problem. The problem of having a way in each field of sorting out the important research from the merely interesting (or indeed the mistaken) is one that remains to be sorted, OA or not OA.

Robin Osborne[6]

While in the US OA efforts are relatively dispersed, in the UK there has been a centralized, state-driven effort to encourage OA. One significant event was the 2012 UK government sponsored "Finch Report" on "expanding access to published research findings" (Finch Group 2012), which built upon recommendations anticipated by the House of Commons in 2004. The UK government enacted the main recommendations and they are now being implemented by, among others, Research Councils UK and the Higher Education Funding Council for England, which mandated that any post-2014 Research Excellence Framework[8] submissions must be published OA in some form.

The Finch Report and its subsequent formalization in policy encourage universities and publishers to move away from the subscription model towards an "article processing charge" (APC) system. In this system, authors or their funders pay the publishers an upfront fee and as soon as the article is published, digital copies are made freely available to the public on the publisher's website. This is referred to as the "gold model", and all of the major publishers have adopted some version for at least some of their journals. The most common strategy is to convert journals from subscription-only to a "hybrid" model where some articles are published gold OA, but access to the vast majority of the journal is kept behind a subscription paywall. While there is not room here to discuss it, hybrid journals present an entirely different set of problems surrounding "double dipping" or the "total cost of ownership" (see Lawson 2015), something the UK public body JISC has been attempting to quantify.[7]

The gold model has other problems beginning with the upfront cost to authors or their funding agencies. US$3,000 per article is not uncommon, and some have argued that this restricts academic freedom by limiting some publication outlets to those who can afford the APCs. But there are a number of other issues. Most importantly, after publication the publisher is no longer directly incentivized to promote their published materials. Instead the publisher is paid a flat fee by the author to publish the article, and henceforth has no opportunity to collect revenue. As Eve (2014: 59) explains, "In this inverted model, publishers are paid for the services they render and not in return for making sound judgments in a sales environment". Furthermore, publishers are no longer directly incentivized to encourage production of a quality product. Instead, the more articles they publish the more they are paid. In other words, "the scale of success flips from quality to quantity. Any amplification effect becomes one based on volume [of articles published], and a linear relationship takes over" (Anderson, 2013). Presumably editors, and even publishers, are still interested in the quality of their journals—something Eve (2014) emphasizes—but the point is that the relationship between quality and profit is no longer straightforward. Instead of producing scarcity, in the gold model publishers are directly incentivized to produce abundance.

The Finch Report also supports the "green" OA model where universities construct institutional repositories for their researchers' "pre-prints"—usually the final accepted version of a paper before it is typeset by the publisher. There are at least three problems with the "green" model. First, green versions of copyrighted papers are typically subject to embargo periods, usually between 12 and 24 months, prior to which they cannot be released to anyone. Second, because it does not include a peer review or editorial procedure, much of the legitimacy of a green version is dependent upon the existence of a final published version in a subscription journal, which means that subscription journals are still necessary to the process.[8] Third, while this landscape is shifting quickly, most green repositories are diverse, disconnected, and expensive to establish and maintain. Consider that for every green paper, universities are now responsible for managing compliance with an array of copyright and embargo rules and regulations. Particularly in the social sciences and humanities, repositories are not typically organized by learned societies, or by disciplines, but by individual university librarians and technical staff. Being disconnected means they are difficult to search and cross-reference. Not surprisingly, the publishing industry recognizes the challenges universities face with regard to the green model, and they are selling repository management software as well as contributing to efforts to standardize OA search across institutions.[9]

Open access is entangled with all sorts of other confusions and contradictions. For instance, despite the oft-referenced suggestion that open access articles attract more attention, meta-studies of this phenomenon are inconclusive (see Suber 2012: 178, note 6). There is widespread belief that OA articles have a "citation advantage", but these studies miss the most obvious explanation of self-selection—that the best research draws the most research funding needed to pay the expensive[10] gold open access fees (Davis 2014). As such, there should be little surprise that the best-funded science attracts the most attention, and thus the most clicks, downloads, and citations.

OA is also lauded for its tendency to provide faster publication. As Randy Scheckman argues in relation to his open access journal, *eLife*, one of the key benefits of OA is speed of distribution of research to other scientists.[11] But this should not be separated from the recent drastic increase in the number of published scientific findings that are retracted (Anderson 2014). In other words, while not exclusively a problem of openness, there is a legitimate question whether the impulse to speed up science also increases the sloppiness of science.

4 Overcrowded knowledge

For many proponents of openness, however, neither retraction nor revision is a problem. In fact, the possibility of a stable record of science is under increasing pressure by those advocating a transition to what Steven Harnad (2014) has called the "crowd sourcing" of peer review. Instead of the conventional peer review model based on *filtering first and publishing second*; this is a model of *publishing first and filtering second*. This is best exemplified by arguments to transition away from pre-publication peer review, which is seen as opaque, slow, and overly politicized, if not utterly corrupt (see Ferguson, *et al.* 2014, Fitzpatrick 2011, Eve 2014). Instead, academics are encouraged to "publish" their work when they see fit via the medium of their choice, and let peers and the wider public decide what is useful after the fact (Gauntlett 2012). Take for instance, the online journal *F1000Research*, which advertises that it is "open for science" and offers "immediate publication… without editorial bias". In this model there is little consideration of a "version of record" as authors are "strongly encouraged" to "address the reviewers' criticisms and publish revised versions".[12] The massive, interdisciplinary OA science journal *PLoS One* does not go this far, but it does ask peer reviewers to focus on whether a paper is "technically sound", regardless of uniqueness, significance, or the potential to be impactful. While not explicit, Taylor & Francis's new interdisciplinary OA journals under the brand "Cogent" seem to have a similar model.[13]

In the publish first-filter second model the best science or scholarship is assumed to float to the top, while the rest sinks into what Kirby (2012: 259) has called the "celestial jukebox". Irrelevant papers, or those from "niche fields or areas that have yet to gain any prominence" should still be published, but discovered "if and only if the seeker desires" (Eve 2014: 145). This process of crowd sourcing the quality of academic knowledge may remove "editorial bias", but it also relies on the objectivity of the World Wide Web to identify academic knowledge without bias, or to somehow filter knowledge without actually filtering it. It furthermore assumes that the "crowd" has equal access to the field of scholarly content, which serves as a tautological justification for expanding open access.

By design this model questions the importance of scientific expertise and academic autonomy, but if you extend the logic of the crowd as a filtering process there is an even deeper contradiction: any pre-publication filtering, editing, or curation presumably adulterates the objectivity of the "review" process, or at least unjustifiably limits the size of the sample for what sounds a lot like a digitally-mediated popularity contest. Consider the similar movement toward "big data", where the abundance of the data itself is assumed to improve its validity (Gitelman 2013). Of course, no one argues that post-publication-reviewed scholarship should be left completely unfiltered prior to publication, but at a very basic level this model suggests that the quality of research output should no longer be subject to the scrutiny of an academic community, but to that of the broader public (Nik-Khah, this volume).

Put differently, the "publish first" model seeks free access to much more than what would otherwise be behind a paywall. Rather than opening up that which was closed, it is more about breaking down *any* wall that restricts the retrieval of *any*thing that *any* author decides to "publish" in *any* medium. One might even extend this logic to the author. Consider that the decision as a potential author to *not publish* something is limiting access to that knowledge, and as such ought to be discouraged.

We ought to ask whether the publish first–filter second model contradicts the very purpose of open access, which above all else is supposed to provide society and economy meaningful and useful research and scholarship. Without rigorous editing and peer review, or any discernible archive, is academic output really *knowledge*, or is it rather more like modestly filtered information? This is a particular problem for the humanities and the "softer" social sciences where well-referenced, thoughtfully argued, and clearly written text constitutes the value of the work (see Slaughter and Wulf 2014). Even those in favor of deepening and formalizing universities' commitments to the "knowledge economy" ought to question the value of this kind of post-publication "reviewed" scholarship. An obvious neoliberal solution would be to establish a new sort of knowledge market to decide what is valuable and what is not. As we will see below, this may already be happening, but if a market is the filtering device does this really constitute openness?

This growing abundance of knowledge—or just information—makes qualitative assessment increasingly difficult, which is problematic given the increasing emphasis on assessment and accounting metrics for universities. So far the solution has been to establish easier-to-manage quantitative benchmarks, indicators, and rankings. There may be no better example than the UK's Research Excellence Framework (REF), the very existence of which betrays the inability of the public and the state to assess the value of academic knowledge production without endless quantitative comparisons.

These conditions have led the sociologist Andrew Abbott to the sad conclusion that "the majority of scholarly publication in the social sciences and humanities today serves no purpose other than providing grist for evaluation" (Abbot 2015). Exaggeration or not, we ought to at least consider this "Simmelian dichotomy" (Featherstone 2000), where the massive increase in the amount of, and access to, information also means that it is much more difficult to discern meaning from that archive. It should be no surprise that all sorts of "altmetrics", such as "mentions" on social media, are becoming popular measurements of the value and impact of research. The problem with what is increasingly becoming an ideology of OA (Golumbia 2016) is that it encourages (over)abundance without appreciating the challenges that come with it. Put another way, too much of the OA discourse is obsessed with *accessing* the archive without considering how researchers, the public, and "the economy" *come to understand the archive as meaningful, significant, and useful.*

I have argued so far that the movement to open up access to knowledge is both analytically and empirically entangled with three things. First are the growing opportunities and incentives within the academy to simply produce *more* knowledge. Second, the process of creating the commodity that is the subscription-bound journal article—the commodity that OA seeks to abolish—is at the same time the process of filtration that creates meaningful knowledge. It is of course possible to create meaningful knowledge without commodifying it, but this is more difficult than many suspect, particularly when the underlying conditions of knowledge production in the academy are becoming more, not less privatized and marketized (Lave, *et al.* 2010). Third, the economy of scarcity in publishing—which OA seeks to reverse—is transitioning to an economy of abundance. In the next section of the paper I will analyze a few of the strategies that for-profit publishers are employing to construct this economy to their advantage, all within the context of an increasingly marketized higher education sector.

5 Publishers or data aggregators?

The OA movement must be considered in the context of a politics of economic development that is obsessed with the production of knowledge and knowledge producing bodies (Pfotenhauer, this volume; Jessop 2008). Higher education plays a crucial role in this "knowledge economy". It is assumed to be a driving force of innovation, economic competitiveness, and the accumulation of wealth (Best and Rich, this volume. Moreover, higher education itself is quickly turning into an economic sector (McGettigan 2013). In the UK in particular, there is intense pressure from the state to turn higher education into a service sector motivated by and organized around competition, profit seeking, and national economic development (Jessop 2008, McGettigan 2013).

Furthermore, with the high costs of research, teaching, and administration—not to mention the pressures engendered by economic crisis—there is a desire to eliminate "waste" and force universities to operate more efficiently, or at least according to a clear financial calculus. But this requires economic value judgments and measurement of processes and people that have not previously been subject to processes of calculation and economizing (De Angelis and Harvie 2009). Obscured in these measurements is a translation of research and knowledge from something previously valued according to political, cultural, or disciplinary standards into something that is largely monetary in nature (see Birch, Johnson and Rampini, and Pagano and Rossi, this volume; Robertson and Muellerleile, 2017). At the same time, fueled by processes like OA, the research process is becoming more vast, disparate, and unwieldy, all of which make it more difficult to measure and quantify, something Woelert (2013) calls the "paradox of effective research governance".

Academic publishers are aware of this paradox and are producing tools to make sense of this new world. These tools serve two broad functions, although they are often co-constitutive. First, publishers are developing technologies that categorize, codify, and measure research and researchers. And second, publishers are using these tools to enclose and sell meta-data about research. Through an evolution of internet media provision, what Mansell (1999) calls the "scarcity-abundance dialectic", the largest academic publishers are losing control of content, but at the same time enclosing information about content and those who produce it. Not unlike Facebook, Google, or Amazon, they are becoming massive data aggregating conglomerates.

Over the past 10–15 years the publishing industry has sponsored the development of a global digital infrastructure composed of identification systems called digital object identifiers or DOIs. Many readers will be familiar with DOIs, which are attached to most published journal articles, but this is just the beginning. CrossRef is a DOI system for academic citations, linking articles to each other across publishing platforms. CrossMark is a DOI system that attaches identifiers to every version of an academic text, giving "scholars the information they need to verify that they are using the most recent and reliable versions of a document".[14] FundRef is a DOI system linking academic bodies and research outputs to funding agencies. And finally, ORCID is a DOI system attached to researchers' bodies themselves, and universities now routinely encourage their researchers to establish a unique identifier. ORCID has the capability to track an individual academic through their labor as an author, peer reviewer, or grant writer.

Not surprisingly these are all "free" services, and they are marketed by their associations and foundations as beneficial to research and researchers because they make knowledge production more standardized, networked, orderly, efficient, and attributable. But they are also designed to facilitate data collection, digital rankings, surveillance, and more importantly, to enforce copyright and intellectual property. It is only a matter of time before DOIs will, for instance, enable the automatic enforcement of embargo periods for "green" OA versions of articles, or the instantaneous ranking of a researcher against their peers based on grant applications, citations, various impact factors, or whatever the next fashionable "altmetric" might be.

Fueled by bibliometrics, ranking is nothing new. Thomson Reuters, which owns the ISI/Web of Knowledge databases, works closely with publishers to identify, categorize, and track the "impact" of particular journals. Publishers of all sizes compete fiercely to convince ISI to include their journals in the database. Through 2014 ISI data drove the Times Higher Education (THE) Global University Rankings (see Robertson and Olds 2012), although THE has recently announced that it will now partner with Elsevier, using their products Scopus and SciVal (ISI competitors) to help them assemble the "largest and most comprehensive database of university data in the world" (*THE* 2014). Reflecting on this new partnership, Nick Fowler, a managing director at Elsevier, said, "We are thrilled to partner with THE…They support university and industry leaders in setting strategic priorities and making investment decisions, and they help governments shape national policy" (ibid.). This is consistent with Elsevier's overall strategic direction. For instance, their "Research Intelligence" unit, which includes SciVal and Scopus, promises to "answer the most pressing challenges researchers and research managers face, with innovative solutions that improve an institution's and individual's ability to establish, execute and evaluate research strategy performance".[15]

Elsevier makes for an interesting, if not paradigmatic example of the transformation of large academic publishers. Over the last 15 years, but particularly in the last five, the company has shifted its focus from managing subscription-based paper journals to managing digital data, of which journals are just one small piece of the puzzle. Of course, of all the large (it is the largest) for-profit publishers, Elsevier is also a locus of scorn by many academics. In 2012 a group began a boycott of Elsevier called "The cost of knowledge". Protesting their restrictive "big deal" subscriptions and substantial profit margins, close to 15,000 academics have now agreed that they will not edit, review, or publish in Elsevier journals. Adding fuel to the fire, Elsevier has recently been aggressively demanding that scholars remove unauthorized copies of articles posted on Academia.edu and other websites (*The Economist* 2014).

It may seem like Elsevier is fixated on protecting its subscription journal model, but behind the scenes the company is transforming itself into a data aggregation platform. Following are a few examples of Elsevier's new data-oriented businesses, much of which is constituted by acquisitions of smaller companies. In 2012 Elsevier acquired Atria, a Danish software company, whose main product was PURE, a sort of catch-all database or "dashboard" tool used by universities to keep track of and order information about academics, research, projects, grants, and most importantly the networks between them. Its goal, according to Elsevier, is to provide university administrators with a "complete picture of the research enterprise" so they may more efficiently "focus and manage resources in order to achieve their desired research outcomes" (Elsevier 2012). One of the key functions of PURE in the UK is to standardize information and data about publications, grants, student supervision and impact across disciplines to ease the next Research Excellence Framework assessment. PURE is just one of many Current Research

Information Systems (CRIS), which have quickly become a necessary component for the management of a research university.

Along the same lines, Elsevier is currently assisting eight of the largest UK research intensive universities in constructing a new system of meta-data metrics called "Snowball Metrics". The stated goal of the Snowball project is to "achieve a shared understanding and buy-in of a set of high-level measures of academic research, across the spectrum of inputs, throughputs and outputs (such as grant applications and awards, research income, and bibliometric indicators), to enable benchmarking across institutions" (Snowball Metrics 2012). Elsevier is not charging any fees for its participation in this project, but it seems pretty obvious that it will benefit greatly from working with university administrators and technology staff to understand what meta-data universities need and the challenges involved in producing them.

In 2013 Elsevier bought the online research collaboration and reference manager tool and company, Mendeley, which among other things codifies academic social networks. More recently, in January of 2015, Elsevier purchased a London-based start-up called Newsflow, which uses algorithms to analyze content from 55,000 English-language news outlets with the goal of determining which researchers and research output are creating an impact (Clark 2015). These two acquisitions/products will be housed together in Elsevier's London-based Big Data Analytics and ScienceDirect offices, where they will be used in tandem to help academics and universities measure the impact of their research across the sprawling global spaces of digital information.

A University of Glasgow Professor recently said of Elsevier, "I think Elsevier's role as the bogieman of science publishing, while probably deserved, misses the point. They aren't really publishers – they are a knowledge company" (Shaw 2013). This is reminiscent of Foucault's suggestion that it isn't any particular unit of knowledge that is powerful, but the assumptions and conditions through which that knowledge becomes legitimate that are run through with power (see Wyly 2015). The point is that while academic texts may increasingly be open and free, finding meaning or use in this ever less filtered world is more difficult and quite possibly more expensive. Elsevier recognizes that academics and universities, not to mention states and funding agencies, are in dire need of (meta)data that will help them understand what research is significant given this new environment of openness, and they are finding willing buyers especially among universities that are forced to constantly justify their existence.

6 Conclusion: the qualities of knowledge

The assumption built into most advocacy of open access is that scientific knowledge must be free for the public to read, if not free to put to use in any way they see fit. On the surface this seems reasonable.[16] But in order to achieve this within the present technical-economic conjuncture, it will be necessary to break apart the existing structures that organize knowledge and make it impactful to the very people on behalf of whom open access campaigners claim to advocate.

Open Access advocates might argue that in a world of open and abundant knowledge and data, a simple Google search will solve the filtering problems by identifying the most popular, well-connected, or most trusted research. The problem is that the for-profit publishers are ahead of this game. They are working very hard to set the rules by which Google or Mendeley or Scopus will identify the "best" academic research on any given topic. Put another way, the information structures of the internet are not flat (Ransom *et al.*, this volume). They are always already filtered, curated, and uneven—or put another way, en*closed*. Furthermore, the algorithms that control these searches are increasingly hidden from human view, or are too complicated for humans (e.g. academic researchers, academic administrators, the broader public) to understand without the aid of digital technology (Gitelman 2013).

We may have different opinions on what large for-profit publishers are up to in all of this. But in some ways they are doing what they have always done—what Bhaskar (2013) calls "filtering, framing, and amplifying" knowledge—and in the process making a profit. I am not attempting to justify or legitimate the subscription or for-profit model, but the important point is that open access is not removing publishers and their profits from the process. In fact, it may be contributing to an environment where they are more necessary than ever. Open access to knowledge may be better than an environment where much academic knowledge is closed, but focusing too closely on the openness may be distracting us from the ways that capital is sneaking in the back door and enclosing the very tools we need to make sense of this new world (Harrison *et al.*, this volume).

Notes

1 Funding for this research was provided by the European Union as part of its FP7 Marie Curie Actions for the project Universities in the Knowledge Economy (UNIKE). Previous versions of this paper were presented at the UNIKE Conference at the University of Auckland in February of 2015, the Association of American Geographers Conference in Chicago in April of 2015, and at the Global Conference on Economic Geography at the University of Oxford in August 2015. I am grateful to John Morgan, Christian Rogler, Chris Newfield, Rebecca Lave, and Sam Randalls for helpful edits and suggestions on previous drafts. I am, however, solely responsible for any errors or omissions.

2 Elsevier had profit margins of 37 per cent, 37 per cent, and 38 per cent in 2014, 2013, and 2012 respectively. For Elsevier in 2014 this represents £762 million in profits on £2.05 billion in revenue. Informa/Taylor & Francis had profit margins of 29 per cent, 30 per cent, 30 per cent in the same years. In 2014 this represents £334 million in profits on £1.14 billion in revenue (author's calculations based on publicly available annual corporate reports). See also Bernstein Research (2014).

3 See www.doaj.org.

4 Publishers, and groups representing them, will often respond to this accusation by admitting that prices have increased, but argue that the libraries attain access to a larger volume of content, thus driving down the cost per article (cf. Gantz 2012).

5 See Mike Taylor's argument on immorality in the *Guardian*: www.theguardian.com/science/blog/2013/jan/17/open-access-publishing-science-paywall-immoral.

6 Osborn, a Cambridge professor of ancient history, is a strong critic of OA most notably in an essay he wrote as part of an extended debate published by the British Academy www.britac.ac.uk/openaccess/debatingopenaccess.cfm). The quote here is taken from an interview by Richard Poynder, Dec. 23, 2013, http://poynder.blogspot.co.uk/2013/12/robin-osborne-on-state-of-open-access.html.

7 See Ken Anderson's discussion of 'double dipping': http://scholarlykitchen.sspnet.org/2013/01/29/in-praise-of-double-dipping-fairness-affordability-vitality-and-sustainability/; and the mathematician Timothy Gower's discussion including some links to one OA advocate's related argument with Elsevier: https://gowers.wordpress.com/2014/04/24/elsevier-journals-some-facts/.

8 There is no necessary reason why the green version must be followed by the "version of record"—see below on the publish first–filter second model. Nevertheless, at least in the UK (or in the US in the University of California policy), the green model is almost always framed as a way to access papers that are otherwise behind publisher paywalls.

9 See for instance Elsevier's recent partnership with the University of Florida www.insidehighered.com/news/2016/05/25/university-florida-elsevier-explore-interoperability-publishing-space; or the broader CHORUS infrastructure in the US, which is sponsored by for-profit publishers http://scholarlykitchen.sspnet.org/2015/11/30/chorus-gets-boost-but-implementation-tricky/.

10 See here for a recent study of the costs of OA article processing charges paid by German universities: https://github.com/njahn82/unibiAPC.

11 See http://elifesciences.org/about.

12 See *F1000Research*'s "About" page: http://f1000research.com/about.

13 See http://cogentoa.tandfonline.com/.

14 See www.crossref.org/crossmark/.

15 See Elsevier's Research Intelligence unit's website. Accessed March 18, 2016: www.elsevier.com/research-intelligence.

16 One topic I did not address here is the question of whether academic knowledge *should* be free. In an environment of increasing "precarity" of academic labor, we ought to ask whether academics have a right to be compensated for their work. This is a complex issue, and I will not attempt to parse it here—but see Chapter 2 of Eve (2014) and Golumbia (2016).

References

Abbott, A. (2015) "Futures for Library Research", *Library as Laboratory: A Symposium on Humanities Collections and Research*. Paper 3. h5p://elischolar.library.yale.edu/libraryaslaboratory/3

Anderson, K. (2013) "The Conversations We're Not Having—Overcoming Uncertainty, Chilling Effects, and Open Access Complacency", blog post on *The Scholarly Kitchen*, September 9, 2013, accessed on January 23, 2015: http://scholarlykitchen.sspnet.org/2013/09/09/the-conversations-were-not-having-overcoming-uncertainty-chilling-effects-and-open-access-complacency/

Anderson, K. (2014) "Slow and Steady—Taking the Time to Think in the Age of Rapid Publishing Cycles", blog post on *The Scholarly Kitchen*, November 13, accessed on December 20, 2014: http://scholarlykitchen.sspnet.org/2014/11/13/taking-the-time-to-think-in-the-age-of-rapid-publishing-cycles/

Bernstein Research (2014) "Reed Elsevier: Goodbye to Berlin—The Fading Threat of Open Access (Upgrade to Market-Perform)", September 24, accessed via Richard Poynder's website on December 8, 2014: www.richardpoynder.co.uk/Aspesi.pdf

Beverungen, A., Bohm, S. and Land, C. (2012) "The poverty of journal publishing", *Organization*, 19(6)

Bhaskar, M. (2013) *The Content Machine*, London: Anthem

Bjork, B.C. (2017) "Gold, green, and black open access", Learned Publishing, early view online: http://onlinelibrary.wiley.com/doi/10.1002/leap.1096/abstract

Ciancanelli, P. (2007) "(Re)producing universities: Knowledge dissemination, market power and the global knowledge commons", included in Epstein, D., Boden, R., Deem, R., Rizvi, F., and Wright, S. (eds.) *World Yearbook of Education 2008*, New York: Routledge

Clark, L. (2015) "Elsevier acquires London startup Newsflow", Wired.co.uk, 12 January, accessed on January 20, 2015: www.wired.co.uk/news/archive/2015-01/12/elsevier-acquires-newsflo

Davis, P. (2014) "Is Open Access a Cause or Effect?", blog post on *The Scholarly Kitchen*, August 5, accessed on December 20, 2014: http://scholarlykitchen.sspnet.org/2014/08/05/is-open-access-a-cause-or-an-effect/

De Angelis, M. and Harvie, D. (2009) "'Cognitive Capitalism' and the Rat-Race: How Capital Measures Immaterial Labour in British Universities", *Historical Materialism*, 17: 3–30

The Economist (2014) "No Peeking…", January 11, accessed on January 28, 2015: www.economist.com/news/science-and-technology/21593408-publishing-giant-goes-after-authors-its-journals-papers-no-peeking

Elsevier (2012) "Elsevier Acquires Atria, a Provider of Research Management Solutions", press release on Elsevier's website, accessed on January 28, 2015: www.elsevier.com/about/press-releases/science-and-technology/elsevier-acquires-atira,-a-provider-of-research-management-solutions

Eve, M.P. (2014) *Open Access and the Humanities*, Cambridge: Cambridge University Press

Featherstone, M. (2000) "Archiving Cultures", *British Journal of Sociology*, 51(1): 161–184

Ferguson, C., Marcus, A. and Oransky, I. (2014) "Publishing: The peer-review scam", *Nature*, 515, November 27: 480–482

Finch Group (2012) "Accessibility, sustainability, excellence: how to expand access to research publications", Working Group on Expanding Access to Published Research Findings, accessed on January 24, 2015: www.researchinfonet.org/publish/finch/

Fitzpatrick, K. (2011) *Planned Obsolescence: Publishing, Technology, and the Future of the Academy*, New York: New York University Press

Gantz, P. (2012) "Digital Licenses Replace Print Prices as Accurate Reflection of Real Journal Costs", *Association of American Publishers Professional Scholarly Publishing Bulletin*, 11(3)

Gauntlett, D. (2012) "How to move towards a system that looks to 'publish, then filter' academic research", a blog post on the LSE Impact Blog, July 10, accessed on January 27, 2015: http://blogs.lse.ac.uk/impactofsocialsciences/2012/07/10/publish-then-filter-research/

Gitelman, L. (ed.) (2013) *"Raw Data" is an Oxymoron*, Cambridge, MA: MIT Press

Gitelman, L. (2014) *Paper Knowledge: Toward a Media History of Documents*, Durham, NC: Duke University Press

Golumbia, D. (2016) "Marxism and open access in the humanities: turning academic labor against itself", *Workplace*, 28: 74–114

Harnad, S. (2014) "Crowd-Sourced Peer Review: Substitute or supplement for the current outdated system?", The Impact Blog, London School of Economics and Political Science, accessed on March 5, 2016: http://blogs.lse.ac.uk/impactofsocialsciences/2014/08/21/crowd-sourced-peer-review-substitute-or-supplement/

Jessop, B. (2008) "A Cultural Political Economy of Competitiveness and its Implications for Higher Education", in Jessop, B., Fairclough, N. and Wodak, R. (eds.), *Education and the Knowledge-Based Economy in Europe*, Rotterdam: Sense Publishers, pp. 13–39

Kirby, A. (2012) "Scientific communication, Open Access, and the publishing industry", *Political Geography*, 31: 256–259

Laakso, M., Welling, P., Bukvova, H., Nyman, L., Bjork, B. and Hedlund, T. (2011) "The Development of Open Access Journal Publishing from 1993 to 2009", *PLOS One*, available online: http://journals.plos.org/plosone/article?id=10.1371/journal.pone.0020961

Lariviere, V., Haustein, S. and Mongeon, P. (2015) "The Oligopoly of Academic Publishers in the Digital Era", *PLoS ONE* 10(6): e0127502. doi:10.1371/journal.pone.0127502

Larsen, P.O. and Ins, M. (2010) "The rate of growth in scientific publication and the decline in coverage provided by Science Citation Index", *Scientometrics*, 84: 575–603

Lave, R., Mirowski, P. and Randalls, S. (2010) "Introduction: STS and Neoliberal Science", *Social Studies of Science*, 40(5): 659–675

Lawson, S. (2015) "'Total cost of ownership' of scholarly communication: managing subscription and APC payments together", *Learned Publishing*, 27: 9–13

Mansell, R. (1999) "New media competition and access: the scarcity-abundance dialectic", *New Media and Society*, 1(2): 155–182

McGettigan, A. (2013) *The Great University Gamble: Money, Market and the Future of Higher Education*, London: Pluto Press

OECD (2007) "OECD Principles and Guidelines for Access to Research Data from Public Funding", Organisation for Economic Co-Operation and Development, accessed on January 24, 2015: www.oecd.org/science/sci-tech/38500813.pdf

Robertson, S.L. and Muellerleile, C. (2017) "Universities, the Risk Industry and Capitalism: A Political Economy Critique", in Normand, R. and Derouet, J.L. (eds.) *A European politics of Education? Perspectives from Sociology, Policy Studies and Politics*, London and New York: Routledge

Robertson, S.L. and Olds, K. (2012) "World university rankings: On the new arts of governing (quality)", in J-É Charlier, S. Croché et B. Leclercq (eds.) *Contrôler la qualité dans l'enseignement supérieur, Louvain-la-Neuve (Belgique): Editions Academia*, pp. 195–214

Shaw, C. (2013) "Elsevier buys Mendeley: your reaction", *Guardian* online, April 10, accessed on January 28, 2015: www.theguardian.com/higher-education-network/blog/2013/apr/10/elsevier-buys-mendeley-academic-reaction

Slaughter, E. and Wulf, K. (2014) "Open Access for the Humanities: A View from the William and Mary Quarterly", paper presented at McNeil Center for Early American Studies, February 21, 2014, accessed on 15 March 2016: https://oieahc.wm.edu/about/Slauter_Wulf_OA_MCEAS.pdf

Snowball Metrics (2012) "Statement of Intent", October 2012, accessed on November 17, 2014: www.snowballmetrics.com/metrics/statement-of-intent/

Stiglitz, J. (1999) "Knowledge as a Public Good", in Kaul, I, Gruenberg, I. and Stern, M.A. *Global Public Goods: International Cooperation in the 21st Century*, Oxford: Oxford University Press

Suber, P. (2012) *Open Access*, Cambridge, MA: MIT Press, accessed on December 26, 2014: http://mitpress.mit.edu/books/open-access

Tenopir, C. and King, D.W. (2009) "The growth of journals publishing", in Cope, B. and Phillips, A. (eds.) *The Future of the Academic Journal*, first edition, London: Chandos

THE (2014) "Times Higher Education announces reforms to its World University Rankings", *Times Higher Education*, November 19, accessed on January 22, 2015: www.timeshighereducation.co.uk/world-university-rankings/news/times-higher-education-announces-reforms-to-world-university-rankings

Woelert, P. (2013) "The 'Economy of Memory': Publications, Citations, and the Paradox of Effective Research Governance", *Minerva*, 51: 341–362

Wyly, E. (2015) "Where is an author?", *City*, 19(1): 5–43

10

THE POLITICAL ECONOMY OF HIGHER EDUCATION AND STUDENT DEBT

Eric Best and Daniel Rich

A global transformation is underway in the political economy of higher education. Dramatic shifts are taking place in what, where, how, by whom, and to whom higher education services are provided and funded. The transformation will intensify in strength and complexity over succeeding decades, driven by new technology, shifting educational costs, and the changing policies and strategies of nations and universities. Cutting across these forces are new patterns of supply and demand and major changes in both public and private investment that impact who bears the burden of higher education costs. In the industrialized nations of the Global North, a growing portion of that burden has shifted from government to the students who are expected to be the prime beneficiaries of higher educational opportunities.

In the United States and other nations of the Global North, the new political economy challenges some of the underlying features of the higher education system created over the previous half century. In response, many public universities have pursued strategies that emphasize greater self-reliance, privatization, and entrepreneurship, expecting that the levels of public funding they received in the past will not be available in the future. By contrast, China, India, South Korea, and other nations in the Global South have dramatically increased public investment in higher education, expecting that the growth of higher education capacity is critical to advancing national goals in an increasingly knowledge-based global political economy (Xu and Ye, this volume). Universities in these nations are expected to accept a larger public responsibility than in the past, focused on ameliorating social and economic challenges while at the same time supporting the innovation and labor force development needed for economic prosperity.

We review how this transformation differs from the dramatic changes in the political economy of higher education in the second half of the 20th century. We also distinguish features and implications of these changes for higher education in the Global North and the Global South, focusing especially on the impacts of these changes on student debt. While Global North institutions are the envy of the world, higher education is increasingly considered a private good, leading to a system of financing and loan repayment that appears unsustainable.

The 20th-century transformation

The political economy of higher education in the Global North underwent a transformation in the second half of the 20th century that dramatically increased higher education capacity and student access, introduced programs to respond to an expanding vision of the public role of universities, promoted rapid growth of graduate and professional degree programs, and, most importantly, created the modern research university. The leading edge of the transformation was in the United States.

The rapid expansion of the U.S. higher education system in the second half of the 20th century reflected a growing recognition of higher education as a public good and a priority for public investment. After World War II, higher education was seen as a major factor in the development of a larger and more prosperous economic middle-class, and a means of entry into that class for millions of citizens. This view fueled both federal and state investment in the rapid expansion of colleges and universities, including the development of entire new state-supported higher education systems. For example, the State University of New York (SUNY), established in 1948 through the initial consolidation of a number of smaller campuses, and the subsequent expansion and addition of campuses through state funding, is now the largest state university system in the U.S., with 64 campuses and nearly a half million students. Much of this growth in scale was driven by policies and investments in what John Thelin calls "higher education's golden age: 1945–1970," which reshaped American higher education to support mass access to college enrollment and simultaneously increased the scope of advanced academic programs, including highly selective professional schools and doctoral programs (2004:260).

One of the key steps was taken in the midst of World War II, when the federal government passed legislation, the Servicemen's Readjustment Act of 1944 (popularly known as the G.I. Bill), which enabled returning military service veterans to pursue higher education rather than enter the post-war labor market (although that access was not equally distributed across the population of veterans) (Onkst, 1998); the result was a remarkable growth in enrollments at colleges and universities of all types. "By the time the original GI Bill ended on July 25, 1956, 7.8 million of the 16 million World War II veterans had participated in an education or training program" (U.S. Department of Veterans Affairs, 2013). Before World War II, only about 5 percent of the U.S. college-aged population attended college. Because of the G.I. bill, enrollments increased to 15 percent of the college-aged population, and it has been increasing ever since.

> In 1939–40, total student enrollment at all colleges and universities was just under 1.5 million ... By 1949–50, total student enrollments had ballooned to almost 2.7 million – an increase of 80 percent in one decade. This was no aberration, for the figure increased to about 3.6 million in 1960 and then doubled again over the next decade, reaching over 7.9 million in 1970.
>
> *(Thelin, 2004:261)*

In the decades between 1940 and 1970, growth rates of higher education were 80 percent, 33 percent and 119 percent, compared to population growth rates of 14 percent, 18 percent, and 13 percent (U.S. Census, 1940–1970). College enrollments continued to outpace population growth for most of the second half of the 20th century; by 2012 about 66 percent of high school graduates went on to higher education (U.S. Department of Labor, 2013). That growth was fueled by decades of increased public funding that was predicated on expectations that a college-educated labor force was essential to both economic prosperity and national security. The result is a higher education system that in 2016 is designed (in finances, faculty, support staff, and physical facilities) to support 20 million enrolled students each year.

The development of U.S. higher education also was driven by a model that connected investment in research and advanced graduate and professional programs with the achievement of national goals. Universities were viewed as having a central role in helping to solve critical social and economic challenges – ranging from the cold war to civil rights, from improved government services to improved business practices, and from the wars on poverty and drugs to the weapons to wage war in Korea, Vietnam, and even later, in Iraq. The underlying view was expressed in 1945 by Vannevar Bush, science advisor to President Truman, who called upon the federal government to recognize that the applied research needed to solve national problems would not be sustained without federal investment in basic research. The idea embedded in his case was that the U.S. would rely on federal support of universities to provide this capacity rather than investing primarily in government research laboratories.

The concept of the modern research university, energized and subsidized by federal funding of both basic and applied research, began with Vannevar Bush's report, entitled "Science: The Endless Frontier" (U.S. Office). From his report was born the National Science Foundation, and also the expectation that federal mission agencies (U.S. Department of Defense, Department of Energy, National Institutes of Health, National Aeronautical and Space Administration) had a major responsibility to support university research. Over succeeding decades, the boundaries between basic and applied research began to blur, and in some regards, vanish. The age of big, expensive science was launched.

Without question, the core argument driving the ramp-up of federal funding for research and development was national security (see chapter by Thorpe, this volume). In the "cold war" environment after World War II, national public leaders increasingly expected that, just as university scientists and engineers had been mobilized to help win the war, they should now be relied upon to help preserve the peace.

Universities invested in programs, research facilities, and infrastructure to attract the federal funding doled out to help address the challenges of cold war brinksmanship. Indeed, federal funding of research and development at U.S. universities continued to grow through the end of the 20th century, long after the fall of the Berlin Wall. In constant 2000 dollars, annual federal funding grew from $9 billion to $18 billion between 1970 and 1990, and almost doubled again to $32 billion by 2008, with much of this investment going to a concentrated group of research universities, which Clark Kerr called "federal grant universities" (Kerr, 1963:52–53).

A half century of public investment created a vast and diverse higher education sector in the U.S. In 2013, there were about 4,400 degree-granting higher education institutions, which annually enrolled nearly 20 million students and carried out $60 billion dollars of externally funded research and development, with most of the funding going to 200 major research universities (U.S. NCES). Higher education institutions offer a range of programs that affect communities at all levels, from neighborhoods to the nation. The prosperity and global economic leadership of the U.S. in the second half of the last century was due, above all else, to the long-term public investment in higher education.

It is also clear that the higher education industry was designed to be dependent upon continued public investment from both direct state funding of operations that kept student tuition and fees low, and federal funding of research and development. For the most part, the expanding public responsibilities and funding were accepted with enthusiasm by universities, which reshaped their policies, programs, facilities, and faculty to match them. For research universities, this entailed an entire institutional make-over that shifted the internal balance of priorities towards a greater investment in graduate and professional programs and large-scale research and development capacities. The shift was so dramatic that, in 1998, the national Boyer Commission argued that undergraduates were being neglected at many research universities (1998).

The 21st century transformation

In the 21st century, the higher education system in the U.S. and Western Europe, shaped over the previous half a century, has faced dramatic challenges arising from a new and more global transformation in the political economy of higher education. Across the Global North, the political priority of public investment in higher education has declined, even though the role of universities as assets for economic development has become better recognized than it was a half century ago. Within the U.S., funding from individual state governments - the primary source of governmental revenue for operating expenses – has been a declining fraction of the budgets of most public colleges and universities since the 1990s. These state governments are required to invest in formula-driven programs, such as elementary and secondary education and Medicaid (health insurance for the poor), leaving less available for higher education and other discretionary spending. At the same time, the global economic recession between 2008 and 2013 reduced government revenues, and state budget allocations to universities were cut along with other government obligations. The Center on Budget and Policy Priorities reports that state governments spent, on average, 28 percent less per student on higher education in 2013 than they did in 2008; over that same period, per student funding was cut by more than one-third by eleven states, and more than half by two states (Center for Budget and Policy Priorities, 2013). For some public universities, state funding now represents single-digit percentages of their total budgets; for example, in 2013, state support of the University of Virginia, one of the oldest and most distinguished public universities, was less than 7 percent of the total university budget.

For many of the 200 major U.S. research universities, reduced state funding has been accompanied by increased federal research and development funding. To a significant extent, state government dependency has been swapped for federal government dependency. However, the level of federal R&D funding has been relatively flat in the last decade (AAAS, 2016). A larger number of universities are competing more intensely for a relatively fixed amount of federal support; those that receive a greater share and ramp up to higher levels of research infrastructure then need to keep up the pursuit of federal dollars simply to sustain their previous level of operation.

In the competition for federal research and development funding, the traditional distinctions between public and private universities, which historically relate to university governance and direct state funding, have become irrelevant. In fact, major private research universities are increasingly dependent on federal funding. The university with the highest annual federal research expenditures and therefore the greatest dependence on public funding is Johns Hopkins, a private university, which had $1.9 billion in federal research funding in 2011 (NSF, 2013). More than half of the 40 universities with the highest federal research expenditures are private universities (NSF, 2013).

This blurring (and in some regards elimination) of public and private differences is an increasingly important feature of higher education globally. U.S. universities that have traditionally been classified as private are non-profit institutions that represent a diverse array of over 1,800 four-year colleges and universities. Indeed, the U.S. has more private than public four-year colleges and universities, and another 600 two-year private colleges. While many of these institutions are quite small, private higher education includes some of the largest, most prestigious, and richest universities in America, such as Harvard, Yale and Stanford. These have major private endowments, but there are no stockholders and no profit-takers, as such.

The same is not true for the new breed of for-profit universities that has proliferated in recent decades, largely as a result of the diffusion of online technologies. The University of Phoenix, which initially was focused on serving working adults, is now the largest for-profit, private university in the U.S., with 350,000 students, most studying online. Between 1998 and 2008, student enrollments at for-profit institutions tripled, reaching about 2.4 million students; three-quarters of those students are at institutions owned by publicly traded stock corporations and private equity firms (Lewin, 2012). As the market for new students in the United States slows and student loan access is exhausted, the University of Phoenix and other for-profit, online providers now market internationally and to students in Africa, Asia, and Latin America as well as North America and Europe. None of this transformation would have been possible, however, without the shift to student debt as an increasingly key form of funding for higher education institutions.

The entrepreneurial university and the political economy of student debt

In the U.S. and other nations of the Global North, the response of universities, particularly research universities, has focused on how to translate the turbulent, competitive, and threatening political economy of higher education into an environment of opportunity for universities that desire to become engines of innovation in a knowledge-based global economy. In this view, universities must become more self-reliant, self-directed, and self-conscious of their competitive identity and position in an increasingly global market for their services (Rich, 2013). Fulfilling these roles requires a new calculus for evaluating priorities and performance. As more institutions compete for research funding, programs are increasingly judged based on return on investment. Investments must be focused on supporting initiatives likely to produce high-impact innovations that confer a competitive advantage in the higher education marketplace and beyond.

The vision of the Entrepreneurial University is particularly appealing to universities that have experienced a significant disinvestment of public funds and have essentially been forced to adopt a more "private" orientation to their operational support. The connection of this shift with the rising levels of student debt is incontestable. In the U.S., as state funding of colleges and universities has declined, the cost of traditional higher education has continued to increase, driven by increased expenses for facilities, technology, administration, and salaries and wages. In response, public colleges and universities have increased tuition charges and fees and some issue debt to finance long-term goals. The average annual tuition at four-year public colleges and universities, adjusted for inflation, has grown by 27 percent ($1,850) between the onset of the economic recession in the 2007–2008 academic year and the 2012–2013 academic year, with two states increasing tuition by more than 70 percent and seven states increasing tuition by more than 50 percent (Center for Budget and Policy Priorities, 2013). The tuition and fees at private (non-profit colleges and universities), which already were much higher across the nation than at public institutions, have also increased. Over the decade ending in 2010–2011, undergraduate tuition and room and board, adjusted for inflation, increased by 42 percent at public colleges and universities and by 31 percent at private colleges and universities, with an average annual cost for the latter of over $36,000, more than twice as much as public institutions, $13,600 (NCES, 2013).

The entry of for-profit institutions has added complexity to the pricing structures, since tuition and fees of for-profit, online programs are lower than at public and private programs and the increase over the decade ending in 2010–2011 was only 5 percent. The incremental cost for additional students is often low once online programs are established. However, rather than representing a bargain for students, for-profit institutions have been quite the opposite. For-profit universities have a poor record of graduating the students they enroll. They attract a significant level of federal government higher education loans for students who never complete their degrees, accumulate high levels of debt, and rarely find a job that enables them to pay back their loans (U.S. Senate Committee, 2010). In fact, a new study shows that dropouts outnumber graduates by so much that on average, salaries actually decline after attendance at for-profit undergraduate programs (Cellini and Turner, 2016). A U.S. Senate report indicates that the University of Phoenix received $1.2 billion in federally funded student Pell grants in 2010–2011, but most of the students left the program without earning a degree, and a majority of the subset that does graduate earns certificates or associate's degrees, not four-year degrees (Miller, 2014). Further, among 30 for-profit providers, the study reports that "an average of 22.4 percent of revenue went to marketing and recruiting, 19.4 percent to profits and 17.7 percent to instruction"; the colleges had 32,496 student recruiters compared with 3,512 career-services staff to assist students in finding a job (Lewin, 2012:2; for other critical work on for-profit colleges see Mettler, 2014).

While precise estimates vary, the consensus is that total U.S student loan debt reached or exceeded $1 trillion in 2012, exceeding total U.S. credit card debt, and representing indebtedness of 37 million borrowers, including two-thirds of students who earn four-year bachelor's degrees, and representing one household in every five across the United States (Fry, 2012). Most of this debt, over $860 billion, is in outstanding federal government student loans, with the remainder in outstanding loans from private sources, such as banks, often packaged together and used as collateral in student loan asset-backed securities (SLABS). Recently, forgiveness programs in the United States are causing concerns to holders of securities backed by student debt as original loan maturity dates may no longer be honored (Shenn and Scully, 2015). The Pew Research Center reports that the average household student debt in 2012 was nearly $27,000 and 10 percent of households have student debts that exceed $60,000 (Fry, 2012:1). These circumstances document the increasing displacement of the earlier vision of a college-educated nation as a "public good" by a contrary vision that college education is primarily a "private good" with benefits received by individuals and to be paid by individuals who must repay accumulated loans from future earnings - presumably made possible by their higher education (Hebel, 2014, Best and Best, 2014).

The challenge posed by this shift in vision is daunting. As the cost of college attendance and the expectation of debt increase, enrollment demand will likely decline or shift from more expensive on-site four-year programs to less expensive online alternatives, or two-year community college programs with much lower tuition and fees. Indeed, the U.S. community college system has been a growing component of higher education for many years, featuring non-residential programs and two-year degrees, open admission, and comparatively low tuition rates. Further, demographic projections of the U.S. college-age population indicate that the total pool of high school graduates is expected to decline over the next decade (U.S. NES). Rates of college application will likely increase from low-income students (especially since increasing those rates is a national policy priority), but these students are often unable to pay the higher tuition rates and require financial aid or discounted rates in order to enroll and graduate. Not surprisingly, a 2012 survey of U.S. colleges and universities by Moody's financial services indicated that nearly half expected enrollment declines in full-time students, and a third expected tuition revenue to decline or to grow less than the rate of inflation (Martin, 2013).

Internationally, in the countries where loan programs are normal and there are frequent cases of graduates struggling with college debt, income share agreements are popular. Today, there are several countries that have income-based repayment programs, including Australia and the United Kingdom, which have almost universal income share agreement programs for students who borrow (Australian Government 2016, UK Government 2016). While these are two of the oldest and most mature income-based repayment systems, they are not without problems, and in both cases programs are getting more restrictive as the cost of education and total loan balances grow. In Australia, current projections indicate that about 20 percent of student loans will be unrecoverable, leading to worry that the country will return to a cap on total higher education enrollment (Norton 2014, Jump 2013). In the UK, many universities are charging the maximum allowed tuition and the loan portfolio is growing rapidly leading to concerns about future repayment (Paton 2014, Bolton 2015). Most recently, Japan is experiencing issues with repayment and the government is suing large number of borrowers for repayment for the first time (Japan Press Weekly, 2016, Kikuchi 2016).

Higher education and global economic development

The changing configuration of U.S. providers is just one facet of a truly global transformation in the topography of higher education. The drive of many nations in Asia and the Global South to develop higher education systems through massive public investment is a distinctive feature of the 21st century transformation. Ironically, these nations have invested in higher education as a public good – even at the expense of other priorities – at the same time that the U.S. and the other nations of the Global North have reduced public investment and embraced the idea of higher education as a private good.

The nations of the Global North and Global South seem unanimous, however, that the prosperity of nations within the knowledge-based global economy of the 21st century is dependent upon a more highly educated labor force and the capacity to generate new knowledge and translate that knowledge into commercial advantage. The underlying assumption is that universities (and university systems) are essential for sustaining economic development: generating new intellectual property that may lead to commercialization; strengthening the science and technology labor pool; incubating and jump-starting new businesses that attract investment and create jobs; mobilizing the knowledge assets of universities to address emerging challenges of a global political economy; and serving as a hub of 21st-century innovation and culture. Universities, especially research universities, also are essential to attract what Richard Florida calls the "creative class": those people with advanced skills and imagination who are critical to innovation and who tend to aggregate in locations that provide amenities associated with the environment surrounding universities (Florida, 2012). What differs, therefore, is the understanding of how to achieve these goals, and the role of government funding in that process, given existing levels of 'achievement' of these metrics.

Some nations in the Global South have responded to this vision with massive public investments in the development of a higher education capacity, a strategy reminiscent of the path taken in the U.S. and other industrialized nations a half century ago. China and India greatly surpass the U.S. in total university graduates per annum (although they lag in graduates per capita) and are investing aggressively in expanding the size, quality, and research capacity of their higher education sector (Cheng, 2010) (see chapter by Suttmeier, this volume). America ranks tenth among nations in the percentage of citizens aged 25–34 with postsecondary degrees (Christensen and Horn, 2011:1). China has launched a $250 billion-a-year investment in human capital, much of it directed to produce college graduates in numbers never seen before. "Just as the United States helped build a white-collar middle class in the 1940s and early 1950s by using the G.I. Bill to help educate millions of World War II veterans, the Chinese government is using large subsidies to educate tens of millions of young people as they move from the farms to the cities" (Bradsher, 2013). Other Global South nations are at risk of falling even further behind the educational divide due to lack of investment in higher education (Torres and Schugurensky, 2002).

The global change in post-secondary education is not only quantitative. While the vast majority of top-ranked universities are in the U.S., Western Europe and other developed regions, that dominance may be diminishing. India, China, South Korea and other nations are making immense investments in developing major research universities. Indeed, in the short term, the U.S. is helping that process. Since the 1960s, U.S. and European universities have been training international graduate students to be researchers and university faculty members. In the past, that process resulted in a "brain drain" from other nations; now the process is quite different. Indeed, the global competition for advanced knowledge and degrees, especially in science and engineering, is more acute than ever before and will likely intensify as nations restrict the drain of their "brain power" to other parts of the globe (Saxenian, 2005). In this competition, the U.S. and Europe retain an advantage because of their concentration of major research universities and the established institutional partnerships and infrastructure to support advanced research across a broad range of fields. Yet, this advantage may be temporary, especially since public investment in higher education and research and development is lagging in the U.S. and Europe and growing dramatically in other nations. Over the next few decades, the global restructuring of the higher education industry promises to be as wrenching as those experienced in the U.S. automobile and steel industries in the second half of the 20th century.

Despite general increases in the percentage of students participating in higher education into the 21st century, there are still sizable differences in tertiary educational attainment rates across the world (The World Bank, 2016). While enrollment rates from domestic students may be expected to decline in U.S. and Global North universities, there remains a steady flow of students from the Global South to the Global North either through online programs or onsite matriculation. The Institute for International Education reports that in the 2011–12 academic year more than three-quarters of a million international students were enrolled at U.S. colleges and universities, marking the sixth consecutive year of enrollment increases, with the largest numbers from China and India (Abrams, 2012).

One attribute that may eventually make Global North educations less desirable is that many countries now ask for contributions from students for universities that used to be almost completely subsidized (Berman et al., 2007). As costs rise for individuals, student loan programs follow. Countries that traditionally financed very high levels of tertiary education have adopted student loan systems, including Canada, Denmark, France, Germany, Ireland, Japan, the Netherlands (begun in Fall 2015), New Zealand, Norway, Sweden and the UK. With the exception of Norway and Sweden, both of which have relatively small inbound and outbound educational programs, these Global North countries (along with massive hosts Australia, the UK, and the US) host many more international students than they send abroad (UNESCO, 2016a).

For now, according to data from the United Nations Educational, Scientific and Cultural Organization, about 90 percent of all tertiary students studying outside of their home country are educated in the Global North, as defined by the United Nations (UNDP, 2016, UNESCO, 2016b). Among students that study internationally outside of their home continent, about 94 percent are educated in Europe, North America, Australia, and New Zealand. Overall, students in the Global North are almost certain to remain in other Global North countries for international educational experiences, while students from the Global South also show a strong preference for Global North educations.

Instead of improving the diversity of student bodies across the globe, increasing international education is contributing to a centralization of the best students in the Global North. The education advantage that Global North countries already enjoy will not disappear until universities in the Global South are considered international destinations, attractive not only to a nation's best students, but also to those from other countries – though it is unclear how or when this could happen. In the meantime, high-performing students from around the world will migrate to the Global North to study, and some will stay long after school ends, leading to an even higher concentration of highly educated people in the countries with the most advanced education systems.

The developing world is making commendable progress increasing access to higher education, but the gap in the overall percentage of population with access to higher education is increasing because of larger gains in the Global North (Barro and Lee, 2013). While many Global South countries attempt to increase their educated populations and generally do so with heavy public subsidies largely avoiding massive student debt problems, international mobility of the best students and faculty members presents a problem for economies attempting to catch up to established premier higher education systems (Altbach, 2013).

The path ahead

The transformation of the political economy of higher education will intensify in the decades ahead. The global marketplace for higher education will likely grow significantly, driven by the requirements for both individual and collective prosperity in an increasingly knowledge-based economy and facilitated by global access to online resources and technologies. The concentration of higher education opportunities will not replicate earlier patterns. While the size of the traditional U.S. and European college-bound pool of students is flattening (and in places declining), the number of college-bound students in Africa, Asia, and South America will continue to grow as their governments increase investments in the human capital needed for the 21st-century economy. Beyond the traditional college-age population, the demand for advanced graduate degrees and certifications by those in mid-career also will increase to keep pace with the growing knowledge demands of careers in all sectors. A key challenge for these expanding national systems is to match the growth in scale with an equivalent growth in the quality of education, research, and scholarship. It is difficult to see how this improvement in quality can have significant effect unless it is broad-based, not just limited to the most globally competitive and attractive institutions that will necessarily only serve a tiny percentage of students.

Under virtually any future scenario, competition will grow as additional providers, including online, for-profit, and blended (on-site and online) programs enter the global marketplace. The sorting out process among delivery systems both within and across nations will continue for decades. One may anticipate the market entry of multinational online universities that provide global access to top flight faculty from many nations as well as a vast array of program options, far beyond what any single institution now delivers on site or online. In this environment, the scramble for resources and students will almost surely intensify.

Because we are still at the early stages of experience with online programs, we can only speculate on their long-term impacts. More online higher education programs are added each year, including programs from traditional providers as well as from for-profit suppliers. In some fields, online programs provided by major universities may displace weaker local programs. Massive Open Online Courses (MOOCs) have the potential to provide students around the globe with free access to a scope and quality of advanced instruction that could be truly revolutionary. It is clear that these applications of new technologies not only could greatly enhance higher education capacities, but also make possible a level of customized learning that would otherwise be unavailable or prohibitively expensive. But significant questions remain about how, or the extent to which, these kinds of courses can be integrated into degree-awarding schemes as well as about how they will be funded.

In Global North countries, the general progression from public financing to loan programs to concern about high debt levels to forgiveness programs suggests that the structure of higher education is very much evolving. While working to catch up in per capita tertiary education, Global South nations would be wise to watch the fallout of these current transitions.

There is no reason to assume that universities that have been the academic leaders of the past inevitably will remain global centers of knowledge and imagination for the next century. Indeed, at least some of the new universities developing in great numbers in nations in Africa, Asia, and South America have the opportunity to produce faculty and organize them as communities of scholars in ways that are much less encumbered by the inertia of entrenched academic structures, and can be much more responsive to societal needs and to the emerging competitive demands of the global marketplace of higher education. Yet the truly successful universities in the 21st century almost surely will be partnerships among institutions in many nations, including traditional and new institutions, and they will be notable as innovators who are engaged in addressing the cardinal challenges of our times on a truly global scale.

References

Abrams, T. (2012, November 15). "China and India top list of international students attending U.S. colleges". *The New York Times*. Retrieved from http://india.blogs.nytimes.com/2012/11/15/chinese-enrollment-soars-as-more-international-students-attend-u-s-colleges/?_r=0.

Altbach, Philip G. (2013). "Globalization and forces for change in higher education". In: *The International Imperative in Higher Education*. Boston: Sense Publishers, pp. 7–10.

American Association for the Advancement of Science (AAAS). (2013). "R&D budget and policy program". Retrieved from www.aaas.org/spp/rd/guihist.shtml.

American Association for the Advancement of Science (AAAS). (2016). "Historical Trends in Federal R&D". Retrieved from www.aaas.org/page/historical-trends-federal-rd.

Association of Public and Land-grant Universities. (2013). "About APLU". Retrieved from www.aplu.org/page.aspx?pid=203.

Australian Government. (2016). "StudyAssist". Retrieved from http://studyassist.gov.au/sites/StudyAssist.

Barro, Robert J. and Jong Wha Lee. (2013). "A new data set of education attainment in the world, 1950–2010". *Journal of Development Economics* 104(2013): 184–198.

Bennett, M.J. (1996). *When dreams came true: the GI Bill and the making of modern America*. McLean, VA: Brassey's, Inc.

Berman, Edward H., Simon Marginson, Rosemary Preston, and Robert F. Arnove. (2007). "The political economy of educational reform in Australia, England, and the United States". In: Arnove, Robert F. and Carlos Alberto Torres. Eds. *Comparative education: the dialectic of the global and the local*. Third edition. New York: Rowman & Littlefield, pp. 217–256.

Best, Joel and Eric Best. (2014). *The student loan mess: how good intentions created a trillion-dollar problem*. Berkeley: University of California Press.

Bolton, Paul. (2015, October 5). "Student loan statistics". House of Commons Library Briefing Paper. Number 1079.

Boyer Commission. (1998). "Reinventing undergraduate education: a blueprint for America's research universities". New York: Carnegie Foundation for the Advancement of Teaching.

Bradsher, K. (2013, January 16). "Next made-in-China boom: college graduates". *The New York Times*. Retrieved from www.nytimes.com/2013/01/17/business/chinas-ambitious-goal-for-boom-in-college-graduates.html?pagewanted=all&_r=0.

Cellini, Stephanie Riegg and Nicholas Turner. (2016). "Gainfully Employed? Assessing the employment and earnings of for-profit college students using administrative data". National Bureau of Economic Research. Working paper 22287. Retrieved from www.nber.org/papers/w22287.pdf.

Center for Budget and Policy Priorities. (2013). "Recent deep state higher education cuts may harm students and the economy for years to come". Retrieved from www.cbpp.org/cms/?fa=view&id=3927.

Cheng, Kai-ming. (2010). "China: turning the bad master into a good servant, follow-up 2010". In: Rotberg, Iris C. Ed. *Balancing change and tradition in global education reform*. 2nd Edition. New York: Rowman & Littlefield Education, pp. 3–20.

Christensen, C. and M. Horn. (2011). "Colleges in crisis: disruptive change comes to American higher education". *Harvard Magazine*. 7(21), 1–4.

Florida, R. (2012). *The rise of the creative class.* 2nd edition. New York: Basic Books.

Friedman, T. L. (2005). *The world is flat: A brief history of the twenty-first century.* New York: Farrar, Strauss and Giroux.

Fry, R. (2012). "A record one-in-five households now own student loan debt". Pew Research Center. Retrieved from www.pewsocialtrends.org/2012/09/26/a-record-one-in-five-households-now-owe-student-loan-debt/.

Hazen, Helen D. and Heike C. Alberts. (2006). "Visitors or immigrants? International students in the United States". *Population, Space, and Place.* 12, 201–216.

Hebel, Sara. (2014, March 2). "From public good to private good: How higher education got to a tipping point". *Chronicle of Higher Education.* Retrieved from http://chronicle.com/article/From-Public-Good-to-Private/145061.

Japan Press Weekly. (2016, February 17–23). "Young people in Japan are struggling with repayment of so-called 'scholarship' loans". Social Issues.

Jump, Paul. (2013, March 7). "Australia's academy faces day of reckoning over student loans". *Times Higher Education.* Retrieved from www.timeshighereducation.com/news/australias-academy-faces-day-of-reckoning-over-student-loans/2002256.article.

Kerr, C. (1963). *The uses of the university.* Cambridge, MA: Harvard University Press.

Kikuchi, Daisuke. (2016, January 28). "Japan's student loans system seen falling short, but change underway". *The Japan Times.* Retrieved from www.japantimes.co.jp/news/2016/01/28/national/japans-student-loans-system-seen-falling-short-change-underway/#.V1rmMfkrK5O.

Lewin, T. (2012, July 29). "Senate committee report on for-profit colleges condemns costs and practices". *The New York Times.* Retrieved from www.nytimes.com/2012/07/30/education/harkin-report-condemns-for-profit-colleges.

Martin, A. (2013, January 10). "Downturn still squeezes colleges and universities". *The New York Times.* Retrieved from www.nytimes.com/2013/01/11/business/colleges-expect-lower-enrollment.html.

Mettler, Suzanne. (2014). *Degrees of inequality: How the politics of higher education sabotaged the American dream.* New York, NY: Basic Books.

Miller, Ben. (2014, October 9). "The college graduation rate flaw that no one's talking about". New America Foundation EdCentral. Retrieved from www.edcentral.org/graduation-rate-flaw/.

National Academies of Science, Engineering and Medicine. (2005). "Rising above the gathering storm: Energizing and employing America for a brighter future", Washington, D.C.: The National Academies Press.

National Conference of State Legislatures. (2013). "For-profit colleges and universities". Retrieved from www.ncsl.org/issues-research/educ/for-profit-colleges-and-universities.aspx.

National Science Foundation (NSF). (2013). "Universities report highest ever R&D spending of $65 billion in 2011". Retrieved from www.nsf.gov/statistics/infbrief/nsf13305/.

Newfield, C. (2008). *Unmaking the public university: The forty-year assault on the middle class.* Cambridge, MA: Harvard University Press.

Norton, Andrew. (2014). "Doubtful debt: The rising cost of student loans". Grattan Institute Report. Published April 2014.

Onkst, David H. (1998). "'First a negro… incidentally a veteran': Black World War Two veterans and the G.I. Bill of Rights in the Deep South, 1944–1948". *Journal of Social History,* 31(3), 517–543.

Paton, Graeme. (2014, August 22). "More students charged maximum £9,000 tuition fees". *The Telegraph.*

Population Reference Bureau (PRB). (2015). "2015 World Population Data Sheet". Population Reference Bureau and United States Agency for International Development. Retrieved from www.prb.org/pdf15/2015-world-population-data-sheet_eng.pdf.

Rhodes, F. H. T. (2001). *The Creation of the future: The role of the American university.* Ithaca, N.Y.: Cornell University Press.

Rich, D. (2013). "Public affairs programs and the changing political economy of higher education". *Journal of Public Affairs Education,* 19(2), 263–283.

Saxenian, AnnaLee. (2005). "From brain drain to brain circulation: Transnational communities and regional upgrading in India and China". *Studies in Comparative International Development,* 40(2), 35–61

Shenn, Jody and Matt Scully. (2015, July 15). "$40 billion worth of AAA student loans are at risk of becoming junk". Bloomberg. Retrieved from www.bloomberg.com/news/articles/2015-07-15/america-s-student-loan-crisis-risks-turning-aaa-debt-into-junk.

Thelin, J. R. (2004). *A History of American Higher Education.* Baltimore, MD: Johns Hopkins University Press.

Thorp, H. and Goldstein, B. (2010). *Engines of innovation: The Entrepreneurial University in the twenty-first century*. Chapel Hill, NC: University of North Carolina Press.

Torres, Carlos Alberto and Daniel Schugurensky. (2002). "The political economy of higher education in the era of neoliberal globalization: Latin America in comparative perspective". *Higher Education*, 43(4), 429–455.

United Kingdom Government (UK). (2016). "Student finance". Retrieved from: www.gov.uk/student-finance/overview.

United Nations Development Programme (UNDP). (2016). "South-South cooperation". UNDP Special Unit for South-South Cooperation. Retrieved from http://ssc.undp.org/content/dam/ssc/documents/exhibition_triangular/SSCExPoster1.pdf.

United Nations Educational, Scientific and Cultural Organization (UNESCO). (2016a). "Global flow of tertiary-level students". UNESCO Institute for Statistics. Retrieved from www.uis.unesco.org/Education/Pages/international-student-flow-viz.aspx.

United Nations Educational, Scientific and Cultural Organization (UNESCO). (2016b). "Education: Inbound internationally mobile students by continent of origin". UNESCO Data Centre. Retrieved from http://data.uis.unesco.org/index.aspx?queryid=169.

United States Census Bureau. (1940–1970). "Decennial Censuses, 1940–2010". Retrieved from www.census.gov/prod/www/decennial.html.

United States Department of Labor. (2013). "College enrollment and work activity of 2012 high school graduates". Retrieved from www.bls.gov/news.release/hsgec.nr0.htm.

United States Department of Veterans Affairs. (2013). "The G.I. Bill's history". Retrieved from www.gibill.va.gov/benefits/history_timeline/index.html.

United States National Center for Education Statistics (NCES). (2011). "Statistical abstract of the United States: 2011". Retrieved from www.census.gov/compendia/statab/.

United States National Center for Education Statistics (NCES). (2013). "Tuition costs of colleges and universities". Retrieved from http://nces.ed.gov/fastfacts/display.asp?id=76.

United States Office of Scientific Research and Development. (1945). "Science, the endless frontier: a report to the President by Vannevar Bush". Washington, D.C.: U.S. Government Printing Office.

United States Senate Committee on Health, Education, Labor and Pensions. (2010). "The return on the federal investment in for-profit education: debt without diploma". Washington D.C.

The World Bank. (2016). "Gross enrolment ratio, tertiary, both sexes (%)". World Bank IBRD IDA Data Center. Retrieved from http://data.worldbank.org/indicator/SE.TER.ENRR.

11

CHANGES IN CHINESE HIGHER EDUCATION IN THE ERA OF GLOBALIZATION

Honggang Xu and Tian Ye

1 Introduction

The domination of free-market economies, predominance of supranational institutions, and the formation of a consumer culture across the globe, in addition to rising costs of public services in general and the evolution of the knowledge-based economy, have all contributed to dramatic changes in the character and function of higher education (HE) around the world (Ohmae 1990; Waters 2001; Sklair 1999; Burbules and Torres 2000; Mok and Welch 2003). Higher education systems in many countries have recently been going through significant restructuring processes to enhance their competitiveness and hierarchical positioning within their own countries and in the global education market, with governments attempting to transform their higher education systems to reflect an image of "world-class" universities (Deema *et al.* 2008).

In this competitive context, higher education is increasingly tied to national economic prowess, resulting in increased privatization, strategic interactions between higher education and industry, and more managerial forms of governance (Marginson 2013a). Education as a tradable service commodity is clearly stated in the WTO's general agreement (Shields 2013). The emphasis on incorporation, privatization, accountability and limited government intervention has led to a significant shift away from the social democratic values that previously governed higher education (Rizvi and Lingard 2009). Meanwhile, with increased global mobility, the number of potential students aiming for higher education has expanded from local and national markets to international ones. This global expansion of access to higher education has increased the demand for academic quality and has led to the development of university ranking systems or league tables in many countries (Dill and Soo 2005) as well as internationally.

Since bringing in "open door" economic policies in the late 1970s, China has been participating in the globalization process of higher education (see also chapters by Suttmeier; Delvenne and Kreimer; Tyfield, this volume), and a series of education reforms has been conducted in order to provide increased human capital and increase competitiveness in the global higher education market. Two substantial changes have been observed: growth in the numbers of higher education institutions; and the emergence of more world-class research-oriented universities. As a result of this, China has turned into one of the world's biggest providers of higher education, and more and more Chinese research universities are entering the ranks of the world's top universities. However, due to China's special political, economic and social environment, this reform of higher education presents a striking contrast with many Western countries, since Chinese higher education institutions (HEIs) are still under the strong control of the central state. In contrast to Western countries, active participation in global competition by HEIs is a top-down process; in addition, individual institutions face significant marketization pressure. This paper aims to explore the restructuring process of Chinese higher education in this era of globalization, as well as its implications.

2 A short history of modern Chinese higher education

2.1 The planning system

The classical Chinese education was based on Confucian ideas in the form "Sishu", which was focused on moral teaching, history and writing, while mathematics and science were barely taught. After the First Opium War (1839–1842), China's doors began to open to the rest of the world. Chinese scholars discovered the numerous Western advances in science and technology and started to copy education programs from the Western world (Zhu 1997). By the end of the century this culminated in the establishment of a handful of prominent universities, such as Peiyang University in Tianjin (now Tianjin University) in 1895, Nanyang Public College in Shanghai (now Shanghai Jiaotong University) in 1897, and Imperial University (now Peking University) in 1898. Over time, these universities turned into the leading educational institutions in the country, and by 1949 205 universities had been founded.[1]

In the early 1950s, after the establishment of the People's Republic of China, Soviet influence caused all higher education to be brought under the planning system. The government controlled the number of higher education institutions, their extent, programs, jobs for graduates and funding. Specialized higher education institutions were established and promoted. There was a total of about 60 government ministries, each operating its own higher education institutions. For instance, the Ministry of Agriculture would establish special agricultural universities in different regions inside China, and each agricultural university would supply human resources for the agriculture sector for each particular region. These universities were focused on teaching, and only a few universities, like Peking University and Fudan University, were comprehensive universities, although even here only limited research was carried out. Research was mainly carried out by the Institute of Chinese Academy, set up in the 1950s, a separate system from higher education.

From 1967 to 1976, Chinese higher education was devastated by the Cultural Revolution more than any other significant sector of the economy. All the institutions were closed during the early stages, and later only enrolled certain students selected by the workers' unions. The number of postsecondary students dropped from 674,400 to 47,800 (below 1 percent of 18–21 year-olds). During this period, many teachers and intellectuals also suffered violence from the workers' unions and were forced to quit. Take one medical college of the Ministry of Public Health, for example: over 500 of the total of 674 professors and associated professors were framed and persecuted.[2] Higher education was restricted for political purposes, and the decline in educational quality was profound (Liu 2009).

2.2 Higher education in transition

With the implementation of the "open-door policy" in the 1970s, Premier Deng Xiaoping proclaimed a reorientation of higher education to meet the needs of modernization. He first revived the National Higher Education Entrance Examination (*gaokao*) in 1977, a national test still taken across the country on the same day by high school graduates and the sole basis for admission to universities. The "Decision on Reform of the Education System", launched in 1985 by the Chinese Communist Party, was seen as a milestone of the reform era through its emphasis on the importance of higher education in China's independent scientific and technological development, and in the solving of major theoretical and practical problems in the process of modernization. Teaching and research were then both emphasized in universities (Liu 2009). In 1992, another key policy, "Points Regarding How to Expedite Reforms and Vigorously Develop General Higher Education", was issued by the State Education Commission, which indicated that higher education institutions should be "autonomous entities", and private and enterprise-run educational institutions were permitted to be built. The "Outline for Education Reform and Development in China", issued in 1993, encouraged competition between universities and further accelerated the process of decentralization, marketization, diversification of management, and financing of higher education.

As the reforms picked up pace, Chinese higher education developed rapidly. In 2014, the number of Chinese National Higher Institutions reached 2,824, including 2,529 National General colleges and universities and 295 adult higher institutions, and the number of college students, including undergraduate, master's and PhD students, rose to 34.89 million in 2014.[3] More than 377,000 foreign students from 203 countries or regions enrolled in over 775 Chinese universities and other institutions in 2014.[4] In addition, the number of Chinese students overseas increased to 459,800 in the same year.[5]

Although the reform indicated that higher education should respond to the demand for human resources in Chinese national development, a centralized and hierarchical educational system resulted, as shown in Figure 11.1, where the Ministry of Education controlled all higher education institutions through policy-making, legislation, planning, funding, and evaluation. According to the ownership-based categories of HEIs in China, higher education can be divided into state-owned and non-state-owned entities. State-owned HEIs include Regular HEIs, independent institutions, higher vocational colleges and adult HEIs (Minban Colleges) (Zhu and Lou 2011). These institutions can also be divided into several types including "multiversities" (e.g., Peking University, a familiar "university" across all disciplines), science and technology universities, normal colleges (i.e. higher education for those going into teaching), financial universities, art colleges and so on. According to the particular missions involved, the Chinese higher education system can be divided into four levels: research-based universities, whose main mission is to do scientific research and cultivate high-level scientific manpower (i.e., postgraduate education); teaching and research-based universities, which pay the same attention to cultivating talent as to doing scientific research; teaching-based colleges, focusing on undergraduate education; and vocational-technical colleges, which mainly train technicians and workers (Han and Guo 2015).

In this system, all universities are placed in a steep hierarchy, which developed gradually through the national programs. In 1999, the 985 Project, which was intended to develop a number of Chinese universities into world-class universities, was launched. Universities selected for this project could obtain substantial support, including financial support, from the Education Ministry, and were given more autonomy in their management. Thirty-nine universities were selected for this project. These universities are now considered the top universities. In 1995, the 211 Project, which attempted to build around 100 quality universities, was launched. Up to now there have been 112 universities selected for this project. These universities are also given priority in terms of financial and other resources. Although the 985 Project universities are included in the 211 Project lists, they can still get access to additional resources and are given priority. All of the 985 and 211 Project universities are public. As well as being differentiated according to their 985 or 211 Project categorization, universities are

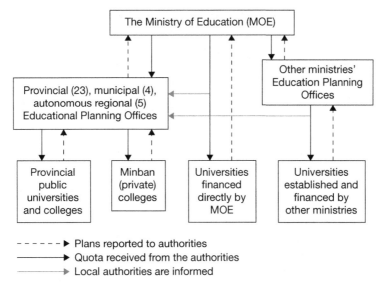

Figure 11.1 The planning system for Chinese higher education recruitment
Source: Huang (2005)

also designated as first-level, second-level, or third-level universities for student recruitment, reflecting the order of their prioritization. This difference in recruiting students also reinforces the concepts of the hierarchical university system. Almost all first- and second-level universities are public universities.

Different from private universities in the Western world, China's private education institutions are in the initial stage of development and are intended to complement public universities in order to meet the needs of those who fail their college entrance examinations or who cannot afford the fees to study abroad. Few private universities and colleges can gain as much prestige as public institutions. Most of them lack financial support, and their degrees are not acknowledged in some local government bureaucratic systems. In addition to the institutional barriers, the culture that "academic knowledge is more elegant than technology" also inhibits young people and their families from selecting private education institutions, which tend to focus on vocational and operational training. Only when they cannot succeed in gaining admittance to public institutes do Chinese students choose private institutes, which also have higher tuition fees (Han and Guo 2015). Overall, the private HEIs exist in an awkward position.

3 Chinese higher education in the globalization process

3.1 Pressure for world-class universities

Since the late 1990s, China has been more and more involved in global competition in many aspects. Global competition is used as a policy instrument, and being "world-class" with regard to universities has become a signifier of national productivity, power and prestige (Hazelkorn 2008). The development of world-class universities and disciplines is now of great importance to the Chinese government. Chinese President Jiang Zemin declared that "China must have a number of first-rate universities of international advanced level".[6] The Academic Ranking of

World Universities (ARWU, also called the Shanghai Jiaotong ranking) was instituted in China in 2003 by the Center for World-Class Universities and Institute of Higher Education of the Shanghai Jiao Tong University. The ARWU was initially created to benchmark Chinese universities against others worldwide (Amsler and Bolsmann 2012). Such a ranking mechanism is both a result and a driver of further competition in the global higher education market (Portnoi and Bagley 2011), driven by the promise that highly ranked institutions could enjoy benefits such as increased funding and student enrollment (Amsler and Bolsmann 2012).

Entering the 21st century, Chinese research universities tended to be keener on joining the ranks of world-class universities than when the 985 and 211 Projects were initially started. To participate actively in this global competition and to restructure the higher education system, a series of reform measures was conducted in China. In 2010, a National "Outline for Medium- and Long-term Education Reform and Development (2010–20)" statement was issued to shape the country's education system for the next ten years, which put great emphasis on the improvement of higher education competitiveness. It stressed that "The international status, influence and competitiveness of our country's education should be promoted. We must cultivate a large number of talents with international vision, familiar with international rules, able to participate in international affairs and competitions."

With the aim of transforming the university system into an image of "world-class" higher education, in 2015 the State Council of China formally issued "The Overall Plan to Promote the Development of World-Class Universities and Disciplines". This was aimed at developing a number of world-class universities and leading disciplines to make China a powerful country in higher education by 2050. Great importance is therefore attached to HEIs' performance evaluations and the reform of education management systems in building a competitive framework for HEIs.

In the world academic university rankings published by Shanghai Jiaotong University in 2015, there are four Chinese universities in the top 150: Peking University, Shanghai Jiaotong University, Tsinghua University and Zhejiang University.[7] Recently, in 2016, U.S. News released the "Best Global Universities Rankings", in which Peking University, Tsinghua University, Fudan University and Shanghai Jiaotong University ranked 25th, 41st, 59th and 96th, respectively.[8] The QS World University Discipline Ranking (evaluated by research publications and graduates' employment competitiveness) in 2016 showed that five disciplines in China have entered the world top ten. In particular, Tsinghua University ranked first in the world in engineering. However, it is still noted that compared to some powerful higher education nations like the U.S., there is still a big gap.[9]

3.2 The increasing importance of research

With the intention of performing well in global university competitions, universities in many nations adopt different measures to enhance their competitiveness. Knowledge and knowledge production have been seen as a kind of national competitiveness, leading both governments and HEIs to place increased emphasis on building research capacity for human capital development and national economic advancement (Rizvi and Lingard 2009). The primacy of research is grounded in day-to-day practices for the research universities, supplying the material know-how and symbolic capital that help keep them at the "cutting edge" (Bagley and Portnoi 2014).

This emphasis on research has intensified in the 21st century, when international position-seeking has become more systematic with the appearance of a number of ranking systems. Rankings are often based on visible and measurable variables such as publications, grants, applications for doctoral studies, etc., which are often related to the output of researchers and programs (Amsler and Bolsmann 2012). Higher education institutions participating in the global market have to give a high priority to international rankings nowadays, as these have the capacity to enhance their reputation and increase their competitiveness in student enrollment, research funding and academic staff recruitment. Indicators of educational attainment in terms of citations and publication of papers feed directly into annual performance indicators for universities and their faculties in an ongoing process that goes substantially beyond the tenure-for-life system.

Since developing world-class universities has been regarded as a national priority, Chinese higher education institutions are now subject to extraordinary pressures to upgrade themselves in terms of quantitative evaluations and rankings, and research capacity is gaining more importance in performance evaluations. To some extent, the emphasis on research in Chinese universities may be more intense than their international partners, and this is supported by examining the ARWU. The emphasis of the ARWU is on institutional reputation and research performance as measured in a quantifiable way rather than on localized student needs (Marginson 2007). Scores are calculated through "objective indicators", which include the numbers of Nobel Prize and Fields Medal winners, Thomson Reuters highly cited researchers, articles published in *Nature and Science*, articles indexed in the Science and Social Sciences citation indices, and performance in relation to the size of the institution (Amsler and Bolsmann 2012). The ARWU relies on Thomson Reuters for much of its data, but does not include teaching, learning and subjective experiences (Marginson 2007). It is very clear that these indicators are very selective and favorable to those universities which have strong science and technology programs and have the capacity to publish in English-language publications.

Rather than competing for international students in the global market, Chinese universities actually place top priority on gaining research funding from the government, which is substantial, especially in fields of key importance to national-level development priorities as defined by the government. In other words, their participation in global competition is more a result of the national top-down process than from pressure for marketization, as HEI research capacity has been given great importance by the state to build world-class universities and disciplines. Special funds are to be provided by central government, and their allocation will be more performance-oriented, as indicated in the "Overall Plan to Promote the Development of World-Class Universities and Disciplines". However, due to the hierarchical system of Chinese higher education, state-owned HEIs, particularly the elite universities, have more resources and always maintain an advantageous position in these processes. This has led to the increasing gap between different institutions, and consequently resources and opportunities for students, which will be discussed in the following section.

3.3 The increasing gap between different institutions

Participating in the global education market and emphasizing research has led to an increasing gap between different institutions in several aspects, such as funding, faculties' priorities, and the structure of academic programs. In the Chinese public higher education system, the number of first-level colleges and universities accounts for about 6 percent of all regular HEIs, and these HEIs have 32 percent of the country's undergraduate students, 69 percent of master's students, and 84 percent of doctoral students, sharing 72 percent of the country's scientific research funds and 54 percent of the instruments and equipment, and covering 96 percent of the country's state key laboratories and 85 percent of the nation's key disciplines (Fei 2007).

The majority of Chinese universities are state-owned, and financial support from the government, in most cases, decides each university's development, varying dramatically among different universities. There are special funds limited to the 112 affiliated universities of Project 211 approved by the Ministry of Education, while the rest, totaling approximately 2,000 local colleges and universities, are excluded from this system (Fei 2007). According to the data from the PRC Ministry of Education for 2009 to 2013, the total government research funding for 39 Project 985 institutions was 13.9 billion RMB, with 73 Project 211 institutions at approximately 5.1 billion RMB, and the rest, 670 regular undergraduate colleges, at only 7.9 billion RMB. Among the Project 985 universities, Peking University and Tsinghua University got the highest funding, at 1.8 billion RMB in the first phase, while Chinese Ocean University only received 300 million RMB, one-sixth of the other two (Liu 2015). In 2013, Tsinghua University had a total budget of 3.031 billion RMB for scientific research, with government funding comprising 2.775 billion of that, accounting for about 91.5 percent. By contrast, China Southwest Petroleum University obtained 460 million RMB, which was the highest among regular universities (i.e., non-Project 211), including 120 million RMB of government funding, which accounted for 26.1 percent (Liu, 2015). This means that Tsinghua University received 23 times the funding that China Southwest Petroleum University did. This unbalanced distribution in funding deepens the gap between Project 211 universities and regular public universities, as well as the gaps between Project 211 universities themselves. Institutes at higher levels do not have to be anxious about funding because they can obtain generous funds from the government and also produce revenues through their own endeavors, while institutes at lower levels usually fall into the dilemma of having insufficient funds, which hinders their development (Han and Guo 2015). As for private universities, funding for them depends largely on students' tuition fees, which often leaves them short of money, making their development even more difficult.

Administered by the Ministry of Education, the colleges and universities of Project 211 and Project 985 form an elite that is favored in the selection of students via the college entrance examinations (the *gaokao*), and effectively gain a monopoly on the enrollment of top students. When students are enrolled in higher-ranked universities, they also enjoy stronger national financial support, preferential government policies and more abundant school resources, and are thus able to access better living conditions, more advanced scientific instruments, more comfortable working environments, and more exchange opportunities for international learning, which in turn helps in attracting excellent teachers and better-known professors. With these great advantages, elite universities usually have higher research performance and attract brighter students, and therefore accumulate prestige which is further leveraged to raise public and private monies to hire highly paid faculty and sustain their research programs.

In this process, universities and students develop into a closed circle of a mutually beneficial community. Universities as producers compete for "preferred customers", i.e., students with the highest entry scores; and students, as the customers, compete for entry to preferred institutions (Amsler and Bolsmann 2012). The bigger the distance between elite universities and the others, the more society values those elite universities, which is the logic of a winner-take-all market (Frank 2001). In other words, the prestige of universities at higher levels sustains high student scores, contributing to better graduation outcomes and the maintenance of good reputations, which in turn strengthens their dominant positions and leads to a reinforcement of the hierarchy (Amsler and Bolsmann 2012). This reinforcing effect is further exaggerated in the Chinese social system, wherein the social mobility of university graduates remains inflexible, a situation which will be discussed in the following section. The outcome of this process is a steep pyramidal system that generates intense pressure among both career academics and prospective students in order to support the international rankings of a handful of elite universities.

3.4 Social mobility of graduates

The role of education in promoting social mobility is among the central issues in contemporary sociological and political debates (Iannelli and Paterson 2005). In modern societies, education has become an increasingly important factor in determining which jobs people enter and in determining their social class, and has been considered to be the easiest and most popular avenue for upward mobility (Mulligan 1952). A nation's colleges and universities are expected to promote the goal of social mobility in order to make it possible for anyone with ability and motivation to succeed (Zhang and Hao 2006). However, the situation in China has become far more complex, as social mobility in general has slowed down (Mok and Wu 2016). People from wealthier families and the upper classes have more opportunities to receive a quality higher education, causing social class solidification to be strengthened to a high degree (Liu and Liu 2013). Indeed, higher education in China is increasingly a vehicle of entrenched social privilege rather than of social mobility and meritocracy. Thus, the ranking system has begun to show profound impacts on students' mobility. Students who are in 211 Project universities get more chances to be enrolled in graduate programs and to obtain scholarships to study abroad. Employers think more highly of students from Project 211 universities than they do of those from provincial colleges. Some job advisements clearly indicate that they only consider those who have graduated from Project 985 universities. Meanwhile, according to the investigation on university graduate employment (Report on college graduates' employment investigation, 2015),[10] graduates from Project 211 universities (including Project 985) get the highest average starting salary (5,571 RMB), while graduates from Regular HEIs earn 3,944 RMB, and the starting salary of those from Higher Vocational Colleges (2,597 RMB) and Minban colleges and independent institutions (2,993 RMB) is much lower. These barriers for social mobility from the university system create great pressure on Chinese families to be engaged in strenuous competition in their children's education from the time they are very young.

Faced with such a situation, getting admission to a high-level university is seen by most families as access to a better employment in the future for their children, leading to both students and parents working hard for the *gaokao*. As a result, families have to find extra resources to enable their children to be enrolled in good kindergartens, premier schools and high schools. That is to say, higher-income parents can make enormous efforts toward ensuring their children's academic success, while children of poorer parents begin the "college education game" later and with fewer resources. This process begins from early childhood, and depends upon the parents' financial resources – e.g., to be able to afford apartments in catchment areas for the best schools in major cities (where the best universities are located, with admissions skewed to city residents), an intensely competitive and increasingly expensive process.

Xie and Wang (2006) conducted a survey and found there is a gap in the recruitment opportunities for the rich classes (representing 9.3 percent of the national population) and the low-income classes (representing 76.4 percent of the national population). Students from high-income families are 4–18 times more likely than students from low-income families to attend HEs directly financed by the MoE, which are normally 211 Project universities.

Since the rapid expansion of higher education in the late 1990s, the proportion of rural students in Chinese key universities has been also falling. In Peking University, the proportion of rural students fell from 30 percent to 10 percent; and in Tsinghua University, only 17 percent of students in 2010 were from rural areas, although rural students accounted for 62 percent of the candidates participating in the *gaokao* that year (Liu and Liu 2013). This phenomenon is becoming more and more obvious in HEIs, particularly in elite universities. In 2011, an article entitled "Poor children have no bright prospect? Why are they moving further away from the first-level colleges and universities?"[11] sparked a nationwide discussion about the impact of class gaps on the fairness of education in China. The reporter conducted interviews and investigations into the phenomenon of there being fewer and fewer rural students in elite universities, and commented that "the lower the class the youth is from, the lower the quality of the university he is admitted to", a trend that is intensifying and being solidified. "The better the family background, the more opportunities to find a job, to pursue further study, and the higher the starting salary". Overall, ranking HEIs reinforce the disparity among students with different family backgrounds.

Ironically, however, it is not clear that this cycle of privilege through elite universities necessarily produces the best qualified graduates, even from the best universities. Since it is primarily *admission* to a high-level university that makes the difference to one's job prospects, not the degree class of the resulting degree, many staff at these universities complain that their students work themselves extremely hard for the *gaokao*, but then, if admitted to a top university, do not apply themselves to their degree. This is compounded by pressure on the staff to pass them so as not to harm the university's reputation. Moreover, anecdotal evidence suggests a gender bias in this regard, with male students in particular not working hard once admitted, but instead spending their time busily forging social connections (or *guanxi*) or accumulating the work experience needed to get the best jobs on graduation. This leads to the second issue we consider here, regarding gender inequalities.

3.5 Gender issues in higher education

The effects of these far-reaching reforms on Chinese higher education (and broader political economy and society) as regards gender equality are complex, but largely regressive. On the one hand, the greater access to higher education in the past decade has resulted in a growing number of women obtaining degrees and entering professional fields, and education opportunities for women have been very much improved. This may be due to the one-child policy in cities, and to parents' tendency to strive for the best education for their children. However, once these young female researchers begin their academic careers at universities or research institutions, the increasing pressure in the academic world for research has brought additional barriers for them in obtaining the same status as men.

According to data from the PRC Ministry of Education, in the last ten years the percentage of female students in undergraduate, master's and doctoral programs has been steadily increasing. The number of female master's students exceeded that of males in 2010, and in 2011 female undergraduate students also outnumbered males. Also, while male students at the postgraduate level still remain the majority, the number of female postgraduate students is increasing year by year, and the gap is being narrowed.

Table 11.1 Number of students in different programs in 2004 and 2014

Degree	Doctoral		Master's		Undergraduate	
Year	2014	2004	2014	2004	2014	2004
Total	312,676	165,600	1,535,013	654,300	15,410,653	7,378,500
Female	115,459 (36.93%)	51,900 (31.37%)	792,828 (51.65%)	288,900 (44.15%)	8,084,728 (52.46%)	3,238,400 (43.89%)
Male	197,217 (63.07%)	113,700 (68.63%)	742,185 (48.35%)	365,400 (55.85%)	7,325,925 (47.54%)	4,140,100 (56.11%)

Sources: Education Statistical Yearbook of China, 2005 and 2015

The number of female teachers has been growing at a faster rate than that of males. In higher vocational colleges, female teachers exceeded males in 2011, and in independent institutions female teachers outnumbered males in 2014. However, although the gap is being narrowed, females are still a minority in HEIs offering degree programs at higher levels.

Although the proportion of female teachers in HEIs is rising rapidly, their male colleagues still dominate in terms of professional titles. The higher the professional title, the fewer the number of females, with the lowest rate being female professors (senior) (see Table 11.3). Female teachers with mid-level titles outnumber males, and teachers with low-level or no titles are still mainly women.

A similar situation appears with regard to post-graduate supervisors. From 2003 to 2013, the percentage of female supervisors increased, but the overall difference between numbers of females and males became larger (see Table 11.4). Men still play the dominant role in higher education, and the gap in elite universities is even more severe. Based on the statistics up to 2006 for male and female supervisors (master's and PhD) for 37 Project 985 universities, the percentage of female supervisors in Jilin University was the highest, at 30.83 percent, and the lowest was East China Normal University, at 14.38 percent.[12] In the highest-level universities in China, over half had less than 20 percent female supervisors. In terms of high-level leadership, according to research conducted in 2013, there were only 45 female leaders among 38 Project 985 universities, accounting for less than 10 percent of the total number (Wang *et al.* 2014). Most of them were deputy leaders, and 42 of them were ten years or more older than the average age of the universities' presidents (Wang *et al.* 2014).

Table 11.2 Number of teachers in different kinds of regular HEIs

HEI	HEIs Offering Degree Programs		Independent Institutions		Higher Vocational Colleges	
Year	2014	2004	2014	2004	2014	2004
Total	1,091,645	575,300	136,303	35,400	438,300	193,400
Female	509,163 (46.64%)	236,800 (41.17%)	68,945 (50.58%)	15,300 (43.17%)	227,608 (51.93%)	87,800 (45.39%)
Male	582,482 (53.36%)	338,500 (58.83%)	67,358 (49.42%)	20,100 (56.83%)	210,692 (48.07%)	106,500 (55.61%)

Sources: Education Statistical Yearbook of China, 2005 and 2015

Table 11.3 Number of full-time teachers and their titles in HEIs in 2014

	Total	Senior	Sub-senior	Middle	Junior	No-ranking
Total	1,566,048	190,528	458,388	627,233	201,440	88,459
Female	755,423 (48.24%)	56,219 (29.51%)	203,953 (44.49%)	333,144 (53.11%)	114,475 (56.83%)	47,632 (53.85%)
Male	810,625 (51.76%)	134,309 (70.49%)	254,435 (55.51%)	294,089 (46.89%)	86,965 (43.17%)	40,827 (46.15%)

Source: Education Statistical Yearbook of China, 2015

Table 11.4 Number of post-undergraduate supervisors in 2003 and 2013

Year	2013	2003
Total	150,798	128,652
Female	31,472 (20.87%)	25,651 (19.94%)
Male	119,326 (79.13%)	103,001 (80.06%)
Doctoral Supervisors	11,065	10,620
Female	1,141 (10.31%)	1,104 (10.40%)
Male	9,924 (89.69%)	9,516 (89.60%)
Master's Supervisors	115,774	99,727
Female	27,876 (24.08%)	22,721 (22.78%)
Male	87,898 (75.92%)	77,006 (27.28%)
Doctoral and Master's Supervisors	23,959	18,305
Female	2,455 (10.25%)	1,826 (9.98%)
Male	21,504 (89.75%)	16,479 (90.02%)

Sources: Education Statistical Yearbook of China, 2004 and 2014

The above analysis shows that although Chinese females have made significant gains in education at all levels because of expanding enrollment, they are still under-represented in higher education, especially in the senior, more influential levels of the university hierarchy. Few women presidents exist in Chinese universities, and most department leaders are male. While, culturally, male bias puts women at a disadvantage for promotion to higher management and for participation at the higher levels of the bureaucracy or leadership, the evaluation criteria, which emphasize competition and research, have also hampered young women. Since the time for research for Chinese academics often requires incursions into their leisure time, and women are generally still burdened with more family responsibilities (including to in-laws) given prevailing gender norms, the time that women academics can devote to research, bid for funds and publish is comparably less than their male counterparts. As a result, women generally perform less well than men in terms of these indicators and are in a weak position promotion-wise compared to their male colleagues. Consider the field of tourism as an example. Tourism is a subject in which there is a high percentage of female researchers. However, when searching the CNKI (China National Knowledge Internet, an important database containing e-journals, newspapers, dissertations, proceedings, yearbooks, reference works, etc.) for papers published in the *Tourism Tribune* (the best domestic journal in this area) from 1986 to 31 January 2016, it was found that there were only six females in the top forty scholars in terms of publications, and that the top ten were all men.[13]

As Chinese HE becomes an ever-steeper pyramid, all the intense competition that has come with it has created a system characterized by an ever-growing army of surplus academic labor which is predominantly female in the low-paying and junior-level jobs, and relatively few men who will continue to dominate the ranks of the few elite winners that the system is explicitly designed to produce.

4 Conclusions

Since the implementation of the "Reform and Opening-up" policies, a series of reforms has been conducted to move the higher education sector from a unified, centralized and closed system to one that allows openness and diversification. Development of higher education has met with considerable success, and Chinese higher education has experienced a great expansion. Especially in recent years, various universities have ceaselessly expanded enrollment and have constructed new campuses for higher education. The proportion of China's college-age population in higher education has now increased to over 20 percent, from 1.4 percent in 1978.

With China's growing exposure to international competition and the world-class university movement, the state has taken it as a national priority to develop a few top universities to rise above the waters into the "sunshine" of a global reputation. However, the continuing strong control by the central state over the HE sector has made the pyramid system even deeper, as the apex of the Chinese HE pyramid gets ranked highly under the effect of government policy committed to intense concentration of resources. The consequent disadvantages of this strong competition and ranking are worrisome. The overemphasis on competition and rankings may damage the very essence of Chinese universities, which is to improve social equality through education. This concern is being raised in Chinese society now, since social equity is now considered a priority issue. However, whether, and how, balance can be achieved between providing an equal opportunity to all and supporting "excellence" is still far from certain.

Notes

1 Data source: China Statistical Yearbook 1985, Beijing.
2 http://view.news.qq.com/a/20130822/001787.htm.
3 Data source: China Education Yearbook, 2015.
4 Data source: China Education Yearbook, 2015.
5 Data source: Blue book of international talent: report on overseas study development in China (2015).
6 Project 985 and 211 (www.chinaeducenter.com/en/cedu/ceduproject211.php).
7 www.jyb.cn/high/sjts/201604/t20160407_656711.html.
8 www.jyb.cn/high/sjts/201604/t20160407_656711.html.
9 http://mt.sohu.com/20160406/n443411937.shtml.
10 http://gongwen.cnrencai.com/diaochabaogao/41321.html.
11 www.infzm.com/content/61888.
12 http://learning.sohu.com/20110926/n320556864.shtml.
13 http://epub.cnki.net/kns/brief/result.aspx?dbprefix=scdb&action=scdbsearch &db_ opt=SCDB, 2016.2.1.

References

Amsler, S. S. and Bolsmann, C. 2012. "University ranking as social exclusion". *British Journal of Sociology of Education*, 33(2): 283–301.

Bagley, S. S. and Portnoi, L. M. 2014. "Setting the stage: global competition in higher education". *New Directions for Higher Education*, 168: 5–11.

Burbules, N.C. and Torres, C.A. eds. 2000. *Globalization and Education: Critical Perspectives*, London: Routledge.

Cai, Z. M. 2014. "Globalization of higher education in China: current situation, problems and countermeasures" [中国高等教育全球化的现状, 问题与对策]. *Modern Education Management*, 1: 8–17.

Clark, B. R. 1983. *The Higher Education System*. Berkeley. CA: University of California Press.

Cooper, D., Hersh, A. and O'Leary, A. 2012. "The competition that really matters: comparing U.S., Chinese, and Indian investments in the next-generation workforce". *Center for American Progress*, August 21.

Deem, R., Mok, K. H. and Lucas, L. 2008. "Transforming higher education in whose image? Exploring the concept of the 'world-class' university in Europe and Asia". *Higher Education Policy*, 21(1): 83–97.

Dill, D.D. and M. Soo. 2005. "Academic quality, league tables, and public policy: A cross-national analysis of university ranking systems". *Higher Education*, 49: 95–533.

Fei, X. 2007. "Behind the scale expansion: The stratification of higher education and the fracture of society" [规模扩张的背后——分层的高等教育和断裂的社会]. *Heilongjiang Research Higher Education*, 9: 1–5.

Frank, R. 2001. "Higher education: The ultimate winner-take-all market?" In Devlin, M. and Meyerson, J. eds. *Forum Futures: Exploring the future of higher education*. Forum Strategy Series Vol. 3. Jossey-Bass.

Han, M. J. and Guo, C. 2015. "The hierarchical structure of Chinese higher education system". *US–China Education Review*, 5(12): 825–830.

Han, M. and Zhang, D. 2014. "Structural changes in Chinese higher education system: Public and private HE mix". *International Journal of Comparative Education and Development*, 16(2): 212–221.

Hazelkorn, E. 2008. "Learning to live with league tables and ranking: The experience of institutional leaders". *Higher Education Policy*, 21(2): 193–215.

Huang, L. H. 2005. *Elitism and Equality in Chinese Higher Education*. Institute of International Education, Stockholm University.

Iannelli, C. and Paterson, L. 2005. *Does Education Promote Social Mobility?* Centre for Educational Sociology.

Liu, Y. 2009. "Historical review on China's higher educational development" [中国高等教育发展历史述评]. *Journal of Nanyang Normal University Social Sciences*, 8(2).

Liu, Q. 2015. "Reflections on the controversy over the necessity of the '211 Project' and the '985 Project'" [关于 "211 工程" "985 工程" 存废之争的思考]. *Journal of Higher Education Management*, 9(3): 90–93.

Liu, H. W. and Liu, Y. F. 2013. "Analysis of social capital in the curing of higher education" [高等教育助推阶层固化的社会资本分析]. *Higher Education Exploration*, 4: 124–127.

Marginson, S. 2010. "Higher education in the global knowledge economy". *Procedia-Social and Behavioral Sciences*, 2(5): 6962–6980.

Marginson, S. and Van der Wende, M. 2007. "To rank or to be ranked: The impact of global rankings in higher education". *Journal of Studies in International Education*, 11(3): 306–329.

Mok, K. H. 2003. "Globalisation and higher education restructuring in Hong Kong, Taiwan and Mainland China". *Higher Education Research and Development*, 22(2): 117–129.

Mok, K.H. and Welch, A. eds. 2003. *Globalization and Educational Restructuring in the Asia Pacific Region*, Basingstoke, Hampshire: Palgrave Macmillan.

Mulligan, R. A. 1952. "Social mobility and higher education". *The Journal of Educational Sociology*, 25(8): 476–487.

Ohmae, K. 1990. *The Borderless World: Power and Strategy in the Interlinked Economy*, New York: Harper Perennial.

Pan, M. and Dong, L. 2009. "Research on the classification, orientation and characteristic development of colleges and universities". *Educational Research*, 2: 33–38.

Rizvi, F. and Lingard, B. 2009. *Globalizing Education Policy*. Routledge.

Shields, R. 2013. "Globalization and international student mobility: A network analysis". *Comparative Education Review*, 57(4): 609–636.

Sklair, L. 1999. "Globalization". In *Sociology: Issues and Debates*, Edited by: Taylor, S. 321–345. London: Macmillan.

Wang, Y. H., Yu, K., and Yue, Q. 2014. "Women above glass ceiling: images of group of women in high-level leadership of '985 Project' universities in China" [超越天花板的女性——我国"985"高校中的女性高层领导群像]. *Education Research Monthly*, 2: 30–35.

Waters, M. 2001. *Globalization*, London: Routledge.

Wen, D. 2005. "The impacts of SES on higher education opportunity and graduate employment in China" [家庭背景对我国高等教育机会及毕业生就业的影响]. *Peking University Education Review*, 3(3): 58–63.

Xie, Z. X. and Wang, W. Y. 2006. "The difference in higher education access opportunity of the children in different strata in China in the context of the popularization of higher education" [高等教育大众化视野下我国社会各阶层子女高等教育入学机会差异的 研究]. *Journal of Educational Studies*, 2(2): 65–74.

Yang, R. 2000. "Tensions between the global and the local: A comparative illustration of the reorganisation of China's higher education in the 1950s and 1990s". *Higher Education*, 39(3): 319–337.

Zhang, X. M. and Hao, F. L. 2006. "Giving up education: some rural families' helpless choice" [教育放弃: 部分农村家庭无奈的抉择]. *Journal of Higher Education*, 27(9): 57–60.

Zhu, G. R. 1997. "The spread of higher education in the West and the formation of higher education in modern China" [西方高等教育的传播与中国近代高等教育的形成]. *Journal of Higher Education*, 4: 79–85.

Zhu, H. Z. and Lou, S. 2011. *Development and Reform of Higher Education in China*. Elsevier.

12

FINANCING TECHNOSCIENCE

Finance, assetization and *rentiership*

Kean Birch

Introduction

Science was officially turned into an *asset* in 2008. How? In that year, the United Nations Statistical Commission adopted a new *Systems of National Accounts* (henceforth SNA 2008) in which research and development (R&D) spending – as well as expenditure on creative arts – was redefined as fixed investment. Previously, R&D spending was treated as an expense incurred during the production process – that is, as an expenditure incurred in the creation of products (or services) ranging from pharmaceutical drugs through cellphones to medical procedures. Following the SNA 2008 decision, then, R&D spending would be reframed as an investment because it produced an asset, in this case *scientific knowledge*. The USA's Bureau of Economic Analysis outlined the change as follows:

> Expenditures for R&D have long been recognized as having the characteristics of fixed assets - defined ownership rights, long-lasting, and repeated use and benefit in the production process. Recognizing that the asset boundary should be expanded to include innovative activities, such as R&D, the NIPAs will record private and government expenditures for R&D as investment.
>
> *(BEA 2013: 14)*

As the Bureau of Economic Analysis note, the "asset boundary" was extended as a result of the SNA changes, thereby creating a new *asset class* comprising the knowledge outputs of research activities. The implications of this change will likely be as profound for social studies of science, technology and innovation – or science and technology studies (STS) – as they are for research and innovation policy-making and business.[1] The SNA informs the development of national accounting systems that each country uses it to measure the "economic" activity (e.g. output, expenditure, income) undertaken within their borders. Specifically, the SNA changes imply that R&D costs will be capitalized rather than expensed at the time of "investment". R&D spending will now be understood as creating an asset with annual depreciation costs, or *capitalized property*, meaning that the value of R&D spending will stretch beyond its immediate contribution to production. The extension of the "asset boundary", in its rather bland terminology, can be seen more simply as the further extension of private property into scientific knowledge (Frase 2013). This move reinforces the approach taken by "neoliberal economists" to delegitimize the treatment of scientific knowledge as a public good (Mirowski 2011: 61); this is done through the extension of legal rights and the creation of knowledge assets. And, in the extreme, it represents an end to the scientific "commons" altogether – however idealized that may be – as governments, businesses, universities and others are all incentivized to find ways to stop sharing "their" research and innovation (see Delfanti, Harrison et al., Johnson and Rampini, Muellerlisle; Pagano and Rossi; Randalls, this volume).

A key issue with the creation of knowledge assets is how to value them. The extension of the "asset boundary" suggests that more and more scientific research will fall within the remit of intellectual property (IP). Of particular importance, in this regard, is the fact that the "science business", in Gary Pisano's (2006) terms, involves the monetization of such IP rather than the development of new products and services. In the life sciences, for example, the early entrants like Genentech showed "that intellectual property could be packaged and sold independently of the final product" and that "IP was an asset that could be monetized" (ibid.: 142). Existing literature on the changing political economy of research and innovation (CPERI) highlights the particular – and peculiar – valuation logics, knowledges and practices in the business of science (e.g. Mirowski 2012; Birch and Tyfield 2013; Mittra 2016; Birch forthcoming). Primarily, this centres on the expected future earnings of IP rights like patents, copyright, trademark, and suchlike. However, it is also dependent on the (re)configuration of the financial system supporting the business of science, especially venture capital and capital markets. Consequently, the expansion of knowledge assets resulting from the SNA 2008 changes leads inevitably to the increasing monetization of scientific knowledge, necessitating, on the side of STS scholars, a significant engagement with finance, financial markets and financialization processes in order to understand the political economy of technoscience.

My aim in this chapter is to illustrate, in a small but hopefully useful way, how to pursue this sort of engagement. In one sense, I am arguing that STS scholars need to develop yet another competency in their research, particularly in understanding the financing of the scientific enterprise. Without developing this expertise, it is likely that scholars will miss some of the critical changes happening in the evolution of technoscience, of all shapes and sizes. In another sense, I am arguing that STS scholars also need to engage with finance on a normative level in order to challenge the negative implications of finance for technoscience, which I come back to in the conclusion. Before that, I provide a brief outline of the relationship between finance and technoscience. Then I discuss several key financial logics, knowledges and processes that impact technoscience. I illustrate these arguments with reference to the life sciences sector, before concluding.

Finance, assetization and *rentiership*

Finance has been a research topic in STS and cognate disciplines for some time now, especially in social studies of finance (e.g. MacKenzie 2009). This literature largely turns an STS gaze on finance and financial markets in order to understand how technoscience configures them. It is not my intention to get into these debates here, but rather to focus on how finance and financing come to configure technoscience. In this regard, I define *finance* primarily in terms of the financing of (scientific) business organizations, which includes equity investment (i.e. shares and shareholding), debt (i.e. loans), and other more exotic financial instruments (e.g. securities). Although it might appear as a neutral or insignificant aspect of science and innovation, as Mirowski (2011), Tyfield (2012a, 2012b) and others in this volume point out, the financing of science comes to shape science in important ways. Of relevance to this chapter, for example, are the claims that finance has come to dominate management and research strategies since the

1970s, especially as the pursuit of shareholder value (i.e. share price) has supplanted other concerns (Lazonick et al., this volume, Lazonick and O'Sullivan 2000). The dominance of finance and financial thinking has been defined as a process of *financialization* by a number of scholars: first, Krippner (2005: 174) defines it as "a pattern of accumulation in which profits accrue primarily through financial channels"; Leyshon and Thrift (2007: 102) define it as the "growing power of money and finance within economic life"; and Pike and Pollard (2010: 30) define it as "the growing influence of capital markets, their intermediaries, and processes". Simply put, financialization can be seen as the influence of financial logics, practices, and knowledges on other activities (Chiappello 2015), in this case, technoscience.

Much of the existing research on the financing of science has been centred on the importance of inter-organizational collaboration and relationships to learning and innovation in high-tech sectors like the life sciences, in particular, the relationship between research-based firms and capital providers (e.g. venture capital). Examples of this literature include: Pisano (1991), who presents a range of different governance structures in the biotech industry, such as vertical or horizontal integration and collaborative partnerships; Powell et al. (1996), who argue that the "locus of innovation" is in the networks between firms and other institutions, since no single organization could acquire the capacity needed to develop new products; Powell et al. (2002), who argue that biotech firms and venture capital are co-located in particular places (e.g. San Diego, CA); and Pina-Stranger and Lazega (2011), who argue that personal ties between biotech firms and venture capital are critical to learning processes in firms. However, despite its insights, this literature does not really do much to analyse how finance shapes science.

A number of scholars in STS and related fields have sought to make these conceptual connections. Early work by Coriat et al. (2003) on the emergence of "new science-based innovation regimes" emphasized the importance of institutional inter-dependencies and complementarities in the expansion of high-tech sectors. For example, they explain how the outsourcing of research to universities is tied to the extension of strong IP regimes and the financing of private firms through venture capital, all of which helped turn research into a "product" and IP rights into an "asset" (ibid.: 17, 19). A number of other scholars have stressed the importance of new IP regimes to the emergence and expansion of high-tech sectors, especially the life sciences, noting the extent to which value "creation" is now underpinned by monopoly rents enabled by the expansion of IP rights (e.g. Serfati 2008; Tyfield 2008; Zeller 2008; Birch forthcoming). More recently, Andersson et al. (2010) argue that high-tech firms have adopted a "financialized business model" in which financing is driven by a relay of investment and exit decisions made by financiers; none of these decisions, it is important to note, necessarily entail the marketing of a final product. Similarly, Hopkins et al. (2013) provide a detailed account of the biotech financing process, highlighting the fact that finance has a significant influence on strategic decisions inside firms. Others, like Lazonick and Tulum (2011) and Styhre (2014, 2015), stress the impact of restructuring capital markets and corporate governance on the financing of sectors like the life sciences. For example, Lazonick and Tulum argue that financing focuses on shareholder value over and above research, while Styhre notes the relationship between finance and "rentier capitalism", to which I return below.

This focus on finance means it is important to analyse *science* as a business, which means understanding what science is "selling". As others note (e.g. Pisano 2006; Mirowski 2012), the science business does not necessarily entail the research and development of new products or services, which mainstream theories of innovation and entrepreneurship generally emphasize (Godin 2012). Rather, it involves the creation of assets. This "assetization" process, as I call it (Birch 2015, forthcoming), is an emerging topic in the STS literature. A number of scholars have sought to analyse the socio-economic implications of assets in the bio-economy (e.g. Birch and Tyfield

2013; Cooper and Waldby 2014; Lezaun and Montgomery 2015; Martin 2015), while others have sought to analyse how assets are constituted and constitute particular valuation practices (e.g. Muniesa 2012, 2014; Ortiz 2013; Doganova and Karnøe 2015; Doganova and Muniesa 2015). Almost anything can be turned into an asset with the right techno-economic configuration that enables the "transformation of something into property that yields an income stream" (Birch forthcoming). This transformation involves the construction of property rights so *the thing* – e.g. IP, business model, artefact, land, resource, skill, bodily function, personal popularity, pollution, building, infrastructure, life form molecule, etc. – can be enclosed and owned, using monetization technologies so it can be alienated and traded, and discounting practices so it can be capitalized and valued. As such, assetization involves both tangible materiality and intangible knowledge.

The focus on assets might sound overly technical, but it has significant implications for understanding the political economy of science (Birch forthcoming). In part, these implications result from the distinctiveness of assets, especially knowledge assets (e.g. IP rights), from commodities (i.e. products and services). First, knowledge assets (e.g. IP rights) give owners exclusion rights *and* use rights for copies derived from the asset; for example, when we buy a music CD we do not have the right to reproduce and distribute it. Second, assets are constructs of law and regulation, being dependent on the state for the enforcement of property rights. Third, assets have a distinct supply and demand logic because they are generally unique and full or quasi-monopolies; as a result, assets tend to rise in price as demand rises because new producers cannot enter a market (e.g. there is only one copyright to the music of Metallica). Fourth, as a result of being monopolies, assets generate monopoly and other forms of economic rent (Fuller 2002; Zeller 2008). Fifth, while the demand logic may entail rising asset prices, this does not preclude owners from seeking to decrease their value, transform an asset from one form to another, to transfer ownership, and so on. Finally, it should be obvious that asset prices are highly dynamic and dependent on active management of their value.

The discussion of assets, especially as they relate to scientific knowledge, highlights one key aspect that conceptually differentiates assets from commodities: they entail forms of rent-seeking, or *rentiership*, as opposed to entrepreneurial activity (e.g. developing new products, services, markets, etc.). As a concept, rentiership is underpinned by a number of theoretical assumptions. First, knowledge is a social process – à la social epistemology (Fuller 2002) – rather than an idea in our heads; as such, it entails our "habits of life", to use Veblen's (1908) terms, or the "general intellect" to use Marx's (1993). Second, since knowledge is a social process, it can only be turned into an asset through specific techno-economic configurations – including legal-political rights and regulations, socio-technical instruments, and knowledge practices – that enable the extraction (cf. creation) of value through the reification and enclosure of knowledge. Profits thus stem from limiting access to an existing thing, rather than producing anything new (Fuller 2013). Third, and as alluded to already, this assetization entails rent-seeking rather than profit-making (Zeller 2008). Fourth, rent-seeking, however, is not intrinsic to assets; instead, rent-seeking involves a range of knowledges and practices that often involve a temporal or serial accrual of revenues (Andersson et al. 2010), in which the original creators do not necessarily benefit. Finally, rentiership is dependent on specific forms of social organization and governance, especially those relating to private business (Mirowski 2012).

Valuation, corporate governance, and the financialization of the life sciences

In order to understand the implications of finance, assetization and rentiership on science, it is important to unpack a range of political-economic organizational forms, practices, and knowledges. Here, when I use "political-economic", I do so as a descriptive rather than analytical term to define the kinds of political-economic activity often sidelined in STS perspectives, such as the allocation and distribution of societal resources. In this section, for example, my intention is to consider three political-economic aspects of science that are frequently black-boxed in the STS literature: financing, valuation, and organizational governance. I unpack these political-economic aspects of science in order to understand how finance and financialization come to configure the life sciences, which I use as an example of a "science business" (Pisano 2006).

Finance and financing in the life sciences

Several STS scholars have raised serious questions about the purported revolutionary nature of the life sciences; for example, Nightingale and Martin (2004) call the "biotech revolution" a "myth" (see also Birch 2006; Hopkins et al. 2007). Such claims often reflect technoscientific developments (or the lack thereof), rather than political-economic ones. For example, it is interesting to note that in 2014 the global market capitalization (i.e. total share value) of public "biotech" firms reached over US$1 trillion (Ernst and Young 2015), having risen from around US$400 billion in the immediate aftermath (2008–11) of the global financial crisis. The huge rise in market capitalization between 2011 and 2014 seems incongruous when put in relation to the revenues and profits of those same firms, as illustrated in Figure 12.1. First, the ratio of market capitalization to revenues fell from 6–7 before the GFC to around 4 afterwards, and since then it has risen to 7–8 in 2013 and 2014. This means that the share value of these firms has fallen and risen in response to factors other than revenues and profits derived from products and services. Second, the global "biotech" industry as a whole only became profitable for the first time in 2009 (ibid.). Unpacking these numbers in more detail reveals that, first, only ten predominantly American "biotech" corporations represented around 60 percent (i.e. US$600 billion) of that global market capitalization; and second, only the largest 10–15 corporations were actually profitable in 2011 (see Figure 12.1). In light of these revenue and profit numbers, the valuation of the biotech industry on public capital markets seems contradictory.

Other scholars have raised similar questions about the extent to which biotechnology has lived up to the expectations that many people have had of it over the years – e.g. policy-makers, investors, business people, academics, etc. Pisano (2006: 94, 112) argues that the biotech industry is characterized by poor returns on R&D investment, when judged on the introduction of new products and services, and by poor returns on financial investment, when judged on the aggregate share value performance of public corporations. Moreover, Pisano argues that returns on private investment (e.g. venture capital) have also been poor and that without Amgen the whole industry would have "sustained steady losses throughout its history" (ibid.: 114). However, and illustrating why biotechnology is interesting, this has not halted increasing levels of government funding and private and public capital investment in the sector over the years. As Figure 12.2 illustrates, the level of funding fell briefly after the global financial crisis, but subsequently rose again; the main difference has been an increasing reliance on financing through partnering and debt.

Part of the reason for this disjuncture between investment and returns can be explained by the financing process in the life sciences. Generally, life sciences businesses are dependent on "patient capital", or long-term financial investments that can accommodate long product development times (e.g. 10–20 years) (Birch and Cumbers 2010; Hopkins et al. 2013). However, most private and public market investments are short-term. Private investment, like venture capital, for example, is driven by the time horizon of their managed funds, which is four to six years. This is because the source of these funds is institutional investors (e.g. pension, insurance, mutual funds), which need regular returns on their investments (Hopkins 2012). As a result, most life sciences financing is intrinsically configured as a relay or serial process in

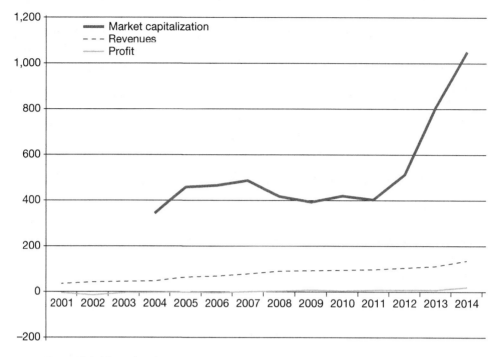

Figure 12.1   Global biotech industry: market capitalization ($b)
Sources: Lähteenmäki and Lawrence (2005); Lawrence and Lähteenmäki (2008, 2014); Huggett et al. (2009, 2010, 2011); Huggett and Lähteenmäki (2012); Huggett (2013); Morrison and Lähteenmäki (2015); reproduced with permission.

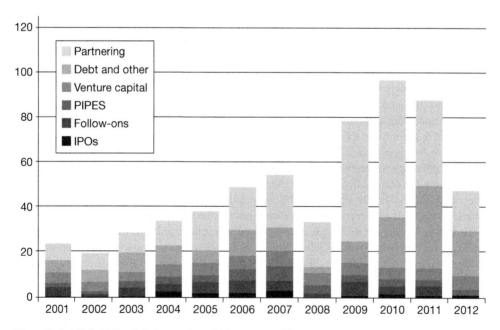

Figure 12.2   Global biotech industry: financial investment ($b)
Sources: Lähteenmäki and Lawrence (2005); Huggett and Lähteenmäki (2012); Yang (2013); data for partnerships for the years 2009–12 includes global deals; reproduced with permission.

which a financier is driven by the need for an exit before a business is necessarily profitable or even revenue-generating (Andersson et al. 2010). Consequently, a range and number of different financiers (e.g. business angels, venture capital, strategic venture funds, etc.) need to find an exit to recoup their investment and are largely reliant on finding other financiers to pick up the "baton" (Hopkins 2012). Each financier's primary concern in this process is the dilution of the value of their investment which successive rounds of investment might engender; that is, an increase in the number of (private) shareholders who own shares in a business, but not in the value of the business itself. Hence, it is often "cleaner" at each refinancing stage for new financiers to replace rather than supplement existing financiers. How value is determined is itself an important question (see below). This short-term, serial process configures the research and business strategies that life sciences firms can actually undertake, and explains why scientific knowledge – protected by suitable IP rights – has become such an important asset. On the one hand, it is how firms generate revenues through partnerships, out-licensing, royalty arrangements, etc., and, on the other hand, it is how firms represent their *fundamental* value – a tricky concept in itself (Styhre 2014).

Financial practices and logics of valuation in the life sciences

Having considered the financing trends and patterns in the life sciences, it is now important to consider how this financing is translated into value by various political-economic actors. A starting point is to unpack the financial logics and practices that drive valuation decisions. The key social actors in this regard are financiers and investors, rather than a firm's managers, scientists, etc. Consequently, it is important for STS analyses to engage with these political-economic actors, as much, if not more than, technoscientific actors (Birch forthcoming). This means, though, that STS scholars have to engage with a new set of knowledges, practices, logics, etc., sometimes in areas where they feel less intellectually comfortable.

It is difficult to judge the value of a life sciences business without a set of political-economic knowledges and practices to make and manage valuations (Ortiz 2013; Birch forthcoming). Here I want to discuss valuation practices and then consider the conceptual implications of these logics. First, there is a range of rather prosaic "valuation methods" that financiers can use. Bratic et al. (2014) split these among an "asset approach", "income approach" and "market approach". An *asset approach* involves valuing a business's assets and liabilities at "fair market prices" – or, prices that would be received in a market exchange at that point in time; an *income approach* involves valuing (expected) future revenues; and a *market approach* involves valuing a business in relation to other businesses in terms of its market share, market position, market growth, etc. Each entails a set of judgements and practices that informs, or *performs*, the valuation of a business (Muniesa 2012). For example, IP rights might represent an asset, but they could also represent a risk from a litigation perspective, as others may challenge them in court, leading to significant legal costs. The point I want to get across here is that the valuation of a business is a complex social practice that involves particular financial logics; there is no objective way of determining what a business is worth outside of social conventions and practices for doing so.

Another example is represented by the work of STS scholars on "valuation devices", which include business models and business revenue formulae (e.g. Doganova and Eyquem-Renault 2009; Baden-Fuller and Morgan 2010; Perkmann and Spicer 2010). These models and formulae are particularly important in new, high-tech sectors like the life sciences for at least two reasons: first, value is not intrinsic in new technoscientific sectors since future revenues are uncertain (at best) (Perkmann and Spicer 2010); and second, models and formulae provide a means to establish – or "perform" – new markets and valuations (Doganova and Muniesa 2015). For example, such models and formulae are used to define and frame the expected customer base, revenue streams, value capture, etc., which help financiers and investors to work out what the value of a business entity *should* be if it is going to return the investment made in it. There are numerous business models according to Baden-Fuller and Morgan (2010), each with their own rationales, expectations, activities, etc., for example Wal-Mart, with low prices but high throughput; Google, with free services but targeted advertising; McDonald's, with franchising but standardized products; etc. In some senses, a business model can even be considered a fetishistic representation of business activity, used to establish valuations on the basis of particular techno-economic organizational structures and relations, which I come back to below.

These valuation practices reflect certain financial logics, especially the logic of capitalization as outlined by STS scholars like Muniesa (2012, 2014), as well as others (e.g. Nitzan and Bichler 2009; Chiappello 2015). Working within a tradition which treats finance and capital as social practices – cf. Marxist perspectives that emphasize capital as a set of social relations embodied by commodity production – capitalization is underpinned by the idea that value is not inherent in a thing or relation. Rather, the concept of capitalization refers to the social practice of discounting future revenues to determine current valuation, for example calculating current share price on the basis of future earnings that a shareholder can expect to reap through dividend payments. According to Muniesa (2012), this is a dual process in which the construction of "value" (i.e. earnings) occurs simultaneously with the construction of the thing being "valued" (i.e. business entity). In the case of the life sciences, this entails valuing the future earnings of a business entity by valuing it as a "going concern" with the potential for a certain market share (ibid.). It involves an assessment of the value that can be "created" or "captured" from the creation of a business entity through particular business models (Doganova and Muniesa 2015), which, in light of the theoretical discussion above, ends up conflating entrepreneurship (i.e. creation of value) with *rentiership* (i.e. extraction or capture of value). For example, a life sciences business may have been created as a venture-backed, dedicated biotech firm with the goal of developing new biopharmaceutical products, but might actually capture value, for financiers and investors at least, through the strategic threat it represents to incumbents, leading to a buy-out by the incumbent or its competitors.

Financial organization and governance in the life sciences

As the discussion above illustrates, value and valuation are not intrinsic to particular assets, activities (e.g. product sales), or entities (e.g. businesses); some scholars, like Ortiz (2013), argue that value and valuation are not automatic or inherent processes, they are always necessarily (at least partially) subjective. The way political-economic actors, especially financiers and investors, value a business is driven by a set of financial logics and practices, and these can often conflict with or contradict the logics and practices of other social actors (e.g. scientists, managers, policy-makers, etc.). In the case of the life sciences, this process is reflected in the organizational structure and relations of financing and its governance. In particular, it is evident in the dominant narrative of the dedicated biotech firm as an entrepreneurial entity that creates value. This perspective is simplistic, if not downright inaccurate, on a number of levels.

To start with, the financial practices and logics of value and valuation I outlined above are embodied in the business entity itself, rather than in the production or other process. That is, the thing being valued, in financial terms, is the business; one of the primary reasons for this is that a business has a lifespan that enables capitalization, or the discounting of future earnings, whereas other entities or different processes do not facilitate this. It is helpful here to turn to the arguments of Philip Mirowski (2012) on the life sciences businesses; he explicitly defines biotech firms as financial artefacts rather than integral to any production process. According to Mirowski, this is because "most biotechs never produce a drug or other final product" (ibid.: 295). In this sense, he goes on to argue, the biotech firm is really a "Ponzi scheme" designed "to lure exponentially increased investment and then to cash out before the inevitable collapse ensues" (ibid.: 296). I have interviewed informants from the venture capital world who have said exactly the same thing: "it is a bit of, can be a bit of a Ponzi scheme which is, you know, [phone rings], 'I pay this for it, so that's what it's worth'" (see Birch 2016: 122 fn1). With this in mind, it is important to integrate this aspect of high-tech firms into STS analyses in order to avoid the conceptual ambiguity around notions of technoscientific promise, expectations, and suchlike; to financiers and investors, high-tech firms can represent nothing more than a *financial* return.

In order to achieve this return, however, financiers and investors are reliant on certain forms of corporate governance. Corporate governance has become an important academic, business, and policy issue since the 1970s as the result of the rise of the idea that corporate governance *should* maximize shareholder value (Lazonick and O'Sullivan 2000). As a concept, corporate governance refers to both an area of academic and legal research *and* a set of legal and economic mechanisms that centre on resolving the separation of "ownership" (i.e. shareholder) and "control" (i.e. manager). As an area of academic research it is mainly concerned with the "way in which suppliers of finance to corporations assure themselves of getting a return on their investment" according to one influential review (Shleifer and Vishny 1997: 737). But as this definition illustrates, it can be considered as a highly normative area of study focusing on how one group (i.e. investors) can best control another group (i.e. managers) on the basis of assumptions about who can and should control the societal allocation of capital (i.e. it should be investors because they are most efficient at allocating capital because they have the most to lose) (Styhre 2015). As a legal and economic mechanism it is less clear-cut who does and who should control business entities (Stout 2012). When it comes to the life sciences, Pisano (2006: 136) points out different forms of investment involve different forms of corporate governance: for example, venture capital involves more than an investment of capital, it also involves "close oversight" through "representation on the board of directors, covenants and contractual restrictions, incentive arrangements, and the staging of capital infusions". Others, like Styhre (2015), note the difference in goals between financiers/investors and founders, in that the former are more concerned with selling their stake and the return they get than with product development. As such, they may represent rentiers, but they "are by no means passive" ones (ibid.: 161). How different social actors understand the rationale and mechanism of corporate governance has an enormous impact on the configuration of technoscientific businesses, especially in high-tech sectors like the life sciences.

An important aspect of this whole organization and governance of high-tech businesses is the dominance of finance and investment returns over other considerations (e.g. research spending). In his work over the years, William Lazonick and collaborators have demonstrated how shareholder value has come to dominate business strategies and decisions in high-tech sectors (e.g. Lazonick and O'Sullivan 2000; Lazonick and Tulum 2011; Lazonick and Mazzucato 2013; Lazonick et al., this volume). Starting with the incongruity between financing levels and lack of product development which others have highlighted (e.g. Nightingale and Martin 2004; Pisano 2006; Hopkins et al. 2007), Lazonick and Tulum (2011) examine the phenomena of stock repurchases (or buy-backs) in the life sciences. These stock repurchases are decisions by corporations to use their profits to buy shares back from shareholders and thereby boost share prices as fewer shares end up being traded on the market. For example, in drawing on Lazonick and Tulum's work, Mazzucato (2013: 26) notes that Amgen, the leading light of the life sciences sector, "has repurchased stock in every year since 1992, for a total of $42.2 billion through

2011". Moreover, the fact that Amgen borrows billions to repurchase stock distorts the seemingly "healthy" financing picture in Figure 12.2. As Lazonick and Mazzucato (2013: 1097) argue, this repurchasing activity represents the extraction of the value that is generated in organizations (e.g. life sciences businesses) through markets. Repurchasing and other market mechanisms do nothing to increase the investment in science or innovation; rather, they represent forms of rent-seeking enabled by policy changes in scientific, innovation, and market institutions.

Conclusion: Implications of financialization for the life sciences

In concluding this chapter, I want to consider the practical and theoretical implications of the various issues I have covered in the discussion above. In particular, I want to develop the notion of *rentiership* introduced in the theoretical section. I start here with the conceptual implications before addressing some of the broader policy implications not already mentioned above.

First, in terms of conceptual implications, it is worth developing the notion of *rentiership* as an analytical tool for understanding contemporary capitalism, especially varieties underpinned by (technoscientific) sectors like the life sciences. Theoretically this necessitates a renewed interest in intellectual property (IP) rights, although more attention needs to be focused on how IP rights are *used* by different social actors rather than assuming that they represent something of value. For example, IP rights are themselves both socio-technical configurations and part of broader configurations that enable the monetization and capitalization of knowledge as an asset. Consequently, value and valuation need to be rethought, as I have sought to do elsewhere (Birch forthcoming). My main point here would be to emphasize that value in knowledge-based economies is not constituted, conceptually speaking, by commodity relations; it is, rather, constituted by the turning of knowledge into assets (i.e. assetization). As a result, value is extracted, rather than created, through various forms of proactive rent-seeking (e.g. ownership, regulations, standards, etc.).

Second, the policy implications are broad when considering the political economy of science. However, I want to focus on one issue to do with the alignment of innovation policy and financial markets, which has been pursued in jurisdictions like the European Union (Birch and Mykhnenko 2014). Certain kinds of finance (e.g. venture capital) are frequently associated with innovation and high-tech sectors. For example, European policy debates and changes (e.g. *Lisbon Agenda, Horizon 2020*) have been shaped by the innovation imaginaries of *and* from the USA (Birch 2016). In particular, European policy-makers fetishized the financial markets in the US as an especially important component of the innovation "ecosystem" there. As a result, European policy-makers have promoted the restructuring of European financial markets and regulations to stimulate innovation. Whether it has succeeded in this regard is subject to debate. According to Birch and Mykhnenko (2014), for example, these financial policy changes have merely led to the financialization of the European economy, as well as the financialization of research and innovation. The implications of this financialization could be profound, in that rentiership comes to drive research and innovation towards particular areas that are easier to exclude, easier to alienate, easier to turn into capitalized property (Kapcyzynski 2014), and away from science in and for the public or global interest. For example, so-called "patent trolls" (or "non-practising entities") have found that a profitable and relatively low-risk strategy for extracting value is to buy intellectual property (IP) and then sue possible infringers, especially in contrast to the risks and uncertainties related to developing new products or services (Chien 2013). Consequently, there are incentives to do research that can be easily turned into IP assets and sold to "non-practising entities", rather than research that is complex and time-consuming precisely because it has uncertain and global implications (e.g. climate science).

Acknowledgements

Thanks to the editors for their helpful suggestions on an earlier draft.

Note

1   Personally, I think that this would make a fantastic PhD project for someone; there is a real need for an examination and analysis of the SNA 2008 changes as they relate to science, technology, and innovation.

Bibliography

Andersson, T., Gleadle, P., Haslam, C. and Tsitsianis, N. 2010. "Bio-pharma: A financialized business model". *Critical Perspectives in Accounting*, 21: 631–641.

Baden-Fuller, C. and Morgan, M. 2010. "Business models as models". *Long Range Planning*, 43: 156–171.

BEA 2013. *Preview of the 2013 Comprehensive Revision of the National Income and Product Accounts: Changes in Definitions and Presentations*. Washington, DC: Bureau of Economic Analysis.

Birch, K. 2006. "The neoliberal underpinnings of the bioeconomy: The ideological discourses and practices of economic competitiveness". *Genomics, Society and Policy*, 2.3: 1–15.

Birch, K. 2015. *We Have Never Been Neoliberal*. Winchester: Zero Books.

Birch, K. 2016. *Innovation, Regional Development and the Life Sciences: Beyond Clusters*. London: Routledge.

Birch, K. forthcoming. "Rethinking value in the bio-economy: Corporate governance, assets and the management of value". *Science, Technology and Human Values*.

Birch, K. and Cumbers, A. 2010. "Knowledge, space and economic governance: The implications of knowledge-based commodity chains for less-favoured regions". *Environment and Planning A*, 42.11: 2581–2601.

Birch, K. and Mykhnenko, V. (2014) "Lisbonizing vs. financializing Europe? The Lisbon Strategy and the (un-)making of the European knowledge-based economy". *Environment and Planning C* 32.1: 108–28.

Birch, K. and Tyfield, D. 2013. "Theorizing the Bioeconomy: Biovalue, Biocapital, Bioeconomics or… What?" *Science, Technology and Human Values*, 38.3: 299–327.

Bratic, W., Blok, J. and Gostola, M. 2014. "Valuation of early-stage companies in the biotechnology industry". *Journal of Commercial Biotechnology*, 20.2: 51–58.

Chiapello, E. 2015. "Financialization of valuation". *Human Studies*, 38.1: 13–35.

Chien, C. 2013. "Startups and patent trolls". *Stanford Technology Law Review*, 17: 461–505.

Cooper, M. and Waldby, C. 2014. *Clinical Labor: Tissue Donors and Research Subjects in the Global Bioeconomy*. Durham NC: Duke University Press.

Coriat, B., Orsi, F. And Weinstein, O. 2003. "Does biotech reflect a new science-based innovation regime?" *Industry and Innovation*, 10.3: 231–253.

Doganova, L. 2011. "Necessarily untrue: On the use of the discounted cash flow formula in valuation of exploratory projects". 7th Critical Management Studies Conference, Naples, Italy.

Doganova, L. and Eyquem-Renault, M. (2009) "What do business models do? Innovation devices in technology entrepreneurship". *Research Policy* 38: 1559-1570.

Doganova, L. and Karnøe, P. 2015. "Clean and profitable: Entangling valuations in environmental entrepreneurship", in Berthoin Antal, A., Hutter, M. and Stark, D., eds. *Moments of Valuation: Exploring Sites of Dissonance*. Oxford: Oxford University Press: 229–248.

Doganova, L. and Muniesa, F. 2015. "Capitalization Devices: business models and the renewal of markets", in Kornberger, M., Justesen, L., Mouritsen, J. and Koed Madsen, A., eds. *Making Things Valuable*. Oxford: Oxford University Press: 109–215.

Ernst and Young 2015. *Biotechnology Industry Report 2015: Beyond Borders*. Boston MA: EY LLP.

Frase, P. 2013. "We have always been rentiers". www.peterfrase.com: www.peterfrase.com/2013/04/we-have-always-been-rentiers/.

Fuller, S. 2002. *Knowledge Management Foundations*. Woburn MA: Butterworth-Heinemann.

Fuller, S. 2013. "On commodification and the progress of knowledge in society: A defence". *Spontaneous Generations: A Journal for the History and Philosophy of Science* 7.1: 6–14.

Godin, B. 2012 "'Innovation studies': The invention of a specialty". *Minerva*, 50: 397–421.

Hopkins, M. 2012. "Exploring funding routes for therapeutic firms", in O' Neill, M. and Hopkins, M., eds. *A Biotech Manager's Handbook*. Oxford: Woodhead Publishing: 131–155.

Hopkins, M., Martin, P., Nightingale, P., Kraft, A. and Mahdi, S. 2007. "The myth of the biotech revolution: An assessment of technological, clinical and organisational change". *Research Policy*, 36.4: 566–589.

Hopkins, M., Crane, P., Nightingale, P. and Baden-Fuller, C. 2013. "Buying big into biotech: Scale, financing, and the industrial dynamics of UK biotech, 1980–2009". *Industrial and Corporate Change*, 22.4: 903–952.

Huggett, B. 2013. "Public biotech 2009 – the numbers". *Nature Biotechnology*, 31: 697–703.

Huggett, B. and Lähteenmäki, R. 2012. "Public biotech 2011 – the numbers". *Nature Biotechnology*, 30: 751–757.

Huggett, B., Hodgson, J. and Lähteenmäki, R. 2009. "Public biotech 2008 – the numbers". *Nature Biotechnology*, 27: 710–721.

Huggett, B., Hodgson, J. and Lähteenmäki, R. 2010. "Public biotech 2009 – the numbers". *Nature Biotechnology*, 28: 793–799.

Huggett, B., Hodgson, J. and Lähteenmäki, R. 2011. "Public biotech 2010 – the numbers". *Nature Biotechnology*, 29: 585–591.

Kapczynski, A. 2014. "Intellectual property's Leviathan". *Law and Contemporary Problems*, 77.4: 131–145.

Krippner, G. 2005. "The financialization of the American economy". *Socio-Economic Review*, 3: 173–208.

Lähteenmäki, R. and Lawrence, S. 2005. "Public biotechnology 2004 – the numbers". *Nature Biotechnology*, 23: 663–671.

Lawrence, S. and Lähteenmäki, R. 2008. "Public biotech 2007 – the numbers". *Nature Biotechnology*, 26: 753–762.

Lawrence, S. and Lähteenmäki, R. 2014. "Public biotech 2013 – the numbers". *Nature Biotechnology*, 32: 626–632.

Lazonick, W. and Mazzucato, M. 2013. "The risk-reward nexus in the innovation-inequality relationship: Who takes the risks? Who gets the rewards?" *Industrial and Corporate Change*, 22.4: 1093–1128.

Lazonick, W. and O'Sullivan 2000. "Maximizing shareholder value: A new ideology for corporate governance". *Economy and Society*, 29.1: 13–35.

Lazonick, W. and Tulum, O. 2011. "US biopharmaceutical finance and the sustainability of the biotech business model". *Research Policy*, 40.9: 1170–1187.

Leyshon, A. and Thrift, N. 2007. "The capitalization of almost everything: The future of finance and capitalism". *Theory, Culture and Society*, 24: 97–115.

Lezaun, J. and Montgomery, C.M. 2015. "The pharmaceutical commons: sharing and exclusion in global health drug development". *Science, Technology and Human Values*, 40.1: 3–29.

MacKenzie, D. 2009. *Material Markets*. Oxford: Oxford University Press.

Martin, P. 2015. "Commercialising neurofutures: Promissory economies, value creation and the making of a new industry". *BioSocieties* doi:10.1057/biosoc.2014.40.

Marx, K. 1993. *Grundrisse*. London: Penguin Books.

Mazzucato, M. 2013. *The Entrepreneurial State*. London: Anthem Press.

Mirowski, P. 2011. *ScienceMart*. Cambridge MA: Harvard University Press.

Mirowski, P. 2012. "The modern commercialization of science as a Passel of Ponzi schemes". *Social Epistemology*, 26: 285–310.

Mittra, J. 2016. *The New Health Bioeconomy*. Basingstoke: Palgrave Macmillan.

Morrison, C. and Lähteenmäki, R. 2015. "Public biotech 2014 – the numbers". *Nature Biotechnology*, 33: 703–709.

Muniesa, F. 2012. "A flank movement in the understanding of valuation". *Sociological Review*, 59: 24–38.

Muniesa, F. 2014. *The Provoked Economy: Economic Reality and the Performative Turn*. London: Routledge.

Nightingale, P. and Martin, P. 2004. "The myth of the biotech revolution". *Trends in Biotechnology*, 22.11: 564–569.

Nitzan, J. and Bichler, S. 2009. *Capital as Power*. London: Routledge.

Ortiz, H. 2013. "The limits of financial imagination: free investors, efficient markets, and crisis". *American Anthropologist*, 116.1: 38–50.

Perkmann, M. and Spicer, A. 2010. "What are business models? Developing a theory of performative representations". *Research in the Sociology of Organizations*, 29: 269–279.

Pike, A. and Pollard, J. 2010. "Economic geographies of financialization". *Economic Geography*, 86.1: 29–51.

Pina-Stranger, A. and Lazega, E. 2011. "Bringing personalized ties back in: Their added value for biotech entrepreneurs and venture capitalists interorganizational networks". *The Sociological Quarterly*, 52: 268–292.

Pisano, G. 1991. "The governance of innovation: Vertical integration and collaborative arrangements in the biotechnology industry". *Research Policy*, 20.3: 237–249.

Pisano, G. 2006 *Science Business*. Boston: Harvard Business School Press.

Powell, W., Koput, K. and Smith-Doerr, L. 1996. "Interorganizational collaboration and the locus of innovation: Networks of learning in biotechnology". *Administrative Science Quarterly*, 41: 116–45.

Powell, W., Koput, K., Bowie, J. and Smith-Doerr, L. 2002. "The spatial clustering of science and capital: Accounting for biotech firm-venture capital relationships". *Regional Studies*, 36: 291–305.

Serfati, C. 2008. "Financial dimensions of transnational corporations, global value chain and technological innovation". *Journal of Innovation Economics and Management*, 2: 35–61.

Shleifer, A. and Vishny, R. 1997. "A survey of corporate governance". *The Journal of Finance*, 52.2: 737–783.

Stout, L. 2012. *The Shareholder Value Myth*. San Francisco: Berrett-Koehler Publishers.

Styhre, A. 2014. "Coping with the financiers: Attracting venture capital investors and end-users in the biomaterials industry". *Technology Analysis and Strategic Management*, 26.7: 797–809.

Styhre, A. 2015. *Financing Life Science Innovation*. London: Palgrave Macmillan.

SNA 2008. *Systems of National Accounts 2008*. New York: United Nations: http://unstats.un.org/unsd/nationalaccount/sna2008.asp.

Tyfield, D. 2008. "Enabling TRIPs: The pharma-biotech-university patent coalition". *Review of International Political Economy*, 15.4: 535–566.

Tyfield, D. 2012a. "A cultural political economy of research and innovation in an age of crisis". *Minerva*, 50: 149–167.

Tyfield, D. 2012b. *The Economics of Science: A Critical Realist Overview* (Volume 1 and 2). London: Routledge.

Veblen, T. 1908. "On the nature of capital: Investment, intangible assets, and the pecuniary magnate". *Journal of Economics*, 23.1: 104–136.

Yang, W. 2014. "2013 – biotech back in the saddle". *Nature Biotechnology*, 32.2: 126.

Yang, W. 2016. "2015 – another banner year for biotech". *Nature Biotechnology*, 34.2: 127.

Zeller, C. 2008. "From the gene to the globe: Extracting rents based on intellectual property monopolies". *Review of International Political Economy*, 15.1: 86–115.

13

THE ETHICAL GOVERNMENT OF SCIENCE AND INNOVATION

Luigi Pellizzoni

Introduction

Science and technology are expected to provide generalized social benefits and to be respectful of human dignity and well-being and, increasingly, the dignity and well-being of animals and the nonhuman world in general. Medical science has progressed at an astonishing pace since World War II, from antibiotics to kidney dialysis, from organ transplants to tissue regeneration. In agriculture, thanks to genetic technologies, new kinds of pesticides and herbicides have been produced, new species have been created and existing species have been cloned. Technologies that deploy algorithmic calculation are becoming ubiquitous, from biometric profiling to 'data-driven' research. Nanotechnology offers the possibility to improve the performance of materials (for example, in cosmetics, antibacterial materials based on nanosilver) and to target drugs to specific parts of the body. In these and many other fields, unprecedented opportunities have opened up which reconfigure humans' relationships with one another, with nonhuman entities and with themselves, raising important ethical questions. Resonant dilemmas are posed, for example, by the utilization of human cells and tissues for research purposes, or by the storage and use of sensitive personal data. Long-debated issues, such as volunteer informed consent or animal involvement in experiments, become increasingly salient.

That the ethical review of science and technology has gained growing relevance seems therefore understandable and laudable. Yet, the meaning and import of the process have significantly changed along the way. From a traditional field of philosophy, ethics has become 'a decisive level of reflection and legitimization for the regulation of fundamentally contested societal-political questions' (Bogner and Menz 2010: 890). This shift is important. As cultural political economy scholarship stresses, symbolic and discursive elements are entwined with, and of no less relevance than, structural factors in accounting for societal dynamics, affecting the sense-making of goals, interests, problems and solutions (Jessop 2010a; Tyfield 2012). 'Governmental ethics regimes' (Braun et al. 2010) are not exclusive to science and technology but perform therein a prominent role, as an alleged means to improve the rationale and rationality of public decisions. For critics, however, such a role corresponds by and large to neutralizing political issues, introducing norms outside the traditional process of law-making, staging public inclusion while building on expert processes, and protecting the market from criticism and debate (see Ottinger and Pinto, this volume; Felt and Wynne 2007). In an historical conjuncture, where innovation has become a discourse and a policy category filled with eschatological expectations against ever-worsening environmental challenges and economic crises, ethics seems to fulfil the task of containing any politicization of science and technology that might undermine or slow down its pace.

The aim of the chapter is to discuss this triangulation of science, ethics and economy. The first step is to clarify why ethics cannot be a substitute for politics, their respective problem fields being profoundly different. The second step is to shed light on the institutionalization of ethics as an instrument for governing science and technology. The basic move has been to reframe ethics as a self-standing issue capable of a rational, 'scientific' treatment. In this way ethics has penetrated regulation as a companion to the technical assessment of the risk, safety and efficacy of innovation. The third step is to show that this process is inscribed in the ruling neoliberal governmental logic of the last decades, to the extent that such logic builds on the depoliticization of public issues and on the 'responsibilization' of individuals as self-disciplining agents. I will conclude by arguing that an effective assessment of science and innovation has to address their political aspects – which means their embroilment with choices that can never be fully inclusive and justified.

Ethics and politics

The relationship between ethics and politics has been traditionally framed in terms of 'political ethics': how to deal morally with power. As Max Weber (1958 [1919]) famously argued, adopting an 'ethics of principles', unconditionally following an ideal, may have blameworthy implications. Think, for example, of the innocent victims of religious fundamentalism. On the other hand, adopting an 'ethics of responsibility', that is caring for the foreseeable consequences of decisions, may lead to cynical or technocratic realism devoid of principled motivations. The latter, as the recent vicissitudes of the European Union suggest, are no less crucial to political effectiveness. The appropriate balance between idealism and realism remains an open question. Of particular relevance today, however, is another issue: not the ethical *grounds* of politics, but ethics as a *target* and *means* of political action.

It is important to see why politics should not be confused with or replaced by ethics. The sociologist Niklas Luhmann (e.g. 1989) notes that ethics and politics use different semantics, respectively based on good/bad and coercion/non-coercion codes. The first code applies to what, as an intentional agent, I 'ought to do' according to a moral obligation towards others or, sometimes, myself. Should I buy cheap clothes even if they come from sweatshops? Should I eat meat, knowing industrial farming methods? Should I take a drug to enhance my strength or intelligence? The second code applies to compelling decisions concerning a given community. The questions above become: Should we ban meat or at least forbid certain breeding methods? Should we sanction certain working conditions, or the use of some drugs? Therefore, contrary to the dyadic structure of ethical relationships (the subject and the object of a moral obligation), political relationships have a triadic structure: they concern me, you and certain affected others (see e.g. Dewey 1984; Lévinas 2000). Said differently, politics has to do with establishing, reaffirming or changing a social order.

A crucial issue is whether a polity can ever be completely harmonious and unified. Liberal thought has contested traditional appeals to shared identities (blood, culture, religion...) as a source of unity, pointing instead to the idea of universal reason as the basis for fair compromise among competing interests or consensus over selected goals. However, for radical democratic theorists, such as Jacques Rancière (1998) and Chantal Mouffe (2013), no social order can be fully inclusive or rationally justifiable. It always entails decision, in the literal sense of 'cutting away', divisive choice. For example, no answer to the questions above is likely to be approved by each and every citizen of a state (though we may expect everyone to accept decisions they do not agree with as long as those decisions are made according to the agreed upon procedural rules).

In sum, ethical questions do not coincide with political questions. Ethics is the field of the unconditional. Politics is the field of the conditional, which crucially includes science and technology, to the extent that these do not proceed simply by virtue of rational operations over given 'facts' but also as a result of choices regarding what is to be considered a fact, which facts are relevant, and to what purposes. This, as we shall see, is systematically obscured by the saturation of public discourse with claims about scientific soundness and ethical correctness.

From technology assessment to the government of ethics

The rise of the governmental role of ethics has coincided with the establishment of a narrative by which ethics constitutes a field relevant to, but separated from, social, economic and political issues related to science and technology.

Early traces of this process can be found in the institutionalization of bioethics. Though its origins are as ancient as the Hippocratic Oath, the rise of bioethics has been spurred by crucial events before, during and after World War II, including experiments in Nazi camps and the eugenic programs (such as compulsory sterilization) pursued also by democratic countries such as Sweden and the US. The Nuremberg Trials led to the Nuremberg Code (1947), a ten-point document outlining the rights of subjects in human experiments, followed by other ethical guidelines such as the Helsinki Declaration (1964, last updated in 2013) and the Belmont Report (1979).

The institutionalization of bioethics as a distinct disciplinary and professional field is usually seen to begin with the birth of two interdisciplinary academic bodies in the US: the Hastings Center (1969) and the Kennedy Institute of Ethics (1971). Institutionalization, however, gained real momentum in the 1990s with a flourishing of advisory councils and committees, most of which operating at the national level (Fuchs 2005). Up to this moment the dominant approach to the governance of science and innovation had been technology assessment, which incorporated ethical aspects as one of many concerns. A salient example is the US Office for Technology Assessment (OTA). Established in 1972, OTA had the mandate of providing Congress with 'competent, unbiased information concerning the physical, biological, economic, social, and political effects of [technological] applications' (Technology Assessment Act 1972, SEC 2 (d)). OTA provided a model that several other countries followed.[1] Blamed for being 'too politicized', the OTA was discontinued in 1995, almost simultaneously with the establishment of the National Bioethics Advisory Committee (NBAC), the first permanent US presidential ethics body (replaced in 2001 and 2009 by similar bodies under the G.W. Bush and Obama administrations).

Ethics, as said, committees proliferated internationally in the 1990. In Canada, the Biotechnology Advisory Committee was formed in 1999. In Italy, the National Committee for Bioethics was set up in 1990. In the UK, the Nuffield Council on Bioethics began in 1991. In Germany, the first permanent national-level ethics commission was created in 1994, and the National Ethics Council was founded in 2001. Many other examples could be listed. While there have been significant national variations in the way ethics was institutionalized and professionalized depending on, among the other things, the balance of power between physicians and bioethicists and the relative separation between clinical practice and public policy issues (De Vries et al. 2009), the trend is generalized. Furthermore, over the years, ethics committees have tended to expand their scope beyond biotechnology issues. For example, the

Group of Advisers on the Ethical Implications of Biotechnology (GAEIB), set up in 1991 by the European Commission, was replaced in 1997 by the European Group on Ethics in Science and New Technologies (EGE), whose mandate, renewed several times up to the present, covers all areas of science and technology.

The triangulation of science, ethics and economy

A straightforward explanation of the flourishing of ethical advice on science and technology policy is that it represents a logical reply to rapid progress in research and innovation in a cultural and political context increasingly emphasizing people's rights of information and control. This account, however, obscures three key aspects. First, as argued above, the creation of bodies tasked specifically with performing an ethical review of science and technology entails the isolation of ethical issues from other questions that could (and arguably should) be asked. Second, this process coincided with a shift in the institutional position of expert advice, 'from advising a parliament to shaping opinions aimed at legitimizing governmental decisions' (Tallacchini 2009: 286). An example of this simultaneous transition is provided by the replacement of OTA with NBAC in the US. Third, the purification of ethical issues from other kinds of social questions corresponds to its entrenchment with the case for 'sound science' as transcending values and interests to provide objective answers to policy problems (Moore et al. 2011).

Early evidence of this process is offered by a 1991 Communication of the European Commission on *Promoting the Competitive Environment for the Industrial Activities Based on Biotechnology Within the Community*. Biotech legislation and product marketization, the Commission says, should be assessed through objective scientific evaluation according to three criteria: safety, quality and efficacy. Consideration of 'broader socio-economic needs … (for example, consequences on agricultural production)', is ruled out, since adding a fourth 'hurdle' would create uncertainty, which in its turn 'could result in a diversion of investment and could act as a disincentive for innovation and technological development by industry' (European Commission 1991: 8). Ethical issues, identified as those pertaining to human life and identity, animal welfare and 'other value-laden issues', have instead to be addressed, as this is necessary to avoid confusion that 'can adversely influence the whole climate for industrial development of biotechnology' (European Commission 1991: 10–11).

We find here outlined a triangulation among science, ethics and economy that has increasingly characterized the dynamics of research and development, whereby 'ethics' is separated from 'risk' and both are demarcated from socio-economic issues and invested with the task of 'optimizing' innovation, assumed as unquestionably socially beneficial, in view of its commodification. The evolution of US and European ag-biotech policies, for example, shows that, in spite of important institutional differences (for instance in regard to the regulatory capacity of US agencies, such as the Food and Drug Administration, compared with the advisory competences of the European Food and Safety Agency), a common rationale has been to rule out consideration of socio-economic implications. Emblematic is the case of recombinant bovine growth hormone (rBGH) – the first ag-biotech product to be successfully commodified. The ag-biotech industry started to request market authorization in the mid-1980s. While final permission was granted in the US (in 1993) but not in the EU, in both cases contentions about the need to consider socio-economic implications, especially on traditional farming and small producers, were rejected largely as a result of pressures from the ag-biotech industry. Under WTO rules, argued the European Court of Justice, rBGH marketization could be forbidden only if it were proved harmful. Eventually Europe banned rBGH on ethical grounds, namely on concerns about animal suffering, as supported by scientific studies (Kinchy et al. 2008).

Similar reasons for rejection were used in Canada, Japan, Australia and elsewhere. Whatever the destiny of rBGH around the world (after the US it has been approved in various countries), its story confirms the alliance between technical and ethical assessment, scientific arguments having been used to legitimize ethical ones (ascertainment of animal suffering) and vice versa ('sound science' as duly premised on policy decisions), while relevant political and distributive issues were marginalized.

The same downplaying of socio-economic aspects can be found elsewhere, from the transport and use of genetically modified organisms (Cartagena Biosafety Protocol) (Kinchy et al. 2008) to biofuels policies (Levidow et al. 2012). Nor is this limited to biotech. A similar trend characterizes a number of fields, from nanotechnologies to Information and Communications Technologies (ICTs) and big data. Be it a matter of formal or, more frequently, 'soft' regulation (voluntary codes of conduct, best practices and so on), any reference to political and distributive aspects of innovation is kept to a minimum, or avoided entirely. For example, reading the EU's Code of Conduct for Responsible Nanosciences and Nanotechnologies Research, one finds the same narrative met above: controversies over new technologies are generated by 'worries about risks to health and the environment, as well as for ethics and the respect of fundamental rights' and should be dealt with by ensuring that research is undertaken 'in a safe, ethical and effective framework' (European Commission 2009: 7, 13). Similar discourses are produced also in regard to the ethical handling of algorithms, despite acknowledgment of the major governmental power residing in their capacity to 'structure possibilities' (Ananny 2016) through selection and association of information about issues such as genetic risk factors (Mitchell and Waldby 2010) or for surveillance purposes (Amoore 2009).

Staging participation

One of the main justifications within policy and academia for strengthening the role of ethical review is the need to establish a more intense and open dialogue between science and society, in response to evidence of growing 'public unease' with science and technological innovation (the vicissitudes of ag-biotech in Europe offer a resonant lesson in this regard). Technology assessment was often blamed for its technocratic orientation, despite attempts to make it more participatory and inclusive. Ethics, then, is portrayed as a way to make citizens' values and concerns count, in the framework of a dialogue among policy makers, researchers, industry, expert committees, civil society organizations and society at large.

However, critics argue that in ethics committees, public participation is more staged than realized. These committees are composed of appointed experts (physicians, philosophers etc.) allegedly able to represent relevant viewpoints and concerns, or, when 'lay' people are involved, to guide their reflections and interpret their inputs. Ethics is portrayed as a neutral technique capable of producing 'a single, correct solution for each ethical problem which is largely independent of person, place or time' (Bosk 1999: 63). Correspondingly, ethics committees are depicted as 'a "neutral" normative tool, endowed with the potential to speak for rationality' (Tallacchini 2009: 281). Ethics, in other words, is framed as a 'science', the equivalent in the normative realm of the function that natural sciences and technical expertise perform in the realm of facts.

Ongoing innovation and its contribution to the welfare of the whole society, usually through appropriate marketization, are generally taken for granted (Braun et al. 2010). Discussions rarely address questions of 'whether or not' and 'for the benefit of whom', focusing instead on questions of 'how'. The trading and exchange of values is normalized and legitimated. As Salter and Salter remark, 'through the enunciation and application of a set of principles, standardized rules are established that enable the translation of different moral positions to a common metric capable of facilitating, usually on a cost-benefit basis, choices and decisions' (2007: 560). Especially when lay people are engaged in ethical debates, emergent counter-narratives are either included as variations internal to a shared framework or, if incompatible with the latter, marginalized or stigmatized as ignorance or prejudice. And when ethical review is not the formal remit, as with many 'public dialogues' on sciences and technologies, the debate is typically tailored to the apolitical, cognitively naïve but ethically committed lay citizen, while the politically engaged one is marginalized (Wynne 2001).[2]

In short, ethics is framed as setting appropriate limits to techno-scientific advancement, yet these limits are continuously expanded by that advancement itself. The room for political and distributive questions shrinks dramatically, with a systematic exclusion of conflicting world views, questions of justice and inequality, and the interweaving of science, technology and society at large. For example, a strictly ethical framing of donation of biological material for medical and pharmaceutical purposes obscures how bodies are increasingly integrated, as 'clinical labour', into the production of value. Moreover, waged forms of such labour, from drug experimentation to sperm and oocyte markets, typically entail unequal terms of exchange between poor vendors and wealthy purchasers (Sunder-Rajan 2006; Fisher 2009; Mitchell and Waldby 2010; Cooper and Waldby 2014).

From ELSI/ELSA to AG/RRI

The same picture appears from the perspective of the so-called ELSI/ELSA programs developed in the US, Canada, Europe and the Far East since the 1990s. These acronyms refer to research and interaction activities (stakeholder dialogues, education etc.) aimed at anticipating and addressing ethical, legal and social implications/aspects of emerging sciences and technologies. In this context, concerns that public controversy could hinder innovation are even more explicit. The claim is that strategies need to be enacted to assess and orient its development at a stage early enough to forego future public resistance and facilitate its social embedding.

For critics this approach shows various 'pathologies' (Zwart et al. 2014; Wickson et al. 2015). First, ELSI/ELSA inquiry is often pre-formatted by the research programs it aims to study. Second, the usual framework of 'risk' and 'ethics' dominates, with issues of harm prevention and individual autonomy and privacy prevailing over questions of identity, justice and so on. Third, the focus is on single cases rather than the broader socio-economic framework of innovation. Fourth, the so-called 'Collingridge dilemma' is very relevant: at an early stage of development it is easier to shape technologies, but it is also far more difficult to predict their impact.

Various attempts have been made to overcome these limitations. One example is the 'midstream modulation' approach (Schuurbiers and Fisher 2009), which builds on collaboration at the laboratory level between natural and social scientists. The purpose is to adjust research decisions according to wide-ranging societal considerations. Inquiry, however, is explicitly limited to 'how' questions, without touching 'why' issues.

A more decisive step towards a (re)politicization of science and innovation is possibly represented by the recent rise of a discourse offered in two main versions: 'anticipatory governance' (AG) and 'responsible research and innovation' (RRI). AG emerged in the US in the early 2000s, in the context of nanotechnology policy debates. It is defined as 'a broad-based capacity extended through society that can act on a variety of inputs to manage emerging knowledge-based technologies while such management is still possible' (Guston 2008: vi). RRI (see Stilgoe and Macnaghten, this volume) arose a few years later in Europe (to a remarkable extent it is the offspring of expertise internal to the European Commission). It is described as 'a transparent, interactive process by which societal actors and innovators become mutually responsive to each other with a view to the (ethical) acceptability, sustainability and societal desirability of the innovation process and its marketable products (in order to allow a proper embedding of scientific and technological advances in our society)' (von Schomberg 2013: 63). AG is purported to entail foresight (building scenarios of plausible futures), engagement of lay publics and integration of different views and concerns (Guston 2014). Likewise, RRI is claimed to comprise anticipation, reflexivity, inclusion and responsiveness (Stilgoe et al. 2013). Similarly to ELSI/ELSA, the idea is to shape innovation before technological 'lock-in' sets in. However, the focus is not only on research and development but also on production and distribution. Moreover, the stance is more proactive. The emphasis is on innovation more than risk, and ethics and other 'normative anchors' (such as the principles included in the EU Treaty: sustainability, competitiveness, environmental protection, social inclusion etc.) are treated as triggers rather than constraints. Finally, questions concerning the purpose of innovation (rationale, distributive effects, alternatives) fall within the scope of inquiry.

A lot of public money is being invested in developing and applying AG and RRI. It is too early to say what this will eventually produce. A radical departure from the ruling governmental approach is, however, unlikely. One may even argue that AG and RRI represent a further intensification of that approach. Not only is the lexicon of AG/RRI still basically ethical, but social divisions elicited by innovation are often depicted in a depoliticized way – as between technological initiates and technological laypeople, rather than between contrasting interpretations of the public good (see Grinbaum and Groves 2013). Assumptions fundamental to deciding what are the 'right' social impacts and processes to realize them (for example, whether marketization should be the rule unless proven unsuitable) remain unspoken. And major prominence is given to the economic valorization of innovation and the speeding up of the transfer from bench to market (Zwart et al. 2014). AG/RRI is therefore likely to legitimate a further emphasis of industrial agendas over distributive concerns.[3]

The neoliberal underpinnings of the ethicization of science governance

Neoliberalism is clearly implicated in the tightening interlinkage of ethics, science and economy and its underlying governmental logic. There are many definitions of neoliberalism, but for the purposes of this chapter we can consider neoliberal those approaches which loosely build on the following interlinked tenets (see Mirowski 2013; Dardot and Laval 2014):

- humans are competitive, entrepreneurial beings;
- the market is the only institution capable of processing information effectively;
- state regulation is instrumental to disseminating and strengthening market rationality in any social field; and
- the space of politics should be restricted, transferring as many issues as possible to private or technical spheres.

Adopting this definition, robust evidence emerges of widespread, comparable patterns of institutional change in recent decades (Baccaro and Howell 2011). After the deregulation and the dismantling of the welfare state of earlier years, from the 1990s onwards market-guided state re-regulation, public–private partnerships and promotion of non-market metrics and social capital become the dominant strategy for restoring the social grounds for capital accumulation (Peck and Tickell 2002). The rise of ethics as a crucial means for a 'science-society dialogue', mainly understood in terms of removing obstacles to the acceptance of innovation, corresponds with this phase.

It is important to consider that neoliberalism does not, as liberalism did, conceive of the human agent as a unit whose motivations are exogenous to economy and impenetrable by power, but as an optimizer of resources, beginning with the valorization of oneself as capital (Foucault 2008; Feher 2009; Lazzarato 2009). This agent is thus eminently governable through 'soft', symbolic and discursive interventions premised on values, such as individual autonomy, self-fulfilment and responsibility, which are deeply entrenched in modern, and especially late modern, culture. Many scholars have stressed how the new accumulative phase of capitalism begun in the 1970s has integrated critical discourses and practices that emerged in previous years, against the hierarchies and rigidities of the Fordist mode of production. The values of freedom, autonomy and creativity have been translated into flexibility, networking, communication, and permanent education (Boltanski and Chiapello 2005; Hartmann and Honneth 2006; Mouffe 2013).

Accordingly, burgeoning forms of advice conveyed by various types of expertise (medical, psychological, financial, managerial, etc.) offer 'a means of exercising power that is ethical because it has as its basis not an external truth, but an internal truth, one essential to each individual person over whom it is exercised' (Rose 1998: 92).

This logic can be easily detected in the governance of science and technology. Scientific knowledge and technological artefacts stem from and incorporate imaginaries and visions of the 'good', implicit and often prescriptive models and assumptions about the existing or desirable social order (Brown and Michael 2003; Welsh and Wynne 2013). However, innovation is increasingly framed in ethical terms by both developers and students (see e.g. Shilton 2012; Van de Poel 2012; Steen 2015). The figure of the citizen/consumer is also increasingly endowed with ethical connotations, from supporting traditional farming (Gottlieb and Joshi 2010) to using genetic testing kits (Rose 2007) and 'smart meters' for gauging everyday habits (Marres 2011), to buying carbon credits to take them off the market and raise costs for polluting industries (Blok 2012). The very blurring of designer and user in the 'prosumer' figure, till now relevant especially to the ICTs but increasingly involving other fields, such as biotech (Delfanti 2011), is mainly framed ethically, be it a matter of entrepreneurial self-fulfilment or of activist engagement in accomplishing a collective goal (free software etc.).

The 'productive' character of power as eliciting rather than constraining behaviours, long stressed by Michel Foucault, is therefore witnessing an unprecedented intensification with regard to science and innovation, as is the role of ethics in this process. Some scholars – Nicholas Rose (2007) is an example – adopt a descriptive tone where risks (of manipulation) and opportunities (of choice, prudence and responsibility) of burgeoning possibilities of intervention on human and nonhuman matter are given a balanced (or anodyne) treatment. Others, instead (e.g. Lemke 2004; Raman and Tutton 2010), combine Foucauldian and political economy perspectives to contend that we are hardly confronted with a broadening space for freedom and self-actualization, but rather with an extension of disciplinary powers, perhaps softer but also more constraining than in the past.

Indeed, self-entrepreneurialism and political activism are becoming increasingly difficult to disentangle. Is GM food rejected because it is considered lower quality and unhealthy, or out of environmental and socio-economic concerns? Is one practising DIYbio to challenge the monopoly of universities and pharmaceutical companies, or to realize low-cost (and marketizable) products? The intensification of indirect forms of government building on the ethicization of agency is directly relevant to these (self-)interpretive dilemmas.

It is worth noting how not only 'advanced liberal' readings of present and prospective impacts of innovation, such as Rose's, but also the post-Marxist constellation is receptive to the lure of ethics. For Alain Touraine (2014), a prominent scholar of social movements, globalization has destroyed all institutions and society itself. What remains is just the individual. Actors no longer are qualified according to their social relations, but according to their relation to themselves and their own legitimacy, and single-issue mobilizations based on moral claims prevail over encompassing economic claims. For Paolo Virno (who, like Antonio Negri, belongs to the 'autonomist' strand of radical post-Marxism), the subject of resistance today is neither the class nor the people of the old nation state, but a network of singularities: the multitude. This is mainly composed of the mass intellectuality that constitutes the basic productive force of the knowledge-based economy. Engaged in 'virtuous', uncontrollable forms of creative labor, this new collective subject 'presents itself on the public stage as an ethical movement' (2009: 103; see also 2004). Similarly, for Simon Critchley (2007), the dislocating effects of capitalism bring ethics to the forefront, as a 'metapolitical moment', which provides motivation and propulsion to action.

What is missing in the arguments above is a consideration for how single-issue mobilizations and appeals to 'rethink politics' are consonant with neoliberal discourses and imaginaries (Harvey 2005; Mouffe 2005; Jessop 2010b); how the ethicization of engagement corresponds by and large to a 'neoliberalization of activism' (Roff 2007), where contentious politics is increasingly subsumed to a narrative of 'active', 'responsible' citizenry, concerned with the quality, safety and availability of innovation; and how even anti-capitalist networks, such as those operating in the open source and hacking movements, can be easily integrated into, or subjugated to, the logic of capital (Suarez-Villa 2009; Ottinger 2013; Söderberg and Delfanti 2015).

This convergence between ethicization of science governance and ethicization of social mobilizations and academic critique highlights once more how 'ethics' has become a pervasive horizon of meaning and driver of de-politicization.

Conclusion

Early reflections on the governmental role of ethics in relation to science and technology have been proposed by Hans Jonas (1984). For him, the unprecedented capacities of destruction that today reside in the hands of humanity raise an 'imperative of responsibility' for each and every person, calling for a new ethics for the technological age. The critical potential present in this position, however, has been increasingly neutralized by a 'post-political' drift focused on the consensual acknowledgment of the inevitability of capitalism, market cosmopolitanism and insecurity, which finds a powerful trigger in narratives of global environmental challenges, adaptive strategies and technological fixes (Swyngedouw 2010). Contrary to Weber's forecast, and disguised behind resonant appeals to reason and responsibility, the contemporary political landscape is dominated by a peculiar version of the ethics of principles: innovation as an undisputable imperative.

That the triangulation of science, ethics and economy has been saturating the space of public discourse – or, in Foucauldian terms, has been defining the current problematization of science and innovation, dictating both the relevant questions and the scope of disagreement about the answers – is exemplified by the debate over human enhancement (that is, the improvement of bodily and mental capacities: memory, reasoning, temperament, longevity, immunity to diseases, strength etc.). Both supporters and detractors (e.g. Agar 2004; Sandel 2007) tend to focus on the risks and desirability of individual access to, and freedom of choice about, enhancing technologies. What remains generally neglected is the role of cultural and market pressures in selecting particular 'genetic services', and the actual room people have for opting out of what is going to become a new category of positional goods, similar to education or professional qualification (Pellizzoni 2012).

In a context where ethics has become a major depoliticizing device, recalling the fundamental difference between ethics and politics and the relevance of a cultural political economy of science and technology (that is, of an inquiry into the ideas, values, assumptions and narratives underpinning the conception, realization, justification and marketization of research and innovation) is important. Criticisms of radical democratic approaches take issue especially with their key tenet of politics as the realm of discord. It is, however, significant that, in providing alternative accounts, critics often adopt an ethicized language. Rancière and Mouffe claim that social order lacks ultimate foundations; as a consequence, conflict cannot be eliminated, though its destructiveness can be kept at bay by translating hostility into a struggle between reciprocally respectful adversaries. This argument is questioned according to a moral lexicon, based on self-legitimating notions like care, responsibility, receptivity, or 'otherness' – the latter understood as a given, rather than the result of the divisive character of any social ordering (see e.g. Barnett 2004). This is a further confirmation that today, even unwittingly, ethics fulfils the task of hollowing out politics. Only a major effort to resist the hegemonic lure of ethics can support an effective assessment of science and innovation in the present historical condition.

Notes

1   A significant European example is the Danish Board of Technology (DBT), which started its life as an experiment in the 1980s becoming permanent in 1995 as a self-governing body connected with the parliament. Years after the demise of OTA, DBT has met with a somewhat comparable destiny. After successfully pioneering public debates and developing related methodologies, it suffered reductions in funding that led it to increasingly operate as a consultancy company, a trend reinforced when in 2011 it was closed and re-established as a foundation.
2   A well-documented example of this strategy is the GM Nation? deliberative process on agricultural gene technologies organized in the UK in 2003 (see Irwin 2006).
3   This trend is well exemplified in Europe by the Innovative Medicines Initiative (IMI). Defined as 'Europe's largest public–private initiative aiming to speed up the development of better and safer medicines for patients', IMI deals with 'pre-competitive' research and development, getting huge money from the EU's Horizon 2020 program (€1.638 billion for the period 2014–24), with EFPIA (European Federation for Pharmaceutical Industries and Associations) companies defining the topics of the calls for project proposals and contributing 'in kind' to their realization (for example by donating their researchers' time or providing access to research facilities or resources). See www.imi.europa.eu/content/home [accessed 12 January 2016].

References

Agar, N. 2004. *Liberal Eugenics: In Defence of Human Enhancement.* Oxford: Blackwell.
Amoore, L. 2009. 'Algorithmic War: Everyday Geographies of the War on Terror'. *Antipode*, 41(1), 49–69.
Ananny, M. 2016. 'Toward an Ethics of Algorithms: Convening, Observation, Probability, and Timeliness'. *Science, Technology, & Human Values*, 41(1), 93–117.
Baccaro, L. and Howell, C. 2011. 'A Common Neoliberal Trajectory: The Transformation of Industrial Relations in Advanced Capitalism'. *Politics & Society*, 39(4), 521–563.
Barnett, C. 2004. 'Deconstructing Radical Democracy: Articulation, Representation, and Being-With-Others'. *Political Geography*, 23(5), 503–528.
Blok, A. 2012. 'Configuring the Homo Carbonomicus: Carbon Markets, Calculative Techniques, and the Green Neoliberal', in Pellizzoni, L. and Ylönen, M., eds. *Neoliberalism and Technoscience: Critical Assessments.* Farnham: Asghate: 187–208.
Bogner, A. and Menz, W. 2010. 'How Politics Deals with Expert Dissent: The Case of Ethics Councils'. *Science, Technology & Human Values*, 35(6), 888–914.
Boltanski, L. and Chiapello, E. 2005. *The New Spirit of Capitalism.* London: Verso.
Bosk, C.L. 1999. 'Logical Professional Ethicist Available: Logical, Secular, Friendly'. *Daedelus,* 128(4), 47–68.
Braun, C., Herrmann, S.L., Könninger, S. and Moore, A. 2010. 'Ethical Reflection Must Always Be Measured'. *Science, Technology & Human Values*, 35(6), 839–864.
Brown, N. and Michael, M. 2003. 'A Sociology of Expectations: Retrospecting Prospects and Prospecting Retrospects'. *Technology Analysis & Strategic Management*, 15(1), 3–18.
Cooper, M. and Waldby, C. 2014. *Clinical Labor.* Durham, NC: Duke University Press.

Critchley, S. 2007. *Infinitely Demanding: Ethics of Commitment, Politics of Resistance*. London: Verso.

Dardot, P. and Laval, C. 2014. *The New Way of the World: On Neoliberal Society*. London: Verso.

De Vries, R., Dingwall, R. and Orfali K. 2009. 'The Moral Organization of the Professions: Bioethics in the United States and France'. *Current Sociology*, 57(4): 555–579.

Delfanti, A. 2011. 'Tweaking Genes in Your Garage: Biohacking Between Activism and Entrepreneurship', in Sützl, W. and Hug, T., eds. *Activist Media and Biopolitics Critical Media Interventions in the Age of Biopower*. Innsbruck: Innsbruck University Press: 163–178.

Dewey, J. 1984. 'The Public and Its Problems', in Bodyston, J.A., ed. *The Later Works of John Dewey, Volume 2*. Carbondale: Southern Illinois University Press: 235–372.

European Commission. 1991. *Promoting the Competitive Environment for the Industrial Activities Based on Biotechnology Within the Community*. Commission Communication. Brussels: SEC(91)629 final.

European Commission. 2009. *A Code of Conduct for Responsible Nanosciences and Nanotechnologies Research*. Commission Recommendation. Luxembourg: Office for Official Publications of the European Communities.

Feher, M. 2009. 'Self-Appreciation: Or, the Aspirations of Human Capital'. *Public Culture*, 21(1), 21–41.

Felt, U. and Wynne, B. eds. 2007. *Taking European Knowledge Society Seriously*. Report for the European Commission. Luxembourg: Office for Official Publications of the European Communities.

Fisher, J.A. 2009. *Medical Research for Hire: The Political Economy of Pharmaceutical Clinical Trials*. New Brunswick, NJ: Rutgers University Press.

Foucault, M. 2008. *The Birth of Biopolitics. Lectures at the Collège de France 1978–1979*. Basingstoke: Palgrave Macmillan.

Fuchs, M. 2005. *National Ethics Councils*. Berlin: Nationaler Ethikrat.

Gottlieb, R. and Joshi, A. 2010. *Food Justice*. Cambridge, MA: MIT Press.

Grinbaum, A. and Groves, C. 2013. 'What Is "Responsible" About Responsible Innovation? Understanding the Ethical Issues', in Owen, R., Bessant, J. and Heintz, M., eds. *Responsible Innovation. Managing the Responsible Emergence of Science and Innovation in Society*. Chichester: Wiley: 119–142.

Guston, D. 2008. 'Preface', in Fisher, E., Selin, C. and Wetmore, J.M., eds. *The Yearbook of Nanotechnology in Society: Presenting Futures, vol. 1*. New York: Springer: v–viii.

Guston, D. 2014. 'Understanding "Anticipatory Governance"'. *Social Studies of Science*, 44(2), 218–242.

Hartmann, M. and Honneth, A. 2006. 'Paradoxes of Capitalism'. *Constellations*, 13(1), 41–58.

Irwin, A. 2006. 'The Politics of Talk: Coming to Terms with the "New" Scientific Governance'. *Social Studies of Science*, 36(2), 299–320.

Jessop, B. 2010a. 'Cultural Political Economy and Critical Policy Studies'. *Critical Policy Studies*, 3(3–4): 336–356.

Jessop, B. 2010b. 'From Hegemony to Crisis? The Continuing Ecological Dominance of Neoliberalism', in Birch, K. and Mykhnenko, V., eds. *The Rise and Fall of Neoliberalism*. London: Zed Books: 171–187.

Jonas, H. 1984 *The Imperative of Responsibility: In search of an Ethics for the Technological Age*. Chicago: University of Chicago Press.

Kinchy, A., Kleinman, D. and Autry, R. 2008. 'Against Free Markets, Against Science? Regulating the Socio-Economic Effects of Biotechnology'. *Rural Sociology*, 73(2), 147–179.

Lazzarato, M. 2009. 'Neoliberalism in Action: Inequality, Insecurity and the Reconstitution of the Social'. *Theory, Culture & Society*, 26(6), 109–133.

Lemke, T. 2004. 'Disposition and Determinism – Genetic Diagnostics in Risk Society'. *Sociological Review*, 52(4), 550–566.

Levidow, L., Papaioannou, T. and K. Birch. 2012. 'Neoliberalizing Technoscience and Environment: EU Policy for Competitive, Sustainable Biofuels', in Pellizzoni, L. and Ylönen, M., eds. *Neoliberalism and Technoscience: Critical Assessments*. Farnham: Asghate: 159–186.

Lévinas, E. 2000. *Entre Nous: Essays on Thinking-of-the-Other*. New York: Columbia University Press.

Luhmann, N. 1989. *Ecological Communication*. Cambridge: Polity.

Marres, N. 2011. 'The Costs of Public Involvement: Everyday Devices of Carbon Accounting and the Materialization of Participation'. *Economy and Society*, 40(4), 510–533.

Mirowski, P. 2013. *Never Let a Serious Crisis Go to Waste: How Neoliberalism Survived the Financial Meltdown*. London: Verso.

Mitchell, R. and Waldby, C. 2010. 'National Biobanks: Clinical Labor, Risk Production, and the Creation of Biovalue'. *Science, Technology, & Human Values*, 35(3), 330–355.

Moore, K., Kleinman, D., Hess, D. and Frickel, S. 2011. 'Science and Neoliberal Globalization: A Political Sociological Approach'. *Theory and Society*, 40(5), 505–532.

Mouffe, C. 2005. *On the Political*. London: Routledge.

Mouffe, C. 2013. *Agonistics*. London: Verso.

Peck, J. and Tickell, A. 2002. 'Neoliberalizing Space'. *Antipode*, 34(3), 380–404.

Ottinger, G. 2013. *Refining Expertise: How Responsible Engineers Subvert Environmental Justice Challenges*. New York: New York University Press.

Pellizzoni, L. 2012. 'Strong Will in a Messy World: Ethics and the Government of Technoscience'. *NanoEthics*, 6(3), 257–272.

Raman, S. and Tutton, R. 2010. 'Life, Science, and Biopower'. *Science Technology & Human Values*, 35(5), 711–734.

Rancière, J. 1998. *Disagreement*. Minneapolis: University of Minnesota Press.

Roff, R.J. 2007. 'Shopping for Change? Neoliberalizing Activism and the Limits to Eating Non-GMO'. *Agriculture and Human Values*, 24, 511–522.

Rose, N. 1998. *Inventing Our Selves*. Cambridge: Cambridge University Press.

Rose, N. 2007. *The Politics of Life Itself*. Princeton, NJ: Princeton University Press.

Salter, B. and Salter, C. 2007. 'Bioethics and the Global Moral Economy: The Cultural Politics of Human Embryonic Stem Cell Science'. *Science, Technology, & Human Values*, 32(5), 554–581.

Sandel, M. 2007. *The Case Against Perfection: Ethics in the Age of Genetic Engineering*. Cambridge, MA: Harvard University Press.

Schuurbiers, D. and Fisher, E. 2009. 'Lab-scale Intervention: Science & Society Series on Convergence Research'. *EMBO Reports*, 10(5), 424–427.

Shilton, K. 2012. 'Values Levers: Building Ethics into Design'. *Science, Technology, & Human Values*, 38 (3), 374–397.

Steen, M. 2015. 'Upon Opening the Black Box and Finding it Full: Exploring the Ethics in Design Practices'. *Science, Technology & Human Values*, 40(3), 389–420.

Stilgoe, J., Owen, R. and Macnaghten, P. 2013. 'Developing a Framework for Responsible Innovation'. *Research Policy*, 42(9), 1568–1580.

Suarez-Villa, L. 2009. *Technocapitalism*. Philadelphia: Temple University Press.

Sunder-Rajan, K. 2006. *Biocapital: The Constitution of Postgenomic Life*. Durham, NC: Duke University Press.

Swyngedouw, E. 2010. 'Apocalypse Forever? Post-Political Populism and the Spectre of Climate Change'. *Theory, Culture & Society*, 27(2–3), 213–232.

Tallacchini, M. 2009. 'Governing by Values. EU Ethics: Soft Tool, Hard Effects'. *Minerva*, 47(3), 281–306.

Touraine, A. 2014. *After the Crisis*. Cambridge: Polity Press.

Tyfield, D. 2012. 'A Cultural Political Economy of Research and Innovation in an Age of Crisis'. *Minerva*, 50(2), 149–167.

Van de Poel, I. 2012. 'Can We Design for Well-Being?', in Brey, P., Briggle, A. and Spence, E., eds. *The Good Life in a Technological Age*. New York: Routledge: 295–306.

Virno, P. 2004. *A Grammar of the Multitude*. Los Angeles: Semiotext(e).

Virno, P. 2009. 'Natural-Historical Diagrams: The "New Global" Movement and the Biological Invariant'. *Cosmos and History: The Journal of Natural and Social Philosophy*, 5(1), 92–104.

Von Schomberg, R. 2013. 'A Vision of Responsible Research and Innovation', in Owen, R., Bessant, J. and Heintz, M., eds. *Responsible Innovation: Managing the Responsible Emergence of Science and Innovation in Society*. Chichester: Wiley: 51–74.

Weber, M. 1958 [1919]. 'Politics as Vocation', in Gerth, H. and Wright Mills, C., eds. *From Max Weber*. New York: Oxford University Press: 77–128.

Welsh, I. and Wynne, B. 2013. 'Science, Scientism and Imaginaries of Publics in the UK: Passive Objects, Incipient Threats'. *Science as Culture*, 22(4), 540–566.

Wickson, F., Strand, R. and Kjølberg, K.L. 2015. 'The Walkshop Approach to Science and Technology Ethics'. *Science and Engineering Ethics*, 21(1), 241–264.

Wynne, B. 2001. 'Creating Public Alienation: Expert Discourses of Risk and Ethics on GMOs'. *Science as Culture*, 10, 1–40.

Zwart, H., Lendeweerd, L. and van Rooij, A. 2014. 'Adapt or Perish? Assessing the Recent Shift in the European Research Funding Arena From "ELSA" to "RRI"'. *Life Sciences, Society and Policy*, 10(11), 1–19.

14

THE POLITICAL ECONOMY OF MILITARY SCIENCE

Chris Langley and Stuart Parkinson

Introduction

The world today faces many grave problems – including escalating armed conflict and regional poverty, climate change, resource depletion and increasing inequality. Such challenges are important in themselves but also exacerbate national and global insecurity. For example, resource scarcity and climate change can lead to the mass movement of people, resulting in armed conflict. It is important, while considering the role of Science, Engineering and Technology (SET) in shaping the security and military agendas, to realise that these terms are highly contested. For many, the notion of 'security' involves deploying major military technologies, thereby threatening and using force rather than taking a broader perspective, which seeks to understand and deal with the roots of conflict. Indeed, an influential view today is that the use of conventional military force constitutes a practical tool of foreign policy post-Cold War (Stone 2004).

A number of SET areas, like microelectronics, computer science, nuclear technology and artificial intelligence, owe much of their historical origin to significant military funding, with further development being in the hands of civilian companies - a process continuing today. SET are also integral players in the 'knowledge economy' and are expected to provide solutions to an ever-growing array of global problems within a low carbon framework. The political economy of (military and non-military) SET is shaped and influenced by a wide range of interacting societal and political factors, which include:

- economic globalisation coupled with a widespread neoliberal worldview; thereby creating a concomitant mindset which questions the overarching value and function of SET;
- the emergence of global innovation networks and internationalised R&D and other SET collaborations;
- a matrix of issues concerning dual-use,[1] technology transfer and research integrity;
- the post-Cold War rise of influential and policy-related narratives of 'failed states' and wide-ranging discussions of security, especially regarding terrorism;
- national and international alliances and economic power;
- issues relating to the actual process of SET – including funding bias, 'irreversibility' (the growing understanding that we cannot 'undo' technological approaches over time[2]), data reliability, plus a variety of ethical dilemmas (Rappert and McLeish 2007; Langley 2005).

Such interrelated issues pose a number of questions, both normative and pragmatic, concerning the reliability, integrity and effectiveness of SET. Currently the rate of change and development and the pervasive nature of SET, together with the resultant powerful new technologies, call for professional codes and ethical guidelines which recognise potential or pressing security aspects of SET research (including the use of data and experimental techniques by state militaries and non-state armed groups) and the need for public accountability (Rappert and McLeish 2007). Unfortunately, this recognition has not been well developed within SET research culture (Kuhlau et al. 2008; Somerville and Atlas 2005). A number of research publications from the SET community (especially the biomedical sector) have raised possible dual-use security concerns (James 2006; Rappert 2006); however, there is a paucity of material which addresses issues entailed specifically by SET militarisation (Langley 2005).

The combination of global security threats, rapid development of new technologies and the increasing commercialisation of universities helps to generate a markedly problematic militarisation of SET and of society itself. This trend creates a pronounced need for in-depth analysis of militarised SET. Many have argued that changes within SET practice and funding have also reduced the space for 'blue skies' research (Linden 2008). As Schroeer has pointed out, 'The impact of technology goes far beyond the hardware it creates. ... technology is the source of a way of looking at the world through faith in technological solutions' (Schroeer 1997). These trends are a major focus of this chapter.

Military research and innovation have undoubtedly been extremely influential in the wider history of socio-technical change. This has led to the largely unexamined assumption that funding such work is good for broader civilian economies. Innovation pathway(s) from military funding to civilian spin-out technologies tend to be long and involved (Stone 2004). Studies have shown that military-related R&D investment has very low rates of social return (Lichtenberg 1984). The cost-effectiveness of pathways from militarised investment to civilian or military utility is in need of further analysis.

The research environment – the UK as a case study

Most Organisation for Economic Co-operation and Development (OECD) nations fund R&D budgets for specified 'needs', such as health, security, energy and transport. Globally, neoliberal views have changed the ways in which research is funded and directed, and how European and US universities (in which fundamental SET expertise lies) are perceived and supported (Mirowski 2011). The commercialisation and privatisation of knowledge production, including academic SET research, is one of the key elements of the neoliberal project and is described in *Science in the Private Interest* (Krimsky 2003; see also Mirowski 2011 and this volume).

The UK is a useful country in which to examine militarised SET because, in expenditure terms, it lies between those highly militarised industrial nations such as the USA, China and Russia and other significantly less militarised countries of the EU, as well as Japan, Australia and Brazil. In addition, the UK, especially in the last twenty years, has undertaken a variety of changes to SET funding and the R&D process which are shaped by the neoliberal worldviews just mentioned. UK governments, with the active participation of university managers, have also normalised the involvement of universities (in particular, the high-intensity research ones) in a range of collaborative ventures with commercial 'partners' (Langley 2008).

The changing environment in which military R&D is undertaken and the political decisions which underscore an increasing reliance on SET to address security challenges help produce militarised SET embedded in the research, teaching and training culture in the UK, some other European countries and the USA.

Commercialised universities have grown markedly since the 1980s. In the UK, a large number of government publications from the 1990s to the present have stressed closer collaborations between universities and business (see Langley 2005, pp. 19–20; BIS 2014). This follows trends in the USA where federal policy has actively encouraged university–industry collaboration since the 1970s (Mowery 1998). Universities serving as major players in R&D are more common in the UK and US than other OECD countries, with broad implications for the political economy and ethos of SET (Langley 2008).

As others in this volume describe in detail, SET is not simply value-free, objective and ethically unproblematic (see also Wilsdon et al. 2005). With the globalised nature of research and innovation growing, the funding process especially, in its global context and end-points, has been shown to introduce both obvious and more subtle biases, especially where commercial actors are involved. Such biases have been described in commercially supported research in pharmacology, clinical trials, biotechnology and tobacco (see Abraham 1995; Langley and Parkinson 2009), but to date military collaboration has not been subjected to similar in-depth scrutiny. A plethora of guidelines and discussions have been published to address SET research integrity and core standards, but guidelines specifically for those embarking on military-funded partnerships are few (Langley 2014).

During the 1970s and 1980s there was considerable discussion about whether the priorities of academic researchers were being influenced by military funding (Smit 1995). Smit pointed out that SET practice was starting to pose interesting questions about the major influences over the construction of research funding processes in general (Smit 1995). Additionally, distinctions between 'basic' and 'applied' research are highly problematic and unhelpful in understanding the role of SET in knowledge production (see Ziman 2000, pp. 12–27). Rappert et al. (2008) discuss the historic role of SET in the security agenda and point out that developments in international affairs and diplomacy raise questions about the efficacy of military intervention. Many believe that heavy dependence upon militarised SET has led to a decrease in national security (however that is defined) since national security is basically a political rather than a purely technological issue (see Parkinson et al. 2013; Schroeer 1997; UNDP 2015).

Militarised SET today is not a new phenomenon but is arguably more far-reaching because it is globally undertaken within a context dominated by attention to fears about 'security' in a highly unstable world; and where there is a growing dependence on 'knowledge intensive' innovations deriving from a deeply commercialised SET. Here disinterested (non-commercial or governmental) 'expertise' is marginalised, and public accountability of SET and its practices is limited (Langley and Parkinson 2009).

Spending and goals – from the UK to the European context

For over a century, and especially during the Cold War and up to the present day, achieving superiority in technology and innovation in military operations has become a predominant theme in industrialised countries (Langley 2005). The development of the atomic bomb showed that SET held a pivotal role in supporting political and economic power.

Globally, total military expenditure in 2015 was estimated at $1.68 trillion (SIPRI 2016) – likely to be an underestimate - with many highly industrialised countries allocating large sums of their 'defence' budgets to the procurement of sophisticated technological weapons systems, to upgrade existing systems and also to maintain and sustain a military high-technology R&D effort. The USA is the dominant military spender, but the UK and other European countries play a significant role too.

Collecting data on military R&D spending in industrialised nations – even democratic ones – is highly problematic, but vital given the changes in the nature of SET in the military context.

Data from public sources is often of poor quality; countries vary in their definitions of R&D; funders are reluctant to provide information; and the pathways leading to innovation are complex, with national variation (Mowery 2010; SIPRI 2016; Perlo-Freeman, personal communication 2016). There exists no single and widely accepted source of international data on military R&D, and the accounting and governance of military research globally is hugely variable. Parkinson et al. (2013) discuss some of the specific problems in the UK situation. Extra complexity occurs because of changing trends in overall government spending on R&D. One trend of note for militarised SET is that of UK governments progressively reducing direct spending on undertaking public-sector R&D, whilst at the same time increasing funding to UK business – thereby stimulating a commercialised environment for militarised SET (see for example NAO 2013).

Historically, public funding of R&D in the UK has been dominated by the Ministry of Defence (MoD). In the 1980s, it provided half of all public money for R&D, but this fell significantly in the two decades following the end of the Cold War (Parkinson et al. 2013). This fall was arrested following the release of the National Security Through Technology White Paper (NSTT) by the MoD in 2012 (Ministry of Defence 2012). The NSTT superseded the Defence Industrial Strategy (2005) and the Defence Technology Strategy of 2006 – without actually replacing either. The NSTT described the intended procurement process and the resultant SET policies. These policies were to support future MoD activities and to provide the latest weapons systems and related platforms for the UK armed forces and for export (Parkinson et al. 2013). A key issue in the NSTT was a fundamental reliance on SET to achieve the strategy's six critical security objectives (Parkinson et al. 2013).

A detailed assessment by Parkinson et al. (2013) – using data obtained through Freedom of Information requests – found that in the period 2008–11 R&D expenditure by the MoD averaged approximately £1.8 billion a year and was dominated by projects focused on nuclear weapons systems (including submarines) and combat aircraft. Other UK government departments spent varying sums of money on 'security' too – including the Home Office on areas like cybersecurity.

The MoD, in the latest National Security Strategy (Ministry of Defence 2015), places further emphasis on using SET expertise within and outside universities to provide for the nation's 'defence'. An additional £165 million was to be allocated to a Defence and Cyber Innovation Fund. A cross-government Emerging Technology and Innovation Analysis Cell (see later discussions on emerging technologies) was also planned, drawing upon academic SET expertise.

Most funding for military R&D in the UK goes either directly to the commercial military sector or to entities like the Defence Science and Technology Laboratory (DSTL a trading fund of the MoD). Additionally, UK Research Councils and higher education establishments also fund from taxpayer sources a variety of R&D, including that with broadly 'security' objectives, though it is all but impossible to estimate the sums involved.

UK government policy over the past thirty years has been to encourage the private sector to increase its investment in R&D to stimulate economic growth. Noteworthy here is that military R&D has a number of specific features not found in civilian R&D, a main difference being that government is the major customer for the military technologies developed. The MoD's annual spending levels discussed above amount to more than one-sixth of all UK public R&D expenditure per year (Parkinson et al. 2013). Dorman et al. point out that the UK has retained a 20 per cent share of the global 'defence' export market over the last decade and currently remains the second highest world 'defence' exporter, behind the USA, with orders of £9.8 billion (in 2013). The authors go on to say that they 'recognize that there are security, economic and ethical implications of defence exports which render them a contested area of UK public policy' (Dorman et al. 2015).

Dorman et al. (2015) also point out:

> the Ministry of Defence (MoD) has significantly reduced the scope and coverage of statistics and data in three areas: i. on MoD expenditure with the UK defence industry, ii. on the wider domestic economic and employment impact of that expenditure and iii. on the security and economic benefits of defence exports. This impacts on how a robust analysis can be undertaken on the UK military sector, especially given the well described difficulty of examining commercial data.

Langley also discusses these issues (see Langley 2005, 2008). In the 2000s the UK MoD set up a number of consortia (with a variety of funding partners including UK Research Councils, DSTL and QinetiQ) involving 29 universities to undertake joint research and training programmes in SET.[3] Many of these collaborating universities still 'partner' with the military sector (for example in sensor engineering – Langley 2005). A cost-benefit analysis of these various schemes has not been undertaken. The UK Home Office has a variety of 'liaisons' with academic researchers for programmes at its Centre for Applied Science and Technology (Home Office 2015). A detailed study published in 2005 showed the complex and interconnected nature of university-military sector collaboration in the UK (Langley 2005). This collaboration is difficult to map in detail because of the commercialised nature of the UK university sector and the opacity of MoD R&D funding but has indirect effects that are discussed later and which have been elucidated by Kleinman (Kleinman 2010). Nevertheless, the available data suggests that it is likely that currently the overwhelming majority of UK universities accept research and/or teaching funding from both government and corporate sources (Parkinson 2015).

Other European countries have put in place similar partnerships. In Sweden, for instance, the country's largest military company, Saab AB, collaborates with and offers funding to the three largest technical universities to run research projects (including LinkLab[4]), supporting training and teaching, as well as collaborating with other Swedish universities.

The US Department of Defense (DOD) currently funds military research in Europe, for instance at twenty-two German universities, and has 'formally encouraged' (in the Multidisciplinary University Research Initiative) UK academic researchers to apply for research funds in order to 'accelerate progress…' (Malakoff 2015). NATO also supports a variety of SET-directed programmes linking university researchers with the commercial military sector (NATO 2015).

Such complex collaborative programmes of partnerships involving UK and European universities, other governments and the 'defence' companies address the R&D 'needs' of government and the participating companies and are closed to scrutiny. These collaborations raise a number of questions, including the degree of emphasis placed on projects useful to the military, dual-use (especially in development), the sidelining of other, non-military ways of addressing global security challenges, and intellectual property concerns (in both research and development). The lack of openness means that one is unable to fully assess how public funding of military projects impacts across SET and the technologies developed (in particular how is oversight maintained and who benefits from the end products of such investment?) (Langley 2005). Mowery discusses how important complementarities exist between R&D and procurement programmes which in the USA and probably the UK help shape the direction of innovation (Fabrizio and Mowery 2005). Additionally, technology transfer from UK MoD establishments to the civilian sector has been shown to be poor (Spinardi 1992; Dorman et al. 2015).

Fabrizio and Mowery have shown that civilian benefits from military funding of development are most significant in early developmental stages of new technologies, where overlap between civilian and 'defence' requirements for applications are most likely. Maturing technologies tend to have divergent requirements and civilian benefit from such spinoffs drops (Fabrizio and Mowery 2005). These authors also showed that procurement policy (which often stresses performance above other needs) can shape the end product and reduce civilian utility without further investment (Fabrizio and Mowery 2005).

In addition to university–industry collaboration in R&D, with its potential to compromise open-ended enquiry and to import a business ethos, SET militarisation also involves the training of future SET personnel through corporate-directed schemes (within universities) and the 'normalisation' of militarised SET via outreach programmes run by corporations such as BAE Systems, Rolls-Royce and GKN Aerospace in UK schools. Historically, BAE Systems has joined with Rolls-Royce Technology Centres to pursue joint education ventures (Langley 2005); many are still ongoing. These activities pose questions about the values and worldviews covertly imported into the learning and training contexts by such partnerships and whether dissenting views of militarism and the narrowing of options to deal with 'security' are available to participants in these programmes. BAE Systems and Rolls-Royce have their own laboratories which actively partner with UK Research Councils, to undertake a wide swathe of both military- and civilian-directed SET research with universities (Langley 2005; Street and Beale 2007).

EU spending on 'security' research has become a dominant theme in the last five years with the creation of the EU Security Research Programme (EU SRP). The creation of this security-industrial programme (embedded in the Horizon 2020 Programme) has come about at the same time as the boundaries between the military, the security services and law enforcement have eroded (Hayes 2006). The EU SRP was established in 2003 by the creation of the High Level Group of Personalities (including CEOs from the major 'defence', information technology companies and EU officials; see Hayes 2006). The European Commission's Joint Research Centre was to provide support for the SRP. The Group considered that the funding the US government provided to US military companies economically disadvantaged European military multinationals, and that high technology funding by the EU would 'level the playing field' (Hayes 2006).

As is the case across the military-industrial landscape there is little information on the meetings of the Group of Personalities or how decisions were arrived at. The SRP is an integral part of the re-named Framework Programme to support research and innovation and calls upon research expertise within and outside companies – including in universities (EU 2016; Bigo and Jeandesboz 2010). Recently the Group of Personalities announced that the maintenance of military advantage across the EU as a whole was crucial, adding:

> defence-related research is pivotal in maintaining the technological edge that ensures military advantage, European investment in defence R&D has declined by more than 29 % since 2006.
>
> *(EU 2016)*

Horizon 2020 facilitates active industrial-university collaboration and sets in place high technology as a key element in innovation including in the security sphere. During the last eight years the building of a 'Fortress Europe' mentality, with concomitant strengthening of surveillance and EU law enforcement agencies, militarises internal and external security, placing advanced technology at the centre of such security. The Framework Programme (FP) goals are thus shifted from looking at problems of socio-economic importance impacting upon the general public, as detailed in previous FPs, to those of a more 'securitised' nature, increasing the exposure of European academic researchers to military influence.

Corporate presence in the universities – the UK experience

After the end of the Cold War (especially through the 2000s) the UK SET environment started to change as the government began a wholesale privatisation of its research laboratories. During the 1980s and 1990s a far more commercial environment had been promoted within British universities, where the majority of fundamental SET research is situated. This meant more 'commercial-led rather than military-led "solutions" to military problems' (Rappert et al. 2008; Mackenzie and Pottinger 1997). These changes, heralded by a series of funding and oversight processes, gradually re-configured universities to become highly economically significant entities in the UK (Langley 2005) – a process that is ongoing, as the recent White Paper Educational Excellence Everywhere confirms (Department of Education 2016). These trends were in addition to the closure or amalgamation of a number of UK university engineering departments, thereby limiting the available engineering expertise and increasing the pressure from the commercial (military and non-military) sectors on those remaining centres of engineering expertise.

The formation of commercialised universities in the UK and US was linked closely to notions of the knowledge economy and the commodification of knowledge (see Pagano and Rossi this volume). Innovation was seen as flowing from university expertise and migrating into start-up companies incubated in science parks (Langley 2005). Academic researchers in OECD countries working with business often create the main pathways by which new technologies and practices are distributed within society. But, according to Nightingale and Coad, university spin-outs, commercial licensing and science parks show poor performance, and technology transfer (one of the key elements in university-military collaboration) is similarly weak (Nightingale and Coad 2014).

A number of studies in the past two decades examining a range of public- and private-funded military research and training/teaching programmes in SET in the UK showed significant levels of military involvement in the 59 UK universities examined (Parkinson 2015; Langley 2005; Street and Beale 2007). Using Freedom of Information requests, it was found that universities receiving the highest levels of military-sector funding included Cambridge, Cranfield, Imperial College London, Oxford, and Sheffield (Langley 2005; Parkinson 2015; Street and Beale 2007).

A 2014 study (Langley 2014) looked in detail at collaborative funding involving UK universities and the Atomic Weapons Establishment (AWE), which maintains, develops and 'delivers' the UK's nuclear warheads. The study found that 50 UK universities received funding from AWE during the period 2010–2012. Furthermore, five of these universities – Bristol, Cambridge, Cranfield, Heriot-Watt and Imperial College London – had formed an 'alliance' with AWE and obtained a total of £15m (about $24m) over the three-year period. These kinds of collaborations not only involve funding streams (often modest) but also import indirectly a business ethos and 'securitisation' into the university research sphere, touched on earlier (Langley 2014; Kleinman 2010).

Researchers obtaining corporate funds are often perceived as bringing prestige to the department or university which can thereafter attract further support from both corporate and non-corporate sectors (Hildyard 1998; Washburn 2005; Anon personal communication 2006). This process potentially shapes the research culture and agenda by prioritising often short-term economic end-points, and can compromise freedom of research and openness (Langley 2005; Langley 2008). However, some university academics receiving military funding in the UK claimed that open-ended research was not compromised (Langley 2014).

Mechanisms which help to build and maintain the military UK R&D agenda (and hence a militarised SET) are complex and multilayered and space does not allow their detailed description here. In a 2005 study Langley found that the UK MoD relied on advice from groups such as the National Defence Industries Council and the Defence Scientific Advisory Council as well as having inter-departmental groups like the National Defence and Aerospace Committee input on SET R&D areas as well as the security agenda. There was also a tier of teams advising the then Department of Trade and Industry on civil and military aerospace. The military industry was heavily represented in these advisory bodies. The working practices, sources of information and opinion and output from these groups were opaque and lacked public accountability (Langley 2005; Street and Beale 2007).

Braun et al. (2015) have recently described how military technology (autonomous vehicles), when transferred to a civilian context, co-imports specifically militarised discourses for its use and control, especially concerning privacy and security. They described how the development of 'drones' by the military put relatively low importance on privacy when operating such devices, whilst in the civilian realm privacy is accorded higher importance, individuals objecting to covert surveillance without their knowledge. Such 'lock-in' has been found in other areas too (nuclear reactor design for instance Cowan 1990; Cavoukian 2009; Feenberg 2002; Langley 2005), and calls for more discussion of normative processes (Braun et al. 2015). Noble (1985) has also discussed how technological development has been markedly influenced by military and political bias toward forms of hierarchical control (his main example being machine tool development in the USA).

In the UK, government funding from the seven research councils has become far more directed at 'economic end-points' with a concomitant denigration of the Haldane Principle.[5] Research Council-funded research (and training) within universities and Research Council establishments now has a heavily business focus and partnering with a wide range of commercial entities is the norm. The UK government also supports SET research through other entities such as the Defence Science and Technology Laboratory (DSTL – a trading fund of the MoD), the National Physical Laboratory (owned in part by Serco) and the Central Science Laboratory (still a 'public-sector' laboratory) – often partnering with university researchers (Langley 2005; Langley and Parkinson 2009). Such research support, demanding economic outcomes, narrows open-ended and disinterested investigations and imports a business mindset and conservatism into universities. Furthermore, militarised SET has the added burden of 'national security' which can compromise academic freedoms.

It has been shown that commercialised academic research and that which has security implications requires high levels of personal responsibility and professional codes to ensure integrity and reliability (Kuhlau et al. 2008; Langley 2005; Salter and Martin 2001). In recent surveys of those receiving military sector funding we found a reluctance to engage with other members of the SET community or with the informed public about the non-classified research they were engaged in (Langley 2005; Langley et al. 2008). Despite an extensive literature describing the potential for bias and poor levels of transparency in university–business partnerships, a 2015 publication from the UK government (BIS 2015) extols ever more collaboration between universities and small businesses for innovation, without pointing out the potential for problems such as bias, lack of openness and short-term research goals (Langley 2005; Collini 2012).

The US context – on a grand scale

The Gulf War of 1990–1, in which the USA played a leading role, demonstrated a range of new advanced military technologies which would become central in 21st-century warfare, as well as shaping ideas about building security (National Priorities Project 2015).

The US Department of Defense (DOD) is the largest contributor to US federal R&D spending through the Department's research, development, testing and evaluation (RDT&E) budget, which extends from basic research through to systems evaluation. The DOD is responsible for more than half of the US's public R&D spending (Parkinson et al. 2013). In terms of academic R&D funding, generally only the National Institutes of Health and the National Science Foundation surpass the DOD.

DOD R&D funding goes to a variety of public and private institutions. The overwhelming majority of external funding is destined for industrial contractors for the development of weapons systems and other military technologies. The RDT&E basic and applied research budgets also support a broad engineering and science programme at US universities and colleges (AAAS 2016). Similarly, researchers in around sixty armed services laboratory centers, divisions and directorates are supported by DOD.

DOD supports the Defense Advanced Research Projects Agency (DARPA), which has been especially active in the past decade in artificial intelligence (AI) and robotics, technologies which are instrumental in autonomous vehicle design. DOD also funds research in biomedicine through the Biological Technologies Office (begun in 2001) (Reardon 2015). DARPA has seven programmes spanning SET from electronics to human–machine interfaces (Russell 2015).

Projects supported by DARPA do not go through formal peer review in order to receive funding, and DARPA does not allow chosen investigators to follow interesting avenues arising during the course of DARPA funding. DARPA programme managers approach potential applicants and shape a research project with team members. These features colour the research process and its oversight and outcome, and create a lack public accountability (Mervis 2016).

The DOD also supports social science research in universities (some of which has been controversial) through the Minerva Research Initiative (Minerva 2015). The CIA has also been engaged with the SET community in developing programmes of psychological warfare (Roberts 2007), the implications of which are discussed later.

The 21st-century context for military R&D

The terrorist attacks of September 11, 2001 have unsurprisingly been cited by many as the key to understanding how global military paradigms have changed in the 21st century, increasingly drawing upon sophisticated technologies to deal with such problems as cyberthreats and information warfare wherever they arise. Many changes in foreign policy globally have been predicated on what was termed the 'War on Terror' (Richmond and Franks 2005), with concomitant SET-promoted surveillance and information technology developments. However, other events have been important too in paradigm shaping, such as the interdependent globalisation of R&D and the formation of powerful Information and Communication Technologies (ICT) – in civilian and military areas.

Powerful ICT developments can narrow state sovereignty, impacting on politics, finance, civil freedoms and trade. The convergence of civilian and military autonomous vehicle development and overarching surveillance systems[6] can compromise both internal and external security. One consequence of these trends is that, for many nations, multinational companies and lobby groups have taken over the determination of security stances,[7] as we discuss later.

The reliance on high technology interconnected ICT networks, linking weapons systems and related platforms with a networked centre, lies at the heart of 'Command, Control, Communications and Intelligence' systems (C3I) (Larkin 2006; Klahr and Waterman, 1986; O'Hanlon 2000) – the contemporary orthodoxy of military strategy. C3I is integral to the *Revolution in Military Affairs* (RMA) (Black 2004; O'Hanlon 2000), and depends upon SET expertise, supported by a variety of funders within and outside universities (Larkin 2006; O'Hanlon 2000), an example being a Systems Engineering for Autonomous Systems Defence Centre set up by the UK MoD in 2002.

C3I currently uses remotely piloted vehicles and information technology (IT) systems within and outside the battlespace (Langley 2005; Street and Beale 2007). C3I is also linked historically to nuclear weapons infrastructure and the ill-fated Strategic Defense Initiative (which in the 1980s intended to cement US domination of space using space-mounted weapons systems able to destroy Soviet missiles and weapons; Baucom 1992; Black 2004). Remotely piloted systems have been extended to border and civil space surveillance within national and across international borders, and aerial 'drones' are now commercially available in the UK – prompting questions about privacy and basic human rights (see discussions in Halpin et al. 2006; Braun et al. 2015).

It is assumed that C3I systems are highly safeguarded and impenetrable but a number of commentators have questioned their dependability and expense and have shown that other sophisticated US surveillance and communications systems have failed in the battlespace (Larkin 2006).

In 2012 a three-year programme in electronic surveillance R&D was launched in the UK involving QinetiQ (a company formed in 2001 when the UK MoD privatised the larger part of the publicly owned Defence Evaluation and Research Agency) and university researchers. Developments in this and other cutting-edge areas with security implications such as nanotechnology and synthetic biology have rapidly developed without full in-depth public or specialist SET scrutiny (see the work of the Oxford Research Group – ORG 2016 – and Scientists for Global Responsibility – SGR 2016). Additionally, recent disclosures of global surveillance by the US National Security Agency (NSA) and UK Government Communications Headquarters (GCHQ) – both agencies are linked to covert military activities – of private individuals' electronic interactions underscores the largely unchallenged drift of the militarised mindset into civilian life (MacAskill 2015).

This brief survey of SET-based R&D for broadly military goals in Western Europe (especially UK) and the US indicates that funding derives from national and transnational governmental and commercial bodies and is used to support research and teaching by commercial and university SET practitioners. Military-sector funding of R&D carries important implications for the nature (especially the openness) of the research enterprise, the role of universities in society and how staff see their roles. In many nations security is largely about power projection and high-technology weapons and support systems rather than other, more nuanced methods. Analysis has shown that the UK spent much more of these funds on developing offensive weapon systems (with the capability of projecting force at large distances) than on defensive systems in the period 2008–11 (Parkinson et al. 2013).

Non-military basic SET research potentially can impact negatively on national or international security. For example, work on infectious disease can pose challenges for biosecurity as discussed on the Global Security website (Global Security 2015; Rappert and McLeish 2007). New developments in software programming have attracted the attention of US Homeland Security, and nanotechnology could be used in various weapon applications (Gsponer 2002). The lack of public scrutiny in these areas is of concern.

The opportunity costs of militarised SET research (a key area of public accountability) and the impact of such spending on economic growth and the political economy of SET are rarely examined in detail in major economies (Dunne and Uye 2009; Fabrizio and Mowery 2005; Mowery 2010). However, Parkinson et al. (2013) have attempted to compare UK public spending on military R&D with that on furthering the understanding of the roots of conflict. The latter work included research on climate change, poverty alleviation and a range of other social and environmental problems. They found that between two and seven times as much R&D spending was directed towards military ends as on non-military alternatives, depending on how those alternatives were defined.

Social scientists in militarised SET

It is not just the physical and biological sciences that have been instrumental in the development of warfare. The behavioural, social sciences and cognate disciplines like geography have also played a key and problematic role in framing the military agenda and providing combat tools. The involvement of such disciplines can be seen to 'normalise' methods of warfare, such as torture, and raise serious ethical and legal questions (see Roberts 2007).

In the US, RAND Corporation social scientists played a primary role in human–machine interface research, which underpins autonomous vehicles (mentioned earlier). It is an area which has further proliferated thanks to government support (particularly in the UK, USA and Israel). The RAND Corporation was instrumental in developing 'psychological warfare' (RAND 2015) and the Corporation continues today to provide research expertise, international funding programmes for universities, and policy advisors for various security and military purposes.

The American Psychological Association initially worked with the military in various benign ways, broadening into a highly dubious collaboration during the Cold War: the 'mind-control' programme – MKUltra – involved psychologists aiding the CIA to test mind-altering techniques (Roberts 2007; Anon 2015). The Association continues a close relationship with the military today and a recent report (APA 2015) indicates the role of psychologists with post-9/11 torture and the so-called War on Terror. Without close ethical oversight the integrity and independence of SET in these militarised circumstances can easily be compromised (Anon 2015).

Government funding for research in the social sciences and humanities in the UK has been severely reduced in the last decade and it is conceivable that psychologists and other social scientists will be drawn to military funding.

Militarised SET – summarising the key issues

This chapter has briefly focused on several clearly emerging themes from increasing global militarisation of SET. A more thorough understanding is hampered by the paucity of in-depth research examining global SET militarisation. Such research is severely limited not only by the commercialised environment in which SET is increasingly embedded, but also by narrow notions of 'national security' used to prevent a debate on wider issues. Furthermore, the neoliberal agenda makes data acquisition and transparency problematic. Transparency and public accountability of UK government departments' R&D funding in the last five years has worsened, as Dorman et al. mention (Dorman et al. 2015). This increase in opacity comes at a time when commercialised universities and their various partnerships with the corporate sector in the UK are increasing.

A number of problems accompany militarised SET and colour the political economy of SET. These include:

- military support for new and powerful technologies – such as IT, robotics and autonomous engineering, nanotechnology and synthetic biology – is widespread globally. The military sector plays a key and largely unacknowledged role in the governance of SET used for 'security' purposes and does so without full and informed public scrutiny;
- military funding of SET in those areas examined tends to produce militarised products with little civilian utility without further funding to overcome the embedded militarised nature of

the product – thus creating problems of 'irreversibility'. Additionally, it is questionable that military support for R&D has any net economic benefits, especially in 'mature technologies';

- security involves understanding complex and multilayered challenges – which include resource depletion, global power relations, poverty, ethnic and religious issues, economic and social inequalities, and climate change – and is not simply about using high technology force to 'overcome' violence or dissent. There is some recent evidence from the UK that the public funding of military R&D is markedly larger than that for broader security areas;

- militarised SET produces high-technology weapons and associated platforms which have export value and play a part in exacerbating international arms proliferation, thus reducing security;

- military SET is central to the continued development and deployment of nuclear weapons, thus prolonging the risk of nuclear war;

- procurement practices together with public investment in military R&D impact on SET research, especially in emerging technologies, and tends to favour 'lock-in', thereby reducing civilian benefit without further investment;

- in the UK and USA an increasingly commercialised SET involving collaboration with privatised universities can potentially compromise long-term or open-ended independent research. Such a trend has been shown to import various forms of bias widely described in pharmaceutical, biotechnology and tobacco R&D. To date, we only have a limited understanding of the impact that the militarisation of SET has on university research, teaching and training in the UK;

- obtaining robust and detailed information from the UK MoD and Home Office concerning militarised SET research and the part played by the university sector has become very difficult;

- in many of the UK university SET departments examined, commercial objectives and short-term contracts with commercial partners have become the norm.

In summary, global security threats, the rapid and pervasive development of new technologies and increasingly privatised universities give rise to a highly problematic militarised SET, where challenges such as exacerbation of international arms proliferation, the continued deployment of nuclear weapons and the diversion of funding from better understanding the root causes of insecurity and conflict arise. A deeply commercialised SET also poses dilemmas such as funding bias, lack of transparency and conflicts of interests. In such a climate SET practitioners face difficulties in constructing a research and teaching environment without compromising academic freedoms. The use of ethical codes may help, but it is hard to escape the conclusion that a reduction in spending on military R&D, in favour of increased spending on alternatives, would be part of the solution. One thing is clear, however – there needs to be much more recognition of these problems, more transparency and much more effort directed to trying to solve them.

Acknowledgements

The authors would like to warmly thank the reviewers and editors of the Handbook for their constructive and valuable advice, comments and criticisms on the various drafts of the chapter; any shortcomings or omissions are entirely those of the authors.

Notes

1 Traditionally, dual-use refers to techniques and developments that can have a civil and possible military application. Dual-use has a number of dimensions – equipment, products, techniques and research knowledge, including its dissemination, which might be used for purposes other than that

intended, especially in the hands of military or terrorist groups, or those intent on causing harm (Atlas and Dando 2008).
2   For more on 'irreversibility' see Callon (1991).
3   The consortia were the Defence Technology Centres, Towers of Excellence and the Defence and Aerospace Partnerships. Funders included the Ministry of Defence, industry and the UK research councils. The Joint Grants Scheme was also a partnership between the Ministry and some of the research councils. The DSTL now offers PhD schemes in security and defence. A Freedom of Information request indicated that the Ministry of Defence has no data on the effectiveness or research output from these schemes.
4   The universities are Stockholm-Kungliga Tekniska Hogskolan, Gothenburg-Chalmers and Linkoping. More on LinkLab at: www.linklab.se/.
5   The Haldane Principle can briefly be described as 'decisions about what to spend research funds on should be made by researchers rather than politicians'. Although never formally described by Lord Haldane in his Report of 1918 on the mechanisms by which research supported the First World War effort, the principle has guided successive governments in the UK as to the best way to support SET research. For more detail see Langley and Parkinson (2009, p. 14).
6   A collaboration involving a number of military corporations including QinetiQ and UK universities in 2012 entitled 'Communications and Cross-cutting Electronic Surveillance' will investigate novel methods to collect security 'procurements' – QinetiQ (www.qinetiq.com/media/news/releases/Pages/Three-year-programme-in-electronic-surveillance-research-and-development-underway.aspx, accessed 15 November 2015).
7   For more detail see Langley (2005).

References

AAAS. (2016). 'American Association for The Advancement of Science'. *Department of Defense*. [Online]. Available from: www.aaas.org/fy16budget/department-defense [accessed 13 May 2016].

Abraham, J. (1995). *Science, Politics and the Pharmaceutical Industry: Controversy and Bias in Drug Regulation*. London, UK: UCL Press.

Anon. (2015). 'Editorial: Unholy alliance'. *Nature* 523 (7561), 255.

APA. (2015). 'American Psychological Association. Report to the special committee of the Board of Directors of the American Psychological Association Independent Review relating to APA ethics guidelines, national security interrogations and torture'. [Online]. Available from: http://apa.org/independent-review/APA-FINAL-Report-7.2.15.pdf [accessed 15 November 2015].

Atlas, R.M. and Dando, M.R. (2006). 'The dual-use dilemma for the life sciences: Perspectives, conundrums and global solutions'. *Biosecurity and Bioterrorism: Biodefense, Strategy Practice and Science*. 4, 276–286.

Baucom, D.R. (1992). *The Origins of SDI, 1944–1983*. Lawrence, USA: University Press of Kansas.

Bayer, M. (2006). 'Virtual violence and the real war. Playing war in computer games: The battle with reality'. In Halpin, E., Trevorrow, P., Webb, D. and Wright, S. (eds.) (2006) *Cyberwar, Netwar and the Revolution in Military Affairs*. Basingstoke: Palgrave Macmillan.

Bigo, D. and Jeandesboz, J. (2010). 'The EU and the European security industry: Questioning the "Public–Private Dialogue"'. *INEX Policy Brief* 5; February 2010. [Online] Available from: www.ceps.eu/publications/eu-and-european-security-industry-questioning-%E2%80%98public-private-dialogue%E2%80%99 [accessed 15 November 2015].

BIS. (2014). *Our Plan for Growth*. Cm 8980. [Online] Available from: https://www.gov.uk/government/uploads/system/uploads/attachment_data/file/387780/PU1719_HMT_Science_.pdf [accessed 13 November 2015].

BIS. (2015). 'The Dowling review of business-university research collaborations'. BIS/15/352. [Online] Available from: www.gov.uk/government/uploads/system/uploads/attachment_data/file/440927/bis_15_352_The_dowling_review_of_business-university_rearch_collaborations_2.pdf [accessed 12 December 2015].

Black, J. (2004). *War since 1945*. London, UK: Reaktion Books.

Braun, S., Friedewald, M. and Volkenburg, G. (2015). 'Civilizing drones: Military discourses going civil?' *Science & Technology Studies*. 28 (2), 73–87.

Callon, M. (1991). 'Techno-Economic Networks and Irreversibility'. *Sociological Review*. 38, 132–161.

Cavoukian, A. (2009). *Privacy by Design: Take the Challenge*. Toronto, Canada: Information and Privacy Commissioner of Ontario.

Collini, S. (2012). *What are Universities for?* London, UK: Penguin Books.

Cowan, R. (1990). 'Nuclear power reactors: A case of technological lock-in'. *The Journal of Economic History*. 50 (3), 541–667.

Department of Education (2016). 'Educational excellence everywhere'. [Online]. Available from: www. gov.uk/government/uploads/system/uploads/attachment_data/file/508447/Educational_ Excellence_Everywhere.pdf [accessed 13 May 2016].

Dorman, A., Uttley, M. and Wilkinson, B. (2015). *A Benefit Not a Burden: The Security, Economic and Strategic Value of Britain's Defence Industry*. London, UK: Kings College Policy Institute.

Dunne, J. P. and Uye, M. (2009). 'Military spending and development'. *Ideas* [Online]. Available from: http://carecon.org.uk/DPs/0902.pdf [accessed 13 December 2015].

EU. (2016). 'High-level Group of Personalities on defence research issues statement'. [Online]. Available from: www.eda.europa.eu/info-hub/press-centre/latest-news/2015/06/18/high-level-group-of-personalities-on-defence-research-issues-statement [accessed 14 May 2016].

Fabrizio, K.R. and Mowery, D.C. (2005). 'Defense-related R&D and the growth of the post-war information technology industrial complex in the United States'. *Revue d'economie industrielle*. 112 (1), 27–44. [Online] Available from: www.persee.fr/doc/rei_0154-3229_2005_num_112_1_3123 [accessed 10 December 2015].

Feenberg, A. (2002). *Transforming Technology: A Critical Theory Revisited*. Oxford, UK: Oxford University Press.

Global Security. (2015). *Bird Flu/Avian Flu*. [Online] Available from: www.globalsecurity.org/security/ ops/hsc-scen-3_bird-flu.htm [accessed 13 December 2015].

Gsponer, A. (2002). 'From the lab to the battlefield? Nanotechnology and fourth-generation nuclear weapons'. *Disarmament Diplomacy* 67 Opinion and Analysis. [Online]. Available from: www.acronym. org.uk/dd/dd67/67op1.htm [accessed 13 December 2015).

Halpin, E., Trevorrow, P., Webb, D. and Wright, S. (eds.) (2006). *Cyberwar, Netwar and the Revolution in Military Affairs*. Basingstoke: Palgrave Macmillan.

Hayes, B. (2006). *Arming Big Brother: The EU's security research programme*. Amsterdam, the Netherlands: Transnational Institute/Statewatch.

Hildyard, N. (1998). *Scientific Research for Whom?* [Online] Available from: www.thecornerhouse.org.uk/ resource/scientific-research-whom [accessed 12 December 2015].

Home Office. (2015) *Centre for Applied Science & Technology*. [Online]. Available from: /www.gov.uk/government/ collections/centre-for-applied-science-and-technology-information [accessed 15 November 2015].

James, A.D. (ed.) (2006). *Science and Technology Policies for the Anti-Terrorism Era*. Manchester, UK: IOS Press.

Klahr, P. and Waterman, D.A. (1986). 'Artificial intelligence: A Rand perspective'. *AI Magazine*. 7 (2), 54–64.

Kleinman, D.L. (2010). 'The commercialization of academic culture and the future of the university'. In Radder, H. (ed.), *The Commodification of Academic Research: Analyses, Assessments, Alternatives*. Pittsburgh, USA: University of Pittsburgh Press.

Krimsky, S. (2003). *Science in the Private Interest*. Maryland, USA: Rowan & Littlefield.

Kuhlau, F., Eriksson, S., Evers, K. and Hoglund, A.T. (2008). 'Taking due care: Moral obligations in dual use research'. *Bioethics*. 22 (9), 477–487.

Langley, C. (2005). *Soldiers in the Laboratory: Military Involvement in Science and Technology – and Some Alternatives*. Folkestone, UK: Scientists for Global Responsibility.

Langley, C. (2008). 'Universities, the military, and the means of destruction in the United Kingdom'. *The Economics of Peace and Security Journal*. 3 (1), 49–55.

Langley, C. (2014). *Atoms for Peace: The Atomic Weapons Establishment and UK Universities*. Reading: Nuclear Information Service.

Langley, C and Parkinson, S (2009). *Science and the Corporate Agenda: The Detrimental Effects of Commercial Influence on Science and Technology*. Folkestone, UK: Scientists for Global Responsibility.

Larkin, B.D. (2006). 'Nuclear weapons and the vision of command and control'. In Halpin, E., Trevorrow, P., Webb, D. and Wright, S. (eds.) *Cyberwar, Netwar and the Revolution in Military Affairs*. Basingstoke: Palgrave Macmillan.

Lichtenberg, F. (1984). 'The relationship between federal contract R&D and company R&D'. *American Economic Review*. 74, 73–78.

Linden, B. (2008). 'Basic blue skies research in the UK: Are we losing out?' *Journal of Biomedical Discovery and Collaboration* 3. doi:10.1186/1747-5333-3-3.

Macaskill, E. (2015). 'The spooks have come out of the shadows – for now'. *The Guardian*. [Online] 15 October Available from: www.theguardian.com/uk-news/2015/oct/28/snowden-surveillance-and-public-relations [accessed 12 November 2015].

Mackenzie, D. and Pottinger, D. (1997). 'Mathematics, technology and trust: Formal verification, computer security and the U.S. military'. *Annals of the History of Computing, IEEE* 19 (3), 41–59.

Malakoff, D. (2015). 'Pentagon funding program opens door to U.K. collaboration'. *Science* doi 10.1126/ science.aab0266. [Online]. Available at: http://news.sciencemag.org/education/2015/03/pentagon-funding-program-opens-door-u-k-collaboration [accessed 12 March 2015].

Mervis, J. (2016). 'What makes DARPA tick?' *Science*. 351. (6273), 549–553.

Minerva. (2015). *The Minerva Project: Program history and overview* [Online]. Available from: http://minerva. dtic.mil/overview.html [accessed 13 November 2015].

Ministry of Defence. (2012). *National Security through Technology: Technology, Equipment, and Support for UK Defence and Security*. White paper. Cm 8278. [Online] Available from: www.gov.uk/government/ uploads/system/uploads/attachment_data/file/27390/cm8278.pdf [accessed 15 December 2015].

Ministry of Defence. (2015). *National Security and Strategic Defence and Security Review* Cm 9161. [Online] Available from: www.gov.uk/government/uploads/system/uploads/attachment_data/file/478933/52309_ Cm_9161_NSS_SD_Review_web_only.pdf [accessed 15 November 2015].

Mirowski, P. (2011). *Science-Mart: Privatizing American Science*. Cambridge, MA, USA: Harvard University Press.

Mowery, D.C. (1998). 'Collaborative R&D: How effective is it?' *Issues in S & T*. [Online] Available from: www.issues.org/15.1/mowery.htm [accessed 12 September 2015].

Mowery, D.C. (2010). 'Military R&D and innovation'. In Hall, B.H. and Rosenberg, N. (eds). *Handbook of the Economics of Innovation*. Volume 2. Amsterdam, the Netherlands: Elsevier.

National Priorities Project. (2015). *Military Spending in the United States*. [Online]. Available from: www. nationalpriorities.org/campaigns/military-spending-united-states/ [accessed 10 August 2015].

NAO. (2013). *Research and Development Funding for Science and Technology in the UK*. [Online] Available from: www.nao.org.uk/wp-content/uploads/2013/07/Research-and-development-funding-for-science-and-technology-in-the-UK1.pdf [accessed December 2015].

NATO. (2015). *Science for Peace and Security*. [Online]. Available from: www.nato.int/cps/en/ natolive/87260.htm [accessed 13 November 2015].

Nightingale, P. and Coad, A. (2014). 'The myth of the science park economy'. *Demos Quarterly* 2, Spring. [Online] Available from: http://quarterly.demos.co.uk/article/issue-2/innovation-and-growth/ [accessed 9 December 2015].

Noble, D.F. (1985). 'Command performance: a perspective on the social and economic consequences of military enterprise'. In Smith, M. R. (ed). *Military Enterprise and Technological Change: Perspectives on the American Experience*. Cambridge, MA: MIT Press.

O'Hanlon, M. (2000). *Technological Change and the Future of Warfare*. Washington, DC, United States of America: Brookings Institution Press.

ONS. (2013). 'UK Gross National Domestic Expenditure on R&D 2012'. [Online] Available from: www.ons.gov.uk/ons/rel/rdit1/gross-domestic-expenditure-on-research-and-development/2013/ stb-gerd-2013.html#tab-Key-Points [accessed 13 August 2015].

ORG. (2016). The Oxford Research Group. [Online]. Available from: http://remotecontrolproject.org/ [accessed 7 January 2016].

Parkinson, S. (2015). 'Military-University Collaborations in the UK – an Update'. [Online] Available from: www.sgr.org.uk/resources/military-university-collaborations-uk-update [accessed 31 May 2016].

Parkinson, S., Pace, B. and Webber, P. (2013). *Offensive Insecurity: The Role of Science and Technology in UK Security Strategies*. Folkestone, UK: Scientists for Global Responsibility.

RAND. (2015). *Psychological Warfare*. [Online] Available from: www.rand.org/topics/psychological-warfare.html [accessed 13 December 2015].

Rappert, B. (2006). 'National security, terrorism and the control of life science research'. In *Science and Technology Policies for the Anti-Terrorism Era*. James, A.D. (ed.) Manchester, UK: IOS Press.

Rappert, B., Balmer, B. and Stone, J. (2008). 'Science, technology and the military: Priorities, preoccupations and possibilities'. In *The Handbook of Science and Technology studies*. Third Edition. Hackett, E.J., Amsterdamska, O., Lynch, M.E. and Wajcman, J. (eds.) London, UK: MIT Press.

Rappert, B. and Mcleish, C. (eds.) (2007). *A Web of Prevention: Biological Weapons, Life Sciences and the Governance of Research*. London, UK: Earthscan.

Reardon, S. (2015). 'The military-bioscience complex: The US Department of Defense is making a big push into biological research – but some scientists question whether its high-risk approach can work'. *Nature*. 522 (7555), 142–144.

Richmond, O. and Franks, J. (2005). 'Human security and the war on terror'. In *Human and Environmental Security: An Agenda for Change*. Dodds, F. and Pippard, T. (eds) London, UK: Earthscan.

Roberts, R. (ed.) (2007). *Just War: Psychology and terrorism*. Ross-on-Wye, UK: PCCS Books.

Russell, S. (2015). 'Take a stand on AI weapons'. *Nature*. 521 (7553), 415–417.

Salter, A.J. and Martin, B. (2001). 'The economic benefits of publicly-funded basic research: A critical review'. *Research Policy*. 27, 394–396.

Schroeer, D. (1997). 'The future of high technology in military affairs'. In *The weapons legacy of the Cold War: Problems and opportunities*. Schroeer, D. and Pascolini, A. (eds.). Aldershot, UK: Ashgate.

SGR. (2016). [Online] Available from: http://sgr.org.uk [accessed 7 January 2016].

SIPRI. (2016). Perlo-Freeman, S., Fleurant, A., Wezema, P. and Wezeman, S.T. *Trends in World Military Expenditure 2015* SIPRI Fact Sheet. [Online] April 2016. Available from: http://books.sipri.org/files/FS/SIPRIFS1604.pdf [accessed 31 May 2016].

Smit, W. (1995). 'Science, technology and the military: Relations in transition'. In Jasanoff, S., Markle, J., Peterson, J. and Pinch, T. (eds). *Handbook of Science and Technology Studies*. Revised edition. Thousand Oaks, CA, USA: Sage Publications Inc.

Somerville, M. and Atlas, R.M. (2005). 'Ethics: A weapon to counter bioterrorism'. *Science*. 307, 1881–1882.

Spinardi, G. (1992). 'Defence technology enterprises: A case study in technology transfer'. *Science and Public Policy*. 19, 198–206.

Stone, J. (2004). 'Politics, technology and the revolution in military affairs'. *The Journal of Strategic Studies*. 27, 408–427.

Street, T. and Beale, M. (2007). *Study War No More: Military Involvement in UK Universities*. Campaign Against Arms Trade/Fellowship of Reconciliation. Available from: www.studywarnomore.org.uk/.

UNDP. (2015). *Human Development Report 2015: Work for Human Development*. [Online] Available from: http://report.hdr.undp.org/ [accessed 30 May 2016].

Washburn, J. (2005). *University Inc*. New York, USA: Basic Books.

Wilsdon, J., Wynne, B and Stilgoe, J. (2005). *The Public Value of Science: Or How to Ensure that Science Really Matters*. London, UK: Demos.

Ziman, J. (2000). *Real Science: What it is, and What It Means*. Cambridge, UK: Cambridge University Press.

PART III

Fields of science

15

GENETICALLY ENGINEERED FOOD FOR A HUNGRY WORLD

A changing political economy

Rebecca Harrison, Abby Kinchy, and Laura Rabinow

Introduction

Genetic engineering has revolutionized the science of plant breeding and transformed agricultural systems by allowing plant breeders to create plants with characteristics that would have been difficult or impossible to develop through traditional breeding methods. Genetic engineering techniques are increasingly wide-ranging, including not only the creation of transgenic organisms, but also the use of emerging tools in synthetic biology (see chapter by Rossi, this volume) and gene editing. Genetic engineering has been used to impart numerous traits to agricultural crops, including resistance to diseases and drought, tolerance to herbicides, increased nutrient content, and the ability to repel insect pests. While genetic engineering for agriculture (ag-biotech) holds tremendous promise, particularly as climate change makes food production increasingly (if unevenly) precarious, there are also significant reasons to remain critical about its effects on social-ecological systems, rural economies, and scientific research cultures.

Ag-biotech has been under intense scrutiny by social scientists, activists, and journalists from the time the first genetically engineered organism was patented in the early 1980s. Since then, food and hunger advocacy organizations have helped to lay the groundwork for a global movement in opposition to ag-biotech. Key dimensions of concern about the new technologies include: corporate control of genetic resources; the commercialization of university science; and food security in the Global South.

In this chapter, we revisit the political economy of ag-biotech, asking whether new and emerging ag-biotech projects and products complicate previous theoretical understandings. We discuss two notable cases. The first is the American Chestnut Research and Restoration Project, a university-based project that aims to bring new life to a tree that has become all but extinct in North America, due to disease. The second case is Water Efficient Maize for Africa, a non-profit public–private partnership that aims to develop seeds for small-scale farmers in a number of African states. Both cases involve new arrangements for funding biotechnology research and for creating and sharing intellectual property. It is unclear whether our cases are in fact representative illustrations of the current tensions in the field, but, as we will show, they demonstrate both significant shifts and stabilizations of earlier configurations.

We will address these questions more specifically by considering what these two cases show about new models of research funding. Historically, intellectual property has allowed researchers and companies to extract funding in the form of profit. In our first case, university scientists have declined to patent their discoveries and used crowdfunding to help support their research; in the latter case, companies like Monsanto have "donated" patented traits while philanthropic organizations and agricultural research institutions have provided the necessary funding and infrastructure. We have not chosen these particular cases explicitly to compare and contrast the two—the first speaks to the storyline of academic capitalism, while the second extends the Green Revolution narrative. We will, however, compare the two institutional settings by examining how funding arrangements and research agendas have and have not changed, and the interplay between the two.

Critical analysis of ag-biotech: three dimensions

Corporate control of genetic resources

Rural sociologists, drawing on Marxist theoretical traditions in the study of agriculture, anticipated that new biotechnologies would increase corporate control over food production and shift power away from farmers (Kloppenburg [1988] 2005; Busch 1991; Goodman, Sorj, and Wilkinson 1987; Buttel 1995; Buttel et al. 1984; Kenney and Buttel 1985; Buttel and Belsky 1987). One focus of concern was the application of patent protection to genetic material and engineered organisms. Critical scholars observed that patent law would enable seed companies to force farmers to purchase improved seeds every season instead of using seeds saved from the previous harvest (Shiva 1997). Earlier innovations in plant breeding—such as hybridization—had also limited seed saving (for both biological and legal reasons), and astute observers interpreted plant patents as the latest stage in the commodification of plant genetic material (Kloppenburg 1988; Lacy, Lacy and Busch 1988). One of the most significant outcomes of the development of patents for genes and organisms has been the concentration of the seed industry (Howard 2009).

These changes have been met with resistance from a diverse global movement to defend farmers' seed saving rights. For nearly two decades, civil society groups have successfully opposed the introduction of "genetic use restriction technologies" (GURTs), also known as "Terminator" genes, that confer sterility on the seeds of plants grown from engineered seeds. Advocacy groups such as the Center for Food Safety have investigated and criticized Monsanto for its aggressive use of patent litigation against farmers who try to reduce their costs by using farm-saved seeds. Seed saving projects, such as seed libraries and "open source" seeds, have gained popularity in the United States, while the global peasants' movement, Via Campesina, has tirelessly campaigned to defend the right to save seeds as a key dimension of food sovereignty.

Commercialization of university research

Ag-biotech has also had a central role in broader shifts in the political-economy of academic science in the United States (Busch 1991). While, as Kleinman (2003) points out, the American university has never been an "ivory tower" (see also chapter by Edgerton, this volume), there have been significant changes in the economy of university patronage, particularly in relation to biotechnology and plant breeding. In the 1980s, federal and state initiatives encouraged new partnerships between universities and commercial firms, often in the emerging field of biotechnology. Advocates of these relationships argued that they "would foster the flow of knowledge and technology from the university to the private sector, while also generating increased basic research funding" (Lacy et al. 2014, p. 457).

Henry Etzkowitz (1998), for example, argues that while entrepreneurial activities by scientists are not new phenomena, per se, something is changing in science: No longer does science condemn profit-making motives as it did traditionally, but rather a new "norm" of science is emerging that embraces them. Even as early as the mid-1980s, industry provided over one-third of all funding for university-based biotechnology research (Blumenthal et al. 1986). Legislation, such as the Bayh-Dole Act of 1980, encouraged university scientists to patent and commercialize their discoveries. Some university scientists formed start-up biotech companies, entering directly into the world of commerce, while others contributed to the growth of the ag-biotech industry by doing research that would enable life science firms to bring new products to market (Berman 2012).

Critics identified potential consequences of these new arrangements, including:

(1) a shift in disciplinary emphasis in the research community to molecular biology, (2) reduction of research on systems, ecology, and the social sciences, (3) increased concentration of research funds at a small number of institutions, (4) reduction of long-term research in the public sector, (5) increased collaboration between industry, government and universities with a restriction of scientific communication, and a potential for conflict of interest, favoritism and increased scientific misconduct, [and] (6) a change of the primary goals and agenda of the public sector research community.

(Lacy, Lacy, and Busch 1988, p. 3)

Of particular concern to many observers were the diminishing opportunities to do research in areas with limited commercial viability, such as improving crops that are primarily consumed by the rural poor, or discovering non-chemical methods of controlling insect pests. Some researchers have concluded that areas of research with potentially great public value are being neglected because they do not have ag-biotech's potential to generate revenue for universities (Glenna et al. 2011).

Solving hunger and environmental crisis?

Defenders of ag-biotech have often sought the moral "high ground" by framing the technology as a solution to world hunger and as a means to address the challenges of the rural poor (Kleinman and Kloppenburg 1991). Claims about the benefits of biotechnology for the poor have been vigorously debated in both academic and popular literature (Glover 2008; Goodman, Sorj and Wilkinson 1987; Altieri and Rosset 1998). Robert Paarlberg (2009) and Calestous Juma (2011), in addition to other scholars, have forcefully argued that ag-biotech seeds are a pro-poor technology that needs more vigorous promotion in Africa.[1] The debate about the role of ag-biotech as a solution to poverty, hunger, and environmental challenges has been further complicated by global climate change. Some argue that genetic engineering can speed up research on crops that are tolerant to new climate-related stresses, providing another tool for farmers to adapt to climatic changes (Ronald 2011).

A major critique of the pro-biotech position is that the seeds cannot solve world hunger because they do not address its root cause: poverty (Lappé, Collins, and Rosset 1998); rather, they deflect attention away from structural inequalities facing small farmers (Mayet 2007). Another criticism is that the agricultural systems that benefit most from ag-biotech seeds on the market are ecologically unsustainable, relying on chemical inputs and monocultures that are harmful to small-scale food producers who rely on healthy ecological systems for their livelihoods (Altieri 1999). Anthropologist Glenn Davis Stone (2010) goes so far as to suggest that "The claim that transgenic technologies are 'just another tool for the farmer' is true only in the studiously myopic sense that the textile mills in England's Industrial Revolution were 'just another tool for making cloth'" (395).

Critics of today's efforts to improve crops for low-income regions of the world have often drawn parallels with India's "Green Revolution" during the 1960s. Agro-chemical companies had a marked influence on the Green Revolution, and the high-yielding crop varieties developed depended on chemical inputs, such as synthetic fertilizers and pesticides. Scholars and activists concerned with the negative impacts of the Green Revolution pointed not only to ecological degradation as a result of more soil intensive monoculture farming practices, but also to socio-economic hardships, such as significant debt tied to the obsolescence of seed varieties and continual costs of new inputs (Shiva 1991; Lappé et al. 1998).

Major new philanthropic efforts to fund crop improvement for the poor lend some credibility to the argument that the benefits of ag-biotech are not limited to industrial agriculture, but these efforts have also faced criticism.[2] Many of the same companies and institutional structures that had active roles in the 1960s' Green Revolution continue their work towards addressing food security, today with a new—though not dissimilar—pro-poor narrative. Proponents of emerging ag-biotech tell a "Good GMO" story that addresses "hidden hunger" and micronutrient deficiencies (Kimura 2013), climate change mitigation, and environmental restoration through public-private partnerships and philanthropy. We explore this Trojan Horse narrative, and the other themes discussed above, in the following case studies.

American Chestnut Research and Restoration Project

Like many new generations of biotechnologies, such as those intended to produce drugs or control invasive species, the case of American chestnut restoration moves the debate about ag-biotech beyond questions of food security and rural livelihoods. Furthermore, the case illustrates a shift in focus from intellectual property and commercialization of biotechnology to crowd source funding efforts to mobilize "public" engagement and support for "publicly funded" research.

In the 1870s, a shipment of foreign chestnuts from Japan to the United States harbored *Cryphonectria parasitica*, or chestnut blight, a fungal pathogen to which Asian trees had long evolved resistance—while their American relatives had not. Since its discovery in the Bronx in 1904, this pathogen has eradicated 3–5 billion American trees, which now only exist as small saplings and stumps. The fungus releases oxalic acid, which causes cankers to grow, restricting flow of vital water and nutrients through the plant's vascular system. For decades, scientists have used biochemistry and plant breeding in efforts to bring this heritage tree back to the United States.

This case study will focus on the work of the American Chestnut Research and Restoration Project at the State University of New York College of Environmental Science and Forestry in Syracuse, NY. Lead biotechnologists William Powell and Charles Maynard have, after decades of collaboration, identified that the single oxalate oxidase gene found in wheat can be used to "detoxify" oxalic acid released by the cankers of infected trees, raising blight resistance with one single gene already consumed by humans on a daily basis. As of 2015, the team is beginning the process to obtain deregulated status for the engineered trees.

Biotechnology projects such as tree restoration create a unique case study of plant biotechnology, which is likely to be received by the public in ways that differ from the products currently on the market. For example, tree crops—especially framed as restoration projects— have symbolic and emotional resonance in a way industrial crops like feed corn do not; the narrative Powell and Maynard have constructed around "restoration" creates a new importance of chestnuts for a generation of people whose interaction with the nut is predominantly with literature, songs, and street signs—not as an ingredient in every food they eat. In addition, genetic modification of trees differs from annual field crops in breeding methods and time required to mature to harvest. This longer timeframe to production complicates the current regulatory framework for the regulation of biotechnology products given its relatively short requirements for field testing and evaluation of subsequent generations of the crop.

Powell and Maynard are anticipating public rejection of their products, rooted in fears of corporate control of agricultural and forestry systems (interviews by Harrison). Groups such as the Global Justice Ecology Project, the Center for Biological Diversity, and the Center for Food Safety have led campaigns against the genetic modification of trees, especially those with the "express intent" of being released into wild forests, as advanced by powerful interests such as ArborGen and Duke Energy (Bennington 2014). At a time when many university scientists seek out patents and commercialization for their discoveries, Powell and Maynard have taken a different route. "Independent" academic researchers play an important role in building public support for trust in biotechnology (Lipton 2015). Thus, to head off objections, Powell and Maynard have promoted their work as a "not-for-profit endeavor" by making explicit their lack of interest in patenting the disease-resistant tree—or using genes without a free-use license (Zimmer 2013).

Additionally, Powell and Maynard have used crowdfunding to secure public "buy-in" (literally) to their project, emphasizing the narrative that they aim to restore a native tree that is culturally and historically important. In November 2014, the American Chestnut Research and Restoration Project held a crowdfunding campaign to "help bring back the American chestnut tree." It raised over $100,000. This crowdfunding project not only raised money, but also served as a public engagement tool: If one made a donation of $100 or more, they received wild-type (unmodified) American chestnut seedlings to grow at home. If successfully grown to maturity, the genetic material from these trees can become "mother" trees for future breeding with blight resistant trees. These researchers' focus is on giving the "public" ownership and agency in this seemingly public project to restore "our" tree. Powell and Maynard's research fundamentally relies on the willingness of volunteers to plant mother tree seedlings for diverse genetics, and this is one way simultaneously to build enthusiasm around their product, raise money, and establish genetic diversity.

Though the formal crowdfunding campaign is over, the team continues to accept "tax-deductible charitable donations," and publicly lists donors, which include individuals, foundations, and companies such as ArborGen LLC and the Monsanto Fund. Accepting funding from the public has also opened a new door for ag-biotech companies to associate themselves closely with this "Good GMO" that improves public perceptions of ag-biotech. Similar efforts through "philanthropic" projects can be seen in the case of Golden Rice, or the Water Efficient Maize for Africa public–private partnership, discussed below (Stone and Glover 2016). Independent university scientists like Powell and Maynard have the appearance of neutral, non-political actors, when, in fact, they are lobbying for the acceptance of their own technology and, perhaps inadvertently, providing a public relations opportunity for ag-biotech firms.

The incorporation of public fundraising complicates the traditional academia–industry funding relationship by giving the public direct access to it for the first time—even if only an inconsequential percentage. At this time, crowdfunding is not a viable means to fund expensive, important scientific research fully, but it is a way to cultivate a sense of public participation (whether illusory or not) while representing an attempt by scientists to challenge traditional university research funding models developed through academic capitalism and close industrial ties.

Powell and Maynard have interpreted their crowdfunding success as a sign of significant public support for the transgenic American chestnut; however, public funding campaigns risk only targeting individuals in close proximity, creating an unrepresentative positive feedback loop within their network. In an interview, for example, Forest Health Initiative Science Advisory Committee Chair Steven Strauss (University of Oregon) suggests that, while Powell and Maynard have received largely positive feedback about their project, some organizations such as the Forest Health Service and Nature Conservancy "Don't want the team to proceed right to commercial release. They're really worried their constituencies are going to object with them having any role in this. They're not ready for it."

Does the rise of crowdsourcing indicate potential for future, dramatic shifts in the political economy of biotechnology? Not only does clear not-for-profit intentionality play an important role in gathering unlikely support for this biotechnology project, but also defining one's research initiative as "publicly funded" (here meaning by private individuals not via public or state institutions) becomes a convenient rhetorical device. The two (very deliberate) tactics, in tandem, connote independence, without exclusion of all corporate influence. In this way, the American Chestnut Research and Restoration Project responds to some widely held criticisms of agricultural biotechnology, and circumnavigates others—namely patenting and close industrial ties. We next consider the case of Water Efficient Maize for Africa, a philanthropic effort that takes a different approach to, on the surface, addressing similar criticisms of corporatized agriculture.

Water Efficient Maize for Africa

Water Efficient Maize for Africa (WEMA) began in 2008 as a public–private partnership coordinated by the African Agricultural Technology Foundation (AATF) with the aim of developing biotechnologies for smallholder farmers on the continent. While AATF is a non-profit foundation, it aims to create public–private partnerships that facilitate access to "appropriate" agricultural technologies. WEMA is in some ways a continuation of earlier funding structures and relationships, but it also represents a shift in the political economy of ag-biotech.

As noted above, public–private partnerships among university, industry, and philanthropic organizations have long existed in the plant breeding arena. WEMA strongly appears to reproduce earlier arrangements of ag-biotech research, development, and commercialization. AATF works with the International Maize and Wheat Improvement Centre (CIMMYT) (a central player in the Green Revolution) as well as with partners at national research institutes in the five countries across which the project operates: Kenya, Mozambique, South Africa, Tanzania, and Uganda. Aside from these partners, the project is jointly funded by the Bill and Melinda Gates Foundation, the Howard G. Buffett Foundation, and the United States Agency for International Development (USAID). In addition to these funding sources, the project receives in-kind contributions from Monsanto in the form of technical expertise and "donations" of germplasm with patented drought-tolerant and pest-resistant traits.

The public–private partnership (PPP) uses conventional breeding, marker-assisted breeding, and biotechnology to produce new varieties of maize. Marker-assisted breeding is a method in which genetic markers, or identifiable DNA sequences that indicate the presence of certain desirable or undesirable traits, are used to select those plants for the next generation, effectively speeding up the selection process compared to conventional approaches (Reece and Haribabu 2007). Development and distribution of these new varieties will occur through market-oriented mechanisms. That is, they will be reproduced and sold by breeding companies and agro-dealers. The new varieties are intended for what WEMA refers to as "smallholder farmers"—generally understood to be those working on two hectares of land or less, but also variably used, as the United Nations' Food & Agriculture Organization notes, to refer to a person with "limited resource endowments relative to other farmers in the sector." Escobar

(1995) observes that the term "smallholder" has long been used by such organizations as a reductive linguistic mechanism that makes possible a technological solution for a distilled conception of a problem or person. In this case, WEMA appears to conceptualize "smallholders" as both consumers and entrepreneurs.

WEMA's intention is to create an "appropriate technology" in the form of "drought-tolerant and insect-protected maize varieties [that] will provide valuable economic, agronomic and environmental benefits to millions of farmers by helping them produce more reliable harvests" (Water 2016). *Appropriate technology* (AT) is typically set in contrast to the practice of *technology transfer*—taking a technology designed or intended for one context and applying it to another (often, problematically, from the Global North to the Global South). WEMA frames its products as appropriate technology, as the organization is trying to adapt crops to local climates, but much of its work fits squarely within the conception of a technology transfer project. The germplasm it draws on, as in the case of Golden Rice, was developed in and intended for other geographies and climates. The projects' focus on maize—albeit a current staple food in many of the places WEMA operates—further underlies its work as technology transfer, since maize is a non-native crop to all of its locations.

WEMA's organizational structure as a public–private partnership draws directly on those arrangements established by the earlier Golden Rice project and the somewhat concurrent Drought Tolerant Maize for Africa (DTMA) project. All of these projects were co-funded by the Bill and Melinda Gates Foundation and all were projects that sought to address food availability in the Global South through a market-based approach. WEMA also reflects earlier international agricultural research and development projects pertaining to the Green Revolution. First, its goals are based around the "scalability" and "transferability" of technologies and technological knowledge. And second, it frames such goals as effectively addressing issues of world hunger. Sally Brooks (2015) compares WEMA to the earlier Golden Rice project, finding that WEMA places a greater focus on technology, rather than scientific knowledge, as the medium to be transferred; it reframes farmers as the consumers of products, rather than as the recipients of aid; and it has conceptualized its administration under AATF as an "African led" project (109). Thus, while there are continuities with the past, WEMA represents a new set of political-economic arrangements for crop improvement.

The donation of patented genetic material by agribusiness companies is a notable emergent feature of projects like WEMA. The apparent philanthropic nature of the endeavor, however, deserves some scrutiny. While the donation of patented germplasm by Monsanto (and other companies) means that farmers do not have to pay the royalty fee to the seed company each season, it does not mean the germplasm comes without patents that are retained by the company, nor does it mean that farmers will not have to repurchase seeds each season due to the lack of trait fidelity in second generation seeds (Brooks 2013).

A similar licensing arrangement exists for the Golden Rice Project through Syngenta. Research institutes that are breeding for provitamin A traits to address nutritional deficiencies can obtain a "humanitarian license" for free from the Syngenta Foundation. Food sovereignty advocates, like the Southeast Asia Regional Initiatives for Community Empowerment (SEARICE), have pointed out, however, that Syngenta's retention of the exclusive commercial license puts the future of farmers using Golden Rice-derived seeds in a precarious place (SEARICE 2013). Likewise, Brooks notes that the particular institutional and financial arrangements of WEMA mean that germplasm "donations" are not as free (from intellectual property rights) as the term might suggest. More broadly, Brooks (2015) argues that such "institutional experiments"—characterized as *philanthrocapitalism*—serve to shift public debates around ag-biotech, "reframing questions of 'access' to technology in terms that valorize the technology 'donor'; and advocating regulatory systems that 'enable' more rapid approval of new technologies" (108).

Scholars of agriculture, echoing past critiques of the Green Revolution and first-generation ag-biotech, have raised further questions about the acquisition of local, national, and regional seed companies by foreign or multinational companies. This kind of consolidation has happened internationally in the transgenic crop industry since the mid-1990s (Howard 2009). Monsanto, for example, has an "estimated 39% market share for vegetable seeds in the US, 24% in the EU, and 26% globally" (1276). Such concerns lend to framings of projects like WEMA as a Trojan horse, helping to establish a market for products that larger companies can later acquire access to by purchasing smaller companies.

Regulatory systems for new ag-biotech products have also been a particular matter of concern. Advocacy organizations like the African Centre for Biodiversity have looked skeptically at the regulatory contexts that are emerging. They argue that "WEMA is a Trojan horse [used] to pressurise participating governments to pass weak biosafety regulations and open the door to the proliferation of GMOs (genetically modified organisms) that will undermine food sovereignty." Likewise, social scientists have questioned who will benefit from the current trajectory of ag-biotech development in African countries given dominant trends in the regulatory environment. Schnurr (2015) notes that in the Ugandan context,

> Experimentation and legislation have not come from farmers or even public representatives but rather as a result of a large volume of investment and support from external interests. The outcome of this investment and support has been to produce a permissive regulatory environment that is dominated by scientists deeply embedded not only in the research of GM crops but also in their promotion and evaluation.
>
> *(68)*

This and other studies (e.g. Kingiri 2010) raise doubts that the new technologies will benefit their intended users.

In summary, the WEMA project represents some notable shifts and continuities with regard to earlier instantiations of ag-biotech research, development, and commercialization. The public–private nature of the project reflects a continuation of existing structures related to research, development, and commercialization—particularly with respect to the institutional arrangements related to the Green Revolution. Some of the particular characteristics of WEMA's organization, however, may reflect salient differences from earlier phases of crop improvement. For example, leadership of AATF is primarily located in Africa. As such, WEMA challenges notions that the interests served by this project are solely extra-local or corporate ones (see also chapter by Delvenne and Kreimer). Such structuring makes it difficult to discern which actors most benefit from these arrangements. However, global agribusiness companies may potentially benefit from these arrangements in significant ways through future patent rights and the acquisition of smaller companies. Even less certain are which companies, under whose ownership or control, will stand to benefit most; and, if the technologies produced by those companies will in fact benefit "smallholders," given the socio-economic and political arrangements in which they are produced.

Discussion and conclusion

To what extent do these seemingly disparate case studies represent a new way of marketing ag-biotech products in an increasingly precarious political economy of science? The cases of American chestnut restoration and Water Efficient Maize for Africa illustrate evolving arrangements of corporate control of genetic resources and subsequent commercialization of research. The cases also challenge and extend the narrative of food security and hunger that ag-biotech historically appropriates. Herein, we see attempts by scientists to push back on the dominant political economies of ag-biotech.

These cases demonstrate not so much a rejection of intellectual property as a recognition that the base genetic resources involved in developing new agricultural biotechnologies are on the whole property of large corporations. In the former case, rejection of traditional property arrangements will decrease the barriers to widespread planting of approved, engineered chestnut trees—the fundamental goal of the publicly funded restoration project. In the latter, the philanthropic donation approach to drought-resistant seed technology gives the impression of humanitarianism rather than corporate profit from seed royalties. At least in the short-term, some farmers and communities may be better able to cope with changing environmental and socio-economic conditions because of WEMA's public–private–philanthropic partnership. However, as in earlier instantiations of ag-biotech, these products may also lock farmers into a system which necessitates the continual (re)purchase of varieties—varieties that may not be forever royalty-free, and whose intellectual property ownership has the potential to shift.

As our review suggests, ag-biotech has traditionally been at the center of a dominant, popularized narrative of food security and hunger. WEMA's significant emphasis on public benefit continues to echo and extend Green Revolution technology development narratives. While WEMA appears to have more focus on local adaptation than the Green Revolution, the extent to which this adaptation is then done in the interests of farmers—especially small-scale farmers—is questionable and variable at present (Schnurr 2015). The case of the American chestnut, however, complicates this narrative by using the same recombinant DNA technology in a non-food (at least in its predominant use), functional crop. The American chestnut restoration case instead perpetuates the "restoration" narrative that leads one to believe that the scientists' efforts are responsible and environmentally conscious—and this simply because they are "scientists" and "publicly funded." The broader ag-biotech community has capitalized on this uniquely positive silviculture project as justification of genetic engineering's potential for positive societal impact.

It is still unclear to us if these cases represent actual changes, or merely superficial attempts to do plant breeding *in the public interest*. Through new philanthropic endeavors, ag-biotech corporations have sought to shake off critiques of their work during and following the Green Revolution (also see Vessuri, this volume). It appears that scientists involved in these projects are genuinely committed to challenging the dominant frameworks of intellectual property—but the constraints of academic capitalism and narratives of Green Revolution humanitarian philanthropy are still felt, regardless of the personal intentions of those involved. Further comparison between political, historical, and economic contexts and the work of the new generation of ag-biotech researchers is a key research area for future work.

Notes

1 Some studies of genetically engineered cotton in the Global South have suggested that "smallholder farmers" have benefited from the plants' bollworm resistance (Brookes and Barfoot 2006; Gomez-Barbero and Rodriguez-Cerezo 2006; James 2008). However, such conclusions have been strongly criticized. Dominic Glover (2010), for instance, argues that the cotton studies are seriously flawed, reflecting comparative gains with regard to relatively short-term gross margins and lacking consideration for (among other factors): longitudinal outcomes, such as the further consolidation of land ownership; large variations in farm family experiences, particularly between those more and less socio-economically advantaged; and methodological issues with the calculation of wage labor. Nonetheless, such studies have contributed to the persistence of the "pro-poor success" narrative (Glover 2008, 2010).

2   In response to the consumer "crises of confidence" in ag-biotech in the 1990s (particularly in Europe), Monsanto created the short-lived (2000-2) Technology Cooperation and Smallholder Programmes (SHP). These programmatic efforts were heavily publicized, in part, as a means to present an alternative narrative about ag-biotech. However, as Glover's (2008) study of the SHP demonstrates, it was also seen by company executives as a means for opening new markets and asserting that their technologies were both appropriate to such contexts and sustainable. While some of the more philanthropic and socially oriented aims of the SHP may have been genuine, Glover notes that fitting the SHP into the broader corporate structure of Monsanto "meant that the special characteristics of the programme were steadily undermined" (2007).

References

Altieri, M. and Rosset, P. (1998). "Ten reasons why biotechnology will not ensure food security, protect the environment and reduce poverty in the developing world". *AgBioForum* 2(3&4): 155–62.

Altieri, M. and Rosset, P. (1999). "Strengthening the case for why biotechnology will not help the developing world: a response to McGloughlin". *AgBioForum* 2(3&4): 226–36.

Bennington, W. (2014, January 15). "The emperor's new clothes: genetically engineered trees and the bioeconomy". *The Peak Magazine*.

Berman, E.P. (2012). *Creating the Market University: How Academic Science Became an Economic Engine*. Princeton University Press.

Blumenthal, D., Gluck, M., Louis, K., Soto, A. and Wise, D. (1986). "University-industry research relations in biotechnology: implications for the university". *Science* 232 (June 13): 1361–1366.

Brookes, G. and Barfoot. (2006). "Global impact of biotech crops: socio-economic and environmental effects in the first ten years of commercial use". *AgBioForum* 9(3): 139–151.

Brooks, S. (2013, July 18). "Investing in food security? On philanthrocapitalism, biotechnology and development". *Open Democracy*, accessed 16 February 2017 at www.opendemocracy.net/sally-brooks/investing-in-food-security-on-philanthrocapitalism-biotechnology-and-development.

Brooks, S. (2015). "Philanthrocapitalism, 'pro-poor' agricultural biotechnology and development". In Morvaridi, B. (Ed.). (2015). *New Philanthropy and Social Justice: Debating the Conceptual and Policy Discourse*. Policy Press. pp. 101–116.

Busch, L. (1991). *Plants, Power, and Profit: Social, Economic, and Ethical Consequences of the New Biotechnologies*. Cambridge, Mass: B. Blackwell.

Buttel, F.H. (1995). "The global impacts of agricultural biotechnology: a post-Green Revolution perspective". In *Issues of Agricultural Bioethics*, ed. T. B. Mepham, Gregory A. Tucker, and Julian Wiseman, pp. 345–360. Nottingham: Nottingham University Press.

Buttel, F.H. and Belsky, J.M. (1987). "Biotechnology, plant breeding, and intellectual property: social and ethical dimensions". *Science, Technology, and Human Values* 12(1): 31–49.

Buttel, F.H., Cowan, T.J., Kenney, M. and Kloppenburg, J. (1984). "Biotechnology in agriculture: the political economy of agribusiness reorganization and industry-university relationships". In *Research in Rural Sociology and Development*, ed. Harry Scharzweller, 1: 315–348. Greenwich, CT: JAI Press.

Escobar, Arturo. (1995). *Encountering Development: The Making and the Unmaking of the Third World*. Princeton University Press.

Etzkowitz, H. (1998). "The norms of entrepreneurial science: cognitive effects of the new university-industry linkages". *Research Policy*, 27(8): 823–833.

Glenna, L.L., Welsh, R., Ervin, D., Lacy, W.B. and Biscotti, D. (2011). "Commercial science, scientists' values, and university biotechnology research agendas". *Research Policy*, 40(7): 957–968.

Glover, D. (2007). *The Role of the Private Sector in Modern Biotechnology and Rural Development: The Case of the Monsanto Smallholder Programme*. University of Sussex.

Glover, D. (2008). "Made by Monsanto: the corporate shaping of GM crops as a technology for the poor". STEPS Working Paper 11, Brighton: STEPS Centre.

Glover, D. (2010). "Is Bt Cotton a pro-Poor Technology? A Review and Critique of the Empirical Record". *Journal of Agrarian Change* 10(4): 482–509.

Gómez-Barbero, M. and Rodríguez-Cerezo. (2006). *Economic Impact of Dominant GM Crops Worldwide: A Review*. Office for Official Publications of the European Commission, Joint Research Centre.

Goodman, D., Sorj, B. and Wilkinson, J. (1987). *From Farming to Biotechnology: A Theory of Agro-Industrial Development*. New York: Basil Blackwell.

Howard, P.H. (2009). "Visualizing consolidation in the global seed industry: 1996–2008". *Sustainability* 1(4): 1266–1287.

James, C. (2008). "Global status of commercialized biotech/GM crops: 2008. ISAAA Brief No. 39". ISAAA: Ithaca, NY.

James, C. (2014). "Global status of commercialized biotech/GM crops: 2014. ISAAA Brief No. 49". ISAAA: Ithaca, NY.

Juma, C. (2010). *The New Harvest: Agricultural Innovation in Africa*. Oxford University Press.

Kenney, M. and Buttel, F.H. (1985). "Biotechnology: prospects and dilemmas for Third World development". *Development and Change* 16(1): 61–91.

Kimura, A.H. (2013). *Hidden Hunger: Gender and the Politics of Smarter Foods*. Cornell University Press.

Kinchy, A.J., Kleinman D.L. and Autry, R. (2008). "Against free markets, against science? Regulation the socio-economic effects of biotechnology". *Rural Sociology* 73(2): 147–179.

Kingiri, A. (2010). "Experts to the rescue? An analysis of the role of experts in biotechnology regulation in Kenya". *Journal of International Development* 22(3): 325–340.

Kleinman, D.L. and Kinchy, A.J. (2003). "Why ban bovine growth hormone? Science, social welfare, and the divergent biotech policy landscapes in Europe and the United States". *Science as Culture* 12(3): 375–414.

Kleinman, D.L. (2003). *Impure Cultures: University Biology and The World of Commerce*. University of Wisconsin Press.

Kleinman, D.L. and Kloppenburg, J. Jr. (1991). "Aiming for the discursive high ground: Monsanto and the biotechnology controversy". *Sociological Forum* 6(3): 427–447.

Kloppenburg, J.R. (1988). *Seeds and Sovereignty: The Use and Control of Plant Genetic Resources*. Durham: Duke University Press.

Lacy, W.B., Lacy, L.R. and Busch, L. (1988). "Agricultural biotechnology research: practices, consequences, and policy recommendations". *Agriculture and Human Values* 5(3): 3–14.

Lacy, W.B., Glenna, L.L., Biscotti, D., Welsh, R. and Clancy, K. (2014). "The two cultures of science: implications for university-industry relationships in the US agriculture biotechnology". *Journal of Integrative Agriculture* 13(2): 455–466.

Lappé, F.M., Collins, J. and Rosset, P. (1998). *World Hunger: 12 Myths*. Grove Press.

Lipton, E. (2015, Sept. 5). "Food industry enlisted academics in G.M.O. lobbying war, emails show". *New York Times*, p.1.

Mayet, M. (2007). "The new Green Revolution in Africa: Trojan horse for GMOs". In Nærstad, Aksel, ed. *Africa Can Feed Itself*, Oslo: The Development Fund, 158–165.

Paarlberg, R. (2009). *Starved for Science: How Biotechnology is Being Kept out of Africa*. Cambridge, Mass.: Harvard University Press.

Reece, David J. and Haribabu, Ejnavarzala. (2007). "Genes to feed the world: the weakest link?" *Food Policy* 32(4): 459–479.

Ronald, Pamela. (2011). "Plant genetics, sustainable agriculture and global food security". *Genetics* 188(1): 11–20.

Schnurr, M.A. and Gore, C. (2015). "Getting to 'Yes': governing genetically modified crops in Uganda". *Journal of International Development* 27(1): 55–72.

Schumacher, E.F. (1973). *Small is Beautiful: Economics as if People Mattered*. New York, Perennial Library.

Shiva, V. (1991). *The Violence of Green Revolution: Third World Agriculture, Ecology and Politics*. Zed Books.

Shiva, V. (1997). *Biopiracy: The Plunder of Nature and Knowledge*. Boston: South End Press.

Southeast Asia Regional Initiatives for Community Empowerment. (2013). "Going against the golden grain: a primer on golden rice", accessed 16 February 2017 at http://searice.org.ph/wp-content/uploads/2013/09/GoingAgainstTheGoldenGrain_screen.pdf.

Stone, G. (2010). "Field vs. farm in Warangal: Bt cotton, higher yields, and larger questions". *World Development* 39(3): 387–398.

Stone, G. D. and Glover, D. (2016). "Disembedding grain: Golden Rice, the Green Revolution, and heirloom seeds in the Philippines". *Agriculture and Human Values* 34(1): 87–102.

Water Efficient Maize for Africa (2016) "Frequently asked questions". Retrieved from www.aatf-africa.org/userfiles/WEMA-FAQ.pdf.

Zimmer, C. (2013, March 11). "Resurrecting a forest". *National Geographic (Blogs)*. Retrieved from http://phenomena.nationalgeographic.com/2013/03/11/resurrecting-a-forest/.

16

BIODIVERSITY OFFSETTING

Rebecca Lave and Morgan Robertson

1 Introduction

The tension between promoting economic development and protecting the environment has deep roots. One way to require that development projects address the costs of environmental impacts is known as *mitigation* – reducing or compensating for environmental damage from development projects – and dates back to at least 1958. Mitigation first appeared in amendments to the US Fish and Wildlife Coordination Act, and initially it was limited to the US Fish and Wildlife Service's non-binding comments on the environmental effects of other federal agency projects. But with the advent of the major US environmental protection laws in the 1970s, the US and many other countries began to use the concept of mitigation to put more serious weight on the environmental side of the scale in attempt to bring economic and environmental goals into better balance. In the US usage, "mitigation" includes reducing the *gross* or total impacts from a development project. But as the economic costs of reducing environmental impacts became apparent through the 1970s and 1980s, the practice developed of achieving *net* reductions by allowing impacts to occur, and requiring compensation to offset them.

Compensation using offsets has proved to be an attractive, but also controversial, way to balance the goal of environmental quality with the need for economic development, and there are numerous and ongoing attempts to harmonize economic and environmental goals using required or suggested compensation activities. Today, one of the most widely promoted approaches is known as biodiversity offsetting.[1] The core idea of offsetting is that some environmental impacts from development projects such as timber harvesting or mining are unavoidable even with the best project planning. In order to prevent the gradual erosion of biodiversity, ecological function, and ecosystem services, regulations should require compensation for – should *offset* – those impacts through the restoration or creation of sites or ecological functions of comparable environmental value. Advocates argue that this will enable continued economic growth and resource use while ensuring that the environment experiences no *net* loss of functions and values. Critics argue that offsetting is simply putting a green face on business as usual and constitutes a "license to trash." This phrase has become a sometimes successful rallying cry for the environmental movement in opposition to offsets policy,[2] alongside the claim that offsets do not in fact fully compensate for lost ecosystem qualities and therefore resemble a fee paid by polluters for permission to damage the environment. Despite these critiques, biodiversity offsetting is widely promoted in international environmental policy circles (Metcalfe & Vorhies 2010; GDI 2013), although implementation is limited to the national scale (e.g., Collingwood Environmental & IEEP 2014). Countries that have developed and implemented biodiversity offsetting policies include the US, Australia, Germany, South Africa, and the UK.

In this chapter, we first describe biodiversity offsetting in theory and in practice. We then address the role of science and knowledge producers more broadly in promoting this policy framework, and thus in justifying continuing capital accumulation and development, arguing that the neoliberalization of knowledge production plays a central role in the neoliberalization of nature (Lohmann, this volume).

2 What is biodiversity offsetting?

Definitions of biodiversity offsetting vary somewhat across countries and documents. Perhaps the most commonly used definition comes from an international NGO called BBOP: the Business and Biodiversity Offsets Program, a strong advocate of offsetting. According to BBOP, biodiversity offsets are "measures taken to compensate for any residual significant, adverse impacts that cannot be avoided, minimised and/or rehabilitated or restored, in order to achieve no net loss or a net gain of biodiversity" (BBOP 2012). The explicit goal of offsetting is to address the conflict between economic development and environmental quality described above, "to go beyond traditional environmental-impact mitigation measures and help relieve tension between conservation and development by enabling economic gains to be achieved without concomitant biodiversity losses" (Gardner et al., 2013, p.1255). Implicit in the grammar of BBOP's definition is the assumption that the developer will have "avoided, minimised and/or rehabilitated or restored" to the extent possible *before* resorting to the purchase or creation of an offset. This provision, typically referred to as the mitigation hierarchy, is explicit and mandatory in the context of some offsets policy (e.g., the US), while in other settings it is not always clear that such a demonstration *must* precede offsetting (see Collingwood Environmental & IEEP 2014, 51). The perception that promises of compensation affect the decision about whether or not to allow the impact lies at the heart of the public controversy over offsets. Without such a requirement, offsets can be accused of being offered *instead* of expensive and inconvenient efforts to reduce impacts, rather than *in addition* to them (Spash 2015). An offset purchased in lieu of conducting a thorough analysis of low-impact alternatives is easily framed as a "license to trash" (Howarth 2013).

In countries that allow offsetting, such as the US, Germany, and Australia, the process works like this. When a project is proposed, its potential environmental impacts are evaluated by regulatory agency staff – in the US, this typically occurs under the aegis of the Clean Water Act or the Endangered Species Act, and the agencies involved are, respectively, the US Army Corps of Engineers and the US Fish and Wildlife Service. If staff find that the project would have impacts to environmental features protected by regulation, project proponents can be required to rework their plans by following "the mitigation hierarchy" of avoidance, minimization, and compensation mentioned above. First, proponents must redesign the project to avoid environmental damage; then they must minimize any impacts that cannot be avoided. Only then are they allowed to purchase or create compensation offsets for unavoidable environmental impacts. Often this occurs by paying to restore or recreate ecologically equivalent habitat elsewhere.

In practice, however, it has proven possible for project proponents to circumvent the avoidance and minimization requirements of the mitigation hierarchy. Savvy developers propose more impact than they require, and accede to a reduction in impact, achieving "avoidance." The minimization step is often honored in the breach: developers point to the lack of any regulatory definition of what "minimization" actually means. Since neither avoidance nor minimization is politically palatable to enforce, compensatory mitigation is the most common result of the use of the mitigation hierarchy (Houck 1989, Bean and Dwyer 2000, Hough and Robertson, 2009).

To provide this compensatory mitigation, project proponents typically purchase offset credits produced by a public, non-profit, or for-profit "mitigation bank" that has acquired rights to environmentally degraded land and restored it in advance to produce particular kinds of offsets. In some cases, the preservation of areas of high environmental quality is allowed to constitute an offset, but generally agencies prefer to see some managed uplift of environmental values at the offset site in order to prevent net loss of biodiversity. Biodiversity offsetting is thus considered to be a Market-Based Instrument for promoting environmental protection, since it attempts to internalize the environmental costs of economic development through a transactional relationship between the polluter and a service commodity provider. Because of the heavy government involvement – the government requires that credits be purchased, it certifies credit producers, and sometimes it even produces the credits for sale – offsetting is typically referred to as a regulatory market, rather than a free market (Shabman et al. 1994; King 2002).

Even staunch supporters of offsetting agree that there are some kinds of biodiversity or ecosystem services that are so rare or difficult to restore or recreate that impacts to them cannot be offset, and thus should not be allowed (e.g. ten Kate et al. 2004, Kiesecker et al. 2010, Quétier and Lavorel 2011, Gardner et al. 2013, Pilgrim et al. 2013). However, supporters argue that for many ecosystems, particularly those that can be reliably restored in relatively short time periods, offsetting can provide much needed support for environmental protection. Critics and supporters alike agree that successful offsetting policy must address a number of key issues, including equivalence, additionality, and uncertainty.

Discussions of *equivalence* address the widespread concern that the environmental benefits from management or restoration actions at a compensation site may not actually be equivalent to the environmental impacts they are intended to offset. To know whether there is equivalence between ecological "debits" and "credits" we need a metric that quantifies them, converting ecological complexity into a simplified set of characteristics that can be measured, regulated, and sold. This in turn requires paring away the ecological specificity of both impact and compensation sites to define an ecologically and economically coherent core indicator (or set of indicators). This standardized, measurable commodity-like credit is the "offset" for sale (Lave et al. 2010a). Developing the metrics that establish ecological equivalence is thus a crucial and highly fraught task of environmental science (Ransom et al., this volume). For example, in attempts to offset impacts on the red-cockaded woodpecker, an endangered species in the US, will offsets be defined on the basis of breeding pairs displaced from the development site and replaced at the compensation site, or on the basis of the physical area of their habitat destroyed or restored? This question is not trivial, either ecologically or economically, as it sets the envelope of possibilities for biodiversity conservation and the basic conditions that will allow the regulatory market in woodpecker offsets to function or collapse (Quetiér and Lavorel 2011, Bull et al. 2013, Curran et al. 2014).

A second area in which environmental science plays a central role in enabling markets for biodiversity offsetting is *additionality*. The question at stake here is whether the proposed compensation would provide additional ecological value over what would have happened without the proposed project, under existing regulatory requirements. Without additionality, there is little chance that offsetting would prevent net loss of biodiversity, a key concern of both advocates and critics of offsetting. Measuring additionality requires the development of detailed scenarios determining the baseline against which the proposed compensation actions should be measured. As with the metrics described above, developing these baselines is a task of environmental science, without which the basic criteria for offsetting markets could not be met (McKenney and Kiesecker 2010, Gillenwater 2011, Quétier et al. 2014).

A third area in which the viability of offsetting markets depends upon environmental science regards the question of *uncertainty,* an overarching issue that could undermine biodiversity offsetting entirely. In the case of offsetting, uncertainty stems from both human and ecological factors, such as whether regulatory frameworks might change with shifts in political parties, whether compensation sites will be competently monitored and managed over the long-term, whether actual environmental impacts can be adequately measured, and whether larger systemic issues such as climate change could undo compensation efforts. The task of environmental science here is to attempt to reduce uncertainty, and to quantify it sufficiently that regulators can adjust offset credit definitions accordingly (King & Price 2006, Quétier and Lavorel 2011, Maron et al. 2012, Bull et al. 2013, Curran et al. 2014).

A functional offsetting market requires all three of these (as well as a number of other scientific products), and thus is fundamentally dependent upon methods and claims of scientific knowledge.

The continuing support for biodiversity offsetting in international policy circles suggests that many believe that these tasks of environmental science – developing metrics, establishing additionality, and defining baselines – are doable projects (Fujimura 1987), and thus that offsetting is a viable practice that can indeed meet both environmental and economic goals. It is worth noting, however, that there is very little data on whether offsetting is actually achieving any of its conservation goals (e.g. Fox and Nino-Murcia 2005, Robertson and Hayden 2008, Bull et al. 2013, Rayment et al. 2014, Curran et al. 2015). This is particularly worrisome given the mounting body of evidence that the ecological restoration practices on which offsetting depends are fraught with uncertainty and catastrophic project failures (Moilanen et al. 2009, Palmer and Filoso 2009, Maron et al. 2012, Curran et al. 2014). As Curran et al. remark, "There is clearly a need for more empirical data at both the local (i.e., the performance of individual trades) and policy scale (i.e., isolating the effect of offset policies on overall trends in biodiversity)" (Curran et al. 2015, p.1744).

Despite the lack of evidence that biodiversity offsets actually have positive ecological results (and the high likelihood that they are failing, given the uncertainties associated with restoration), use of offsetting is growing, enabling development to continue even in jurisdictions with relatively strong environmental protection legislation. In the long run of environmental policy, the growth of offsetting has allowed governments to replace the regulatory "no's" that were originally intended to prevent environmental harm with the concept of a regulatory "yes, with conditions" (Walker et al. 2009), intended to prevent *net* environmental harm.

3 The role of science and scientists in biodiversity offsetting

The literature on biodiversity offsetting and markets for ecosystem services more broadly consistently assumes that science can produce the metrics and accounting tools needed to make offsetting work (e.g. ten Kate et al. 2004, Kiesecker et al. 2010, Wissel and and Wätzold 2010). But physical scientists have not exactly been leading the charge for ecosystem service markets, as several commentators have noted (ten Kate et al. 2004, p.73; Hrabanski 2015, p.147). In most of these markets (with the exception of carbon offsetting) university- or public agency-based scientists have been trailing along behind policy advances, offering cautionary notes but rarely engaged in policy development. In some cases, scientists seem to be entirely absent from the discussion, as in stream mitigation banking in the US (Lave et al. 2010a, Lave 2014), or the

European Commission's No Net Loss Working Group which, though tasked with evaluating the potential of biodiversity offsetting to achieve no net loss of biodiversity in the EU, did not include university- or public agency-based scientists.

Scientists who are engaged with offsetting and its relatively rapid adoption take a variety of stances towards it. Some seem to be generally supportive of the concept of offsetting, but critical of its implementation so far. They thus produce earnest explorations of the general ecological principles needed to make offsetting work (or at least work better) (e.g. Kremen 2005, Bruggeman et al. 2005, Moilanen et al. 2009, Bull et al. 2013, Gardner et al. 2013) that recycle a shared set of concerns without discernibly contributing to the evolution of biodiversity offsetting policy. In addition to the concerns about metrics, additionality, and uncertainty raised above, these papers typically call out issues with time lag (the gap between when habitat is lost and when it is restored, which can create fatal problems for species that temporarily have no available habitat), duration (the need for compensation sites to be protected for as long as the development site is impacted, typically in perpetuity), scale (the distance of compensation sites from impact sites), type (whether offsetting is allowed only in kind (e.g. turtle habitat traded for turtle habitat) or whether out-of-kind trades are allowed to improve ecological outcomes), monitoring (the need for independent third-party monitoring to verify ecological outcomes), and enforcement (the need to enforce mitigation and long-term management requirements).

Responding more concretely, some physical scientists have developed specific metrics or tools intended to improve the ecological outcomes of offsetting. However, offset metric developers have noted that there is generally a trade-off between the ecological precision of the metric and its usability in policy (Treweek 2009). These tools have, at least thus far, a level of ecological specificity and rigor that interferes with the generalizability needed for a commodity definition for market purposes (e.g. the RobOff model developed by Pouzols and Moilanen 2013).

Other scientists are leading the charge against offsetting, raising objections from natural science (e.g. Gibbons and Lindenmayer 2007, Palmer and Filoso 2009, Bekessy et al. 2010, Clare et al. 2011, Maron et al. 2012, Curran et al. 2014, Maron et al. 2015, Moreno-Mateos et al. 2015, Moilanen and Jussi 2016), social science (Ruhl and Salzman 2006, BenDor and Brozovic 2007, Büscher and Fletcher 2014, Sullivan 2013, Lockhart 2015, Spash 2015) and integrated perspectives (Walker et al. 2009, Bekessy et al. 2010). These critiques run the gamut from practical to theoretical. Some scientists argue that, as implemented to date, offsetting policy and implementation fail to address the central ecological concerns laid out in the previous paragraph, such as protecting compensation sites over the long term, or preventing time lag between when impacts occur and when compensation sites are ready. Others point out that offsetting has important social equity impacts, since compensation sites are typically distant from impact sites (Ruhl and Salzman 2006, BenDor and Brozovic 2007). Residents of a neighborhood that loses a cherished woodland bordering their homes, critics argue, cannot be adequately compensated for their loss by a restored forest which may be in the same biogeographic region, but 40km or even 100km away.

Some critics argue that offsetting fatally undermines existing environmental protections by giving agency staff far more politically palatable alternatives to denying environmentally damaging permit applications. Where regulators are firmly required to evaluate the impact on its merits, before considering compensation, this is less of a problem. But otherwise, instead of requiring permit applicants to do no harm, agency staff can allow developers to move forward with their projects as long as they pay for offsets to compensate for the losses they cause. This relaxation of environmental standards is of particular concern to critics because, as noted above, there is no guarantee that management and restoration actions at compensation sites will replace the biodiversity lost in development projects. Critics point out that offsetting is deeply dependent on ecological restoration to produce net biodiversity gain, and argue that this is a fatal flaw given that restoration itself is highly uncertain and often unsuccessful.

Still other critics argue that offsetting is part of a broader commodification or financialization of nature that is intrinsically unacceptable. To these critics, the environment should not be subjected to the capitalistic logic which provides the core rationale for offsetting and other Market-Based Initiatives, and the entire paradigm of selling nature in order to save it (Mcafee 1999) should be avoided (Sullivan 2013, Büscher and Fletcher 2014; see also Lohmann, this volume).

Market-Based Initiatives such as offsetting are highly dependent on environmental science to define many key market parameters, such as establishing equivalence between impact and compensation sites, assessing the additionality of proposed compensation projects, and addressing the deep human and ecological uncertainties offsetting necessarily entrains. And yet, despite the fact that university- and agency-based scientists are not playing their expected role in offsetting markets by providing the assessment tools needed to make them ecologically credible, there are many offsetting markets up and running worldwide. If not academic or agency-based scientists, who is filling this gap and providing the needed scientific frameworks? Consultants and scientists at private firms and NGOs.

4 Privatizing ecological knowledge production

Even a quick scan of the commonly cited peer review and gray literature on biodiversity offsetting shows that consultants and staff at environmental NGOs play a pivotal role within it. Instead of university- or agency-based scientists, private-sector knowledge producers are the ones developing the broadly cited justifications for biodiversity offsetting, as well as the practical metrics and assessment tools needed to make it work (or so they hope). And they seem to be viewed consistently as scientifically authoritative sources despite the fact that they are not employed by universities, that many do not hold PhDs, and that in some cases they are subject to commercial conflicts of interest as they promote approaches from which they also profit.

For example, stream mitigation banking, an offsetting market in the US, depends almost entirely on the work of two consultants: Dave Rosgen and Will Harman. Rosgen developed the classification system most states use to establish equivalence between impact and compensation sites, and is widely considered to be the most influential stream researcher in the US (Lave 2012a). When binding federal requirements for mitigation banking were established in 2008, states had to assess impact and compensation sites based not on the comparatively simple physical assessments of condition used in Rosgen classification, but on the far more complex basis of actual ecological function. This opened up possibilities for academics and agency-based scientists, many of whom are deeply frustrated by their exclusion from stream mitigation policy and practice, to step in and begin to develop market tools for establishing functional equivalence. Instead, however, the work needed to link Rosgen classifications to the new functional standards is being done by consultants, in most cases by Harman, a Rosgen protégé (Lave 2014).

In the related field of wetland assessment, nearly every important technical manual used by regulators to define wetlands was produced either by a private-sector consultant (e.g. Adamus et al. 2010, Lee et al. 1997) or by state agency staff who have an abundance of field experience and graduate training but who often lack doctoral degrees (e.g., Ohio EPA 2001, Minnesota BWSR 2010). There are hundreds of such assessment methods in circulation, many of them created by the state and nearly all of them funded by the state through grants or contracts. Their prevalence is a testament to the power of the privatization of knowledge but also to the simultaneously deep involvement of the state in that privatization.

The international policy community supporting biodiversity offsetting seems to be similarly dependent on a small, tightly linked group of private sector knowledge producers. The most highly cited articles and reports supportive of offsetting come from a handful of consultants and NGO staff, most notably Kerry ten Kate (a former lawyer who is now head of BBOP), Jo Treweek (an environmental consultant), and Fabien Quétier (a Ph.D. ecologist turned ecological entrepreneur). The most practical metrics and assessment tools for offsetting come from consultants such as John Pilgrim (e.g. Pilgrim et al. 2013) and scientists employed at NGOs, such as John Kiesecker (Kiesecker et al. 2009 and 2010). Although these offsetting advocates lack many of the traditional trappings of scientific expertise such as PhDs and/or academic jobs, they are routinely cited as authoritative voices and even challenge more conventionally legitimate scientists critical of offsetting in peer-reviewed journals (e.g. a recent exchange in *Ecological Applications*: Curran et al. 2014, Quétier et al. 2015, Curran et al. 2015). Their work is amplified and publicized through non-profit organizations rather than academic institutions: Forest Trends, www. ecosystemmarketplace.com, and the books of market-environmentalist popularizers such as Gretchen Daily (1997), Geoffrey Heal (2000), Tony Juniper (2013), and Joe Whitworth (2015).

This is a striking illustration of what many commentators have described as the increasing horizontality of knowledge production: as the authority of academic science declines, the authority of scientific knowledge producers outside the academy has risen. While the professionalization of science in the 1800s more or less entirely delegitimized non-academic or agency-based scientists (Reingold 1976, Keeney 1992, Secord 1994) what might be described as extramural scientists (e.g. producers of local knowledge, indigenous knowledge, amateurs, citizen science, etc.) came roaring back into view in the 1980s on a renewed wave of bioprospecting (Brush and Stabinsky 1996, Shiva 2001, Hayden 2003), rising activism around environmental justice (Brown 1990, Allen 2003), and increasing inclusion of indigenous knowledge in environmental management (Nadasdy 1999). With this visibility has come a rise in prestige and legitimacy. Activists and indigenous groups are increasingly consulted in environmental policy (Fairhead and Leach 2003, Cohen and Ottinger 2011, Ottinger 2013) in ways that were unthinkable until very recently.

Particularly relevant to biodiversity offsetting, consultants and other private sector scientists have successfully claimed the mantle of scientific authority (Briske et al. 2011, Lave 2012a and 2015). While in recent decades their knowledge claims were seen as called into question, or even contaminated, by financial conflicts of interest, they are increasingly seen as *legitimated* by market forces rather than compromised by them; if people are willing to pay for their expertise, they must be right. Thus, rather than dismissing the work of Pilgrim, Quétier, Treweek, and others as subject to financial conflicts of interest when they are hired to advise on the development of policy frameworks they promoted, they are seen instead as the most authoritative figures on offsetting.

This resurgence of private sector scientific authority is one consequence of the increasing emphasis on the privatization and commercialization of knowledge production under neoliberal science policies (Lave et al. 2010b, Randalls 2010, Mirowski 2011, Lave 2012b, Tyfield 2010), which is visible also in trends such as the striking expansion of intellectual property protections. Instead of producing freely available knowledge for the public good, university-based scientists are increasingly encouraged to both privatize and sell their knowledge claims via patents, Material Transfer Agreements (MTAs), and copyrighting of previously shared materials (Nowotny et al. 2001, Coriat and Orsi 2002, Nowotny 2005, Biagioli 2006, Nedeva and Boden 2006, Geiger and Sa 2008, Popp-Berman 2008, Tyfield 2010, Mirowski 2011). This clearly legitimates private-sector knowledge production by association: with academic scientists encouraged to privatize their knowledge, the stigma of privately produced knowledge claims erodes.

While the resurgence of private sector knowledge production stretches across academic fields, it is particularly pronounced in the environmental sciences. The development of fields on which offsetting depends, such as ecological restoration and biodiversity conservation, has been catalyzed by a sense of crisis rather than more organically through scientific breakthroughs. These fields are thus cobbled together from pre-existing pieces, leaving far more obvious seams and contradictions than in better developed disciplines. In addition, most environmental sciences emphasize the particularity, complexity, and interconnectedness of the systems they study, which produces high levels of uncertainty, opening up their results to determined questioning. Further, environmental disciplines often touch on areas in which market actors have powerful interests (via climate securities and ecosystem service markets, for example), which can lead them to intervene in scientific debates. Lastly, many environmental sciences concentrate on topics about which people without formal scientific training have substantial knowledge. Taken together, these vulnerabilities leave many environmental scientists less able to defend their authority against knowledge producers outside the academy (Lave 2012b), as we see in biodiversity offsetting.

What we seem to be seeing, then, is the neoliberalization of knowledge production playing a central role in attempts to neoliberalize nature. Without metrics that abstract the ecological specificity of particular ecosystems into easily measurable, comparable units, market-based environmental management approaches such as biodiversity offsets could not function. Creating these market-enabling metrics is thus a critical task of "science in the service of capital" (Robertson 2006). In this case, as in many other markets for ecosystem services, that science is produced primarily outside the academy.

5 Implications

As of this writing, it is not entirely clear where biodiversity offsetting is going. On the one hand, offsetting and other Market Based Instruments are still strongly promoted tools of pro-market segments of the international environmental policy community, and have been for some time. Offsetting can now be found on every continent except Antarctica, and the volume of articles and reports promoting it outweighs that of critiques by at least an order of magnitude, perhaps several. In the US, for example, no environmental group opposes compensatory mitigation via offsetting, not even more radical groups such as Greenpeace that one might expect to line up against the financialization of nature.

But a funny thing happened on the way to ubiquity. Offsetting and similar Market Based Instruments have been repeatedly blocked in international negotiations over implementation of the CBD (Dempsey 2016). And civil society groups in the EU seem to have at least temporarily blocked the formalized introduction of offsetting at the EU level. A broad coalition of environmental groups rallied their supporters and successfully opposed what appeared to be the pre-ordained inclusion of offsetting in EU environmental policy. Weighing in on the debate, the European NGO FERN began the first of three briefing documents with a sarcastic, scathing critique of marketization:

> The term biodiversity offsetting is echoing round environment ministries across the EU – and slipping off the tongues of money market speculators. In its most crude manifestation, biodiversity offsetting involves the pricing and swapping of one area of biodiversity for another in order to facilitate development. You want to build houses on a field rich with flora and fauna? Merely find another field of roughly equal size a distance away and replace or offset one lot of nature with another. To facilitate the process, you contact middlemen or brokers who organize the process for you: money is made, deals are done and biodiversity levels remain. What could be simpler?
>
> *(FERN 2015, p.1)*

The briefing document raised a variety of arguments, but among them were concerns that the complexity and interconnectedness of ecosystems makes them difficult and expensive to measure, much less put a price tag on, that it underplays the deep uncertainties associated with restoration, that there is not sufficient institutional capacity for long-term monitoring and enforcement needed to protect compensation sites in perpetuity, and that offsetting raises unfixable social equity issues because of the distance between impact and compensation sites.

The critique of marketization is explicit, frequent, and trenchant – and is grounded in issues of scientific knowledge concerning the adequacy of offsets. It also seems to have been highly effective. Interviews in 2015 and 2016 indicate that at least for the time being, offsetting is "a poisoned term",[3] with even policy advocates referring to it as "toxic".[4] EU policy debates and the controversies around them have claimed the career of at least one UK minister, who was seen to be too enthusiastic about the ability of offsetting to address the environmental consequences of economic development.[5] Thus while we have demonstrated that the neoliberalization of scientific knowledge production plays a strong role in the neoliberalization of nature, the debate over biodiversity offsetting also demonstrates a striking counter-trend. Here, opposition to the financialization and privatization associated with neoliberalism more broadly has catalyzed opposition to the neoliberalization of the environment.

Offsetting is not permanently dead, though. In response to opposition, advocates for offsetting and other Market Based Instruments have begun the process of repackaging them under different names (see the failed Green Development Mechanism in CBD negotiations, which is now the Green Development Initiative, and the switch from "offsetting" to "compensation" in England), and different organizations (e.g. the IUCN). It remains to be seen whether this zombie form of offsetting will be more successful in its newly risen form.

Notes

1   1974 U.S. federal regulations on implementation of the Clean Air Act contain the first reference to 'offsetting' air pollution impacts through reducing other emissions at the same facility, a different application of the same general concept of mitigation. Although in the US context, *mitigation* tends to refer to expenditures that create environmental improvements, while *offsetting* tends to refer to expenditures that avoid environmental impairments, globally the two terms have become roughly synonymous, broadly applied to a range of policies that require polluters to compensate for their impacts in order to balance economic development with environmental health.
2   See http://naturenotforsale.org/. Last accessed May 25, 2016.
3   Personal communication, NGO staff member, 18 November 2015.
4   David Hill, deputy chair of UK agency Natural England, apparently used the term at the Westminster Energy and Environment Transport Forum on 21 April 2016, as reported on Twitter by several attendees (@keasdenkate and @MilesKing10).
5   In July 2014, UK Defra Minister Owen Paterson was dismissed after suggesting that biodiversity offsetting could be used to replace 'ancient woodland:' www.telegraph.co.uk/news/earth/environment/10550482/Ancient-woodland-could-be-bulldozed-for-housing-suggests-Owen-Paterson.html.

References

Adamus, P., Morlan, J. and Verble, K. 2010. *Manual for the Oregon Wetland Assessment Protocol (ORWAP) Version 2.0.2.* Salem, OR: Oregon DSL.
Allen, B. 2003. *Uneasy Alchemy: Citizens and Experts in Louisiana's Chemical Corrido Disputes.* Cambridge, MA: MIT Press.
BBOP. 2012. "Standards on biodiversity offsets". Washington, D.C.: Business and Biodiversity Offsets Programme.
Beck, U. 1992. *Risk Society: Towards a New Modernity.* Thousand Oaks, CA: Sage Publications.

Bean, M.J. and Dwyer, L.E. 2000. "Mitigation banking as an endangered species conservation tool". *Environmental Law Reporter* 7:10537–10556.

Bekessy, S., Wintle, B., Lindenmayer, D., Mccarthy, M., Colyvan, M., Burgman, M., and Possingham, H. 2010. "The biodiversity bank cannot be a lending bank". *Conservation Letters* 3.3:151–158. doi: 10.1111/j.1755-263X.2010.00110.x.

BenDor, T. and Brozovic, N. 2007. "Determinants of spatial and temporal patterns in compensatory wetland mitigation". *Environmental Management* 40.3:349–364.

Biagioli, Mario. 2006. "Patent republic: specifying inventions, constructing authors and rights". *Social Research* 73.4:1129–1172.

Briske, D., Sayre, N., Huntsinger, L., Fernandez-Gimenez, M., Budd, B., and Derner, J. 2011. "Origin, persistence, and resolution of the rotational grazing debate: integrating human dimensions into rangeland research". *Rangeland Ecology & Management* 64.4:325–334.

Brown, P. and Mikkelsen, E. 1990. *No Safe Place: Toxic Waste, Leukemia, and Community Action*. Berkeley: University of California Press.

Bruggeman, D., Jones, M.L., Lupi, F., and Scribner, K. 2005. "Landscape equivalency analysis: methodology for estimating spatially-explicit biodiversity credits". *Environmental Management* 36.4:518–534.

Brush, S. and Stabinsky, D., eds. 1996. *Valuing Local Knowledge: Indigenous People and Intellectual Property Rights*. Washington, D.C.: Island Press.

Bull, J., Suttle, K.B., Gordon, A., Singh, N.J., and Milner-Gulland, E.J. 2013. "Biodiversity offsets in theory and practice". *Oryx* 47.3:369–380.

Büscher, B. and Fletcher, R. 2014. "Accumulation by conservation". *New Political Economy*. doi: http://dx.doi.org/10.1080/13563467.2014.923824.

Canaan, J. and Shumar, W. 2008. "Higher Education in the era of globalization and neoliberalism", in *Structure and Agency in the Neoliberal University*, Canaan J., and Shumar, W., eds., London: Routledge.

Clare, Shari, Naomi Krogman, Lee Foote, and Nathan Lemphers. 2011. "Where is the avoidance in the implementation of wetland law and policy?" *Wetlands Ecology and Management* 19.1:65–182.

Cohen, B. and Ottinger, G., eds. 2011. *Technoscience and Environmental Justice*. Cambridge, MA: MIT Press.

Collingwood Environmental & IEEP. 2014. *Evaluation of the Biodiversity Offsetting Pilot Programme. Final Report; Vol. 1*. London: Collingwood Environmental Planning Ltd.

Coriat, B. and F. Orsi. 2002. "Establishing a new intellectual property rights regime in the United States". *Research Policy* 31:1491–1507.

Curran, M., Hellweg, S., and Beck, J. 2014. "Is there any empirical support for BO policy?" *Ecological Applications* 24.4:617–632.

Curran, M., Hellweg, S., and Beck, J. 2015. "The jury is still out on biodiversity offsets: reply to Quétier et al.". *Ecological Applications* 25.6:1741–1746.

Daily, G. 1997. *Nature's Services: Societal Dependence on Natural Ecosystems*, Washington, DC: Island Press.

Dempsey, J. 2016. *Enterprising Nature*. Wiley-Blackwell.

Fairhead, J. and Leach, M. 2003. *Science, Society and Power: Environmental Knowledge and Policy in West Africa and the Caribbean*. Cambridge: Cambridge University Press.

FERN. 2014. "Briefing note 1: What is biodiversity and why is it important?" FERN. Brussels.

Fox, J. and Nino-Murcia, A. 2005. "Status of species conservation banking in the United States". *Conservation Biology* 19.4:996–1007.

Fujimura, J. 1987. "Constructing 'Do-Able' problems in cancer research: articulating alignment". *Social Studies of Science* 17.2:257–293.

Gardner, T., Von Hase, A., Brownlie, S., Ekstrom, J., Pilgrim, J., Savy, C., Stephens, R.T.T., Treweek, J., Ussher, G., Ward, G., and ten Kate, K. 2013. "Biodiversity offsets and the challenge of achieving no net loss". *Conservation Biology* 27.6:1254–1264.

GDI [Green Development Initiative]. 2013. "The Green Development Initiative: Biodiversity Management in Practice". Presentation for the International Dairy Federation/Sustainable Agriculture Initiative Platform, Workshop on Biodiversity in the Dairy Sector, 18 September 2013, Brussels.

Geiger, R. and Sa, C. 2008. *Tapping the Riches of Science: Universities and the Promise of Economic Growth*. Cambridge, MA: Harvard University Press.

Gibbons, M., Limoges, C., Nowotny, H., Schwartzman, S., Scott, P., and Trow, M. 1994. *The New Production of Knowledge: The Dynamics of Science and Research in Contemporary Societies*. London: Sage.

Gibbons, Philip, and David B. Lindenmayer. 2007. "Offsets for land clearing: no net loss or the tail wagging the dog". *Ecological Management and Restoration* 8.1:26-31. doi: 10.1111/j.1442-8903.2007.00328.x.

Gillenwater, M. 2011. *What is Additionality? Part 1: A Long-Standing Problem*. Silver Spring, MD: Greenhouse Gas Management Institute.

Hayden, C. 2003. *When Nature Goes Public: The Making and Unmaking of Bioprospecting in Mexico*. Princeton, NJ: Princeton University Press.

Heal, G. 2000. *Nature and the Marketplace: Capturing the Value of Ecosystem Services*. Washington, D.C.: Island Press.

Houck, O. 1989. "Hard choices: the analysis of alternatives under Section 404 of the Clean Water Act and similar environmental laws". *University of Colorado Law Review* 60:773–840.

Hough, P. and Robertson, M. 2009. "Mitigation under Section 404 of the Clean Water Act: where it comes from, what it means". *Wetlands Ecology and Management* 17:15–33.

Howarth, L. 2013. "A license to trash? Why Biodiversity Offsetting (BO) will be a disaster for the environment". *Ecologist*, 9 September 2013. www.theecologist.org/News/news_analysis/2048513/a_license_to_trash_why_biodiversity_offsetting_bo_will_be_a_disaster_for_the_environment.html. Last Accessed 25 May 2016.

Hrabanski, M. 2015. "The biodiversity offsets as market-based instruments in global governance: Origins, success and controversies". *Ecosystem Services* 15:143–151. doi: 10.1016/j.ecoser.2014.12.010.

Juniper, T. 2013. *What Has Nature Ever Done for Us? How Money Really Does Grow On Trees*. Santa Fe, NM: Synergetic Press.

Keeney, E. 1992. *The Botanizers: Amateur scientists in Nineteenth Century America*. Chapel Hill, NC: University of North Carolina Press.

Kiesecker, Joseph M., Holly Copeland, Amy Pocewicz, Nate Nibbelink, Bruce McKenney, John Dahlke, Matt Halloran, and Dan Stroud. 2009. "A framework for implementing biodiversity offsets: Selecting sites and determining scale". *Bioscience* 59.1:77–84.

Kiesecker, Joseph M., Holly Copeland, Amy Pocewicz, and Bruce McKenney. 2010. "Development by design: Blending landscape-level planning with the mitigation hierarchy". *Frontiers in Ecology and the Environment* 8.5:261–6.

King, D. 2002. "Managing environmental trades: lessons from Hollywood, Stockholm, and Houston". *Environmental Law Reporter* 32:11317–11320.

King, D. and Price, E. 2006. *Developing Defensible Wetland Mitigation Ratios: Standard Tools for 'Scoring' Wetland Creation, Restoration, Enhancement, and Conservation*. Report submitted to Office of Habitat Protection, National Oceanic and Atmospheric Administration. August 15, 2006.

Kremen, C. 2005. "Managing ecosystem services: what do we need to know about their ecology?" *Ecology Letters* 8:468–479.

Latour, B. 2004. "Why has critique run out of steam? From matters of fact to matters of concern". *Critical Inquiry* 30:225–248.

Lave, R. 2012a. *Fields and Streams: Stream Restoration, Neoliberalism, and the Future of Environmental Science*. Athens: University of Georgia Press.

Lave, R. 2012b. "Neoliberalism and the production of environmental knowledge". *Environment & Society: Advances in Research* 3.1:19–38.

Lave, R. 2014. "Neoliberal confluences: the turbulent evolution of stream mitigation banking in the U.S.". *Political Power and Social Theory* 27:59–88.

Lave, R. 2015. "The future of environmental expertise". *Annals of the Association of American Geographers* 105.2:244–252.

Lave, R., Doyle, M., and Robertson, M. 2010a. "Privatizing stream restoration in the U.S.". *Social Studies of Science* 40.5:677–703.

Lave, R., Mirowski, P., and Randalls, S. 2010b. "Introduction: STS and neoliberal science". *Social Studies of Science* 40.5:659–675.

Lee, L., Brinson, M., Kleindl, W., Whited, M., Gilbert, M., Nutter, W., Whigham, D., and DeWald, D. 1997. *Operational Draft Guidebook for the Hydrogeomorphic Assessment of Temporary and Seasonal Prairie Pothole Wetlands*. Seattle, WA: The National Wetland Training Cooperative.

Lockhart, A. 2015. "Developing an offsetting programme: tensions, dilemmas and difficulties in biodiversity market-making in England". *Environmental Conservation* 42.4:335–344. doi: 10.1017/S0376892915000193.

Maron, M., Hobbs, R., Moilanen, A., Matthews, J., Christie, K., Gardner, T., Keith, D., Lindenmayer, D., and McAlpine, C. 2012. "Faustian bargains? Restoration realities in the context of biodiversity offset policies". *Biological Conservation* 155:141–148.

Mcafee, K. 1999. "Selling nature to save it? Biodiversity and green developmentalism". *Environment and Planning D: Society and Space* 17.2:133–154. doi: 10.1068/d170133.

McKenney, Bruce A., and Joseph M. Kiesecker. 2010. "Policy development for biodiversity offsets: a review of offset frameworks". *Environmental Management* 45:165–76.

Metcalfe, J. and Vorhies, F. 2010. "Making the business case for a Green Development Mechanism". *Business: A Magazine on Business and Biodiversity* 5.1:33.

Minnesota BWSR [Board of Water and Soil Resources]. 2010. *MnRAM 3.4 for Evaluating Wetland Functions*. St. Paul, MN: BWSR.

Mirowski, P. 2011. *Science-Mart: Privatizing American Science*. Cambridge, MA: Harvard University Press.

Moilanen, A., van Teeffelen, A. Ben-Haim, Y., and Ferrier, S. 2009. "How much compensation is enough? A framewok for incorporating uncertainty and time discounting when calculating offset ratios for impacted habitat". *Restoration Ecology* 17.4:470–478.

Moilanen, A. and Laitila, J. 2016. "Indirect leakage leads to failure of avoided loss biodiversity offsetting". *Journal of Applied Ecology* 53:106–11. doi: 10.1111/1365-2664.12565.

Moreno Mateos, David, Virginie Maris, Arnaud Bechet, and Michael Curran. 2015. "The true loss caused by biodiversity offsets". *Biological Conservation* 192:552–559. doi: DOI: 10.1016/j.biocon.2015.08.016.

Nadasdy, P. 1999. "The politics of TEK: power and the 'integration' of knowledge". *Arctic Anthropology* 36.1–2:1–18.

Nedeva, M. and Boden, R. 2006. "Changing science: the advent of neoliberalism". *Prometheus* 24.3:269–281.

Newfield, C. 2008. *Unmaking the Public University*. Cambridge, MA: Harvard University Press.

Nowotny, H., Scott, P., and Gibbons, M. eds. 2001. *Rethinking Science: Knowledge and the Public in an Age of Uncertainty*. Cambridge: Polity Press.

Nowotny, H., Pestre, D., Schmidt-Assman, E., Schultze-Fielitz, H., and Trute, H. eds. 2005. *The Public Nature of Science Under Assault: Politics, Markets, Science and the Law*. Berlin: Springer.

Ohio EPA [Environmental Protection Agency]. 2001. *Ohio Rapid Assessment Method for Wetlands, v. 5.0.* Columbus, OH: OEPA.

Ottinger, G. 2013. *Refining Expertise: How Responsible Engineers Subvert Environmental Justice Challenges*. New York: New York University Press.

Palmer, M.A. and Filoso, S. 2009. "The restoration of ecosystems for environmental markets". *Science* 325.5940:575–576.

Pilgrim, John, Susie Brownlie, Jonathan Ekstrom, Toby Gardner, Amrei von Hase, Kerry ten Kate, Conrad Savy, R.T. Theo Stephens, Helen Temple, Jo Treweek, Graham Ussher, and Gerri Ward. 2013. "A process for assessing the offsetability of biodiversity impacts". *Conservation Letters* 6.5:376–384.

Popp-Berman, E. 2008. "Why did universities start patenting? Institution Building and the road to the Bayh-Dole Act". *Social Studies of Science* 38.6:835–872.

Pouzols, F. and Moilanen, A. 2013. "RobOff: Software for analysis of alternative land-use options and conservation actions". *Methods in Ecology and Evolution* 4:426–432.

Quétier, F. and Lavorel, S. 2011. "Assessing ecological equivalence in biodiversity offset schemes: key issues and solutions". *Biological Conservation* 144:2991–2999.

Quétier, F., Regnery, B., and Levrel, H. 2014. "No net loss of biodiversity or paper offsets? A critical review of the French no net loss policy". *Environmental Science & Policy* 38:120–131.

Quétier, F., van Teeffelen, A., Pilgrim, J., von Hase, A., and ten Kate, K. 2015. "Biodiversity offsets are one solution to widespread poorly compensated biodiverisity loss: a response to Curran et al.". *Ecological Applications* 25.6:1739–1741.

Randalls, Samuel. 2010. "Weather profits: Weather derivatives and the commercialization of meteorology". *Social Studies of Science* 40.5:705–730.

Rayment, M., Haines, R., McNeil, D., Conway, M., Tucker, G., and Underwood, E. 2014. "Study on specific design elements of biodiversity offsets: Biodiversity metrics and mechanisms for securing long term conservation benefits". Report prepared for European Commission. London: ICF International.

Reingold, N. 1976. "Definitions and speculations: the professionalization of science in America in the nineteenth century", in *The Pursuit of Knowledge in the Early American Republic*, Oleson, A., and Brown, S., eds, 33–70. Baltimore, MD: Johns Hopkins University Press.

Robertson, M. 2006. "The nature that capital can see: science, state and market in the commodification of ecosystem services". *Environment and Planning D: Society and Space* 24.3:367–387.

Robertson, M. and Hayden, N. 2008. "Evaluation of a market in wetland credits: entrepreneurial wetland banking in Chicago". *Conservation Biology* 22.3:636–646.

Ruhl, J.B., and J. Salzman. 2006. "The Effects of Wetland Mitigation Banking on People". *National Wetlands Newsletter* 28.2:1.

Secord, A. 1994. "Science in the pub: artisan botanists in early 19th century Lancashire". *History of Science* 32.3:269–315.

Shabman, L., Scodari, P., and King, D. 1994. "National Wetland Mitigation Banking Study: Expanding Opportunities for Successful Mitigation: The Private Credit Market Alternative". Alexandria, VA: US Army Corps of Engineers Institute for Water Resources.

Shiva, V. 2001. *Protect or Plunder? Understanding Intellectual Property Rights*. London: Zed Books.

Spash, C. 2015. "Bulldozing biodiversity: the economics of offsets and trading-in Nature". *Biological Conservation* 192:541–551.

Sullivan, S. 2013. "Banking nature? The spectacular financialization of environmental conservation". *Antipode* 45.1:198–217.

ten Kate, K., Bishop, J., and Bayon, R. 2004. *Biodiversity Offsets: Views, Experience, and the Business Case*. Cambridge: IUCN.

Treweek, J. 2009. "Scoping study for the design and use of biodiversity offsets in an English context". Report to UK Department of Environment, Food and Rural Affairs, April 2009.

Tyfield, D. 2010. "Neoliberalism, intellectual property and the global knowledge economy", in Birch, K. and Mykhenko, V., eds, *The Rise and Fall of Neoliberalism: The Collapse of an Economic Order?*, 60–76. London: Zed Books.

Walker, S., Brower, A., Stephens, R.T.T., and Lee, W. 2009. "Why bartering biodiversity fails". *Conservation Letters* 2:149–157.

Whitworth, J. 2015. *Quantified: Redefining Conservation for the Next Economy*. Washington, DC: Island Press.

Wissel, S. and Watzold, F. 2010. "A conceptual analysis of the application of tradable permits to biodiversity conservations". *Conservation Biology* 24.2:404–411.

17

DISTRIBUTED BIOTECHNOLOGY

Alessandro Delfanti

In the last two decades, an array of do-it-yourself biology groups, biotech start-ups and community labs have emerged in Europe, America, and Asia. These groups and spaces share the vision of a "distributed biotechnology" and are part of broader transformations of the relation between technological and scientific change and society. Distributed biotechnology includes amateurs as well as an emergent set of companies that provide laboratory equipment and digital platforms designed to foster citizen contribution to biotechnology research. It differs from traditional forms of citizen science (see Ottinger, this volume) as it draws on elements from hacker cultures and adopts molecular biology as its main scientific framework. The term "distributed" means that actors envision a biotechnology free from centralized control. They imagine biotechnology as personal, and the aggregation of individual efforts as technically and socially meaningful. Thresholds to access are relatively low, as distributed biotechnology's spaces are open to amateurs and its techniques sometimes rudimentary. Finally, connections between different actors are created and maintained through the circulation of people, materials, and information.

Regardless of the hype that surrounds it, the output of distributed biotech tends to be relatively far from any "revolutionary" scientific breakthrough. What makes it worthy of analysis is the way it imagines and implements practices that construct biotechnology as *open*, *personal*, and oppositional towards biomedical research incumbents. Distributed biotech is characterized by a perceived, and in some cases sought-after, independency from incumbent institutional actors, such as corporate and university labs. Indeed, different actors share the goal of broadening life science research beyond the limits of traditional institutional laboratories. Yet, distributed biotechnology seems to emerge out of a complex relation with institutional actors, rather than in opposition to them. Also, it intersects deeply with the broader neoliberal economy of science and its innovation and justification regimes. The definition of "distributed" aims at unpacking some of these ambivalences, as it signals a plural approach to biotechnology while avoiding the lexicon of democracy implicit in definitions such as "participatory" or "citizen" science. The term also highlights how the aggregation of individual scientific and technological practices is seen as increasingly efficient, which resonates with neoliberal ideas about the market's spontaneous order. While distributed biotech affects relations of power within the life sciences, in many cases its endeavors are hardly emancipatory. Rather, they are geared towards the creation of new forms of value. This reminds of contemporary open science's role as a site where new forms of appropriation of the value produced by scientific research are experimented with and established (Birch 2012, Tyfield 2013; see chapters in this volume by Pagano and Rossi; Rossi; Stilgoe and Macnaghten).

Citizen and amateur science have long been used as examples of the permeable boundaries of scientific knowledge production. Yet it is only since the first draft of the human genome was sequenced and published in 2000 that the diffusion of equipment for DNA extraction, sequencing, recombination, and eventually synthesis has become available and affordable. Furthermore, distributed biotechnology emerged from political and cultural transformations. In fact, it is based on the availability of relatively cheap and accessible equipment such as PCR machines, centrifuges, vectors, or microscopes; the emergence of community laboratories explicitly directed towards amateurs; the broad availability of shared information, such as biotech protocols or genetic sequences, through open access databases; and the influence of digitally mediated participatory cultures within science. The actors that compose it are arguably quite diverse and heterogeneous, but they tend to co-evolve within networks that exchange resources and information. Community labs allow individuals to tinker with basic molecular biology processes, such as DNA extraction or bacteria genetic modification. Some labs have access to more advanced equipment, such as polymerase chain reaction machines or genetic sequencers. Start-ups might aim at engineering yeast to produce commercially interesting molecules such as THC, or develop web-based platforms for distributed genetic research. Groups work to produce molecules as different as insulin and hormones in order to escape the monopoly of pharmaceutical companies.

These phenomena have been described using terms such as "craft." This highlights the scalability of biotech towards small-scale interventions; these are characterized as low-cost and accessible to amateurs, in opposition to the professionalization of mainstream biotech (Roosth 2011). Concepts such as "kitchen" or "garage" biology touch upon the same idea while contributing to the understanding of how these forms of amateur biology are gendered (Jen 2015). Scholars have referred explicitly to DIY biology as a step towards an increased democratization of biotechnology. For example, through processes of "domestication" or "demystification" that question the separation between expert and amateur (Frow 2015, Meyer 2013, Wolinsky 2009). Since the mid-2000s, scholars analyzing the rise of phenomena such as DIY biology have also focused on the relation between distributed biology and hacking, thus adopting the term "biohacking" as an umbrella term referring to different forms of distributed intervention in the life sciences (Davies et al. 2015, Delfanti 2013, Kelty 2010). This designation reflects the self-ascribed genealogy that many DIY biologists or entrepreneurs construct. Furthermore, it allows scholars to highlight the ambivalent relation that DIY biologists and entrepreneurs have with scientific and biomedical research institutions and corporations. Hacker cultures encompass a diverse set of practices and values. What they have in common is a playful approach to information technologies, undaunted by hierarchies and organized around the idea that the skilled many can achieve change through a politics of technology (Coleman 2012, Söderberg 2013). Using the term biohacking, actors and scholars alike draw parallels between biotechnologies and computers, imagining technology that intervenes in living matter will become "personal" and open to a mass market. In the 1970s, the personal computer emerged out of attempts at liberating computing technologies from the control of academic, military and industrial actors. This "liberation" was aimed at the political appropriation of communication tools. But it was also geared towards the creation of a new market for mass-produced computers (Turner 2006). Ideologies of technodeterminism and libertarianism emerging from the Silicon Valley influenced advanced capitalism at large with their visions of the free technological entrepreneur as the engine of progress and wealth creation (Barbrook and Cameron 1996). The groups, companies and spaces that compose distributed biotech have emerged out of parallel histories. They share a dissatisfaction with the current political economy of biomedical research and the idea that it can be overcome by making biotech open, personal and distributed. In this sense, they imagine that incumbents such as Monsanto or Novartis may be today's biotech equivalent of what IBM was for 1970s hackers: bureaucratic monopolies that can be disrupted through an expansion of both technologies and markets.

Distributed biotech has been imagined and practiced in artistic milieus that aim at opening up recombinant DNA techniques to critique the dominance of multinational corporations in the biotechnology sector. In a parallel genealogy, distributed biotechnology has also been constructed as a form of "personal" technology by actors from the industrial and academic world. This created a wave of community labs first, and start-up companies that attempt to foster a new market for biotech equipment and services later. The development of "openness" as a set of organizational and political characteristics, such as open source information exchange, open citizen participation, and open markets, is a crucial foundation of distributed biotech. The above factors aim at providing new sources of public trust for biotechnology – *re-moralizing* it – by constructing it as consumer-friendly, non-proprietary and participatory. By creating new entrepreneurial subjects and exploiting outsourced labor, distributed biotech may contribute to broader phenomena of market and labor deregulation. Finally, distributed biotech is subject to processes of institutionalization that integrate its technologies and practices within new contexts while also diluting their political potential. As it matures, it is increasingly participating in a reconfiguration of the relation between practices of knowledge production and the social order.

Critique of the biotech industry

Since the early 2000s the possibility of re-appropriating biotech through distributed and participatory research has been explicitly presented as a critique of the political economy of corporate biotechnology. *Bioart* has long been used as either an educational tool or a celebration of biotech development through the engagement of different publics. In other cases, artists aimed at using biotech tools and practices to criticize the biotechnological industry for its lack of transparency, reliance on intellectual property rights, and environmental impact. Groups related to hacker cultures struggled to create permeable spaces where political and artistic explorations of biology could express confrontational practices that addressed the power of the industrial and academic sectors.

Among other artists and collectives using biotech-based art as a form of political intervention, the Critical Art Ensemble (CAE), a United States art collective, stands out as one of the most influential cases. In the early 2000s, CAE designed several citizen science performances that were explicitly framed as oppositional to the biotechnological industry. CAE called for the emergence of a "contestational biology" as a tool to challenge the structures of power within market relationships and the role of biotechnology in today's capitalist societies – in their words, "molecular capitalism" (2002). During CAE's *Free Range Grain* public performance, for example, the art collective allowed the public to test foods through basic molecular biology techniques. Distributing the means to search for genetically modified crop contamination was meant to counter the disempowerment produced by the role of multinational corporations in agrobiotech. In its proposal for new forms of "fuzzy biological sabotage," CAE envisioned that genetic hacking could provide activist groups with tools to challenge the structures of power and the role of biotechnology in today's capitalist societies. These politicized activities in the artistic sphere continue nowadays, especially in Europe and Asia. Art collectives such as the Switzerland-based group Hackteria routinely organize workshops that aim at re-appropriating biotech. The processes used within these practices can be quite basic. For example, they may rely on teaching to build a DIY gel electrophoresis chamber in an IKEA Tupperware. Yet, these groups tend to represent the political economy of biotech as a site of conflict and contestation, while its re-appropriation through DIY approaches is constructed as a form of tactical intervention (Magrini 2014). Activism in this field tends to be concerned with the politics and hierarchies that characterize the biotech industry, as well as the possible emancipatory uses of re-appropriated biotech processes and materials, such as citizen environmental research. Feminist groups emerging out of hacker and punk cultures, especially in Europe, are mostly concerned with the collective appropriation of biotech to create spaces of autonomy from state-controlled medical systems. Groups such as GynePunk or Gaudi Labs, for example, attempt to produce open source tools that can be used to perform gynecological medicine. Other projects, such as Open Source Gendercodes, engineer tobacco plants to produce hormones that can be used to cross gender boundaries and that are "collectively owned".[1]

Other forms of critique emerge from claims for a new kind of scientific universalism based on people's access to biological research. Written in the US in 2010, the *Biopunk Manifesto* introduces critiques of the monopoly of institutional biotech while implementing the idea that freedom of research should be equal to freedom of speech: "We reject the popular perception that science is only done in million-dollar university, government, or corporate labs; we assert that the right of freedom of inquiry, to do research and pursue understanding under one's own direction, is as fundamental a right as that of free speech or freedom of religion" (Patterson 2010). This and other, similar, documents point out a problem in the distribution of power in biology. At the same time they somewhat conflate the democratization of science with access to its technologies and knowledge. This rhetoric has been inspirational for subsequent waves of biohackers. Yet the role of these attempts at critiquing the political economy of contemporary biotechnology should not be overrated. Based on ethnographic research, scholars have balanced descriptions of a politicized distributed biotech, highlighting areas of political ambivalence (Delfanti 2013, Tocchetti 2012). Through somewhat ironic definitions such as "outlaw biology," scholars have recognized a willingness to perform participatory biotech outside of established institutional frameworks, meanwhile stressing its limited scope and nuanced genealogy (Kelty 2010). For example, through the construction of the need for biosafety regulation, distributed biotechnology has been prompted to engage in negotiations with state actors to confront issues of environmental safety. This is the case for the DIYbio network in the United States and the relationship it built with the Federal Bureau of Investigation (FBI) in the early 2010s in order to present DIY activities as legitimate and safe. This scenario generated frictions with certain European groups. Yet, it also helped construct distributed biotechnology as a promissory field while redefining the risks associated with it as scientific and financial rather than, for example, linked to bioterrorism (Tocchetti and Aguiton 2015).

Biotechnology becomes personal

Distributed biotechnology is rooted in attempts at transforming molecular biology into a *personal* technology by making biotech equipment, processes and knowledge accessible to individuals. The idea of making technology personal is strictly tied to utopian visions of a decentralized, egalitarian and free society that resonate with the idea of a "digital utopianism" that is hegemonic in Silicon Valley cultures (Turner 2006). Distributed biotech constructs biology as produced by and for the people, and thus envisions "unlimited participation" in science (Reardon 2013, Tocchetti 2014). Yet the scope and goals of distributed biotech are not unlimited but rather geared towards certain groups and specific ends. Furthermore, personal biotechnology produces neoliberal entrepreneurial subjects whose proactive and individualized approach to biotech, based upon exchange freed from centralized command (Foucault 2008), becomes meaningful through the aggregation of plural contributions into an emergent order rather than through collective deliberation practices.

In the mid-2000s, a new wave of efforts to imagine and practice forms of distributed biotechnology emerged in academic departments. It then spread to both amateur communities and entrepreneurial milieus. This genealogy is based on the construction of new mechanisms that intervene in living matter, a broadened inclusion of new constituencies, and the growth of an infrastructure of distributed biotechnology laboratories, tools, and digital platforms. Such efforts are founded upon attempts dating back to the early 2000s that sought to construct biological matter as a composition of standardized, interchangeable parts. These early processes came to define what we now call "synthetic biology" (see Rossi, this volume). The Registry of Standardized Biological Parts is a database of BioBricks: genetic parts that can be assembled into full DNA sequences. Proposed by US technologists and geneticists such as Tom Knight and Drew Endy, this project was coupled with platforms for open information exchange, such as the OpenWetWare wiki. The latter is an online service for sharing information about synthetic biologicy protocols and materials. These approaches tackle DNA and living matter not just as information, but also as pliable material which, like software, can be made hackable and shareable (Calvert 2010, Roosth 2011). This is related to a broader shift of the scientific enterprise towards computation as a core tool for life science research, as well as a cultural framework with epistemic value (Kay 2000). Early synthetic biology was also the result of a willingness to challenge the idea that biotech must be based on the strict enforcement of exclusive intellectual property rights. Furthermore, attempts at standardizing biological matter components into interchangeable parts are part of a project of further industrialization of biotechnology. Finally, these changes fostered the opening of synthetic biology to distributed contributors (Hilgartner 2012, Bogdanov 2016). For example, the International Genetically Engineered Machine (iGEM) competition, hosted by MIT since 2003/2004, is an international competition in which teams of students from universities or countries use BioBricks to generate synthetic organisms. The aim of iGEM is the "open and transparent development of tools"[2] for biotech. Inspired by free and open source software and yet geared towards molecules and cells rather than bits, such sites were foundational in the birth of contemporary synthetic biology (Roosth 2011). Combined, the informatization, standardization, and open sourcing of synthetic biology provided a foundation for its expansion towards distributed forms of biotechnology and also fostered its commodification. Scholars have argued that experiences such as iGEM have spread a neoliberal entrepreneurial culture among participants (Aguiton 2014). This newfound culture cultivated an approach to living matter aimed at its transformation and commercialization.

Later, the idea of expanding access to synthetic biology included opening it up to new actors, such as individual entrepreneurs. In a 2005 *Wired* article, the US biotechnologist Robert Carlson called for new forms of distributed biotechnology that he referred to as "garage biotech" – referencing the Silicon Valley garage, depicted in many accounts of the history of computers as a core site of disruptive innovation (Carlson, 2005). Carlson's article, along with other conceptualizations of biotech as accessible from non-institutional spaces, such as garages or backyards, were based upon the idea that biology had witnessed the emergence of the same premises that have allowed for the existence of online peer-to-peer production. Such premises included the availability of affordable hardware in forms of equipment and machinery; an online infrastructure for sharing protocols and data; collaborative software services; the broad availability of easily accessible public data and information; copyleft licenses that allow content reuse, modification and redistribution; and a culture of participation (Delfanti 2013, Meyer 2012).

Under this banner, early attempts such as the 2007 Open Biohacking Kit or the website biopunk.org (Bogdanov 2016) preceded the birth of DIYbio (do-it-yourself biology), a loose network of amateur biologists launched in Boston in 2008. DIYbio's founders were already actively involved in projects such as the iGEM competition and the Personal Genome Project. With the launch of DIYbio, they aimed at fulfilling the idea of a distributed, citizen biology led by non-experts – a "science without scientists" (Bobe 2008). Initially organized around a local group and a website, DIYbio has grown to represent the most significant early example of a distributed biotechnology community. DIYbio was formed to make biology accessible to *anyone*, regardless of formal education, technical skills or institutional affiliation. Under its umbrella, distributed biotech has indeed attracted a flow of individuals to biotechnology and other forms of life science research. Following its launch, a series of spaces for the development of distributed biotech started emerging in urban environments. Predominantly white and male, at least initially, amateur biologists have formed groups in many cities in North America and Western Europe, with a recent expansion in Asia and South America (Kera 2012, Meyer 2013). These groups now tend to include individuals with varying backgrounds. In many cases, a core constituency is composed by biology students, while other participants are computer programmers interested in applying information science to living matter. A minority of individuals are interested in art and design. In a significant number of cases, DIYbio participants seem to be biologists frustrated with the hierarchies and lack of freedom experienced in their professional lives (Delfanti 2013, Delgado 2013, Grushkin et al. 2013, Landrain et al. 2013). Since the foundation of DIYbio, participants have constructed this form of distributed biotechnology as independent from, although not opposed to, scientific institutions.

While early rhetoric depicted distributed biotech or biohacking as happening in kitchens, garages or backyards, the spaces of early laboratories were rather community spaces or hackerspaces. Such labs include GenSpace in New York (2010), Biologigaragen in Copenhagen (2010), Biocurious in Sunnyvale, California (2011), La Paillasse in Paris (2011) and Counter Culture Labs in Oakland (2014) (Delfanti 2013, Meyer 2013). In many cities, such as Seattle, Los Angeles, Copenhagen or Toronto, DIY biolabs were initially formed as "wet" corners within existing hackerspaces or makerspaces. Although characterized by different local and political cultures, the shared goal of these and other *biohackerspaces* is to provide community-run labs where non-professionals can have access to basic equipment such as glassware, centrifuges, polymerase chain reaction machines, or gel electrophoresis for biological research. In most cases these spaces are self-funded through donations or participants' monthly fees. However, some early labs were equipped with scrap or second-hand equipment. Activities can be quite diverse and include basic biology experiments, such as cell cultures, as well as more advanced processed based on recombinant DNA, such as the engineering of bioluminescent bacteria or the production of "real" vegan cheese obtained by engineering yeast to produce milk protein. DIYbio participants and an emerging network of start-up companies soon started designing and producing open source lab equipment for recombinant DNA technologies, such as the early flagship projects Open Gel Box or OpenPCR. This DIYbio open source technical equipment, now expanded to include many DIY machines produced by biohacker groups, is designed to be directly transformable by individual users and based on shared protocols (Kera 2012). Further technological evolutions have produced affordable and consumer-friendly DIYbio tools that are not technically open source and thus more difficult to transform, upgrade and reproduce, while aimed at broader constituencies. This is the case of portable, laptop-sized biotech labs commercialized in the mid-2010s: Bento Lab includes a PCR machine, a centrifuge and a gel electrophoresis unit and presents itself as part of "a mission to make bio available to all;"[3] and the Amino is a unit for cell cultures that runs pre-determined "apps," that is, kits for synthetic biology production. Companies such as The Odin commercialize lab supplies and equipment such as yeast or bacteria CRISPR kits that allow DIY precision genome editing. Since early attempts at producing open source tools, distributed biotech has thus been enriched by the launch of start-up companies that have tapped into an emerging, albeit limited, market for personal biotech products (Palmer and Jewett 2014).

Although it first emerged out of an academic context, the idea of a personal biotechnology is the product of a more complex history that includes its relationship with the maker movement. *Make Magazine*, arguably one of the flag-bearer publications of the US maker movement, has been instrumental in constructing biology as a personal technology offered to new constituencies (Tocchetti 2012). This mirrors discourses about the 1970s as a time when it was first imagined that computers could be personal technologies fit for mass commercialization rather than technologies targeted at bureaucratic institutions, such as the military or universities (Turner 2006). Due to the inclusion of DIY biology within a broader maker culture, biohacking has become a site in which biotechnological interventions on life are based on small-scale technology and bestowed upon the hands of a new entrepreneurial subject, the maker (Tocchetti 2012). This change, embodied by a series of start-up companies working within distributed biotech, contributes to claims that a personal biotech should be constructed as complementary, rather than in opposition to, corporate and academic incumbents. In this renewed context, the political economy of corporate biotech is to be challenged only insofar as it is tackled as a problem of industry concentration. Actors tend to comply with state regulations on environmental and laboratory safety while expressing grievances towards obstacles to market-based interventions.

Openness as a new moral ground

Distributed biotech adopts a specific set of forms of "openness" as the main framework that governs decisions about which information must be circulated freely, who can access DIY labs, and who should be able to design and commercialize biotech artifacts or services. Spilling from free and open source software into areas as heterogeneous as technological development, journalism, and politics, openness has come to represent a crucial driver of legitimization of contemporary societies (Tkacz 2015). In science, this is hardly a radical change. Through the idea of a *moral economy* of openness that underpins scientific research, modern science has been conceptualized as based upon a set of social values that underlie and govern exchange within a scientific community. In particular, this relates to property, credit, and access (Kohler 1994). These values have influenced contemporary research. For example, the exchange of genetic parts in open source synthetic biology is an evolution of earlier moral economies that underpinned the 20th century exchange of basic tools of research, such as model organisms like *drosophila* (Kelty 2012). Modern "open" science is also the result of a specific social contract, with its incentives and arrangements aimed at sustaining and legitimizing the scientific enterprise (David 2000). This contract includes references to the boundaries and role of public participation to scientific research. The increasing use of computational technologies for contemporary research in biotechnology implies not only an epistemic change, but also a reconfiguring of how morality is constructed through openness. Thus, the moral economy of openness that sustains distributed biotech seems to represent a further step towards the construction of public legitimization.

Openness, in other words, has become a crucial *test* of public morality (Boltanski and Thevenot 2006). The re-moralization of the biotech industry, particularly in the case of synthetic biology (Tyfield 2013), occurs in the wake of political contestations over research privatization and corporate monopolies in both agrobiotech and medical biotech, especially resulting from the introduction of mass-produced GM organisms in agriculture in the 1990s (Bauer and Gaskell 2002). The resulting crisis of public trust in biotech was related to the rise of intellectual property rights owned by multinational corporations, the commodification of knowledge produced by public universities, and a lack of political control of biotech's goals and methods. On the contrary, the exchange of information, tools and materials underpins distributed biotechnology, albeit in different forms, on three complementary dimensions of openness: open source information, open participation, and open markets. The idea that a new kind of biotechnology could be modeled after free and open source software meant that it could be distributed not only by adopting technical open source arrangements such as open licenses, but also by including new, non-expert individuals. Thus, on the one hand, openness refers to the use of alternative forms of property and control, adapted from the software world, that help make information and processes available to distributed individuals. On the other hand, broad new groups of participants are created through a political form of openness that grants access to distributed biotech while making power susceptible to scrutiny and transformation, thus reinventing the somewhat lost universalism of contemporary biotechnology (Kelty 2010).

The final form of openness refers to the creation of open markets for consumer-friendly products that new economic actors can develop and commercialize. These actors include start-up companies or community-based actors that compete against the market concentration that pharmaceutical and agrobiotech corporations represent. Thus, openness is a multifaceted element rooted in technical, legal and moral decisions (Bogdanov 2016). Through its use of openness, distributed biotech is constructed as non-proprietary, participatory, transparent, and user- and consumer-friendly, as well as opposed to monopolies and market concentrations. This makes distributed biotech a site where tensions towards a collective and participatory biology coexist with forms of commercialization within a common framework of public morality. While several authors have denounced the ambivalence of this project (Birch 2012, Deibel 2014, Delfanti 2013, Tyfield 2013), the incorporation of these multi-faceted forms of openness into the moral economy of distributed biotechnology has left the field relatively prone to new reconfigurations.

Institutionalization and commercialization

Despite recurrent rhetorics that construct distributed biotech as autonomous from corporate and academic institutions, processes of increasing institutionalization are at play. Contrary to accounts that present new forms of distributed biotech, such as DIY biology or biohacking, as a re-appropriation of life science research, some authors state that the trajectory of distributed biotech is one of further integration within the industrial, academic, and educational sectors. Indeed, distributed biotechnology is intertwined with academic and corporate laboratories, and it remains technologically dependent from its mainstream counterpart (Delgado 2013). For example, DIYbio communities rely on these labs for skills, equipment, and tools. According to surveys and ethnographic accounts alike, many DIYbio practitioners also work in academic, corporate or government labs (Grushkin et al. 2013, Seyfried et al. 2014). These members constitute a core group that provides skills and resources while leading the development of biohackerspaces, community labs and start-ups. Also, academic institutions appear to have a growing interest in funding DIY biology or establishing partnerships with it, following a trend of inclusion that is increasingly common among forms of citizen science (Grushkin et al. 2013, Landrain et al. 2013).

Processes of institutionalization typically studied in social movements have been observed in groups that use alternative technological innovation as a tool for social change. These alternative technologies and processes are often developed with the help of companies that work in close relation to non-market actors. The technologies are eventually incorporated by the industry, which transforms and adapts them according to its needs (Hess 2005). One standard example is the rise of open source software as a market-friendly evolution of free software. Institutions tend to partially adopt alternative technologies and socio-technical practices while simultaneously altering and neutralizing them. These dynamics of co-option are at play with hacking, which evolves in symbiosis with industry partners and experiences cycles of institutionalization (Söderberg and Delfanti 2015). Organizational practices geared towards the fostering of distributed innovation and derived from hacker cultures, such as hackatons, are subject to uptake by institutional actors, as they can be used to produce and celebrate a neoliberal entrepreneurial subjectivity that resonates with Silicon Valley cultures (Irani 2015).

The emergence of start-up companies inspired by biohacking, especially in the US, reflects broader market-based shifts, as science and health are increasingly mediated by private corporations through processes of individual consumption. In fact, distributed biotech builds upon phenomena such as direct-to-consumer genetic testing and personalized genomics while providing a cultural and technological infrastructure for synthetic biology research. Early examples of this transformation towards commercialization include companies that design web-based platforms for distributed synthetic biology, inviting connected individuals to participate in drug development. Accelerators such as IndieBio, based in both the US and EU, fund "independent" biotech start-ups and help them position themselves on the market. The appearance of distributed biotech companies fosters further mobilization of new active contributors to biotech research. Yet, it also guarantees that these same groups can participate in the commercialization of products deriving from their contributions. For example, contributors to distributed drug development projects represent deregulated, outsourced laborers as well as potential consumers (Cooper and Waldby 2014, Lupton 2014). On the other hand, the emergence of distributed biotech start-ups is also part of an ongoing process of financial risk outsourcing in which pharmaceutical and biotech corporations harness value in the form of intellectual property or services created by new companies. While these start-up companies tend to require a relatively low initial capital, they also tend to absorb all risk of failure. This indicates that distributed biotechnology might abandon technical openness in favor of traditional intellectual property rights when adopted by market-based actors (Delfanti 2013).

Finally, some of the practices, equipment, and aesthetics stemming from DIYbio and other forms of biohacking are adopted and repurposed by educational institutions, such as universities and museums. Examples of the adoption of distributed biotech as a form of public communication includes a number of citizen laboratories opened by European universities, museum exhibitions on DIYbio, and collaborations between DIYbio community labs and schools to provide biotech-related student activities. Portable labs, such as Bento or The Amino, are commercialized as suitable for schools, while community labs, such as New York's GenSpace, collaborate with science teachers to provide scientific education programs. Distributed biotechnology's emphasis on enabling citizens to directly carry out scientific research through hands-on approaches resonates with the increasingly common educational goal of outlining the processes that underpin biotech rather than its final results (Davies et al. 2015). Similarly, European groups have been involved in EU-funded research projects aimed at testing new forms of citizen participation under the umbrella of the European bioeconomy. Within these new frameworks, distributed biotech's goal of creating new and accessible spaces for biotechnological processes seems to dissipate the possibility of an independent, let alone oppositional, biotech. This goal has become part of a standard narrative regarding the need for an increased consensus around biotech. In these cases, distributed biotech aims at creating "domesticated" publics through the interaction with its transparent processes rather than the opaque results of biotechnological research.

Conclusions

Although it could be considered marginal if compared to major fields such as agrobiotech or pharmaceutical research, distributed biotechnology has been central to recent political transformations in the relationship between biology and society. Distributed biotech is comprised of different actors that exchange people, material and information. DIY biology groups, biohackerspaces, start-ups, incubators, and education and academic institutions all encompass this diverse field. Its current configuration is the historical and political product of a number of genealogies that combine actors of cultural and social diversity who have in common a dissatisfaction with the political economy of mainstream biotechnology. Distributed biotech is constructed through a complex entanglement of technical, political, and economic *openness*. Also, it fosters the idea that biotechnology can be a *personal* technology that individuals can appropriate for processes of consumption and entrepreneurship. Visions of a *distributed* biotechnology tend to present scientific progress as the result of the aggregation of free individual contributions. This is depicted as more efficient than centralized and bureaucratized research. Yet, while actors in distributed biotechnology communities or companies tend to construct their activities autonomously from mainstream biomedical research, processes of dependence and increased institutionalization are at play.

Practitioners, pundits, and scholars alike have explicitly linked the trajectory of biohacking, DIY and distributed biotechnology to that of personal computers in the 1970s. Under the influence of post-1968 countercultures, hackers first imagined that the computer could become personal: first, a community-based tool used for collective liberation, and later, an individual tool for mediated communication. This led to the commercialization of computers as personal technologies designed for mass consumption, breaking a monopoly held by corporations that viewed computers as tools for experts and institutions. This story is often told as an edifying narrative of democratization and economic success. And yet a more nuanced analysis reveals the contestations, ambivalences and tensions that characterized the rise of personal computers within a new ideological framework as well as corporate system. Similarly, distributed biotechnology aims at disrupting current monopolies within biological research. Yet while representing a change in the current balance of power in biotechnology, it contributes to the transformation of living matter into pliable, modifiable material that can be subject to industrial processes and further commodification. Furthermore, it presents the individual as the main subject that can produce a socially meaningful biology, either alone or through the aggregation of plural contributions into an emergent order. Nevertheless, the existence of groups that aim at re-appropriating its processes and techniques for collective and autonomous purposes signals that, within this general framework, distributed biotech can be tweaked towards quite different ends. The political and technological evolution of distributed biotech is still open.

Acknowledgements

This chapter has been shaped by many conversations. I would like to thank Ana Delgado, Clare Jen, Gabby Resch, Gabriela Sanchez, Bruno Strasser and the Rethinking Science and Public Participation research group, as well as many other friends and colleagues, for their comments and help. I am particularly indebted to Sara Tocchetti for letting me borrow (and distort) some of the ideas developed here.

Notes

1 http://opensourcegendercodes.com, accessed July 2016.
2 http://igem.org, accessed July 2016.
3 http://bento.bio, accessed July 2016.

References

Aguiton, S., 2014. *La Démocratie des Chimères: Gouvernement des Risques et des Critiques de la Biologie Synthétique, en France et aux États-Unis*. PhD dissertation. Paris: Institut d'Études Politiques de Paris.

Barbrook, R. and Cameron, A., 1996. "The Californian Ideology". *Science as Culture* 6.1: 44–72.

Bauer, M., and Gaskell, G. (eds.), 2002. *Biotechnology: The Making of a Global Controversy*. Cambridge: Cambridge University Press.

Birch, K., 2012. "An Open Biotechnology Revolution?" *Science as Culture* 21.3: 415–419.

Bobe, J., 2008. "Science Without Scientists". http://diybio.org/blog/science-without-scientists, accessed February 2016.

Bogdanov, R., 2016. "Practices of Openness in Biohackers". Preprint.

Boltanski, L. and Thévenot, L., 2006 *On Justification: Economies of Worth*. Princeton: Princeton University Press.

Calvert, J., 2010. "Synthetic Biology: Constructing Nature?" *The Sociological Review* 58.s1: 95–112.

Carlson, R., 2005. "Splice It Yourself". *Wired*. www.wired.com/wired/archive/13.05/view.html?pg=2, accessed January 2016.

Coleman, G., 2012. *Coding Freedom: The Ethics and Aesthetics of Hacking*. Princeton: Princeton University Press.

Cooper, M. and Waldby, C., 2014. *Clinical Labor: Tissue Donors and Research Subjects in the Global Bioeconomy*. Durham: Duke University Press.

Critical Art Ensemble, 2002. *The Molecular Invasion*. New York: Autonomedia.

David, P., 2005. "From Keeping 'Nature's Secrets' to the Institutionalization of 'Open Science'". In Ghosh, R., *Code: Collaborative Ownership and the Digital Economy*. Cambridge: MIT Press: 85–108.

Davies, S., Tybjerg, K., Whiteley, L., and Söderqvist, T., 2015. "Co-Curation as Hacking: Biohackers in Copenhagen's Medical Museion". *Curator: The Museum Journal* 58.1: 117–131.

Deibel, E., 2014. "Open Genetic Code: On Open Source in the Life Sciences". *Life Sciences, Society and Policy* 10.1: 1–23.

Delfanti, A., 2013. *Biohackers. The Politics of Open Science*. London: Pluto Press

Delgado, A., 2013. "DIYbio: Making Things and Making Futures". *Futures* 48: 65–73.

Foucault, M., 2008. *The Birth of Biopolitics: Lectures at the Collège de France, 1978–1979*. New York: Springer.

Frow, E., 2015. "Rhetorics and Practices of Democratization in Synthetic Biology". In Wienroth, M., and Rodrigues, E., *Knowing New Biotechnologies: Social Aspects of Technological Convergence*. New York: Routledge: 174–187.

Grushkin, D., Kuiken, T., and Millet, P., 2013. *Seven Myths and Realities About Do-It-Yourself Biology*. Washington: Woodrow Wilson International Center for Scholars.

Hess, D., 2005. "Technology- and Product-oriented Movements: Approximating Social Movement Studies and Science and Technology Studies". *Science, Technology & Human Values* 30.4: 515–535.

Hilgartner, S., 2012. "Novel Constitutions? New Regimes of Openness in Synthetic Biology". *BioSocieties* 7.2: 188–207.

Irani, L., 2015. "Hackathons and the Making of Entrepreneurial Citizenship". *Science, Technology & Human Values* 40.5: 799–824.

Jen, C., 2015. "Do-It-Yourself Biology, Garage Biology, and Kitchen Science". In Wienroth, M., and Rodrigues, E., *Knowing New Biotechnologies: Social Aspects of Technological Convergence*. New York: Routledge: 125–141.

Kay, L., 2000. *Who Wrote the Book of Life? A History of the Genetic Code*. Stanford: Stanford University Press.

Kelty, C., 2010. "Outlaw, Hackers, Victorian Amateurs: Diagnosing Public Participation in the Life Sciences Today". *Journal of Science Communication* 09.01.

Kelty, C., 2012. "This is not an Article: Model Organism Newsletters and the Question of 'Open Science'". *BioSocieties* 7.2: 140–168.

Kera, D., 2012. "Hackerspaces and DIYbio in Asia: Connecting Science and Community with Open Data, Kits and Protocols". *Journal of Peer Production* 2: 1–8.

Kohler, R., 1994. *Lords of the Fly: Drosophila Genetics and the Experimental Life*. Chicago: University of Chicago Press.

Landrain, T., Meyer, M., Perez, A.M., and Sussan, R., 2013. "Do-it-yourself Biology: Challenges and Promises for an Open Science and Technology Movement". *Systems and Synthetic Biology* 7.3: 115–126.

Lupton, D., 2014. "Critical Perspectives on Digital Health Technologies". *Sociology Compass* 8.12: 1344–1359.

Magrini, B., 2014. "Hackteria: An Example of Neomodern Activism". *Leonardo Electronic Almanac* 20.1: 58–71.

Meyer, M., 2012. "Build your Own Lab: Do-It-Yourself Biology and the Rise of Citizen Biotech-Economies". *Journal of Peer Production* 2.

Meyer, M., 2013. "Domesticating and Democratizing Science: A Geography of Do-It-Yourself Biology". *Journal of Material Culture* 18.2: 117–134.

Palmer, M. and Jewett M., 2014. "Enabling a Next Generation of Synthetic Biology Community Organization and Leadership". *ACS Synthetic Biology* 3.3: 117–120.

Patterson, M., 2010. *A Biopunk Manifesto.* http://maradydd.livejournal.com/496085.html, accessed February 2016.

Reardon, J., 2013. "On the Emergence of Science and Justice". *Science, Technology and Human Values* 38.2: 176–200.

Roosth, S., 2011. *Crafting Life; A Sensory Ethnography of Fabricated Biologies.* PhD dissertation, Cambridge: Massachusetts Institute of Technology.

Seyfried, G., Pei, L., and Schmidt, M., 2014. "European Do-It-Yourself (DIY) Biology: Beyond the Hope, Hype and Horror". *Bioessays* 36.6: 548–551.

Söderberg, J., 2013. "Determining Social Change: The Role of Technological Determinism in the Collective Action Framing of Hackers". *New Media & Society* 15.8: 1277–1293.

Söderberg, J. and Delfanti, A., 2015. "Hacking Hacked! The Life Cycles of Digital Innovation". *Science, Technology & Human Values* 40.5: 793-798.

Tkacz, N., 2015. *Wikipedia and the Politics of Openness.* Chicago: University of Chicago Press.

Tocchetti, S., 2012. "DIYbiologists as 'Makers' of Personal Biologies: How MAKE Magazine and Maker Faires Contribute in Constituting Biology as a Personal Technology". *Journal of Peer Production* 1.2.

Tocchetti, S. and Aguiton, S., 2015. "Is an FBI Agent a DIY Biologist Like Any Other? A Cultural Analysis of a Biosecurity Risk". *Science, Technology & Human Values* 40.5: 825–853.

Turner, F., 2006. *From Counterculture to Cyberculture: Stewart Brand, the Whole Earth Network, and the Rise of Digital Utopianism.* Chicago: University of Chicago Press.

Tyfield, D., 2013. "Transition to Science 2.0: 'Remoralizing' the Economy of Science". *Spontaneous Generations: A Journal for the History and Philosophy of Science* 7.1: 29–48.

Wolinsky, H., 2009. "Kitchen biology". *EMBO Reports* 10.7: 683–685.

18

TRANSLATIONAL MEDICINE

Science, risk and an emergent political economy of biomedical innovation

Mark Robinson

On April 3rd, 2012, Ian Chubb, Australia's Chief Scientist and former Vice-Chancellor of the Australian National University, delivered the keynote speech at a summit of the Biomelbourne Network, a meeting of the country's most prominent biotechnology leaders and investors. During the summit's serendipitously named, "Biobreakfast," Chubb addressed an important new area in biomedical research called *translational medicine*. The keynote responded to two questions: First, should Australia jump on the global trend towards translational research; and, second, could it afford to do so? Chubb, only a year into his policy role as Chief Scientist, argued that Australia indeed needed to refocus its scientific efforts towards "translational research." He cited a multitude of reasons, including the need to develop new medicines for the world's sick and the importance of translational research for Australia's competitiveness. However, he also framed the need for translational research using an economic rationale:

> Funding research is all about return on investment. By funding basic research, we have seen that there is usually little return, certainly very little immediate return. Basic research is rarely developed in a practical way for doctors, hospitals or pharmaceutical companies…But if we invest in translational research, the wealth of knowledge available will be amplified since it all of a sudden has clinical applications.
>
> *(Chub 2012, p. 2)*

Invoking the language of finance – of investments, wealth and return, translational research is presented here as a means of activating existing knowledge, accelerating that knowledge's applicability and producing a "return" for various Australian publics on national investments in science and technology. As Chubb continues, he moves from the language of investment into explicit economic invocation:

> A small investment in translational research, could lead to huge outcomes stemming from the basic research. Translational research, economically speaking, has a multiplier effect. Investing in translation leverages the investments made in biomedical science.
>
> *(Chub 2012, p. 2)*

The notion of a "multiplier effect," itself economic policy parlance, reflects the larger economic thesis that informs the justification of government investments in Translational Science and Medicine (TSM). For Chubb and others, this new field both contains and exemplifies a classic linear model of science and innovation. According to this model, debunked by scholars such as Philip Mirowski (2011) and others, there is some sequential, "natural" pathway from basic science and technology research to inevitable, national economic growth (Etzkowitz 2007). Similarly, proponents argue that state investment into TSM will yield outsized economic "returns" from the nation's scientific assets. At the same time, translational medicine is framed as the ultimate means through which investments in science will usher in transformative medical innovations for patients. Thus, TSM in this view solves multiple problems ranging from social policy (as it pertains to public spending and national science and technology policy) to the problem of biomedical innovation.

As a means to privatize the products of publicly funded science research, reorganize knowledge activities according to market agendas, and insert clear economic objectives and a set of overarching values into the aims of biomedical research, TSM is the apotheosis of the neoliberal transformation at work in science via the university (Lave et al. 2010). That TSM is the manifestation of neoliberal aims is no surprise given the increasing market-oriented transformation of higher education globally (Nedeva and Boden 2006, Canaan and Shumar 2008, Mirowski 2011). What one finds in Chubb's keynote – and what this chapter explores – is the harnessing of particular narratives regarding the economics of innovation to justify the reorganization of academic biomedical research towards TSM. As I show in this chapter, the economic and biomedical narratives attached to TSM obfuscate a much more complicated history of privatization, risk, and failure that marks the recent rise and expansion of translational medicine.

What is Translational Medicine?

Translational Science, Translational Medicine, Clinical Translation and Translational Research are all monikers used to represent a common set of overlapping concepts that coalesce around a central notion: to entirely redesign biomedical research in order to accelerate the process whereby publicly funded science is turned into applications and especially products. Thus, "translation" is used to refer a rather wide set of activities, projects, and initiatives that stem from this abstract notion.

One finds this diversity of outputs on the face of a website for the Clinical and Translational Science Institute at Tufts University in the U.S.: "Accelerating translation of research into clinical use, medical practice, and health impact."[1] Among many elements, one often finds that translational definitions tend to highlight *application*. The application of scientific research is the hallmark of the definition offered on the website for the journal *Science Translational Medicine*, created in 2009:

> **Translational medicine defined:** Often described as an effort to carry scientific knowledge "from bench to bedside," translational medicine builds on basic research advances – studies of biological processes using cell cultures, for example, or animal models – and uses them to develop new therapies or medical procedures.
>
> *(Science Translational Medicine 2016)*

Because the aims of translational research often focus on developing medicines such as pharmaceuticals, biotechnologies, therapies and diagnostics, Translational Medicine is increasingly used as an umbrella term to refer to large swaths of translational research. Additionally, because

Figure 18.1 The website for the Clinical and Translational Science Institute at Tufts University in the U.S. (accessed in 2016)

nationally funded biomedical research is largely housed at or developed in partnership with universities, the university and the academic medical center are key players in the *translational supply chain*. I use the term "translational supply chain" to refer to the long, complicated pathways and associated institutions, policies and actors thought to be involved in the movement of laboratory science or basic biological research into market-ready medicines for patients. From clinical research programs at university hospitals to new translational graduate programs, the most visible manifestation of the translational shift is found at universities.

Thus, TSM must be understood in multiple ways: as ethos and newly formalized academic discipline, as well as a set of concrete objects: TSM funding brought about an explosion of TSM centers, institutes, translation-focused laboratories, faculty and graduate student funding lines, buildings, conferences, academic journals, software, cross-disciplinary collaborations, terminology, and new professional pathways for scientists and clinicians (Nathan 2002). In this heterogeneity and in the broad claims made about innovation under TSM's reorganizations, one can see that TSM is also, therefore, a thesis about the nature of innovation – one which assumes that a re-engineered infrastructure, including uncluttered collaboration, appropriate incentives, and application-oriented scientific imagination (Robinson, forthcoming) – would yield, almost organically – a rise in innovation. This theory of innovation is evident even in the descriptions and mission statements of TSM centers. Consider the language used on the website of the Center for Integrative and Translational Neuroscience at the University of Nebraska Medical Center, where translation is distinguished by interdisciplinarity, epistemological linking, and an acceleration of the processes through which science can be turned into medicines:

> The Center for Integrative and Translational Neuroscience is the link between basic science discoveries and translational implementation in the [medical/hospital] clinic. It will take the fruits of neurodegenerative research from the [scientific laboratory] bench to the [patient] bedside. The center brings together basic research faculty with clinicians in neurology, psychiatry, pediatrics, radiology, medicine and surgery. This joint effort will move new discoveries rapidly out of the lab and into the clinic...[2]

As can be seen from this description and others, TSM is also marked by the problematization of current biomedical research (Vignola-Gagné 2013). However, the focus on activating existing underutilized or "disconnected" research and the development of new products therefrom essentially frames science as something akin to an under-leveraged asset, and translation as a means to recapture dormant scientific value. The notion of underutilization also reveals the way that TSM, by its constitution, injects clear imperatives regarding application-oriented scientific thinking.

Of course, the emergence of TSM must be understood as part of a larger current marked by the increasing commercialization (Berman 2012; Bok 2005; Shore and Wright 2000; Shumar 1997), commodification (Nedeva and Boden 2006) and privatization (Brown 2000) of the modern university, and the emergence of a unique brand of academic capitalism (Etzkowitz 2007), enabled, in part, by the passage of a series of legislative actions and the enactment of various reforms (Loewenberg 2009; Mirowski 2011; Pagano and Rossi, this volume), including the Bayh-Dole Act of 1980, a U.S. policy that allowed the private patenting of intellectual property developed from publicly funded sources. While TSM achieves something similar in terms of creating a pathway for the private commercialization of state-funded research, TSM is distinct because of how it brings with it an ecosystem that includes both infrastructure and most importantly, a culture. If Bayh-Dole constituted a key architecture for the bringing of private interests to university research, the emergence of TSM installed within it a mechanism: an *ethos* alongside an associated infrastructure.

While commercialization lay at the heart of TSM, this aspect is, interestingly, rarely part of TSM centers' mission statements. From the outset, TSM was framed in public discourses as a largely scientific and clinical intervention that was – at its heart – about failed public investments in research, the needs of the world's suffering patients, and the promise of transformative innovation in health.

The histories of translational medicine

A panoply of approaches precedes TSM. The emergence of federal programs dedicated to speeding up the commercialization of publicly funded science, such as Bayh-Dole, is a part of this history. However, history also has seen the formalization of multiple scientific and institutional approaches designed to refocus scientific research towards applications. Some scholars point to oncological research in 1990s as flashpoint in this history (Cambrosio, et al. 2006). Other observers point to other fields such as Molecular and Experimental Medicine and Clinical Pharmacology (FitzGerald 2005) or Molecular Pathology (Royer 1972) as spaces where prior "translational" efforts met with new energies and attempts at formalization. Yet, TSM's sustained focus on the commercialization of knowledge – including formalized partnerships with private firms and investors, which I discuss in ensuing sections – reveals the explicitness regarding commercialization that renders TSM distinct (Robinson 2010; Robinson forthcoming). In fact, I suggest that one key element that distinguishes TSM from older, similar models of application-oriented work is both TSM's formalization of pathways to commercialization and a concomitant explicitness regarding the need for academic medical center faculty, students and clinicians to be engaged in the work of product discovery and, in the words of one TSM proponent, the "increasingly efficient commercialization of their intellectual property" (FitzGerald 2005, p. 817).

By 2012, the year of Ian Chubb's keynote referenced earlier, TSM had already emerged as a zeitgeist in the West, shaping science and public health policymaking, including the agendas of national research funding bodies. In this way, TSM had already begun to impact the work of university scientists, some of whom barely knew what TSM actually meant. In a 2014 blog from a website dedicated to trends in Australian research, the authors discussed the infiltration of all things translational into Australia's research infrastructure under Ian Chubb's new science strategy:

> It feels like translation is the new buzz word in research, or at least that's how it could be taken in the Australian context. Over the last couple of years and particularly the last 12 months, the term "translation" has been thrown into everything...Australia's national health funding agency, the National Health and Medical Research Council, has embedded the term "translation" and "translational" within its strategic plan, on fifty-two occasions.[3]

Nevertheless, by 2014, Australia was already playing "catch up" according to TSM's proponents. As a discrete set of named policies and initiatives, one can point to the U.S. National Institutes of Health (NIH) as one key birthplace for the *institutional* emergence and growth of TSM.[4] Nearly a decade earlier, in 2005, Elias A. Zerhouni, the director of the NIH, outlined his vision for TSM in the piece "Translational and Clinical Science – Time for a New Vision", published in the *New England Journal of Medicine*. According to Zerhouni (2005), the NIH started in 2002–2003 to create a series of collaborative discussions with scientists, clinicians, industry, universities, entrepreneurs, patients and other stakeholders. From these dialogues emerged the NIH Roadmap for Medical Research in 2003. From this roadmap, the NIH launched a program in 2005 to fund Clinical and Translational Science Awards (CTSAs) to U.S. universities. CTSA was the program that gave institutional birth to TSM on a large scale in the U.S. According to Zerhouni (2005),

> We now aim to stimulate the development of a brighter vision for translational and clinical research, to ensure that these disciplines remain powerful engines of creativity. We offer the opportunity for change to those who share a vision and commitment to innovation and experimentation.
>
> *(pp. 1621–1623)*

Suddenly, starting in 2006–2007, universities across the U.S. began to erect new centers with the term, "translational" therein, such as the University of Alabama's UAB Center for Clinical and Translational Science, and the UCLA Clinical and Translational Science Institute at the University of California, Los Angeles. Awards also facilitated the creation of multi-institution centers such as the Georgetown-Howard Universities Center for Clinical and Translational Science in Washington D.C., and the Atlanta Clinical and Translational Science Institute (Atlanta-CTSI), a network connecting Emory University, Morehouse School of Medicine, Georgia Institute of Technology and Children's Healthcare of Atlanta. These centers received funding to produce new translational programs consisting of degree programs, faculty and graduate student funding lines, and physical and digital infrastructures to support these new research centers. In total, more than 60 new institutions across 30 states and Washington, D.C., were created with one fell funding swoop.

In 2011, the NIH went a step further and established the National Center for Advancing Translational Sciences (NCATS). According to NCATS, "The Center strives to develop innovations to reduce, remove or bypass costly and time-consuming bottlenecks in the translational research pipeline in an effort to speed the delivery of new drugs, diagnostics and medical devices to patients."[5] In essence, and with an enormous effort, the NIH created its own separate and permanent center (akin to the National Institutes of Mental Health) to facilitate all national translational activities, including the CTSA program. A priority of the NIH Director, the NIH's budget request for NCATS totaled $574.7 million in 2012, $639 million in 2013, and $685.417 million in funding for 2017.[6]

While the NIH catalyzed TSM in the West, the globalization of TSM had already begun. Shanghai Jiatong University spearheaded the formalization of TSM in China, creating the Med-X Institute of Translational Research by 2007 and the Academy of Translational Medicine in 2011. By 2014, China had more than 50 TSM institutions (Dai, Yang and Gan 2013), with stated intentions to build another five institutions in 2014. By 2010, a group of European countries created the European Advanced Translational Research Infrastructure in Medicine (EATRIS), with the goal of developing TSM centers (Shahzad, et al. 2011). In the U.K., the Wellcome Trust Scottish Translational Medicine and Therapeutics Initiative connected four academic medical centers in Scotland, while Cambridge and Oxford Universities created TSM centers soon thereafter. TSM projects emerged in the Netherlands as well as Austria, Australia, South Korea and India. By 2014, TSM had become an inextricable part of a global biomedical modernity.

Yet, if TSM was billed as a solution to address the entire supply chain of laboratory-to-patient innovation, then TSM's interventions necessarily had to include the creation of sustainable pathways for the commercialization of translational outputs. And indeed, the partnering of academic institutions and private industry (including private investors) appears as a principal hinge in the conceptualizations of TSM, or what I call "the translational imaginary." From university laboratories to new public–private partnerships, TSM brought about new partnerships between university TSM arms and external private interests – pharmaceutical companies, startups, investors and venture capital firms, corporate sponsorship programs and idea competitions (see chapters by Sismondo; Lazonick et al., this volume) – charged with helping to develop and commercialize the products of translational efforts. Though sidelined in official historiographies, which tend to emphasize the new medicines that TSM will create, the underlying commercial mechanics of TSM are a key part of the translational imaginary and the resulting redesign of academic biomedical research.

Translation and the language of economic salvation

In what follows, I show how TSM's proponents use promises of TSM's resulting economic productivity to justify the reorganization of biomedical research. While this paper is concerned with tracing the use of economic narratives in the move to reshape scientific infrastructures, the analytical importance of these narratives lay beyond concerns about the mere intrusion of commercial interests into scientific work.

Indeed, tracing the economic arguments used to help realize TSM is important in mapping its global emergence and the promises upon which these initiatives are leveraged. However, this line of analysis is also important for another reason: for its proponents, the importance of TSM lay not merely in the stream of new medicines that it was to create, but also in the institutional transformations of science and research towards a more linear scientific model, producing outputs that were more conducive to application and resulting economic development. Here, TSM is part of a radical "cultural change," using the language with which Chubb (2012) ended his keynote. In this way, TSM and its rise show the way that the embedding and expression of specific *value*(s) – economic and political values in the case of TSM – are another intended product (Dussage et al. 2015) of TSM's reconfiguration of research. Therefore, in tracing how economic justifications are used to enroll various publics into the project of TSM – especially as they are embedded within new TSM-oriented legislative, administrative and funding practices, we are also mapping coordinated attempts at value transformation around science.

I offer two examples in which we find the use of economic models of innovation to justify the reorganization of scientific infrastructures towards TSM. The first example returns to the keynote speech with which I began this chapter. The second example delves into the justificatory language from economic policy reports about TSM and economic development. In both examples, TSM is framed as both economic opportunity and national imperative.

Ian Chubb's "biobreakfast" keynote occurred during a pivotal moment in 2012. In late 2011, the National Institutes of Health (NIH) founded NCATS (the National Center for Advancing Translational Science), a center that consolidated all of the translational efforts of the NIH. The founding of NCATS as a permanent NIH center signaled the prioritization of TSM as a strategic and permanent direction for U.S. biomedical research. In his speech, Chubb made reference to the importance of TSM for Australia by directly addressing the issue of international competitiveness:

> Translational research is a priority, and the more our international competitors invest in it while we lag behind, the more challenges face us in the future. ... By contrast, the US and Europe have invested heavily in translational research. In the US, the NIH have invested $480 million in its Clinical and Translation[sic] Science Awards, and another $500 million in a National Centres for Advancing Translational Sciences. And in the UK, they have recently invested 900 million pounds setting up a system similar to the US.
>
> *(Chubb 2012)*

Perhaps Chubb's international comparisons were a pretext designed to neutralize critics' concerns about TSM's cost. Indeed, throughout his keynote, TSM's cost was the "elephant in the room," especially given the fact that Australia's research funding had been cut under recent austerity measures. Thus, the question that also composed the keynote's title, "Can Australia afford to fund translational research?" signaled the fact that Chubb's speech also required making an economic argument about TSM. After assuring the audience that embracing TSM wouldn't spell a complete defunding of other research, he then went on to offer an economic argument about TSM that I included earlier, and which I offer again below:

> But let me go back to a point I made earlier. Funding research is all about return on investment. By funding basic research, we have seen that there is usually little return, certainly very little *immediate* return. Basic research is rarely developed in a practical way for doctors, hospitals or pharmaceutical companies (and it leaves the door open to those who might argue that we should just buy in what we need). But if we invest in translational research, the wealth of knowledge available will be amplified since it all of a sudden has clinical applications. A small investment in translational research, could lead to huge outcomes stemming from the basic research. Translational research,

economically speaking, has a multiplier effect. Investing in translation leverages the investments made in biomedical science.

This argument – that TSM, despite its costs, inexorably leads to new innovations and thus is the key to national economic output and innovation – constituted a classic rejoinder about the economics of innovation, and one that had become nearly canonical by 2010. In the years that followed Chubb's 2012 speech, a flurry of reports emerged focused on "the problem" of Australian innovation. In each report, the central focus presented the problem of innovation in economic terms. One report, "Translating Research for Economic and Social Benefit: Country Comparisons" (Bell, et al. 2015), combined a large number of analyses of international TSM efforts with the goal of identifying potential approaches for Australia. Drawing together a number of analyses from other countries, the authors emphasized the importance of turning "public sector knowledge capital" into "private sector productivity" (Ibid., p.29). In this view, we again see that untranslated science gets framed as an underleveraged asset and universities/researchers as a valuable national resource:

> Improved performance in research translation and business–researcher collaboration in Australia is of concern to government, business and the research sector. Government is increasingly emphasising the importance of demonstrating the impact of research as part of public sector expenditure accountability. Improved research translation and business‑researcher collaboration benefits through the access to ideas and knowledge, equipment and talent that they would not otherwise possess and which gives them commercial advantage. The benefits to universities lie in not only new sources of income but also in active involvement of their researchers in the complex, interesting, and valuable problems that businesses face.
>
> *(Ibid., p. 30)*

For proponents of TSM, a fully realized translation-focused ecosystem necessarily requires engineering sustainable pathways from the public to the private and vice versa; new public–private partnerships between universities and private firms flourish under TSM. In its framing as an economic opportunity, such partnerships are necessarily part of the logic of the linear model of innovation, which goes as follows: after redirecting publicly funded research at universities towards application-oriented ends such as applications, patents, and ideas, partnerships with private industry or connections to venture capital and other funding would, in this model, allow for these outputs to be further developed and turned into products, intellectual property and companies that would nourish an innovation-based economy. According to economists, policy scholars, and other proponents of TSM, such collaborations are the bedrock and the primary means of mobility for TSM-enabled innovation:

> In a modern knowledge-based economy, boosting the ways in which new ideas are applied in practice is an important priority and can be facilitated by measures such as increasing the levels of collaboration between researchers, businesses, not-for-profit, and government sectors. There is the opportunity for Australia to leverage the skills and knowledge in universities through sponsored research, bringing about closer collaboration between publicly funded researchers, industry, government and the community.
>
> *(Ibid., p.28)*

Understanding the role of partnerships under TSM is important for tracing the on-the-ground dynamics of TSM. Toward the end of his speech, buried in a section justifying the costs of

TSM, Chubb mentioned a relatively new Australian public–private partnership funded by the National Health and Medical Research Council [NHMRC] in the area of translational oncology, a field focused on accelerating the development of pharmaceuticals, devices and treatments focused on diagnosing and treating cancer. As indicated in his speech, TSM, and the public–private partnerships that they engender embody the kinds of "collaboration" understood to be necessary under TSM, no matter the costs:

> The organisers asked me to address the question of whether Australia can afford to fund translational research. The cogs have already started turning. This year the NHMRC has committed $52 million to the cause in support of partnership programs and research grants. One particular success story is the Translational Oncology Research Collaborative Hub, bringing together pharmaceutical giant Pfizer with university and public funds. But let me say that the economic situation in the US and UK is a catastrophe compared to Australia. But they have prioritized translational research…the consensus is that no matter how bad the economy is, this is something we need to invest in.
>
> *(2012)*

Chubb's use of the term "success" in his description of the Translational Oncology Research Collaborative Hub here likely refers to the mere creation of the partnership suturing "pharmaceutical giant" Pfizer, Australian universities, and public funds. After all, as of the publication of this chapter, no notable product has emerged out of this collaboration, which began in 2008. In fact, there are few notable successes that have emerged from the translational shift.[7] Chubb also addressed this issue of a TSM's few successes, conceding, "Of course for the moment, all of this is fairly hypothetical. There have been a few translational research success stories…It's too early to tell how successful they will be, and the onus is on the investigators to come up with success stories" (Chubb 2012). While earlier in the keynote Chubb articulated TSM as something that would accelerate the yield from the economic investment in science, here he seems to suggest that even despite existing economic problems facing Australia and other countries as well as the dearth of "success stories," TSM is still important. Here we see how TSM is, aside from any new scientific outputs, about the installation of values.

Nevertheless, the notion of the great economic and innovation-related opportunities that TSM will portend are part of a productive set of economic narratives used in order to justify the investment in, development of, and nurturing of TSM (and while I focus on Australia here, one finds these economic development narratives and justifications across global efforts to bring about TSM). The push of TSM is also, importantly, about the installation of a specific set of values and valuation systems around science and innovation. Yet, TSM is also a story about privatization, risk and corporate restructuring. As I argue in what follows, TSM's triumphalist narratives hide a much more complicated picture about the emergence and function of TSM between 2006 and 2010.

The divestment in corporate R&D and the sudden emergence of TSM

Despite a relatively minimal mention, the cancer research collaboration that Chubb references in his keynote has an interesting backstory – one that I believe gets at the heart of a larger reality that informs the growth of TSM, and which is rendered invisible amidst the bright economic growth narratives and shimmering medical promises used to justify the reshaping of biomedical research towards TSM.

The NMHRC's push towards TSM produced the Peter MacCallum Pfizer Translational Oncology Research Collaborative Hub (which they acronymized into TORCH), which was founded in 2008 in Melbourne. Indeed, TORCH amalgamated important institutional players around a central, important focus of cancer research. As per the playbook for TSM, it tethered university laboratories and researchers, state funding and a prominent corporate partner and co-funder, Pfizer. Yet, what is missing from Chubb's account as well as the many press releases that accompanied its founding, was how the very emergence of TORCH intricately connected to specific internal crises occurring at Pfizer at around the same time. The situation was elucidated in an article about Pfizer's new head of oncology published in 2008:

> The recovery of Pfizer, the world's biggest pharmaceutical company, rests largely on how well Nicholson, 53, can get cancer-fighting drugs out of its research labs and into doctors' offices... Pfizer needs to convince investors it can withstand the loss of the U.S. patent of cholesterol-fighter Lipitor... analysts predict that by 2015 generic competition for Lipitor and other big sellers will chop 25% out of Pfizer's present revenue stream...Chief Executive Jeffrey Kindler has cut 10,000 jobs and put new executives in charge of research, finance and global marketing. ...Now Kindler says he is putting "Pfizer's full scope and scale" behind a push into the cancer market... Cancer-fighting drugs can reach the market twice as fast as the average medicine, and companies can charge as much as $50,000 for a single course of treatment. The oncology drug market is forecast to grow 50% to $85 billion by 2013 as more effective and expensive drugs are launched.[8]

Here one can see how the emergence of TORCH functioned in a context of Pfizer's "recovery." Pfizer's decision to venture into translational oncology is inextricable from a larger strategy motivated, in part, by shareholder concerns over an impending market-share loss, an imperative to capitalize on existing drug pipelines, as well as need to respond to its depressed share price. Thus, while TORCH may have represented a success in Chubb's larger vision, this translational oncology partnership, which used Australia's already "scarce" public funding, was actually a means through which Pfizer sought to solve a specific set of its own problems. In this view, TSM was not merely a means to capitalize on state investments in science, or an opportunity to move existing research towards medical applications, but also enabled state intervention into what was by 2008 a risky life sciences market.

The problems at Pfizer were part of a long line of industry-spanning restructurings among biopharmaceutical research & development (R&D) departments. Starting in 2005, large pharmaceutical companies began massive layoffs of staff across their corporate structure. Soon thereafter, these firms began to systematically divest from risky research areas (Riordan and Cutler 2011), closing down their own internal laboratories. Early-stage pharmaceutical research and development (R&D) was hit especially hard. Part of a larger strategy of cost savings, companies slashed headcount and R&D costs. Between 2007 and 2008, large pharmaceutical firms announced layoffs totaling nearly 100,000 people.[9] The layoffs and divestments continued well into 2011. By December 2012, several big pharmaceutical companies – AstraZeneca, Merck, and GlaxoSmithKline (GSK) – significantly downsized or entirely closed their research divisions in certain disease categories (Cressey 2011).

While this divestment occurred, all of the companies mentioned here – AstraZeneca, Merck, GSK and Pfizer – entered into partnerships with universities under the aegis of TSM. In many cases, university partners were working on projects that had been under the tutelage of private firms. State agencies such as NCATS, the NIH's translational office, actually facilitated new partnerships between universities and pharmaceutical companies in which universities would work on research formerly belonging to now leaner pharmaceutical companies.

I first learned of the relationship between corporate R&D restructuring and the emergence of TSM during my fieldwork at annual biotechnology investment and partnering summits, private events focused on showcasing newly developed drugs and biotechnologies, spurring new partnerships between investors and new biotechnology companies, as well as learning about the latest trends in life sciences-related investing and business development. During one such event, in Boston in 2010, I spoke with pharmaceutical executives who shared their own fears about the changing landscape for biopharmaceutical innovation. For many executives, the solution to this changing landscape hinged on the development of public–private partnerships. During one panel conversation, a Johnson & Johnson executive discussed his company's partnership with a prominent research university.

> We have created partnerships with Johns Hopkins and our attempt is to capture this innovation at its earliest stage. …So we have external discovery engines to afford us the opportunity to offload the overflow from our academic collaborations. In the past, we signed a deal with Vanderbilt and…we looked at external development partnerships and we're looking to capture the innovation of academics and we're looking to increase our partnerships. One of our objectives is to increase early stage partnering [so that] … we're able to come in at a lower cost.

Evidenced in the case of both the Pfizer collaboration in translational oncology and in the words of the executive commenting about reducing costs through public–private partnerships, we see a more complex reality that underlay the public-facing discourses surrounding TSM. TSM must be understood – at least in one sense – as something that specific companies sought out with an eye towards diverting the costs of early stage R&D onto the public domain, a fact that is only visible through an analysis of the on-the-ground articulations of TSM, including its emergent partnerships as well those partners' corporate histories and reconfigurations. Of course, this strategy of offshoring the risks and costs of early stage research onto universities via TSM creates questions: Are universities equipped to absorb the risks of R&D that had formerly belonged to large firms and to do so without comparable financial reserves? Also, if the payoff from early-stage R&D is too anemic for pharmaceutical companies to continue servicing internally, what does that do to the narratives of economic development upon which public state investments in TSM are leveraged? Lastly, what are the implications of importing corporate R&D strategies into university laboratories.

Under the translational shift, market concerns – i.e. Pfizer's need to respond to an impending market share loss or Johnson & Johnson's cost-lowering strategy – become a necessary pre-condition for the way that biomedical research is funded, designed, crafted and assessed. Rather than a simple linear model, in which untapped scientific research is simply monetized, the Pfizer and Johnson & Johnson examples show how TSM's partnerships can enable private firms to solve their own market problems using the public sector – in the form of state funding, the use of university resources, and commercialization agreements that protect the capacity of firms to have the first right of refusal in monetizing potential discoveries.

We are also brought to take seriously the corporate configurations that increasingly shape the tenor and agendas of national biomedical research programs. Pfizer shareholders' concerns about a diminishing market share and a decision to downsize its internal R&D workforce mean that the rapid pursuit of public–private partnerships must be seen as something more than merely a means for university research to be funneled into market-ready outcomes. Bolstered by new institutional partnerships and configurations, TSM functions as a means by which cost and risk from R&D get re-socialized onto the public and then re-privatized in cases where there are monetizable developments from TSM laboratories.

The discursive work of translation

Nevertheless, it is clear that TSM functions as a grand space of discourse-making about the nature of innovation. In fact, that the narratives attached to TSM frame it as a mere knowledge–action problem (Greenhalgh and Wieringa 2011), intellectual and economic opportunity (FitzGerald 2005), and, in light of the world's patients (Zerhouni 2005), a moral obligation.

Indeed, the narratives accorded to TSM exploit economies of expectation regarding medical innovation, especially as they pertain to economic development. However, they also obfuscate very particular corporate histories of divestment and shareholder anxiety regarding R&D risk. In so doing, TSM offers both an opportunity and a methodological caution about the work that narratives regarding economics of innovation both achieve and obscure. The case of TSM here also shows the importance of tracing the "political, economic and disciplinary roots" of "global health institutions, epistemes and programs" (Biehl and Petryna 2013, p. 25) and the special importance of analyzing "corporate reconfigurations" (Birch 2013, p. 52) as they increasingly shape global scientific landscapes.

Indeed, compared to the kind of economic justifications exemplified in Chubb's keynote referenced earlier, in which "investing in translation leverages the investments made in biomedical science," or the framing that treats TSM as a means through which to make state-funded science more beneficial for the larger public, an on-the-ground analysis shows a more complicated picture regarding the economics of innovation under TSM. Rather than merely a platform through which the market can – in some naturalistic way – help translate science into economic gains, TSM actually functions as a state-initiated market intervention on the part of pharmaceutical partners and investors in the life sciences and a means by which private firms have externalized the risks and costs of early-stage research and innovation. Ironically, inasmuch as it intends to remedy the problems of shaky biotechnology innovation markets, it at the same time promotes the view that the solution to problems of national scientific and medical innovation is a market-based reorganization (Lave, et al. 2010; Randalls, this volume) of national knowledge infrastructures.

In thinking through the mechanics of narratives in the management of public perceptions regarding new biomedical initiatives, cases such as that of TSM show the importance of understanding the role of biotechnology markets and especially private firms and corporate histories in the enunciation of new knowledge regimes and in the reorganization of biomedical infrastructures in the name of innovation in medicine.

Notes

1   www.tuftsctsi.org/.
2   www.unmc.edu/pharmacology/integrative_translational_neuroscience.htm.
3   www.ktaustralia.com/making-sense-of-translation-in-health-research/.
4   The history of TSM is not a straightforward one. Some locate the beginning of TSM within Canadian oncological research and others, who include general developmental research under the category of TSM, point to a variety of developments as the start of TSM. Additionally, the terms "translation" and "translational" were used with some regularity as early as the 1990s, but it is unclear that this usage aligns with more recent formalized usage and conceptualizations.
5   www.ctsacentral.org/about-us/ctsa.
6   http://officeofbudget.od.nih.gov/.
7   Judah Folkman's research is commonly alluded to as an example of successful translational research (Fischer 2012) and several other observers (Fitzgerald and Fitzgerald 2013; Kringelbach, et al. 2007) have used historical discoveries that they argue highlight an example of what they believe comprises successful translation. However, thus far, few notable developments have emerged out of the global institutionalization of TSM.

8 www.forbes.com/forbes/2008/0602/044.html.
9 "Top Layoffs in 2009," Fierce Pharma www.fiercepharma.com/special-reports/top-10-layoffs-2009, and related articles for 2007 and 2008.

References

Bell, J., Dodgson, M., Field, L., Gough, P. and Spurling, T. (2015). "Translating Research for economic and social benefit: country comparisons". Report for the Australian Council of Learned Academies, wwww.acola.org.au.

Berman, E. P. (2012). *Creating the Market University: How Academic Science Became an Economic Engine*. Princeton: Princeton University Press.

Biehl, J., and Petryna, A. (2013). "Therapeutic markets and the judicialization of the right to health". In J. Biehl and A. Petryna (Eds.), *When People Come First: Critical Studies in Global Health* (edition I). Princeton University Press.

Birch, K. (2013). "The political economy of technoscience: an emerging research agenda". *Spontaneous Generations: A Journal for the History and Philosophy of Science*, 7(1).

Bok, D. C. (2005). *Universities in the Marketplace: The Commercialization of Higher Education*. Princeton: Princeton University Press.

Brown, J. R. (2000). "Privatizing the university – the new tragedy of the commons". *Science*, 290(5497), 1701–1702.

Brown, N. (2003). "Hope against hype – accountability in biopasts, presents and futures". *Social Studies of Science*, 16(2), 3–21.

Cambrosio, A., Keating, P., Mercier, S., Lewison, G., and Mogoutov, A. (2006). "Mapping the emergence and development of translational cancer research". *European Journal of Cancer*, 42(18), 3140–3148.

Canaan, J. E. and Shumar, W. (eds). (2008). *Structure and Agency in the Neoliberal University* (edition I). New York: Routledge.

Chubb, I. (2012, April). "Can Australia afford to fund translational research? Keynote address presented at the Biomelbourne Network, Australia". Retrieved from www.chiefscientist.gov.au/2012/04/can-australia-afford-to-fund-translational-research/.

Clinical and Translational Science Awards. (n.d.). "About the CTSA consortium". Retrieved April 3, 2014, from www.ctsacentral.org/about-us/ctsa.

Cressey, D. (2011). "Psychopharmacology in crisis". *Nature News*.

Dai, K.-R., Yang, F., and Gan, Y.-K. (2013). "Development of translational medicine in China: Foam or feast?" *Journal of Orthopaedic Translation*, 1(1), 6–10.

Dussauge, I., Helgesson, C.-F., Lee, F., and Woolgar, S. (2015). "On the omnipresence, diversity, and elusiveness of values in the life sciences and medicine". In I. Dussauge, C.-F. Helgesson, and F. Lee (Eds.), *Value Practices in the Life Sciences and Medicine* (1 edition). Oxford, United Kingdom: Oxford University Press.

Etzkowitz, H. (2007). *MIT and the Rise of Entrepreneurial Science*. London: Routledge.

Fischer, M. M. J. (2012). "Lively biotech and translational research". In K. S. Rajan (Ed.), *Lively Capital: Biotechnologies, Ethics, and Governance in Global Markets*. Durham: Duke University Press.

FitzGerald, G. A. (2005). "Anticipating change in drug development: the emerging era of translational medicine and therapeutics". *Nature Reviews Drug Discovery*, 4(10), 815–818.

Fitzgerald, D. J. and FitzGerald, G. A. (2013). "Historical lessons in translational medicine cyclooxygenase inhibition and p2y12 antagonism". *Circulation Research*, 112(1), 174–194.

Greenhalgh, T. and Wieringa, S. (2011). "Is it time to drop the 'knowledge translation' metaphor? A critical literature review". *Journal of the Royal Society of Medicine*, 104(12), 501–509.

Jogalekar, S. (2011). "Lost in translation". *Current Science*, 101, 12.

Kringelbach, M. L., Jenkinson, N., Owen, S. L. F., and Aziz, T. Z. (2007). "Translational principles of deep brain stimulation". *Nature Reviews Neuroscience*, 8(8), 623–635.

Lave, R., Mirowski, P., and Randalls, S. (2010). "Introduction: STS and Neoliberal Science". *Social Studies of Science*, 40(5), 659–675.

Loewenberg, S. (2009). "The Bayh–Dole Act: A model for promoting research translation?" *Molecular Oncology*, 3(2), 9193.

Mirowski, P. (2011). *Science-Mart*. Harvard University Press.

Nathan, D. G. (2002). "Careers in translational clinical research - historical perspectives, future challenges". *JAMA*, 287(18), 2424–2427.

Nedeva, M. and Boden, R. (2006). "Changing science: the advent of Neo-liberalism". *Prometheus*, 24(3), 269–281.

Riordan, H. and Cutler, N. (2011). "The death of CNS drug development: overstatement or omen?" *Journal for Clinical Studies*, 3(5), 12–15.

Robinson, M. (2010). "The privatization of neuroscience: the university, the state and the moral aims of science". *Anthropology News (Association for Political and Legal Anthropology)*, 54(5-6), 789–797.

Robinson, M. (2016). "Engineering the translational imagination: instrumentalism and ideation in translational research" (manuscript in preparation).

Royer, P. (1972). "Medical applications and therapeutic prospects deduced from knowledge in molecular pathology". *Biochimie*, 54(5–6), 789–797.

Science Translational Science. (2016). Retrieved February 2, 2016, from www.sciencemag.org/site/marketing/stm/.

Shahzad, A., McLachlan, C. S., Gault, J., Cohrs, R. J., Wang, X., and Köhler, G. (2011). "Global translational medicine initiatives and programs". *Translational Biomedicine*, 2(3).

Shore, C. and Wright, S. (1999). "Audit culture and anthropology: neo-liberalism in British higher education". *The Journal of the Royal Anthropological Institute*, 5(4), 557–575.

Shumar, W. (1997). *College for Sale: A Critique of the Commodification of Higher Education*. London; Washington, D.C.: Falmer Press.

Vignola-Gagné, E. (2013). "Gaps, pitfalls and the valley of death: translational research and the reform of biomedical innovation". DPhil dissertation. University of Vienna.

Zerhouni, E. A. (2005). "Translational and clinical science – time for a new vision". *New England Journal of Medicine*, 353(15), 1621–1623.

19

ARE CLIMATE MODELS GLOBAL PUBLIC GOODS?

Leigh Johnson and Costanza Rampini

As global climate change became an issue of major international concern beginning in the 1990s, models that accurately replicate observed climate trends and make projections of future changes have become increasingly important tools for both scientists and policy makers. These global and regional models require large investments and major computing power, and have been developed by a handful of government-sponsored institutions and universities, primarily located in the Global North.[1] Over this same timeframe, many other scientific fields have undergone large-scale institutional reorganization, prioritizing research leading to privatizable commercial innovations (Mirowski, 2011, Lave et al., 2010, Lave, 2012; see chapters by Delfanti, Harrison et al., Lave and Robertson, Robinson, and Rossi, this volume).

In this context, several characteristics of global climate modeling make the field appear an exceptional case that has escaped neoliberal imperatives for commercialization: it has remained largely government funded; it has retained a focus on "basic" science rather than being packaged for end-user commercial applications; and the legitimacy of modeling depends on open-source code that allows models to be scrutinized by any researcher with sufficient computing power. As such, climate models might arguably be placed in the category of "global public goods", a term from the fields of economics and political science used to refer to goods whose use are "nonrival and nonexcludable" on the global scale. This is to say, their use by one actor does not prevent others from using them; it is difficult to exclude any actor from reaping benefits from their existence; and their benefits accrue to an ostensibly "universal" public rather than to citizens of a particular nation (Kaul et al., 1999, Sandler, 1997).

In this chapter, we explore the genealogy and recent uses of climate modeling to evaluate whether the field can be considered a global scientific public good. We question this premise, demonstrating the exclusionary terms under which global models have been developed and the commercial purposes to which downscaled regional climate models have been put. We draw on these examples to problematize the simplistic notion of global scientific public goods, demonstrating that the benefits of such goods do not inevitably or inherently accrue at an explicitly global scale nor to an especially vulnerable or worthy "public". In the case of climate modeling, the form of knowledge produced is largely too global to matter to the most vulnerable, and is often used for private profit-making purposes when it is in fact localized enough. But this need not mean that all modeling for public purposes is inevitably exclusionary or co-opted for private ends. We close by pointing out the democratic possibilities that new modeling techniques for attributing instances of extreme weather to anthropogenic emissions may hold, allowing Least Developed Countries to make redistributive claims against wealthy historically high-emitting nations. We emphasize that global public goods are *fashioned* by actors with particular imaginations of the publics whose interests should be prioritized. Rather than conceptualizing all models as inherent public goods, we call for actively recognizing their embeddedness in political economic structures and cultivating their potential to help envision alternative decarbonized futures.

A global public good?

The concept of public goods has a long history in economics and political science, where scholars have interrogated the conditions under which actors such as states provide for the "common good", and have theorized that such goods are typically subject to underprovision ("market failure") by the rational actors envisioned by neoclassical economics and international relations (e.g. Samuelson, 1954, Hardin, 1968). To this basic conception, scholars and policy makers have appended "global" to refer to infrastructures and outcomes with ostensibly global benefit, applying the concept loosely to conditions as disparate as environmental quality, global security, and global financial stability, as well as the international regimes providing common frameworks for achieving these outcomes (cf. Sandler, 1997). An influential volume published by the UNDP defines global public goods as "outcomes or intermediate products that tend towards universality in the sense that they benefit all countries, population groups and generations. At a minimum, a global public good['s] ... benefits extend to more than one group of countries and do not discriminate against any population group or any set of generations, present or future" (Kaul et al., 1999, 16). The same authors tellingly categorize public goods as "the world outside the market places" (ibid., 2). With respect to science, the status of global and/or regional public goods has been assigned to outputs of applied scientific research such as epidemiological surveillance and disease control (Chen et al., 1999), biodiversity conservation (Rands et al., 2010), agricultural research and extension, and weather monitoring and forecasting (Cook and Sachs, 1999; Randalls, this volume). Rather than uncritically employing the concept, we test the term "global public goods" here as an exercise to explore both the characteristics of the climate modeling field and the sufficiency of the concept of global public goods.

A genealogy of climate modeling

Since World War II, the field of climate modeling has depended on national and supra-national funding regimes, and especially defense funding, to develop the global infrastructure, governance and technology needed to produce global climate knowledge. World War II military efforts produced vast amounts of new weather data and the digital computer technology that transformed weather forecasting from an observational to a computational science. These developments provided the impetus for standardizing and integrating national and regional weather systems into a single global system, under the United Nations' World Meteorological Organization (WMO), established in 1950 (Edwards 2010). The international cooperation needed for establishing a weather internetwork – a network of networks behaving as a single unified system (Edwards 2010) – through which meteorological information could be communicated near instantaneously across national boundaries was also a political exercise in the reorganization of international relations in the post-war era (Miller 2001). The WMO provided meteorological assistance to newly independent nations by training meteorologists and building national weather services (Edwards 2010). At the same time, cold war politico-military competition spurred the

U.S., Europe and the Soviet Union to develop meteorological satellites and link them with surface-based observing systems, data processing and communication networks through the World Weather Watch program, beginning in the early 1960s (Landis 1999, Edwards 2010). While geopolitical competition led the world superpowers to underwrite most of the costs and technical burdens of this global weather infrastructure, it also enrolled them in scientific cooperation through infrastructure integration and data sharing. Overall, World War II computer technology and weather data along with Cold War fears of climatological warfare and politico-military competition combined to create a global climate infrastructure, governance structure, and consciousness that led to the emergence of a climate modeling epistemic community – a transnational network of knowledge-producers united across Cold War boundaries around common beliefs and capable of influencing policymakers through their scientific authority (Haas 1990).

After the launch of the Soviet Sputnik satellite in 1957 as part of the International Geophysical Year, the U.S. government reacted by significantly increasing its support for scientific research and education. U.S. institutions came to dominate the field of climate modeling in the 1950s, as post-war military and civilian weather services funding supported the development of the first general circulation model (GCM) in 1955 by scientists at Princeton University, and led to the establishment of the Geophysical Fluid Dynamics Laboratory (GFDL) (Edwards 2011). By 1969, thanks to significant improvements in computer power, GFDL scientists had developed the first coupled atmosphere–ocean general circulation model (AOGCM). Coupled GCMs divide the earth system into several thousands of three-dimensional grid boxes, and for each grid-box they perform hundreds of thousands of complex calculations based on known physical principles about the movement of energy to simulate future climate. By the mid-1970s, GFDL scientists began experimenting with carbon dioxide doubling simulations (Edwards 2011). The 1950s and 60s saw the emergence of two other pioneering climate research groups at the University of California, Los Angeles and at the U.S. National Center for Atmospheric Research, and by the 1970s global climate modeling efforts had spread from these three U.S. institutions to several others in Europe and Japan (Edwards 2011). Between the 1960s and 1980s, rising atmospheric and environmental concerns about a nuclear winter, acid rain, and the ozone hole helped bring anthropogenic climate change into the political arena and cemented the role of general circulation models as indispensable for understanding global climate change (Edwards 2010). Since the 1990s, climate modeling advances have made it possible to incorporate new chemical and biological processes in global climate simulations, including land surface and hydrology, ecosystem responses and socio-economic dimensions such as population growth, energy use, and land cover change.

Despite the transnational collaboration involved, the Cold War defense orientation of early climate modeling endeavors dictated that the weather observation infrastructure and models developed during that time should benefit individual nations' security. These were thus *national* public goods. In contrast, the current use of AOGCMs to address questions of global environmental concern arguably makes them global public goods (where the national/global identity of the good is differentiated by criteria of use and intent, rather than any inherent or immutable characteristic of the infrastructure or model).

Although, to our knowledge, no one has claimed that climate modeling itself represents a global public good, this seems a reasonable extrapolation to make based on classical definitions. The climate modeling field was consolidated by the establishment of the IPCC as an international regime in 1989 – under the sponsorship of the World Meteorological Organization and the United Nations Environment Program – which requires periodic model intercomparison efforts and produces comprehensive assessments of climate model simulations for policymakers

(Edwards 2010; 2011). Though current and particularly future generations could benefit from the knowledge generated by global climate models, developing each model requires tremendous investment. Yet because model outputs are freely available – non-rivalrous and non-excludable – this makes them subject to the so-called "free-rider" problem of collective action, in which actors avoid investing in common goods but nonetheless reap the benefits of them.

Casting the problem in these terms raises a set of questions that we endeavor to answer in the remainder of this chapter: Does modeling benefit "all countries, population groups, and generations"? Is modeling subject to underprovision? To what extent do climate modeling practitioners and outputs function "outside the market places"? And how might the answers to these questions prompt us to revise the concept of "global public good" to better reflect the political economy of science?

Universal benefit?

Observing the international fora organized to produce and authorize knowledge about climate change and govern nations' emissions, one might assume that model outputs are operating outside the forces of the market, and for the benefit of all populations. The reports of the IPCC, the international body charged with reviewing and drawing conclusions about climate change research to inform policy making, rely heavily on the perpetually updated models of the major research institutes and their projections about future climate conditions under various emissions scenarios. These models generate a range of plausible future climate conditions such as temperature, precipitation, and sea level rise by applying scenarios reflecting different future concentrations of greenhouse gases. Despite the uncertainties and limitations of projections, improvements in GCMs between the fourth and fifth IPCC Assessment Reports have further consolidated epistemic consensus over the 2°C to 5°C range in equilibrium climate sensitivity, which is the expected increase in global average surface temperature in response to a doubling of carbon dioxide concentrations from pre-industrial levels (Flato et al. 2013). Model projections are what allow the IPCC to warn that zero net CO_2 emissions must be reached by 2070 to avoid "dangerous warming" (IPCC, 2014). These alarming projections also constitute a major rationale for taking action through international governance regimes such as the UN Framework Convention on Climate Change (UNFCCC), through which the 196 UN-recognized countries agreed on new emissions reduction targets to keep warming "well below" 2°C at the December 2015 Conference of Parties.[2] When the text of the historic Paris climate deal refers repeatedly to using the "best available science" to guide emissions reductions (UNFCCC, 2015), it is referring primarily to outputs from climate models.

Modeling has also gained political traction outside of international fora. Calls by activists and public intellectuals to divest from fossil fuel companies and levy carbon taxes on all fossil fuels extracted (cf. McKibben, 2012) deploy the bleak picture of coastal flooding, drought, and storms that could result from even 2 degrees of warming (cf. Hansen et al., 2015) as a central rationale for their proposals. In these cases, evidence from climate modeling is marshaled in an explicit attempt to keep heedless capital accumulation from sending the planet's radiative balance and ecosystems into catastrophic disarray (cf. Klein, 2014).

Political economic and institutional pressures

But the fact that climate modeling has been pivotal in crafting international agreements and legitimating activist calls for transformation of the carbon economy does not necessarily mean that the knowledge produced functions as a global public good. Significant political economic and institutional pressures have circumscribed the application of this knowledge such that it is far from yielding universal and non-excludable benefits. For instance, the UNFCCC used model projections to develop "stabilization targets" (to constrain warming to 2°C and atmospheric CO_2 concentrations at 450–550 parts per million), a move critiqued by the climate justice movement for its minimization of the uncertainties and dangers surrounding even 2 degrees of warming. The very concept of *stabilization* is telling: in its focus on calculating the quantity of allowable emissions and required reductions, it orients policy-making towards maintaining the current socioeconomic order, rather than advocating concerted decarbonization of the economy or robust adaptation measures (Boykoff et al., 2010). The concept of allowable emissions – the quantity of greenhouse gases that can be "safely emitted" without leading to "dangerous warming" – has been a cornerstone in the creation of the multi-billion dollar carbon trading market for companies and countries exceeding their allocated allowable quantities (Liverman, 2009). The practice of compensating for excess emissions in the Global North with carbon offsetting projects in the Global South inscribes a new form of inequality – sustaining affluent consumption in the North while dispossessing atmospheric rights and livelihood strategies in the Global South (Lovell et al., 2009, Bumpus and Liverman, 2008; see also Lohmann, this volume).

The practice of climate modeling itself is far from a globally distributed or accessible good. The computational and personnel requirements of developing climate modeling programs, comparable only to those of nuclear weapons research and high-energy physics, have confined climate modeling efforts to a few national research centers, weather services and well-funded institutions (Edwards 2010; 2011). Only a few dozen modeling groups around the world have the financial and technological resources to build, refine and run GCMs with the help of government funding (Lahsen 2005). The supercomputers required need tremendous computational power to reiterate calculations and re-compute the state of the entire atmosphere at repeated time intervals (Lahsen 2005, Miller and Edwards 2001). Improving model resolution or increasing the number of climate processes and components included in GCMs leads to enhanced model complexity and accuracy, but also to higher computational costs (Flato et al. 2013).

For instance, the U.S. National Center for Atmospheric Research's (NCAR) latest supercomputing center, which opened in October 2012 in Cheyenne, Wyoming, cost between $95 and $105 million dollars, including $25 to $35 million for IBM's latest supercomputer system (UCAR 2016). The U.S. National Science Foundation and the State of Wyoming largely funded the new laboratory, but the cost of building the facility and its computing systems are only a portion of the overall cost of running the center. For instance, the Wyoming Center's power consumption averages an extraordinary 1.8 to 2.1 megawatts of electricity (UCAR 2016); at Wyoming's average unsubsidized[3] commercial rate of 8.88 cents per kilowatt hour (U.S. Energy Information Administration 2015), this would yield a daily electricity bill of nearly $4,000!

Given such enormous costs, it is not surprising that – with the exception of a handful of modeling centers in China and Korea – all other global climate-modeling efforts have been undertaken by groups in the U.S., Europe, Canada, Australia, Russia, and Japan (Flato et al. 2013). The requirements for such programs are not simply computational: a tremendous amount of accumulated human capital is required over many years to develop and run models and continue improving them. Thus the expertise to design models, frame research questions, and interpret results is also located in these countries, limiting their accessibility to the majority of the world and drawing into question their status as a "non-excludable" global public good.

The "universal benefit" of models is also drawn into question by institutional and technological requirements dictating their development and orientation towards a "global" scale. Under the aegis of the IPCC, climate modelers face institutional and political pressures to produce a global knowledge and an epistemic consensus that can guide international climate negotiations and influence national policies regarding climate adaptation and mitigation (Hulme and Mahoney 2010, van der Sluijs et al. 1998). Meanwhile, the development of state-of-the-art GCMs is limited by the economic and technological requirements of supercomputers. The overall result is that GCM projections are most useful to a particular user group – national governments and government-sponsored institutions – focused on a global-scale response to climate change. The general public can only benefit from the knowledge produced by GCMs to the extent that outputs are successful at influencing national and international policies.

Ironically, while GCMs may succeed at producing the global climate knowledge that serves as the organizing basis for a broad political coalition (Wynne 2010), they cannot produce the local climate knowledge that is urgently needed by a vast, heterogeneous, and globally dispersed group of potential users whose everyday decisions could benefit from knowledge about climate variations (Agrawala et al. 2001). Uncertainties in modeling the earth's climate include the internal stochasticity (randomness) of the climate system, responses of the climate system to anthropogenic emissions, and the structural limitations of GCMs, particularly their limited resolution (Giorgi 2005). Amongst other things, the simulation of clouds, mountains, coastlines, and extreme events with localized effects or short durations remains difficult, constraining predictive power at smaller spatial and temporal scales (Flato et al. 2013). For this, regional downscaling is required. Regional climate models able to capture mesoscale features like topography, coastlines, and vegetation characteristics can be used to project regional climate change, including impacts on agriculture; to make seasonal predictions; and to run other local models, such as ecosystem, hydrology, and ocean sea ice models (Leung et al. 2003). Regional higher-resolution predictions are more relevant to the needs of the most vulnerable groups and countries (Huntingford and Gash 2005).

Yet since downscaling groups tend to favor simulating their "home" region first (Giorgi et al. 2009), regional understandings of climate change impacts are uneven. Most notably, though Africa is deemed particularly vulnerable to climate change for a variety of socio-economic reasons, it has historically received relatively little attention from downscaling efforts and future projections are especially uncertain (Hulme et al. 2001; Giannini et al. 2008). International efforts are underway to include scientists from lower-income countries in regional modeling networks by providing scientific training and making regional models more flexible, portable and user-friendly, while also encouraging existing downscaling groups to prioritize Africa (Giorgi et al. 2009; Pal et al. 2007). Meanwhile, outputs from regional downscaling have been eagerly embraced by commercial interests for profit-oriented uses.

Commercializing modeling

At the outset of this chapter, we observed that, in comparison to many other scientific fields, the field of global climate modeling has remained remarkably insulated from imperatives to create commercializable science. We suggested the "non-rival and non-excludable" character of the field might qualify it as a global public good. While this is true, it is also misleading: since GCMs make projections at such coarse resolutions and over such long timescales, their outputs are of little relevance to most commercial operations. The same does not necessarily hold for regional impact forecasting, and here we examine several examples of regional downscaling conducted with the involvement of commercial firms that trouble the simple dichotomy between public and commercial goods.

The insurance industry has long been one of the most vocal sectors regarding the potential risks of climate change (e.g. Geneva Association, 2009), and has invested substantially in developing geoscientific expertise to quantify these risks in monetary terms (Johnson, 2010). Within the industry, reinsurance companies – who underwrite insurers in case of major losses that would otherwise send them into bankruptcy – have spearheaded research to determine whether and how climate change signals should be incorporated into current pricing. A 2011 study of industry practices found that, out of eight major reinsurers, only one – the second largest global reinsurer, Swiss Re – claimed to concretely account for climate change in any of its current pricing (Johnson, 2011). The firm's ability to implement and legitimize these pricing changes grew from a collaborative research project with climatologists at the Swiss Federal Institute of Technology (ETH) and the Swiss Federal Office of Meteorology. The study simulated insured losses from European winter storms through the year 2085 using two regional climate models and two atmospheric GCMs (ultimately published as Schwierz et al., 2010). As a result, beginning in 2006, the company applied a per annum surcharge of 0.5 percent for German windstorm coverage. All else being equal, by 2085 this will generate 50 percent higher premium rates compared to 2006 (Johnson, 2011).

Further regional and "near term" applications of climate model outputs have been made by catastrophe modeling firms, the third-party technical companies that build models used by insurers and reinsurers to estimate potential losses from catastrophic events (Grossi and Kunreuther, 2005). Such commercial interests are typically concerned with the impacts of climate change over shorter time frames of one to ten years rather than the 50- to 100-year timescales analyzed in most modeling studies. For instance, in order to integrate climate change impacts into a forecast of the frequency and severity of North Atlantic hurricanes in the coming five years, in 2013 the market-dominant catastrophe modeling firm Risk Management Solutions used outputs from a public global multi-model ensemble[4] to predict sea surface temperatures in the North Atlantic's Main Development Region for tropical cyclones (Wilson, 2014, Laepple et al., 2008). This resulted in a four to five percent increase in the company's estimate of land-falling U.S. hurricanes between 2013 and 2017, and thus higher estimates of annual monetary losses to storms, which ultimately translated into higher rates for catastrophe reinsurance coverage (Wilson 2014, 22, Johnson, 2015). As in the reinsurance case, the company's collaboration with a scientist at a public research institute – in this case the German Wegener Institute – vouched for the legitimacy of such adjustments.

Agribusiness is another sector that has availed itself of possibilities created by public investment in climate monitoring and modeling. The agribiotech firm Monsanto acquired the Google-spinoff Climate Corporation for nearly a billion dollars in October 2013 to offer farmers new monitoring, analytics and risk-management products (Monsanto 2013). The Climate Corporation combines local weather and agronomic conditions with historical weather data to create field-level weather projections for farmers (www.climate.com). Every day, it processes 50 terabytes of new and historical weather data, mostly from the National Weather Service's radar stations and the U.S. Department of Agriculture (Callen 2014). Monsanto's aim is to commercialize downscaled weather predictions to enable farmers – particularly those in key corn-growing regions – to make timely decisions and minimize losses in the face of increasingly "volatile weather".

The Climate Corporation's reach is enormous: by June 2015, U.S. farmers had already adopted the company's free basic online service on nearly 45 percent of corn and soybean fields in the country (Monsanto 2015). Their premium service has also been adopted on over 5 million acres across the U.S at three dollars per acre. The company's digital platforms can now also be connected in real-time with a variety of John Deere precision agriculture large equipment (John Deere Company 2015). For our purposes, what is significant is the way such firms use climate data to proliferate financial instruments for hedging and speculating on hyper-localized weather conditions – capitalizing on a rising consciousness of extreme weather events and their implicit link to a changing climate.

These cases demonstrate that, rather than simply operating as a non-commercial public good, the public nature of climate data, climate models, and the expertise embedded in public institutions are enabling preconditions for the appropriation of climate knowledge for private use. They illustrate precisely what Moore castigates in the uncritical discourse of global public goods, namely that it cloaks the "collective activities needed to pave the way for original [i.e. primitive] accumulation", meaning the creation of a class of owners of private property via the expropriation of the commons (Moore, 2004, 101). For climate and weather risks to become commodities that can be hedged against or speculated upon, a great deal of preexisting weather knowledge and data is required (cf. Randalls, 2010, Thornes and Randalls, 2007). The public nature of climate research over the last 50 years has made such knowledge widely available at little or no cost and generated a pool of highly trained experts, setting the conditions for the private sector to create these fully "rivalrous" and "excludable" goods whose benefits are decidedly non-universal.

Extreme event attribution

Yet, like other infrastructures of environmental surveillance and prediction, climate models can support multiple uses and needs (Benson, 2012). They are not always appropriated for exclusionary private ends, and there are cases where the benefits of model output may also accrue to the marginalized populations most vulnerable to climate change. These include efforts to develop community-directed adaptation plans – informed by model projections – prioritizing livelihoods and equity (cf. Tschakert et al., 2014). In these cases the knowledge generated by climate models may be a necessary but alone insufficient condition for robust and equitable adaptation (Weaver et al., 2013).

A less visible but potentially highly significant application of climate modeling for public good comes from an "upstream" body of research that attempts to estimate the extent to which past anthropogenic greenhouse gas emissions are responsible for current extreme events such as droughts, floods, and heatwaves (e.g. Allen, 2003, Stott et al., 2013). Such estimates are constructed by using ensembles of climate models to compute the probability of the occurrence of extreme events under current conditions and in a "world which might have been" without anthropogenic emissions (Otto et al., 2015). Some scientists championing these efforts, termed probabilistic event attribution, explicitly frame their research as one method of accounting for climate change "loss and damage" sustained by least developed countries (Parker et al., 2015). Their intent is to provide scientific grounds on which calls for adaptation financing and compensation to these countries could be based (James et al., 2014). Although UNFCCC parties adopted a framework to address loss and damage associated with climate change impacts in 2013, the mechanisms by which such losses will be adjudicated remains contested. Least Developed Countries and island states have advanced redistributive claims against wealthy, historically high-emitting nations, whose negotiators typically reject the principle of "compensation" (Huq et al., 2013).

There is a great deal of scientific and political uncertainty surrounding such attribution studies and their plausible policy impact (Parker et al., 2016), not to mention whether such loss and damage mechanisms could ever accomplish just or transformative change or account for non-economic losses (Wrathall et al., 2015). These are all valid concerns. Nevertheless, we highlight the studies above to point out how climate scientists themselves may acknowledge the political nature of their inquiries upstream in the research process. Politics is not something that happens *to* the model simulations after the fact, but rather one of the framing rationales for the research questions being asked.

The infrastructure on which the simulations are run also has a political character: the bulk of probabilistic event attribution research is based at the University of Oxford but modeled through the distributed volunteer computing project Climateprediction.net. The project uses the spare capacity of thousands of personal computers whose users have volunteered their machines to run small parts of larger ensemble models in the absence of supercomputing capacity large enough to conduct such "super ensembles" (Stainforth et al., 2002). Such infrastructure uses an open-source platform whose developers frame the significance of volunteer computing in explicitly democratic terms: "Volunteer computing power can't be bought; it must be earned. A research project that has limited funding but large public appeal can get huge computing power" (BIONC 2014).

The volunteered computing capacity running extreme event attribution studies, as well as many other global and regional climate modeling experiments at Climateprediction.net, alert us to the need to reframe the standard conceptualization of "global public goods" as provisioned by beneficent states. And contrary to the neoclassical assumptions of freeriding and underprovision of public goods, the project has amassed over 600,000 individual computer "hosts" providing spare computing capacity (BIONCstats 2016). Whether such a distributed modeling project is broadly replicable and representative of a new form of public good – a global network good – is a question we can only begin to pose; however, the project's decade-long existence and considerable scientific impact illustrate larger points about climate modeling and global public goods with which we conclude.

Conclusions

We have used the case of climate modeling to illustrate how we might rethink the concept of global public goods to better reflect the political economy of science. Our point is that climate models – like "global public goods" more generally – are not inevitably beneficial for one purpose or population or another. Rather, they are *made* so by planning, framing, and prioritization of research questions, as well as by the surrounding institutional and financial orders governing the production and distribution of data.

One weakness of the concept of public goods is that it does not allow us to distinguish *between* the various publics that may benefit under different conditions, nor does it suggest how we might evaluate which publics should be prioritized. The concept is "ideologically unmoored" (Moore 2004, 102): a global public good may be lauded by classical liberals for creating the enabling conditions for the development of private markets, such as weather risk markets, or it may be championed by those with social democratic sensibilities for promoting global redistributive transfers, such as loss and damage claims.

This ambivalence means that characterizing climate modeling as a global public good is too simplistic. There are clear cases in which huge private profits may be reaped by "enclosing" the knowledge and expertise of climate research generated in the public domain, particularly in downscaled regional contexts. But it is likewise too cynical to maintain that the benefits of climate modeling entirely bypass the global publics that are most vulnerable to climate change impacts; the case of probabilistic event attribution is just one example of how climate science may directly intervene in political debates to promote cross-generational redistributive climate justice.

Ultimately, climate models and modelers are inevitably embedded in political economic structures that shape how climate science can be put to use. But scientists themselves have some agency in directing both their research (and employment) priorities and the ways their outputs are represented and used. Though some climate modeling knowledge and data are undeniably employed for private profit-oriented purposes, there is also something profoundly radical about modeling's ability to explore the counterfactual world "as it might have been", as well as a range of future possible worlds given different emissions scenarios. We close with a call for modelers to actively cultivate the plurality of responses to climate change that modeling may allow us to envision, always with the recognition of the political economic ramifications of such work.

Notes

1   For instance, the U.S. National Center for Atmospheric Research, the NASA Goddard Institute for Space Studies, the U.K. Met Office Hadley Center, the Max Planck Institute for Meteorology in Germany, and more recently the Beijing Climate Center.
2   Targets which, as critics have bitterly noted, are still not legally binding. Rather, countries' "intended nationally defined contributions" to emissions will likely yield a warming of at least 2.7 degrees – an estimate also derived from climate modeling (UNFCCC Secretariat, 2015).
3   Of course, NCAR's rate is likely heavily subsidized by the state, which bears the costs instead.
4   Freely available from the World Climate Research Programme's Coupled Model Intercomparison Project (CMIP3), compiled to facilitate scientists' drafting of the IPCC Fourth Assessment Report.

References

Agrawala, S., K. Broad, and Guston, D. 2001. "Integrating climate forecasts and societal decision making: Challenges to an emergent boundary organization". *Science, Technology, and Human Values*, 26(4): 454–477.

Allen, M. 2003. "Liability for climate change". *Nature*, 421, 891–892.

Benson, E. 2012. "One infrastructure, many global visions: The commercialization and diversification of Argos, a satellite-based environmental surveillance system". *Social Studies of Science*, 42(6): 843–868.

BIONC. 2014. "Volunteer Computing, Berkeley Open Infrastructure for Network Computing". Retrieved from http://boinc.berkeley.edu/trac/wiki/VolunteerComputing.

BIONCstats. 2016. "Detailed stats: Climate Prediction". Retrieved from: http://boincstats.com/en/stats/2/project/detail/.

Boykoff, M., Frame, D. and Randalls, S. 2010. "Discursive stability meets climate instability: A critical exploration of the concept of 'climate stabilization' in contemporary climate policy". *Global Environmental Change-Human and Policy Dimensions*, 20: 53–64.

Bumpus, A. G. and Liverman, D. M. 2008. "Accumulation by Decarbonization and the Governance of Carbon Offsets". *Economic Geography*, 84: 127–155.

Callen, J. 2014. "The value of government weather and climate data. Economics and Statistics Administration", United States Department of Commerce. Retrieved from www.esa.doc.gov/economic-briefings/value-government-weather-and-climate-data.

Chen, L. C., Evans, T. G. and Cash, R. A. 1999. "Health as a global public good". In: Kaul, I., Grunberg, I. and Stern, M. A. (eds.) *Global public Goods: International Cooperation in the 21st Century*. Oxford: UNDP/Oxford University Press: 284–304.

Cook, L. and Sachs, J. 1999. "Regional public goods in international assistance". In: Kaul, I., Grunberg, I. and Stern, M. A. (eds.) *Global public Goods: International Cooperation in the 21st Century*. Oxford: UNDP/Oxford University Press: 436–449.

Edwards, P. 2010. *A vast Machine: Computer Models, Climate Data, and the Politics of Global Warming*. Cambridge, MA: MIT Press.

Edwards, P. 2011. "History of climate modeling". *WIREs Climate Change*, 2(1): 128–139.

Flato, G., et al. 2013: "Evaluation of Climate Models". In: Stocker, T.F., D. Qin, G.-K. Plattner, M. Tignor, S.K. Allen, J. Boschung, A. Nauels, Y. Xia, V. Bex and P.M. Midgley (eds.) *Climate Change 2013: The Physical Science Basis. Contribution of Working Group I to the Fifth Assessment Report of the Intergovernmental Panel on Climate Change*. Cambridge and New York, NY: Cambridge University Press.

Geneva Association 2009. *The Insurance Industry and Climate Change – Contribution to the Global Debate*, Geneva, The Geneva Association for the Study of Insurance Economics.

Giannini, A., M. Biasutti, I. Held, and Sobel, A. 2008. "A global perspective on African climate". *Climatic Change*, 90(4): 359–383.

Giorgi, F. 2005. "Climate change prediction". *Climatic Change*, 73(3): 239–265.

Giorgi, F., C. Jones, and Asrar, G. 2009. "Addressing climate information needs at the regional level: The CORDEX framework". *World Meteorological Organization Bulletin* 58(3): 175–183.

Grossi, P. and Kunreuther, H. 2005. *Catastrophe Modeling: A New Approach to Managing Risk*, New York, Springer.

Haas, P. 1990. "Obtaining international environmental protection through epistemic consensus". *Journal of International Studies* 19(3): 347–363.

Hansen, J., Sato, M., Hearty, P., Ruedy, R., Kelley, M., Masson-Delmotte, V., Russell, G., et al. 2015. "Ice melt, sea level rise and superstorms: evidence from paleoclimate data, climate modeling, and modern observations that 2° C global warming is highly dangerous". *Atmospheric Chemistry and Physics Discussions*, 15, 20059–20179.

Hardin, G. 1968. "The tragedy of the commons". *Science*, 162: 1243–1248.

Hulme, M., R. Doherty, T. Ngara, M. New and Lister, D. 2001. "African climate change: 1900–2100". *Climate Research*, 17(2): 145–168.

Hulme, M. and Mahony, M. 2010. "Climate change: What do we know about the IPCC?" *Progress in Physical Geography*, 34: 705–718.

Huntingford, C. and Gash, J. 2005. "Climate equity for all". *Science*, 309: 1789.

Huq, S., Roberts, E. and Fenton, A. 2013. "Loss and damage". *Nature Climate Change*, 3: 947–949.

IPCC 2014. *Climate Change 2014: Synthesis Report Summary for Policymakers. Contribution of Working Groups I, II and III to the Fifth Assessment Report of the Intergovernmental Panel on Climate Change*, Geneva, Switzerland, IPCC.

James, R., Otto, F., Parker, H., Boyd, E., Cornforth, R., Mitchell, D. and Allen, M. 2014. "Characterizing loss and damage from climate change". *Nature Climate Change*, 4: 938–939.

John Deere Company. 2015. "John Deere and The Climate Corporation expand options for farmers". [Press Release]. Retrieved from www.deere.com/en_US/corporate/our_company/news_and_media/press_releases/2015/corporate/2015nov03-corporaterelease.page.

Johnson, L. 2010. "Climate Change and the Risk Industry: The multiplication of fear and value". In: Peet, R., Robbins, P. and Watts, M. (eds.) *Global Political Ecology*. London: Routledge: 185–202.

Johnson, L. 2011. *Insuring Climate Change? Science, Fear and Value in Reinsurance Markets*. PhD, Department of Geography, University of California Berkeley.

Johnson, L. 2015. "Catastrophic fixes: cyclical devaluation and accumulation through climate change impacts". *Environment and Planning A*, 47: 2503–2521.

Kaul, I., Grunberg, I. and Stern, M. A. 1999. "Defining global public goods". In: Kaul, I., Grunberg, I. and Stern, M. A. (eds.) *Global Public Goods: International Cooperation in the 21st Century*. Oxford: UNDP/Oxford University Press: 2–19.

Klein, N. 2014. *This Changes Everything: Capitalism vs. the Climate*, Simon & Schuster, New York.

Laepple, T., Jewson, S. and Coughlin, K. 2008. "Interannual temperature predictions using the CMIP3 multi-model ensemble mean". *Geophysical Research Letters*, 35.

Lahsen, M. 2005. "Seductive simulations? Uncertainty distribution around climate models". *Social Studies of Science*, 35(6): 895–922.

Landis, R. 1999. "Lessons learned about IGOS through the World Weather Watch. Integrated Global Observing Strategy, UN System-wide Earthwatch Coordination", UNEP Geneva. Retrieved from: www.un.org/earthwatch/about/docs/igusland.htm.

Lave, R. 2012. "Neoliberalism and the production of environmental knowledge". *Environment and Society: Advances in Research*, 3: 19–38.

Lave, R., Mirowski, P. and Randalls, S. 2010. "Introduction: STS and neoliberal science". *Social Studies of Science*, 40: 659–675.

Leung, L., Mearns, L., Giorgi, F., and Wilby, R. 2003. "Regional climate research: Needs and opportunities". *Bulletin of the American Meteorological Society*, 84: 89–95.

Liverman, D. M. 2009. "Conventions of climate change: constructions of danger and the dispossession of the atmosphere". *Journal of Historical Geography*, 35: 279–296.

Lovell, H., Bulkeley, H. and Liverman, D. 2009. "Carbon offsetting: sustaining consumption?" *Environment and Planning A*, 41: 2357–2379.

McKibben, B. 2012. "Global warming's terrifying new math". *Rolling Stone*.

Miller, C. 2001. "Scientific internationalism in American foreign policy: The case of meteorology, 1947–1958". In *Changing the Atmosphere: Expert Knowledge and Environmental Governance*. Eds. Miller, C. A. and P. N. Edwards. Cambridge, MA: MIT Press: 167–218.

Miller, C. and Edwards, P. 2001. *Changing the Atmosphere: Expert Knowledge and Environmental Governance*. Cambridge, MA: MIT Press.

Mirowski, P. 2011. *Science-Mart*, Harvard University Press.

Monsanto. 2013. "Monsanto to acquire The Climate Corporation, combination to provide farmers with broad suite of tools offering greater on-farm insights". [Press Release]. Retrieved from http://news.monsanto.com/press-release/corporate/monsanto-acquire-climate-corporation-combination-provide-farmers-broad-suite.

Monsanto. 2015. "The Climate Corporation announces record adoption of digital agronomic services platform". [Press Release]. Retrieved from http://news.monsanto.com/press-release/climate/climate-corporation-announces-record-adoption-digital-agronomic-services-platf.

Moore, D. 2004. "The Second Age of the Third World: From primitive accumulation to global public goods?" *Third World Quarterly*, 25: 87–109.

Otto, F., James, R., Parker, H., Boyd, E., Jones, R., Allen, M., Mitchell, D., et al. "Developing research about extreme events and impacts to support international climate policy". EGU General Assembly Conference Abstracts, 2015. 1711060.

Pal, J., et al. 2007. "Regional climate modeling for the developing world: The ICTP RegCM3 and RegCNET". *Bulletin of the American Meteorological Society*, 88: 1395–1409.

Parker, H. R., Boyd, E., Cornforth, R. J., James, R., Otto, F. E. and Allen, M. R. 2016. "Stakeholder perceptions of event attribution in the loss and damage debate". *Climate Policy*, 1–18.

Parker, H. R., Cornforth, R. J., Boyd, E., James, R., Otto, F. E. and Allen, M. R. 2015. "Implications of event attribution for loss and damage policy". *Weather*, 70: 268–273.

Randalls, S. 2010. "Weather profits: Weather derivatives and the commercialization of meteorology". *Social Studies of Science*, 40: 705–730.

Rands, M. R., Adams, W. M., Bennun, L., Butchart, S. H., Clements, A., Coomes, D., Entwistle, A., et al. 2010. "Biodiversity conservation: Challenges beyond 2010". *Science*, 329: 1298–1303.

Samuelson, P. A. 1954. "The pure theory of public expenditure". *The Review of Economics and Statistics*, 36: 387–389.

Sandler, T. 1997. *Global Challenges: An Approach to Environmental, Political, and Economic Problems*, Cambridge, Cambridge University Press.

Schwierz, C., Köllner-Heck, P., Zenklusen Mutter, E., Bresch, D., Vidale, P.-L., Wild, M. and Schär, C. 2010. "Modelling European winter wind storm losses in current and future climate". *Climatic Change*, 101: 485–514.

Stainforth, D., Kettleborough, J., Allen, M., Collins, M., Heaps, A. and Murphy, J. 2002. "Distributed computing for public-interest climate modeling research". *Computing in Science & Engineering*, 4: 82–89.

Stott, P. A., Allen, M., Christidis, N., Dole, R. M., Hoerling, M., Huntingford, C., Pall, P., et al. 2013. "Attribution of weather and climate-related events". *Climate Science for Serving Society*. Springer: 307–337.

Thornes, J. E. and Randalls, S. 2007. "Commodifying the atmosphere: pennies from heaven?" *Geografiska Annaler: Series A, Physical Geography*, 89: 273–285.

Tschakert, P., Dietrich, K., Tamminga, K., Prins, E., Shaffer, J., Liwenga, E. and Asiedu, A. 2014. "Learning and envisioning under climatic uncertainty: an African experience". *Environment and Planning A*, 46: 1049–1068.

UNFCCC 2015. "Adoption of the Paris Agreement, United Nations Framework Convention on Climate Change 21st Conference of Parties", 12 December.

UNFCCC Secretariat 2015. "Synthesis report on the aggregate effect of the intended nationally determined contributions". United Nations Framework Convention on Climate Change, 21 Conference of Parties. FCCC/CP/2015/7.

U.S. Energy Information Administration. 2015. "Historical average annual electricity prices by state by type of electricity provider. Frequently Asked Questions: Does EIA publish electric utility rate, tariff, and demand charge data?" Retrieved from www.eia.gov/tools/faqs/faq.cfm?id=20&t=3.

University Corporation for Atmospheric Research. 2016. "NCAR-Wyoming Supercomputing Center Fact Sheet. NCAR UCAR AtmosNews". Retrieved from www2.ucar.edu/atmosnews/news/nwsc-fact-sheet.

van der Sluijs, J., van Eijndhoven, J., Shackley, S., and Wynne, B. 1998. "Anchoring devices in science for policy: The case of consensus around climate sensitivity". *Social Studies of Science*, 28(2): 291–323.

Weaver, C. P., Lempert, R. J., Brown, C., Hall, J. A., Revell, D. and Sarewitz, D. 2013. "Improving the contribution of climate model information to decision making: The value and demands of robust decision frameworks". *Wiley Interdisciplinary Reviews: Climate Change*, 4: 39–60.

Wilson, P. 2014. "North Atlantic Hurricanes". *Catastrophe Modelling and Climate Change*. London: Lloyd's.

Wrathall, D. J., Oliver-Smith, A., Fekete, A., Gencer, E., Reyes, M. L. and Sakdapolrak, P. 2015. "Problematising loss and damage". *International Journal of Global Warming*, 8: 274–294.

Wynne, B. 2010. "Strange weather, again: Climate science as political art". *Theory Culture & Society*, 27(2–3): 289–305.

20

RENEWABLE ENERGY RESEARCH AND DEVELOPMENT

A political economy perspective

David J. Hess and Rachel G. McKane

Introduction

There are many benefits associated with shifting from an energy system based primarily on fossil fuels to one based on renewable energy and energy efficiency (REEE) and other low-carbon sources. In addition to the reduction in greenhouse gases, countries and subnational regions can benefit from reduced air pollution, from a more secure energy supply, and from economic development if the new energy sources displace imported energy.

Because the benefits are clear, one might expect that an energy transition would occur quickly, but progress at all levels of governance—from cities, provinces, states, and countries to global arrangements—has been slow. Technical factors have impeded the transition, among them the high cost of solar energy; the problem of transmission for wind resources, which are often located far from population centers; the intermittency of solar and wind energy and the expense of energy storage; and the problem of integrating distributed energy into electricity grids that are based on stable baseload power and centralized distribution. But there are also political-economic factors that impede a more rapid energy transition. In many cases corporations associated with the existing energy regime—fossil fuel producers, utilities, and companies in industries that are heavily reliant on fossil fuels—view energy-transition policies as a threat to their profitability and existing models of business. In some cases the incumbent actors have mobilized in the political field to block policies in support of REEE and decarbonization, and their political opposition has included reduction of support for scientific research on climate change and REEE.

A political economy perspective can allow the robust interpretation and explanation of the emergence of opposition to energy transition policies. In this chapter we will describe our approach to the political economy of science and technology, then discuss how it works using data drawn from changes in state government policies with respect to REEE in the United States.

Conceptual background

The term "energy transition" will be used here to refer to changes in energy technologies that lead to a reduction in greenhouse gas emissions. Although there are various types of greenhouse gas emissions, the focus here will be on carbon dioxide and an energy transition primarily understood as decarbonization. The outcome of an energy transition entails a fundamental change across various industries, including electricity, transportation, agriculture, buildings, and manufacturing. The focus in this study will be on the electricity industry. There are various terms in use to describe an alternative to an electricity system that is heavily reliant on fossil fuels, which in most countries means a combination of coal and natural gas. REEE is a narrow category represented primarily by hydropower, solar, wind, and geothermal energy and by energy efficiency technologies. In turn, REEE is one type of low-carbon energy, which can include nuclear energy and fossil fuels when configured with carbon sequestration and with energy-efficient technologies such as combined heat and power. The focus here will be on greater reliance on REEE rather than on the full range of low-carbon energy technologies.

Some industrial transitions take place largely through marketplace processes, but in the case of a heavily regulated industry, such as electricity, government policy is especially important. Government policy sets the conditions for a transition by providing funds for research, incentives for the development of new technologies, and regulatory support for them to scale up. Because of the importance of government policy, the industrial transition can be a highly political process. Coalitions of industrial incumbents can emerge to slow or block transition policies, and likewise transition coalitions can emerge to support those policies.

A political economy approach provides one important framework for understanding the politics of energy transitions. We understand "political economy" broadly as the study of how political and economic institutions and actors influence each other. Two of the most central points of reference in an adequate political economy framework are social structure and institutional structure. Social structure refers to the enduring relations of inequality categorized by class, race, ethnicity, gender, sexuality, global position, and other aspects of social structure (Hess et al. 2016b). In the case of low-carbon energy transitions, lack of support for environmental policy is often linked to the capacity of sectors of the dominant class to oppose stronger environmental regulations. However, energy-transition politics can also involve conflicts within the dominant class. For example, there have been some instances of support for energy transition policies by the technology and investment industries in the U.S. (Hess 2016a).

The second main point of reference in a political economy approach involves institutions, or the enduring areas of social action that have their own roles, rules, values, and cognitive categories (Powell and DiMaggio 1991). Examples of social institutions that are relevant to this project are government, industry, science, and civil society. Institutions are nested and interacting; for example, government regulation occurs at multiple scales, from cities to global treaty frameworks. Interactions across institutions occur through a variety of mechanisms, such as when actors bring their different forms of capital—for example, the social capital of networks or their financial capital—to bear on their strategies within different fields. We draw on field theory as a framework for analyzing action and strategies within and across institutions (Bourdieu 2001, Fligstein and McAdam 2012). This approach emphasizes how actors accumulate and spend various types of capital and how they acquire and change a system of meanings that inform their dispositions for action.

To understand how scientific and technological change occurs in institutions and fields, we also draw on transition studies, a body of research that has its roots in work on large technical (or technological) systems (LTSs). An LTS is a heterogeneous ensemble of natural resources, a sociotechnical system (organizations, laws, practices, infrastructure, products, consumers), and a cultural system of cognitive and normative categories. An LTS is generally associated with an industrial system such as transportation, electricity, and food production, and LTSs undergo changes or transitions from one configuration to another. The case of electricity as an LTS was historically important in science and technology studies because of Hughes's work (1983, 1987) on the transition of urban lighting systems and buildings from gaslight to electricity. We are interested in the transition of the electricity system from a configuration based on the use of fossil fuels for stable electricity generation (or "baseload power") from centralized power plants to a configuration that includes a much larger role for distributed generation (such as rooftop solar that is connected to the grid), energy storage and "smart grid" technologies, and the use of renewable energy and other low-carbon energy sources.

Whereas Hughes developed a phase model of the transition of LTSs, subsequent work on industrial transitions has emphasized conflict among actors. This work has tended to focus on institutional structure and to emphasize relations of conflict and cooperation between incumbents and challengers in an industrial field. Although social structural factors such as class and gender can be included, they tend to be addressed via a residual category known as the "landscape"(Geels 2011). The incumbents are associated with a configuration of the LTS known as a regime, whereas challengers often begin as relatively minor actors located in niches of the LTS. The actors who support the development and scaling up of niches can be scientists and entrepreneurs with funding from venture capital or government agencies, or they can be part of the research and development efforts of large corporations. Niches can be symbiotic with the industrial regime, in which case their innovations can be incorporated into the regime with little conflict, or they can generate deep institutional conflict (Geels and Schot 2007). These conflicts can take the form of large, established organizations versus smaller start-ups (e.g., the electricity utilities versus the solar installation firms). However, in the case of electricity there are also conflicts between utilities and firms in countervailing industries, such as finance, that support the scaling-up of the niches, such as rooftop solar.

In our case, the incumbents include both the utilities, which favor a stable system of centralized power, and fossil-fuel production firms, which provide a particular form of centralized, baseload power. An energy transition away from reliance on centralized, baseload power toward distributed REEE threatens the utilities because it could lead to the growth of off-grid electricity generation (Kind 2013). For example, households and businesses could build on-site energy storage for their solar power and effectively disconnect from the grid. Because of this potential for REEE to be deeply disruptive, the utilities prefer to slow the transition and, as the innovations develop, to steer them toward the dominant configuration, such as by building centralized solar farms instead of enabling the development of rooftop solar. The coal industry is also threatened because electricity is the main source of demand for coal, and an energy transition could mean the bankruptcy of firms. For the natural gas industry, there could be a sharp decline in demand as the market becomes restricted to the heating of buildings rather than including the use of natural gas to power large electricity generation facilities.

When incumbents form a political alliance to block a transition and to support the existing regime, they engage in "regime resistance." In transition studies, this topic is not yet well developed, but there is increasing interest in it (Geels 2014; Hess 2016a, 2016b). Regime resistance can focus on specific policies that the incumbents attempt to block, but it can also involve more general alliances with other industrial groups. In the U.S. these regime coalitions have constructed an institutional field of public relations firms, lobbyists, think tanks, campaign spending organizations, and organizations that create a "corral" around the government (Barley 2010). Supported by large corporations and by wealthy donors, of whom some of the most prominent have ties to the fossil fuel industry, this institutional field has shifted political discourse toward conservative (neoliberal) and anti-regulatory policy preferences. Regime resistance can include this general, long-term historical development, but for our purposes the focus will be more on the specific, short-term dimensions of regime resistance associated with opposition to specific REEE policies.

Although the economic resources of regime actors tend to make conflicts between incumbents and challengers over industrial transitions a David and Goliath struggle, the challengers associated with transition coalitions have various options that they can use to overcome regime resistance. Among the options are the mobilization of countervailing industrial power and ideological judo. For example, wealthy donors in California associated with the finance and technology sectors provided significant funds to support the state's global warming law against a ballot initiative that was sponsored by out-of-state fossil-fuel firms and that would have rolled back the law. Similar countervailing industrial power can be found in other political conflicts over energy transitions in state governments in the U.S. (Hess 2014). Ideological judo refers to the translation of pro-transition policies into policy instruments that are consistent with conservative values (Hess 2016b). REEE policies that are configured to reduce government regulation, such as "red tape"that makes it hard to gain solar photovoltaic permits, tend to gain higher levels of support than renewable portfolio standards, which require utilities to produce a specified percentage of REEE by a given date, such as 25 percent by 2025 (Hess et al. 2016a, Hess 2016a).

The analysis that follows will explore the political and economic factors that impede a more rapid energy transition on a global level, then it will use a comparative analysis of U.S. state government policy to examine how regime resistance occurs through the alliance of political conservatives with pro-fossil fuel regime actors. The case of electricity transition politics in the U.S. provides a good basis for developing general knowledge about regime resistance, the politics of transitions, and the political economy of science and technology.

Energy transitions in global perspective

During the 2008 U.S. presidential elections, both Republican and Democratic presidential candidates acknowledged the existence of global warming and the need to have a policy to mitigate greenhouse gas emissions. However, after the Republican Party gained control of the U.S. House of Representatives in 2011, opportunities to pass legislation to mitigate greenhouse gas emissions ended in the federal government. Republicans in Congress frequently expressed climate denialism and began a campaign to reduce funding to science research that addressed climate change and energy transition issues. They proposed and sometimes achieved cutbacks in climate-related and REEE research in a wide range of government agencies (Morello et al. 2011, U.S. House of Representatives 2011). By attacking not only energy transition policy but also scientific research programs, conservative political leaders linked the issue of energy transition policies to the scientific field and to the politics of research funding. In turn, this strategy created a situation of undone science, or the systematic underproduction of research due to lack of support from political and industrial elites (Hess 2016b; also see Fernández Pinto, this volume).

Although the U.S. is arguably the world leader in climate denialism and opposition to REEE research and development, similar opposition has appeared from conservative governments in Australia, Canada, and the U.K. (Carter and Clements 2015, Young and Coutinho 2013). For example, Canadian Prime Minister Stephen Harper withdrew from the Kyoto Protocol and ended the government's National Round Table on the Environment and the Economy, which reports on climate-related issues. The government also censored its own scientists and cut funding for climate-related research (Ogden 2015). In Australia, Prime Minister Tony Abbot's government repealed the country's carbon tax, ordered the government's Clean Energy Fund to stop investments in wind and small-scale solar energy, proposed cuts of 69 percent to the Australian Climate Change Science Program, and eliminated some environment-related agencies (Dayton 2014). In the U.K. the conservative government increasingly turned against

REEE development (Carter and Clements 2015). Although climate change denialism is particularly influential in the neoliberal, Anglophone countries, it has also spread to other areas of the world (Dunlap and McCright 2015, Tranter and Booth 2015).

Even in countries where there is relatively strong support for energy transition policies from parties across the political spectrum, there can be significant differences of views on what the ideal pace of the transition should be and on what its effects and side effects have been. For example, in Germany support for the feed-in tariff for solar energy came mainly from the Green Party and Social Democratic Party, whereas opposition came from the more conservative Christian Democratic Party and Liberal Democratic Party (Hoppman et al. 2014). Although the conservative parties supported renewable energy under the Energiewende policy, they also sought to weaken the feed-in tariff law and the growth of solar energy. The changes came in response to concerns raised by the utilities about the growth of distributed solar energy, which was being produced by independent organizations and was undermining utility profitability, and with general concerns about the cost of electricity and economic competitiveness.

There is little information on political conflict and green energy transition policies in other countries. Our comparative analysis of 18 Asian countries found that countries with relatively low levels of policy support for renewable energy were poorer, more authoritarian, and more heavily endowed with fossil fuels (Hess and Mai 2014). The study also found that some of the countries had a high reliance on hydropower and were likely to reduce the percentage of renewable energy as they grow their electricity system to meet increased demand. Because some of the countries are adding generation capacity by increasing the level of fossil fuel production, they are actually engaged in an energy transition toward fossil fuels. In general, in the smaller and poorer developing countries, the primary focus is still on electrification and on meeting demand growth, and the severe budgetary constraints of these countries have tended to make REEE a luxury that they perceive as unaffordable.

From a greenhouse gas emissions perspective, policy reform in the large industrializing countries is important because of their growing contribution to emissions. Although the goals set in the Conference of Parties 21 in Paris in 2015 do not represent binding commitments, leading industrialized countries did agree to intended Nationally Determined Contributions (iNDCs). For example, Brazil set the goal of reducing economy-wide greenhouse gas emissions by 43 percent by 2030 from 2005 levels; China announced that it will achieve peak greenhouse gas emissions by 2030 and will reduce its carbon intensity by 60–65 percent below 2005 levels; India announced the similar goal of reducing its carbon intensity by 30 percent below 2005 levels by 2030; and Mexico announced that it will reduce its emissions by 22 percent by 2030 relative to business as usual and will reduce black carbon (soot) by 51 percent (United Nations 2015). Although such proposals are a welcome development, they will likely be far from adequate for the goal of reducing global emissions at a pace required to prevent the worst risks predicted by climate scientists. In many developing countries, growth in emissions has to date outpaced decarbonization efforts, and goals are still framed in terms of energy intensity rather than the reduction of total emissions. Even so, we do not see the same level of organized resistance to REEE policies from the fossil fuel sector that is evident in some of the industrialized Anglophone countries. It is possible that the high projected growth of energy production in industrializing countries reduces the potential threat to the existing regime, and it is also possible that the transition to solar and wind energy is not as advanced as it is in some of the wealthier, industrialized countries. If these are the correct explanatory factors for the relative lack of opposition in the industrializing economies, then opposition may emerge when demand growth slows and the non-hydro REEE portion of the energy mix increases. We would especially expect opposition if renewable energy growth is not owned and controlled by the regime actors, such as the utilities.

REEE policy in the American states

As the country with the highest level of opposition from industrial incumbent organizations to decarbonization policies, the U.S. provides a good laboratory for a detailed examination of the political economy of REEE. The specific focus here will be on the issue of regime resistance that has emerged in the political field as part of the alliance among the utilities, donors associated with the fossil fuel industries, and conservative political leaders. We focus on state governments because much of REEE policy in the U.S. is developed and implemented at that level. The analysis that follows is based on the assumption that one avenue for examining the political economy of REEE is through the effects of party changes on policy. In many cases, political party conflicts in the U.S. have become closely aligned with support for fossil fuels (higher in the Republican Party) versus support for decarbonization policies (higher in the Democratic Party). The campaign finance system facilitates the influence of utilities and fossil fuel companies by allowing firms and wealthy donors to affect campaigns through donations and independent spending. The 2010 U.S. Supreme Court decision of *Citizens United v. the Federal Election Commission* opened the floodgates for political spending in what was already an important pathway of influence between the industrial and political fields.

In the 2010 mid-term elections, the conservative wing of the Republican Party defeated moderates in the primary elections, and support of moderate Republicans for energy transition policies was a divisive issue in some campaigns. In addition to the shift within the Republican Party that purged moderates, the party also gained control of the U.S. House of Representatives and several governors' offices and state legislative bodies that had been controlled by Democrats. In other words, the 2010 election was largely regarded as a rout against the Democrats, but it also represented a shift within the Republican Party toward hardened opposition to REEE policies. Increasingly, the elected officials of the Republican Party in both the federal and state governments opposed REEE legislation, many also voiced climate denialism, and in some state legislatures Republicans attempted to repeal renewable energy portfolio standards, including laws that had passed with bipartisan votes only a few years earlier. Likewise, whereas Republican governors prior to 2008 had in some cases supported a cap-and-trade approach to carbon regulation and other policies favorable to a "green economy," they increasingly opposed such proposals and supported the development of fossil fuels such as natural gas fracturing technologies. Although some Republican leaders maintained support for REEE policies, they became a minority within the party. Candidates for office in the Republican Party became acutely aware of the risks that such support could entail to re-election campaigns, where spending from the network of pro-fossil fuel donors could support primary challenges from candidates whose views were stridently opposed to climate science and REEE.

In the section that follows we examine the effects of the changes of political party on REEE policy, with a focus on policies that support research, economic development, or industrial growth for the REEE sector. We selected states that had a change of the party of the governor between 2010 and 2015. We did not include Florida, where Governor Crist began as a Republican but switched parties to become an independent. We began with a baseline analysis of state government policies in support of REEE, conducted with a team of students in 2010 (Hess et al. 2010). This analysis identified a range of REEE policies, including programs that supported REEE research and development. McKane then analyzed state government web sites and news reports to examine to what extent the programs were still in effect. This provided a beginning inventory of shifts in REEE policy directly related to research and development. Additional searches of news reports for the governor and REEE policy were conducted to identify other examples of how the shift from Democratic to Republican governors was associated with important changes in REEE policy.

The result is an inventory of the most significant examples of REEE policy shifts associated with changes in the political party of the governor during the specified period. Often Republican Party control of the governor's office coincided with control of both houses of the legislature by the Republican Party, but our focus is on the governors. In most cases Republican governors opposed the Environmental Protection Agency's proposed Clean Power Plan, which proposed to regulate carbon dioxide emissions from electricity power plants. Because opposition to the Clean Power Plan was widespread, we do not include it in the analysis. We grouped the presentation of policy changes by the four U.S. Census Bureau regions (see Table 20.1).

The summary of the REEE policy changes associated with a change from a Democratic to a Republican governor indicates that in many cases there were attempts to roll back REEE policies (see Table 20.2). An exception was Governor Bransted of Iowa, but Iowa has well-developed wind and biofuels industries that are supported by powerful rural constituencies, and these forms of REEE tend to have bipartisan support. Furthermore, the governor had served a previous term and had supported REEE policies, and he was not part of the wave of anti-environmental "Tea Party" Republicans. The state also has a split legislature, a condition that means that bipartisan efforts are required in order to approve legislation.

Table 20.1 Shift from Democratic to Republican Governor, 2010–15

Region	State	Date	Outgoing Democrat	Incoming Republican	Legislative Composition, Governor's First Year
Midwest	Illinois	2015	Quinn	Rauner	Both Democrat
	Iowa	2011	Culver	Bransted	Split (House R., Senate D.)
	Kansas	2011	Parkinson	Brownback	Both Republican
	Michigan	2011	Granholm	Snyder	Both Republican
	Ohio	2011	Strickland	Kasich	Both Republican
	Wisconsin	2011	Doyle	Walker	Both Republican
Northeast	Maine	2011	Baldacci	LePage	Both Republican
	Massachusetts	2015	Patrick	Baker	Both Democratic
	New Jersey	2010	Corzine	Christie	Both Democratic
	Pennsylvania	2011	Rendell	Corbett	Both Republican
South	Arkansas	2015	Beebe	Hutchinson	Both Republican
	Maryland	2015	O'Malley	Hogan	Both Democratic
	N. Carolina	2013	Perdue	McCrory	Both Republican
	Oklahoma	2011	Henry	Fallin	Both Republican
	Tennessee	2011	Bredesen	Haslam	Both Republican
West	New Mexico	2011	Richardson	Martinez	Both Democratic
	Wyoming	2011	Freudenthal	Mead	Both Republican

Table 20.2 Summary of major REEE policy shifts in states with a change to Republican Governor, 2010–15

Region	State	Policy Changes under Republican Governor
Midwest	Illinois	• Budget for 2016 proposes cuts to REEE programs (legislature rejected): end to Energy Efficiency Portfolio Standard Fund and Renewable Energy Resources Trust Fund
	Iowa	• Governor signs S.F. 2340, 2014: triples solar tax credits • Governor signs S.F. 2343, 2014: extends wind tax credits • Governor supports ethanol and national renewable fuels standard • Governor does not defend Iowa Energy Center when utility threatens to withhold funding
	Kansas	• Governor signs HB 2101, 2014: reduces payments to net metering customers • Governor signs SB 91, 2015: changes state's renewable portfolio standard from mandatory to voluntary
	Michigan	• Centers for Energy Excellence, established under previous Democratic governor, does not approve additional REEE projects • Advanced vehicle battery manufacturer credit ended • Alternative fuel and vehicle research, development, and manufacturing credit ended • Governor opposes 2012 ballot initiative for a 25% renewable portfolio standard (initiative failed)
	Ohio	• Governor signs S.B. 310, 2014: freezes Ohio's RPS for two years, creates Energy Mandates Study Committee to evaluate effectives of the RPS • Governor opposes indefinite freeze of RPS • Ohio Third Frontier (business development program) shifts from fuel cells and advanced energy to start-up programs
	Wisconsin	• Governor ends Green to Gold Fund (energy-efficiency improvements) • Governor opposes implementation of Wind Siting Rules (PSC 128), which leads to withdrawal of wind energy projects • Governor's 2015 budget cuts $8 million for bioenergy research
Northeast	Maine	• Governor vetoes LB 1252, 2014: tax to support solar energy (legislative override) • Governor vetoes LB 1263, 2015: to create a stakeholder group to develop an alternative to net metering (legislative override)
	Massachusetts	• Governor appoints former fossil fuel lobbyist to lead energy policy • Governor signs S1979, 2016: raises net metering cap but lowers payment to 60% of retail rate • Governor supports natural gas and hydropower development
	New Jersey	• Governor withdraws state from Regional Greenhouse Gas Initiative • Governor's 2011 Energy Master Plan has cutbacks for REEE and support for natural gas development • Governor signs SB 2036, 2010: supports offshore wind, but his Regulatory Committee creates hurdles for wind development

	Pennsylvania	• Governor supports natural gas resource development • Governor dismantles programs that support REEE (Green Government Council and Office of Energy Management) • Alternative Energy Development Program of Ben Franklin Technology Partners unfunded as of 2015
South	Arkansas	• No changes identified
	Maryland	• Governor blocks regulations to reduce coal plants' nitrogen-oxide emissions because of concerns he had with the effects on costs • Governor downsizes Maryland Energy Administration • Governor opposes raising utility rates to expand energy efficiency efforts • Governor signs SB 323, 2016: to reduce greenhouse gas emissions by 40% from 2006 levels by 2030 • Governor vetoes HB 1106, 2016: bill to increase RPS
	N. Carolina	• 2013 state government budget cuts funding completely for Biofuels Center • The Department of Energy and Natural Resources removes information on climate change from its web site and reassigns officials who worked on climate change
	Oklahoma	• Governor supports climate denialism • Governor signs SB 1456, 2014: authorizes monthly charge for electricity customers with solar panels
	Tennessee	• Governor signs HB 62, 2013: increases taxes on solar and wind facilities • Governor reduces solar investment policies of Democratic predecessor • Governor supports HB 1268, 2013: supports energy efficiency for state government buildings
West	New Mexico	• Governor fires Environment Improvement Board • Governor appoints climate change denier to run Energy, Minerals, and Natural Resources Department • Governor prevents publication of a rule to require a 3% reduction in greenhouse gas emissions • Governor ends Energy Innovation Fund for solar and biofuels • Governor vetoes HB296 (2015): to extend solar tax credits • Governor vetoes funding for Renewable Energy Transmission Authority in 2015
	Wyoming	• In 2013 governor unveils energy policy focused on development of fossil fuels

Notes: Key: HB=house bill, RPS=renewable portfolio standard, REEE=renewable energy and energy efficiency, SB=senate bill

In states with Democrat-controlled legislatures, there is no consistent pattern of gubernatorial policy. Massachusetts is a very Democratic state with a history of strong support for REEE policy under Democratic Governor Patrick, and Republicans in the state tend to be more moderate than in other regions of the country. Consistent with this moderate position, Governor Baker supported a compromise solar law, but the law had a crucial feature of ending net metering policy (payment for rooftop solar generation at the retail rate), which the utilities have been seeking in many states. He also indicated the need to expand energy sources by including more natural gas and hydropower, but he signaled willingness to expand hydropower if there was no or weak political support for natural gas. In other states with shifts to Republican governors and Democrat-controlled legislatures (Illinois, Maryland, New Jersey, and New Mexico), the governors generally attempted to dial back the strong support that energy transition advocates had enjoyed under previous Democratic governors.

There is also a pattern in the types of REEE policies that were targeted. First, there was no new development of renewable portfolio standards or regional carbon trading regimes under the newly elected Republican governors. Our interviews with state government legislators and their aides indicated that Republicans view these policies as unwanted government mandates (Hess et al. 2016a). In Kansas, the renewable portfolio standard was changed to voluntary; in Michigan the governor opposed a ballot initiative that would have supported a constitutional change in favor of REEE; in Ohio the governor supported a temporary freeze on the standard, and in New Jersey the governor withdrew from the regional greenhouse gas cap-and-trade agreement. In contrast, there are several cases where the newly elected Republican governors explicitly supported more natural gas development while they blocked supportive programs for wind energy and for solar. In the case of solar, the utilities were engaged in a comprehensive campaign to weaken net metering laws and other support for distributive solar energy, and Republican governors often supported these policy changes. Republican governors also downsized government agencies associated with REEE and cancelled funds in support of REEE research and development.

Discussion

The sharp differences between Republicans and Democrats on energy transition policies in the U.S. are symptomatic of the broader polarization on issues in American politics (McCright et al. 2014; Shor and McCarty 2011). The causes of the polarization trend are complex, but there is arguably a connection with political economy in the sense of the concentration of wealth, the weakening of labor unions, and other dimensions of class conflict. The mobilization of wealthy conservatives and large corporations to build the institutional field to influence government as described above has led to an increasing rightward drift of the Republican Party and a drift in the political center to the right. In the case of environmental policy, one dimension of this institutional field, political spending by interest groups, clearly favors the fossil fuel sector. For example, whereas donations from the alternative energy sector favor Democrats slightly, the much higher level of donations from the oil and gas, coal, and utility industries strongly favored Republicans (Center for Responsive Politics 2015). Sociologists have also documented the flow of funding from conservative donors, of whom some have connections with the fossil fuel sector and conservative foundations (Brulle 2014). Furthermore, the American Legislative Exchange Council (2015), a conservative organization that supports the dismantling of REEE policies, has claimed support from more than one-fourth of all state legislators.

A political economy perspective based on class power and industrial influence provides a good explanatory framework for the general pattern of polarization that is evident in energy policy in the U.S. The perspective can also help to explain variation in the degree of support from Republicans for energy transition policies, such as the cases in which Republican governors have been relatively supportive of such policies. In addition to the case of Iowa, discussed above, a similar pattern of support for REEE policy occurred in California and New York, where former Republican Governors Schwarzenegger and Pataki were relatively supportive of REEE policy. The mobilization of regime resistance by industrial incumbents is likely to be particularly effective if the economy associated with the state government has strong fossil fuel resources and/or fossil fuel employment. Conversely, as the REEE sector grows and catalyzes a strong political constituency (e.g., farmers in Iowa or the clean technology sector in California), this constituency will tend to override the regime resistance of the fossil fuel sector and utilities. At the other extreme is Wyoming, a conservative state with a high level of fossil fuel employment. Neither the Democratic nor the Republican governor showed much support for wind energy, even though the state has significant wind energy resources and the capacity to export the energy to other states. Thus, there are variations in the mobilizing capacity of the industrial incumbents that affect the political opportunities for advocates of deepened energy transition policies. Various studies indicate that the endowment of fossil fuel resources is a predictor of policy support for REEE among state governments (e.g., Coley and Hess 2012, Vasseur 2014), and this factor also can explain some variation across countries (Hess and Mai 2014).

An additional perspective based on institutional and field theory can also bring out some complexities in the relationship between the Republican Party and support or opposition for REEE. Research that our group conducted on Republican-controlled legislatures indicates that there are some types of REEE policy that still garnered bipartisan support during this period (Hess et al. 2015, 2016a). Specifically, if the policies use instruments that are consistent with conservative values, they can gain support from conservative legislators. One example is support for building efficiency standards for government (not private-sector) buildings, a policy that can reduce government spending and inefficiency. An example from Table 20.2 is Tennessee's HB 2013, which supports energy efficiency measures in government buildings. In some cases Republican-controlled legislatures also provided support for solar and wind tax credits, a measure that benefits the private sector and also is consistent with conservative views that support tax reduction. However, in New Mexico the Republican governor vetoed a bill that would have extended solar tax credits, and in Tennessee the state government approved a law to increase solar and wind taxes. Thus, a solar tax credit is not a guarantee of bipartisan support, but it is one pathway to gaining support in some cases. Republican-controlled legislatures also supported legislation in support of property-assessed clean energy, or PACE, which allows businesses and homeowners to obtain financing for REEE improvements with support of funds from local bond initiatives. Although there are sometimes pockets of opposition to PACE laws, in general the laws are seen as market-enabling and therefore consistent with conservative philosophies of government (Hess et al. 2016a).

This approach is consistent with STS research on the politics of design, which draws attention to the political meanings of different types of design configurations of LTSs (Winner 1986, Hess 2016b). Applied to REEE politics, policy instruments that use mandates are the most likely to clash with conservative values and tend to be the ones that conservatives will try to roll back. Republican governors have also cut funding for programs that support REEE research and development, a policy move that is consistent with conservative opposition to government subsidies and to the problem of "picking winners and losers" that is associated with industrial policy. In contrast, more market-enabling policy instruments, such as tax credits and PACE laws, are less controversial.

Conclusion

There is great value in an approach to the political economy of science and technology that begins with structural inequality associated with class conflict and corporate power. We have indicated the importance of such classical political economy factors at play in the energy transition politics of the U.S. Wealthy donors and powerful corporations have formed an immensely influential political mobilization that has supported a fossil fuel regime as an important element of the broader neoliberalization of the political field. However, the political field has some degree of autonomy, and a classical political economy perspective anchored in social structure can be made more effective when used with insights from institutional and field theory. The interests of elites are translated and redefined as they are expressed in the political field, where distinctions among types of policies are important. These distinctions in turn depend on the systems of meaning that orient action in the field, specifically the clash between conservative and progressive ideologies. The partial autonomy of the political field from influence by powerful industrial firms and donors makes it possible for some forms of support for REEE to continue even in the context of roll-backs and mounting opposition. Thus, it is still possible to find some kinds of support for REEE policies from conservatives in a polarized political environment. The goal of regime resistance is refracted by the institutional logics of the political field, and differences among policy instruments can create opportunities for some bipartisan agreement.

The conflict between challengers and incumbents in an industrial field is primarily an institutional rather than social structural conflict. The challengers include coalitions of environmentalists, some labor unions, consumer groups, and other actors associated with social movements, but they also include entrepreneurs, venture capitalists, technology firms, and other segments of industry, some of which include representatives of powerful countervailing industrial firms (see chapters by Delfanti; Harrison et al.; Rossi, this volume, for a comparison with biotech). The case of energy transition policy conflicts therefore has broader implications for the study of the political economy of science and technology. We have shown that there is considerable value for a perspective on the political economy of science and technology that brings together conflicts of institutional and social structure by drawing on insights from institutional, field, and transition studies.

References

American Legislative Exchange Council. 2015. "Membership." www.alec.org/membership/.

Barley, Stephen. 2010. "Building an Institutional Field to Corral a Government: A Case to Set an Agenda for Organization Studies." *Organizational Studies* 31(6): 777–805.

Bourdieu, Pierre. 2001. *Science of Science and Reflexivity*. Chicago: University of Chicago Press.

Brulle, Robert. 2014. "Institutionalizing Delay: Foundation Founding and the Creation of U.S. Climate Change Counter-Movement Organization." *Climatic Change* 122: 681–694.

Carter, Neil and Ben Clements. 2015. "From 'Greenest Government Ever' to 'Get Rid of the All the Green Crap': David Cameron, the Conservatives, and the Environment." *British Politics* 10(2): 204–225.

Center for Responsive Politics. 2015. "Energy and Natural Resources." www.opensecrets.org/industries/indus.php?ind=E.

Coley, Jonathan and David Hess. 2012. "Green Energy Laws and Republican Legislators in the United States." *Energy Policy* 48(1): 576–583.

Dayton, Leigh. 2014. "Australian Budget Hits Science Jobs." *Nature*, July 1. www.nature.com/news/australian-budget-hits-science-jobs-1.15492.

Dunlap, Riley and Aaron McCright. 2015. "Challenging Climate Change: The Denial Movement." In Riley Dunlap and Robert Brulle (eds.), *Climate Change and Society: Sociological Perspectives*. New York: Oxford: 300–332.

Fligstein, Neil and Doug McAdam. 2012. *A Theory of Fields*. Oxford University Press.

Geels, Frank. 2011. "The Multilevel Perspective on Sustainability Transitions: Responses to Seven Criticisms." *Environmental Innovation and Societal Transitions* 1(1): 24–40.

Geels, Frank. 2014. "Regime Resistance against Low-carbon Energy Transitions: Introducing Politics and Power into the Multi-level Perspective." *Theory, Culture, and Society* 31(5): 21–40.

Geels, Frank and Johan Schot. 2007. "Typology of Sociotechnical Transition Pathways." *Research Policy* 36(3): 399–417.

Hess, David J. 2014. "Sustainability Transitions: A Political Coalition Perspective." *Research Policy* 43(2): 278–283.

Hess, David J. 2016a. "The Politics of Niche-Regime Conflicts: Distributed Solar Energy in the United States." *Environmental Innovation and Societal Transitions* 19: 42–50.

Hess, David J. 2016b. *Undone Science: Social Movements, Mobilized Publics, and Industrial Transitions*. Cambridge, MA: MIT Press.

Hess, David J. and Quan D. Mai. 2014. "Renewable Electricity Policy in Asia: A Qualitative Comparative Analysis of Factors Affecting Sustainability Transitions." *Environmental Innovation and Societal Transitions* 12: 31–46.

Hess, David J., David Banks, Bob Darrow, Joe Datko, Jaime D. Ewalt, Rebecca Gresh, Matthew Hoffmann, Anthony Sarkis, and Logan Williams. 2010. *Building Clean-Energy Industries and Green Jobs: Policy Innovations at the State and Local Government Level*. Troy, NY: Science and Technology Studies Department, Rensselaer Polytechnic Institute.

Hess, David J., Jonathan S. Coley, Quan D. Mai, and Lucas Hilliard. 2015. "Party Differences and Energy Reform: Fiscal Conservatism in the California Legislature." *Environmental Politics* 24(2): 228–248.

Hess, David J., Quan D. Mai, and Kate Pride Brown. 2016a. "Red States, Green Laws: Ideology and Renewable Energy Legislation in the United States." *Energy Research and Social Science* 11: 19–28.

Hess, David J., Sulfikar Amir, Scott Frickel, Daniel Lee Kleinman, Kelly Moore, and Logan Williams. 2016b. "Structural Inequality and the Politics of Science and Technology." In Rayvon Fouché, Clarke Miller, Laurel Smith-Doerr, and Ulrike Felte (eds.), *Handbook of Science and Technology Studies*. MIT Press: 319–347.

Hoppmann, Joern, Joern Huenteler, and Bastien Girod. 2014. "Compulsive Policy-Making: The Evolution of the German Feed-in Tariff System for Photovoltaic Power." *Research Policy* 43: 1422–1441.

Hughes, Thomas. 1983. *Networks of Power: Electrification in Western Society, 1880–1930*. Johns Hopkins University Press.

Hughes, Thomas. 1987. "The Evolution of Large Technological Systems." In Wiebe Bijker, Thomas Hughes, and Trevor Pinch (eds.), *The Social Construction of Technological Systems*. MIT Press: 51–82.

Kind, Peter. 2013. *Disruptive Challenges: Financial Implications and Strategic Responses to a Changing Retail Electric Business*. Washington, D.C.: Edison Electric Institute.

McCright, Aaron, Chenyang Xiao, and Riley Dunlap. 2014. "Political Polarization on Support for Government Spending on Environmental Protection in the USA, 1974–2012." *Social Science Research* 48 (Nov.): 251–260.

Morello, Lauren, Dina Fine Maron, Lisa Freidman, and Saqib Rahim. 2011. "Republicans Gut EPA Climate Rules, Slash Deeply into Climate Research, Aid and Technology Programs." *New York Times* (ClimateWire) Feb. 14: n.p. Retrieved Dec. 30, 2013 (www.nytimes.com/cwire/2011/02/14/14climatewire-republicans-gut-epa-climate-rules-slash-deep-87716.html?pagewanted=all).

Ogden, Leslie. 2015. "Feeling Ignored by Government, Canadian Academics Offer their Own Climate Policy." *Science*, March 18.

Powell, Walter and Paul DiMaggio, eds. 1991. *The New Institutionalism in Organizational Analysis*. Chicago: University of Chicago Press.

Shor, Boris and Nolan McCarty. 2011. "The Ideological Mapping of American Legislatures." *American Political Science Review* 105(3): 530–551.

Tranter, Bruce, and Kate Booth. 2015. "Skepticism in a Changing Climate: A Cross-National Study." *Global Environmental Change* 33: 154–164.

United Nations. 2015. "INDCs as Communicated by Parties." www4.unfccc.int/submissions/indc/Submission%20Pages/submissions.aspx.

U.S. House of Representatives. 2011. "Discretionary Spending Recommendations Offered by the Following Members of the House Committee on Science, Space, and Technology: Rep. RalphM. Hall, Rep. F. James Sensenbrenner, Rep. Lamar Smith, Rep. Judy Biggert, Rep. W. Todd Akin, Rep. Michael McCaul, Rep. Steven Palazzo, Rep. Andy Harris, and Rep. Randy Hultgren." October 14.

Retrieved Dec. 30, 2013 (http://science.house.gov/sites/republicans.science.house.gov/files/Letter_to_Joint_Select_Committee.pdf).

Vasseur, Michael. 2014. "Convergence and Divergence in Renewable Energy Policy in U.S. States from 1998 to 2011." *Social Forces* 92(4): 1637–1657.

Winner, Langdon. 1986. *The Whale and the Reactor: A Search for Limits in an Age of High Technology.* Chicago: University of Chicago Press.

Young, Nathan and Aline Coutinho. 2013. "Government, Anti-Reflexivity, and the Construction of Public Ignorance about Climate Change: Australia and Canada Compared." *Global Environmental Politics* 13(2): 89–108.

21

SYNTHETIC BIOLOGY

A political economy of molecular futures

Jairus Rossi

Introduction

In August of 2015, Intrexon, a synthetic biology firm, acquired Oxitec for $160 million for its genetically modified (GM) male *Aedes aegypti* mosquitos (Intrexon 2015). These mosquitos were engineered to pass a sterility gene on to their offspring. Earlier that year, Oxitec initiated field trials in Piracicaba, Brazil, which successfully reduced the population of this dengue and Zika vector by 80 percent (Pollack 2016). Prior to this acquisition, Intrexon's share price had been dropping precipitously due to its lack of tangible revenue-generating products. Following the recent outbreak of the Zika virus, however, investors have regained interest in Intrexon (Williams 2016). Oxitec has expanded its GM mosquito production facilities in Brazil in response. If successful, Oxitec's mosquito might prove to investors that biotechnology can finally produce viable, valuable commodities (Pollack 2016). Similarly, by potentially stemming an epidemic, Intrexon might give a skeptical global public evidence that genetically modified organisms are not monstrous, and instead have a social and ecological value. In this way, synthetic biology offers to make good on unfulfilled promises of the previous generation of genetic technology to produce valuable innovations.

Synthetic biology (synbio) centers on the design of organic machines by editing their genomes using techniques drawn from electrical engineering and computer science (Calvert 2010; Endy 2005; Rossi 2013). Synbio allows biologists to streamline biological functioning in organisms, genomes, and other organic systems by treating DNA as programmable information. This differs from previous-generation recombinant DNA technologies, which rely on inserting already-existing genes from one species to another. By designing and producing custom gene sequences, instead of harvesting them from existing organisms, synthetic biologists break down barriers to commodification that inhibited the commercial viability of previous generation (i.e. recombinant) genetic technologies (Church et al. 2014). These barriers include the unpredictable functioning of genes in different cellular contexts, scalar inefficiencies in research, and general public resistance to transgenics.

While synbio represents the novel convergence of digital and genetic technologies, synbio firms still draw from resources and technological advances made available by recombinant DNA firms. For instance, Intrexon's AquaBounty Technologies uses recombinant DNA technology to insert two genes from different species into a Chinook salmon to create a rapidly growing commodity (US FDA 2015). This GM salmon was approved by the FDA for human consumption despite vehement protests from many environmental groups and promises by major grocery chains to not sell this product (Dennis 2015).

Intrexon's acquisition of Oxitec and AquaBounty – small firms which produce innovative diverse consumer-oriented products – represents both a transformation and continuation of the biotech industry in terms of its application of technology as well as its product development and investment approaches. In this chapter, I detail four general themes emerging in the current political economic landscape of synbio as a result of this transformation.

First, synbio differs from previous generation biotechnologies through its attempts to control and simplify biological systems using emerging gene editing and cellular engineering technologies. Synbio firms promise precision that allows engineered products to be free from the functional quirks and limits of biology – a hyperbolic aim of the recombinant era (see Cooper 2008; Rajan 2006). In other words, product development is streamlined and more radically open to the imagination. Additionally, with more precise biological design, firms characterize synbio products as less risky and more environmentally friendly than recombinant products (Rossi 2013; Zhang 2015c). This positioning is crucial toward generating investor interest and public acceptance.

Second, despite the radical technological differences between synbio and recombinant DNA in terms of how the former embraces engineering and information technologies, synbio firms still draw from many intellectual, technical, informational, and material resources developed from previous-generation recombinant technologies.

Third, its political economy is highly inclusive. This inclusivity is driven by biotech firms' experience with commercially unsuccessful ventures of the recombinant DNA era as well as the flexibility of synbio technologies. Firms have attracted investment from large government entities, major oil companies, military interests, internet firms, architects, agricultural biotech giants, large medical companies, venture capitalists, and crowd-sourced collectives (Burgess 2015a; Estes 2015; Fairs 2013; Kuiken 2015). Consequently, synbio firms' choices regarding what innovations to pursue are not restricted or determined by narrow funding regimes. Synbio's technological flexibility allows firms to rapidly shift the focus of their product development. The industry, then, is rather decentralized in terms of firm ownership and the types of innovations firms pursue.

Finally, synbio promises commercial viability due to demonstrated speed and scale efficiencies gained by (1) technological advances that streamline organismal and genetic functioning, (2) scaling down, digitizing, and automating moments in genome design, construction, and analysis, (3) accessing genetic resources compiled and characterized during the recombinant era (1980s to early 2000s), and (4) emphasizing open-source sharing of genetic resources.

Continuities between synbio and recombinant approaches

Despite widespread hopes to produce novel pharmaceuticals, biofuels, and medical innovations, recombinant molecular technologies are limited by their source materials. AquaBounty's GM salmon aside, innovations and commodities have been slow to develop since a geneticist must first collect and characterize genes from existing organisms before determining genes' possible uses. This search for useful gene sequences produced an extensive bioeconomy based on the compilation of biodiversity and the selling of firm potential (Cooper 2008; Hayden 2003; Parry 2004; Rajan 2006). In the 1980s and 1990s, firms and research institutions initiated massive speculation efforts which produced large collections of vegetal, animal, fungal, and microbial biodiversity.

Molecular biologists, plant chemists, and other scientists extracted genetic material from these collected organisms and analyzed these materials for bioactivity and potential function (Hayden 2003; Parry 2004). Only once a gene's functions were defined could a biotech firm or research group determine if and where this gene might have a potential application. Yet, even when characterized and annotated, genes' functions are highly contextual. DNA expression is shaped by poorly understood epigenetic, cellular, and environmental factors that differ between individuals and species (Jablonka and Lamb 2002; Stallins 2011).

Due to these complexities, recombinant genetic technologies trace a jumbled path from idea to market. Innovations are based on and thus limited by the material particularities of collected and characterized molecules. This limits what problems are eligible for molecular solutions. Many biotech companies also focused on innovation in profitable, but highly regulated industries such as energy and pharmaceuticals. These industries have a very long gap between product development and commercial application. As such, the recombinant biotech economy produced few viable commodities (Firn 2003; Li and Vederas 2009). Firms were instead valued for their ability to distill, translate, compile, and transmit genetic information. Some firms achieved market prominence by patenting genetic sequences and then leasing the information to other firms. Others became valuable for sifting through this large amount of data to provide a narrower set of molecules with which to experiment. The firms purchasing these molecules and their information then gained market value by selling a vision that future advances would address industrial society's biggest issues (Parry 2004; Rajan 2006; also see Harrison et al., this volume).

Synbio as a response to commercial failings of recombinant technologies

Synthetic biology firms seek to remedy the commercial shortcomings of the recombinant era through more efficient genetic modification technology. Instead of relying on genetic information and material from currently existing organisms, synthetic biology is centered on writing, editing, designing, and producing customized organisms (Arkin 2008; Calvert, 2010; Collins 2012; Keller, 2009). At the same time, the synthetic bioeconomy retains many connections with the intense endeavors of collection, sequencing, and characterization of molecules from global biodiversity in the 1980s and 90s. For instance, while synthetic biology is premised on the *de novo* creation of gene sequences and cell lines, firms will still create and mine sequence archives for new molecule ideas (Kim et al. 2015; Rusch et al. 2007).

In endeavors such as the Minimal Genome Project (Glass et al. 2006; Schwille and Diez 2009) and the BioBricks (Mooallem 2010),[1] synthetic biologists identify already existing organismal assemblages that can serve as the potential building blocks for new synthetic systems. Additionally, many synbio firms are designing interventions into extant organisms, such as gene-editing based therapies for human cancers (see Begley 2015; Kalos and June 2013). To understand how the synthetic objects/organisms of these interventions will interact with systems, bodies, and environments, scientists draw from efforts to characterize molecular pathways in different organisms. So, while synbio is hyped as a radical break from traditional genetic approaches, gene sequence archives are used as templates for cell and genome design.

Firms which have attained huge stores of biodiversity over the past 30 years can still bend these resources to the purposes of synthetic biology. For instance, J. Craig Venter, an early visionary for genome sequencing (Parry 2004) and synbio (Rose 2007), has long sought ways to compile, control, and derive value from genetic resources by extracting and patenting gene sequences from (1) oceanic microbe genomes collected in international waters (Rusch et al. 2007), (2) humans during the Human Genome Project (HGP) in the 1990s, and (3) diverse biological materials collected by the National Cancer Institute (Rajan 2006).

Drawing from these pre-synbio efforts, Venter's various research institutions and companies have developed extensive material resources and technological innovations. These resources enable a variety of research endeavors in synbio. For instance, the J. Craig Venter Institute (JCVI)[2] initiates primary research on medical, energy, and agricultural applications of synbio while also developing new analytic methods and studying the policy/regulatory environment of this new technology. JCVI's research is spun off into for-profit companies. Synthetic Genomics, Inc.[3] is developing synthetic biofuels, while Human Longevity, Inc.[4] attempts to extend human life and develop novel cancer therapies. Venter also formed Agradis, a plant genomics company that was subsequently acquired by Monsanto (SGI 2015a), and Human Genome Science, a drug development company purchased by GlaxoSmithKline (GSK 2012). Venter's diversification strategy reflects a broader approach by synbio entrepreneurs to create relationships with large multinational corporations, tying primary research labs to narrowly targeted commercial startups, and creating larger firms that investigate diverse applications of synbio.

Harvard geneticist George Church has an even longer history in genetic technology and its commercialization. Church was part of a research team that developed the technique of multiplexing – sequencing large amounts of genetic data quickly (Church 1984). By reducing the time and cost of sequencing, his efforts facilitated the collection, extraction, and compilation of numerous gene sequences – and by extension, the recombinant bioeconomy in the 1980s and 1990s. This expertise was carried forward into synbio by developing new analytic techniques and by co-founding a number of synbio firms. He has co-founded Editas, which offers gene editing services (Temple 2016), Joule, a biofuel company (*The Economist* 2014), and Gen9, which produces raw base pairs for other synbio firms (Matheson 2015). In contrast to Venter, Church is a strong proponent of open access to genetic information (Temple 2016).

The key thing to note here is that the main trends in the political economy of synbio are conditioned by many actors' experience with promises and shortcomings of the recombinant era. The commercialization of synbio thus relies on the following trends: (1) managing biological contingencies through technological interventions, (2) product diversification through technological pluripotency and firm decentralization, and (3) creating scale and speed efficiencies. I examine these trends and detail particular firms' contributions to each.

Decreasing contingency in biological function

Synbio is premised on reducing or removing the messy contingencies of interactions between organisms, their DNA, and complex environments (Calvert 2010; Keller 2009). Instead of working with the genomes and bodies provided by existing organisms, synthetic biologists are able to design novel genetic constructs on a computer and then print out the material version of this code (SGI-DNA 2016). Other firms produce customized cell bodies to directly express this code into proteins in a desired format (Collins 2012). Additionally, biologists can now insert designed sequences into any existing organism using the revolutionary CRISPR-Cas technology – a protein/promoter combination that can target any site on a genome (Burgess 2015b). Through these technologies, synbio allows researchers to start from a particular problem and then design a synthetic organism or organic machine to address this problem.

For example, in June of 2015 a child in London was treated for leukemia using a gene editing tool called TALEN (LePage 2015). This approach makes two edits in the genes of a healthy T-cell – one to insert a synthetic gene for a receptor that finds and destroys cells with a protein specific to the cancer and a second to make sure the host's immune system does not attack the edited T-cell. Conceivably, synthetic biologists could design and insert any sequence into a human cell that would recognize other types of cancer. Or they could replace illness-causing mutations in any part of the genome, thereby streamlining organismal functioning.

Custom code, however, will only work if its conditions of expression are controlled. Synthetic biologists have made advances in identifying and producing custom cells that predictably express synthetic DNA sequences (Calvert 2010). While scientists using recombinant technologies have relatively controlled cell lines, yeast, and bacterial models, these models still have idiosyncratic interactions with inserted DNA sequences. Synbio's aim is to design synthetic cells that further reduce this complexity (Benner and Sismour 2005).

Synbio, then, is unique in that both the genetic software and cellular hardware are modified or created *de novo* in order to create biological production systems conducive to digital design. The reduction of biological complexity allows the synbio industry to more tightly harmonize with computer/engineering approaches (Rossi 2013). This goal of writing genetic code as if it were computer code has attracted big investments from individuals associated with Google, Microsoft, Facebook, and Paypal (Burgess 2015a; Hayden 2015). I detail how contingency is managed by different biotech firms to generate scalar efficiencies in the production of commercial products.

Managing genetic contingencies

Gene editing firms have emerged to serve as the technical base for more efficient design of synthetic genomes and organisms. The two most prominent firms are CRISPR Therapeutics and Editas. CRISPR Therapeutics was co-founded by Emmanuelle Charpentier while Editas was created by Jennifer Doudna and Feng Zhang – each a member of the research team that originally developed this technology (see Doudna and Charpentier 2014). Both have received sizable investments and partnerships (Pollack 2015). Bayer purchased a majority stake in CRISPR Therapeutics for $35 million and has promised $300m for developing medical treatments (Ramsey 2015). Editas received $120m in 2015 from investors including the Gates Foundation, Google, and various venture capital firms (Chen 2015). Editing startups Caribou and Intellia were also recently created to take advantage of this technology's pluripotency (Guo 2015). Other firms such as Intrexon, Zymergen, and Synthetic Genomics offer big data approaches to sequencing, designing, synthesizing, and analyzing genetic data. This includes Zymergen's attempts to develop a programming language for DNA design, supported by $44m in investments from infotech companies (Konrad 2015).

Other companies draw from gene editing companies' advances to design and produce customized organisms and gene sequences. For instance, Ginkgo Bioworks advertises a gene/cell editing 'foundry' that can produce organismal products with attributes specified by a client.[5] Ginkgo currently focuses on fermenting synthetic versions of natural products such as perfumes, flavors, sweeteners, and cosmetics. By developing quickly commodifiable consumer products, Ginkgo is building the technological and financial resources for use in longer-term product development in the health and energy sectors (Jacobs 2015b). Originally founded with funding from DARPA to develop probiotics for soldiers (Stinson 2015), Ginkgo is also designing carbon-capture organisms and microbes that attack antibiotic resistant bacteria (Jacobs 2015b).

Ginkgo is an important example to consider for many reasons. First, they received $54 million in funding from diverse sources, including DARPA and investors associated with Facebook. They also have been seeded with venture capital from Y-Combinator (and Viking Global), which has focused many of its investments in internet companies such as Airbnb, Reddit, and Dropbox (Jacobs 2015b; Stinson 2015; Zhang 2015b). Ginkgo thus illustrates the convergence of digital and biological technologies in both funding and application.

Second, Ginkgo's co-founder Tom Knight began his career as an engineer and computer scientist, worked on the development of ARPANET, and eventually explored molecular approaches to computing issues. In the process, he began modifying biological systems to mimic circuit boards, stripping down and simplifying molecular interactions (Bluestein 2012). This research became the foundation for BioBricks – standardized biological parts which are common in and crucial to synbio research. Often compared to Legos, BioBricks can be assembled in a predictable manner by individuals of diverse skill sets. BioBrick designs are housed in an open source repository – the 'Registry of Standard Biological Parts'.[6] This Registry is designed to build a common functional vocabulary for synbio that makes biology more predictable and streamlined (Rossi 2013).

Finally, Ginkgo has recently purchased 100 million base pairs of DNA from Twist Bioscience. This transaction is the largest single purchase of synthetic DNA. To fulfill this obligation, Twist and Ginkgo raised $100 million to scale up base pair production (Graham 2015; Segran 2015). While Twist is one of the few companies, along with Gen9, to produce the raw materials for the synthetic construction of genomes (Matheson 2015), Ginkgo's purchase from Twist indicates that the technological barriers to producing DNA at an economically viable level are quickly falling. At a threshold of 10 cents per base pair, diversely scaled genome synthesis and editing companies will be able to participate in product development (Leproust 2015).

While synbio firms manage genetic contingency by editing and streamlining genes and genomes, many firms are also attempting to produce fully synthetic cell lines that express synthetic genes in a predictable manner. In other words, synthetic biologists consider genomes and organisms together when designing products and interventions. At this point, however, firms still draw from recombinant DNA techniques to modify existing cell types within which they then insert synthetic genetic material. Again, synbio maintains distinct connections with the previous era of biotechnology.

Synthetic Genomics Inc. (SGI) – developed to commercialize Venter's many research endeavors – is an important example of this synergy (SGI 2015b). SGI also promotes its cell engineering capacities based on the success of Venter's separate research institution in developing the first fully synthetic cell in 2010. Researchers designed a genome on a computer containing the most basic functions required for a self-replicating organism, printed this code out via synthetic molecules, and then inserted it into a fully synthetic cell designed to mimic a yeast cell (Gibson et al. 2010). Caribou Biosciences offer similar cell engineering services as SGI.[7] In general, however, fully synthetic cells and organisms (i.e. with no existing organismal analog) have yet to be rolled out commercially.

Synbio's pluripotency encourages firm diversity and decentralization

The development of CRISPR-Cas and other gene editing tools has opened up biology to radical rearrangements and creations. Synbio is pluripotent – it can be advanced to address diverse challenges. Like the recombinant era, synbio promised innovations that address high priority global issues. Some firms attempt to address climate change and the energy crisis through synthetic microbes which would capture atmospheric carbon and convert it to a usable biofuel (Estes 2015; Georgianna and Mayfield 2012; Robertson et al. 2011). Researchers are also tackling pressing medical issues such as cancer (Chen et al. 2012; Kalos and June 2013) and developing strategies to increase agricultural productivity (Ort et al. 2015; Harrison et al., this volume). Others see possibilities for synthetic organisms to remediate industrial/nuclear pollution (Fairs 2013), enhance the gut microbiome (Church et al. 2014), develop quasi-living building materials and textiles (Armstrong 2012; Jacobs 2015a), produce animal meat from plants (Estes 2015), and eradicate disease-carrying vectors in bodies and ecosystems (Gantz et al. 2015). Some even suggest addressing challenges of space travel and the terraforming of uninhabited planets (Menezes et al. 2015).

Synbio's pluripotency, then, has captured the imagination and money of diverse investors from energy, agriculture, military, information technology, and medical industries. While many firms and startups are involved in biofuel development and pharmaceutical/medical technologies, some have recognized that these longer-term goals must be augmented by quicker marketable innovations in areas with a broader consumer base, such as food, textiles, and consumer products (Hayden 2015). Additionally, larger firms tend to purchase promising start-ups to build their portfolios even as these startups often (but not always) have very specific aims (Burgess 2015a; Zhang 2015a).

Gene editing technologies allow firms to diversify aims

Caribou Biosciences is one firm that applies CRISPR-Cas technology to diverse ends. Infused with $11.5 million in 2015 from Novartis and two venture capitalists, Caribou aims to develop anti-microbial therapies using gene editing techniques (Caribou 2015; Estes 2015; Novartis 2015). Additionally, they formed a strategic agreement with DuPont to develop beneficial modifications in selected row crops (DuPont 2015). This multiplex approach to product development is common in synbio firms since gene editing technologies are less limited by species boundaries than recombinant techniques.

Intrexon is a more prominent example of how firms diversify their approaches. As mentioned, Intrexon's acquisitions of Oxitec and AquaBounty were part of a broader strategy to have commercial research interests in all major sectors. In terms of agriculture, Intrexon owns Okanagan Specialty Fruits, a company that developed a GM apple that does not turn brown and Trans Ova Genetics, a subsidiary focused on bovine reproduction. Additionally, Intrexon's in-house labs experiment with various organisms that circumvent disease resistance, increase yields in commercial crops, produce biofuels, remediate polluted environments, and create plastic substitutes.[8]

Intrexon also has a health division that designs a wide range of interventions into gut health, fertility, diabetes, auto-immune conditions, and cancers. This range of potential products partially explains why Intrexon reached a near-$6 billion market cap in mid-2015 (Chatsko 2015) and has accumulated over $300 million in investments over the past ten years (Estes 2015). Yet as mentioned in the introduction, Intrexon's market cap is volatile, dropping rapidly to $3 billion in 2015 and then partially recovering on Oxitec's GM mosquito solution to Zika. This volatility indicates that synbio companies, like their recombinant progenitors, are subject to a gap between expectation and realization of their technical capabilities.

Agricultural and natural product substitutes

Other firms have narrower objectives such as producing consumer products that substitute traditional natural resources (petroleum, timber, etc.) with synthetically produced items. By appealing to sustainability, these firms discursively rebrand synbio as a potential protector or producer of biodiversity (Fairs 2013). By actively counteracting negative associations with GMOs (Zhang 2015c), synbio firms attempt to make their products palatable to or desired by a skeptical public.

One branch of recent start-up interest involves the 'post-animal bioeconomy' – creating animal products from microbe- or plant-based sources (Estes 2015). Beyond Meat and Impossible Foods grow meat and cheese proteins using plants, while Clara Foods, Muufri, and Modern Meadow use microbes to create milk, eggs, and other animal products. These ventures are attracting a lot of interest. Beyond Meat and Modern Meadow have received investments of $17 million and $11 million. Impossible Foods raised $183 million in two years from UBS, Viking Global, Bill Gates, and the Hong Kong-based Horizons Ventures (Burgess 2015a; Loizos 2015). Google also attempted to buy Impossible Foods for $250 million in the summer of 2015 as part of their restructuring as Google Alphabet (Burgess 2015a).

In addition to these interventions, conventional agriculture biotech corporations are developing synbio capacity through acquisitions and collaborations. Collaborations between Novozymes and Monsanto (Novozymes 2016), as well as Syngenta and DSM (Syngenta 2015), are aimed at producing unique microbial products that aid in pest control and soil fertility. Monsanto has also acquired Agradis, Craig Venter's SGI subsidiary, which engineers microbial approaches to crop productivity (SGI 2015a).

The continued lure of biofuels

Synbio firms are still seeking to develop a competitive fossil fuel alternative, since the ramifications (and profits) would be incredible. Synthetic oils could replace fossil fuel-based consumer products and provide a mechanism for adapting to or slowing climate change (Georgianna and Mayfield 2012; Ort et al. 2015; Robertson et al. 2011). Joule Unlimited has received $190 million in investments to create a biofuel/carbon capture microbe. They expect this process to become commercially viable before 2020 (Lane 2015) by producing fuel at a cost of $50 per barrel. Ginkgo and SGI both have a long-term objective to produce a similar microbe that produces both food and biofuels (Jacobs 2015b; Venter 2013), although Exxon's $100 million investment into SGI's innovation in 2009 was deemed a commercial failure (Herndon 2013).

Despite this failure, firms such as SGI and Ginkgo both offset the risks and difficulties of competing with fossil fuels in the energy sector by developing niche consumer products (Hayden 2015; Jacobs 2015b; Zhang 2015b). Conversely, firms with a narrow focus on developing fuel substitutes to compete with conventional fuels have experienced numerous issues. TerraVia (formerly Solazyme), Gevo, and Amyris – all publicly-traded synthetic biofuel companies – have encountered rapid drops in value over the past three years (Grushkin 2012; Nanalyze 2015; Wesoff 2015). While Solazyme has garnered over $145m in investments from Chevron, Morgan Stanley, and others since 2010 (Schrek 2008; Solazyme 2010), its stock price has dropped from $25 to around $2 since its IPO (Lane 2014). As a response, Solazyme rebranded as TerraVia. It now produces algae-based oil for food and cosmetic products. Like Solazyme, Amyris has placed biofuel development in the background. Its focus is to develop anti-malarial drugs using $417m in funding from the Gates Foundation and others (Grushkin 2012).

Despite these difficulties, many companies still invest in microbial biofuel startups. Investors representing BP and Sime Darby Berhad – a Malaysian conglomerate – have infused Verdezyne with over $48m for research into petroleum replacements (Verdezyne 2014). Similarly, Cargill, Shell, and Honda are part of a suite of investors contributing to Virent Energy Systems (Content 2010). The persistence of companies pursuing bio-based fossil fuel replacements – despite the mixed history of success – indicates that the potential windfall awaiting innovations that solve some of the world's largest crises without disrupting the fundamental basis of the global economic system.

Conclusion: scalar efficiencies and crowd sourcing

While few synthetic products have become commercially viable, the emergence of gene editing technologies has allowed biologists to streamline their design approach – simplifying the functioning of invented biological systems (Canton et al. 2008). Gene editing, DNA synthesis, and genomic analysis advances are reaching a point where synbio firms' products can compete with those of other origins. I conclude with a few thoughts on how synbio is achieving critical thresholds in analytic speed through a few sociotechnical strategies. These temporal and scalar efficiencies are crucial to realizing the unfulfilled promises of the recombinant era.

First, as discussed, researchers streamline complex information–organism–environment relationships using gene editing and cell modification techniques. Biological systems can be assembled through standardized biological parts and devices, and by quickly accessing archives of previously characterized gene sequences (ibid.). Second, the U.S. Supreme Court has made already-existing DNA sequences ineligible for patents, a condition that creates a broadly accessible pool of public-domain gene sequences (Rossi 2013). Additionally, many synbio companies advocate the free sharing of basic information (Galdzicki et al. 2104; Delfanti, this volume). These trends encourage the creation of more complex downstream gene sequences and/or organisms which are still eligible for IP protection.

Third, genomic sequencing and synthesis technologies are rapidly improving. Twist Bioscience and Gen[9] have developed nanowell-based gene synthesis processes that can produce 10,000 different genes on one small silicon plate. Previous synthesis technologies produced one gene per similar size plate with significantly more material and labor (Matheson 2015; Zhang 2015d). Automation and the scaling down of material needs will allow base pair production to drop below ten cents/pair. These synthesis efficiencies will facilitate the scaling-up of product design and production for firms large and small (Leproust 2015). Fourth, digital modeling and data mining technologies allow for researchers to rapidly experiment with and design novel sequences *in silica* and *in vitro*. Researchers can quickly sift through large sequence databases produced and collected over the past 25 years (Church et al. 2014; Kim et al. 2015).

Finally, as synthesis and analysis technologies drop in price, barriers to entering the synbio industry will drop. These efficiencies are already producing a decentralized geography of firms and research institutions with many startups rapidly emerging (Hayden 2015). Investors need only a few million dollars in startup money to create a potentially profitable item or service. Additionally, the open source ethic of synbio has led to an annual design competition, the Registry of Standard Biological Parts, and the Synbio4all9 initiative, all of which provide social networks for identifying genetic resources, lab procedures, and potential collaboration efforts (Suresh 2014). Others are involved in crowd-funding different projects such as the fungal remediation of plastic waste through platforms such as Kickstarter or Experiment[10] (Landrain et al. 2013). DIY biohacking communities are emerging, which involve amateur scientists using and sharing cheap synbio kits to explore new ideas and genetic modifications (Ledford 2015).

Synbio, then, is a powerful approach that is becoming widely accessible (economically and technically) to both experts and amateurs. As knowledge production is distributed widely, tangible applications are likely to come from groups with diverse sources and motivations. Innovations with commercial promise will likely garner funding from larger firms and startups. Additionally, as a nascent technology, synbio is relatively unregulated. As such, it is crucial for scholars, activists, and citizens to continue to understand the relationships among different actors, groups, and their proposed innovations.

Synbio has ramped up in terms of funding and potential in 2015 ($560 million in investments), especially with breakthroughs in gene editing technologies (Zhang 2015b). While the current political economic landscape is dominated by a few large firms, many startups, and connections with research labs and larger multinationals, we may see a rapid rearrangement of these relationships in the next five years as products become viable and as regulation catches up with the technology. Industry analysts predict that the global synbio industry will grow to $13.4 billion by 2019 as its methods and aims evolve (*Industry Today* 2015). What will emerge from these efforts is unclear, but will undoubtedly have tremendous impacts on how we understand and interact with biological systems.

Notes

1 BioBricks are characterized at partsregistry.org – an open-source website for facilitating DIY synbio.
2 http://jcvi.org/cms/home/.
3 www.syntheticgenomics.com/.
4 www.humanlongevity.com/.
5 http://ginkgobioworks.com/foundry/.
6 http://parts.igem.org/Catalog.
7 cariboubio.com/application-areas/biological-research.
8 http://intrexon.com/Markets.
9 Synbio4all.com.
10 https://experiment.com/projects/can-we-use-fungi-to-break-down-our-plastic-and-rubber-waste.

References

Arkin, A. (2008). "Setting the standard in synthetic biology." *Nature Biotechnology* 26, 771–774.
Armstrong, R. (2012). *Living architecture: How synthetic biology can remake our cities and reshape our lives.* TED books.
Begley, S. (2015). "Medical First: Gene-Editing Tool Used to Treat Girl's Cancer." *Stat.* November 4. www.statnews.com/2015/11/05/doctors-report-first-use-gene-editing-technology-patient/. Accessed January 25, 2016.
Bluestein, A. (2015). "Tom Knight, Godfather of Synthetic Biology, On How to Learn Something New." *Fast Company.* August 28. www.fastcompany.com/3000760/tom-knight-godfather-synthetic-biology-how-learn-something-new. Accessed January 24, 2016.
Benner, S. A. and Sismour, A. M. (2005). 'Synthetic biology.' *Nature Reviews Genetics*, 6(7), 533–543.
Burgess, S. (2015a). "Synbio is Booming." *Plos Synbio.* December 28. blogs.plos.org/synbio/2015/12/28/synbio-is-booming/. Accessed January 21, 2016.
Burgess, S. (2015b). "The gene editing tsunami." *Plos Synbio.* December 15. blogs.plos.org/synbio/2015/12/15/the-gene-editing-tsunami-and-the-10-synbio-highlights-of-2015/. Accessed January 21, 2016.
Calvert, J. (2010). "Synthetic biology: constructing nature?" *The Sociological Review* 58(S1): 95–112.
Canton, B., Labno, A., and Endy, D. (2008). "Refinement and standardization of synthetic biological parts and devices." *Nature Biotechnology* 26(7): 787–793.
Caribou Biosciences, Inc. (2015). *SEC Filing - Form D.* March, 24. www.sec.gov/edgar.shtml.
Chatsko, M. (2015). "Why Intrexon Corp. Soared Past a $6 Billion Market Cap Today." *The Motley Fool.* July 28. www.fool.com/investing/general/2015/07/28/timesensitive-why-intrexon-corp-soared-past-a-6-bi.aspx. Accessed January 21, 2016.
Chen, Y.Y., Galloway, K.E., and Smolke, C.D. (2012). "Synthetic biology: advancing biological frontiers by building synthetic systems." *Genome Biol* 13(2): 240.
Chen, C. (2015). "Gates, Google Join $120 Million Funding for Genome Editing Firm." *Bloomberg.* August 10. http://www.bloomberg.com/news/articles/2015-08-10/gates-google-join-120-million-funding-for-genome-editing-firm. Accessed January 26, 2016.
Church, G.M. and Gilbert, W. (1984). "Genomic sequencing." *Proceedings of the National Academy of Sciences of the United States of America* 81(7): 1991–1995.
Church, G.M., Elowitz, M.B., Smolke, C.D., Voigt, C.A., and Weiss, R. (2014). "Realizing the potential of synthetic biology." *Nature Reviews Molecular Cell Biology* 15(4): 289–294.
Collins, J. (2012) "Synthetic biology: bits and pieces come to life." *Nature* 483: S8–S10.
Content, T. (2010). "Virent secures funding from Shell, Cargill, Honda." *Milwaukee Journal Sentinel.* June 8.
Cooper, M. (2008). *Life as Surplus: Biotechnology and Capitalism in the Neoliberal Era* University of Washington Press, Seattle, WA.
Dennis, B. (2015). "The FDA just approved the nation's first genetically engineered animal: A salmon that grows twice as fast." *The Washington Post.* November 19.
Doudna, J. A. and Charpentier, E. (2014). "The new frontier of genome engineering with CRISPR-Cas9." *Science* 346(6213): 1258096.

DuPont. (2015). "DuPont and Caribou Biosciences announce strategic alliance." News release, October 9. www.agprofessional.com/news/dupont-and-caribou-biosciences-announce-strategic-alliance. Accessed January 21, 2016.

The Economist (2014). "Welcome to My Genome." *The Economist.* September 6.

Endy, D. (2005). "Foundations for engineering biology." *Nature* 438: 449–453.

Estes, V. (2015). "Innovation to Tackle Climate Change and Feed a Growing Population: Commercializing Synthetic Biology." *Biofuels Digest.* December 1.

Fairs, M. (2013). "Synthetic Creatures Could 'Save Nature' Says Alexandria Daisy Ginsberg." *Dezeen Magazine.* November 13. www.dezeen.com/2013/11/13/synthetic-creatures-could-save-nature-says-alexandria-daisy-ginsberg/. Accessed January 21, 2016.

Firn, R.D. (2003). "Bioprospecting—why is it so unrewarding?" *Biodiversity and Conservation* 12: 207–216.

Galdzicki, M., Clancy, K.P., ... and Bartley, B.A. (2014). "The Synthetic Biology Open Language (SBOL) provides a community standard for communicating designs in synthetic biology." *Nature biotechnology* 32(6): 545–550.

Gantz, V.M., Jasinskiene, N., ... and James, A.A. (2015). "Highly efficient Cas9-mediated gene drive for population modification of the malaria vector mosquito Anopheles stephensi." *Proceedings of the National Academy of Sciences* 112(49): E6736–E6743.

Georgianna, D.R. and Mayfield, S.P. (2012). "Exploiting diversity and synthetic biology for the production of algal biofuels." *Nature* 488(7411): 329–335.

Gibson, D., Glass, J., Lartigue, C., ... and Venter, J.C. (2010). "Creation of a bacterial cell controlled by a chemically synthesized genome." *Science* 329(5987): 52–56.

Glass, J.I., Assad-Garcia, N., Alperovich, N., Yooseph, S., Lewis, M.R., Maruf, M., ... and Venter, J.C. (2006). "Essential genes of a minimal bacterium." *Proceedings of the National Academy of Sciences of the United States of America* 103(2): 425–430.

GlaxoSmithKline. (2012). "GSK to Acquire Human Genome Sciences for US$14.25 per Share in Cash." News release. July 16. www.gsk.com/en-gb/media/press-releases/2012/gsk-to-acquire-human-genome-sciences-for-us-1425-per-share-in-cash/. Accessed January 24, 2016.

Graham, J. (2015). "Ginkgo's DNA order spirals." *Boston Herald.* November 8.

Grushkin, D. (2012). "The Rise and Fall of the Company That Was Going to Have Us All Using Biofuels." *Fast Company.* August 8. www.fastcompany.com/3000040/rise-and-fall-company-was-going-have-us-all-using-biofuels. Accessed January 26, 2016.

Guo, N. (2015). "CRISPR – The Future of Synthetic Biology." *Lux Capital.* July 7. www.luxcapital.com/blog/crispr/. Accessed January 26, 2016.

Hayden, C. (2003) *When Nature Goes Public. The Making and Unmaking of Bioprospecting in Mexico.* Princeton University Press, Princeton, NJ.

Hayden, E. (2015). "Synthetic biology lures Silicon Valley investors." *Nature* 527: 19.

Herndon, A. (2013). "Exxon Refocusing Algae Biofuels Program After $100 Million Spend." *Bloomberg.* www.bloomberg.com/news/articles/2013-05-21/exxon-refocusing-algae-biofuels-program-after-100-million-spend. Accessed January 21, 2016.

Industry Today. (2015). "Global Synthetic Biology Market to Expand at 32.60% CAGR till 2019 Thanks to Growing R&D Efforts." November 4. www.industrytoday.co.uk/market-research-industry-today/global-synthetic-biology-market-to-expand-at-3260-cagr-till-2019-thanks-to-growing-rd-efforts/42731. Accessed January 20, 2016.

Intrexon. (2015). "Intrexon to Acquire Oxitec, Pioneer of Innovative Insect Control Solutions Addressing Global Challenges." News release, August 10. www.prnewswire.com/news-releases/intrexon-to-acquire-oxitec-pioneer-of-innovative-insect-control-solutions-addressing-global-challenges-300125896.html. Accessed January 24, 2016.

Jablonka, E, and Lamb, M. (2002). "The changing concept of epigenetics." *Annals of the New York Academy of Sciences* 981: 82–96.

Jacobs, S. (2015a). "This company made a jacket out of microbe-made spider silk." *Grist.* November 19. grist.org/business-technology/this-company-made-a-jacket-out-of-microbe-made-spider-silk/. Accessed January 23, 2016.

Jacobs, S. (2015b). "Are microbes about to remake manufacturing? This synthetic biologist thinks so." Grist. grist.org/people/are-microbes-about-to-remake-manufacturing-this-synthetic-biologist-thinks-so/. Accessed January 26, 2016.

Kalos, M. and June, C. H. (2013). "Adoptive T cell transfer for cancer immunotherapy in the era of synthetic biology." *Immunity* 39(1): 49–60.

Keller, E.F. (2009). "What does synthetic biology have to do with biology?" *Biosocieties* 4: 291–302.

Kim, E., Moore, B.S., and Yoon, Y.J. (2015). "Reinvigorating natural product combinatorial biosynthesis with synthetic biology." *Nature Chemical Biology* 11(9): 649–659.

Konrad, A. (2015). "Robots and Microbes: Zymergen Raises $44 Million From Big VCs." *Forbes*. June 15. www.forbes.com/sites/alexkonrad/2015/06/16/zymergen-raises-44-mil-for-robot-microbes/#28ffbf4f59b3. Accessed January 16, 2016.

Kuiken, T. (2015). *U.S. Trends in Synthetic Biology Research Funding*. W. Wilson International Center for Scholars, Washington, DC. September 15.

Landrain, et al. (2013). "Do-it-yourself biology: challenges and promises for an open science and technology movement." *Systems and Synthetic Biology* 7(3): 115–126.

Lane, J. (2014). "What's up with Solazyme? Stock free-falls after Moema ramp-up delayed." *Biofuels Digest*. November 6.

Lane, J. (2015). "Joule Says 'Will Go Commercial in 2017': Solar Fuels on The Way." *Biofuels Digest*. March 23.

Ledford, H. (2015). "Biohackers gear up for genome editing." *Nature* 524(7566): 398–399.

LePage, M. (2015). "Gene Editing Saves Girl Dying from Leukemia in World First." *New Scientist*. November 5. www.newscientist.com/article/dn28454-gene-editing-saves-life-of-girl-dying-from-leukaemia-in-world-first. Accessed January 15, 2016.

Leproust, E. (2015). "Beyond The $1K Genome: DNA 'Writing' Comes Next." *Tech Crunch*. September 18. techcrunch.com/2015/09/18/beyond-the-1k-genome-dna-writing-comes-next-2/. Accessed January 25, 2016.

Li, J. and Vederas, J. C. (2009). "Drug discovery and natural products: end of an era or an endless frontier?" *Science* 325(5937): 161–165.

Loizos, C. (2015). "Impossible Foods Raises a Whopping $108 Million for its Plant-Based Burgers." *Tech Crunch*. October 6. techcrunch.com/2015/10/06/impossible-foods-raises-a-whopping-108-million-for-its-plant-based-burgers/. Accessed January 25, 2016.

Matheson, R. (2015). "Scaling Up Synthetic-Biology Innovation." *MIT News Office*. December 10. www.news.mit.edu/2015/startup-gen9-scales-synthetic-biology-innovation-1211. Accessed January 24, 2016.

Menezes, A.A., Montague, M.G., Cumbers, J., Hogan, J.A., and Arkin, A.P. (2015). "Grand challenges in space synthetic biology." *Journal of The Royal Society Interface* 12(113): 20150803.

Mooallem, J. (2010). "Do-it-yourself genetic engineering." *New York Times*. February 10.

Nanalyze. (2015). "3 of Synthetic Biology's Failing Biofuel Stocks." *Nanalyze*. June 16. www.nanalyze.com/2015/06/3-of-synthetic-biologys-failing-biofuel-stocks/. Accessed January 15, 2016.

Novartis. (2015). "Caribou Biosciences to explore making medicines and drug discovery tools with CRISPR genome editing technology." News release, January 7. www.novartis.com/news/media-releases/novartis-collaborates-intellia-therapeutics-and-caribou-biosciences-explore. Accessed January 25, 2016.

Novozymes. (2016). "The BioAg Alliance readies new microbial solution to improve corn harvests." News release, January 6. www.novozymes.com/en/news/news-archive/Pages/The-BioAg-Alliance-readies-new-microbial-solution-to-improve-corn-harvests.aspx. Accessed January 22, 2016.

Ort, D.R., Merchant, S.S., Alric, J., ... and Moore, T.A. (2015). "Redesigning photosynthesis to sustainably meet global food and bioenergy demand." *Proceedings of the National Academy of Sciences* 112(28): 8529–8536.

Parry, B. (2004). *Trading the Genome*. Columbia Press, New York.

Pollack, A. (2015). "Jennifer Doudna, a Pioneer Who Helped Simplify Genome Editing." *New York Times*. May 11.

Pollack, A. (2016). "A Biotech Evangelist Seeks a Zika Dividend." *New York Times*. March 5.

Rajan, K. (2006). *Biocapital: The Constitution of Post-Genomic Life*. Duke University Press, Durham, NC.

Ramsey, L. (2015). "A Major Gene-editing Company Just got $335 Million to get its technology into people." *Business Insider*. December 21. www.businessinsider.com/crispr-therapeutics-forms-a-335-million-partnership-with-bayer-2015-12. Accessed January 15, 2016.

Robertson, D.E., Jacobson, S.A., Morgan, F., Berry, D., Church, G.M., and Afeyan, N.B. (2011). "A New Dawn for Industrial Photosynthesis." *Photosynthesis research* 107(3): 269–277.

Rose, N. (2007). *The Politics of Life Itself: Biomedicine, Power, Subjectivity, in the Twenty-first Century*. Princeton University Press, Princeton, NJ.

Rossi, J. (2013). "The socionatural engineering of reductionist metaphors: a political ecology of synthetic biology." *Environment and Planning A* 45(5): 1127–1143.

Rusch, D., et al. (2007). "The Sorcerer II global ocean sampling expedition: northwest Atlantic through eastern tropical Pacific." *PLoS Biology* 5: 398–431.

Schrek, A. (2008). "Solazyme Inks Algae Fuel Deal with Chevron." *Toronto Star.* January 22.

Schwille, P. and S. Diez (2009). "Synthetic biology of minimal systems." *Critical Reviews in Biochemistry and Molecular Biology* 44: 223–242.

Segran, E. (2015). "Twist Bioscience Inks Deal to Sell 100 Million Base Pairs of Synthetic Dna." *Fast Company.* November 4. http://www.fastcompany.com/3053065/most-creative-people/twist-bioscience-inks-deal-to-sell-100-million-pairs-of-synthetic-dna. Accessed January 23, 2016.

SGI-DNA. (2016). "SGI-DNA Launches Automated Cloning Module for the BioXp™ 3200 System and Reaches another Instrument Milestone." News release, January 13. sgidna.com/news-item-20160116-BioXp-Automated-Cloning-Module.html. Accessed January 24, 2016.

Solazyme. (2010). 'Solazyme Announces Series D Financing Round of More Than $50 Million.' News release, August 9. investors.solazyme.com/releasedetail.cfm?releaseid=588859. Accessed January 23, 2016.

Stallins, J. A. (2011). Scale, causality, and the new organism–environment interaction. *Geoforum* 43(3): 427–441.

Stinson, L. (2015). "Move Over, Jony Ive—Biologists Are the Next Rock Star Designers." *Wired.* November 18. www.wired.com/2015/11/move-over-jony-ivebiologists-are-the-next-rock-star-designers/. Accessed January 25, 2016.

Suresh, A. (2014). "Crowdsourcing Synthetic Biology." *Discover Magazine.* August 29. blogs.discovermagazine.com/citizen-science-salon/2014/08/29/crowdsourcing-synthetic-biology/#.Vq-M7vkrJD8. Accessed January 15, 2016.

Syngenta. (2015). "Syngenta and DSM to Develop and Commercialize Biological Solutions for Agriculture." News release, November 6. www.syngenta.com/global/corporate/en/news-center/news-releases/Pages/151106.aspx. Accessed January 24, 2016.

SGI (Synthetic Genomics Inc.) (2015a). "Monsanto Acquires Select Assets of Agradis, Inc. to Support Work in Agricultural Biologicals." News release, January 30. www.syntheticgenomics.com/300113.html. Accessed January 24, 2016.

SGI (Synthetic Genomics Inc.) (2015b). "Synthetic Genomics and Gen9 Sign Licensing Agreement for Synthetic Biology Technology Patents." News release, June 11. www.syntheticgenomics.com/06112015.html. Accessed January 26, 2016. www.syntheticgenomics.com/news20151215.html. Accessed January 26, 2016.

Temple, J. (2016). "Meet the Time-Traveling Scientist Behind Editas, the Biotech Company Going Public With Google's Help." *Re/code.* January 5. http://recode.net/2016/01/05/meet-the-time-traveling-scientist-behind-editas-the-biotech-company-going-public-with-googles-help/. Accessed January 24, 2016.

US Food and Drug Administration (2015). "Questions and Answers on FDA's Approval of AquAdvantage Salmon." December 21. www.fda.gov/AnimalVeterinary/DevelopmentApprovalProcess/GeneticEngineering/GeneticallyEngineeredAnimals/ucm473237.htm Accessed January 22, 2016.

Venter, J.C. (2013). "Genomic science coupled with a strong carbon policy can change our energy future." *Sustainability.* March 12.

Verdezyne. (2014). "Verdezyne Formalizes $48 Million Financing at Signing Attended by President Barack Obama." News release, April 28. verdezyne.com/2014/04/28/verdezyne-formalizes-48-million-financing-at-signing-ceremony-attended-by-president-barack-obama/ Ceremony. Accessed January 26, 2016.

Wesoff, E. (2015). "Cleantech IPOs: Predictions Revisited, 2015 Winners, 2016 Picks." *Greentech Media.* December 30. www.greentechmedia.com/articles/read/cleantech-ipos-predictions-revisited-2015-winners-2016-picks. Accessed January 22, 2016.

Williams, S. (2016). "The Likely Reason Behind Intrexon Corporation's Soaring Share Price." *The Motley Fool.* January 14. www.fool.com/investing/general/2016/01/14/the-likely-reason-behind-intrexon-corporations-soa.aspx. Accessed January 22, 2016.

Zhang, S. (2015a). "Intrexon's Billionaire CEO Is Betting on the Most Controversial GMOs." *Wired.* November 10. www.wired.com/2015/11/meet-billionaire-ceo-behind-controversial-gmos/. Accessed January 22, 2016.

Zhang, S. (2015b). "Y Combinator's Sam Altman Is Bullish on Biotech Startups." *Wired.* November, 7. www.wired.com/2015/11/y-combinator-sam-altman-interview-on-investing-in-biotech-startups/. Accessed January 22, 2016.

Zhang, S. (2015c). "Biotech's New Plan: Nobody Say 'GMO'." *Wired.* November 5. www.wired.com/2015/11/synthetic-bio-startups-really-really-dont-want-monsanto/. Accessed January 23.

Zhang, S. (2015d). "Cheap DNA Sequencing is Here. Writing DNA is Next." *Wired.* November 20. www.wired.com/2015/11/making-dna/. Accessed January 22, 2016.

PART IV

Governing science and governing through science

22

TOWARD A POLITICAL ECONOMY OF NEOLIBERAL CLIMATE SCIENCE

Larry Lohmann

Perhaps even more than the other types of "nature" that are said to constitute the subject matters of the sciences, "the climate", "climate change" and "the climate system" are often construed today as monoliths, essentialized and externalized from a similarly block-like "society". Policymakers, environmentalists and flood refugees are commonly understood to be connected to an independently-coherent natural world of climate through interaction points across which biophysical processes are held to impinge on an otherwise relatively self-enclosed social or human world. This is seen to happen in two ways. The first is through brute "external shocks to social and environmental systems" (Taylor 2015: 32; see also Hulme 2011) to which society must "adapt". The second is through representation of those "external" biophysical processes or systems within various "internal cultural frames" (Taylor 2015: 39), notably those of a climate-scientist profession commonly understood to have a privileged method for interpreting signals passing through interfaces with nature (Rouse 2002) while filtering out static from society. Conversely, human influence on climate is seen, as Marcus Taylor puts it, as an "outside 'forcing' to an otherwise coherent model of atmospheric dynamics" (Taylor 2015: 38). Changes in a climate pre-formulated in terms of heat transfers, CO_2 molecules, cloud albedo and methane clathrates are to be collectively "mitigated" via a management gateway through which a sparsely specified "internal" reorganization of society via energy or economic policy can be focused on a separate physical world. Thus it was considered a normal piece of global policymaking for the 2015 Paris climate agreement to set itself up as a passage-point through which a unitary "international community" would be able to formulate ways to hold global average temperature rise in a similarly black-boxed physical climate system to "well below 2° C above pre-industrial levels" (UNFCCC 2015: 21). In this way, the environmentalist homily that society or the economy depends on and subsists within a climate system, "far from marking humanity's reintegration into the world, signals the culmination of a process of separation" (Ingold 2000: 209) involving distinct systems "locked into an endless dance of adaptation" (Taylor 2015: 39).

Today, the theme that climate is a nonhuman "force of nature", interpreted by climatologists, "that enfolds upon a similarly coherent society" that duly returns the favour is "firmly engrained in the politics of mitigation and adaptation at an institutional level" (Taylor 2015: 31). In official discourse, global warming politics is seldom understood as a matter of concrete histories entangling both humans and nonhumans in surplus extraction, neocolonialism, racism, hydrocarbon use, labour discipline and struggles over class (Malm 2014, Huber 2009, The Corner House 2014, Moore 2015) and modes of respect for and dialogue with non-humans (Smith 2007). Instead, it is shrunk into an exercise in the control or "governance" of an external, zombie climate (Boykoff, Frame and Randalls 2010), the indeterminacy of whose antics are reduced to the percentage-point probabilities that the Intergovernmental Panel on Climate Change (IPCC), à la *Star Trek*'s Mr. Spock, is constrained to present as "inputs" to the policy process (IPCC 2013, Lahsen 2005). Experts, states and private corporations become the relevant agents in a centralized, territorial, supposedly science-driven global environmental monitoring and mitigation system of "green governmentality" that moulds "environments to fit the sovereign state" (Kuehls 1998: 49) but also fuses in a "mutually constitutive" combination (Bäckstrand and Lövbrand 2007: 131) with a purportedly decentralized liberal market-environmentalist order that requires climate to be not only measurable, predictable and stabilizable but also cost-optimizable. Far more than other environmentalisms, climate activism tends to rely on the conclusions of scientists about a physical globe as "seen from above" in isolation from experience in the everyday spheres that Tim Ingold (2000) calls "lifeworlds". At official and academic meetings on global warming, climatologists empowered as spokespersons for nature regularly "present the science" and then leave the room to let policymakers or activists empowered as spokespersons for society get on with discussions about how to maintain surplus extraction in a greenhouse world. Climate deniers do their bit toward maintaining the same climate/society, science/nonscience binaries when they profess horror that some scientists might have "cross[ed] a line into policy advocacy" (Broder 2010). Environmentalists such as Bill McKibben chip in when they advocate a politics in which "physics and chemistry call the tune" to which governments dance (Romm 2011; cf. Carey 2014). Scientific panels are meanwhile convened to decide at what point "humanity's" influence on a separate "natural" world became powerful enough to justify the naming of a new, anthropocene geological epoch (Lewis and Maslin 2015). Contemporary climate politics, in short, continues to be characterized by incessant nature/society "boundary work" (Gieryn 1999, Keller 2011, Ramirez-i-Olle 2015), helping to shape both fertile research programmes and productions of ignorance, as well as institutionally embodied notions of knowability, causality and governability (Seager 2009, Israel and Sachs 2013). Under this settlement physical scientists' responsibility to society consists in protecting a privileged apprenticeship to what is construed as nonsocial; their authority and status comes to depend on conjuring (in public, at least) a nature that is predictable, controllable and separated from commons – in short, either dead or irreducibly non-human.

Should the study of the political economy of climate science fall in with this dualism-producing politics? Should it assume that climate science is a "natural kind" (Rorty 1991: 46–62), possessing an essence that places its internal procedures outside politics and economics (Woods 2007)? Should it therefore avoid attempting to trace ways in which knowledge of climate might be one with "those cultural practices and formations that philosophers of science have often regarded as 'external' to knowledge" (Rouse 1996: 239) and instead confine itself to exploring political conditions under which the posited scientific independence is and is not possible? Or – as will be presumed here – should it instead view these binaries as actively produced and themselves subject to investigation and challenge, taking its cue from widespread, longstanding resistance to the settlement exemplified by these very segregations and their associated interfaces? Today, this opposition is manifest above all in indigenous, peasant, feminist, gay rights and anti-racist politics. Examples include small-farmer movements that hold at arm's length conceptions of resources, ecosystem services or natural capital (Confédération Paysanne 2014); Amazonian defences of territory partly grounded in practices that avoid a conception of nature as background objects over which culture is draped (Viveiros de Castro 2004a, 2004b; Kohn 2013); organized challenges to claims of "natural authority" deployed by patriarchists to justify oppression of women; and health and environmental movements that have "played a crucial role in politicizing technical domains that liberal discourse had formerly isolated from the scope of politics" (Thorpe 2008: 75; see also Epstein 1996). This resistance dovetails with various strains of post-1970s academic work in science and technology studies, which have questioned the society/nature binary, and "illustrated in rich detail the enormous problems with presuming there is any such single and definable thing as 'science'" (Tyfield 2012: 46), and insisted that the technosciences both help constitute and are partly constituted by a much broader field including commerce, colonialist history, property law, territorialization, structures of feeling, economic policy, and military, corporate and foundation patronage – all the way down to the most intimate reaches of the relata (Barad 2007), measurements and units of analysis that the technosciences feature and do not feature (Birch 2013, Kleinman 2003, Robertson 2012). Much of this work has consisted of resolutely "local" ethnographies of professional research communities that demonstrate how objects are constituted, transformed and made circulatable, histories erased, methodologies standardized, mechanized and black-boxed, laboratory labour "frozen" into various instruments, fact/value distinctions erected, and knowledge claims negotiated in particular laboratory and field settings according to a shifting variety of criteria that would be considered "non-scientific" according to the settlement sketched above (Latour and Woolgar 1979, Collins 1985, Knorr-Cetina 1981). This ethnographic approach is sometimes seen as consorting with political accommodationism. But once it succeeds in beginning to break down and "distance" the settlement at the level of what Karin Knorr-Cetina calls the "hard core" of science – "its technical content and the production of knowledge" (1995: 140; cf. Bloor 1981) – then there is no reason why it should not be understood as a crucial contribution to the more thoroughgoing political economy of science that many activists are also pursuing. Such a political economy aspires to spell out in detail, and help open up for intervention, the series of links that join even the most quotidian scientific practices with, for example, colonial history, industrial labour exploitation and neoliberalism. In doing so, it extends laboratory ethnographies – often constrained by having to focus on how cooperation among experts is achieved in the creation of transportable "factness" – into a more agonistic arena in which the structures resulting from some collaborations are resisted as threats to livelihood, liberation or survival. One way of viewing researchers as diverse as Daniel Lee Kleinman (2003), George Caffentzis (2013), Emily Martin (1989), Donna Haraway (1989), Peter Galison (2004), Robert Marc Friedman (1989), Londa Schiebinger (2004), Jason W. Moore (2015), and Salvatore Engel-Di Mauro (2014) is as contributors of materials for such a self-consciously activist political economy of science that can delineate and intervene in a contiguous, evolving, heterogeneous field of power that is both direct and indirect, agential and structural, "political" and "scientific".

One obstacle to promoting such an approach to the political economy of climate science is that, instead of being seen as a challenge to the dominant settlement, it is often interpreted according to that settlement's terms, as an attempt either to debunk climatological practice because it is not "pure" or to expose or reduce "bad influences" – such as the privatization of science, or funding for the wrong kind of research programmes – that prevent climate scientists from doing their "proper" job of deploying scientific method to represent the facts of nature correctly to society. An approach unwilling to assume *a priori* dualisms between nature and society or science and nonscience often has to do a lot of heavy lifting to show why it is not contrasting a "situated" (Haraway 1991: 183–201) with an imaginary "unsituated" climate science, but rather distinguishing various actual and possible economically situated sets of scientific practices (and scientifically situated economic or political practices (Shapin and Schaffer 1989, Ezrahi 1990, Mirowski 1992, Kob 2015) and why it might be both possible and liberatory to engage with science and scientists for political change "within" science as well as without.

Making the task all the harder are academic border patrols that attempt to divide political economy of science off *a priori* from science and technology studies; the histories, philosophies and sociologies of science and economics; the economics of science and scientific knowledge; political theory; anthropology; postcolonial theory; political ecology; and most of all environmental activism and social and political movement-building. The fussily proprietary attitude that such boundary work reveals hinders political economists in advance from benefiting from many of the tools and collegial relations that they need if they are to come to terms with what links historical patterns of, say, financial investment, neocolonialism, resource extraction, grant funding, or agrarian class struggle with the concepts, devices and conclusions found in the gathering places of scientists, and vice versa. Indeed, it makes it hard for the study of political economy to understand itself, since it obscures the origins of "the economy" itself, whose historical specificity might have remained relatively unexplored were it not for the work of political scientists, anthropologists and science and technology scholars (Mitchell 2002, Callon 1998). Most important, if political economy of science is to concern itself not with "*whether* there is and/or should be a 'politics' of science", but rather with "securing a more democratic process of deciding *which* politics (and culture) of science dominates [sic]" (Tyfield 2012: 87; see also Kenney 2015, Harding 2004), then it cannot help but overlap with political activism. A political economy of science capable of finding its place among the activities that Joseph Rouse (1996: 237–259) calls the "cultural studies of science" will view the claim that it must be different in kind from, say, political ecology, or from political mobilization, or from science itself, with as much suspicion as it does the claim that all such activities are the same.

What does such a "difficult" political economy of climate science look like? This chapter offers one brief perspective by commenting on two quotations from the relevant scientific literature. One comes from the Intergovernmental Panel on Climate Change (IPCC), the body charged by the United Nations with formulating global scientific consensus on global warming. The other comes from research conducted partly at Resources for the Future, a Washington think tank that has advocated market approaches to environmental policy for many decades (Lane 2015) with the support of corporations such as Duke Energy, Goldman Sachs, BP, Weyerhaeuser, Chevron and Rio Tinto (RFF 2015).

Neither quotation possesses any intellectual distinction or political importance in itself. But both are appropriate platforms for suggesting what the scope of a critical political economy of climate science might be, for three reasons. First, their artless air of common sense (neither statement feels the need to burden itself with argument or evidence), which reveals the entrenched nature of the relations of political and economic domination that they represent, cries out for a political economy approach that achieves not so much an "unveiling" of influences or an opening of a black box as a "generative critique" (Verran 2001: 20–47) continuous with a collaborative crafting of effective points for fresh intervention and resistance. Second, both quotations can be analyzed as occupying intermediate positions in the overall field of political/scientific power, linking the kind of politics conventionally considered as "extra-science" (investment trends, class struggle) to various practices "within" what is conventionally demarcated as science (instrument readings, hypotheses about causal chains). Third, taken together, the two quotations indicate a significant recent transition in the ongoing "co-constitution" (Jasanoff 2004) of capital and climate science.

From enclosure to postwar settlement:
the Intergovernmental Panel on Climate Change

"Underlying all aspects of [our] report," affirms a "Summary for Policymakers" put out by Working Group I of the Intergovernmental Panel on Climate Change, "is a strong commitment to assessing the science comprehensively, without bias and in a way that is relevant to policy but not policy prescriptive" (IPCC 2013: vii).

This classic statement reiterates in one crisp sentence numerous features of a longstanding settlement that attempts to govern how the sciences are supposed to relate to politics and economy and vice versa. The phrase *"the science"*, with its emphatic definite article, implicitly black-boxes science as a bounded article that can influence and be influenced by politics but is constituted by processes that are distinct. It also implicitly channels, in advance, potential challenges to that science into the form of proposals for alternative "objects" that can be fixed or fetishized to a greater or lesser degree (Verran 2001). The term *"comprehensively"* tends to conceal the partial or incomplete structure of knowledge and directs attention away from the various fresh ignorances continually produced in the course of inquiry. *"Without bias"*, in denying the ways climate science necessarily carries within itself attributions of causality, responsibility and property that support some interests and are prejudicial to others, positions the IPCC as a political opponent of social movements that have questioned the possibility of unbiased expertise. *"Relevant to policy but not policy-prescriptive"*, embodied in the IPCC's bureaucratic division of its processes into three tracks dealing with physical sciences, socioeconomic impacts and possible policy responses, works not only to keep alive a fact/value dichotomy under assault for over two centuries but also to reify dominant postwar US structurings of political responsibility. In performing the "god trick" (Haraway 1991) of making climate both representable by knowers removed from politics and manipulable by controllers advised by the knowers, the passage helps keep spaces open for both geoengineering and carbon trading – which is one reason why investigating its political economy is crucial to social movements fighting such initiatives.

One part of this investigation could well zero in on the supercomputer-driven global circulation models (GCMs) that enable and constrain the climatological work of the IPCC (see Johnson, this volume). The "god's-eye view" (Lahsen 2005: 911) characteristic of such models, and their tendencies to reinforce climate determinism (Carey 2014) and accrete ever-increasing volumes of disaggregated physical data to the exclusion of knowledge that cannot be so easily "plugged and played", are neither accident nor conspiracy. They are rooted, rather, in postwar systems analysis, military-spurred digital developments, computer simulations of powered flight and the nonlinear fluid dynamics of nuclear explosions, Cold War-era cybernetics, World War II-era artillery-control servomechanisms and, more remotely, the mechanical feedback-control "governors" required by Industrial Revolution steam engines (Edwards 2013, Elichirigoity 1999; Beniger 1986) and the population "servomechanism" postulated by Thomas Malthus, one of the godfathers of nature/society binaries. Nor is the computerized mapping of energy flows and balances exempt from political economy inquiry. Such mapping would not be possible at all without the prior practices of commensurating heat, force and electromagnetism that resulted in circulatable units of abstract "energy", whose physical and theoretical emergence during the 19th century cannot be separated from the drive to amplify, disaggregate and discipline wage labour in Europe using fossil-fuelled engines and dynamos (Corner House 2014). If GCMs sometimes appear to the innocent eye as capable of dissociating climate change from civilizational politics, allowing it to be "medicalized" instead (Fleming 2014), this is only because they have tended to "disappear" this history into the fetish of all-purpose thermodynamic energy as one aspect of a nonsocial "nature".

Arguably, the project of measuring, modelling and manipulating in a "virtual" way various exchanges of carbon among the atmosphere, oceans, and terrestrial and geological reservoirs is well-funded partly because it invites a view of climate action as the expert governance and placement of molecules globally. Responsibility and property can be assigned according to the geographic jurisdiction from which the molecules originate. Internationally agreed methodologies for accounting for flows of greenhouse gases within state territories via commensuration of biotic and fossil emissions into a uniform CO_2 meanwhile create the possibility of nationally owned carbon sinks (Paterson and Stripple 2007) and ultimately facilitate expert calls for "the intensive management and/or manipulation of a significant fraction of the globe's biomass" (Fogel 2004: 110) by imperial arrangements whose reach matches that of GCMs themselves. Ownership by national "geobodies" (Thongchai 1994) or institutions for the management of global territory under regimes of "green governmentality" then paves the way for ownership by private entities under a worldwide regime of "green growth" (see below).

This vein of political economy of science is continuous with the ongoing work of those social movements for whom the more than half-millennium history of nature/society dualisms associated with enclosure and state and private simplifications and appropriations is a living reality. For example, the study of political economy is well-suited to investigate the roles of GCMs, cost-benefit analysis, neoclassical economics and recent statist politics in the well-documented inability of today's climate modelling/policy complex to come to terms with various indeterminacies and uncertainties (see, e.g., Lahsen 2005, Hulme 2011, Nilsson et al. 2000, Jonas et al. 1999, Jonas et al. 1998, Schulze et al. 2000, Anderson et al. 2001, Randalls 2011, Carey 2014, Schultze et al. 2002, J. A. Nelson 2008). But only an intellectual perspective informed by popular movement work will be able to place the results of such investigations in a wider narrative of the rolling self-defeats that other sciences, too, have experienced historically in performing passive, calculable, controllable, circulatable natures in the face of partly nonhuman peasant or indigenous practices of recreating "complex, heterogeneous ensembles" (Smith 2007) relating to land and labour. These practices – often characterized by cautious respect, propitiation and reciprocity across human–nonhuman boundaries – also illuminate the long history of science, capital accumulation, and accumulation's component others. If political economists studying steam and internal combustion engines as well as industrial and computing machines more generally have learned from labour movements (and vice versa), so too can political economists investigating the science of GCMs learn from many of today's popular struggles for land, forests and the atmosphere (and vice versa). Updating Marx, one might say that the apparatuses (Barad 2007) in which climatologists participate make their own "factnesses" about climate, but not in circumstances of the climatologists' – or the apparatuses' – own choosing (cf. Kleinman 2003, Paterson and Stripple 2007, Hay 1995). It is precisely this black-boxing or "structurizing" at diverse levels, moreover, that necessitates political responses that move beyond technical or moral injunctions directed at the accountability of institutions or individuals toward the building of radical social movements committed to reworking science from "within" as well as "without".

Neoliberal evolution: climate control becomes marketable

Since the 1970s, new elements have been bricolaged onto the historical nature/society settlement in which most climate science is practised. Ecosystem functions – a category partly traceable to colonial-era (Anker 2001) as well as cybernetic postwar US military innovations (Elichirogoity 1999, S. H. Nelson 2015) – have become subject to protective state regulation, and then transformed into ecosystem services, which have become tradeable assets in transactions which are supposed to reduce regulatory costs. These assets have been fashioned and appropriated by the state and business in a process paralleling the more general privatization of public goods that has gained ground under neoliberalism, generating novel kinds of rent (Felli 2014). Advertised as being capable of addressing ecological crisis in "depoliticized" ways that help free business from constraints that might otherwise be imposed on it by environmental movements, planners or conventional regulation, markets in the new assets are also supposed to help relieve the state of much of the increasing expense of an environmental protection that is redefined to be compatible with growth or capital accumulation.

Some of what this means in terms of the content of climate sciences is neatly summarized in a 2007 article in *Ecological Economics* entitled "What Are Ecosystem Services? The Need for Standardized Environmental Accounting Units" by James Boyd of Resources for the Future and Spencer Banzhaf of Georgia State University. Boyd and Banzhaf defend a definition of "ecosystem" that is frankly "derived from a desire for consistency between conventional market accounting units and ecosystem accounting units" (626) so that "one particular set of accounting units is applicable to both of these broad applications" (617).

Boyd and Banzhaf's formulation encapsulated a conflicted movement that had been under way in climate and other sciences since at least the 1980s. For example, the 1992 UN Framework Convention on Climate Change started out by following climatologists in figuring the earth's atmosphere, somewhat in the style of the US environmental laws of the 1970s, as a zone of externalized, potentially regulatable molecules. Atmospheric concentrations of greenhouse gases, it was proposed, were ultimately not to exceed such-and-such a level; those nations not doing their fair share would be punished; and so on. But under pressure from a US regime influenced by a "liberal environmentalism" (Bernstein 2001) spearheaded by politicians, NGOs and economists, the 1997 Kyoto Protocol then converted this agreement to reduce pollutants to a certain level into entitlements to emit them up to that level, and to make those entitlements tradeable. These entitlements – the right to charge rent on this aspect of nature – were then awarded to the states of the industrialized North (Felli 2014). Under the EU Emissions Trading Scheme, such entitlements have been mainly passed on to large industrial corporations. Although many business sectors expressed misgivings early on about the uncertainty and bureaucracy this would involve them in, the potential of carbon trading to provide relief from existing or threatened climate regulation to key corporations while putting new economic assets in circulation could not but be appealing to many at a time when the roster of the ten largest companies of the Fortune Global 500 regularly featured a preponderance of private or national oil companies, car manufacturers and national grids as well as banks bent on expanding into innovative financial products. Broadening the appeal of the shift, state and private-sector entrepreneurs were urged to produce additional circulatable entitlements ("offsets") for sale by expanding the earth's capacity to compensate climatically for fossil fuel emissions. The meaning of "expanding", moreover, was widened to include "preventing a decrease in". The results were twofold. First, entrepreneurs set off on a protracted scramble to annex forest, agricultural and other activities and subsume them, in both formal and real terms, to the sequestration of carbon. Hence pulpwood plantations, forest conservation and "climate-smart agriculture" became potential sources of saleable regulatory relief for industrial carbon dioxide polluters worldwide. Second, state and private entrepreneurs went to work to find or create as many instances as possible in which the causes – and thus legal ownership – of increases in (or purported preventions in the reduction of) the capacity of the earth to "clean up" fossil fuel emissions could be traced to themselves. Having previously been conceptualized as a "natural resource that needed to be defended from the onslaught of industrialism" or as pollution prevention (Hart and Victor 1993: 667–68; cf. Maunder 1970), climate now needed to be capitalized "efficiently" as an ownable service.

At no point can this dynamic be separated out from the evolution of climate science, whether at the level of field methodology, laboratory apparatus or computer processor. For one thing, the new economic units relied for materials on the scientific units of the predecessor settlement. Just as the market in individual transferable quotas in Norwegian fisheries after the 1980s depended on the previous construction of cyborg "fish-as-fit-for-management" and the transformation of fishers working commons into "owners and investors" (Holm 2007: 239–240; Johnsen et al. 2009), so too the emergence of carbon markets depended on the prior development of a cyborg climate of CO_2 molecules. It was merely that the "plug and play" units appropriate for atmospheric circulation models had to be modified to make them pluggable and playable in economic circulation models as well (cf. Robertson 2012: 387; 2007: 503). If the IPCC's contested commensuration of biotic- and fossil-origin CO_2 – together with a half-dozen other greenhouse gases – into a new unit of nature, the "Global Warming Potential" (MacKenzie 2009), was useful (when suitably black-boxed) for the UNFCCC's territorial inventories of responsibility for global warming, it was also crucial (again suitably black-boxed) in increasing the scope for claims that a supposedly unchanging "climate change mitigation" was being more efficiently achieved through climate markets (Lohmann 2014). But the well-funded turn to "efficient" mass production of transferrable tokens of "reduction" set up reciprocal incentives for climate science to seek and perform large numbers of further equivalences capable of expanding the universe of units of an aggregate "mitigation" process untied from any single location, pedigree, time frame, technology or set of historical entailments. Just as species offset markets encouraged the development of scientific methodologies for identifying, measuring and circulating new, species-transcending units of nature called "species-equivalents" (Pawlicek and Sullivan 2012), about which clustered new knowledges and ignorances, carbon offset markets resulted in the proliferation of methodologies for identifying, measuring and transporting greenhouse gas "reductions" that – for example – incorporated both counterfactual and actual molecular flows, creating expanded opportunities for achieving a new, globally averaged pollution and a new aggregate nature of "net zero emissions" (Lohmann 2014, 2016). Such moves tended to intensify the nature/society binaries of the older settlement on which they were built, attempting to perform natures that were even "deader": more stabilizable, more predictable, more externalizable, more fragmentable, more extensively ownable. But they also extended the unstable field of power constituted by these settlements. The nodes forming this field were multiple and diverse but never isolated from each other. They included legal reforms affirming that, while the state had power to manage the climate system from "outside", it was not to venture too far into determining who produced what in which quantities, for whom, and at what price (Felli 2015), as well as innovations encouraging the financial bundling of quantifiable carbon-cycling capacity with other ecosystem services, claims on public subsidies and timber, recreational or mineral leases (Kay 2015). They encompassed institutionalized environmentalism, governmental and foundation funding sources, research institutions, and new types of territorial control, property relations, insurance, colonialist or racist reasoning and modes of militarized repression against communities whose presence interfered with the efficient manufacture and certification of ecosystem service tokens. Not least, they included new regimes of scientific inquiry: the new property and financial settlement, the new colonial settlement and the new epistemic settlement were one.

By the same token, the contradictions and contestations that have dogged the modified settlement, limiting its ability to rescue flagging labour productivity (Moore 2015), are at once political, economic and scientific. When activist groups protest the bankrolling of programs for

Reducing Emissions from Deforestation and Forest Degradation (REDD) by the Norwegian government, the Packard Foundation and others (No REDD Platform 2011), they are also, in effect, entering technical criticisms of the quality of forest offset science. Scientific arguments against the possibility of proving that offsets are quantifiably "additional" to what would have happened without offset projects (e.g., Anderson 2012) are simultaneously blows against the colonialism that reduces "the natives" to a passive background as well as contributions to Marxist praxis. A recent activist call to jettison the EU Emissions Trading Scheme (Scrap the EU ETS Coalition 2013), similarly, resists being parsed into separate scientific and political objections. Nor will the learning necessary to setting aside academic debates that oppose social constructivism to critical realism be as easily achieved without building the committed relationships with indigenous peoples' movements that are needed to undermine the settlement that makes such disputes possible. Just as resistance to patriarchy is less effective if it does not embrace a scientific critique of the limitations of reproductive biology, and vice versa, so too resistance to the organization of industrial society around fossil-fuelled production and circulation will be less effective if it does not self-consciously join with, for example, scientific dissidents contesting the content of the science of "global warming potentials" as a part of the dominant science/politics settlement, and vice versa.

It is central to the intellectual responsibilities of the "difficult" and engaged political economy of climate science that this chapter has defended to affirm, not obscure, these lively and varied connections. Keeping alive the sense that even the most everyday details of scientific practice have a political economy, that this political economy can be both studied and challenged, and that the world need not be treated as if it were "produced by two discrete, interacting substances" called "society" and "nature" (Moore 2015) involves a willingness to treat political and intellectual alliances as one.

References

Anderson, D. et al. (2001). *Taking Credit: Canada and the Role of Sinks in International Climate Negotiations.* Vancouver: David Suzuki Foundation.

Anderson, K. (2012). "Offsetting (& CDM): a guarantee for 100 years or just a clever scam? From a climate change perspective, is offsetting worse than doing nothing?". Manchester: University of Manchester, www.tyndall.manchester.ac.uk/news/Offsetting-Planet-Under-Pressure-Conf-March-2012.pdf.

Anker, P. (2001). *Imperial Ecology: Environmental Order in the British Empire, 1895–1945.* Cambridge, MA: Harvard University Press.

Bäckstrand, K. and Lövbrand, E. (2007) "Climate governance beyond 2012: competing discourses of green governmentality, ecological modernization and civic environmentalism". In Pettenger, M. (ed.) *The Social Construction of Climate Change.* Aldershot: Ashgate. 123-48.

Barad, K. (2007). *Meeting the Universe Halfway: Quantum Physics and the Entanglement of Matter and Meaning.* Durham: Duke University Press.

Beniger, J. M. (1986). *The Control Revolution: Technological and Economic Origins of the Information Society.* Cambridge, MA: Harvard University Press.

Bernstein, S. (2001). *The Compromise of Liberal Environmentalism.* New York: Columbia University Press.

Birch, K. (2013). "The political economy of technoscience: an emerging research agenda". *Spontaneous Generations* 7 (1): 49–61.

Bloor, D. (1981). *Wittgenstein: A Social Theory of Knowledge.* London: Routledge.

Boyd, J. and Banzhaf, S. (2007). "What are ecosystem services? The need for standardized environmental accounting units". *Ecological Economics* 63: 616–626.

Boykoff, M. T., Frame, D. and Randalls, S. (2010). "Discursive stability meets climate instability: a critical exploration of the concept of 'climate stabilization' in contemporary climate policy". *Global Environmental Change* 20: 53–64.

Broder, J. M. (2010). "Scientists taking steps to defend work on climate". *New York Times*, 2 March, www.nytimes.com/2010/03/03/science/earth/03climate.html.

Caffentzis, G. (2013). *In Letters of Blood and Fire*. Oakland: PM Press.

Callon, M. (1998). *The Laws of the Markets*. London: John Wiley.

Carey, M. (2014). "Science, models, and historians: toward a critical climate history". *Environmental History* 19: 354–64.

Collins, H. M. (1985). *Changing Order: Replication and Induction in Scientific Practice*. Chicago: University of Chicago Press.

Confédération Paysanne [Via Campesina France]. (2014). "Statement against climate-smart agriculture". Paris, 18 September.

The Corner House. (2014). *Energy, Work and Finance*. Sturminster Newton: The Corner House.

Edwards, P. (2013) *A Vast Machine: Computer Models, Climate Data, and the Politics of Global Warning*. Cambridge, MA: MIT Press.

Elichirigoity, F. (1999). *Planet Management: Limits to Growth, Computer Simulation, and the Emergence of Global Spaces*. Evanston: Northwestern University Press.

Engel-Di Mauro, S. (2014). *Ecology, Soils and the Left: An Ecosocial Approach*. New York: Palgrave-Macmillan.

Epstein, S. (1996). *Impure Science: AIDS, Activism, and the Politics of Knowledge*. Berkeley: University of California Press.

Ezrahi, Y. (1990). *The Descent of Icarus*. Cambridge, MA: Harvard University Press.

Felli, R. (2014). "On climate rent". *Historical Materialism* 22 (3–4): 251–280.

Felli, R. (2015). "Environment, not planning: the neoliberal depoliticisation of environmental policy by means of emissions trading". *Environmental Politics* 24 (5): 641–60.

Fleming, J. R. (2014). "Climate physicians and surgeons". *Environmental History* 19: 338–345.

Fogel, C. (2004) "The local, the global, and the Kyoto Protocol". In Jasanoff, S. and Martello, M. L. (eds.) *Earthly Politics: Local and Global in Environmental Governance*. Cambridge: MIT Press: 103–126.

Friedman, R. M. (1989). *Appropriating the Weather: Vilhelm Bjerknes and the Construction of a Modern Meterology*. Ithaca: Cornell University Press.

Galison, P. (2004). *Einstein's Clocks, Poincare's Maps: Empires of Time*. New York: Norton.

Gieryn, T. F. (1999). *Cultural Boundaries of Science: Credibility on the Line*. Chicago: University of Chicago Press.

Haraway, D. (1989). *Primate Visions: Gender, Race and Nature in the World of Modern Science*. London: Verso.

Haraway, D. (1991). *Simians, Cyborgs and Women: The Reinvention of Nature*. London: Free Association Books.

Harding, S. (2004). "A socially relevant philosophy of science? Resources from standpoint theory's controversiality". *Hypatia* 19 (1): 25–47.

Hart, D. M. and Victor, D. G. (1993). "Scientific elites and the making of US policy for climate change research, 1957–1974". *Social Studies of Science* 23 (4): 643–680.

Hay, C. (1995). "Structure and agency". In Marsh, D. and Stoker, G. (eds.) *Theory and Methods in Political Science*. Basingstroke: Macmillan: 189–208.

Holm, P. (2007). "Which way is up on Callon?" in MacKenzie, D., Muniesa, F. and Siu, L. (eds.) *Do Economists Make Markets? On the Performativity of Economics*. Princeton: Princeton University Press.

Huber, M. T. (2009). "Energizing historical materialism: fossil fuels, space and the capitalist mode of production". *Geoforum* 40 (1): 105–115.

Hulme, M. (2011). "Reducing the future to climate: a story of climate determinism and reductionism". *Osiris* 26 (1): 245–266.

Ingold, T. (2000). *The Perception of the Environment*. London: Routledge.

Intergovernmental Panel on Climate Change (IPCC). (2013). "Climate change 2013: the physical science basis. Summary for policymakers". Bonn: IPCC.

Israel, A. L. and Sachs, C. (2013). "A climate for feminist intervention: feminist science studies and climate change". In Alston, M. and Whittenbury, K., *Research, Action and Policy: Addressing the Gendered Impacts of Climate Change*. Dordrecht: Springer. 33–52.

Jasanoff, S. (ed.) (2004) *States of Knowledge: The Co-Production of Science and Social Order*. London: Routledge.

Johnsen, J. P. et al. (2009) "The cyborgization of the fisheries: on attempts to make fisheries management possible". *Maritime Studies* 7 (2): 9–34.

Jonas, M. et al. (1999) "Verification times underlying the Kyoto protocol: global benchmark calculations". Interim Report IR-99-062. Laxenburg: International Institute for Applied Systems Analysis.

Jonas, M. et al. (1998) *Land-use change and forestry in Austria: a scientific assessment of Austria's carbon balance in light of Article 3 of the Kyoto Protocol*. Interim Report IR-98-028. Laxenburg: International Institute for Applied Systems Analysis.

Kay, K. (2015). "A hostile takeover of nature? Placing value in conservation finance". Paper presented at the Financialization of Nature Conference, University of Sussex, 19–20 March.

Keller, E. F. (2011). "What are climate scientists to do?" *Spontaneous Generations: A Journal for the History and Philosophy of Science* 5 (1): 19–26.

Kenney, M. (2015). "Counting, accounting and accountability: Helen Verran's relational empiricism". *Social Studies of Science* 45 (5): 749–771.

Kleinman, D. L. (2003). *Impure Cultures: University Biology and the World of Commerce*. Madison: University of Wisconsin Press.

Knorr-Cetina, K. (1981). *The Manufacture of Knowledge: An Essay on the Constructivist and Contextual Nature of Science*. New York: Pergamon Press.

Kob, J. J. (2015). "Getting the trembling mountain to the market – a history of catastrophe modelling and the emergence of a new disaster risk market". Paper presented at the Financialization of Nature Conference, University of Sussex, 19–20 March.

Kohn, E. (2013). *How Forests Think*. Berkeley: University of California Press.

Kuehls, T. (1998). "Between sovereignty and the environment: an exploration of the discourse of government". In Litfin, K. (ed.) *The Greening of Sovereignty in World Politics*. Cambridge: MIT Press. 31–53.

Lahsen, M. (2005). "Seductive simulations? Uncertainty distribution around climate models". *Social Studies of Science* 35 (6): 895–922.

Lane, R. (2015). "The costs and benefits of nature". Paper presented at the Financialization of Nature Conference, University of Sussex, 19–20 March.

Latour, B. and Woolgar, S. (1979). *Laboratory Life*. London: Sage.

Lewis, S. L. and Maslin, M. A. (2015). "Defining the Anthropocene". *Nature* 519: 171–180.

Lohmann, L. (2016). "What is the 'green' in 'green growth'?" In Dale, G., Mathai, M. and Puppim de Olivera, J., *Green Growth: Ideology, Political Economy and the Alternatives*. London: Zed Books.

Lohmann, L. (2014). "Performative equations and neoliberal commodification: the case of climate". In Fletcher, R., Dressler, W. and Büscher, B. (eds.), *Nature™ Inc: The New Frontiers of Environmental Conservation*. Tucson: University of Arizona Press.

MacKenzie, D. (2009). "Making things the same: gases, emissions rights and the politics of carbon markets". *Accounting, Organizations and Society* 34 (3–4): 440–455.

Malm, A. (2014). *Fossil Capital: The Rise of Steam-Power in the British Cotton Industry c. 1828–1840 and the Roots of Global Warming*. PhD dissertation, Lund University.

Martin, E. (1989). *The Woman in the Body: A Cultural Analysis of Reproduction*. Milton Keynes: Open University Press.

Maunder, W. J. (1970). *The Value of the Weather*. London: Methuen.

Mirowski, P. (1992). *More Heat than Light: Economics as Social Physics, Physics as Nature's Economics*. Cambridge: Cambridge University Press.

Mitchell, T. (2002). *Rule of Experts: Egypt, Technopolitics, Modernity*. Berkeley: University of California Press.

Moore, J. W. (2015). *Capitalism in the Web of Life: Ecology and the Accumulation of Capital*. London: Verso.

Nelson, J. A. (2008). "Economists, value judgments, and climate change: a view from feminist economics", *Ecological Economics* 65 (2008): 441–7.

Nelson, S. H. (2015). "Beyond *The Limits to Growth*: ecology and the neoliberal counterrevolution". *Antipode* 47 (2): 461–80.

Nilsson, S. et al. (2000). "Full carbon account for Russia". Interim Report IR-00-021. Laxenburg: International Institute for Applied Systems Analysis.

No REDD Platform (2011). "Open letter of concern to the international donor community about the diversion of existing forest conservation and development funding to REDD+", http://wrm.org.uy/all-campaigns/open-letter-of-concern-to-the-international-donor-community-about-the-diversion-of-existing-forest-conservation-and-development-funding-to-redd/.

Paterson, M. and Stripple, J. (2007). "Singing climate change into existence: on the territorialization of climate policymaking". In Pettenger, M. (ed.), *The Social Construction of Climate Change: Power, Knowledge, Norms, Discourses*. Aldershot: Ashgate. 149–172.

Pawliczek, J. and Sullivan, S. (2011). "Conservation and concealment in SpeciesBanking.com,US: an analysis of performance in the species offsetting service industry". *Environmental Conservation* 38 (4): 435–44.

Ramirez-i-Olle, M. (2015). "Rhetorical strategies for scientific authority: a boundary-work analysis of 'climategate'". *Science as Culture* 24 (4): 384–411.

Resources for the Future. (2015). *2014 Annual Report*. Washington: RFF.

Robertson, M. (2012). "Measurement and alienation: making a world of ecosystem services". *Transactions of the Institute of British Geographers* 37 (3): 386–401.

Robertson, M. (2007). "Discovering price in all the wrong places: the work of commodity definition and price under neoliberal environmental policy". *Antipode* 39 (3): 500–526.

Romm, J. (2011). "Bill McKibben and Betsy Taylor on the merger of 350.org and 1Sky". *Climate Progress* website, 7 April, http://thinkprogress.org/climate/2011/04/07/207849/bill-mckibben-betsy-taylor-merger-350-org-1sky/?mobile=nc.

Rorty, R. (1991). *Objectivity, Relativism and Truth*. Cambridge: Cambridge University Press.

Rouse, J. (2002). "Vampires: social constructivism, realism and other philosophical undead". *History and Theory* 41: 60–78.

Rouse, J. (1996) *Engaging Science: How to Understand its Practices Philosophically*. Ithaca: Cornell University Press.

Schiebinger, L. (2004). *Nature's Body: Sexual Politics and the Making of Modern Science*. New Brunswick: Rutgers University Press.

Schultze, E.D. et al. (2002). "The long way from Kyoto to Marrakesh: implications of the Kyoto Protocol negotiations for global ecology". *Global Change Biology* 8: 505–518.

Schulze, E.-D. et al. (2000) "Managing forests after Kyoto". *Science* 289: 2058.

Scrap the EU ETS Coalition. (2013). "It is time to scrap the ETS". Available from www.tni.org/files/download/scrap_the_ets18feb.pdf.

Seager, J. (2009). "Death by degrees: taking a feminist hard look at the 2° climate policy". *Kvinder Køn & Forskning* 3–4: 11–2.

Shapin, S. and Schaffer, S. (1989). *Leviathan and the Air-Pump: Hobbes, Boyle, and the Experimental Life*. Princeton: Princeton University Press.

Smith, W. D. (2007). "Presence of mind as working climate change knowledge: a Totonac cosmopolitics". In Pettenger, M. (ed.), *The Social Construction of Climate Change: Power, Knowledge, Norms, Discourses*. Aldershot: Ashgate. 217–34.

Taylor, M. (2015). *The Political Ecology of Climate Change Adaptation: Livelihoods, Agrarian Change and the Conflicts of Development*. New York: Routledge.

Thongchai Winichakul. (1994). *Siam Mapped*. Honolulu: University of Hawaii Press.

Thorpe, C. (2008). "Political theory in science and technology studies". In Hackett, E. J. et al. (eds.), *The Handbook of Science and Technology Studies*. Cambridge, MA: MIT Press. 63–82.

Tyfield, D. (2012). *The Economics of Science: A Critical Realist Overview. Volume 2: Towards a Synthesis of Political Economy and Science and Technology Studies*. London: Routledge.

United Nations Framework Convention on Climate Change. (2015). "Adoption of the Paris Agreement. Proposal by the President. Draft decision -/CP.21". Bonn: UNFCCC.

United Nations Framework Convention on Climate Change. (2013). "Climate change: the physical science basis". Bonn: UNFCCC.

Verran, H. (2001). *Science and an African Logic*. Chicago: University of Chicago Press.

Viveiros de Castro, E. (2004a). "Perspectival anthropology and the method of controlled equivocation". *Tipití* 2 (1): 3–22.

Viveiros de Castro, E. (2004b). "Exchanging perspective: the transformation of objects into subjects in Amerindian ontologies". *Common Knowledge* 10 (3): 463–84.

Woods, B. (2007). "Political economy of science". In Ritzer, G. (ed.) *Blackwell Encyclopedia of Sociology*. Oxford: Blackwell.

23

COMMERCIALIZING ENVIRONMENTAL DATA

Samuel Randalls

Introduction

In Scott's (1998) classic account of government, *Seeing like a State*, he argues that state power is established through an administrative vision that enables government to track, monitor and record citizens, and engineer policies to enhance economic development. Increasingly, seeing like a state means 'seeing like a market' (a term used in reference to Foucault by Tellmann, 2009 and being developed by Fourcade and Healy, 2013). Markets have become dominant ways of resolving all kinds of policy problems, from CO_2 to water supply, and from energy to healthcare. More fundamentally, the general epistemic warrant given to 'the marketplace' as the best adjudicator of expertise is a core trademark of neoliberal thinking. In the 'marketplace of ideas', the market delivers the best verified and established information, its raw information processing capacity far surpassing the ability of states or intelligent persons (Mirowski, 2011). Markets can be trusted to deliver solutions not simply because they may provide regulatory fixes for a wide range of problems, but because they have the ability to *know* better than a state could. As Mirowski (2012) somewhat bluntly states, a neoliberal agenda does not invest hope in state-funded science, but rather in the "day when all knowledge (and not just science) is comprehensively funded and coordinated by the market, which really means private corporations, and state-organized research is reduced to a pitiful insignificant remnant" (Mirowski, 2012: 306). If states see like markets, then there would be a withdrawal from state funding of science and state intervention into knowledge production. In line with this conclusion, a significant literature on the political economy of science has emerged particularly focusing on innovation, research and development as arenas in which marketization is increasing visible (and as chapters in this book demonstrate). But in Scott's (1998) account, data practices are central to seeing like a state whether through censuses, surveys or maps. Likewise in Mitchell's (2002) account of the formation of national economic management there is a reorganization and transformation of calculative practices (property titling, surveys and maps, national statistics) that is crucial to establishing 'the economy' as an object for development. Data are equally central therefore to seeing like a market.

Debates about the commercialization and marketization of data are familiar within the context of biomedicine and pharmaceutical science, focusing on the loss of the free and open exchange of information, the data agreements that restrict further use, and the studies that are simply obscured or published with limited or misleading findings (Krimsky, 2003). Yet it is not just in the fields of biomedicine that data have become a critical site for governmental intervention in the spirit of market and neoliberal oriented reforms. As Bates (2014) has noted, information policy across government is central to delivering on such neoliberal visions. In the U.K. the settlement in the 1950s–70s whereby data were funded by taxpayers for the general public good, was transformed by the cost recovery programmes of Thatcher's government in the 1980s, a settlement that is being transformed again now by open access. Government agencies have been under pressure to demonstrate and extract the economic value of the data they provide and store. This is as true with the case of environmental, particularly meteorological, data and services as it is with other areas of government remit.

This question of what government should provide has often been considered more broadly in terms of the literature on public goods. In meteorological terms, public goods are often considered to cover basic infrastructure, essential data products and some basic services such as severe weather forecasts, where lives are in imminent danger (Freebairn and Zillman, 2002). They are national public goods as their provision is non-rival and many users benefit from their consumption. But not all data or forecasts would be considered public goods. High-resolution data beyond what publics would regularly use and specialist forecasts (whether more spatially or temporally or weather-specific covering particular industry requests e.g. for frost for creating cement) would be considered to be value-added. In other words, data and services that emanate from the same infrastructure are conceived differentially as public or private goods based on the use to which they are put. As Johnson and Rampini (this volume) point out in the case of global climate models, the models are not built for one purpose or user but they are made to be relevant for purposes or users by the "institutional and financial orders governing production and distribution of data." Likewise in meteorology, I suggest, what is to be defined as a core public good part is not a settled object, but rather an emergent configuration shaped by regulations and ideals. If, as this chapter will suggest, these regulations and ideals are increasingly moulded to commercial and neoliberal ends, then this is a significant area for research within the political economy of science.

It is this chapter's core claim that environmental data in the U.K. and the U.S. are increasing treated as markets rather than as primarily public goods. Yet this is neither a straightforward process towards marketization nor one that leads to outcomes that are always welcomed by commercial actors. Commercialization and marketization are messy processes (Mirowski and van Horn, 2005) and thus seeing like a market is not simply an unfolding story of neoliberal achievement. In the case of meteorology explored here, I first outline a brief history of commercial meteorology to outline some of the market-oriented practices they have suggested, but then in more detail move on to consider how governments have translated the goals of national meteorological providers, particularly the U.K. Met Office, to deliver on the commercial value of meteorological data and services. This is achieved through changes in accountancy practices and regulations and policies that define public and commercial services, but which re-define their objects in new ways. It is the contention in this chapter that these have frequently paralleled neoliberal arguments, but that these have been resisted and transformed too, such that what has been developed reflects a diversity of practices. That said, the fundamental presupposition of the centrality and vitality of the 'marketplace of ideas' is central and it is therefore important to combine studies of complexity in practice as STS scholars are so expert at doing, with a renewed attention to the political economy of science that directs analytical focus to the ways in which science is increasingly seen like a market.

Early arguments for market-oriented meteorology from industry

Meteorology as a discipline has long had a commercial component, particularly in the U.S. A surplus of war-time-trained meteorologists led to the creation of a raft of new commercially oriented meteorological jobs within companies and an emergent consultancy sector. Commercial meteorologists made regular claims for their value and usefulness to society, not least in relation to economic sectors such as agriculture, fisheries, energy, air pollution and importantly aviation. For example, Du Pont offered short-range weather forecasting for construction and to predict storms and tides for plants in vulnerable coastal locations and, in 1953, established a Severe Weather Advisory Service (Collins and Evans, 1958). For Du Pont, the advantage of a private-sector meteorologist was that they intimately knew the company's plant sites and could therefore understand the interactions between weather events and the specific conditions of each bay and inlet, in a way the Weather Bureau could not. As Francis Reichelderfer, Chief of the Weather Bureau, said: "The government cannot possibly handle all the applications of meteorology for aviation and industry. Is it to be left undeveloped because the government cannot handle it?" No; after all, he continued, "Americans believe in private enterprise" (Reichelderfer, 1949: 79).

Commercial meteorology organizations were growing in number, led by people like Malone at the Travelers Insurance Company based in Hartford, Connecticut who headed up the Travelers Weather Research Centre within the company in 1954 (Janković, 2015). Malone estimated a quadrupling of private consultancy companies in the previous ten years (but this would have been from a very low base of fewer than ten in the 1940s) and noted that a new organization was needed, a meteorological equivalent of the National Bureau of Economic Research. Weather knowledge could aid economic growth and profit, not just simply act as an information service. Even university meteorologists were starting to embrace the new commercial operations. David Ludlum, Chairman of the Committee on Industrial, Bureau and Applied Meteorology stated that "It is an unimaginative meteorology professor who walks on campus today without two or three consulting contracts in his pocket" (Ludlum, 1953: 125).

Commercial meteorologists, however, had to work hard to convince doubters of their expertise. A long-running jibe suggested that commercial meteorologists were counterfeiters in that they took public meteorological information and put their own twist or specificity on it, but did not really add anything in terms of expertise (see critiques of this in Courtney, 1979; Smith, 2002). Cheerleading for the commercial meteorologists, on the other hand, were people like Charles Pennypacker Smith, of Pacific Gas and Transmission, who argued that "active, overt, challenging, and financially rewarding competition" was the key to a thriving commercial meteorology (Smith, 1970: 97). Even individuals whose ideas might be considered crazy should be allowed expression, he stated, noting a forecaster in the company who believed that a severe winter storm in the English Channel would be followed a week later by a damaging storm in California. Why should such claims simply be discarded by scientists without seeing if they work economically? The marketplace would decide what would be considered relevant expertise, not some notional scientific expert.

In part as a result of fears that 'crazy' claims might diminish the professionalization of commercial meteorology, a system of Certified Consulting Meteorologists was established by the American Meteorological Society in 1957 to enable a formal process to recognise expertise within the commercial meteorology sector and protect their reputations. A parallel, though not equivalent, marker of expertise emerged from the University of Birmingham, which established an MSc in Applied Meteorology and Climatology in 1963 to enable the development of applied and commercial meteorology (Janković, 2015). During the 1960s the American National

Council of Industrial Meteorologists was organized as a professional body, and about 36 companies featured in lists of applied meteorology in the *Bulletin of the American Meteorological Society*. In the 1970s, some research labs were outsourced (though this was not a universal change) and consultancies emerged to perform the research previously conducted by the in-house teams (see Mirowski and van Horn, 2005, for the general point). By 1971 there were 52 firms offering consultancy work listed in the *Bulletin of the American Meteorological Society*, with 21 having at least one of their personnel trained formally as a Certified Consulting Meteorologist. The number of private meteorology companies listed in BAMS rose to 81 by 1979 and by 1990 it was over 100. Spiegler's (1996) review suggested that there were then over 2,200 private meteorologists by 1996, with their companies having a business volume of $780–1,100 million per year. In the U.S. this proliferation of firms, as compared to the U.K. (Ellig, 1989), has been said to arise from the funding structure of meteorology. To explore the different funding structures and how they have been translated into a market-oriented agenda, I next turn to the government side of this story.

Government interest in the commercial value of meteorology

As meteorology embraced numerical modelling that required ever-faster computing power, the cost to government increased rapidly, leading to much concern to economically justify investment in meteorology especially for publicly funded offices (Janković, 2015). An economic rationale, however, was not uniformly implemented and it is worth briefly contrasting the regulatory cases of the U.S. and the U.K.

In the U.S., the progenitor of the National Weather Service was founded in 1870 under the title of 'The Division of Telegrams and Reports for the Benefit of Commerce' (Fleming, 1990). Concerned with a disciplined telegraph system, it was established under the Department of War, but was renamed the Weather Bureau and transferred to the Department of Agriculture in 1890, where it was sited until transfer to the Department of Commerce in 1940 (Daipha, 2015). The name was changed from the Weather Bureau to the National Weather Service (NWS) in 1970 as it moved under the administration of the National Oceanic and Atmospheric Administration. Except for a brief foray into charging for data in the late 1940s (Spiegler, 1996), the NWS provided data for free, enabling companies to use this to create and tailor forecasts and services to their own needs. This was central to government policy to only provide essential public services and basic infrastructure – what Freebairn and Zillman (2002) classified as public goods – while leaving the rest to commercial operators. As re-iterated in a 1991 government policy statement, the NWS focus was to protect life and property (e.g. severe weather alerts) and, for all else, to provide freely accessible meteorological data which private meteorologists could use to construct their own products (Daipha, 2015; Spiegler, 1996).

While the NWS continued to issue regular forecasts through into the 1990s, they lost out to competition: in media, from television news stations and particularly the Weather Channel for public weather forecasts, especially once news stations acquired their own weather radars from the 1980s; and for specialist forecasts, to commercial weather forecasters, e.g. in 1995 the NWS passed on its agricultural and non-wildfire fire weather services to commercial operators (Daipha, 2015). Private weather companies were establishing "new weather information display techniques, private weather data networks and uses of computer managed databases that rival those being created in the government and, at times, surpassing the capabilities of the federal weather service" (Pearl and Henz, 1980: 280). The NWS's role was to set this market free.

In the U.K. on the other hand, there was a rather different regulatory set-up. Historically, the U.K. Met Office started out in the 19th century within the Board of Trade, but was transferred to defence in the First World War, and remained in the Ministry of Defence until coming round full circle with the transfer to Business, Innovation and Skills in 2011 (Hall, 2015; Walker, 2012). While the Met Office provides public information and forecasts from its own data as with the NWS, it can openly compete with commercial companies in selling more specialized weather services and products too. This has led some private meteorologists to claim that the Met Office can act as a monopoly competitor that forces competition out by inflating data prices and cross-subsidizing its commercial operation from its public expertise (see for example Ellig, 1989). Ironically, therefore, the need to generate a market-oriented meteorology in the U.K. has established a framework in which the monopoly provider is widely criticized for blocking the emergence of competitors i.e. being anti-market at some level. Commercial meteorology was much slower to emerge and generate significant investment, at least in part because of the Met Office's dominant position in the marketplace (Ellig, 1989).

The structure of the government agency for meteorology plays an important role in shaping the prospects for commercial meteorology. As Ellig (1989: 14) puts it, "The British policy attempts to make a government bureau function more like a private business, while the US policy restrains a government bureau so that private businesses can enter the field." While the U.S. approach enabled the NWS to support a market in commercial meteorology, in the U.K. the same organization that provided the public goods (the Met Office) would equally be encouraged to sell commercial services to maximise cost recovery. The arguments in the U.K. and U.S. have strong family resemblances, not least in their desire for marketization, but they are institutionalized and regulated in contrasting ways, what might usefully be termed 'variegated neoliberalism' (Brenner, Peck and Theodore, 2010). Both were based on an interpretation of the arguments about public goods.

Public goods, for economists, are non-rival and non-excludable, benefiting all, and their use by one does not affect their use by another. Meteorological data and forecasts might seem to sit fairly neatly within this definition, except that it prompts a further question – whether the same level of quality and quantity of data and forecasts provided are needed for all users. In other words, do all users benefit equally from enhancements in meteorological capacity? For the U.S. the answer was that only basic data was a public good. The pitfall of this system, for marketeers, was that there was arguably little incentive to improve the quality of basic data if the agency responsible for its construction had no commercial stake in the value that this data received in the marketplace. The challenge with charging for basic data, however, was that there was a monopoly supplier (the national meteorological service) and if that supplier was also competing with value-added suppliers then there was an inequitable competition basis. This prompted a more complex debate in the U.K. about the boundary between public and private goods. This played out through shifting regulatory and accounting environments for the Met Office and it is useful to turn to these next to explore the contradictory dynamics of commercialization.

Making meteorology a commercial activity for government

The Met Office was perceived to be a prime candidate for emerging Trading Fund legislation in the 1970s. Trading Funds would set up a new efficient management for government offices that served public and (potential) commercial goals. The advantages of the Trading Fund designation were seen to be greater accountability for staff, clearer internal management, better cost recovery and a clear demarcation between services that would be provided on a commercial basis and services that needed to be provided on a public basis. Within trading funds, internal accountancy changes would enable better cost recovery through charging end-users for data and services, while maintaining an ideal of public service too. For environmental data, this legislation implies treating science as another kind of bureaucratic concern to deliver on economic goals.

But if the Trading Fund legislation is clear in what it sets out to achieve, in practice it did not simply roll out easily. There were competing arguments about the legislation including concerns about what might happen to data or products which might not attract sufficient commercial value but would still be societally important. Trading Funds did not necessarily mean that services in the public interest would be abandoned where there was no substitute or where they failed to pay their way (Earl of Lauderdale (HL Deb, 1973)), but rather that the designation of Trading Funds would establish an economic rationale for recovering the costs of taxpayer-funded work. Users would be central and enable the marketplace of users to shape the nature of future government work rather than experts always defining what should be provided. But there were concerns:

> the Government are inclined to regard the trading fund device as essentially a managerial device which does not necessarily affect policy, that it … is really only another way of running the Ordnance Survey… I am concerned, as indeed are many people who use maps, that the availability and cost of these maps is likely to be determined much more by a commercial approach.
>
> *(Earl of Lauderdale, (HL Deb, 1973))*

The Earl's angst here was that, for maps, for example, given that the main users would be other public bodies, in essence one part of the government would be trying to extract revenue from another part of government. The 'customer–contractor principle' would mean that information users would pay the relevant cost of access to the information they required. This legislative change needed to be accompanied by an accounting change within organizations like the Ordnance Survey and the Met Office to distinguish public and commercial services.

The key accounting change was from a public service approach to a cost recovery system. As Broadbent and Guthrie (1992: 3) have suggested, public-sector accountancy moved from a concern with "probity, compliance and control…" to one where "the emphasis now is on changing the character of the discourse and technologies to promote what is characterized as efficiency, effectiveness, cost savings and streamlining – managerialism in the public sector" (see also Robins and Webster, 1988). By exploring the full cost of providing public services, management hoped to achieve greater efficiencies within the public sector (Ellwood and Newberry, 2007). Indeed, in the case of the Met Office, which was not formally instituted as a trading fund until 1996, these accountancy changes in the 1980s shaped the organization to behave in a commercially oriented way that steered the organization towards Trading Fund status.

The National Audit Office, which was set up in 1983 with the National Audit Act to aid with privatization programmes (McEldowney, 1991), made two key arguments for a better cost recovery of services. First, they suggested that Met Office's free services restricted growth; that is, they prevented the development of a marketized meteorology. Second, drawing from the work of consultants, they concluded that the Met Office activities were under-priced, which meant that government was not recovering as much money as it could do (National Audit Office, 1986). Cost recovery accountancy, on the other hand, would enable a clearer structure in which the Met Office could become more economically efficient. In practice, cost recovery sent the budget deficit down as private users were charged for information on a commercial basis, but with accountancy changes the expenditure on free services went up as the percentage of overheads attributed to the public services was increased significantly between 1983–5 (Table 23.1).

Table 23.1 Changes in the attribution of costs of respective Met Office services, 1983-5

	1983–4	1984–5
Budget deficit	£8mn	£0.8mn
Expenditure on free public services	10%	28%
Attribution of central overheads:		
Armed forces	46%	40%
Free public services	10%	32.5%
Civil aviation	22.5%	22.5%
General repayment	21.5%	5%

Source: Data from Sharp and Hansford, as synthesized in Wood, 1997

The Met Office needed to generate further revenue. The 1985 Sharp and Hansford report's answer was that data would not be available free of charge since it was not in the public (taxpayers') interest (Sharp and Hansford, 1985) and charging at commercial rates would prove the value of meteorology to government. Equally, prices could not be too high or else customers would rely on that basic, free public weather information and thus not pay for enhanced data or forecasts (National Audit Office, 1986). Charging for data would maximize the public value from taxpayer investment as it would focus attention on those services the 'users' actually wanted. Data would be treated as a market good. The taxpayer would only indirectly reap any benefits from meteorology as the public would not have free access to all the enhanced data or products.

With the promise of more independence for an organization like the Met Office came the unambiguous message that the price of this freedom was an orientation to commercial activity. "The Met Office is in practice a business activity and not a government organization in the usual sense and therefore it should adopt a commercial approach in all its dealings" (Sharp and Hansford, 1985: 14). Internally, the Met Office would have to account for the division of all of its activities: those that served a clear commercial purpose, with products that would be priced at a level the market would bear, and those that were essential for public services such as emergency weather forecast alerts. Met Office staff were less than comfortable with this division, not least as it enforced artificial separation between forecasters' work, and frustrated managers confessed that some parts of the operation paid too little regard to business targets, with the National Audit Office (1995) commenting that managers had resisted changes to traditional ways of working amidst claims that new ways of measuring performance were inadequate. In the 1990-1995 period the Met Office was placed under clear efficiency targets, including stronger engagement in performance management, reduction of costs, and a 6 per cent increase in uptake in services across both the public and commercial sectors with commercial service revenue to increase by 10 per cent (Walker, 2012). This led the Met Office to adopt new commercial activities, though many private meteorological companies complained that the Met Office had an unfair advantage based on its ownership and pricing of the datasets that only the Met Office had the power to collect.

The Met Office was finally established as a trading fund on 1 April 1996 and faced immediate targets to further enhance efficiency, customer satisfaction, model accuracy and a value-for-money index to judge the quality of its services (Walker, 2012). Further bureaucratic performance management measures were enacted to improve efficiency and effectiveness in the new commercial era. Yet, if the trading fund legislation was to encourage competition, there has been a conspicuous lack of serious competition in British meteorology. As Mirowski (2011: 268) notes, "once data provision becomes privatized, it usually follows that a form of oligopolistic competition sets in." Despite some high-profile casualties such as the Met Office losing prestige weather forecast contracts, such as for the BBC, ironically because the BBC was forced to seek out the best value for money (BBC, 2015), the Met Office accounts show that it still receives some 80 per cent of its funding from government sources. So while the Met Office has been made to see the provision of meteorology as like a market, through accounting, legislation and internal targets, the state remains its biggest market.

That said, after the Met Office officially became a trading fund, its then Chief Executive Prof. Julian Hunt argued that the new commercial-like operation would present "great opportunities to be competitive in the growing markets for meteorology and environmental services" (Cited in Walker, 2012: 429). One of its flagship interventions was the 2001 establishment of the company weatherXchange, a joint partnership with a financial brokerage company. WeatherXchange was formed to provide services (data and forecasts) to the emerging weather futures market, an industry that by its very nature transformed meteorological information into a market (Randalls, 2010). It was to enormous embarrassment that weatherXchange went bankrupt with the loss of about £1.5mn of public funds and to even greater discomfort when called out at a parliamentary hearing in 2006 after Met Office executives publicly stated that they had deliberately undercut their joint venture to achieve a greater share of the market and profits themselves (see Randalls, 2010). They had demonstrated in this one incident just how much the Met Office could see like a market. By 2013–14, the Met Office was making an operating profit of £11.2m (Hall, 2015). But there was a new challenge ahead: increasing pressure to free, open access to government data, a campaign that potentially imperilled the cost recovery settlement developed from the 1970s.

Towards open data

In the 2000s, movements for open access data including *The Guardian's* 'Free our Data' campaign put pressure on the U.K. government to release more data to public (and commercial) access. The U.K.'s Department for the Environment, Food and Rural Affairs (hereafter Defra) was set a target to deliver 8000 open datasets by June 2016 for everything from long-term ecological monitoring and environmental quality through to ecological survey data, the national food survey and agricultural statistics (Coley and Newman, 2016; Ross, 2016). Central to this was a concern to put users first and consider how open data might be taken up in productive ways. In principle what this meant was that data are to be adjudicated and valued by the marketplace of users while data providers compete (or in the case of government departments, enhance quality provision) to meet user demands (see the Defra Digital blog, e.g. Kavanagh, 2016). Indeed data releases have been described as being on a 'use it or lose it' basis because government cannot afford to keep producing open data for only a few end-users (personal communication). Data that are of limited user value, but not demonstrably in the public interest, may simply be removed as the new strictures on quality and availability of data restrict the possibility of maintaining everything.

As government agencies are to account for and recover costs from their data and services, yet increasingly be open access, there are real challenges, particularly where a significant data infrastructure is required (Edwards, 2010). Within remote sensing, there has been considerable discussion of the possibilities and pitfalls of open vs commercial satellite system data. Johnston and Cordes (2003) discussed the Landsat satellite system, where new laws in the 1980s were enacted to privatize the operation of weather satellites and the commercialization of remote sensing capabilities. This was intended as a ten-year experiment, but lasted a little less than that and was repealed in 1992 as the commercialization had not been successful. As a result of this,

Landsat data became freely provided with no restrictions on commercial use (Harris and Baumann, 2015). The Iraq war further emphasized the value of government-owned Landsat data and there were few signs that Landsat had the capability to operate as a commercial-only entity (Johnston and Cordes, 2003). That, however, did not prevent debates about whether its data were all essential for providing other public goods and, in an era of cost recovery, whether other government agencies would pay for that data. By 2001 there were competing remote sensing systems generating data for diverse users with commercial systems providing high spatial resolutions. There was concomitantly a significant expansion in private or licensed data.

In the case of satellite data, a series of riders were placed on what kinds of data should be provided free of charge, including exemptions if data were affected by issues of security, law, IP, commercial confidentiality, statistical confidentiality, proprietary interests, availability of resources and so on (Harris and Baumann, 2015). In practice that could cover nearly everything in principle, leaving "both data providers and data users with large uncertainty with regard to individual data sets" (Harris and Baumann, 2015: 53) not knowing if they would be maintained, or access would be continued. For the Met Office, likewise, there were similar problems if taxpayer-funded data were released when users were quite prepared to pay a charge for those services enabling the Met Office to recover its costs (Hall, 2015). Commitments to open data were couched within the economic language of preceding approaches (cost recovery), but as Harris and Baumann (2015: 52) put it, "The supply of data free of charge requires continuing assured long-term public funding," precisely what governments did not want to commit to without seeing direct economic returns. The challenge of opening up access to government data had to be squared with the need to maintain arguments about economic efficiency, recovery of costs and marketplace superiority (see Bates, 2014, and Mullerleile, this volume).

Open access may create alternative possibilities too, but it is important to diagnose the continuing neoliberal rhetoric at the heart of this political economy of science when it comes to seeing like a market for environmental data provision. While commercialization and economization are not specifically new (Berman, 2014; Hall, 2015), there are neoliberal resonances in much of the debate about meteorological data. It is not simply about extracting efficient economic value from government services. It is about opening up that data infrastructure to be reorganized as a market in which the marketplace delivers an assessment of the value of the kinds of data produced. It is the marketplace that should reign supreme in deciding on data, not some notional experts or governments. Government agencies are to be taught to see like a market. The example of open data hints at how determinations of the value of data through the marketplace could have significant consequences on what kinds of data are produced and maintained. If only what is used and valued now is maintained in the marketplace of data, then this has all kinds of consequences for the availability of data that might have been useful for other projects in years to come. "*Après moi le déluge!* is the watchword of every capitalist and capitalist nation" (Marx, 2008: 155).

To return to the example of weatherXchange and the weather futures market, traders are much more concerned with accurate, timely data than with improvements in modelled cleaning of data for the long-term records. This is because weather future contracts pay out on the data provided at a specific meteorological station at a specific time and if data are wrong or an instrument is moved without much notice, there is nothing that can be done about it financially (Randalls, 2010). Correcting historical records after the fact is irrelevant. This is just one commercial interest, of course, and others might compete to have historical smoothing at the heart of Met Office policy. The general point, though, is that if particular users commercially direct the data providers to create data for the market there could be overt or subtle shifts in the kinds of data infrastructures created and maintained, less along scientific lines and more along commercial ones.

Conclusions

Data infrastructures do not exist merely to support commercial ends (Benson, 2012); rather they can support multiple, sometimes competing interests (Edwards, 2010). Even if there is a broadly neoliberal policy infrastructure it does not translate that all users will have neoliberal motivations; witness the clamouring by private meteorologists against the increasingly market-oriented Met Office. But neither does this disprove the argument that these data infrastructures are increasingly organized around market-oriented ideas. The regulatory framework that instructs the Met Office to enhance cost recovery, to increase its revenues, to manage the resources in line with the Thatcherite principles underpinning the auditing of government services from the 1980s: all of this comes to shape the collection, use and accessibility of data. Within the political economy of science it is crucial to focus on what are sometimes seemingly banal, but important accounting principles and procedures that enable the formation of a marketized (and neoliberal) approach to data. Data, in other words, have to be central to considerations of the political economy of science.

At one level, this is intuitive territory for science and technology studies scholars. Scientists do not simply go out and collect 'neutral' data on everything without a reason. On the other hand, it seems uncomfortable to reflect on the ways in which a logic of the marketplace of ideas has informed the changing practices of data collection, collation and use. The economics of information underpinning this has been clearly identified by Mirowski (2011): that science's organization, structure and regulation should be supplied through market-oriented tools such that science is treated as per any other commodity. The Met Office is geared to delivering on the foundations of economic growth and efficiency in public services, hoping to both continue the day-to-day income-generating activities while looking to capture market share in meteorological services. Science (often of very high quality) performs a supporting role to administrative economic reason.

In contrasting ways, the U.K. and the U.S. cases demonstrate how to create a market from and in meteorology. Changes in regulations, accounting techniques and auditing regimes are the banal but significant players training scientists and organizations to see like a market. Marketized logics do not simply represent unfolding neoliberalism; they are also an experimentation in governance too (Law and Williams, 2014). They are a situated and variegated assembling of components (from computers to thermometers, and from accounts to staff audit protocols) that unfold in practice in sometimes coherent and sometimes contradictory ways to unlock the market potential of meteorology.

There is, therefore, a family resemblance to core neoliberal principles. Scientists or government experts are not to know what is best; rather, the marketplace of ideas defines the relevant, useful and efficient information required. While commentators like Morss and Hooke (2005) imply that commercialization can be better regulated or managed to ensure that meteorology does not follow the pitfalls of biomedicine, they neglect the foundational economics of information that underpins the enacting of the marketplace as an ideal bar none. If science is to be seen like a market and to see (work) like a market, then for all the variegation and contextual-specificity outlined in this chapter, there is a fundamental (attempt at) marketization of data infrastructures. That is not to say that all users or uses are neoliberal, but rather that a guiding principle is to unlock the market value of meteorological services for the knowledge economy. For research in the political economy of science, scholarship needs to be aware of these kinds of broader philosophies while still remaining alive to the fact that these are in formation rather than already settled. This kind of work might be considered an awkward encounter between political economy and the diverse sites of science in action, but this Handbook suggests that it is a worthwhile goal.

References

Bates, J. 2014. "The strategic importance of information policy for the contemporary neoliberal state: The case of Open Government Data in the United Kingdom", *Government Information Quarterly*, 31(3): 388–395.

BBC 2015. "Met Office loses BBC weather forecasting contract", www.bbc.co.uk/news/uk-34031785 (last accessed 23rd June 2016).

Benson, E. 2012. "One infrastructure, many global visions: The commercialization and diversification of Argos, a satellite-based environmental surveillance system", *Social Studies of Science*, 42(6): 843–68.

Berman, E.P. 2014. "Not just neoliberalism: Economization in US science and technology policy", *Science, Technology and Human Values*, 39(3): 397–431.

Brenner, N., Peck, J. and Theodore, N. 2010. "Variegated neoliberalization: Geographies, modalities, pathways", *Global Networks*, 10(2): 182–222.

Broadbent, J. and Guthrie, J. 1992. "Changes in the public sector: A review of recent 'alternative' accounting research", *Accounting, Auditing and Accountability Journal*, 5(2): 3–31.

Coley, A. and Newman, A. 2016. "Let's make Defra data driven", available from: https://defradigital.blog.gov.uk/2016/02/01/lets-make-defra-data-driven/ (last accessed 23 June 2016).

Collins, C.A. and Evans, G.F. 1958. "Du Pont Tide and Storm Warning Service", in: *Proceedings of the First National Conference on Applied Meteorology*, Boston: American Meteorological Society, A8–A18.

Courtney, F.E. Jr. 1979. "Trends in industrial meteorology", in: *Conference on Climate and Energy: Climatological Aspects and Industrial Operations of the American Meteorological Society*, Boston, MA: American Meteorological Society, 150–152.

Daipha, P. 2015. *Masters of Uncertainty: Weather Forecasters and the Quest for Ground Truth*, Chicago, IL: University of Chicago Press.

Edwards, P.N. 2010. *A Vast Machine: Computer Models, Climate Data, and the Politics of Global Warning*, Cambridge, MA: MIT Press.

Ellig, J.R. 1989. *Set Fair: A Gradualist Proposal for Privatising Weather Forecasting*, London: Social Affairs Unit.

Ellwood, S. and Newberry, S. 2007. "Public sector accrual accounting: institutionalising neo-liberal principles?", *Accounting, Auditing and Accountability Journal*, 20(4): 549–573.

Fleming, J.R. 1990. *Meteorology in America, 1800–1870*, Baltimore, MA: Johns Hopkins University Press.

Fourcade, M. and Healy, K. 2013. "Classification situations: Life-chances in the neoliberal era", *Accounting, Organizations and Society*, 38: 559–572.

Freebairn, J.W. and Zillman, J.W. 2002. "Funding meteorological services", *Meteorological Applications*, 9(1): 45–54.

Hall, A. 2015. "From the airfield to the high street: The Met Office's role in the emergence of commercial weather services", *Weather, Climate, and Society*, 7: 211–223.

Harris, R. and Baumann, I. 2015. "Open data policies and satellite Earth observation", *Space Policy*, 32: 44–53.

HL Deb, 1973. "Government trading funds bill", 345, 338-69. HMSO: London.

Janković, V. 2015. "Working with weather: Atmospheric resources, climate variability and the rise of industrial meteorology, 1950–2010", *History of Meteorology*, 7: 98–111.

Johnston, S. and Cordes, J. 2003. "Public good or commercial opportunity? Case studies in remote sensing commercialization", *Space Policy*, 19: 23–31.

Kavanagh, M. 2016. "Data Programme Board: putting the user first", https://defradigital.blog.gov.uk/2016/04/27/data-programme-board-putting-the-user-first/ (last accessed, 23/06/2016).

Krimsky, S. 2003. *Science in the Private Interest: Has the Lure of Profits Corrupted Biomedical Research?*, Lanham, MA: Rowman and Littlefield.

Law, J. and Williams, K. 2014. "A state of unlearning? Government as experiment", *CRESC Working Paper 134*, www.cresc.ac.uk/medialibrary/workingpapers/wp134.pdf (last accessed 29 June 2016).

Ludlum, D.M. 1953. "The private practice of meteorology", *Weatherwise*, 6(5): 124–125.

Marx, K. 2008. Edited by Elster, J. *Karl Marx: A Reader*, Cambridge: Cambridge University Press.

McEldowney, J.F. 1991. "The National Audit Office and privatisation", *The Modern Law Review*, 54(6): 933–955.

Mirowski, P. 2011. *Science-Mart: Privatizing American Science*, Cambridge, MA: Harvard University Press.

Mirowski, P. 2012. "The modern commercialization of science is a passel of Ponzi schemes", *Social Epistemology*, 26(3–4): 285–310.

Mirowski, P. 2013. *Never Let a Serious Crisis go to Waste: How Neoliberalism Survived the Financial Meltdown*, London: Verso.

Mirowski, P. and van Horn, R. 2005. "The Contract Research Organization and the commercialization of scientific research", *Social Studies of Science*, 35(4): 503–548.

Mitchell, T. 2002. *Rule of Experts: Egypt, Techno-Politics, Modernity*, Berkeley, CA: University of California Press.

Morss, R.E. and Hooke, W.H. 2005. "The outlook for U.S. meteorological research in a commercializing world: Fair early, but clouds moving in?", *Bulletin of the American Meteorological Society*, 86(7): 921–936.

National Audit Office, 1986. *Ministry of Defence: Financial Arrangements for the Provision of Meteorological Services*, London: HMSO.

National Audit Office, 1995. *The Meteorological Office Executive Agency: Evaluation of Performance*, London: HMSO.

Pearl, E.W. and Henz, J.F. 1980. "On the role of private meteorologists in operational meteorology", in: *8th Conference on Weather Forecasting and Analysis, Denver, CO*, Boston: American Meteorological Society, 278–281.

Randalls, S. 2010. "Weather profits: Weather derivatives and the commercialization of meteorology", *Social Studies of Science*, 40(5): 705–730.

Reichelderfer, F.W. 1949. "Policy with respect to private practice of meteorology", in: *Conference of Weather Bureau Forecasters*, Washington, DC: Weather Bureau, 79–80.

Robins, K. and Webster, F. 1988. "Cybernetic capitalism: Information, technology, everyday life", in: Mosco, V. and Wasko, J. (eds) *The Political Economy of Information*, University of Wisconsin Press: Madison, WI, 44–75.

Ross, H. 2016. "Natural England hits its target early", available from: https://defradigital.blog.gov.uk/2016/03/29/natural-england-hits-its-target-early/ (Last accessed 23 June 2016).

Scott, J.C. 1998. *Seeing Like a State: How Certain Schemes to Improve the Human Condition Have Failed*, New Haven, CT: Yale University Press.

Sharp, K.J. and Hansford, J. 1985. *The Meteorological Office: Financial Management*, Bracknell: Meteorological Office.

Smith, C.P. 1970. "Expanding the usefulness of meteorology in the private sector", in: Caskey, J.E. (ed). *A Century of Progress: A Collection of Addresses Presented at a Joint Symposium Commemorating the Centennial of the U.S. Weather Service and the Golden Anniversary of the American Meteorological Society*, Boston, MA: American Meteorological Society, 95–99.

Smith, M.R. 2002. "Five myths of commercial meteorology", *Bulletin of the American Meteorological Society*, 83(7): 993–996.

Spiegler, D.B. 1996. "A history of private sector meteorology", in: Fleming, J.R. (ed) *Historical Essays on Meteorology, 1919–1995*, Boston, MA: American Meteorological Society, 417–441.

Tellmann, U. 2009. "Foucault and the invisible economy", *Foucault Studies*, 6: 5–24.

Walker, J.M. 2012. *History of the Meteorological Office*, New York, NY: Cambridge University Press.

Wood, A.C.M. 1997. *The Meteorological Office: Trading Fund and Beyond*, MSc Dissertation, School of Defence Management, Cranfield University.

24

SCIENCE AND STANDARDS

Elizabeth Ransom, Maki Hatanaka, Jason Konefal and Allison Loconto

Introduction

Interest in the study of standards and standardization within the social sciences has grown dramatically over the past two decades (Timmermans and Epstein 2010). Prior to that time, standards largely remained in the realm of the technical (e.g. U.S. Standards for Grain). Officially, standards are created to standardize processes (industrial and management), to facilitate trade by both ensuring inter-operability and encouraging competition through differentiation, and to protect consumers by stabilizing product qualities. In doing so, standards are presented as strictly technical details, based on scientific criteria, around which people and things are expected to conform (e.g. standard dress sizes require both fabric and humans to conform to a fixed set of measurements).

Standards and standardization can be found throughout every major social institution including the military (e.g. standard uniforms and weapons), medicine (e.g. the *International Classification of Diseases*, now in its tenth edition), education (e.g. standardized testing), and the economy (e.g. a single standard currency for each nation, usually backed by a state-owned national bank) (see Busch 2011, 93–112). Indeed, only through the standardizing of markets and the economy as a whole has world trade been able to increase (Busch 2011, 112). One area of tremendous growth has been in agriculture and food (agrifood) trade. Without overstating the case, standards and standardization have played a large role in the creation of our globalized food system, in that standards and standardization provide a means of simplifying what could be a very laborious and complex process. Initially, the use of standards and standardization afforded the creation of global grain commodities, as everything from seeds to fertilizer became standardized (Busch 2011). However, in recent years, standards have been used systematically to differentiate products and processes. Within the social sciences, social studies of science approaches in combination with political economic approaches have shed light on the ways in which technical standards are inherently social and part of power struggles, not simply in their formation, but also in their implementation and outcomes.

Three case studies elaborate how a combination of political economic and science studies approaches can illuminate the social, political and economic decisions behind the scientific standards used to create more sustainable agrifood systems. The first focuses on sustainable agriculture standards in the United States and the ways in which the market increasingly influences the standard-setting process and benefits dominant companies in the marketplace. The second examines efforts to construct global "sustainable" beef production standards and the ways smallholder farmers in Southern Africa will not likely benefit from the new standards. The third case study explores a participatory guarantee system, an alternative certification system based on the concept of farmer-led evaluation of farming practices at a local level in Colombia, which seeks to resolve tensions between different types of knowledge in the development and enforcement of standards by creating hybrid practices in organic agricultural production. All three case studies provide a lens for understanding the political economy of standards, notably the privileging of particular types of knowledge and agricultural practices and the ways in which the market shapes standards creation, implementation, and enforcement.

Standards

Standards are agreed-upon criteria for a product or process (Brunsson and Jacobsson 2000; Giovannucci and Ponte 2005). Standards are a ubiquitous part of daily life, whether in the realm of education, health care, or food and agriculture. Yet, far from being strictly technical details, scholars and practitioners alike have increasingly recognized that "standards are intimately associated with power" (Busch 2011, 13). The construction and implementation of standards construct the world in certain ways instead of others (Busch 2000; Brunsson and Jacobsson 2000), and by implication standards are one means by which products, processes, people, and other living entities (e.g. bacteria and animals) are judged.

New types of standards and processes for standards development and implementation have become more important with increased global trade (Giovannucci and Ponte 2005). Specifically, private-sector, voluntary standards have proliferated. Whereas public standards are those criteria created by government authority and enforced through laws and regulations, private standards are any standards created by private interests (e.g. a company, industry, or a non-governmental organization (NGO)) and generally are enforced through market mechanisms (Bain et al. 2013). Private standards are often referred to as voluntary, because there are no laws requiring adoption, but rather adoption becomes *de facto* mandatory in that if a seller wants a company to purchase a product, the seller must conform to various private standards. For example, in 2007, when Unilever announced that it would source only Rainforest Alliance-certified tea by 2015, a seemingly voluntary standard became mandatory for market access because other large tea blenders – Tetley, Twinings, Sara Lee – announced similar policies. Because of concentration in the tea industry, nearly half of all buyers were demanding certified tea and because tea is a blended product most producers sell at least a small percentage of their production to one of these companies. In order to stay in the business, farmers needed to become certified (Loconto 2010).

With globalization and economic liberalization, the agricultural sector has shifted from government regulation to increasingly private or public–private regulation, most of which is occurring via standards creation and implementation. Private standards are not only viewed as a means to overcome the limits of state capacity to regulate food supply chains, but also as an opportunity for states to delegate regulation to private actors (Ponte, Gibbon, and Vestergaard 2011). Yet, far from a complete retreat of the state, some scholars see the use of private standards in combination with public or quasi-public regulation as an example of re-articulated regulation (Utting 2008; also see Ponte, Gibbon, and Vestergaard 2011). By re-articulated regulation, scholars mean that the food system is now governed by a wide range of actors (both human and non-human), including representatives of the state, the private sector and/or civil society. For example, whole sectors are now being governed through standards and these "standards mark a governance field characterized by a complex configuration of deregulation and different modes of re-regulation. It is a political field that poses itself as de-politicized" (Ponte, Gibbon and Vestergaard, 2011, 289). More specifically, Giovannucci and Ponte (2005) argue that standards, particularly sustainability standards, are a new form of a social contract – where the relationship of the state to its citizenry is renegotiated, with NGOs and firms playing a larger role in defining the terms of the relationship.

Political economic approaches have long been critiqued in agrifood studies for their tendency to emphasize the structural to the detriment of local differences and forms of resistance (see Busch and Juska 1997). This can be seen in the case of standards where some studies have assumed "all powerful standards are meaningfully implemented at the local level" thereby "inculcated on to the local" (Ponte 2014, 263). However, we argue that scholars who utilize science studies, particularly Latour (2005), in combination with political economic approaches provide for a much more nuanced understanding of the power of standards. Political economic approaches highlight the power dynamics of standards that arise out of agrifood value chains and identify how these shape the actors that are included and excluded (Ponte 2014). Actor-network theory, which is best known for understanding how actors (human and non-human) interact through networks, affords the ability to identify how power is performed and enacted (Busch 2011; Latour 2005; Loconto 2010). These two theoretical frames when combined provide an additive effect in better understanding the role and impact of standards (Cheyns and Riisgaard 2014).

The three case studies taken up in this chapter all examine sustainability standards. Sustainability standards in agriculture are "flooding" the marketplace (Daviron and Vagneron 2011, 91). While historically standards allowed actors within the agricultural commodities market (e.g. producers, suppliers, and retailers) to agree upon and communicate a set of criteria upon which goods could be bought and sold at a distance, standards for the purposes of creating alternative goods, like organics, were created for a slightly different purpose. While the former focuses on product standards, which are observable qualities, like color and size, the later focuses on so-called process standards (Bingen and Busch 2006). These tend to be qualities that are not directly observable. In addition, many of the newer process standards created in the past 30 years have sought to reduce the commodification of agricultural goods, meaning the standards were put in place to create markets that valued more than simply the price of an agricultural product. These so-called alternative agricultural goods were created using process standards to recognize values such as non-exploitative labor relations, animal welfare, and production practices that do not harm the environment. These sustainability standards have coincided with the expansion of alternative agricultural movements, a broad array of initiatives and practices that are seen as challenging the status quo in our food system (Friedland 2010; Hinrichs and Eschleman 2014). However, as the number of sustainability standards has increased dramatically, it could be argued that these standards are being used to "re-commodify" alternative agricultural goods (Daviron and Vagneron 2011), meaning the market value of the product is driving much of the value chain. Of course, sustainability standards do not automatically denote an alternative agrifood standard and vice versa. For example, locally produced eggs may be part of an alternative food standard (e.g. "buy local"), but this standard is not necessarily a sustainability standard (e.g. local production practices may not qualify as environmentally sustainable).

While social studies of science have been important in drawing academic attention to standards as more than technical specifications, the three case studies in this chapter elaborate on the importance of retaining the analysis of power found in political economic approaches in the study of standards and standardization. The first case study focuses on the creation of agricultural sustainability standards in the United States. Specifically, two sustainability governance initiatives are evaluated for their degree of market embeddedness, revealing the ways in which standards, despite being technical recipes, are always reflections of particular political and economic interests. The second case study expands upon this point, examining why the development of global sustainability beef standards cannot overcome local environments imbued with unique political and economic interests. Finally, once standards are set, the third case study explores how compliance with these standards is assured and the ways in which particular spheres of production and the people that populate these spheres attempt to resist and recreate standards to better fit their needs.

Sustainability metrics and standards for US agriculture

As alluded to earlier, there is a "green frenzy" taking place in which there is "a tooth-and-claw-competition among a growing pack of stakeholders, including environmental activists, think tanks, bloggers, industry associations, consultants … all clamoring to establish and impose their will on green standards" (Unruh and Ettenson 2010, 110). In agriculture, one place this green frenzy is playing out is in the battle over sustainability, with much of the effort to define and operationalize agricultural sustainability now taking place in private settings (Loconto and Fouilleux 2014). In the United States, there are many multi-stakeholder initiatives (MSIs) that have developed metrics and standards for sustainable agriculture. In this section, two of the leading initiatives – Field to Market and National Sustainable Agriculture Standard (LEO-4000) – are discussed.

Begun in 2006, Field to Market was the first agricultural sustainability MSI to emerge in the United States. It was initiated by a group of 12 agribusiness stakeholders and environmental advocacy organizations to develop technology-neutral, science-based metrics for commodity crops. Its membership has since grown to 66 members, with large agribusiness firms and grower associations accounting for a majority of the membership. To date, Field to Market has developed seven environmental metrics, which are land use, soil conservation, soil carbon, irrigation water use, energy use, greenhouse gas emissions, and water quality (Field to Market 2012). They have also developed an online software platform in which farmers can measure their performance using their environmental metrics.

LEO-4000 initially started as an effort by a certifying body, Scientific Certification Systems, to develop a sustainability standard for US agriculture. Recognizing that the standard would have greater legitimacy if developed through a multi-stakeholder process, Scientific Certification Systems transferred the draft standard to the Leonardo Academy, which is an American National Standards Institute (ANSI)-accredited standard development organization. Beginning in fall 2007, consistent with ANSI protocols, the Leonardo Academy advertised the impending standard development process. It then selected a standard development committee of 58 stakeholders, which included "commodity producers, specialty crop producers, agricultural product processors and distributors, food retailers, environmental, labor, and development organizations, NGOs, industry trade associations, government representatives, academics, regulatory officials and certifiers" (Leonardo Academy 2012). After multiple drafts, revisions, and public comment periods, ANSI approved LEO-4000 as the American National Standard for Agriculture. The standard is tiered with multiple levels of certification, applies to all crop agriculture, and includes principles and metrics on social, economic, and environmental sustainability (Leonardo Academy 2013).

Comparing the two initiatives, Field to Market has developed a set of eco-efficiency metrics, that do not threaten the current structure of the food and agriculture marketplace. In contrast, LEO-4000 has developed a standard that, if implemented at the platinum level, would result in significant changes in agricultural practices and thus, threatens to upset the current agrifood marketplace. In brief, LEO-4000 has produced a standard whose objective is transform the current unsustainable practices of agriculture, whereas Field to Market has produced a set of metrics that seek to improve the sustainability of agricultural practices without disrupting the marketplace for food and agriculture. In part, the differences in these two initiatives are an outcome of the different ways each of these initiatives are embedded in the food and agriculture marketplace.

While LEO-4000 initially did include representation of stakeholders from conventional agriculture, following the third annual meeting of the standard committee, in which a series of votes on the principles of the standard largely went against the interests of agribusiness, many of the representatives from conventional agriculture resigned. In a public statement they claimed that "the committee is dominated by environmental groups, certification consultants, agro-ecology and organic farming proponents. These groups have neither the vision nor desire to speak for mainstream agriculture and the 95 percent of farmers who will be materially affected by any resulting standard" (Williams et al. 2010). The resignation of many stakeholders from conventional agriculture tilted the committee towards stakeholders from alternative agriculture and civil society organizations. Reflecting the views of remaining members, the result is a stringent standard that categorizes much of existing agriculture as unsustainable.

Whereas the membership of LEO-4000 was selected to be representative of all stakeholders interested in food and agriculture, the membership of Field to Market has been strategically constructed along much narrower lines. Stakeholders from conventional agriculture constitute the overwhelmingly majority of the membership. In 2012 when it released its second report outlining its metrics, 31 of the 44 members were either grower associations, or companies or organizations associated with the input, processing, or retailing industries. The result is that a majority of Field to Market's membership benefits from current market arrangements. Furthermore, the environmental advocacy organizations that are part Field to Market, such as the World Wildlife Fund and Environmental Defense, have a history of working cooperatively with industry. Thus, they have tended to utilize approaches that work within current market structures and practices to solve environmental problems (Dowie 1997). The outcome is a set of quantitative metrics that focus largely on eco-efficiencies and do not specify what sustainable agriculture actually entails or set sustainability benchmarks.

The cases of LEO-4000 and Field to Market also indicate that the market embeddedness of governance initiatives may affect the implementation of metrics and standards. Despite being approved by ANSI as the national sustainability standard for US agriculture, the LEO-4000 standard is unlikely to be widely adopted at this time. Contestation of LEO-4000 by stakeholders from conventional agriculture has resulted in little support for the standard from many of the dominant companies in the agrifood marketplace. As noted by stakeholders from conventional agriculture, it appears that it will be a "niche" standard at best in the near future. In contrast, given the widespread support of Field to Market by agribusiness companies and grower associations, Field to Market's metrics are likely to see significant adoption. This is because, as they have done with other standards, actors such as Walmart and Kellogg can use their power in supply chains to encourage or require producers to use Field to Market's metrics.

The above analysis illustrates some of the ways that the development and adoption of metrics and standards are embedded in political economies. Thus, while metrics and standards are often understood as technical recipes they also reflect specific political and economic interests. In the case of sustainability metrics and standards for US agriculture, the above case studies demonstrate that lead market actors can use their power and resources to channel metrics towards more conservative options that do not threaten political economic arrangements, and de-legitimate metrics and standards that may be counter to their interests. Additionally, given that there are often multiple standards competing with each other, standards are increasingly understood as market goods. Hence, as the case of sustainability standards in the US indicates, market actors can use their power and resources to both facilitate and hinder the adoption of specific metrics and standards.

Global sustainable beef production and Southern Africa[1]

There is a new global sustainable beef initiative being organized by the private sector, both industry and non-governmental organizations, that seeks to reduce the environmental harms caused by beef production. The initiative, the Global Roundtable on Sustainable Beef (GRSB), focuses on multiple regions of the world, including Southern Africa. The GRSB mission is "to advance continuous improvement in sustainability of the global beef value chain through leadership, science and multi-stakeholder engagement and collaboration" (GRSB n.d.), and to date the group has developed a set of five principles, with each principle having four to nine criteria, which are "a set of conditions or processes by which a system characteristics can be evaluated" (GRSB Annual Report 2014, 15). For example, principle one states that the "global beef value chain manages natural resources responsibly and enhances ecosystem health", after which there are nine criteria, which include, for instance, "practices are implemented to improve air quality" (ibid., 19).

To date, the GRSB has deliberately avoided developing more context-specific levels of indicators, metrics or practices. Instead the GRSB intends to work with national and regional groups to ensure that the more context-specific indicators, metrics and practices that are developed will fit into the overarching principles and criteria of GRSB. As with all standards development, the development of context-specific indicators, metrics and practices, is highly dependent upon who participates. This process is especially complicated in regions of the world that have heterogeneous producers and production systems, like that of Southern Africa.

There is a long history of dual agricultural systems in South Africa and Namibia, where there is a small percentage of well-developed, primarily white farmer-owned farms and a much larger percentage of the population who are primarily indigenous smallholders and largely subsistence farmers. The dual economies found within the agricultural sector are directly linked to past colonial and apartheid policies, which among other things included removal of indigenous people from the majority of agricultural lands, and policies that "encouraged" indigenous populations to seek work in formal, white-controlled, labor markets (see Ransom 2015). The vast majority of cattle in Southern Africa is owned by smallholders, but for a variety of reasons many of these cattle are not sold in the formal marketplace. Over the past decade, smallholders have been the target of numerous development projects that seek to formalize smallholders' production systems and bring these cattle into the marketplace, and this includes current efforts on the part of Solidaridad and the World Wildlife Fund, two of the founding members of GRSB. These two founding members, in addition to Walmart, have also been founding members of two of the first "roundtable" initiatives, the Roundtable on Sustainable Palm Oil (RSPO) and the Roundtable on Responsible Soy (RTRS). This is important, because as with the previous case study of Field to Market, this suggests a certain degree of market embeddedness of GRSB. Other founding members of GRSB include: Cargill, Elanco, JBS, McDonald's, and Merck Animal Health.

Based on analysis of the two previous roundtables along with several other sustainability councils, the academic literature suggests several things about the future development and outcomes of GRSB (Ponte 2014; Schouten et al. 2012). First, GRSB is likely to have a market impact, as some of the biggest purchasers of beef are involved in its founding. Yet, the final indicators, metrics or practices are not likely to represent a wide range of producers' interests, especially smallholders. Rather, these standards will most likely represent the largest, most industrialized and well-capitalized farming operations, especially feedlots, which in South Africa produce over 70 percent of all beef consumed in the marketplace. Second, in general, roundtables are not highly inclusive (Schouten et al. 2012). In the case of GRSB, industry represents 50 percent of all voting members, and producer groups are primarily national organizations that tend to represent the interest of the larger, most industrialized farmers. Governments and governmental agencies are limited to observer status. While GRSB is more global in representation than previous roundtables, the geographical representation remains fairly lopsided, with only a few members who have any ties to Southern Africa and no membership affiliation for Asia. Finally, GRSB is likely to be similar to other roundtables in that roundtables exclude radical solutions, opting for pragmatic solutions to environmental problems (Schouten et al. 2012).

There is also another problem regarding the GRSB's approach to sustainability. Despite the group or collective dynamic of MSIs, the standards (indicators, metrics or practices) that get promulgated from these groups largely focus on individual farmers' responsiveness. In other words, standards tend to privilege individual farmers, as opposed to the collective identity of farmers (e.g. smallholders versus feedlots) (Blowfield et al. 2008). While GRSB at least in theory recognizes the need to allow sustainability criteria to be developed to fit local circumstances, the target of the standards remains individual producers. Therefore, despite organizations like Solidaridad acknowledging the unique circumstances and challenges facing smallholders in Southern Africa, the goal within sustainability standards is to work to change individual smallholders, as opposed to working to change the structure within which smallholders operate. In summary, as this case shows, political economic approaches to standards bring into focus specific power relations unique to local spaces, even as the goal of standards is to transform the particular into a global commodity that eclipses the local.

Providing participatory guarantees for standards

Another important component of the political economy of standards revolves around the means through which compliance with standards is assured. The notion of compliance is a term that comes from a rules-based approach to standards whereby rule-makers establish the rules, rule-takers comply with these rules, and specific actors are authorized to ensure compliance (Mattli and Buthe, 2003). The separation of these roles into independent and 'objective' organizations is the hallmark of the tri-partite standards regime (TSR), which is the dominant governance model in the global political economy of standards (Hatanaka and Busch, 2008; Hatanaka et al., 2012; Loconto and Busch, 2010; Loconto et al., 2012).

While third-party certification dominates in the political economy of standards, alternatives, such as the participatory guarantee system (PGS), are growing in use. PGS is a recent re-emergence and rethinking of the original second-party certification model that was used in organic farming in the 1970s in the US, France, Japan and Brazil. These pioneers felt that in order to be in line with the environmental ethics of organic farming, the expertise of the farmer who knows the land was the most trustworthy (cf. Freyer and Bingen, 2014). This approach to certification began to erode in the 1980s as organic farming became integrated into national legislations and international trade systems (Fouilleux and Loconto, 2016). In developing countries, PGS reemerged over the past 10-15 years in organic farming in response to protestations against the dominant paradigm of standard-setting by corporate and Northern NGO actors. Third-party certification systems were seen as too costly for many small-scale producers and not applicable to local agro-ecological and socio-technical conditions.[2]

The contemporary PGSs are networks created within local communities and consist of farmers, experts, public sector officials, food service agents, and consumers. "They certify producers based on active participation of stakeholders and are built on a foundation of trust, social networks and knowledge exchange" (IFOAM, 2016). PGSs serve to provide a direct guarantee, through the formation of a local market, for sustainably produced food and agriculture products. In Bolivia, Peru and Brazil we see the state re-entering the TSR through the certification window and not only as standards-setters. In these cases, government officials are involved in the guarantee committees that are set up for each PGS at the municipal level. Here the public actors are involved not only in providing extension services to farmers, but they also act as a member of the PGS.

An internationally supported PGS governance framework was first established in a workshop in Latin America in 2004, where international non-governmental actors (e.g. IFOAM, the Latin American Organic Agriculture Movement, Centro Ecologico in Torres, Rio Grande do Sul in Brazil, FAO) convened to develop a "Shared Vision and Shared Ideals" for PGSs around the world. This shared vision contests the 'detached' compliance approach of third-party certification, which focuses their governance efforts on mechanisms of 'social control'.

> In stark contrast to existing certification programs that start with the idea that farmers must prove they are in compliance to be certified, PGS programs use an integrity based approach that starts with a foundation of trust. It builds from there with an unparalleled transparency and openness, maintained in an environment that minimizes hierarchies and administrative levels.
>
> *(Källander, 2008, 7)*

However, PGSs have only become a priority for the International Federation of Organic Agriculture Movements (IFOAM) advocacy at the international level since 2009 (IFOAM, 2014), after many years mainly focused on harmonization of standards and on third-party certification. PGSs pose a clear alternative to the dominant model of third-party certification as they are now legally recognized by an increasing number of national regulations. As of 2015, there were 123 functioning PGS initiatives and another 110 under development. These PGSs are spread over 72 countries, are endorsed by the state in Bolivia, Brazil, and India, and are being adapted to local contexts by hundreds of thousands of farmers on all continents. However, they are being promoted only for domestic or local markets and rely upon direct sales and short value chains. The main importers of organic products from developed countries still refuse to recognize them as credible systems of control, partly because of the legal structures that require third-party certification, partly because of concerns over conflicts of interest in PGSs, and also because of the dominance of the economic power of the organizations that promote TSRs (Fouilleux and Loconto, 2016).

PGSs challenge the dominant political economy of standards by democratizing knowledge in the oversight systems for compliance with standards among producers, experts and consumers who collectively ensure that the techniques are adopted (IFOAM 2016). This process is exemplified by the case of the Familia de la Tierra[3] (FdT) network in the Bogotá region of Colombia. This group is instituting an interesting approach to resolving tensions between traditional and expert knowledge in the development and enforcement of standards through their PGS.

Before the creation of the FdT network in 2009, the 35 peasant farmers were not able to sell their agro-ecological products or would be forced to sell them as conventional products through the black market (as commercial production was not authorized in the peri-urban area of Bogotá). When this group of families began to collectively sell their native and traditional foods, they were met with stiff resistance from organic shops, restaurants and consumers in general, who did not trust that the products were indeed agro-ecological. A strong network between consumers in the city and producers in the peri-urban region was missing and knowledge about the capacities and interests of both groups was non-existent. FdT took this up as a means to rethink its food system model (Nieto, 2016: 88).

They overhauled the linearity of the 'value chain' to create a cyclical paradigm for production and consumption. This began with FdT members nourishing the soil with micro-organisms and natural enzymes; they then began to produce their own seed (mostly native and creole varieties); third, they became the owners and producers of their own inputs; they learned to process food, design its packaging and market it, all as one collaborative, simultaneous and complementary unit. To close the cycle, not only did the organic waste need to be returned to the soil in terms of composting, but the final consumer had to be reconnected with the land, seed and food. FdT members did this with a locally adapted PGS that allowed them to develop a different kind of trading relationship with consumers and created empathy that cemented ties with responsible consumers. The certification process conducted on the farms of the FdT network includes the collection of socio-economic and environmental information about the farms, diagnosis by 'coffee filter' soil chromatography,[4] visits by consumers and the delivery of certificates to the farms based on the approval of the network, which includes 18 restaurants, seven eco-shops and a responsible consumption network (Nieto, 2016).

There are a few key elements that make this PGS unique and well adapted to the local environment: first, the reproduction, saving and use of native seeds by farmers is the foundation of the certification. Second, the integration of famer expertise as a form of social control empowers farmers to maintain their own expertise, and the use of a simple chromatographic analysis using coffee paper enables non-scientists (consumers, producers, intermediaries) to test the soil for pollutants and provides an independent measure of control. Finally, the collaboration between the urban and periphery families has had positive effects on the families and on their ability to mobilize others in the area as a number of changes have been occurring in the political economy of the city. Given concerns over the Bogotá watershed, the FdT network was effective in negotiating an agreement whereby the peasants living in the peri-urban area were given the right to farm – only if they practiced agro-ecological production – as a means to protect and improve the quality of water that entered into the urban area. This was possible only because of the horizontal alliances that the network made through their focus on the local market and the use of a locally bounded certification tool – rather than a positioning towards an export market and the independent authority of third-party certification.

Conclusion

Latour (1987) helps us best to understand that standards are fundamentally about acting at a distance, in that they are created to facilitate transactions between actors in distant locations. Yet, in the cases of the sustainable beef initiative and PGS, efforts are underway to develop standards that are sensitive to local heterogeneity. A political economic analysis of standards enables us to see that in the case of sustainable beef, even if GRSB is successful in creating standards sensitive to heterogeneity, the types of heterogeneity captured in the standards are not likely to be representative of all the local producers, but rather those producers with market power. Moreover, regardless of the standards that are developed, they will require individual producers to conform, without regard to the unique challenges the groups of smallholders experience in terms of access to markets in Southern Africa. In contrast, PGS provide an example of actors completely opting out of the dominant market standards and their accompanying audits and certification. Instead, actors have opted to recreate standards that better fit their own value chains and to build alternative markets and, in doing so, they have also opted to reintroduce and privilege their own experiential knowledge as farmers, retailers and consumers. This, however, does have costs as the PGS actors are excluded from mainstream markets because of powerful political economic actors who do not trust the certification mechanism. Similarly, the case study in the United States alerts us to the ways in which market embeddedness can blunt the impact of efforts to create sustainability in agriculture. All three cases reveal that the more embedded sustainability standards are in the dominant market structure, the more conservative the standards tend to be in disrupting the status quo, which in this case are unsustainable practices in the global agrifood system.

We observe that all three case studies highlight the pursuit of sustainability standards that are backed by scientific criteria, as appeals to scientific criteria help to establish and maintain credibility (Bain, Ransom and Worosz 2010). However, which scientific criteria are utilized and for what purposes is strategic, in that appeals to scientific criteria can also prevent political debates. For example, appealing to a narrowly defined problem of identifying practices that improve air quality within sustainable beef standards precludes debate over the broader topic of the types of production systems that are better for the environment, including the air. Similarly, PGS and LEO-4000 are evidence that *not* all scientific knowledge is accepted equally or openly. Rather, scientific knowledge that challenges the dominant market structures tends to be marginalized or completely blocked from consideration in the marketplace. In the case of PGS, we also see that more accessible forms of knowledge, such as experiential knowledge, are discounted in favor of what is deemed more scientifically rigorous knowledge. Utilizing scientific knowledge that is certified by special equipment and trained experts is also a mechanism for maintaining the legitimacy of a specific set of standards.

Research utilizing social studies of science approaches bring into focus how non-human actors like standards are enrolled and can enact power in global value chains. Political economic approaches call our attention to institutional structures that shape the day-to-day lives of people. When combined, these two perspectives accentuate the fluidity of power in the formation, implementation and outcomes of standards. The results are far from fixed, but they are also not infinitely flexible. This is why, despite the growth of standards, social science research must continue to examine the consequences of a wide range of standards within specific social contexts (Timmermans and Epstein 2010). Such analysis is true for all types of standards, whether in the field of education, medicine, or global agrifood systems.

Notes

1   The United Nations defines Southern Africa as consisting of five countries: Botswana, Lesotho, Namibia, South Africa, and Swaziland. The bulk of this discussion directly pertains to primarily Botswana, Namibia, and South Africa, although there could be long-term relevance for Lesotho and Swaziland.
2   Interview with IFOAM president, February 20, 2014.
3   Family of the Earth.
4   This is a simple technique whereby famers can use coffee filters to determine the mineral and microflora content of the soil in order to determine whether or not synthetic inputs have been used.

References

Bain, C. E. Ransom, V. Higgins. (2013). "Private agri-food standards: contestation, hybridity and the politics of standards". *International Journal of Sociology of Agriculture and Food* 20, 1–10.
Bain, C., E. Ransom, M. Worosz. (2010). "Constructing credibility: using technoscience to legitimate strategies in agrifood governance". *Journal of Rural Social Sciences* 25(3): 160–192.
Bingen, J. and Busch, L. (2006). *Agricultural Standards*, Springer, Dordrecht, the Netherlands.
Blowfield, M. E. and Dolan, C. S. (2008). "Stewards of virtue? The ethical dilemma of CSR in African agriculture". *Development and Change* 39, 1–23.
Brunsson, N. and Jacobsson, B. (2000). *A World of Standards*, Oxford University Press, Oxford/New York.

Busch, L. (2011). *Standards: Recipes for Reality*, MIT Press.

Busch, L. (2000). "The moral economy of grades and standards". *Journal of Rural Studies*, 16(3), 273–283.

Busch, L. and Juska, A. (1997). "Beyond political economy: actor networks and the globalization of agriculture". *Review of International Political Economy*, 4, 688–708.

Cheyns, Emmanuelle and Lone Riisgaard. (2014). "Introduction to the symposium". *Agriculture and Human Values*, 31, 409–423.

Daviron, B. and Vagneron, I. (2011). "From commoditisation to de-commoditisation … and back again: discussing the role of sustainability standards for agricultural products". *Development Policy Review*, 29, 91–113.

Dowie, Mark. (1997). *Losing Ground: American Environmentalism at the Close of the Twentieth Century*. Cambridge, MA: MIT Press.

Field to Market. (2012). *Environmental and Socioeconomic Indicators for Measuring Outcomes of On-Farm Agricultural Production in the United States: Second Report*. Available at www.fieldtomarket.org.

Fouilleux, E. and Loconto, A. (2016). "Voluntary standards, certification and accreditation in the global organic agriculture field: a tripartite model of techno-politics". *Agriculture and Human Values*, 1–14. DOI: 10.1007/s10460-016-9686-3.

Friedland, W. H. (2010). "New ways of working and organization: alternative agrifood movements and agrifood researchers". *Rural Sociology*, 75: 601–27. doi:10.1111/j.1549-0831.2010.00031.x.

Freyer, B. and Bingen, J. (2014). *Re-Thinking Organic Food and Farming in a Changing World*, Dordrecht, Netherlands: Springer.

Giovannucci, D. and Ponte, S. (2005). "Standards as a new form of social contract? Sustainability initiatives in the coffee industry". *Food Policy*, 30, 284–301.

Global Roundtable for Sustainable Beef (GRSB). (2014). "Sustainable beef: a journey of continuous improvement (Annual Report 2014)". Available from http://grsbeef.org/Resources/Documents/GRSB_annualreport_singleF4.pdf. [26 September 2015].

GRSB (n.d.). "About GRSB". Available from http://grsbeef.org/AboutGRSB. [26 September 2015].

Giovannucci, D. and Ponte, S. (2005). "Standards as a new form of social contract? Sustainability initiatives in the coffee industry". *Food Policy*, 30, 284–301.

Hatanaka, M., Bain, C., and Busch, L. (2005). "Third-party certification in the global agrifood system". *Food Policy*, 30, 354–369.

Hatanaka, M. and Busch, L. (2008). "Third-party certification in the global agrifood system: an objective or socially mediated governance mechanism?" *Sociologia Ruralis*, 48, 73–91.

Hatanaka, M., Konefal, J. and Constance, D. (2012). "A tripartite standards regime analysis of the contested development of a sustainable agriculture standard". *Agriculture and Human Values*, 29, 65–78.

Hinrichs, C. and J. Eshleman. (2014). "Agrifood movements: diversity, aims, limits". In: C. Bailey, L. Jensen and E. Ransom (eds) *Rural America in a Globalizing World: Problems and Prospects for the 2010s*. Morgantown, WV: West Virginia University Press, 138–55.

IFOAM. (2016). "Participatory guarantee systems for organic agriculture". Available from www.ifoam.bio/pt/organic-policy-guarantee/participatory-guarantee-systems-pgs [30 January 2016].

IFOAM. (2014). "Support the PGS newsletter on betterplace.org". *The Global PGS Newsletter*, 4(6) (accessed 28 April 2014).

Källander, I. (2008) "Participatory Guarantee Systems – PGS". Stockholm: Swedish Society for Nature Conservation.

Latour, B. (2005). *Reassembling the Social: An Introduction to Actor-Network-Theory*. Oxford: Oxford University Press, 316.

Latour, B. (1987). *Science in Action: How to Follow Scientists and Engineers Through Society*. Cambridge, MA: Harvard University Press.

Leonardo Academy. (2012). "Standards committee members". Retrieved on March 12, 2012 from https://sites.google.com/site/sustainableagstandards/standards-committee-members-1.

Leonardo Academy. (2013). *Draft: National Sustainable Agriculture Standard LEO-4000*. Madison, WI: Leonardo Academy.

Loconto, Allison. (2010). "Sustainably performed: reconciling global value chain governance and performativity". *Journal of Rural Social Science*, 25(3), 193–225.

Loconto, A. and Busch, L. (2010). "Standards, techno-economic networks, and playing fields: Performing the global market economy". *Review of International Political Economy*, 17, 507–536.

Loconto, Allison and Eve Fouilleux. (2014). "Politics of private regulation: ISEAL and the shaping of transnational sustainability governance". *Regulation & Governance*, 8, 166–185.

Loconto, A., Stone, J.V., and Busch, L. (2012). 'Standards, certifications and accreditations'. In: Ritzer G (ed) *The Wiley-Blackwell Encyclopedia of Globalization*. Malden, MA: Wiley-Blackwell, 2044–2051.

Mattli, W. and Buthe, T. (2003). "Setting international standards: technological rationality or primacy of power?" *World Politics*, 56, 1–42.

Nieto, O. (2016). "Familia de la Tierra participatory guarantee system: business innovation as a tool for social and productive change". In: Loconto, A., Poisot, A.-S., and Santacoloma, P. (eds) *Innovative Markets for Sustainable Agriculture: Exploring how Innovations in Market Institutions Encourage Sustainable Agriculture in Developing Countries*. Rome: Food and Agriculture Organization of the United Nations, 85–94.

Ponte, S. (2014). "'Roundtabling' sustainability: lessons from the biofuel industry". *Geoforum*, 54, 261–271.

Ponte, S., Gibbon, P. and Vestergaard, J. (2011). "Governing through standards: an introduction". In Ponte, Gibbon, Vestergaard (eds.), *Governing Through Standards: Origins, Drivers and Limitations*, Palgrave Macmillan, New York, 1–24.

Ransom, E. (2015). "The political economy of agriculture in Southern Africa". In Bonanno, A. B., and Busch, L. (eds.), *The Handbook of International Political Economy of Agriculture and Food*. Northampton, MA: Edward Elgar Press.

Schouten, G., Leroy, P., and Glasbergen, P. (2012). "On the deliberative capacity of private multi-stakeholder governance: the roundtables on responsible soy and sustainable palm oil". *Ecological Economics*, 83, 42–50.

Timmermans, S. and Epstein, S. (2010). "A world of standards but not a standard world: toward a sociology of standards and standardization". *Annual Review of Sociology*, 36(1), 69–89.

Unruh, Gregory and Gregory Ettenson. (2010, November). "Winning in the green frenzy". *Harvard Business Review*, 110–116.

Utting, P. (2008). "The struggle for corporate accountability". *Development and Change*, 39, 959–975.

Williams, R., J.T. Allan, R. Moore, et al. (2010). "Resignation letter, letter to Mr. Arny". Retrieved on March 9, 2011 from www.bio.org/sites/default/files/Resignation_Letter_of_ Ag_Leonardo_Academy.pdf.

25

AGNOTOLOGY AND THE NEW POLITICIZATION OF SCIENCE AND SCIENTIZATION OF POLITICS

Manuela Fernández Pinto

Introduction

If science was once seen as rendering neutral hard facts about the world, thus providing objective and impartial solutions to public policy issues, decades of strengthening the relation between science and politics have ironically diminished the authority of both. On the one hand, the political pressure over science to produce quick and accurate results has uncovered limitations of scientific research, the uncertain nature of scientific results, and the value-ladenness of scientific practice. As science loses its authority as a neutral and objective arbitrator, a door opens for the use of science for partisan interests: the funding and performance of scientific research with specific policy targets and the strategic or selective utilization of available data to favor certain policy lines. This ideological use of scientific research, where results are cherry-picked with political aims in mind, has led to the current *politicization of science* (Cozzens and Woodhouse 1995; Sarewitz 2004; Thorpe 2007). On the other hand, assigning a special role to science in policy making threatens the democratic process. If scientific expertise holds a privileged position in solving policy controversies, scientific values would likely undermine other, cultural, religious, political, and ethical values relevant for the decision-making process in liberal democracy. The conception of science as the only source of legitimate knowledge for policy making has led in turn to the current *scientization of politics* (Hoppe 2005; Fischer 2003; Sarewitz 2004).

The scientization of politics and the politicization of science are two sides of the same coin (Hoppe 1999; Weingart 1999). As more resources are channeled to the development of policy-relevant scientific research, more knowledge becomes available for policy making, and more knowledge is demanded to deal with new policy issues. The resulting inflationary use of scientific expertise ends up delegitimizing the democratic process and diminishing the authority of science (Weingart 1999, 160). This dialectical process of scientizing politics and politicizing science has characterized the science–policy nexus since the end of the Second World War.

In recent decades, however, we have witnessed the transition towards a new regime of science organization that has reshaped the political economy of science (Slaughter and Rhoades 2004; Davies et al. 2006; Lave et al. 2010). In this new regime of globalized privatization (Mirowski and Sent 2007), the political economy of science has become increasingly private and commercial. More importantly, this new regime has promoted a new understanding of scientific knowledge; it has fostered its own epistemology of science (Mirowski 2009). Through an understanding of "knowledge" as a market product, this neoliberal epistemology has had significant consequences for the dialectical process of politicizing science and scientizing politics. Following the recently developed approach of *agnotology* (Proctor and Schiebinger 2008), this chapter focuses on one of these consequences: the practices of *ignorance production* emerging with the globalized privatization of science.

The chapter is divided into four sections. Following the introductory section, the second section briefly describes the new political economy of science and its underlying epistemology. The third section presents the literature on agnotology and examines the ignorance-productive practices encouraged in two of the most allegedly burgeoning sectors of commercially driven research today: clinical research on pharmaceuticals and agricultural research on genetically modified organisms (GMOs). The fourth section analyzes the different consequences for the science–policy nexus that result in these cases of ignorance production. The conclusion highlights the importance of agnotology, for understanding the new political economy of science.

The globalized privatization of science and its neoliberal epistemology

With the end of the Cold War and the advent of the "globalized world," a new regime of science organization also came into place, the globalized privatization of science regime (Mirowski and Sent 2007). By the end of the 1970s, the fear of losing competitiveness in the global market led to major changes in research and development (R&D) strategies in the US, which included major structural and legislative transformations. The emergence of new research structures, such as the contract research organization (CRO) and the think tank, together with a series of legislative acts promoting stronger intellectual property rights and weaker antitrust laws, allowed for commercial exploitation of publicly funded research, as well as new R&D strategies, such as the outsourcing and off-shoring of research, all contributing to consolidating a more flexible social organization of science for the globalized world (Mirowski 2011). With the restructuring of the institutional and legislative frameworks, the steady privatization of scientific research unfolded. Today, the vast majority of US R&D is both performed and funded by the private sector. According to the latest indicators, the corporate sector performs 69 percent of US total R&D and funds 63 percent (NSB 2014).

The globalized privatization of science can be characterized as part of the global trend towards neoliberalism (see, e.g., Davies et al. 2006; Irzik 2007; Lave et al. 2010; Mirowski 2011). While many regard neoliberalism as either an economic or a socio-political doctrine, some have uncovered the importance of its epistemological dimension. Mirowski, for example, claims that "what holds neoliberals together first and foremost is a set of *epistemic* commitments, however much it might be ultimately rooted in economics, or politics, or even science" (2009, 417, emphasis his). In particular, neoliberals understand the market as an "ideal information processor," making "every successful economy a knowledge economy" (Mirowski 2011, 29). Following Hayek, neoliberals replace the traditional problem of resource allocation in the market with the epistemological problem of knowledge distribution:

> The economic problem of society is thus not merely a problem of how to allocate "given" resources … It is rather a problem of how to secure the best use of resources known to any of the members of society, for ends whose relative importance only these individuals know. Or, to put it briefly, it is a problem of the integration of knowledge which is not given to anyone in its totality.
>
> *(Hayek 1945, 519–20)*

Thus, neoliberals start with an epistemological view of the economy, one in which knowledge is a commodity, i.e., a quantifiable thing or "good," tradable in the market. And while neoliberals praise knowledge as "the chief good," they also have an idealized view of the market as knowing better than any particular individual. In Hayek's words, "there is not much reason to believe that, if at any one time the best knowledge which some possess were made available to all, the result would be a much better society. Knowledge and ignorance are relative concepts" (Hayek 1960, 378).

The epistemological position behind neoliberalism is thus relativistic: knowledge and ignorance are concepts relative to the market. The traditional understanding of knowledge as justified true belief is transformed as knowledge becomes whatever information the market renders. In this way, the quality of the knowledge/information is left aside, leaving us with the idea that any accumulation of knowledge/information is always positive: "just as there are no 'negative' prices, there is putatively no such thing as negative information" (Mirowski, 2011: 318). Hence, the more information the market processes, the more knowledge it acquires.

A neoliberal epistemology currently guides the political economy of science. To begin with, the privatization of scientific research, with its strong intellectual property rights and its weak antitrust laws, goes hand in hand with the belief that science in the "free market" will thrive as the market provides the best possible scientific knowledge. Along with this privatization, the creation of new research structures, the commercial profit of academic research, and the offshoring of research, all go hand in hand with the idea of making research facilities more flexible and more efficient. Last but not least, the neoliberal conception of knowledge as relative to the market is also having profound consequences for the traditional epistemic standards within scientific communities today. In particular, the traditional epistemic aims of scientific research—explaining, predicting, understanding, etc.—have been transformed to fit new aims—e.g., efficiently producing a profitable medicine that successfully treats the symptoms of patients (who can pay). And, as shown in the next section, with the change of aims, a change of practice follows.

Agnotology and the social construction of ignorance in commercially driven research

The aim of this chapter is to examine the emergence of practices of ignorance production as one of the many consequences of the current political economy of science. Agnotology, or the study of ignorance, introduces a new perspective to the social studies of science, one in which the social construction of ignorance becomes relevant for understanding scientific practice today. Challenging the traditional conception, agnotology advocates a more complex understanding of ignorance taking into account its social dimensions:

> We need to think about the conscious, unconscious, and structural productions of ignorance, its diverse causes and conformations, whether brought about by neglect, forgetfulness, myopia, extinction, secrecy, or suppression. The point is to question the *naturalness* of ignorance, its causes and its distribution.
>
> *(Proctor 2008, 3)*

Strictly speaking, *agnotology* is the study of ignorance, broadly conceived. As Proctor acknowledges, "there must be as many kinds for ignorance as of knowledge—perhaps more, given how scant is our knowledge compared to the vastness of our ignorance" (2008, 3). As I noticed, however, the innovative part of Proctor's conception of ignorance is related to its social dimensions. In this sense, I will be concerned with the study of the *social construction of ignorance*.

Although the project of agnotology is not restricted to studies of commercialized science—see, for example, the growing research on government secrecy (Galison 2010; Kuchinskaya 2014)—research done for the private interest has certainly been an important area for agnotology (Michaels 2008; Oreskes and Conway 2010; Proctor 2012; Mirowski 2013; Nik-Khah 2014). Starting with the paradigmatic case of ignorance production, i.e., the tobacco industry's campaign to obscure scientific research on the health hazards of smoking, agnotology has uncovered different practices implemented by the private industry to shape the process of scientific knowledge production in favor of commercial gain. In fact, a close analysis of the cases shows that similar strategies of ignorance production have been implemented in cases ranging from tobacco to global warming (Oreskes and Conway 2010), including even the 2008 financial crisis (Mirowski 2013).

Practices of ignorance production in such cases include an emphasis on scientific uncertainty, support of friendly research, recruitment of distinguished scientists, publicity in mass media, and attacks to unfavorable scientific research (Fernández Pinto, forthcoming). Notice that these are all practices traditionally tied to the process of knowledge production—scientists know that their results are uncertain, research centers support research that contributes to their goals, research teams aim at recruiting distinguished scientists, scientists want to disseminate their research results widely, and scientific research is held to high standards of criticism—but they have been reshaped to fulfill commercial purposes. Two salient cases in this respect are the pharmaceutical industry's funding of clinical trials and the agrochemical industry's funding of research on GMOs.

The pharmaceutical industry's funding of clinical trials

Through publication planning strategies (Sismondo 2009), massive funding of industry-friendly clinical research (Michaels 2008), and the reform of the classification systems of disease, especially mental disorders (Whitaker and Cosgrove 2015), pharmaceutical companies have been able to speed up the release of new drugs, to maintain hazardous drugs in the market—think for example of Merck's infamous Vioxx scandal—and to obtain approval for remarketing old drugs for new purposes—e.g., Eli Lilly's rebranding of Prozac as Sarafem to treat PMDD. Through these practices, pharmaceutical companies have shaped the process of knowledge production to suit their commercial interests, and in some cases they have deliberately shaped the production of scientific knowledge.

Take for example the practice of ghostwriting, which has become customary in the pharmaceutical industry for the marketing of new drugs. CROs and medical education and communications companies (MECCs) openly advertise ghostwriting services, often called "medical writing services," i.e., "anonymous science writers who draft scientific articles to be signed by prominent scientists who are paid handsomely for lending their reputations and a modest amount of their time and effort" (McGarity and Wagner 2008, 24). Pharmaceutical companies hire these services so that ghostwriters produce drafts customized to the company's needs, drafts that are in turn submitted for revision, and in many cases just for signing, to a prominent academic scientist, who, in exchange for a fee, signs as the main author of the document, while the ghostwriter and the pharmaceutical company remain hidden (Moffatt and Elliott 2007). For instance, a major CRO, committed to "deliver accurate, timely, and cost effective documents to the highest ethical and scientific standards," advertises on its website a wide arrange of "medical writing services," including "conference materials (abstracts, poster presentations and slide sets), manuscripts, journal/conference submission, medical marketing reviews and reports, literature reviews…" (www.quanticate.com).

Through ghostwriting practices, pharmaceutical companies are reshaping the process of knowledge production to suit their commercial interests: they are actively changing crucial communication venues of scientific research, such as conference presentations, literature reviews, and more importantly, peer-reviewed articles. However, they are not merely changing these venues. As I argue, they are also transforming traditional practices of knowledge production into practices of ignorance production.

It is no secret that financial conflicts of interest take a toll on scientific research. As has been broadly documented, researchers working for private companies are more likely to obtain results favorable to their sponsors (Bekelman et al. 2003; Lexchin et al. 2003; Sismondo 2008). On one account, "company-sponsored research is roughly four times more likely to report results favorable to the company than is independent research" (Sismondo and Doucet 2009, 278). Consequently, industry-sponsored research is more likely to conceal the risks and to portray inaccurately the benefits of medical treatments (Moffatt and Elliott 2007). Infamous litigation cases have made evident the harms of hiding financial conflicts of interest through ghostwriting practices.

Documents obtained during a litigation case against Redux, one of the main components of the diet pill Fen-Phen, have shown that the pharmaceutical company Wyeth hired the "medical writing services" of the MECC Excerpta Medica to ghostwrite a number of articles on the treatment of obesity for journal publication, with the aim of marketing Redux (Sismondo and Doucet 2009, 276). Excerpta Medica produced around half a dozen papers, charging Wyeth between $15,000 and $20,000 per article, and paying "authors" a $1,500 honorarium for signing (Mundy 2002, 163). Customized to fit the pharmaceutical company's needs, the papers explicitly left out any safety concerns. It was not until September 1997, when Fen-Phen was withdrawn from the market for causing heart valve abnormalities and primary pulmonary hypertension, that Fen-Phen users started filing lawsuits against the pharmaceutical company, and, in turn, that Wyeth's ghostwriting practices were uncovered (Nik-Khah 2014, 11–12). Wyeth's Redux case illustrates the ways in which hiding financial conflict of interest through ghostwritten articles misleads doctors regarding the harms and benefits of specific treatment, and ends up compromising patients' health. And this is hardly an isolated case. Similar stories have been uncovered in the case of Merk's Vioxx, Park-Davis's Neurotin, and Pfizer's antidepressant Zoloft, among others (Moffatt and Elliott 2007). In this way, ghostwriting practices affect the process of scientific knowledge production, hiding financial conflicts of interests that have been proven to influence the results of research, which in turn have significant ethical and social consequences, misleading doctors and harming patients.

Notice, however, that the success of ghostwriting depends directly on the apparent reliability of the traditional process of knowledge production, and in particular, on the credibility of renowned scientists and well-established academic journals. Traditional standards of academic writing and authorship presuppose that every author has made a significant contribution to the research. The author's name serves as credence for the quality of research results, and so does the journal name, later on, when the article is published. Pharmaceutical companies are not interested in changing these standards as such: they need them for ghostwriting practices to work. Instead, they are building façades to recreate those standards, while hiding profound conflicts of interests that are likely to disqualify research results if they were brought to light.

The same practice traditionally used to guarantee the quality of research, in this case having a well-known academic scientist as main author, is manipulated to create the impression that results are in good standing, when the standard is clearly not fulfilled, i.e., the renowned scientists did not make any relevant contribution to the research and the ghostwriter has clear financial conflicts of interest. So, the specific results that the ghostwritten paper is trying to put forth, i.e., the piece of information that would qualify as "scientific knowledge," does not bear the relevant credentials for being so. Still, it is taken as such. In this way, pharmaceutical companies are actively engaged in producing ignorance, instead of knowledge.

The agrochemical industry's funding of research on GMOs

In a similar vein, agrochemical companies, such as Monsanto and Syngenta, have increasingly used patent protection to selectively encourage industry-friendly research, while discouraging, and sometimes actively suppressing, scientific research on the health hazards of GMOs and their corresponding herbicides. As the recent controversy over the carcinogenicity of glyphosate (the main active ingredient of the world's most popular herbicide, Monsanto's Roundup®) illustrates, Monsanto has actively fought the World Health Organization (WHO) and the International Agency for Research on Cancer (IARC) for reporting the health hazards of glyphosate (*Monsanto News* 2015). In the meantime, a Monsanto employee was caught up acknowledging during a talk at Oregon State University that Monsanto has "an entire department dedicated to 'debunking' science which disagreed with theirs" (Hampton 2015).

In March 2015, the IARC gathered a panel of international experts to assess the carcinogenicity of five pesticides, glyphosate included. Based on the available evidence of carcinogenicity in humans and animals, and on independent mechanistic evidence, the panel classified glyphosate as "probably carcinogenic to humans" (Guyton et al. 2015). The fact that the panel considered the evidence was overall sufficient to classify glyphosate as carcinogenic is, however, remarkable, given the efforts of the agrochemical industry to obstruct scientific research on the health hazards of GMOs and their corresponding herbicides.

In February 2009, 24 corn insect scientists working in the public sector submitted a statement to the EPA complaining about the lack of legal access to study biotech crops, due to the technology/stewardship agreement that anyone buying GM seeds is required to sign, and which explicitly prohibits the buyer from conducting scientific research on the seeds. Accordingly, these scientists complained that "As a result of restricted access, no truly independent research can be legally conducted on many critical questions…" (Sappington et al. 2010, 55). Research on GM seeds is only possible under restricted circumstances. Academic institutions have to seek permission from agrochemical companies, which involves approval of the experimental design as well as of the resulting publications (Waltz 2009).

Agrochemical companies have been able to develop technology/stewardship agreements because their GM seeds are patent-protected, which provides companies with intellectual property rights over GM seeds. The strong IP rights protecting GM seeds are not rare under the current globalized privatization of science. They were granted after 1980, when the United States Supreme Court ruled in *Diamond v. Chakrabarty*, for the first time in history, that a genetically modified life form could be patented. Since then, patent protection has become a major tool for agrochemical companies to restrict scientific research on GMOs, particularly regarding their health hazards (Biddle 2014).

Two early reviews of the publicly available literature on GMO safety found that papers about experimental investigations on the safety of GM foods/plants were scant (Domingo 2000; 2007). A more recent review acknowledges that, while the number of papers on GMOs has considerably increased since 2007, "the number of studies specifically focused on safety assessment of GM plants is still limited" and, more significantly, "most of the studies demonstrating that GM foods are as nutritional and safe as those obtained by conventional breeding, have been performed by biotechnology companies or associates, which are also responsible for commercializing these GM plants" (Domingo and Bordonaba 2011, 741).

In 2012, Séralini and his colleagues published a crucial study concerning the health hazards of GMOs, particularly of Monsanto's GM corn variety NK603 (Séralini et al. 2012). They studied the effects of NK603 corn with and without Roundup, and also the exposure of Roundup alone, in rats for two years. In all these cases females died more frequently and more rapidly than controls, and they also developed large mammary tumors more often than controls. The researchers also found toxicity in multiple organs, especially severe liver and kidney damage, for both sexes. The study was especially controversial given that it used a protocol similar to the one used by Monsanto in a study for FDA approval. There was a fundamental difference, however, while Monsanto ended the study after ninety days, Séralini et al. conducted the study for two years, the average lifetime of rats. Tumors and toxicity only appeared after four months of exposure, a time that the Monsanto study did not document (Fagan et al. 2014). Séralini's study was strongly attacked by agrochemical companies, to the extent that the peer-reviewed journal where the research appeared retracted the article. As Fagan et al. clearly state, this is hugely problematic for the process of scientific knowledge production: "Instead of doing more research to verify or disprove the findings of Séralini, they did 'science by press release'. They used their huge financial resources to mount a media campaign attacking not only the research but also Séralini personally. These *ad hominem* attacks are standard practice among the GMO proponents and are a serious deterrent to any scientist who considers entering this area of research" (Fagan et al. 2014, 60).

Notice then the profound conflicts of interest that surround the evaluation of GMOs' safety. To begin with, the companies profiting from the commercialization of GMOs have the right to prohibit research on GM seeds, given patent protection, and even when scientists are granted permission to conduct research, this is done under strict surveillance from the companies. It is no surprise then that the literature on the safety of GMOs is scant. Furthermore, as in the case of pharmaceutical research, scientists conducting research for agrochemical companies are more likely to obtain results favorable to their sponsors (Biddle 2014, 17), just like Domingo and Bordonaba (2011) have documented. Thirdly, and perhaps even more worrisome, the few studies reporting the health hazards of GMOs are subjected to strong opposition from the industry, which does not follow the process of scientific critical engagement, but instead produces a media campaign to discredit both researchers and research results.

As a consequence, almost two decades after the commercialization of GMOs, there is no scientific consensus on their safety (Krimsky and Gruber 2014). Prohibiting and controlling research on GMOs through patent protection, sponsoring and publicizing research with favorable results, and attacking unfavorable research and researchers, are some of the main strategies implemented by the agrochemical industry to obstruct the process of knowledge production and selectively promote ignorance regarding the safety of GMOs.

As the analysis of these two cases shows, the current political economy of science fosters certain practices of ignorance production, practices implemented by private companies to shape the process of scientific knowledge production according to their commercial interests. As a result, practices that had been traditionally associated with the epistemic goals of science, i.e., practices that aimed at a better understanding of the world around us, have turned into practices to favor the financial goals of the private companies involved, where epistemic achievements are dispensable.

Politicizing science and scientizing politics through ignorance production

Beyond the negative consequences for the epistemic goals of science, practices of ignorance production also have important consequences for the science–policy nexus. As I already mentioned, the politicization of science and the scientization of politics are two sides of the same coin. In their dialectical relation, changes in one process necessarily affect the other and vice versa, and this is not different with practices of ignorance production. What is significantly different is that the concept of "science" has changed. The neoliberal epistemology has transformed the traditional understanding of "scientific knowledge" and its epistemic goals, for a view of "knowledge" tied to the market as an ideal information processor. Moreover, as the social construction of ignorance in commercially driven research shows, despite this alternative understanding of "scientific knowledge," it is also crucial not to destroy completely the traditional view of knowledge and science, tied to particular epistemic goals (empirical accuracy, explanation, prediction, etc.). This new understanding of science comprises both a relativistic epistemology (knowledge relative to the market) and the necessity to simulate the traditional process of knowledge production (to appear to follow the old standards). For only the latter guarantees the success of practices of ignorance production and with it, the apparent success of neoliberal epistemology.

The new politicization of science needs to be understood in this context. The neoliberalization of science together with its practices of ignorance production foster new ways of politicizing science. Beyond the mere use of scientific research to favor certain policy lines, we now see the institutionalization of whole new ways of developing scientific research with clear commercial goals, while at the same time trying to mimic the credibility of the traditional scientific process. Take the case of ghostwriting, for example. Here the science is not only being politicized through the careful planning of peer-reviewed articles customized to industrial needs; it is also being politicized in a more subtle way, by pretending to be something it is not, i.e., by falsely obtaining the credibility of renowned scientists through the use of their names as signing authors. This is a new political move: industry makes sure it obtains the scientific results that it needs, while pretending it is not doing anything in the first place. In this way, industrial interests are politicizing science by actively pretending to show that it is not politicized, that results are obtained following the standards, that researchers are independent and thus exempt from conflicts of interest, etc. This is the new politicization of science uncovered by agnotology.

In turn, the scientization of politics is also transformed. On the one hand, industry continues to buttress the idea that science is the only source of legitimate knowledge for policy making, thus contributing to the scientization of politics as normally portrayed in the literature (Hoppe 2005; Fischer 2003; Sarewitz 2004). A clear example of this is the way in which agrochemical companies have downplayed the experience of farmers with GM seeds as well as the complaints of populations affected by the toxicity of their pesticides, claiming that the evidence is not scientific but anecdotal and, as such, should not be taken into account in regulatory debates. Salient in this respect is the controversy over the introgression of GM corn into Mexican indigenous maize (Delbourne 2008; Kinchy 2012).

But just like with the politicization of science, agnotology also uncovers another dimension of the scientization of politics, for the "science" being privileged as the only legitimate source for policy making is not what it seems. In this case again, private companies aim at promoting their commercial interests in the policy realm and they do so by supplying the relevant scientific research. The research submitted, however, has important shortcomings. Not only because of conflicts of interest, but also because the mechanisms of ignorance production have shaped the research to conceal those conflicts as well as other epistemic flaws. As a result, the process of scientizing politics becomes problematic in a new way. Science is privileged in the policy realm, *apparently* due to its epistemic quality, but *really* because it has previously been shaped to fulfill commercial interests. In this way, the scientization of politics in the current political economy of science becomes another branch of the neoliberalization of politics. A science serving commercial goals, instead of epistemic goals, makes the scientization of politics another tool to further free-market interests in the policy realm. The agnotological analysis again illuminates the way in which the scientization of politics has been transformed through practices of ignorance production.

Conclusion

The aim of this chapter was to examine the ways in which the globalized privatization of science and its underlying neoliberal epistemology have promoted the politicization of science and the scientization of politics through innovative mechanisms of ignorance production. As seen in this chapter, agnotology provides a particularly useful perspective for uncovering new ways in which science is currently politicized and politics are scientized.

Moreover, agnotology also contributes to uncovering the shortcomings of the neoliberal epistemology of science. The mere accumulation of information, i.e., increasing the amount of scientific research funded and performed, is not equivalent to increasing the production of scientific knowledge. Quality of research (not efficiency) matters significantly. In particular, if commercially funded research is qualitatively inferior to independent research, as the epistemic problems emerging from conflicts of interest suggest, then an increase in commercially funded research to the detriment of independent research does not necessarily benefit the production of scientific knowledge. And if, in addition, the epistemic goals of science are being compromised through practices of ignorance production (practices that mimic the process of scientific knowledge production, without actually striving to achieve epistemic goals), then it is even less clear that such research would benefit the production of scientific knowledge. As Mirowski claims, "If the neoliberal reengineering of science has resulted in a vast ramping up of the production of ignorance … then it immediately follows that more expenditure on science does not necessarily result in more scientific output" (2011, 331). In this sense, an agnotological approach to the study of the political economy of science shows an important inherent flaw of neoliberal epistemology.

References

Bekelman, Justin, Yan Li, and Cary Gross. 2003. "Scope and Impact of Financial Conflicts of Interest in Biomedical Research," *JAMA* 289: 454–65.

Biddle, Justin. 2014. "Can Patents Prohibit Research?" *Studies in the History and Philosophy of Science* 45: 14–23.

Cozzens, Susan E. and Edward J. Woodhouse. 1995. "Science, Government, and the Politics of Knowledge." In: S. Jasanoff, G. Markle, J. Peterson, T. Pinch (eds.) *Handbook of Science and Technology Studies*. London: Sage Publications, pp. 533–53.

Davies, Bronwyn, Michael Gottsche and Peter Bansel. 2006. "The Rise and Fall of the Neo-Liberal University." *European Journal of Education* 41(2): 305–19.

Delbourne, Jason. 2008. "Transgenes and Transgressions: Scientific Dissent as Heterogeneous Practice." *Social Studies of Science* 38(4): 509–541.

Domingo, José. 2000. "Health Risks of GM Foods." *Science* 288: 1748–9.

Domingo, José. 2007. "Toxicity Studies of Genetically Modified Plants." *Critical Reviews in Food Science and Nutrition* 47: 721–33.

Domingo, José and Jordi G. Bordonaba. 2011. "A Literature Review on the Safety Assessment of Genetically Modified Plants." *Environment International* 37: 734–42.

Fagan, John, Michael Antoniou, and Claire Robinson. 2014. "Busting the Big GMO Myths." In: S. Krimsky and J. Gruber (eds.). *The GMO Deception*. New York: Skyhorse Publishing, pp. 57–63.

Fernández Pinto, Manuela. (forthcoming). "To Know or Better Not to: Agnotology and the Social Construction of Ignorance in Commercially Driven Research."

Fischer, Frank. 2003. *Reframing Public Policy*. Oxford: Oxford University Press.

Galison, Peter. 2010. "Secrecy in Three Acts." *Social Research* 77: 970–4.

Guyton, Kathryn et al. 2015. "Carcinogenicity of Tetrachlorvinphos, Parathion, Malathion, Diazinon, and Glyphosate." *The Lancet Oncology* 16: 490–1.

Hampton, Stephanie. 2015. "Monsanto's 'Discredit Bureau' Really Does Exist." *Daily Kos* (March 27). Available at: www.dailykos.com/story/2015/03/27/1373484/-Monsanto-s-Discredit-Bureau-Swings-into-Action#.

Hayek, Friedrich. 1945. "The Use of Knowledge in Society." *The American Economic Review* 35: 519–30.

Hayek, Friedrich. 1960. *The Constitution of Liberty*. Chicago: University of Chicago Press.

Hoppe, Robert. 1999. "Policy Analysis, Science, and Politics: From 'Speaking Truth to Power' to 'Making Sense Together'" *Science and Public Policy* 26(3): 201–10.

Hoppe, Robert. 2005. "Rethinking the Science-Policy Nexus: From Knowledge Utilization and Science Technology Studies to Types of Boundary Arrangements." *Poiesis Prax* 3: 199–215.

Irzık, Gürol. 2007. "Commercialization of Science in a Neoliberal World." In: A. Buğra and Kaan Ağartan (eds.). *Reading Polanyi for the 21st Century*. New York: Palgrave, pp. 135–53.

Kinchy, Abby. 2012. *Seeds, Science, and Struggle*. Cambridge: MIT Press.

Krimsky, Sheldon and Jeremy Gruber. 2014. *The GMO Deception*. New York: Skyhorse Publishing.

Kuchinskaya, Olga. 2014. *The Politics of Invisibility*. Cambridge, MA: MIT Press.

Lave, Rebecca, Phil Mirowski, and Samuel Randalls. 2010. "Introduction: STS and Neoliberal Science." *Social Studies of Science* 40(5): 659–75.

Lexchin, Joel, et al. 2003. 'Pharmaceutical Industry Sponsorship and Research Outcome and Quality: Systematic Review'. *British Journal of Medicine* 326: 1167-70.

McGarity, Thomas and Wendy Wagner. 2008. *Bending Science*. Cambridge, Mass: Harvard University Press.

Michaels, David. 2008. *Doubt Is Their Product*. Oxford: Oxford University Press.

Mirowski, Philip. 2009. "Why There Is (as Yet) No Such Thing as an Economics of Knowledge." In Don Ross and Harold Kincaid (eds.). *The Oxford Handbook of Philosophy of Economics*, Oxford: Oxford University Press.

Mirowski, Philip. 2011. *Science-Mart: Privatizing American Science*. Cambridge, Mass: Harvard University Press.

Mirowski, Philip. 2013. *Never Let a Serious Crisis Go to Waste*. London and New York: Verso.

Mirowski, Philip and Esther-Mirjam Sent. 2007. "The Commercialization of Science and the Response of STS." In: E. Hackett, O. Amsterdamska, and M. Lynch (eds.). *The Handbook of Science and Technology Studies*. Cambridge, Mass, MIT Press, pp. 635–89.

Moffatt, Barton and Carl Elliott. 2007. "Ghost Marketing: Pharmaceutical Companies and Ghostwritten Journal Articles." *Perspectives in Biology and Medicine* 50(1): 18–31.

Monsanto News. 2015. "Monsanto Disagrees with IARC Classification for Glyphosate." (March 20). Available at: http://news.monsanto.com/news/monsanto-disagrees-iarc-classification-glyphosate.

Mundy, Alicia. 2002. *Dispensing with the Truth: The Victims, the Drug Companies, and the Dramatic Story behind the Battle over Fen-Phen*. New York: St. Martin's Press.

National Science Board. 2014. *Science and Engineering Indicators*. Arlington VA: National Science Foundation.

Nik-Khah, Edward. 2014. "Neoliberal Pharmaceutical Science and the Chicago School of Economics." *Social Studies of Science* 44: 489–517.

Oreskes, Naomi and Eric Conway. 2010. *Merchants of Doubt: How a Handful of Scientists Obscured the Truth on Issues from Tobacco Smoke to Global Warming*. New York: Bloomsbury Press.

Proctor, Robert. 2012. *Golden Holocaust: Origins of the Cigarette Catastrophe and the Case for Abolition*. Berkeley: University of California Press.

Proctor, Robert, and Londa Schiebinger. 2008. *Agnotology: The Making and Unmaking of Ignorance*. Stanford, Calif: Stanford University Press.

Sappington, Thomas et al. 2010. "Conducting Public-Sector Research on Commercialized Transgenic Seed." *GM Crops* 1(2): 55–8.

Sarewitz, Daniel. 2004. "How Science Makes Environmental Controversies Worse." *Environmental Science and Policy* 7: 385–403.

Séralini, Gilles-Eric et al. 2012. "Long Term Toxicity of a Roundup Herbicide and a Roundup-Tolerant Genetically Modified Maize." *Food and Chemical Toxicology* 50: 4221–231.

Sismondo, Sergio. 2008. "Pharmaceutical Company Funding and its Consequences." *Contemporary Clinical Trials* 29: 109–13.

Sismondo, Sergio. 2009. "Ghosts in the Machine: Publication Planning in the Medical Sciences." *Social Studies of Science* 39: 171–96.

Sismondo, Sergio and Mathieu Doucet. 2009. "Publication Ethics and the Ghost Management of Medical Publication." *Bioethics* 24(6): 273–83.

Slaughter, Sheila and Gary Rhoades. 2004. *Academic Capitalism and the New Economy*. Baltimore: Johns Hopkins University Press.

Thorpe, Charles. 2007. "Political Theory in Science and Technology Studies." In: E. Hackett, O. Amsterdamska, and M. Lynch (eds.). *The Handbook of Science and Technology Studies*. Cambridge, Mass, MIT Press, pp. 63–82.

Waltz, Emily. 2009. "Under Wraps." *Nature Biotechnology* 27(10): 880–2.

Weingart, Peter. 1999. "Scientific Expertise and Political Accountability." *Science and Public Policy* 26(3): 151–61.

Whitaker, Robert and Lisa Cosgrove. 2015. *Psychiatry under the Influence*. New York: Palgrave MacMillan.

26

RECONSTRUCTING OR REPRODUCING?

Scientific authority and models of change in two traditions of citizen science

Gwen Ottinger

Volunteers monitor water quality in streams that may be affected by fracking in the Marcellus Shale (Wilderman 2007; Kinchy et al. 2014). Nature-lovers report the number and species of birds that visit birdfeeders in their back yards (Bonney et al. 2009b; Bonter and Cooper 2012). People go online to help scientists examine telescope images for gravitational lenses that computer algorithms might have missed (More et al. 2016). Residents convinced that oil refinery emissions are making them sick use community-friendly air samplers to document releases of toxic chemicals and demand better regulatory enforcement (O'Rourke and Macey 2003; Ottinger 2010).

These are but a few examples of the wide range of activities that have come to be known as "citizen science." Definitions of the term vary, as will be discussed below; however, in its broadest formulation, citizen science refers to individuals without formal scientific credentials involved in knowledge production activities. Citizen scientists most commonly take on data collection, especially environmental monitoring of various sorts; they may also become involved in coordinated online efforts to interpret images and other large data sets (Bonney et al. 2016).

Although uncredentialed individuals have long participated in the making of scientific knowledge, "citizen science" has gained new legitimacy and recognition in recent years. The Citizen Science Association, active since 2012 as a self-described "community of practice for the field of public participation in scientific research," now has biennial conferences and its own journal (https://citizenscienceassociation.org/). In 2015, the U.S. federal government issued guidance to federal agencies on how to incorporate volunteers in their research, citing benefits to scientific research and STEM education, as well as cost savings (Holdren 2015), and published a "Federal Crowdsourcing and Citizen Science Toolkit" (https://crowdsourcing-toolkit.sites. usa.gov/). Individual agencies have also created their own citizen science programs, such as the Environmental Protection Agency's "Air Sensor Toolbox for Citizen Scientists" (www.epa. gov/air-research/air-sensor-toolbox-citizen-scientists).

As institutionalized in these new initiatives, the label "citizen science" subsumes two distinct traditions of public participation in scientific inquiry (see Lave 2012, 28) that can be described as "social movement-based citizen science" and "scientific authority-driven citizen science." The two traditions, this chapter will show, have different orientations to the existing political-economic order. Social movement-based citizen science not only critiques standard scientific practices but also refuses to separate inquiry from a vision for social change rooted in collective action. Scientific authority-driven citizen science, in contrast, grounds its claims to legitimacy in promises to uphold the standards of (idealized) science, and envisions the facts it produces as contributing to social change by informing public policy-making and individual behavior.

After describing the social movement-based and scientific authority-driven traditions of citizen science in sections 2 and 3, respectively, this chapter shows how definitional work done by researchers in the scientific authority-driven tradition has come to shape the institutionalization of citizen science at the expense of social movement-based citizen scientists' visions of social and scientific change. Section 4 analyzes taxonomies of citizen science that array scientific authority-driven and social movement-based projects on a single spectrum, arguing that considering them all within the same framework mutes fundamental differences between the two traditions' models of change, and fails to recognize the critiques of science entailed in social movement-based citizen science. Built largely on this framing of citizen science, Section 5 suggests, government initiatives recognize the legitimacy of social movement groups' participation in science to an unprecedented extent, but discipline their participation in ways that leave little space for critique of mainstream scientific methods and standards, and that may divert resources from direct action and other activities that seek change outside of formal governmental processes. Fashioning citizen science in the scientific authority-driven model, the chapter concludes, tends to reproduce the relations of power that surround science rather than reconstructing them in a model more amenable to democratic participation.

Social movement-based citizen science

One kind of activity that the term "citizen science" is often used to describe takes place among communities who are both experiencing some negative impact and unsatisfied by official responses, which may deny the existence of a problem. In order to compel authorities to recognize and address the issues, they marshal information—monitoring data, health data, geographic information—that can serve as evidence of the problem and point to its sources. In these contexts, information-gathering is not an end in itself, but is combined with organizing and collective action to change both local conditions and the underlying political structures that created those conditions in the first place. Moreover, community-based knowledge production does not seek merely to reproduce scientific methods in under-studied areas; rather, these citizen projects critique, and offer alternatives to, methods and standards accepted by the scientific mainstream (see Ottinger 2016 for a fuller account of social movement-based citizen science).

The earliest examples of social movement-based citizen science that appear in the academic literature took place in the early 1980s in working class towns in the northeastern United States. In Woburn, Massachusetts, residents who suspected that toxic waste was responsible for an unusually high prevalence of leukemia initiated their own health study, demonstrated that the disease cluster could be linked to water contamination, and mobilized to demand that the companies responsible for the waste be held accountable and the contamination cleaned up (Brown 1992); residents of Love Canal, New York, undertook similar data-collection activities in the course of their ultimately successful campaign for a clean-up (Tesh 2000). In these and other cases of "popular epidemiology," community researchers transgressed scientific norms by not requiring the individuals who conducted health surveys to be disinterested outsiders, and by questioning the high levels of statistical significance necessary to prove the connection between pollution and illness in the eyes of researchers.

Since emerging as a powerful tool in the anti-toxics movement, community-led health surveys have become prominent in the environmental justice (EJ) movement's attempts to demonstrate the disproportionate impacts of industrial pollution on minority and low-income communities. EJ activists have also embraced low-cost air monitors and participatory mapping as means of generating data that can help them persuade decision-makers to take action to protect communities—and, again, in doing so, they challenge scientists' methods, including standard techniques for characterizing air quality or understanding risk (Allen 2000; Corburn 2005; Ottinger 2010).

Other social movements also include citizen science among their strategies. Workers' movements, in conjunction with environmentalist allies, collect data to document the harms of agricultural pesticides (Harrison 2011; Irwin 1995), and "embodied health movements" may systematically track symptoms and other experiences to contest illness categories or seek more effective treatments (Brown et al. 2004; see also Callon et al. 2011). The rise of social movement-based knowledge production efforts is usefully theorized by Irwin (1995), who first dubbed them "citizen science." Grounded in sociological theory and science and technology studies (STS), Irwin's analysis provides a fitting framework for understanding the larger political economic contexts of community engagement in knowledge production. According to Irwin, the rise of scientific activity among communities, social movement groups and other uncredentialed citizens stems from a larger breakdown of modernist faith in a form of science that purports to deliver decontextualized, universal truths through the rigorous application of methods and standards that promise to eradicate human judgment and values from the pursuit of knowledge. The inherent limitations of—indeed, the practical impossibility of—this sort of science have been thrown into sharp relief by the growing prevalence of ecological crises of our own making. If this idealized version of science, which is embraced and institutionalized by universities, professional societies, and government agencies, can no longer be relied upon as the solution to social and environmental problems, then there is a clear, even urgent need for alternative modes of understanding the natural world that are more open to the embodied experience, epistemologies, and judgment of individuals without scientific credentials.

In Irwin's model, then, residents of environmental justice communities who take their own air samples, or disease sufferers who pool their information to make a case for the environmental causes of their conditions, can be seen as contributing to the construction of new forms of knowledge-making that are more responsive to social needs, more transparent about their own limitations, and more embedded in the contexts of concrete decisions and actions. Their efforts are not *anti*-scientific, in that they uphold the idea of basing knowledge claims on measurements and observations. Indeed, many if not most social movement-based knowledge production projects involve scientists as advisors and collaborators, arguably fostering the development of experts better equipped to do context-aware, social needs-oriented science (Ottinger and Cohen 2012). At the same time, they are also not strictly scientific (in the usual sense), in that knowledge claims are animated by more than just empirical data. Moral reasoning and social savvy also play into claims, for example, about what constitutes concerning levels of chemical exposures.

By naming social movement-oriented epistemologies "citizen science," Irwin both asserts the legitimacy of uncredentialed individuals' participation in knowledge-making and suggests the possibility for us all to understand "science" as a more holistic, heterogeneous practice. Accordingly, his notion of citizen science includes public deliberations on issues related to science and technology, and his analysis suggests the possibility that reflective professional scientists participating in the reconstruction of science would also be considered "citizen scientists." But while his choice of terminology is strategic in one sense, the use of the word "science" also risks obscuring the aspects of knowledge-making by citizens, communities, and movements that don't fit with modern, Western ideals of science. Tellingly, "citizen science" is not used uniformly by social scientists writing about cases of knowledge production in the context of social movements. While some of the terms that are used (e.g. "street science" (Corburn 2005) and "civic technoscience" (Wylie et al. 2014)) also attempt to claim the cultural authority of science, others, like "participatory action research" and "community-based participatory research," avoid the term entirely. Regardless of their choice of term, social scientific analyses continue to echo Irwin in pointing out the ways that social movement-based citizen science challenges the cultural authority of science and pioneers new modes of knowledge production that are more responsive to community needs and ways of knowing (e.g. Hemmi and Graham 2014; Wylie et al. 2014).

Scientific authority-driven citizen science

The other archetype of citizen science is represented by projects led by credentialed scientists that operate on the model of research science as it is typically practiced at universities. Scientists establish the research questions based on what are considered important topics by their professional peers and design data collection and interpretation protocols to answer those questions in a manner that will be convincing to their colleagues and suitable for publication in peer-reviewed journals. In contrast to social movement-based efforts, where citizens drive the inquiry, in this form of citizen science people without formal scientific training participate primarily by collecting data in keeping with scientists' protocols, thereby expanding the data sets available to scientists studying large-scale phenomena that manifest at the local level, such as biodiversity loss due to climate change (e.g. Bonney et al. 2009b). Although it is not the norm, amateur participants may also participate in other aspects of the research process, from hypothesis formation to data interpretation (Bonney et al. 2009a). Many definitions of citizen science include online projects in which volunteers contribute by helping to analyze large data sets (Bonney et al. 2016; Wiggins and Crowston 2011), although this may also be referred to as "crowd-sourcing." Unlike social movement-based citizen science, participants do not frame their investigations primarily as challenges to the political or scientific status quo. Rather, uncredentialed citizens help academic scientists create knowledge that conforms to existing scientific standards, and imagine the potential for policy change as built on their authoritative results.

Academic research on citizen science of this sort began to appear around the turn of the 21st century and has been concentrated in natural science, especially environmental science, and science education journals. The literature in this vein traces the origins of citizen science to a centuries-old tradition of amateur naturalist participation in science (see e.g. Dickinson et al. 2010; Dawson 2015; Miller-Rushing et al. 2012). The historical research, however, does more than show that amateurs have long participated in the making of knowledge; it shows that the categories of "lay," "amateur," "professional," and "expert" have evolved over time and have had different meanings in different historical periods. In fact, prior to the professionalization of the sciences in the late 19th and early 20th centuries, amateur—that is, self-funded—researchers were considered in some fields to be the *better* scientists, because they had no pecuniary stake and could thus be more reliable observers (Vetter 2011; Shapin 1994). Those writing about the tradition of amateur science in the context of contemporary citizen science projects rarely acknowledge the shifting nature of their categories. Instead, they use the terms in their post-professionalization sense, taking for granted that credentialed scientists are easily distinguishable from "volunteer" or "amateur" participants, and that amateur status entails a lower level of competence and reliability than that possessed by credentialed scientists.[1]

The participation of amateurs in scientific research today is justified most often in terms of its value to science. Authors stress that the participation of volunteers allows scientists to pursue new lines of inquiry. Because data collection by citizens—for example, reporting bird sightings or cataloging the presence of invasive species—can so greatly extend the geographical and/or temporal coverage of data available to scientists, one research team goes so far as to argue that,

> Citizen science is perhaps the only practical way to achieve the geographic reach required to document ecological patterns and address ecological questions at scales relevant to species range shifts, patterns of migration, spread of infectious disease, broad-scale population trends, and impacts of environmental processes like landscape and climate change.
>
> *(Dickinson et al. 2010, 166)*

Data processing-oriented citizen science projects have similar potential to expand scientists' reach, by helping them "examine and analyze what would otherwise be unmanageable amounts of information" (Bonney et al. 2016, 6), including hours of video footage from "camera traps" set up to capture the movements of mammals (McShea et al. 2016) and large databases of telescope images (More et al. 2016).

The value of citizen science to the production of authoritative scientific results is reinforced by extensive research into the quality of volunteer-contributed data. Researchers compare volunteers' performance to that of credentialed scientists (e.g. Cox et al. 2012; Elbroch et al. 2011), identify and attempt to account for systematic biases such as over-reporting of rare versus common species (Dickinson et al. 2010; Hochachka et al. 2012), and develop methods for validating data collected by citizen scientists (e.g. Bonter and Cooper 2012; Hunter et al. 2013)—all to show that conclusions based on volunteer-collected data can be trusted.

In addition to furthering scientific research, scientific authority-driven citizen science is frequently framed as contributing to the public understanding of science. Citizen science activities are often seen as valuable additions to K-12 and university-level science curricula (e.g. Trautmann et al. 2012); conversely, some researchers argue that developing projects in partnership with educational institutions is the best way to ensure consistency in volunteer engagement (Dickerson-Lange et al. 2016). But even outside the school setting, researchers hypothesize—and find evidence—that participation in citizen science projects improves volunteers' knowledge of and appreciation for science, as well as their ability to think like scientists (e.g. Bonney et al. 2016; Trumbull et al. 2000). It is further imagined that greater understanding of science can produce behavioral change in participants, making them better environmental stewards and more supportive of science-based policy recommendations on issues such as climate change (Dickinson and Bonney 2012; Dickinson et al. 2012; Phillips et al. 2012).

These claims about improvements in citizen scientists' understanding of science are premised on what STS scholars have described as a "deficit model" of the public (Irwin and Wynne 1996); that is, they assume that volunteers' understanding of science is necessarily in need of improvement. The deficit model manifests in scientific authority-driven citizen science in a number of ways, from repeated questioning of whether volunteer contributions can constitute reliable data to the hope expressed in many publications (e.g. Dickinson and Bonney 2012) that, by participating in biodiversity research in their own backyards, citizens will gain a better appreciation of the threats of global climate change and adjust their political activities accordingly. The problem with a deficit model of the public is that it fails to give uncredentialed people credit for what they do know, for example about their local environments or their workplace conditions. Further, in assessing non-scientists' understanding using scientists' measures of comprehension and proficiency, deficit model thinking devalues other ways of knowing. Legitimate challenges to scientists' standards of proof or decontextualized knowledge claims— the sort of challenges advanced by social movement-based citizen science—are thus reframed as incomprehension or ignorance, an approach that serves to reinforce the authority of science as it is currently practiced in academic institutions.

Also in contrast to social scientists' accounts of citizen science, which ground social movement-based practices in the political-economic conditions of the risk society (Irwin 1995) and neoliberalism (Lave 2012; Liévanos et al. 2011), discussions of scientific authority-driven citizen science refer to larger political-economic forces in rather limited ways. Global climate change is mentioned frequently, usually as a major factor affecting ecosystems and necessitating regional-scale research that would not be feasible without volunteer participation. But environmental policy, including climate policy, is often invoked more subtly in researchers' vision that more scientifically literate volunteers will create a polity willing to act on scientific knowledge of the issues (e.g. Dickinson and Bonney 2012).

Although largely neglected in the literature, contemporary political-economic conditions have arguably played a significant role in the rise of this form of citizen science: Lave (2012) shows how knowledge produced by people outside academic settings is consistent with "neoliberal knowledge regimes," in which public funding for universities is cut and researchers are forced to justify their work in terms of its market relevance. Although research in the scientific authority-driven tradition does not refer to neoliberal policies as such, a number of studies do discuss citizen science in the context of the scarcity of resources for scientific research: environmental monitoring by local volunteers is argued to be inexpensive relative to professional monitoring, even once the costs of setting up and maintaining a citizen science program are factored in (Bonney et al. 2009b; Danielsen et al. 2005); costs of replacing volunteer labor for data processing tasks with paid labor are estimated (Sauermann and Franzoni 2015 show a combined value of $1.5 million to seven projects); and, in the most explicit acknowledgment of shrinking budgets for science, Couvet et al. (2008) laud volunteer-based monitoring programs as more resilient than projects relying solely on credentialed researchers in the face of funding cuts.

Although scientific authority-driven citizen science responds to the erosion of public funding for science, as well as to policy stalemate on global climate change and other environmental problems, these political-economic factors do not typically inform the analyses of citizen science in the natural science and science education literatures. Instead, researchers tend to focus on justifying citizen science projects as legitimate contributions to scientific knowledge, and measuring the impacts of participation on the knowledge, attitudes, and behaviors of citizen scientists. Definitions of what constitutes citizen science in this tradition have been expanding to include social movement-based data collection, as will be discussed below, and a few researchers even speculate that scientists may grow personally and professionally as a result of collaborating with volunteers (e.g. Dickinson and Bonney 2012, 11; cf. Ottinger and Cohen 2011). Yet even in this broadening, the critique of science's limitations entailed in social movement-based citizen science continues to go unacknowledged as researchers defend the contributions of amateurs in terms that privilege scientific methods and ways of thinking and imagine social and policy change as stemming from better understanding of authoritative science.

One spectrum for two traditions?

As described above, the term "citizen science" encompasses two distinct traditions of participation by non-scientists in scientific knowledge production: one critiques the universalizing, values-denying model of science that is currently institutionalized in academic and policy spheres; the other strives to extend its authority to scientist-led research projects that incorporate the efforts of uncredentialed individuals. The two traditions have been analyzed in largely separate academic literatures, with studies of social movement-based citizen science concentrated in STS, sociology, geography, and other critical social science venues, while studies of scientific authority-driven citizen science have been published primarily in natural science and science education journals. But whereas the social science literature on citizen science has almost entirely ignored scientific authority-driven citizen science (Kinchy et al. 2014 and Lave 2012 are partial exceptions), the natural science literature on citizen science has worked to include social movement-based activities in its definitions and taxonomies of citizen science.

The earliest definitions of citizen science offered in natural science publications are narrowly circumscribed, and mark the practice as distinctly different from community-driven activities. Cooper et al. (2007) define "the citizen science model" in contrast to the "participatory action research model." The former, in their characterization, "engages a dispersed network of volunteers to assist in professional research using methodologies that have been developed by or in collaboration with professional researchers," while the latter "begins with the interests of participants, who work collaboratively with professional researchers through all steps of the scientific process to find solutions to problems of community relevance" (2). In these definitions, the fundamental difference between the two practices lies in whose concerns—scientists' or the community's—drive the inquiry; potential differences in the kinds of action that might be sought are also hinted at in references to problem-solving in the participatory action research model.

Subsequent literature on citizen science, however, has moved away from the top-down/ bottom-up dichotomy of this early definition and instead proposes a spectrum of activities that constitute "citizen science," based on the number of steps of the scientific process in which non-scientists participate. The most influential of these, from Bonney et al. (2009a), divides citizen science into three categories: contributory, in which volunteers collect data; collaborative, in which they also analyze data and may influence data collection methodologies; and co-created, in which volunteers help define research questions and hypotheses, and participate in data collection, interpretation, and dissemination. Shirk et al. (2012) elaborates the taxonomy with two additional categories—contractual, in which members of the public hire professional scientists to carry out a study, and collegial, in which amateurs effectively conduct independent research as avocational experts—but continues to classify social movement-based projects like environmental monitoring in EJ communities as a form of "co-created" citizen science. Wiggins and Crowston (2011) offer an alternative taxonomy organized by project goals rather than extent of involvement in the scientific process; here, social movement-based citizen science falls into the "Action" category, characterized by grassroots organizing and "encourag[ing] participant intervention in local concerns."

All of these taxonomies recognize a key feature of social movement-based citizen science: that community involvement in—even control over—defining research directions and methods is fundamental to the practice. However, they largely miss social movement-based citizen scientists' interest in challenging the standards, methods, and/or authority of science. Instead, within these taxonomies, social movement-based projects are assessed against scientists' standards and values—and generally found lacking. "Co-created" projects, for example, are said to be "more aligned with social change than scientific precision" (Shirk et al. 2012, 12), and Wiggins and Crowston (2011) observe that the data from "action" projects *could* "provide a foundation for long-term environmental monitoring in a given locale, but the wide variation in methodologies employed by each independent effort creates challenges for the aggregation of data" (5). These analyses do make important points about the limitations of social movement-based citizen science—the EJ movement, for example, would do well to think more about how and whether community-collected air data from multiple sites of petrochemical production could be woven into their larger argument for an end to fossil fuels (but see Macey et al. 2014). However, there is no corresponding reflection on the limitations of the scientific establishment's accepted standards in community contexts. For example, epidemiologists will typically not conclude that they are observing a disease cluster until there is less than a 5 percent chance that it could have occurred randomly; however, the mathematics involved makes this an almost impossibly high bar for studies of the small neighborhoods living closest to hazardous facilities. Social movement-based citizen science highlights limitations like these and advances alternatives—in this case, a lower threshold for "public health significance" to be used instead of scientists' standard threshold for "statistical significance" (Allen 2000).

The change-seeking character of social movement-based projects is also acknowledged by these taxonomies. In fact, the rationale for including social movement-based projects in frameworks classifying different kinds of citizen science is bolstered by the fact that researchers in the scientific authority-driven tradition identify policy and behavioral change as among the goals of their citizen science projects. "Disseminate conclusions/translate results into action" even appears as one of the steps in the scientific process that serves as a rubric to classify types of citizen science, and public participation in that step is one of the key differences between the less participatory "contributory" and "collaborative" projects and the more participatory "co-created" and "collegial projects" (Shirk et al. 2012).

But in acknowledging practical action as among the goals of many citizen science projects, unifying taxonomies mask fundamental differences in the way that "action" and "social change" are understood in the two traditions. Authors writing about the benefits of scientific authority-driven projects imagine that better information and scientific understanding will lead individuals and policy makers to make better decisions, especially in the environmental realm. As Dickinson and Bonney (2012) put it,

> The hope is that citizen science leads to…increased interest in and knowledge about a range of environmental issues, and increased capacity for people to assemble the tools and data needed to move toward a level of scientific understanding that promotes autonomous, informed choice. The hunch is that having an engaged, educated, nature-loving public helping to drive environmental policy is perhaps even more critical to addressing public conservation problems than further research is.
>
> *(12)*

This vision, of better understanding driving better decisions in the personal and policy realm, is widely shared in the literature on scientific authority-driven citizen science. Other authors imagine that participation in particular projects will, for example, lead landowners to make landscape management decisions that better preserve biodiversity in residential areas (Cooper et al. 2007) or encourage local regulators to change land use regulations (Danielsen et al. 2005).

From the standpoint of social scientific analysis, several things are notable about the model of social and policy change embedded in these claims. First, it is highly individualistic—Jordan et al. (2012) argue that citizen science projects should focus on developing "personal agency" and "self-efficacy" of participants as a route to environmental action—and oriented to a notion of "informed choice" that has been shown to reinforce scientific authority and disempower vulnerable populations by willfully ignoring gaps in relevant knowledge and social structural constraints on individual choice (Ottinger 2013a; 2013b). It also suggests that scientific findings lead to public policy actions in a linear way, in contrast to the empirically grounded models advanced by STS researchers that show public policies to be co-constructed alongside scientific findings in iterative, socially negotiated processes that are themselves shaped by political-economic power relations (e.g. Jasanoff 1990). Finally, it imagines governmental decision-making processes, influenced by people through elections and formal consultative processes, to be the primary site of policy change.

Despite their inclusion in taxonomies of citizen science developed by Shirk and others, social movement-based citizen science projects operate with a fundamentally different model of social change. One prominent example is air monitoring by EJ communities with user-friendly "buckets." Like other community-based environmental monitoring efforts, bucket monitoring would be considered "co-created" citizen science. However, the non-profit groups that provide support for bucket brigades—a term which itself highlights the social organization surrounding the device—emphasize that the bucket is first and foremost an "organizing tool." Specifically, it helps bring people together around a common purpose; it helps draw attention to community campaigns; and it helps add momentum to community members' work toward their campaign goals. Education and consciousness-raising, so prominent in the model of change presumed by scientific authority-driven citizen science, are not among the driving logics of bucket monitoring. Nor is it presumed that change will come through community members' well-informed participation in formal political processes. Instead, Overdevest and Mayer (2008) show that communities use bucket monitoring to create change through a variety of mechanisms: "self-collected data" are used to "create more public pressure on both firms and regulators, to build stronger social networks from which they can sometimes leverage additional campaign resources, to increase the accountability of polluters to citizens in their neighborhoods, and to improve regulatory compliance" (1511). The social movement-based citizen science model of change is thus not centered on the formal processes set up by governments; indeed, it recognizes that considerable political pressure has to be generated in order to hold government institutions accountable to disadvantaged communities and thus requires direct action, media attention, alliances with better-resourced groups, and a broad base of community and public support. It also recognizes that firms themselves can be pressured to change their behavior, even in the absence of government intervention.

Consequences of a unified framework for citizen science

Despite their limitations, the frameworks for citizen science developed in the scientific authority-driven tradition have come to dominate both the academic conversation and governments' efforts to institutionalize citizen science. The "Resource Library" offered as part of the U.S. government's Federal Crowdsourcing and Citizen Science Toolkit, for example, draws heavily on publications from the Cornell Lab of Ornithology—the hub of scientific authority-driven citizen science—and features only one article (Ottinger 2010) that recognizes social movements in its analysis. Three community-based projects, all undertaken by communities involved in the environmental health and justice movement, are featured in the Resource Library; significantly, however, these are profiled in short videos produced and narrated by the U.S. EPA.

The institutionalization of a unified framework for citizen science has mixed consequences for social movement-based projects. On one hand, it gives new legitimacy to bucket brigades and other community efforts. Whereas in the early 2000s, community groups fought in each jurisdiction for agency recognition of their findings, federal initiatives like the EPA's Air Sensor Toolbox for Citizen Scientists signal agencies' belief that uncredentialed residents of affected communities can collect data that will inform enforcement and other agency activities. On the other hand, the new initiatives—like the taxonomies described above—assume a linear relationship between better information and better decisions and largely ignore differences between scientists' and community groups' understandings of what would constitute "better information." As a result, the EPA's outreach to potential citizen scientists has focused on educating them on "appropriate" use of low-cost sensors and proper methods of quality control (see www.epa.gov/air-research/air-sensor-toolbox-citizen-scientists).

To some extent, social movement groups are pushing back against this redefinition of their knowledge production efforts. For example, during a question-and-answer period at the EPA's 2015 Community Air Monitoring Training, one activist challenged an EPA scientist about whether citizen science is really going to make a difference for communities. He asserted that people already *know* what's in the air, and that they were most concerned not with generating more data but in getting changes made and making sure that regulators take action on the data they have already submitted. Yet on-going ethnographic observation suggests that federal models for citizen science will shape the research activities of social movement groups, especially in the environmental justice realm. Organizations involved in bucket monitoring are increasingly investing their limited resources in developing extensive quality assurance plans in collaboration with the regulatory agencies they hope will accept and act on their data, and a few EJ groups, seeing the potential to tap into new sources of funding, are reframing their organizing work as informal science education, following the lead of researchers in the scientific authority-driven tradition. While it seems unlikely that social movement groups will alter their models of social change or cease their organizing activities, pressure to make their knowledge-production conform to a scientific authority-driven model of citizen science may divert resources away from other kinds of political action and blunt their critiques of mainstream scientific standards and methods (see chapters by Pellizzoni; Pinto, this volume).

Conclusion

In Alan Irwin's (1995) vision of citizen science, community-based knowledge production activities are one way for people who are not credentialed scientists to point out the limitations of science and contribute to reconstructing sciences that are more in tune with social needs. Instead, citizen science as it is currently being institutionalized largely reproduces traditional hierarchies and power relations between credentialed experts and "lay" citizens. Researchers working in the scientific authority-driven citizen science tradition—which justifies public participation by pointing to the scientific value and validity of the resulting research—have been successful in defining citizen science as a practice that strives to meet scientific standards and informs change through individual choices and formal political processes. Their definitions have subsumed social movement-based citizen science—which critiques scientific standards and pursues change through a variety of governmental and non-governmental means—with the effect of making activists' participation in knowledge-making activities more legitimate while simultaneously making it harder to pursue the reforms of both science and governance that they seek. Environmental justice communities, for example, have been conducting ambient air monitoring as a way of pushing regulators to enforce environmental laws in residential areas around hazardous facilities, to challenge regulators' focus on long-term average chemical concentrations as the most appropriate way of representing community exposures, and to make the argument that repeated, short-term "blasts" of pollution are a systemic problem not addressed by the current structure of ambient air standards (Ottinger 2009). To the extent that community groups embrace the scientific authority-driven model of citizen science and meet regulators' standards for quality assurance, they may become more successful in convincing environmental agencies to take enforcement action. But a focus on conforming to, rather than explicitly challenging, scientific standards is unlikely to result in any reconsideration of the appropriateness of data-collection methods or the adequacy of the regulatory standards used to interpret the data.

Note

1   A few studies acknowledge the possibility that some amateurs will prove to be—or come to be—just as proficient as scientists, but even these claims are offered in contrast to the standard assumptions about volunteers' capabilities (Elbroch et al. 2011; Hames et al. 2012; Wiggins and Crowston 2011).

References

Allen, Barbara L. 2000. "The Popular Geography of Illness in the Industrial Corridor." In *Transforming New Orleans and its Environs: Centuries of Change*, edited by Craig E. Colten, 178–201. Pittsburgh: University of Pittsburgh Press.

Bonney, Rick, Heidi L. Ballard, Rebecca Jordan, Ellen McCallie, Tina B. Phillips, Jennifer Shirk, and Candie C. Wilderman. 2009a. "Public Participation in Scientific Research: Defining the Field and Assessing its Potential for Informal Science Education." In *A CAISE Inquiry Series Report*. Washington, DC: Center for Advancement of Informal Science Education (CAISE).

Bonney, Rick, Caren B. Cooper, Janis Dickinson, Steve Kelling, Tina B. Phillips, Kenneth V. Rosenberg, and Jennifer Shirk. 2009b. "Citizen Science: A Developing Tool for Expanding Science Knowledge and Scientific Literacy." *BioScience* 59 (11):977–984.

Bonney, Rick, Tina B. Phillips, Heidi L. Ballard, and Jody W. Enck. 2016. "Can Citizen Science Enhance Public Understanding of Science?" *Public Understanding of Science* 25 (1):2–16.

Bonter, David N. and Caren B. Cooper. 2012. "Data Validation in Citizen Science: A Case Study from Project Feederwatch." *Frontiers in Ecology and the Environment* 10 (6):305–307.

Brown, Phil. 1992. "Popular Epidemiology and Toxic Waste Contamination: Lay and Professional Ways of Knowing." *Journal of Health and Social Behavior* 33 (3):267–281.

Brown, Phil, Steve Zavestocki, Sabrina McCormick, Brian Mayer, Rachel Morello-Frosch, and Rebecca Gasior Altman. 2004. "Embodied Health Movements: New Approaches to Social Movements in Health." *Sociology of Health and Illness* 26 (1):50–80.

Callon, Michel, Pierre Lascoumes, and Yannick Barthe. 2011. *Acting in an Uncertain World: An Essay on Technical Democracy*. Translated by Graham Burchell. Cambridge, MA: MIT Press.

Cooper, Caren B., Jennifer Shirk, and Benjamin Zuckerberg. 2014. "The Invisible Prevalence of Citizen Science in Global Research: Migratory Birds and Climate Change." *PLoS ONE* 9 (9).

Corburn, Jason. 2005. *Street Science: Community Knowledge and Environmental Health Justice*. Cambridge, MA: The MIT Press.

Couvet, D., F. Jiguet, R. Julliard, H. Levrel, and A. Teyssedre. 2008. "Enhancing Citizen Science Contributions to Biodiversity Science and Policy." *Interdisciplinary Science Reviews* 33 (1):95–103.

Cox, T. E., J. Philippoff, E. Baumgartner, and C. M. Smith. 2012. "Expert Variability Provides Perspective on the Strengths and Weaknesses of Citizen-Driven Intertidal Monitoring Program." *Ecological Applications* 22 (4):1201–1212.

Danielsen, Finn, Neil D. Burgess, and Andrew Balmford. 2005. "Monitoring Matters: Examining the Potential of Locally-Based Approaches." *Biodiversity and Conservation* 14:2507–2542.

Dawson, Gowan. 2015. "Constructing Scientific Communities: Citizen Science in the Nineteenth and Twenty-First Centuries." *Journal of Victorian Culture* 20 (2):246–254.

Dickerson-Lange, Susan E., Karla Bradley Eitel, Leslie Dorsey, Timothy E. Link, and Jessica D. Lundquist. 2016. "Challenges and Successes in Engaging Citizen Scientists to Observe Snow Cover: From Public Engagement to an Educational Collaboration." *Journal of Science Communication* 15 (1).

Dickinson, Janice L. and Rick Bonney. 2012. "Introduction: Why Citizen Science." In *Citizen Science: Public Participation in Environmental Research*, edited by Janice L. Dickinson and Rick Bonney, 2012. Ithaca: Cornell University Press.

Dickinson, Janis L., Jennifer Shirk, David N. Bonter, Rhiannon L. Crain, Jason Martin, Tina B. Phillips, and Karen Purcell. 2012. "The Current State of Citizen Science as a Tool for Ecological Research and Public Engagement." *Frontiers in Ecology and the Environment* 10 (6):291–297.

Dickinson, Janis L., Benjamin Zuckerberg, and David N. Bonter. 2010. "Citizen Science as an Ecological Research Tool: Challenges and Benefits." *Annual Review of Ecology, Evolution, and Systematics* 41:149–172.

Elbroch, Mark, Tuyeni H. Mwampamba, Maria J. Santos, Maxine Zylberberg, Louis Liebenberg, James Minye, Christopher Mosser, and Erin Reddy. 2011. "The Value, Limitations, and Challenges of Employing Local Experts in Conservation Research." *Conservation Biology* 25 (6):1195–1202.

Hames, Ralph S., James D. Lowe, and Kenneth V. Rosenberg. 2012. "Developing a Conservation Research Program with Citizen Science." In *Citizen Science: Public Participation in Environmental Research* edited by Janice L. Dickinson and Rick Bonney, 139–149. Ithaca: Cornell University Press.

Harrison, Jill. 2011. "Parsing 'Participation' in Action Research: Navigating the Challenges of Lay Involvement in Technically Complex Participatory Science Projects." *Society and Natural Resources* 24 (7):702–716.

Hemmi, Akiko and Ian Graham. 2014. "Hacker Science versus Closed Science: Building Environmental Monitoring Infrastructure." *Information, Communication, and Society* 17 (7):830–842.

Hochachka, Wesley M., Daniel Fink, Rebecca A. Hutchinson, Daniel Sheldon, Weng-Keen Wong, and Steve Kelling. 2012. "Data-Intensive Science Applied to Broad-Scale Citizen Science." *Trends in Ecology and Evolution* 27 (2):130–137.

Holdren, John P. 2015. *Addressing Societal and Scientific Challenges through Citizen Science and Crowdsourcing.* Washington, DC: Office of Science and Technology Policy.

Hunter, Jane, Abdulmonem Alabri, and Catharine van Ingen. 2013. "Assessing the Quality and Trustworthiness of Citizen Science Data." *Concurrency and Computation: Practice and Experience* 25:454–466.

Irwin, Alan. 1995. *Citizen Science: A Study of People, Expertise, and Sustainable Development.* London: Routledge.

Irwin, Alan and Brian Wynne. 1996. "Introduction." In *Misunderstanding Science? The Public Reconstruction of Science and Technology,* edited by Alan Irwin and Brian Wynne, 1–17. Cambridge: Cambridge University Press.

Jasanoff, Sheila. 1990. *The Fifth Branch: Science Advisers as Policymakers.* Cambridge, MA: Harvard University Press.

Jordan, Rebecca, Joan G. Ehrenfeld, Steven A. Gray, Wesley R. Brooks, David V. Howe, and Cindy E. Hmelo-Silver. 2012. "Cognitive Considerations in the Development of Citizen Science Projects." In *Citizen Science: Public Participation in Environmental Research,* edited by Janice L. Dickinson and Rick Bonney, 167–178. Ithaca: Cornell University Press.

Kinchy, Abby, Kirk Jalbert, and Jessica Lyons. 2014. "What is Volunteer Water Monitoring Good For? Fracking and the Plural Logics of Participatory Science." *Political Power and Social Theory* 27:259–289.

Lave, Rebecca. 2012. "Neoliberalism and the Production of Environmental Knowledge." *Environment and Society: Advances in Research* 3:19–38.

Liévanos, Raoul S., Jonathan K. London, and Julie Sze. 2011. "Uneven Transformations and Environmental Justice: Regulatory Science, Street Science, and Pesticide Regulation in California." In *Technoscience and Environmental Justice: Expert Cultures in a Grassroots Movement,* edited by Gwen Ottinger and Benjamin R. Cohen, 201–228. Cambridge, MA: MIT Press.

Macey, Gregg P., Ruth Breech, Mark Chernaik, Carolyn Cox, Denny Larson, Deb Thomas, and David O. Carpenter. 2014. "Air Concentrations of Volatile Compounds Near Oil and Gas Production: A Community-Based Exploratory Study." *Environmental Health* 13 (1):82.

McShea, William J., Tavis Forrester, Robert Costello, Zhihai He, and Roland Kays. 2016. "Volunteer-Run Cameras as Distributed Sensors for Macrosystem Mammal Research." *Landscape Ecology* 31:55–66.

Miller-Rushing, Abraham, Richard Primack, and Rick Bonney. 2012. "The History of Public Participation in Ecological Research." *Frontiers in Ecology and the Environment* 10 (6):285–290.

More, Anupreeta, Aprajita Verma, Philip J. Marshall, Surhud More, Elisabeth Baeten, Julianne Wilcox, Christine Macmillan, Claude Cornen, Amit Kapadia, Michael Parrish, Chris Snyder, Christopher P. Davis, Raphael Gavazzi, Chris J. Lintott, Robert Simpson, David Miller, Arfon M. Smith, Edward Paget, Presenjit Saha, Raphael Kung, and Thomas E. Collett. 2016. "Space Warps II: New Gravitational Lens Candidates from the CFHTLS Discovered Through Citizen Science." *Monthly Notices of the Royal Astronomical Society* 455:1191–1210.

O'Rourke, Dara and Gregg P. Macey. 2003. "Community Environmental Policing: Assessing New Strategies of Public Participation in Environmental Regulation." *Journal of Policy Analysis and Management* 22 (3):383–414.

Ottinger, Gwen. 2009. "Epistemic Fencelines: Air Monitoring Instruments and Expert-Resident Boundaries." *Spontaneous Generations* 3 (1):55–67.

Ottinger, Gwen. 2010. "Buckets of Resistance: Standards and the Effectiveness of Citizen Science." *Science, Technology, and Human Values* 35 (2):244–270.

Ottinger, Gwen. 2013a. "Changing Knowledge, Local Knowledge, and Knowledge Gaps: STS Insights into Procedural Justice." *Science, Technology, and Human Values* 38 (2):250–270.

Ottinger, Gwen. 2013b. *Refining Expertise: How Responsible Engineers Subvert Environmental Justice Challenges.* New York: New York University Press.

Ottinger, Gwen. 2016. "Social Movement-Based Citizen Science." In *The Rightful Place of Science: Citizen Science*, edited by Darlene Cavalier and Eric B Kennedy, 89–104. Tempe, AZ: Consortium for Science, Policy, and Outcomes.

Ottinger, Gwen and Benjamin R. Cohen. 2011. *Technoscience and Environmental Justice: Expert Cultures in a Grassroots Movement*. Cambridge, MA: MIT Press.

Ottinger, Gwen and Benjamin R. Cohen. 2012. "Environmentally Just Transformations of Expert Cultures: Toward the Theory and Practice of a Renewed Science and Engineering." *Environmental Justice* 5 (3):158–163.

Overdevest, Christine and Brian Mayer. 2008. "Harnessing the Power of Information through Community Monitoring: Insights from Social Science." *Texas Law Review* 86 (7):1493–1526.

Phillips, Tina B., Rick Bonney, and Jennifer Shirk. 2012. "What is our Impact? Toward a Unified Framework for Evaluating Outcomes of Citizen Science Participation." In *Citizen Science: Public Participation in Environmental Research*, edited by Janice L. Dickinson and Rick Bonney, 82–95. Ithaca: Cornell University Press.

Sauermann, Henry and Chiara Franzoni. 2015. "Crowd Science User Contribution Patterns and their Implications." *Proceedings of the National Academy of Sciences* 112 (3):679–684.

Shapin, Steven. 1994. *A Social History of Truth: Civility and Science in Seventeenth-Century England*. Chicago: University of Chicago Press.

Shirk, Jennifer, Heidi L. Ballard, Candie C. Wilderman, Tina B. Phillips, Andrea Wiggins, Rebecca Jordan, Ellen McCallie, Matthew Minarchek, Bruce V. Lewenstein, Marianne E. Krasny, and Rick Bonney. 2012. "Public Participation in Scientific Research: A Framework for Deliberate Design." *Ecology and Society* 17 (2):29–48.

Tesh, Sylvia Noble. 2000. *Uncertain Hazards: Environmental Activists and Scientific Proof*. Ithaca: Cornell University Press.

Trautmann, Nancy M., Jennifer Shirk, Jennifer Fee, and Marianne E. Krasny. 2012. "Who poses the Question? Using Citizen Science to help K-12 Teachers meet the Mandate for Inquiry." In *Citizen Science: Participation in Environmental Research*, edited by Janice L Dickinson and Rick Bonney, 179–190. Ithaca: Cornell University Press.

Trumbull, Deborah J., Rick Bonney, Derek Bascom, and Anna Cabral. 2000. "Thinking Scientifically during Participation in a Citizen Science Project." *Science Education* 84 (2):265–275.

Vetter, Jeremy. 2011. "Introduction: Lay Participation in the History of Scientific Observation." *Science in Context* 24 (2):127–141.

Wiggins, Andrea and Kevin Crowston. 2011. "From Conservation to Crowdsourcing: A Typology of Citizen Science." Proceedings of the 44th Hawaii International Conference on System Sciences.

Wilderman, Candie C. 2007. "Models of Community Science: Design Lessons from the Field." Citizen Science Toolkit Conference, Ithaca, NY.

Wylie, Sara Ann, Kirk Jalbert, Shannon Dosemagen, and Matt Ratto. 2014. "Institutions for Civic Technoscience: How Critical Making is Transforming Environmental Research." *The Information Society* 30 (2):116–126.

PART V

(Political economic) geographies of science

27

THE TRANSFORMATION OF CHINESE SCIENCE

Richard P. Suttmeier

A series of recent statistical reports have called attention to the rapid rise of China's research and development expenditures and the likelihood that Chinese spending on R&D, in purchasing power parity (PPP) terms, will surpass that of the United States in the not-too-distant future (National Science Board, 2016; Van Noorden, 2016; *R&D Magazine*, 2016). As these quantitative indicators show, there have been significant changes in the Chinese research and innovation systems over the past two decades. Of particular note is the dominant role played by the industrial enterprises sector in the overall national R&D spending account – now more than 70 percent of the total – a major change from the legacy system in which spending by government was the dominant source of funding (Cao, 2015). This shift reflects the influence of state policy intended to make the industrial enterprises sector the core of the national innovation system.

Other signs of progress include increasing numbers of papers published in international journals, increasing numbers of patents, a large and expanding community of scientists and engineers, and the successful completion of demanding research and engineering projects in such fields as space, ocean engineering, supercomputing, transportation, materials science, etc. These indicators all point to considerable success in implementing science, technology and innovation (STI) policies for transforming Chinese science and catching up with international scientific and technological frontiers.

What these success indicators fail to show, though, is that China's policies and institutions for research and innovation have also undergone enormous changes over the past 35 years, changes which help explain the successes alluded to above. But they also fail to indicate that these systems continue to face serious problems, and thus remain targets of further reform. Indeed, the quantitative indicators at times mask these problems. Thus, the "transformation of Chinese science" must be understood as part of a multi-decade process of progress, encounters with serious problems, and reform, the success of which is still elusive.

The initial challenges of transformation

The origins of the "transformation" can be traced back to the late 1970s and the end of the Maoist era in China. We should recall that, during the 1950s and early 1960s, China built up a substantial research system under Soviet influence and with Soviet assistance. These efforts enabled China successfully to develop nuclear weapons and the ability to launch satellites (the so-called *liangdan yixing* or "two bombs, one satellite" achievements). But, in spite of success in the strategic weapons areas, the disruptions caused by the Cultural Revolution (1966–1976) caused serious setbacks in China's research and innovation capabilities.

These setbacks led to a rethinking of China's approach to science and technology during the 1970s, rethinking that was also influenced by China's increasing exposure at the time to the research and innovation systems of the United States and other OECD countries. This exposure, along with perceptions of the increasing technological progress of its East Asian neighbors, reinforced Chinese understandings that the nation's capabilities for research and innovation were falling ever further behind international trends.

In 1978, therefore, the post-Mao Chinese leadership headed by Deng Xiaoping initiated a set of policies to give the nation's science and technology new directions, with science and technology named as one of the "four modernizations", the pillars of modernizing China[1] (Suttmeier, 1980). In doing so, however, it also embraced practices from the Maoist era that were thought to have been successful. This was especially true of state-directed science and technology planning and the centralized mobilization of resources to support national programs for research and innovation, practices which continue today.

Thus at the dawn of the post-Mao era in the late 1970s, the challenges faced by Chinese leaders were seen more as ones of revitalization, rather than transformation. As noted, the radical politics of the Cultural Revolution had resulted in severe disruptions of Chinese scientific research and higher education. As China's leaders sought to rebuild disrupted research and educational institutions, they understandably were guided by pre-Cultural Revolution models and practices, some of which – such as national science planning – were held in high regard. But, as the Deng-era policies of reform (*gaige*) and open-door (*kaifang*) began to take hold, key decision makers began to realize that pre-Cultural Revolution experience would have to yield to new approaches to policy and institutional design. Whereas the pre-Cultural Revolution experience had been strongly inspired by Soviet practices and assumptions about the role of science in a *planned* economy, the China of the Deng era was increasingly taking inspiration from the US and other OECD countries, the policies and institutions of which were seen as driving new scientific discoveries, dynamic technology-based economic progress, and formidable national security technologies. An initial challenge of reform was therefore to transform the science and technology system to one that would be more compatible with the *market* economy assumptions that were beginning to transform the economy.

The role of the outside world

This incipient transformation of Chinese science and technology was not only *inspired by* the experiences of the OECD countries. China also actively exploited the opportunities afforded by the closer contact with these countries made possible by the open-door policy. First, technology transfer to China from the OECD world began to revolutionize China's industrial technology. As China's foreign investment regime liberalized over the course of the 1980s and into the 1990s, foreign direct investment increased dramatically, and led to significant new modalities for technology transfer resulting from a growing number of joint ventures and wholly owned foreign enterprises.

By the middle of the 1990s, foreign companies began establishing R&D centers in China, a trend that continues today.[2] While the nature of the spillover benefits from these foreign invested centers continues to be debated, there is no doubt that their existence, and the other technology transfer experiences that have occurred over the past 30 years, have greatly changed Chinese R&D practices, the level of industrial technology and, perhaps more importantly, the thinking and orientations towards the management of R&D among Chinese managers.

In addition to technology transfer, China's opening to the outside world has also resulted in hundreds of thousands of Chinese students going abroad for advanced education. Those that have returned, especially those at the PhD level, have brought back knowledge of the leading fields of research and cutting-edge research strategies (methods, technology, research organization, etc.) and have often stepped into influential positions in universities and research institutes. Recent returnees have also assumed roles as technical entrepreneurs who started the high technology firms that are often seen as China's most innovative. Those who have not returned – constituting China's substantial brain drain – have nevertheless often contributed to the transformation of Chinese science as well through co-authoring with colleagues in China, by hosting new generations of Chinese graduate students, by establishing their own research groups in China, and through providing advisory and consulting services to Chinese institutions. Those "lost" to the brain drain, thus, have nevertheless served as important bridges between the Chinese research environment and leading centers of research in the US and other countries.

Finally, China has established active programs of cooperation in science and technology with the governments of OECD countries and the EU. These too have provided enabling linkages for the acquisition of foreign knowledge and experience contributing to the enhancement of Chinese scientific and technological capabilities. This is especially true with regard to the STI policies of other governments, and the ways in which government science programs are organized.

The evolution of domestic policies

The transformation of Chinese science and technology over the past 35 years is usefully understood as a combination of a creative exploitation of those resources in the international environment noted above, and an evolving set of domestic policies focusing on the provision of material resources for scientific development and ongoing institutional reform (cf. Fu, Woo and Hou, 2016). These policies began to take shape in the 1980s, as seen, for example, in the institutional reforms of 1985, the initiation of a patent system, the establishment of the Chinese National Natural Science Foundation (inspired in part by exposure to US NSF), the launching of the "863" national high-technology program, the initiation of special high technology zones and more permissive policies for high technology "spin-off" enterprises originating in universities and the Chinese Academy of Sciences (Gu, 1999). During the 1990s, as the Chinese economy continued to develop, wealth accumulated, and expenditures on R&D began to increase steadily. In the course of the 1990s, however, we also begin to see a more complex and nuanced understanding of *innovation* as something "more than R&D," with China beginning to experiment with a series of indirect policy instruments – preferential tax policies, export subsidies, targeted government procurement, growing attention to patents and technical standards, etc., in addition to direct R&D support. By the end of the 1990s, Chinese "science policy" was giving way to a more complex "innovation policy," the transition to which has yet to be completed, as noted further below.

The dawn of the 21st century saw China beginning to question its heavy reliance on foreign technology. Dissatisfaction over licensing fees charged by foreign patent holders, and concerns over the future ability to access more advanced technologies in the face of foreign export control policies and the commercial strategies of foreign companies to protect their core technologies, drove a rethinking of the balance between foreign technology and indigenous innovation. China's accession to the WTO in 2001, and expectations of further liberalization of the foreign investment regime, created the possibility that technology dependency would actually increase. As a result, the leadership began national discussions over research and innovation strategies – now more feasible given the enhancement of human and institutional resources built up over the previous 15 years – that would strengthen Chinese technological sovereignty. These discussions culminated in the launching of the 15-year "Medium to Long-Term Plan (MLP) For Scientific and Technological Development" in 2006 (Cao, Suttmeier and Simon, 2006).

The MLP is an ambitious strategy of development which specifies major R&D projects in basic and applied research and includes a package of tax, trade, and human resource development policies intended to make China an innovative, knowledge-based society by the year 2020, and a major international player in science and technology (OECD, 2008; Schwaag-Serger and Breidne, 2007). The Plan embraces the concept of *zizhu chuangxin*, often translated as "indigenous innovation," a concept that has led to considerable confusion and controversy internationally as well as in China. While the term might better be rendered as "self-directed" innovation, implying a degree of technological independence and strategic control over technological development (Lazonick, Zhou and Sun, 2016), it has led to internationally controversial trade and investment policies which have been seen by foreign stakeholders as protectionist and inconsistent with the spirit of WTO and its provisions (McGregor, 2010).

Current reform initiatives

One of the more curious aspects of scientific and technological development in China since the initiation of the MLP has been that rapid spending increases on research and development have occurred in the face of an institutional environment that has been unsettled and not always well-suited to the effective use of generous funding. In short, the R&D spending surge over the past 15 years has clearly outpaced institutional design, leaving a legacy of problems including considerable derivative research, scientific misconduct, widespread filing of low-quality patents, waste and misuse of R&D funding, and the development of a technical talent pool, a large portion of which seemed to lack the training and socialization needed for original research. And, in spite of calls for "indigenous innovation," reliance on foreign science and technology for major national research and engineering projects remains high, reflecting ongoing problems of technological dependency. Thus, despite the substantial investments China has made in science and technology and the progress these have facilitated, the resulting research accomplishments, technological innovations, and creation of the innovative society envisioned in the MLP and other national plans have been seen as disappointing by key national decision makers. Not surprisingly, therefore, further reforms of the systems for research and innovation are again on the agenda.

In July, 2012, the Chinese leadership convened a new National Conference on Science and Innovation at which then premier Wen Jiabao bemoaned the performance of China's systems for research and innovation and called for further reform. Two months later, in September, 2012, with the issuance of the "Opinions on Deepening the Reform of the Science and Technology System and Speeding up the Building of a National Innovation System," the Chinese Communist Party (CCP) Central Committee and the State Council brought a sharper focus to the need for further institutional reform (Ministry of Science and Technology, 2012). The "Opinions" served as an important aspirational document, offering a comprehensive statement of reform directions that presaged things to come. Clearly, as the second decade of the 21st century began, China's top political leaders were asking hard questions about the efficiency and effectiveness of all the money that was going into science and technology.

During 2014, these hard questions were being converted into a series of science and technology reform initiatives by the new Xi Jinping government, which at the Third Plenum of the 18th Party Congress in November, 2013, announced a comprehensive package of economic reforms, many of which pertained to science and the national innovation system. President Xi Jinping and other Chinese leaders understood that in order to avoid a "middle income trap," China needed an innovation-driven growth strategy which, in turn, directed attention to the effective functioning of a national innovation system. In addition, pressing environmental problems have made environmental sustainability a more important consideration in devising a new growth strategy, prompting calls for innovative energy and pollution control technologies. The STI reform policies growing out of these concerns, therefore, seek to incorporate knowledge from international best practices, rationalize the relationships among budgets, expenditures, and research programs, ensure that there are effective linkages between research and production, clarify the relationships between government and the market, and ensure honesty and integrity in the implementation of STI policies through greater administrative transparency.

The pace of reform announcements quickened in 2014. In March, the State Council issued an important document directed at reforming the financing and financial management of government science and technology programs which was then followed up in December by a more comprehensive reform directive for changing the central government funding system (State Council, 2014a, 2014b). Since the beginning of 2015, the political regime has continued to issue a flurry of reform documents. In March, the challenges of promoting a market-oriented innovation system were addressed in an important industry-focused document proposing a whole series of policies dealing with industry structure, venture capital, intellectual property, government procurement, R&D management, etc. (State Council, 2015). Other important policy statements were also issued, dealing with the funding of research, research management and governance of the research and innovation systems, human resources, local (as opposed to national) innovation strategies, technology transfer regulations affecting relationships between universities and government research institutes and enterprises, international cooperation, and the promotion of "mass innovation" and technical entrepreneurship. The scope of the reforms is therefore very broad and, as a result, some of the reforms are to be phased in over several years.

Progress has already been made in clarifying the legal environment for government STI programs, especially with regard to transparency in the administration of research funding and the conduct of research projects. Project budgeting procedures have been improved by allowing for more rational salary and overhead allowances; whereas salary support from a grant, for instance, had been limited to 5 percent, this has now been increased to 20 percent. This should help discourage investigators from attempting to maximize the number of grants received in order to enhance income, a practice which contributed to insensitivity to research quality and integrity. New web-based procedures have been introduced to make the funding of research, and the results of research, more transparent. Nationwide databases have been established to aid in research administration and to identify qualified scientists and engineers to participate in project selection and evaluation activities.

An especially significant change is the reconfiguration of major government funding programs into five main categories. In the first, the work of the National Natural Science Foundation of China (NSFC), long considered the best administered of the previous funding streams, is reaffirmed, with a significant increase in funding for basic and exploratory research – a longstanding gap in Chinese science and source of continuing criticism. A second category is focused on China's major projects (*da xiangmu*), such as the 16 identified in the MLP (large aircraft, nuclear power plants, advanced manufacturing, space, etc.) The major national R&D programs that had been administered by the Ministry of Science and Technology, and which had come in for considerable criticism – including the 863 high-technology program, the 973 basic science program and the *zhicheng*, or "support" program – have now been reorganized and consolidated into a third category referred to as the "main R&D plan" (*zhongdian yanfa jihua*). Whereas the previous design of these programs – especially 863 and 973 – was based on different segments of the innovation chain, the new approach focuses on the solution of national problems across the spectrum of R&D activities (Hou, 2016).

A fourth category focuses on technological innovation and involves the leveraging of various governmental and non-governmental sources of funding to support innovation in industry and agriculture, including support for the transfer of research achievements from universities and research institutes to industry. Finally, a fifth category focuses on rationalizing the use of facilities (research institutes, engineering research centers, etc.) and infrastructure, and includes support for the development of creative human talents to lead research and innovation initiatives. In this context, there is a new interest in the development of national laboratories in keeping with instructions from President Xi at the Fifth Plenum of the 18th Party Congress in October, 2015 to develop national labs.

Progress has also been made in attacking some of the procedural difficulties that had developed in implementing Bayh-Dole type policies in China that would allow patenting and/ or commercialization of publicly-funded research findings. Good results were received from pilot programs introduced in the high-tech parks in four cities (Beijing, Shanghai, Wuhan, and Hefei) in which research institutes and universities were given clearer rights to the benefits, use, and transferability (*san quan*, or "three rights") of the intellectual property they develop, and in February, 2016, the State Council approved a policy that would allow academics greater freedom to do part-time work with companies. Successful technology transfer experiences would be given greater weight in future evaluations of research institutes and universities, and the latter would be allowed to retain "no less than half of the income earned" from the products resulting from successfully transferred achievements (MOST, 2016). To further stimulate the integration of research and technology with the economy, reforms were introduced to stimulate the growth of an S&T service industry (*keji fuwu chanye*) to include the strengthening of capabilities for the management and utilization of intellectual property.

Adjusting central policy institutions

Not surprisingly, such system-wide reforms will also require changes in the national science and technology bureaucracy. Importantly, a new approach to the inter-ministerial coordination (a perennial bugbear of Chinese government) has been introduced with the establishment of an "inter-ministerial joint conference system" (*bùjì liánxí huìyì zhìdù*) to coordinate and "unify" the government science and technology programs. Leadership for this new inter-agency mechanism is being shared among MOST, the Ministry of Finance and the National Development and Reform Commission (NDRC), with MOST hosting its secretariat and having responsibility for national R&D activities. The Ministry of Finance is expected to establish a stronger organic link among policy, program, and budgeting, with NDRC taking the lead on innovation issues. The importance of this joint conference system can be seen when we consider that a number of mission-oriented ministries (for health, agriculture, environment, information industry, etc.) now play a greater role in government research programs.

In addition, representatives from industry and trade associations are also participating more actively in important national priority setting activities in keeping with the call from the State Council for the establishment of a high-level strategic consulting/policy advisory mechanism (*zhanlue zixun yu zonghe pingshen weiyuanhui*). During 2015, the "Joint Conference" convened a series of meetings to map out priorities for the new "major R&D plan" (*zhongdian yanfa jihua*). This was intended to be an inclusive exercise, with industry well represented, and with the results reviewed by the new high-level advisory mechanisms consisting of 240 experts organized into seven specialized panels. It led to the identification of 59 key national priorities in the seven areas of "modern agriculture," "public health," "strategic perspectives on major scientific issues," "resources and ecological environment protection," "industrial transformation and upgrading," "energy saving and new energy," and "new approaches to urbanization" (Hou, 2016).

Prior to these latest reforms, the administration of research programs was in the hands of officials in Chinese government ministries, especially the Ministry of Science and Technology. This arrangement was the object of considerable criticism from the technical community which alleged that it produced favoritism, a degree of corruption, and inappropriate incentives for high-quality work. An important new development, therefore, has been the decision to take government agencies out of the active administration of research programs and put it into the hands of "professional organizations" (*zhuanye jigou*). As of this writing, seven such organizations have been identified, all of which are quasi-governmental agencies (*shiye danwei*) affiliated with government ministries, but not officially part of the bureaucratic system.[3] These professional organizations, in turn, organize working panels of experts for project selection, review and evaluation, reminiscent of the operation of research councils in Europe. Government ministries, therefore, are supposed to be removed from active management activities, their role changed to that of overseeing and monitoring the operation of the "professional organizations," in keeping with broader reform objectives intended to redefine the role of the state in the nation's innovation system.

"Transforming" CAS

The national reform program, discussed above, carries implications for a variety of research performers, including the Chinese Academy of Sciences, universities, government research institutes, and industry. Reforms in the Chinese Academy of Sciences serve as an interesting case of how the community of research performers are responding to the broader national reform environment. But, in addition, as one of the most prominent legacy institutions from the Soviet-inspired, pre-reform era, it has faced distinctive challenges to redefine its identity in a China characterized by an ever-enlarging university research sector and the expansion of industrial research.

The CAS reform, referred to in English as the "Pioneer (*shuaixian xingdong*) Initiative," has the potential to bring about the most radical changes in the Academy since the 1950s. It grows out of the policy instructions issued by President Xi Jinping during his July, 2013 visit to CAS, and the need to respond to the broader national S&T reform program discussed above. The initiative involves reorganizing CAS's 100+ institutes into four major thematic categories, enhancing its educational missions through the establishment of the University of the Chinese Academy of Sciences, and through reforms in its academician (*yuanshi*) system to strengthening its policy advisory functions. As noted, these changes can be seen as the latest in a series of attempts to overcome long-standing problems of mission definition and management within CAS as it has had to face the significantly different national innovation system in the post-1978 era. But, in addition, the changing expectations from the new central political leadership, reflected in the new national reform program, have given the reform program a new urgency.

The reorganization of CAS institutes is an attempt to clarify Academy missions and devise management and policy strategies appropriate to the functions and capabilities of the numerous and diverse research institutions (Bai, 2014; Chinese Academy of Sciences, 2014). According to the current plan, institutes would be reorganized into one of four categories: centers of excellence; innovation "academies" (*chuangxin yuan*); platforms for large facilities; and centers for supporting national environmental and resource needs and those of local economies. In principle, this categorization is an imaginative approach that recognizes diverse capabilities and functions provided by the institutes and the need, therefore, to develop managerial strategies appropriate for the different missions and competencies. Complicating this reorganization initiative, though, are the broader national STI reform trends, such as the new five-part funding arrangements and the interest in establishing a network of national labs, some of which would undoubtedly be drawing on the resources of CAS institutes.

Conclusion

At a recent national science and technology conference in May, 2016, President Xi Jinping called attention to the many achievements that have been made over the past 35 years. And, indeed, as reflected in both quantitative and qualitative indicators, there is no doubt that the changes in Chinese science and technology are transforming China into a major power in science and technology. At the same time, however, Xi also echoed the elite concerns of the last five years, noted above, about unmet expectations, and issued renewed calls for further changes intended to realize an innovation-based development strategy.

As seen from the discussion above, there is no shortage of reform initiatives being driven from the political center, a phenomenon often referred to as "top-level design" (*dingceng sheji*). Although the current reform program does reflect the influence of the "top-level," it is important to note that the views of the members of the technical community are being sought, and are being reflected in policy statements. At that same May 2016 science conference, for instance, the remarks of Premier Li Keqiang indicated that complaints and criticisms from scientists about STI policies were being listened to, with the new measures announced at the meeting being well received by the technical community (Xinhua, 2016).

That said, there are many questions and uncertainties about current reform initiatives and their implications for further transformation of Chinese science and technology. Apart from the perennial problems of policy implementation in China, there are also questions about the urgency attached to reform by the political leadership. Some argue, for instance, that the trajectory of Chinese scientific and technological development has been a successful one, and that many of the problems with the system are likely to work themselves out as the system continues to mature. For instance, concerns about the relative scarcity of notable qualitative achievements, in the face of impressive quantitative indicators, need not cause alarm, in this view, since trends toward qualitative improvements are evident. That is, there is less need for major structural and policy changes, which are inevitably disruptive of research routines, than there is for a degree of patience as the system becomes more mature and sophisticated, as many trends indicate.

A less sanguine view, however, would point to the difficulties of implementing reform policies, and the resistance and confusion that is evident in doing so. It is clear that some of the long-standing problems with China's innovation system – the weaknesses of R&D in the business enterprise sector, difficulties of transferring research results into production, corruption and misconduct, the intrusive role of the state, etc. – persist and resist solution. While many of the reform initiatives show promise of offering new solutions to these problems, it is unlikely that their solution or amelioration will result from the system's maturation alone. Thus, the importance of reform policies in need of urgent implementation.

Underlying the current reform agenda are two themes which warrant particular attention. As noted above, a fundamental objective of reform since the 1980s has been the redesign of the innovation system to better serve a market, rather than a planned, economy. Hence, the emphasis placed on strengthening R&D in industrial enterprises and on market-oriented approaches to the building of an innovation-driven economy. These themes have been reiterated vigorously by Party leaders in each of the plenary meetings of the 18th Party Congress, and, although the existence of powerful vested interests has made progress much slower than hoped for, there are signs that the Chinese enterprise sector is beginning to discover its potential for technological innovation.

The second theme has gotten less attention in discussions of reform, but arguably identifies a core issue for the future transformation of Chinese science. As we have seen, changes are being made in research administration that give "professional organizations" a prominent new role. The meaning of "professional" in the Chinese context, however, does not quite accord with that used in the West. In particular, Western ideas associate professionalism with high levels of political autonomy reciprocally linked to fiduciary responsibilities, with autonomy seen as necessary for the responsible exercise of expertise expected by society. Since the establishment of the People's Republic of China, however, professional autonomy has been circumscribed, and viewed as antithetical to the political formula of the Chinese Communist Party. Professional scientific societies that had begun to take root in the pre-1949 era, for instance, were in the 1950s brought under the control of the All-China Federation of Scientific Societies, a Party-sponsored "mass organization" (*quntuan zuzhi*), which subsequently became the China Association of Science and Technology, or CAST.[4] And, as noted, the "professional organizations" charged with research administration under the current reforms are all affiliated with ministries. Thus, although the review panels they will convene will represent a step towards greater professionalization and a degree of insulation from the operation of the state, their autonomy from the state is somewhat limited

Interestingly, under the current reforms, new attention is being given to the role of CAST, and the science and engineering societies under it, in enhancing scientific development and the operation of the innovation system. This new policy emphasis further illustrates the puzzles of "professionalism with Chinese characteristics." CAST serves as an umbrella organization for scientific and engineering societies, and also serves as an instrument for the popularization of science and technology; in this sense it is reminiscent of the American Association for the Advancement of Science in the U.S. and similar organizations in other countries. But, as a mass organization in China, CAST is subordinate to the Party, and by design is intended to bring Party control over the technical community. As part of the reforms, CAST has enhanced its in-house technical expertise, built new policy analysis capabilities to become a "think tank" (as called for by Xi Jinping), and is expanding into areas of research and program evaluation as one of a number of "third-party" (*di san fang*) organizations intended to provide more objectivity and transparency to evaluation activities. In addition, it is expanding its organizational reach to universities, research institutes, and enterprises, by establishing CAST "chapters" (or local branches) in these institutions, with the hope that these will provide information to policy makers about conditions at working levels, facilitate greater inter-organizational cooperation and coordination, and promote understanding of STI policies in the interest of more effective policy implementation. These enhancements of CAST activities are in keeping with a wider directive to revitalize mass organizations, thus strengthening the role of the *Party* system in society as part of the broader effort to reduce and redefine the role of *government* (see, Xi, 2015).

To the Western observer, the absence of professional societies enjoying high levels of autonomy from political pressure has long been seen as a fundamental structural problem in China's scientific development efforts. It has contributed to problems of research evaluation and effective peer review mechanisms, helped perpetuate an overly tolerant attitude toward scientific misconduct, impeded the development of a strong and creative basic research tradition, and compromised the objectivity of policy advice from the technical community. These are all problems that the current reform initiatives hope to solve or ameliorate. The legitimation of autonomous professional organizations, however, is not included in this suite of reforms. Instead, while the need for "professionalization" is recognized, the Party's political formula requires that professionalization be pursued through modernized and expertise-infused instruments of political guidance. Whether this approach validates a successful "Chinese model" of scientific development remains to be seen. But it serves as an abiding central issue in the fascinating and complex process of transformation begun in 1978.

Notes

1 The "four modernizations" are agriculture, industry, national defense and science and technology, with the latter seen as the key to the other three.
2 According to a 2014 report in *Forbes*, there are now more than 1,500 foreign R&D centers in China. (Yip and McKern, 20114).
3 Four of these are affiliated with MOST: the China Agenda 21 Management Center, the High Technology Research and Development Center, the China Rural Technology Development Centre, and the China Biotechnology Development Centre. The Agricultural Science and Technology Development Center is affiliated with the Ministry of Agriculture, the National Health and Family Planning Medicine Health Science and Technology Development Research Center and the Ministry of Information Industry and Industry Development Promotion Center are affiliated with the ministries of those name.
4 Mass organizations facilitate Party penetration and control of social groups; others include trade unions, the Communist Youth League, and the All-China Federation of Women.

References

Bai, C.L. 2014. "The Reform of Research Institutes: Which Way to Go?" Retrieved from www.cas. ac.cn/xw/zyxw/yw/201411/t20141117_4253641.shtml.

Cao, C. 2015. China. *UNESCO Science Report, Towards 2030*. Retrieved from http://unesdoc.unesco. org/images/0023/002354/235406e.pdf.

Cao, C., Suttmeier, R. P., and Simon, D. F. 2006. "China's 15-year Science and Technology Plan." *Physics Today*, December, 2006.

Chinese Academy of Sciences. 2014. "Initial Procedures and Common Policies for the Classification of CAS Institutions." Retrieved from www.cas.ac.cn/xw/zyxw/yw/201411/t20141113_4251558.shtml.

Fu, X.L., Woo, W.T., and Hou, J. 2016. "Technological Innovation Policy in China: The Lessons, and Necessary Changes Ahead." Retrieved from http://papers.ssrn.com/sol3/papers.cfm?abstract_id=2798806.

Gu, S.L. 1999. *China's Industrial Technology*. London and New York: Routledge.

Hou, J. G. 2016. "Keējì bù fù bùzhǎng: Guójiā zhòngdiǎn yánfā jìhuà xīn fāng'àn lā kāi kējì xiàngmù gǎigé de xùmù" (Vice Minister of Science and Technology: Key National Research and Development Program Begins a New Program of Reform Projects). Retrieved from http://news.xinhuanet.com/ info/2016-02/17/c_135105980.htm

Lazonick, W., Zhou, Y. and Sun, Y.F. 2016. *China as an Innovation Nation*. Oxford: Oxford University Press.

McGregor, J. 2010. *China's Drive for "Indigenous Innovation."* Retrieved from www.uschamber.com/sites/ default/files/legacy/reports/100728chinareport_0.pdf.

MOST (Ministry of Science and Technology). 2012. "Opinions on Deepening the Reform of the Science and Technology System and Speeding up the Building of a National Innovation System." Retrieved from www.most.gov.cn/eng/pressroom/201211/t20121119_98014.htm.

MOST (Ministry of Science and Technology). 2016. "Zhōnghuá Rénmín Gònghéguó Cùjìn Kējì Chéngguǒ Zhuǎnhuà Fǎ" (Law on the Promotion of Transformation of Scientific and Technological Achievements). Retrieved from www.most.gov.cn/yw/201603/t20160303_124399.htm.

National Science Board. 2016. *Science and Engineering Indicators, 2016*. Washington: National Science Foundation.

OECD. 2008. *OECD Reviews of Innovation Policy*. Paris: Organization for Economic Cooperation and Development.

R&D Magazine. 2016. *2016 Global R&D Forecast*. Retrieved from www.rdmag.com/article/2016/02/2016-global-rd-funding-forecast-0.

Schwaag-Serger, S. and Breidne, M. (2007). "China's Fifteen-Year Plan for Science and Technology: An Assessment." *Asia Policy*, 4: 135–164.

State Council. 2014a. "Guówùyuàn guānyú gǎijìn jiāqiáng zhōngyāng cáizhèng kēyán xiàngmù hézījīn guǎnlǐ de ruǒgān yìjiàn." Retreived from www.gov.cn/zhengce/content/2014-03/12/content_8711.htm.

State Council. 2014b. "Guówùyuàn yìnfā guānyú shēnhuà zhōngyāng cáizhèng kējì jìhuà (zhuānxiàng, jījīn děng) guǎnlǐ gǎigé fāng'àn de tōngzhī." Retrieved from www.gov.cn/zhengce/content/2015-01/12/content_9383.htm.

State Council. 2015. "Zhōnggòng zhōngyāng guówùyuàn guānyú shēnhuà tǐzhì jīzhì gǎigéjiākuài shíshī chuàngxīn qūdòng fāzhǎn zhànlüè de ruǒgān yìjiàn" (CPC Central Committee and State Council on Deepening the Reform of Institutional Mechanisms: Accelerate the Implementation of a Number of Opinions on Innovation-driven Development Strategy). Retrieved from www.gov.cn/gongbao/content/2015/content_2843767.htm.

Suttmeier, R. 1980. *Science, Technology and China's Drive for Modernization*. Stanford, CA: Hoover Institution Press.

Van Noorden, R. 2016. "China by the Numbers." *Nature*, 534: 7608. Retrieved from www.nature.com/news/china-by-the-numbers-1.20122.

Xi, J.P. 2015. "Speech before the Central Party Mass Organizations Work Conference, July, 6–7." Retrieved from http://news.ifeng.com/a/20151103/46096419_0.shtml.

Xinhua. 2016. "Chinese Gov't Slashes Red Tape for Scientific Researchers." Retrieved from www.china.org.cn/china/2016-06/02/content_38585925.htm.

Yip, G. and McKern, B. "Can Multinationals Innovate in China?" *Forbes,* December 17, Retrieved from www.forbes.com/sites/ceibs/2014/12/17/can-multinationals-innovate-in-china/#66ac3e01572f.

28

POSTCOLONIAL TECHNOSCIENCE AND DEVELOPMENT AID

Insights from the political economy of locust control expertise

Claude Péloquin

Scientific and technical knowledge and practice play a key role in international development interventions. Expertise, thus, is a key element of the geographical and historical relations between the colonial and postcolonial cores and peripheries (Vessuri, this volume; Ferguson 1990, 2006, Escobar 1995, Watts 2003), and it has accordingly been the object of a great deal of attention in critical development studies and related fields (Mitchell 2002, Goldman 2005, Li 2007, Mosse 2011). For example, scholars have examined the 'downstream' effects of expert knowledge on populations' subjectivities (Agrawal 2005, Li 2007, Birkenholtz 2008), and how dominant narratives within colonial ventures have contributed to the stabilization and selections of some ways of knowing over others (Fairhead and Leach 1996, Bassett and Bi Zuéli 2000, Davis 2007).

A political economy perspective on science can bring additional and valuable insights into the politics of development expertise by shedding light on the specific institutional mechanisms that contribute to aligning scientific practices in these settings with the broader transnational and transcolonial power dynamics to which they contribute (Cooper and Stoler 1989, Hoogvelt 2001, Venn 2009). This approach can illuminate the professional incentives that development projects and interventions present to experts: whether those incentives differ from the ones encountered, for example, in national public research agencies or private think-tanks in industrialized core countries, and what the implications might be for the type of knowledge and management approaches these conditions favor (Shackley 2001, Kuus 2014, Cashmore *et al.* 2015).

International efforts to prevent and control the swarming of desert locusts in Africa and Asia provide a useful context to examine how the political economy of expertise in development co-evolves with the production, circulation, and application of scientific and technical knowledge in these settings. This agricultural pest insect is extremely mobile, and its occasional upsurges and invasions are difficult to predict and control. Moreover, its management is largely under the purview of actors implicated in international development efforts. In this sense, locust invasions present a development-related environmental problem that is mismatched to management institutions (Folke *et al.* 2007, Treml *et al.* 2015), and whose resolution, therefore, calls for inquiries on what shapes how mandated organizations prefer to 'think' about such problems, and how they select management practices to resolve them (Douglas 1986, Lecoq 2005, Robbins *et al.* 2008).

This chapter stems from my exploration of the institutional processes shaping the place and role of organizational networks linking the regional structures of locust surveillance and control to those of state and international programs of development aid. The analysis brings attention to the strategies that experts and technicians pursue to maintain and augment the legitimacy, relevance, and financial sustainability of their branch of applied science within development networks. It also sheds light on how the imperatives of professional sustainability pertaining to the challenge of monitoring and controlling the populations of this emergent, mobile, omnivorous, and polyphenic pest insect relate to, and partially shape, the stabilization and selection of preferred locust management strategies amongst experts, and in turn how scientific knowledge is favored and valued in applied settings.

I examine debates in this branch of applied entomology in light of the difficulties faced by locust experts to maintain reliable sources of funding and relevancy. My analysis suggests that these debates have been *de facto* resolved not by technical arguments alone, but also in part by the shared conceptual horizon (Pellizzoni 2011) between (1) the discursive and organizational socio-technical by-products of one subset of locust management strategies and (2) development's contribution to a mode of government that operates via a proliferation of mechanisms of social and ecological improvement. This shared conceptual horizon, and the compatibility between the institutional requirements and discursive logics of development programs and the preventive approach to the application of locust science, I argue, produces the primary mechanisms whereby the political economy of development expertise shapes locust science.

Postcolonial technoscience and development aid

Research in science studies and related fields has revealed how the practices, techniques, texts, and quotidian activities by which scientific facts are produced and stabilized, as well as the ways in which technical and scientific practices are adopted and modified as they travel across different settings, and all have serious implications for our understanding of power and social order (Mitchell 2002, Jasanoff 2004, Abram 2005, Goldman *et al.* 2011). In this context, attention to postcolonial technoscience (Anderson 2002, McNeil 2005, Harding 2011, Mavhunga 2011) has demonstrated how scientific practices and discourses in fields such as health, sanitation, planning, and agriculture have co-evolved with the economic and political structures of domination and exploitation linking industrialized societies to non-industrialized societies, from the colonial era to the present. Examples include the use of technoscientific projects to experiment, perform, and represent forms of social order and subjectivities in colonial settings, including the effect of using colonies as laboratories to experiment with modes of government that would later be incorporated in metropolitan governance (Bonneuil 2000, Carroll 2006, Tilley 2011), and the role of local, material, and cultural contingencies, and popular agency, in shaping the actual outcomes of these projects (Hecht 2002, Mitchell 2002, Freed 2010).

Similarly, scholarship in critical development studies has theorized foreign aid and technical assistance interventions as constitutive of a mode of government produced at the junction of post-colonial state-building and transnational governance (Gupta 1998, Callaghy *et al.* 2001, Ilcan and Phillips 2010, Lie 2015). This work helps trace the continuities and ruptures linking different periods of North–South relations by focusing on the governmental rationalities commonly produced during these periods. For example, the 'development and improvement' (*mise en valeur*) phase of the French 'civilizing mission' in Africa was characterized by structures, practices and discourses whose logic and effect exhibit important similarities with the contemporary aid-driven programs of capacity-building linking these two regions, but the latter also evolved to more than just a different version of the former (Conklin 1997, Cooke 2003, Venn 2009, Tilley 2011, Cherlet 2014). In this context, the concept of *developmental governmentality* allows the analysis of the institutional mechanisms designed to improve livelihoods and landscapes by focusing on the *effect*—intended or not—that these mechanisms have in shaping the conduct of social actors as development subjects (Agrawal 2005, Goldman 2005, Li 2007). Investigations of these mechanisms have highlighted how discourses and practice of training, consultancies, reports, and evaluations carried out in the name of development contribute to modes of power that operate via improvement, care, and attention to subjects and populations and that are thus distinct from regimes of rule more limited to negative powers of surveillance and coercive authority (Rose 1993, Rossi 2004).

The question of how the institutional context responsible for development's governmental effect influences the production, circulation, and application of scientific knowledge has received much less attention. A political economy approach to the study of scientific and technical expertise in development can help address this question by drawing attention to the alliances, strategies, and compromises that experts and technicians make to maximize the professional, institutional and financial viability of their specific field (Latour 1987, Clarke and McCool 1996, Rose 1999), how these shape the work of experts and technicians in development-related research and management programs (Keeley and Scoones 2003, Mosse 2011, Cashmore *et al.* 2014), and, by extension, what type of knowledge is likely to be favored by these outcomes.

Locust control as developmentalist science: programs of foreign aid

Populations of desert locusts present an important agricultural pest hazard across vast parts of the African continent, the Arabian Peninsula, and South Asia. This insect most commonly exists in what is called its solitary form, wherein individuals typically avoid one another as they feed on low-density vegetation scattered in desert environments. When rainfall and vegetation create conditions allowing greater locust population density over sustained periods, individuals start to change behavior and, eventually, their appearance, as they gradually enter what entomologists call a gregarious phase. As they become gregarious, locusts seek one another and form groups that grow in size, density, and mobility, eventually traveling to agriculturally productive areas where they feed massively on crops and pastures, sometimes causing catastrophic damage (Van Huis *et al.* 2007). During an upsurge, locust swarms, and plagues—swarms of swarms—can affect thousands of square kilometers in dozens of countries and last for several years.

Despite their great magnitude and impact, locust outbreaks and upsurges are difficult to predict past a very coarse resolution. The condition presented by these phase changes from the initial gregarization in micro-habitats of scattered desert vegetation patches, to the massive and highly mobile plagues that travel across continents, can be understood as one of *bifurcated spatiality and temporality*. In other words, the locust problem calls for management efforts at distinct scales, ranging from the very small to the very large. In each phase the insect is prone to either evade or overwhelm the spatial reach of the institutions responsible for its monitoring and control.

One important challenge to desert locust management capacity is the difficulty of maintaining an effective network of specialized experts and sufficiently trained and equipped technicians across these vast regions. Specifically, long periods of locust recession—when locust populations are almost all in their solitary phase—challenge the professional viability of locust expertise. During these recession periods, state and donor concerns about this pest problem diminish greatly, and consequently locust scientists and technicians struggle to remain institutionally and financially relevant in a context of unreliable interest from their clients. Entomologist Michel

Lecoq (2005) describes this dynamic as a cycle of crisis and oblivion. The institutional challenges posed by this recession–outbreak cycle are made worse by the fact that desert locusts are relatively omnivorous and not associated with specific sites or crops. This pest is not the concern of one agricultural industry in particular, which makes for a diffused constituency for locust experts. Other scientists doing applied research on pest management in tropical agriculture tend to be closely associated with one crop or commodity. For example, some groups of experts concentrate on coffee, bananas, cotton, and so on, and consequently deal with pests in so far as they affect or threaten this specific crop. In most cases, even if pest threats can be cyclical, researchers focusing on pest insects more prone to affect a particular agricultural commodity have a relatively well-established constituency on which to rely, through industrial and commercial interests, to sustain their work. This is not the case for locust experts (or acridologists), whose client agencies lack such consolidation. Put differently, the locust problem is often quite peripheral to the priorities of political authorities and established producer organizations, not only because the solitary insect is so elusive but also because the threat it continues to pose during recession periods does not concern a specific public. In sum, the institutional challenge of monitoring and controlling desert locust populations—an emergent, mobile, omnivorous and polyphenic pest insect—invites inquiries on how locust control experts attempt to sustain their professional relevancy, and the strategies, alliances, and narratives that sustain these attempts.

Since the 1960s, locust control has been increasingly incorporated in the constellations of programs and activities carried out under the rubric of development, which include technical assistance, foreign aid, and humanitarian relief (Baron 1972, Skaf *et al.* 1990). International efforts to control the desert locust have been coordinated by the Food and Agriculture Organization (FAO)—one of the first international agencies dedicated to North–South cooperation and poverty alleviation in the 20th century—since 1955, when the Organization established its Desert Locust Control Committee (DLCC). In the following decades, the locust problem also became a field of intervention for many other development programs and organizations including the World Bank, the African Development Bank, and bilateral aid agencies of France, the Netherlands, Germany, Sweden, Canada, USA, and Japan. This incorporation of locust management in the orbit of development networks has been justified by government officials and development professional alike, for at least three reasons. First, the threat that the desert locust poses to food security and agricultural productivity in underdeveloped countries makes it a humanitarian concern. Second, the transboundary nature of this pest hazard requires transnational coordination, best provided by multilateral, regional, and supranational organizations. Third, the fit of locust management with the demands of technical capacity building, both via training and technical transfer, make it a good fit with the raison-d'être of several development programs. Locust control efforts thus allow us to examine how the institutional logics and imperatives of these development programs shape the production and application of scientific knowledge, and in turn how and why some scientific recommendations and resulting technical practices are favored in development programs.

I studied the institutional dynamics within member agencies of the Western Region of the FAO's Desert Locust Control Committee (DLCC) from 2010 to 2014. This region includes ten countries in western and northwestern Africa, coordinated under the Commission for Controlling the Desert Locust in the Western Region (Clcpro, Commission de Lutte au Criquet Pèlerin en Région Occidentale). My understanding of the institutional dynamics across this regional organization is primarily informed by the interviews and documentary analysis I carried out in a selection of centers that together constitute a fairly representative cross-section of this international network: a French scientific research unit specialized in applied locust science in France, locust control centers and crop protection agencies in Mali, Senegal, Mauritania and Morocco, and at the FAO headquarters in Rome. In these locations, I interviewed scientific advisors and technicians and observed their work, both in the field and in regional and international meetings. I also analyzed policy and technical documents produced and used by these experts and agencies. This chapter focuses on dynamics reported by French-based entomological experts whose primary professional affiliation is with the Locust Ecology and research team of the French Center of International Agricultural Research for Development (Cirad), in Montpellier, France.

Debates in locust control and the institutional preferences of development science

Locust managers are concerned with preventing, responding, and/or adapting to significant increases in gregarious populations, called upsurges (Van Huis *et al.* 2007). The spatial–temporal particularities of locust upsurges allow multiple approaches or orientations to locust control. The most prevalent is the *preventive orientation*, which favors, as the name suggests, early, preventive interventions at the initial stages of locust gregarization. The competing approach, the *curative orientation*, favors delayed interventions.

In practice, preventive and curative orientations are enacted sequentially along a continuum of intervention, and are therefore compatible and complementary. The sequence follows the evolution of outbreaks, upsurges, and plagues: management strategies that focus on earlier stages in this cycle are 'more preventive' than management strategies that focus on later stages in the cycle, which are 'more curative'. That being said, even though these approaches can be thought of as complementary, they are also in competition with one another, because each calls for distinct organizational and technological commitments: increasing investments in preventive capacity takes away from investments in curative capacity, and vice versa.

In 2008 a group of senior acridologists published, in the journal *Crop Protection*, a review article entitled 'Preventive control and desert locust plagues' (Magor *et al.* 2008). The authors argued that the most effective approach to locust management is to prevent upsurge by forecasting and monitoring outbreaks, and chemically terminating gregarizing populations in situ as early as possible to avoid groups of gregarious locusts coalescing and thus becoming too large and mobile to contain. Based on modeling of outbreak dynamics, the authors make the case that intervention right at the outset of upsurges is not only the most effective, but also the most financially and ecologically sound approach to manage this insect. The authors further argue that the adoption of the preventive control orientation as the official strategy by the FAO's Desert Locust Control Committee since the 1960s has been the main reason for the diminishing frequency, extent, and duration of locust upsurges since then. Further, they argue that the strategy's potential effectiveness has not been fully realized because donors and governments are less likely to finance prevention during long periods of recession, a situation they deplore.

This article prompted a short commentary response from another senior acridologist, in the same journal, under the title 'A critique of preventive control and desert locust plagues' (Symmons 2009). Symmons's response stressed that, in a context of competition for limited resources, commitment to proactive preventive control at the FAO and across the locust control apparatus undermine countries' preparedness to respond to severe locust upsurges. Successful locust control, he argues,

> requires the right methods more than the right strategy. These include aerial detection and demarcation of hopper band targets, the treatment of flying swarms, and probably the use of persistent pesticide 'barriers' against marching bands. However, populations suitable for those methods are unlikely to occur until late in an upsurge and so have at best limited relevance for 'prevention'.
>
> *(Symmons 2009, p. 907)*

This view of locust control favors a 'wait and see' approach vis-à-vis locust breeding dynamics, combined with all-out campaigns of swarm suppression, to be waged only after locust groups have reached a given threshold of size, density, coherence, and/or mobility.

Both sides of this debate stress the difficulty of maintaining locust surveillance and management capacity during periods of locust recession as a key factor favoring their preferred strategic orientation over the competing approach. For Symmons, the problem with the preventive strategy is that it requires the maintenance of a large and complex organizational apparatus of locust surveillance and outbreak control during recessions. He argues that given the immensity of the locust recession area and the very low probability that survey teams will come across an outbreak, let alone one of the very few instances of gregarization that can lead to a real upsurge, the preventive approach is inevitably too costly to maintain and requires large teams of technicians whose skills, morale, funding, and equipment are difficult if not impossible to maintain over time.

For Symmons, rather than the diffuse network required by preventive control, what is needed are 'locust units that are small enough to be sustained' (Symmons 1992, p. 211): a small core of highly trained and experienced locust control officers that intervene by air. This in turn requires that interventions be limited to clearly marked target-blocks within which control efforts ought to be concentrated as much as possible. These target-blocks are precisely delineated spaces wherein locust density thresholds warrant powerful measures intended to kill all locusts within the block, and outside which locust population densities are too low to warrant any intervention at all. Survey teams delineate sectors wherein mature and immature groups of locusts are sufficiently concentrated to warrant a target block (Symmons 1992).

The way the curative strategy, as envisioned by Symmons, deals with the challenge of maintaining a viable apparatus in the face of great variability of locust populations and the tendencies for publics and authorities to 'forget' and lose interest in this agricultural pest is by containing said apparatus to a centralized core of professionals that only intervenes when and where there is a significant outbreak, and keeps doing just that. In an ideal situation, this core group would be specialized and mandated to respond to all outbreaks across a very vast area, travelling on demand, by aircraft, to treat well-identified target blocks and then returning to a centralized headquarters thereafter. The curative orientation then, produces an organizational configuration that is relatively small and concentrated. This smaller managerial core, the reasoning goes, is easier to maintain during periods of recession, and because it specializes almost exclusively on campaigns of locust upsurge elimination, skills and equipment necessary for these campaigns remain in use and are maintained over time.

On the opposite side of this debate, proponents of the preventive orientation push for an apparatus of locust surveillance and control that is expansive, pro-active, and nearly constantly involved in monitoring, reporting, and terminating locust outbreaks. As a senior Moroccan locust expert explained to me during a meeting in Bamako:

> preventive control is the surveillance of the gregarization zones of the Desert Locust, the localization and destruction of the first populations that begin their phase transition to avoid that they become hopper bands or swarms. That is preventive control. And for preventive control, the transition phase is of capital importance. What we need to do is train colleagues, prospectors, field agents so that they are clear on the difference between solitary phases and transiens, and that they report transiens populations as soon as they can, before gregarization occurs, before the insects become gregarious.
>
> *(Senior locust control specialist, Bamako, 2011, personal communication)*

Doing so requires a combination of remote-sensing, on the ground surveys, training, and control operations: a proliferation of mechanisms of reporting, production of knowledge, communication channels, teams of prospectors on the ground, networks of satellite, radio, and internet-based databases, maps, and so on. For this preventive strategy to be really successful, proponents contend that locust management capacity must be extended beyond these cores of professionals—the technical services—to include as many people as possible:

> The (locust control) apparatus involves (A) the donors, (B) technical service, and (C) the populations, farmers, producers. But all the burden, in the current situation, is on the technical service. They are the only ones given all the responsibility. That is a problem, that the technical service is both distinct from the local and international levels. (The problem now) is that National Locust Control Units are disconnected from the international level, and from the populations. According to our perception, what is necessary is that locust control exceeds the scope of that technical service.
> *(Senior locust control specialist, Montpellier, 2010, personal communication)*

The preventive orientation calls for combining regular surveillance and intervention missions and various projects of training, evaluation and other similar programs to populate a busy annual schedule for the many organizations active in this domain. Together, these practices contribute to the maintenance and relevancy of scientific and technical expertise and operational teams and equipment despite the absence of locust upsurges, and justify the funding and legitimacy of the work, both of which are necessary for the network to 'stay afloat' (Levine 2007). The preventive control approach thus best aligns locust management with the institutional logic and imperatives of the international development organizations to which it caters, which in turn helps acridologists ensure that their expertise remains relevant and viable.

Moreover, my interviews with pro-preventive control locust experts suggest that this greater fit between locust swarm prevention and the demands of development is neither accidental nor an afterthought. The acridologists I interviewed are aware of this fit, and many explicitly state that their approach's contribution to a more developmentalist, improving type of intervention makes their work more compatible with the benevolent, capacity-building goal of development. It is this contribution, they argue, that makes their favored approach the most defensible, regardless of its merits on technical terms alone:

> The goal is to help these countries develop, in every sense of the word. And where we can intervene is, if we teach them to set up and carry out a prevention strategy against the desert locust, it will allow them to go further in other domains. And we consider this as an entry point, an element we give them, a tool we give them. After that, they will be able to circumvent that philosophy, to use it, and apply it elsewhere, and learn to develop with it. It goes well beyond the problem of the desert locust.
> *(Entomologist researcher, Montpellier, 2010, personal communication)*

A different interview revealed a very similar sentiment:

> Our philosophy in this is that helping the development of countries, through the intermediary of agriculture, through the intermediary of countless things, but to try to give them the keys, the elements that will allow them to build their own development.
> *(Entomologist researcher, Montpellier, 2011, personal communication)*

This 'philosophical' argument for the preventive control orientation accompanies a criticism of the curative, crisis-oriented responses as not only reactive but also as a fatalist policy of substitution that 'gives up' on the goal of development and that is based on the belief that countries considered 'backward' would not be able to gain and sustain the skills and institutional capacity to ensure prevention:

> There is this other policy, (the curative approach) that says: 'anyways, those countries have too many problems of development, and they will not be able to establish a prevention strategy'. (Its proponents) start from the observation that countries will be unable to do their prevention strategy, as they are unable, we must be ready to intervene'. So they say: 'let's not bother spending money on countries that, no matter what, will have too many problems to be able to do prevention; instead, let's prepare an ad hoc team, with aircrafts, that are ready to wage treatment campaigns when invasions do occur'.
>
> *(Entomologist researcher, personal communication, Montpellier, July 2010)*

The pro-prevention locust expert cited above not only does not challenge, but actually recognizes the curative approach's technical merits: 'Yes, you take a team of professionals, you go and do treatments, the upsurge will be controlled, but that's not the goal'. When asked to explain his answer, this expert argued that the proponents of the curative orientation 'consider that we should return to the 1960s, to DDT, to whites that arrive with planes and say: "move over"'. In other words, this approach is considered inadmissible at least in part because of its association with policies of substitutive, top-down rule at a distance, which preventive approach proponents deem outdated and ill-adapted to the contemporary development goals of capacity building and knowledge transfer.

Moreover, to be effective, preventive control efforts rely on a sound understanding of locust ecology, habitat, breeding and phase change dynamics, all required to increase locust outbreak prediction and early detection and monitoring capacity at the basis of upsurge prevention. The curative approach, on the other hand, can do without these complex, diffused sets of knowledge and practices. A curative approach calls for innovation in insecticidal technologies and organizational and communication structures designed to enhance the effectiveness of a centralized anti-locust force. These limited demands offer little promise of sustaining a viable relevancy and constituency for locust science and expertise, and worse, they are a poor fit with the growing tendency among foreign aid agencies since the 1990s to seek, when possible, more participatory, decentralized, and 'greener', more environmentally friendly interventions (Goldman 2005).

By favoring preventive orientations of locust management, acridologists and the institutions that employ them effectively call for a proliferation of mechanisms of surveillance, participation, improvement, reporting, and training. These mechanisms, as they line up with the goals of capacity building and improvement pursued by development programs, not only increase the likelihood that the work of locust control experts and technicians remains of relevance to state and multilateral organizations responsible for the governance of this international hazard: it also gives them 'something to do' during the long periods of 'protracted non-crises' of locust recessions when the locust problem would otherwise fall out of sight for these organizations. This is not to say that preference for the preventive approach amongst key actors in the Western Region of Desert Locust Control is solely, or even primarily determined by the political economic demands of foreign aid agencies and other donors. Scientific and technical arguments formulated by various experts in this field, based on empirical as well as computer modelling experiments (Simpson *et al.* 2005, Magor *et al.* 2008, Sword *et al.* 2010, Cisse *et al.* 2015) do indeed point to justifications that are independent from the political economical dimensions. What the foregoing suggests, however, is that the preventive approach is strengthened, and made institutionally viable, in part due to its greater degree of compatibility with the logic and imperatives of locust science's primary clients.

The preventive approach to locust management yields relatively complex institutional arrangements that expand outward into other spheres of societies as they seek to 'improve', 'build capacity', and foster 'better governance'. In other words, preventive control in locust management contributes to what Whitehead calls, after Foucault, a form of 'government with science' (2009, 14) that integrates expertise about the desert locust into (1) the institutional settings produced at the intersection of post-colonial state agencies and multilateral development organizations, namely development and (2) the political economy of expertise in these settings. This integration best aligns acridology with the logic and mandate of development programs and organizations, which in turn helps maintain a constituency for, and consequently the relevancy of, expertise on this agricultural pest hazard. By contrast, the curative approach leaves very little scope for the expansion of scientific expertise and research, and when it does, this research has a limited fit with the interests of foreign aid agencies.

One interesting implication is that the tendency discussed here is quite distinct from the technological determinism and reductionism commonly attributed to modern development bureaucracies (Cherlet, 2014; Goulet, 1980). Put differently, the preference among development networks and locust control experts for the preventive approach can be associated with an institutional preference for knowledge practices and management approaches that seek, highlight, and work through the complexity and stochasticity of social-ecological interactions, rather than approaches that seek to ignore or minimize this complexity through greater reliance on spatial or temporal simplification, for example. This has implications for the type of fundamental entomological research required, called for, and enabled by this branch of applied science's contribution to development projects. More broadly, these findings also problematize common assumptions about the nature of technical and scientific practices, and their related social-political effects, as determined by a reductionist technocratic rationality adverse to complexity and dynamism.

A political economy of science focus on the social and political factors shaping the work of scientists can provide valuable insights on the nature of the regime of knowledge production (Pestre 2003)—or science regime (Lave 2012)—that characterizes the professional field of development aid. This perspective can help shed light on how the material and financial concerns for the professional viability of scientific expertise produce the specific mechanisms that link and align scientific practices with structures and strategies of political rule to which they cannot be reduced. Doing so, this approach can help overcome some of the most persistent methodological challenges in political ecological analyses of the relationship between science and power, namely a tendency for deterministic functionalism and the difficulty of attributing causality to relationships.

References

Abram, S., 2005. 'Introduction: science/technology as politics by other means'. *Focaal*, (46), 3–20.
Agrawal, A., 2005. *Environmentality: Technologies of Government and the Making of Subjects*. Durham, N.C.: Duke University Press.
Anderson, W., 2002. 'Postcolonial technoscience'. *Social Studies of Science*, 32 (5/6), 643–658.
Baron, S., 1972. *The Desert Locust*. New York: Charles Scribner's Sons.
Bassett, T.J. and Bi Zuéli, K., 2000. 'Environmental discourses and the Ivorian Savanna'. *Annals of the Association of American Geographers*, 90 (1), 67–95.
Birkenholtz, T., 2008. 'Contesting expertise: the politics of environmental knowledge in northern Indian groundwater practices'. *Geoforum*, 39 (1), 466–482.

Bonneuil, C., 2000. 'Development as experiment: science and state building in late colonial and postcolonial Africa', 1930–1970. *Osiris*, 15, 258–281.

Callaghy, T., Kassimir, R., and Latham, R., 2001. *Intervention and Transnationalism in Africa: Global-Local Networks of Power*. Cambridge: Cambridge University Press.

Carroll, P., 2006. *Science, Culture, and Modern State Formation*. Berkeley and Los Angeles: University of California Press.

Cashmore, M., Richardson, T., and Axelsson, A., 2014. 'Seeing power in international development cooperation: environmental policy integration and the World Bank'. *Transactions of the Institute of British Geographers*, 39 (1), 155–168.

Cashmore, M., Richardson, T., Rozema, J., and Lyhne, I., 2015. 'Environmental governance through guidance: The "making up" of expert practitioners'. *Geoforum*, 62, 84–95.

Cherlet, J., 2014. 'Epistemic and technological determinism in development aid'. *Science, Technology, & Human Values*, 39 (6), 773–794.

Cisse, S., Ghaout, S., Mazih, A., Ould Babah Ebbe, M.A., and Piou, C., 2015. 'Estimation of density threshold of gregarization of desert locust hoppers from field sampling in Mauritania'. *Entomologia Experimentalis et Applicata*, 156 (2), 136–148.

Clarke, J.N. and McCool, D., 1996. *Staking Out the Terrain: Power and Performance Among Natural Resource Agencies*. Albany: State University of New York Press.

Conklin, A.L., 1997. *A Mission to Civilize: The Republican Idea of Empire in France and West Africa, 1895–1930*. Stanford: Stanford University Press.

Cooke, B., 2003. 'A new continuity with colonial administration: participation in development management'. *Third World Quarterly*, 24 (1), 47–61.

Cooper, F. and Stoler, A.L., 1989. 'Introduction tensions of empire: colonial control and visions of rule'. *American Ethnologist*, 16 (4), 609–621.

Davis, D.K., 2007. *Resurrecting the Granary of Rome: Environmental History and French Colonial Expansion in North Africa*. Athens, OH: Ohio University Press.

Douglas, M., 1986. *How Institutions Think*. Syracuse: Syracuse University Press.

Escobar, A., 1995. *Encountering Development: The Making and Unmaking of the Third World*. Princeton, NJ: Princeton University Press.

Fairhead, J. and Leach, M., 1996. *Misreading the African Landscape: Society and Ecology in a Forest-Savanna Mosaic*. Cambridge: Cambridge University Press.

Ferguson, J., 1990. *The Anti-Politics Machine: Development, Depoliticization and Bureaucratic Power in Lesotho*. Cambridge: Cambridge University Press.

Ferguson, J., 2006. *Global Shadows: Africa in the Neoliberal World Order*. Durham, N.C. and London: Duke University Press.

Folke, C., Pritchard Jr., L., Berkes, F., Colding, J., and Svedin, U., 2007. 'The problem of fit between ecosystems and institutions: ten years later'. *Ecology and Society*, 12 (1), [online] www.ecologyandsociety.org/vol12/iss1/art30/.

Freed, L., 2010. 'Networks of (colonial) power: roads in French Central Africa after World War I'. *History and Technology: An International Journal*, 26 (3).

Goldman, M., 2005. *Imperial Nature: The World Bank and Struggles for Social Justice in the Age of Globalization*. New Haven and London: Yale University Press.

Goldman, M.J., Nadasdy, P., and Turner, M.D., eds., 2011. *Knowing Nature: Conversations at the Intersection of Political Ecology and Science Studies*. Chicago: University of Chicago Press.

Goulet, D., 1980. 'Development experts: the one-eyed giants'. *World Development*, 8 (7–8), 481–489.

Gupta, A., 1998. *Postcolonial Developments: Agriculture in the Making of Modern India*. Durham, NC: Duke University Press.

Harding, S., 2011. *The Postcolonial Science and Technology Studies Reader*. Durham, N.C. and London: Duke University Press.

Hecht, G., 1998. *The Radiance of France Nuclear Power and National Identity after World War II*. Cambridge, MA: MIT Press.

Hecht, G., 2002. 'Rupture-talk in the nuclear age: conjugating colonial power in Africa'. *Social Studies of Science*, 32 (5–6), 691–727.

Hoogvelt, A., 2001. *Globalization and the Postcolonial World: The New Political Economy of Development*. Baltimore: Johns Hopkins University Press.

Ilcan, S. and Phillips, L., 2010. 'Developmentalities and calculative practices: the Millennium Development Goals'. *Antipode*, 42 (4), 844–874.

Jasanoff, S., ed., 2004. *States of Knowledge: The Co-production of Science and Social Order*. London and New York: Routledge.

Keeley, J. and Scoones, I., 2003. *Understanding Environmental Policy Processes: Cases from Africa*. London and Sterling, VA: Earthscan.

Kuus, M., 2014. *Geopolitics and Expertise: Knowledge and Authority in European Diplomacy*. Chichester, UK: Wiley.

Latour, B., 1987. *Science in Action: How to Follow Scientists and Engineers through Society*. Cambridge (US): Harvard University Press.

Lave, R., 2012. 'Neoliberalism and the production of environmental knowledge'. *Environment and Society: Advances in Research*, 3 (1), 19–38.

Lecoq, M., 2005. 'Desert Locust management: from ecology to anthropology'. *Journal of Orthoptera Research*, 14 (2), 179–186.

Levine, A., 2007. 'Staying afloat: state agencies, local communities, and international involvement in marine protected area management in Zanzibar, Tanzania'. *Conservation and Society*, 5 (4), 562–585.

Li, T.M., 2007. *The Will to Improve: Governmentality, Development, and the Practice of Politics*. Durham, N.C. and London: Duke University Press.

Lie, J.H.S., 2015. 'Developmentality: indirect governance in the World Bank–Uganda partnership'. *Third World Quarterly*, 1–18.

Magor, J., Lecoq, M., and Hunter, D.M., 2008. 'Preventive control and Desert Locust plagues'. *Crop Protection*, 27 (12), 1527–1533.

Mavhunga, C. C., 2011. 'Vermin beings on pestiferous animals and human game'. *Social Text*, 29 (106), 151–176

McNeil, M., 2005. 'Introduction: Postcolonial Technoscience'. *Science as Culture*, 14 (2), 105–112.

Mitchell, T., 2002. *Rule of Experts: Egypt, Techno-Politics, Modernity*. Berkeley and Los Angeles: University of California Press.

Mosse, D., 2011. 'Politics and ethics: ethnographies of expert knowledge and professional identities'. *Policy Worlds: Anthropology and the Analysis of Contemporary Power*, 14, 50–50.

Pellizzoni, L., 2011. 'Governing through disorder: neoliberal environmental governance and social theory'. *Global Environmental Change*, 21 (3), 795–803.

Pestre, D., 2003. 'Regimes of knowledge production in society: towards a more political and social reading'. *Minerva*, 41 (3), 245–261.

Robbins, P., Farnsworth, R., and Jones, J.P., 2008. 'Insects and institutions: managing emergent hazards in the U.S. Southwest'. *Journal of Environmental Policy & Planning*, 10 (1).

Rose, N., 1993. 'Government, authority and expertise in advanced liberalism'. *Economy and Society*, 22 (3), 283–299.

Rose, N., 1999. *Powers of Freedom: Reframing Political Thought*. Cambridge: Cambridge University Press.

Rossi, B., 2004. 'Revisiting Foucauldian approaches: power dynamics in development projects'. *Journal of Development Studies*, 40 (6), 1–29.

Shackley, S., 2001. 'Epistemic lifestyles in climate change modeling'. In: C.A. Miller and P.N. Edwards, eds. *Changing the Atmosphere: Expert Knowledge and Environmental Governance*. Cambridge, MA and London: MIT Press, 107–133.

Simpson, S.J., Sword, G.A., and De Loof, A., 2005. 'Advances, controversies and consensus in locust phase polyphenism research'. *Journal of Orthoptera Research*, 14 (2), 213–222.

Skaf, R., Popov, G.B., Roffey, J., Scorer, R.S., and Hewitt, J., 1990. 'The Desert Locust: an international challenge'. *Philosophical Transactions of the Royal Society of London. Series B, Biological Sciences*, 328 (1251), 525–538.

Sword, G.A., Lecoq, M., and Simpson, S.J., 2010. 'Phase polyphenism and preventative locust management'. *Journal of Insect Physiology*.

Symmons, P.M., 1992. 'Strategies to combat the desert locust'. *Crop Protection*, 11 (3), 206–212.

Symmons, P.M., 2009. 'A critique of "Preventive control and desert locust plagues"'. *Crop Protection*, 28 (10), 905–907.

Tilley, H., 2011. *Africa as a Living Laboratory: Empire, Development, and The Problem of Scientific Knowledge, 1870–1950*. Chicago and London: University of Chicago Press.

Treml, E.A., Fidelman, P.I.J., Kininmonth, S., Ekstrom, J.A., and Bodin, Ö., 2015. 'Analyzing the (mis) fit between the institutional and ecological networks of the Indo-West Pacific'. *Global Environmental Change*, 31 (0), 263–271.

Van Huis, A., Cressman, K., and Magor, J., 2007. 'Preventing desert locust plagues: optimizing management interventions'. *Entomologia Experimentalis et Applicata*, 122 (3), 191–214.

Venn, C., 2009. 'Neoliberal political economy, biopolitics and colonialism: a transcolonial genealogy of inequality'. *Theory, Culture & Society*, 26 (6), 206–233.

Watts, M.J., 2003. 'Development and governmentality'. *Singapore Journal of Tropical Geography*, 24 (1), 6–34.

Whitehead, M., 2009. *State, Science and the Skies: Governmentalities of the British Atmosphere*. Wiley-Blackwell.

29

WORLD-SYSTEM ANALYSIS 2.0

Globalized science in centers and peripheries

Pierre Delvenne and Pablo Kreimer

Introduction

Science is being transformed by a series of technical and organizational changes that profoundly affect the terms of its production and use, thereby reconfiguring its role in contemporary societies. At the national level, these changes have particularly been analyzed in terms of 'modes' (Nowotny et al., 2001), of 'regimes of knowledge production' (Pestre, 2003; Van Oudheusden et al., 2015), of reconfiguration of the relationship between state, science and industry (Etzkowitz and Leydesdorff, 2000; Joerges and Shinn, 2001), of shifting governance and research evaluation (Mustar and Laredo, 2002), or of a renewed relationship between science and society, due to the increase in public controversies involving scientific and technical issues (Latour, 1999). Furthermore, the nature of the production of scientific knowledge is also subject to greater openness, for example to indigenous knowledge, patient associations (Callon and Rabeharisoa, 2003), or other kind of actors (Jasanoff, 2004, Collins and Evans, 2008).

At the international level, even if science always was an 'international enterprise' (Salomon, 2006) during recent decades it has become increasingly globalized and the reorganization of 'international science' presents a growing complex map. Indeed, some authors (Rosemann, 2014; Moya-Anegón et al., 2013; Grauwin et al., 2012; Veugelers, 2010) talk about a new multipolarity, particularly pointing at the decline of the formerly leading nations in the share of international scientific production (especially the US and Western Europe), and the emergence of new regions, like BRICs (Brazil, Russia, India, China). However, there have existed until today very few studies focused on the consequences of these changes on less advanced (semi-peripheral) countries and on the relationships among knowledge production centers, with a critical perspective that takes into account the emerging complex dynamics. Therefore, our aim in this chapter is to suggest an analytical framework and to present empirical data on these dynamics, as well as on the consequences that 'globalization' has on the international organization of science, analyzing the complex relations between centers and peripheries (emphasizing the plural).

We consider, in fact, that a critical 'centers & peripheries' approach—as it were, a world-system analysis 2.0—is more adequate than the currently used concepts like 'North and South', or 'developing countries', because they are not able to show the profound heterogeneities *within* each geographical context. Indeed, even when adopting the plural to designate 'peripheries', we can distinguish three kinds (presented as ideal types) of knowledge production dynamics among countries[1] usually described as 'developing':

a) traditional contexts where research activities are strongly rooted from (at least) the end of 19th century, with particular specialization patterns, a considerable number of scientists in most disciplinary fields (relatively weaker in 'high technological fields'), and often oriented to biomedical research. This is for instance the case in big Latin American countries such as Brazil, Argentina, Mexico, or Chile and in some Northern African countries such as Egypt, Algeria, Tunisia and Morocco;

b) 'non-traditional scientific countries', which have experienced a very significant and rapid growth during recent decades, as well as a strong presence of firms able to industrialize knowledge (examples include India, Korea, Singapore, or even South Africa – even though it may arguably be also a member of the first group); and

c) countries with weak scientific systems, very few scientists clustered in only a few disciplines, no important equipment, etc. like most African and small Latin American countries (see also chapters by Peloquin; Vessuri, this volume).

In the first part of this chapter, we illustrate the context of globalization and internationalization within which science is evolving. Taking stock of these transformations, we will take, as a starting point, the following questions:

• Does globalization imply that diverse regions conduct the same type of scientific activities and, therefore, that specialization patterns are going to disappear?
• Does it imply that knowledge is equally distributed and used in different contexts?

Our answer to both questions is negative, as elucidated in several examples. Considering that local frames and scientific specialization, as well as the important differences in the production, distribution and use of knowledge, are still important within a globalized context, we can raise several questions: does the process of globalization have different impacts on scientific dynamics in these quite different contexts? And what kind of variables can explain these differences? Are the former 'centers' and 'peripheries' still pertinent to understanding today's scientific dynamics? To answer these questions, the second part of the chapter will analyze a case study from a semi-peripheral country, the development of agricultural biosciences and biotechnologies in Argentina, to show the various emerging alliances between new centers and peripheries *within and across* the country (Tyfield and Urry 2009). We conclude by arguing for the theoretical development of a world-system analysis 2.0 to better understand exactly how globalized science makes national action and policies more important but also more difficult as the disparities between scientific disciplines are exacerbated by international scientific cooperation and competition. Globalization and cosmopolitization thus are not reducing the importance of the nation-state.

The production of scientific knowledge: towards new centers and peripheries

Looking at the production of scientific knowledge from an international perspective, there is no doubt that we live in a changing world. But now that scientific production is no longer concentrated in a few 'developed' countries, which formerly dictated the terms of scientific agendas for the rest of the planet, in what direction(s) are these changes going? We answer this question in relation to the distribution of knowledge production and the emergence of 'mega international networks' (Kreimer, 2012).

In recent decades, the distribution of knowledge production on a global scale has begun to change in at least two ways. First, there is a clear shift from a world largely dominated by the more traditional countries, in which most production was concentrated, towards a multipolar, more complex world (Santander 2014; Grauwin et al., 2012; Veugelers, 2010). Second, a change has occurred in the very *modes* of production of knowledge, towards the elaboration of research results that are increasingly the product of international cooperation. However, we argue that this does not mean that so-called 'developing' countries participate in the same way as their 'developed' counterparts in the new organizations of scientific work, nor that collaboration happens on equal grounds (see also Pfotenhauer, this volume).

To understand these shifts, let's briefly step back a couple of decades to look at the articles then listed on Web of Science. During the period from 1993 to 1997, the United States accounted for some 37 percent of international production, while the European Union (then 15 countries) gathered about 35 percent. Japan, Canada, Russia, Australia and Switzerland accounted for 22 percent, so that altogether this group concentrated about 94 percent of total world scientific production (King, 2004, May, 1997). But that concentration was even more marked in terms of citations as an indirect but relevant indicator of the visibility and usefulness that communities of researchers accord the scientific production within their own field. Here, the United States produced more than half of the citations (52 percent), while Europe maintained the same share (35 percent), and all other countries were dramatically lower. Moreover, if one was taking the upper 1 percent of the most cited articles, the US had nearly two-thirds of the world's total (King, ibid.).

Table 29.1 Percent of world publications and citations in selected countries, 1993–7

	1993–1997		
	% of World Publications	*% of World Citations*	*Dif. Pub-Cit*
United States	37.46	52.30	+14.84
EU 15	35.42	36.57	+1.15
United Kingdom	9.29	10.87	+1.58
Germany	8.05	8.63	+0.58
Japan	8.69	7.54	−1.15
France	6.11	6.37	+0.26
Canada	5.05	5.59	+0.54
Italy	3.67	3.71	+0.04
Switzerland	1.73	2.69	+0.96
Netherlands	2.51	3.22	+0.71
Australia	2.69	2.60	−0.09
Sweden	1.91	2.43	+0.52
Spain	2.37	1.96	−0.41
Belgium	1.20	1.39	+0.19
Russia	3.65	1.23	−2.42
China	2.06	0.95	−1.11
South Korea	0.81	0.44	−0.37
India	2.19	0.76	−1.43
Brazil	0.84	0.51	−0.33

Source: OECD: Main Science and Technology Indicators: www.oecd.org/sti/msti.htm

The situation has shifted today. Considering publications for the period 2010–2012 the US has dropped to less than a quarter of the total (24.3 percent), while some newcomers have clearly emerged. Several countries formerly considered as 'developing' markedly increased their share, most notably China (see chapters by Suttmeier; Xu and Ye, this volume), which gathered almost 11 percent of the world's scientific production during that period. Other cases in point are India and South Korea, scoring 3 percent and 4 percent, respectively (see Figure 29.1). On the other hand, there was a slow decline in some traditionally strong countries like Japan—whose international share in knowledge production halved, as well as, for example, Canada and France, both of which reduced their share by more than a third (Levin, Jensen and Kreimer, 2016). Therefore, several authors speak of a new multipolar world of knowledge production (Veugelers, 2010, Grossetti et al., 2012), one that replaces the older picture of a world dominated by only one hegemonic actor (US) and accompanied by several 'leading figures' (Japan, Germany, United Kingdom). The same scholars also stress a decentralizing trend within each country, with a tendency towards greater distribution among cities (Grossetti et al., 2012).[2]

It is necessary to be careful when taking stock of these changes, especially when observing two considerations: first, it does not seem overstated to argue that the primary change is the increased participation of China in the production of international science, along with the not-yet-so-significant emergence of other Asian countries, for instance South Korea. Indeed, if we set China aside, which was ranked 12th in 1987 and has risen to second place in only twenty years (King, 2004, Levin et al. 2016), the rest of the top ten countries with the highest production remained unchanged. Second, these changes are very heterogeneous from one discipline to another. Using a novel methodology, Levin, Jensen and Kreimer[3] have shown that, while the overall participation of China in all disciplines reaches less than 11 percent, in the field of nanoscience and nanotechnology its global share climbs to almost 24 percent, turning it into the world's leader. Something similar can be noted in the case of engineering.[4] Nonetheless, as the second part of the chapter will show, in more historically established areas of research, such as the emblematic case of biomedical sciences or R&D related to the generation of new drugs and treatments, the long-term accumulation processes remain crucial and, consequently, 'traditional' countries largely remain firmly in the lead even though the emergence of new centers has to be acknowledged.

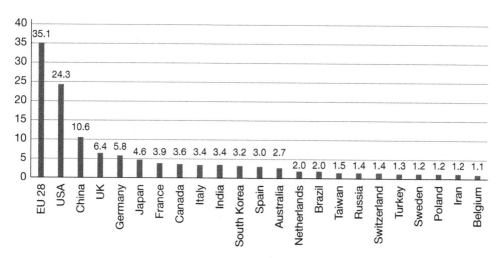

Figure 29.1   Percent of world publications, 2010–2012
Source: Levin, Jensen and Kreimer (2016)

On the other hand, the *scale* of the processes of knowledge production has evolved from national laboratories to the formation of increasingly large networks with participation of a greater number of groups from different countries. This has been clearly influenced by a new set of policies, such as those of the European Union (i.e. the successive Framework Programs, now Horizon 2020), which explicitly promoted these mechanisms, as a reaffirmation of their rivalry with the United States and other regions (CCE, 2007). Several authors (Cambrosio, Keating, and Mogoutov, 2004; Adams, 2012, 2013; Wagner, 2009) attest to the emergence of these networks, which implied a considerable mobilization of resources and an important change in the scale of research: in various fields, standards shifted from the 'group' as a unit of knowledge production to 'large networks' made up of different groups and operating in different national contexts.

These changes in both the modes and scales of knowledge production have different consequences for more advanced research systems and for 'non-hegemonic' ones (Losego and Arvanitis, 2008). Despite the optimistic arguments claiming that greater democratization and new opportunities for formerly excluded groups accompany these changes in processes of knowledge production (Wagner, 2009, Gaillard, 1998), it is important to pinpoint the emergence of a new configuration that has led to a 'new global division of scientific work' (Hwang, 2008, Kreimer and Levin, 2015, Kreimer, 2006). In such a configuration, the elites belonging to countries with important scientific traditions, but which are relatively less developed[5] or 'non-hegemonic', are today actively involved, but their ability to influence the direction of research agendas and, above all, to industrialize the knowledge produced by these networks is still very limited. In recent research, Kreimer and Levin (2015) conducted a survey with almost 1,000 Latin American research leaders who had participated in European projects, and showed that more than a third affirmed that their activities mostly consisted of 'data collection', while another third of researchers stated they were limited to 'data processing'. Another 25 percent stated that they spent their time at 'technical work', and only 10 percent asserted that they took an active part in theoretical development or production.

To present a comprehensive view of current research practices, we need to add one additional piece: the crucial transformation catalyzed by the extension and massification of Information and Communication Technologies (ICTs), especially the Internet and the big databases available 'in a shared cloud'. This has led in several knowledge fields to the creation of 'virtual laboratories' where a great number of scientists from various contexts work together in projects that overcome traditional/national frontiers. International databases shared by a great number of scientists who are at the same time producers and users of data are the mark of a new era of research. However, the access to and application of data is not equally distributed around the world: even when there are not formal restrictions to access, the unequal cumulative capacities in different research groups tend to reproduce the old distinctions between 'centers' and 'peripheries'.

Therefore, the 'globalized science' in emerging countries seems to be working to strengthen knowledge-based industries mostly located in the more advanced countries, but this dynamic is not yet regulated by a new set of policies. To sum up our point so far, current shifts attest to the emergence of a relative multipolarity in terms of knowledge production, but we should be cautious and not take the emergence of multiple centers—and thus of multiple peripheries—as an equalizing trend since major differences and inequalities remain.

Globalized science's dynamics and the joint emergence of centers and peripheries: a case study in Argentina

In most peripheral contexts, a substantial part of knowledge is still being produced by public institutions, with very infrequent participation and relationships with the private/industrial sector—a marked difference to the 'Global North' (see chapters by Edgerton; Pagano and Rossi; Lazonick et al.; Schiller and Yeo, this volume).[6] While the context of neoliberal science (Lave, Mirowski and Randalls, 2010) seems to push research towards industrial needs, at the same time we witness in many countries the (re)emergence of claims favoring a return of the state in a series of domains, including science. This is certainly the case in Argentina, where a long tradition of publicly funded biosciences and biotechnologies today struggles for survival under the new global international division of scientific labor described above.

This leads us to stress a current paradox: in spite of the large scientific community working in Argentina on molecular biology and agricultural biotechnology supported by public funds, scientists' participation in international scientific collaboration has decreased over the last decade (while agriculture decreased its relative relevance for European research collaboration policy with Latin America: see Kreimer and Levin, 2015). Instead, S&T collaborations tend to concentrate on biomedicine or traditional natural sciences (chemistry, physics). Furthermore, in biomedicine there has been a shift from 'local' issues (e.g. tropical diseases) to 'global' ones (tuberculosis, vascular disease or leishmania).

How can we make sense of this paradox? Influential works in the political economy of science and technology address the unfolding of a 'globalized privatization regime' (Mirowski and Sent, 2008), characterized by, among other things, the privatization of publicly funded research, commercial agreements eluding national controls, and a general trend toward the commodification of scientific knowledge (Slaughter and Rhoades, 1996, Tyfield, 2012, Lave et al., 2010). Based on the case study of genetically modified (GM) soybean in Argentina (analyzed in greater detail elsewhere, in Delvenne et al., 2013 and Delvenne and Vasen, 2013), we ask how such a regime has developed in Argentina. Can we point to trends that reflect the general pattern of commercialization of science, or do we see different dynamics, contradicting this general pattern to a certain extent? Are central (corporate and political) power and resources unevenly distributed at the expense of the periphery? To what extent has the peripheral character of Argentina influenced the process of biotechnology's expansion in this country?

Transgenic soy was introduced in Argentina in 1996 as part of the circulation of a global 'technological package', including GM soy and a herbicide whose toxic agent is glyphosate (both were initially produced by Monsanto, the multinational and quasi-hegemonic firm). However, the tremendous expansion of that global technological package coming 'from above' cannot be explained without mentioning its integration with developments coming 'from below', especially no-till farming techniques (see Goulet 2008). While no-till farming started with a group of tinkering farmers in the late 1980s who were seeking productivity gains and concerned by soil's degradation, today Argentina is the world's leading country in no-till farming techniques, with a rate of 92 percent of adopters. The key element is that the massive adoption of no-till farming techniques, the fast development of the national agro-industrial machinery industry to meet the needs of no-till farming (and today of precision agriculture), and the substantial adoption of GM soy *co-evolved* and *co-produced* new centers and peripheries.

In terms of these evolving centers and peripheries, two examples can be highlighted. First, in the late 1990s/early 2000s, GM soy seeds from Argentina (also called 'Maradona soy') were illegally imported to Paraguay and Southern Brazil without significant impediments. The illegal soybean was estimated to represent around 80 percent of the 2003 harvest in the Brazilian state of Rio Grande do Sul (Vara, 2005). This *de facto* situation forced Brazilian Vice-President José Alencar to sign in 2003 an exceptional decree that authorized farmers to plant GM soy, thereby opening the door to a 'transgenic South America' and turning the subcontinent into a global center of GM crop production and export.

Second, in spite of the apparent homogeneity of the national technological package (GM soy, herbicide, no-till farming), the latter doesn't 'work' and deliver its promises equally to small or large-scale farmers. The key to understanding this asymmetry is to consider GM technology as a variable configuration, rather than a stable object or a technique that can be applied in the same manner everywhere. Considering a specific technology as a configuration makes the intimate relationship between technology and its conditions of use and implementation visible. Arza and Van Zwanenberg (2013) make the strong and important claim that the characteristics of farmers' production systems, such as access to capital, agricultural machinery and local seed input markets, are not 'external factors' to an otherwise stable technology, but an inherent part of a technological configuration as it comes into being in concrete situations. Since to be profitable GM soy requires cultivation of large surfaces and the acquisition of expensive machinery, in many cases small and medium-scale farmers were unable to catch up with capitalization and land-scale demands, so they have opted out of production by leasing their land to larger farmers or investors, thus becoming 'rentiers' rejected at the periphery of agricultural production (Gras and Hernandez, 2014).

The seminal work of Kloppenburg (1988) has stressed how much efforts to control the seed have shaped the emergence of the agricultural biotechnology industry. In the case of Argentina, however, there was almost no room for the development of local knowledge associated with GM organisms. The development of the GM soy complex in Argentina has gone through a number of peculiar conditions that render it particularly useful for exploring the ambiguities, complexities and in-between situations that can take place when the globalized neoliberal privatization regime takes root in a semi-peripheral country.

In Argentina, due to contingent circumstances, one can speak of a technological package 'free of patents', embedded in a permissive IP regime (Filomeno, 2013) as well as in a relatively open, non-monopolistic market dominated by private companies and not limited to multinationals. First, the patent of glyphosate had expired in 1991. This has been important because, as Ablin and Paz (2000) note, in the 1980s glyphosate was more expensive in Latin American than in central countries (US$40 per liter), a situation which changed dramatically in the 1990s when the price dropped to US$10, and less than US$3 in 2001—less than one-third of its price in the US. Second, a crucial explanatory element of GM soy's expansion has been that the transnational company Monsanto could not patent the event in Argentina, contrary to what happened in most other countries in the world. This has had huge effects on the cost of the GM soy seeds, which was lower than it would have been had the intellectual property (IP) regime been favorable to Monsanto's interests as has been the case elsewhere with stronger IP regimes.

Argentina's peripheral location therefore facilitated the emergence of different actors from those described in the seminal work of Mirowski and Sent, illustrating the specific configuration of this new phase of the commercialization of science. We especially note two groups of actors. The first group is made of actors that support public–private R&D partnership in biotechnology and claim the importance of a national strategic perspective, as epitomized by the recent alliance of CONICET (National S&T Council) and the company Bioceres for a drought-tolerant event.[7] Unlike NGOs, this group of actors accepts the general terms of an overall privatization regime, but attempts to incorporate perspectives that take advantage of the strategic situation of Argentina, a country that is the world's third largest exporter and producer (after the US and Brazil) of GM crops. At the same time, they acknowledge that the country's peripheral position has forced its companies to enter into alliances with multinational corporations in order to put their products on the market (cf. the example of the US firm Arcadia). As in the framework laid out above, these alliances most often result in situations in which public actors have only very limited influence to steer the industrialized knowledge produced toward social needs of local populations.

The second group is mainly composed of national NGOs (peasants' movements like MOCASE, Via Campesina, or the Rural Reflection Group) and some scientists (e.g. CONICET's molecular biologist Andres Carrasco) who combine a critical look at biotechnology, emphasizing anti-imperialism, the health impacts of herbicide spraying and food sovereignty. During some protest actions, they have been joined by international NGOs such as Greenpeace or Friends of the Earth. In the case of GM soy, the social activists and concerned stakeholders argue that the technological package (made of the GM seed, glyphosate-based herbicides and new farming techniques) dramatically affects public health and the environment. They are especially worried about the impacts of what has been coined as a 'soy-ization' or a 'Pampeanization' of Argentina.

The former term relates to a tendency observed during the last two decades, mainly in the Pampas (a very fertile area of Argentina historically devoted to agriculture), to grow soy instead of any other crop (or instead of cattle raising) because it is more profitable and easier to handle. This led to a lack of crop rotation and to an agriculture that is too intensive, as well as an overuse of agrochemicals and fertilizers, thus decreasing soil quality and increasing erosion. The latter term, 'Pampeanization', refers to the tendency to introduce agro-industrial crops such as soy in other provinces than the ones where such activities usually took place (the humid traditional zones for intensive agricultural production), such as Northern Argentina, which is characterized by extremely dry zones, like the province of Salta. This affects the soil's fertility and disrupts the ecosystems of those regions by displacing indigenous population and increasing deforestation. These conflicting debates and worldviews, we argue, are not context but instead an integral part of the neoliberal governance of globalized science and, as such, can be analyzed in terms of their resulting from, and indirect effects on, the commercialization of science. This point is made in Delvenne et al. (2013: 159), where the authors take a similar approach to Rebecca Lave's (2012) analysis of the different types of environmental knowledge held by extramural science producers (like indigenous people or amateur scientists). Lave argues that those are surprisingly central to neoliberalism, and that it is worth considering them as deeply interconnected in order to see the fine-grained picture of neoliberalism and its effects on knowledge production.

What is interesting to stress here about these two groups is that both have national development objectives of Argentina in their ideological roots, although their conceptions of 'development' are different (industrial development vs. protection of peasants' life and the environment). By contrast, the other actors of the transnational companies (Monsanto, Nidera, etc.) are key players in the global bioeconomy (Delvenne and Hendrickx, 2013), so they see Argentina as a market from which to extract profits rather than a country that should be developed. In this sense, the two local resisting groups mentioned above may share an anti-imperialist imaginary, although from different perspectives, while the transnational companies *represent* that very imperialism. However, a difference lies in the fact that the interests of local actors supporting R&D in biotechnology might overlap with transnational companies' agenda to require a stronger system of intellectual property rights (IPR) protection (this would not be true of national NGOs). So, there is an 'economic cluster', which aims at stimulating a certain pathway of development by turning agricultural biotechnologies into a central axis of the national economy.

To conclude this section, then, we return to our opening paradox. The emergence of new centres and peripheries through the dynamics just described helps us make sense of a situation in which the progression of the hegemonic model of neoliberal science has been dependent on seemingly non-archetypically neoliberal models. With this brief example, we have seen that it is not enough to postulate that the neoliberal globalized privatization regime will just unfold and progressively expand to more countries at the expense of most Southern actors at the periphery. Rather, combined with the commercialization of science, 'peripherality' creates protest, activism and the joint emergence of new centers and peripheries, including through essential antagonisms and tensions within 'Southern' countries. Thus, further research should devote time to address the joint and complex progression of both neoliberal science and its externalities in (semi-) peripheral countries. This can concern cases when scientific knowledge is prevented from circulation by institutionalized means of concentrating knowledge and capital (e.g. patents). But this is also particularly useful to make sense of cases like the one we sketched, in which incorporated scientific knowledge has traveled fast in 'free of patents' technological packages and reconfigured new centers and peripheries within, beyond and across one specific country.

Conclusion[8]

In this chapter we analyzed how the social, political and historical dynamics at play during the developmental, translation and transformation processes of science production are crucial to understanding what happens under conditions of globalized science. We suggest a research agenda building on a critical reexamination of both central and peripheral scientific and technological traditions and policy-oriented approaches. Under this analytical approach, descriptions of 'alternative modernities' and the recognition of hybridities, borderlands and in-between conditions (Anderson, 2002: 643) become important.[9] There is an increased recognition of the need to engage critically in the 'coloniality of power' (Quijano, 2000), but in a more complex and subtle way than the too simple alternative between an uncritical following of Western models on the 'development path', close to the well-known Basalla model (Basalla, 1969) and a purely ideological and totalizing critique of these models. This move implies delving into earlier debates engaging with, and critical of, the dominance of particular institutional models of science and science organization in order to investigate the relations between science and technology traditions in the centers and peripheries and 'study up' from the standpoint of non-OECD cultures (Harding, 2008: 225, Medina, 2011).[10]

To grasp the full texture of the global reconfigurations that we sketched in this chapter, we consider that world-system analysis (Wallerstein, 1974, 2004, 2006; Chase-Dunn and Hall, 1997; Hall 2000) provides an important lens that has been neglected by mainstream science policy and political economic studies of science. But we stress that it needs to be updated to a 2.0 version.

A world-system broadly refers to a matrix made of various institutions: nation-states, the interstate system, corporations, social classes, households, kin, ethnic groups, etc. It relates to the international division of labor, which divides the world into core countries, semi-peripheral countries and peripheral countries. In the 1970s and 1980s, the simple message was that central countries focus on higher skill, capital-intensive production, and the rest of the world focuses on low-skill, labor-intensive production and extraction of raw materials, in ways that are mutually reinforcing. This keeps the 'rich' countries rich and the 'poor' countries under-developed, hence generating enduring and dynamically reproduced 'centers' and 'peripheries'.

In a nutshell, instead of nation-states as the basic unit of social analysis, (traditional) world-system analysis (WSA) stresses that world-systems should be the privileged unit of analysis. In today's multipolar world, we have shown that big countries like India, China, Brazil or Argentina show internal tensions and a blurring of the international division of labor: ICT, nanosciences or agricultural biotechnology introduce other patterns too. Nevertheless, even if some shifting occurs, the earlier pattern of international division of labor is not undermined and it continues constantly to reinforce the dominance of the core countries. So WSA 2.0 is a reason to scrutinize, in each particular case, how and where power relations are enacted and reinforced. But we do not take over a simplistic world-system view on hegemony and domination: to address and analyze the stakes in globalized science, one needs to take the co-production of multiple centers and peripheries into account.

As we noted, innovation institutions, frameworks, and policies have different effects *within* nations—and (so) nations still matter—as much as they do extend *beyond* and *across* nations. Instead of frictions (Tsing, 2005), we see loci of complex interplays and national–international relationships that are to be unfolded (MacLeod 1980). Thus, a WSA 2.0 analytic lens should not only be limited to the national level. A focus on particular institutions, disciplines or topics—like in the example we gave with biotechnologies and GM agriculture—promises particularly interesting findings from a comparative perspective. Indeed, on the one hand, the dynamics observed in one domain in a particular country can vary significantly with other domains in the same country. On the other hand, cross-country comparison of the dynamics related to a specific discipline or domain will show a still different interplay of various centers and peripheries.

In conclusion, we present the various tensions that stem from the emerging situation we have described briefly in this chapter:

Consider the countries of intermediate development, such as those from some Latin American countries, North Africa (and South Africa), and some less developed European countries (Greece, Portugal, Poland), which have solid traditions of research and which have known an increasing international visibility during recent decades. In these countries, most scientific activities continue to be managed by and from the state, with a very low share of R&D to companies, and very little interaction between research and production sectors. Thus, it remains illusory to imagine the application of models such as the National Innovation System or Triple Helix, which have been developed for OECD countries in which the respective shares of public and private research funding show the exact opposite situation. The latter must be taken into account both for analytical purposes and for policy making.

The increasing globalization of S&T activities makes international firms locate within and exploit the comparative advantages of developing countries. However, firms tend only to incorporate scientific and local knowledge to the extent that this is mediated by international scientific networks that include researchers from different regions, but are normally led by Western Europeans and/or North Americans. Indeed, scientists from (semi-)peripheral countries do not control the scientific agendas of the large research networks in which they participate, even though within such networks they collaborate closely with firms from the central countries. The 'optimist' cases of the 'Marburg project' (related to a tropical disease) in Gabon or a fisheries project in Uganda, both in Africa,[11] as presented by Wagner (2009), who emphasizes the benefit of 'open systems' for developing countries, refer to isolated situations and much less scientifically developed countries, thus rendering it difficult to generalize as a structural trend. In addition, international firms continue to appropriate indigenous knowledge (such as the medicinal use of local plants) in order to industrialize it in central countries (see Hayden, 2003, for a brilliant analysis on Mexico), in spite of the recent efforts toward advanced regulations to curb this process of 'cognitive exploitation' of the peripheries (Kreimer and Zukerfeld, 2014).

In terms of multipolarity, what is observed in certain disciplinary or thematic areas—like the case of nanoscience illustrated in Figure 29.2—is a realignment based on the historic domination of 'old leaders' like Western Europe and the United States, which share research and innovation agendas in multiple fields, with a particular strength in biomedical and pharmaceutical applications. On the other hand, a new axis led by China (and, to a lesser extent, by India) concentrates on industrial development and gives a strong weight to engineering. Lastly, a third axis gathers the former socialist countries (close to the Soviet Union), which put a strong emphasis on R&D in energy issues, physics and heavy industries. It is in this context that the less developed countries move around multiple centers. For example, in Latin America, while Mexico and Argentina are closer to an 'OECD model', Brazil seems to be moving towards the pole of expertise led by China.

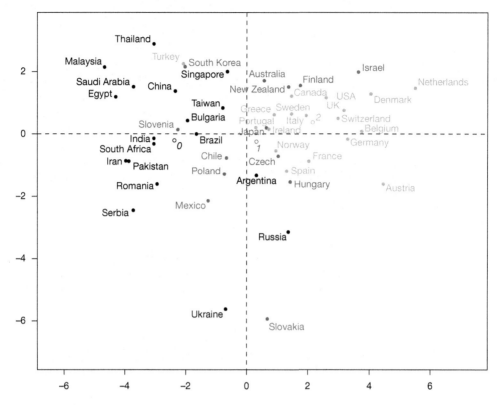

Figure 29.2 World distribution of nanoscience research, 2010–2012

Note: The vertical alignment means that countries in the upper part of the figure are relatively stronger in biomedical and pharmaceutical research, and those relatively stronger in high physics in the lower part. On the left are the countries with a relatively strong engineering research, and on the right, those which are relatively strong in basic research.

Source: Levin et al. (2016)

All these movements along the centers–peripheries axes create the illusion of a greater cosmopolitanism and openness, but we should note that, to date, globalized science's positive effects on the populations from the countries with low or intermediate development is very limited: multipolarity does not increase the chances of directing knowledge to local needs, it simply opens new windows of opportunity for more centers, at the expense of more peripheries.

Notes

1 Notwithstanding both the influence of globalization and the heterogeneities coexisting inside each country, the 'country' remains a crucial level of analysis, both considering national research systems and local research traditions (see e.g. Kreimer, 2010). To be sure, 'globalized' knowledge production dynamics have different effects *within*, *beyond* and *across* nations.

2 However, in the case of Latin America, and analyzing the participation of various cities in international programs, Kreimer and Levin (2015) have shown that, with the exception of Brazil (where programs are distributed in several cities, Sao Paulo, Rio de Janeiro, Campinas, Belo Horizonte, etc.), the bulk of activities remains concentrated in the capital city (Mexico, Buenos Aires, Santiago).

3 The authors have gathered all the nanoscience records from Web of Science (WoS) over three years (2010–2012), allowing for a more general study than previous work, focused in specific subfields. Instead of identifying the relevant subfields for research in nanosciences using standard, predefined

disciplinary categories such as the Journal Subject Categories (JSC) of the WoS, the approach defines subfields through a 'bottom-up' strategy that creates groups of articles that share many references and therefore are close in cognitive space.

4 Zhou and Leydesdorff (2006) had already made the same observations for the nano field, and Glänzel et al. (2008) for engineering.

5 Such as the most advanced countries in Latin America, North Africa and some Asian countries.

6 For instance, public funding for research in Mexico, Argentina and Brazil reaches more than two-thirds of total R&D expenditure (RICYT, 2015), while it is around a half for intermediate-advanced countries (like Spain or Italy) and less than 30 percent for more scientifically advanced countries (the OECD average is around 28 percent; see OECD, 2016).

7 Arcadia Biosciences is an agricultural technology company focused on developing technologies and products that benefit the environment and human health. Bioceres is an agricultural investment and development company owned by more than 230 of South America's largest soybean growers. Together the two companies form Verdeca, a 50–50 joint venture.

8 The conclusion builds on and reinforces the research agenda sketched by Delvenne and Thoreau (2012), whose paper discusses the adequacy of the concept of 'National Innovation System' to non-OECD (Organisation for Economic Co-operation and Development) countries, especially in Latin America, where it is abundantly implemented and tends to be reified, which leads to a situation where relevant contextual elements tend to be ignored.

9 Post-colonial STS (PCSTS) has provided interesting insights to address these issues (see e.g. Anderson, 2002; Anderson and Adams, 2007; Harding, 2008; Harding, 2011; Hecht, 2011, Chakanetsa Mavhunga and Trischler, 2014). We want to stress, however, that to date this subfield has yet mostly neglected the topic of political economy of science and the cultural hegemonism it potentially embeds. Furthermore, many PCSTS studies tend to reify the categories of 'Northern' and 'Southern' countries, whereas we suggest that we will gain analytical precision if we move away from concepts or 'North' and 'South' in order to adopt a 'centers and peripheries' perspective.

10 In an age in which localized political economies and prosperity are increasingly built upon innovation and 'cutting-edge' research, the political economy of *science* is a crucial but under-developed area of contemporary studies (see also Peloquin, this volume)

11 Wagner states, for instance, analyzing the Marburg project, that 'The resulting knowledge was distributed among the project members, as well as to collaborators in Gabon, Africa. In Africa, it could be used to solve or anticipate real problems' (2009). As we can see, there is an asymmetry: in this case, German (or Russian) researchers tackle a scientific problem and try to *offer* a solution to those affected in Gabon.

References

Ablin, E. and S. Paz (2000). *Productos transgénicos y exportaciones agrícolas: Reflexiones en torno de un dilema argentino*. Buenos Aires: Cancillería Argentina.

Adams, J. (2012). 'Collaborations: The rise of research networks'. *Nature*, 490: 335–336.

Adams, J. (2013). 'Collaborations: The fourth age of research'. *Nature*, 497: 557–560.

Anderson, W. (2002). 'Postcolonial technoscience'. *Social Studies of Science*, 32: 643–658.

Anderson, W. and Adams, V. (2007). 'Pramoedya's chickens: Postcolonial studies of technoscience', in *Handbook of Science and Technology Studies*, 3rd ed., eds. Edward J. Hackett, Olga Amsterdamska, Michael Lynch, and Judy Wacjman, 181–204. Cambrige, MA: MIT Press.

Basalla, G. (1967). 'The spread of Western science. A three-stage model describes the introduction of modern science into any non-European nation'. *Science* 156 (3775): 611–22.

Callon, M. and Rabeharisoa, V. (2003). 'Research "in the wild" and the shaping of new social identities'. *Technology in Society* 25: 193–204.

Cambrosio, A., Keating, P. and Mogoutov, A. (2004). 'Mapping collaborative work and innovation in biomedicine: a computer-assisted analysis of antibody reagent workshops'. *Social Studies of Science* 34 (3): 325–364.

CCE (2007). Commission des Communautés Européennes. Livre vert. 'L'Espace européen de la recherche: nouvelles perspectives'. Brussels, April 4, 2007. COM (2007) 161 final.

Chase-Dunn, C. and Hall, T. (1997). *Rise and Demise: Comparing World-Systems*. Boulder: Westview Press.

Chakanetsa Mavhunga, C. and H. Trischler (2014). *Energy (and) Colonialism, Energy (In)Dependence*. Rachel Cansel Center Perspectives.

Collins, H. and Evans, R. (2008). *Rethinking Expertise*. University of Chicago Press.

Dagnino, R. (2009). A construção do Espaço Ibero-americano do Conhecimento, os estudos sobre ciência, tecnologia e sociedade e a política científica e tecnológica. Rev. iberoam. cienc. tecnol. soc. v.4.

Delvenne, P. and Thoreau, F. (2012). 'Beyond the charmed circle of OECD. New Directions for Studies of National Innovation Systems'. *Minerva* 50–2: 205–219.

Delvenne, P. and Hendrickx, K. (2013). 'The multifaceted struggle for power in the bioeconomy'. *Technology in Society* 35(2): 75–8.

Delvenne, P. and Vasen, F. (2013). Lo que los Sistemas Nacionales de Innovación no miran. Una crítica constructiva de las políticas de ciencia y tecnología a partir del 'modelo de la soja transgénica'. In F. Tula Molina, Fernando; Vara, Ana Maria (eds.) *Riesgo, política y alternativas tecnológicas. Entre la regulación y la discusión pública*. Buenos Aires: Prometeo.

Delvenne, P., Vasen, F. and Vara, A.-M. (2013). 'The "soy-ization" of Argentina: dynamics of the "globalized" privatization regime in a peripheral context'. *Technology in Society* 35 (2): 153–162.

Etzkowitz H. and L. Leydesdorff, (2000). 'The dynamics of innovation: from national systems and "mode 2" to a triple helix of university-industry-government relations'. *Research Policy* 29: 109–23.

Filomeno, F. (2013). 'State capacity and intellectual property regimes: lessons from South American soybean agriculture'. *Technology in Society* 35 (2): 139–152.

Gaillard, J. F. (1998). 'Donors "models" for strengthening research capacity building in developing countries'. In M. J. Garrett and C. G. Granqvist (Eds.), *Basic Sciences and Development: Rethinking Donor Policy*, 81–126. Aldershot: Avebury Press.

Glänzel, W., K. Debackere, and M. Meyer (2008). 'Triad or Tetrad? On global changes in a dynamic world'. *Scientometrics* 74 (1).

Goulet, F. (2008). Des tensions épistémiques et professionnelles en agriculture. Dynamiques autour des techniques sans labour et de leur évaluation environnementale. *Revue d'Anthropologie des Connaissances* 2(4): 291–310.

Gras, C. and V. Hernandez (2014). 'Agribusiness and large-scale farming: capitalist globalisation in Argentine agriculture'. *Canadian Journal of Development Studies / Revue canadienne d'études du développement* 35 (3): 339–357.

Grauwin, S. et al. (2012). 'Complex systems science: Dreams of universality, interdisciplinarity reality'. *Journal of the American Society for Information Science and Technology* 63(7): 1327–1338.

Grossetti, M., Eckert, D., Gingras, Y., Jegou L., Lariviere V., and Milard B. (2012). 'The geographical deconcentration of scientific activities (1987–2007)'. 17th International Conference on Science and Technology Indicators (STI), 5–8 September, Montréal.

Hall, T. (2000). *A World-Systems Reader: New Perspectives on Gender, Urbanism, Cultures, Indigenous Peoples and Ecology*. London: Rowman and Littlefield.

Harding, S. (2011). *The Postcolonial Science and Technology Studies Reader*. Chapel Hill, Duke University Press.

Hayden, C. (2003). *When Nature Goes Public: The Making and Unmaking of Bioprospecting in Mexico*. Princeton: Princeton University Press.

Hecht, G. (2011). *Entangled Geographies. Empire and Technopolitics in the Global Cold War*. Cambridge: MIT Press.

Hwang, K. (2008). 'International Collaboration in Multilayered Center-Periphery in the Globalization of Science and Technology'. *Science, Technology & Human Values*, January 33: 101–133.

Jasanoff, S. (2004). 'The idiom of co-production'. In: Jasanoff, S. *States of knowledge: the co-production of science and social order*. London, Routledge.

Joerges, B and Shinn, T. (2001). 'A Fresh look at instrumentation. An introduction'. In Joerges, B. and Shinn, T. *Instrumentation between Science, State and Industry. Sociology of the Sciences Yearbook Nr. 22*. Dordrecht, Kluwer Academic Publishers.

King, D.A. (2004). 'The scientific impact of nations'. *Nature* 430 (6997): 311–316.

Kloppenburg, R. (1988). *First the Seed: The Political Economy of Plant Biotechnology*. Madison: University of Wisconsin Press.

Kreimer, Pablo (2006). ¿Dependientes o integrados? La ciencia latinoamericana y la división internacional del trabajo. *Nomadas*-CLACSO 24.

Kreimer, P. (2010). La recherche en Argentine: entre isolement et dépendance. *Cahiers de la recherche sur l'éducation et les savoirs* 9: 115–138.

Kreimer, P. (2012). Délocalisation des savoirs en Amérique latine: le rôle des réseaux scientifiques. *Pouvoirs Locaux* N° 94 III.

Kreimer, P. and Zukerfeld, M. (2014). La Explotación Cognitiva: Tensiones emergentes en la producción y uso social de conocimientos científicos, tradicionales, informacionales y laborales, in Kreimer, Vessuri et al: *Perspectivas Latinoamericanas en el estudio social de la ciencia y la tecnología*. México, Siglo XXI.

Kreimer, P. and Levin, L. (2013). 'Scientific cooperation between the European Union and Latin American countries: framework programmes 6 and 7', in J. Gaillard and R. Arvanitis, eds. *Research Collaborations between Europe and Latin America Mapping and Understanding Partnership*. Paris: Éditions des archives contemporaines: 79–104.

Latour, B. (1999). *Politiques de la Nature. Comment Faire Entrer les Sciences en Démocratie*, Paris, *La Découverte*.

Lave, R., Mirowski, P., and S. Randalls (2010). 'Introduction: STS and neoliberal science'. *Social Studies of Science* 40 (5): 659–675.

Lave, R. (2012). 'Neoliberalism and the production of environmental knowledge'. *Environement and Society* 3 (1).

Levin, L., Jensen, P., and Kreimer, P. (2016). 'Does size matter? The multipolar international landscape of nanoscience'. *PLOS One* 11 (12): e0166914. doi:10.1371.

Losego, P. and R. Arvanitis (2008). La science dans les pays non hégémoniques. *Revue d'anthropologie des connaissances*, 2 (3), 334–342.

MacLeod, R. (1980). 'On visiting the "moving metropolis": reflections on the architecture of imperial science'. *Historical Records of Australian Science* 5 (3): 1–16.

May, R.-M. (1997). 'The scientific wealth of nations'. *Science Technology & Society*, 275: 793–796.

Medina, E. (2011). *Cybernetic Revolutionaries. Technology and Politics in Allende's Chile*. Cambridge: MIT Press.

Mirowski, P. and Sent, E.-M. (2008). 'The commercialization of science and the response of STS', in E.J. Hackett et al. (eds) *Handbook of Science and Technology Studies*, 3rd edition. Cambridge: MIT Press, 635–689.

Moya-Anegón, F. and V. Herrero-Solana (2013). 'Worldwide topology of the scientific subject profile: a macro approach in the country level'. PLOS ONE, 8(12).

Mustar, P. and P. Larédo (2002). 'Innovation and research policy in France (1980–2000) or the disappearance of the Colbertist state'. *Research Policy* 31: 55–72.

Nowotny, H., Scott, P. and M. Gibbons (2001). *Re-Thinking Science*. Cambridge: Polity Press.

Pestre, D. (2003). 'Regimes of knowledge production in society: towards a more political and social reading'. *Minerva* 41 (3): 245–261.

Quijano, A. (2000). 'Coloniality of power and eurocentrism in Latin America'. *International Sociology* 15 (2): 215–232.

RICYT (2015). *El Estado de la ciencia. Principales indicadores de la ciencia. Iberoamericanos/Interamericanos*. Buenos Aires, RICYT.

Rosemann, A. (2014). 'Multipolar technoscience: clinical science collaborations in a changing world system'. Doctoral thesis (PhD): University of Sussex.

Salomon, J.-J. (2006). *Les Scientifiques. Entre Savoir et Pouvoir*. Paris: Albin Michel.

Santander, S. (2014). 'Competing Latin American regionalisms in a changing world', in M., Telò (Ed.), *European Union and New Regionalism*. London: Ashgate: 187–200.

Slaughter, S. and G. Rhoades (2004). *Academic Capitalism and the New Economy*. Baltimore: John Hopkins University Press.

Slaughter, S. and G. Rhoades (1996) 'The emergence of a competitiveness research and development policy coalition and the commercialization of academic science and technology', *Science, Technology, & Human Values*, 21 (3), 303-39

Tsing, A.-L. (2005). *Friction: An Ethnography of Global Connection*. Princeton: Princeton University Press.

Tyfield, D. (2012), *The Economics of Science: A Critical Realist Overview*. London: Routledge.

Tyfield, D. and J. Urry (2009). 'Cosmopolitan China? Lessons from international collaboration in low-carbon innovation'. *The British Journal of Sociology* 60 (4): 793–812.

Van Oudheusden, M., Charlier, N., Rosskamp, B., and P. Delvenne (2015). 'Broadening, deepening, and governing innovation: Flemish technology assessment in historical and socio-political perspective'. *Research Policy* 44 (10): 1877–1886.

Vara, A.-M. (2005). *Argentina, GM Nation. Chances and Choices in Uncertain Times. Country Case*. New York University Project on International GMO Regulatory Conflicts.

Veugelers, R. (2010). 'Towards a multipolar science world: trends and impact'. *Scientometrics* 82 (2): 439–456.

Wagner, C. (2009). *The New Invisible College: Science for Development*. Washington DC: Brookings Institution Press.

Wallerstein, I. (1974). *The Modern World-System. Volume 1. Capitalist Agriculture and the Origins of the European World-Economy in the Sixteenth Century*. Cambridge: Cambridge University Press.

Wallerstein, I. (2004). 'World-system analysis', in *Encyclopedia of Life Support Systems: Developed under the Auspices of the UNESCO*. George Modelski. Oxford: Eolss Publishers.

Wallerstein, I. (2006). *Comprendre le Monde. Introduction à l'Analyse des Systèmes-Monde*. Paris: La Découverte.

Zhou, P. and Leydesdorff, L. (2006). 'The emergence of China as a leading nation in science'. *Research Policy* 35 (1): 83–104.

30

FROM SCIENCE AS "DEVELOPMENT ASSISTANCE" TO "GLOBAL PHILANTHROPY"

Hebe Vessuri

Introduction

Ever since Francis Bacon at the dawn of the modern age, science has been presented as harboring the promise of providing the solution to the most intractable problems faced by mankind and the natural world. In the course of modern history it has also been targeted as a useful tool in dealings related to the growth of "modern, independent, democratic" societies beyond the West in the post-colonial world. Different from scientific cooperation assumed to take place between relatively equal countries, from the late 19th century onwards, science as development assistance compounded with philanthropy was embraced by Western powers as the royal road contributing to the growth of non-Western country capacities.

In this paper we reconstruct the main lines of evolution of science for development highlighting some initiatives that targeted infrastructure, health, capacity building, natural resources, international trade and competitiveness. The mounting trend of business-foundation collaboration has crystallized in the term "philanthrocapitalism", which tries to sell the idea of the philanthropic largesse and social-entrepreneurial mission of new billionaires of the 1990s as unprecedented and capable of "saving the world". The way the United Nations' platforms came to complement or be subordinated to powerful individual or country programs is briefly reviewed. So is philanthropic science, epitomized by the Rockefeller and Gates Foundations, i.e. the kind of work specifically funded by (and in control of) extremely wealthy Northern individuals. Finally, we consider the increasing role of business philanthropy and charitable investment within the growth of corporate social responsibility (CSR) models and the associated actual and symbolic role of experts and expertise, including the recent multiplication of "think tanks" and consulting work for public policies in developing countries.

A science for development in the waning colonial experience

At the end of the Second World War, the vast regions that constituted the colonial world became the "developing" countries or "Third World". Together with Latin American countries, born of earlier decolonizations, they had to rethink the world and their place in it. "A new intellectual universe and moral community" (Cooper and Packard, 2005) grew up around the world development initiative of the post-World War II era. It carried the conviction

405

that the alleviation of poverty would not occur simply by self-regulating processes of economic growth and social change. It required a concerted intervention by the national governments of both poor and wealthy countries in cooperation with an emerging body of international aid and development organizations. The transfer of knowledge of productive techniques has been key to the whole idea of development, accompanied by foreign aid and investment on favorable terms, health and education improvement, and economic planning.

In the waning of the colonial era in the 1930s and 1940s, the idea of development had already attracted the attention of leaders of both imperial metropolis and colonial outposts. Comparisons between different European versions of empire immediately reveal the complexity of the problem of analysis (MacLeod, 1996), both through time and space. In particular, the British and French colonial experiences of science in the Great War represented an intensification of rational method applied to statecraft and the application of rationality, exemplified in science, to imperial efficiency. In MacLeod's view, that this attitude finds acceptance from India and the white dominions to Latin America and Asia speaks to the persuasive power of the promise of science. At the same time, in the interwar period imperial markets were seen as important sources of replenishment to metropolitan economies depleted by the war. Development became the hallmark of British "constructive imperialism" in the attempts to maintain the empire itself, whatever the cost; while in France, the development project became associated with the planning ideology of the socialist left.

The French segment of the scientific community that generated knowledge and skills for developing countries, similar to their British or Dutch counterparts, was different from the one that addressed northern audiences. The ways that, through the Conseil National de la Recherche Scientifique (CNRS), France dealt with science aimed at Northern audiences, serving the ambitions and demands of metropolitan France, differed from applied science and assistance to Southern countries in their attempt to spawn development through the Office de Recherche Scientifique et Technique Outre-mer (ORSTOM). Eventually this generated distinct forms of knowledge and know-how, which circulated through different international networks of communication and institutions, among semi-academic or non-academic audiences, composed mainly of Third World politicians or administrators, or Third World social and economic groups, international bureaucrats, or other developed-country scientists or their counterparts in the Third World (Ragouet et al., 1997; Bennett and Hodge, 2011; Boomgaard, 2013).

Even in the German case, a latecomer to imperial ventures, a powerful stimulus for supporting overseas investments in the exact sciences occurred when the latter were combined with practical applications. German fears that to withhold support in China or Samoa would open the field to foreign competitors such as the United States emerge clearly from Pyenson's account (1985), which brings out the characteristically modern tension that German scientists already felt between the old ideal of science as an international enterprise above politics and their growing realization that government-supported science must serve political ends. Also nations like Canada (IDRC) and Sweden (SIDA-SAREC), which have no colonial heritage, after World War II developed research agencies with alternative agendas related to development assistance.

From international to global governance in development

In the decades following World War II, a dizzying array of international organizations connected to the development field were founded or revamped, including the World Bank and International Monetary Fund (IMF), UNICEF, FAO and UNDP, numerous international and local governmental and non-governmental organizations (NGOs), humanitarian and advocacy movements, research institutes, private foundations, business groups, and so on. Internationalization, of course, carried with it the idea that it was between or among nations. The basic unit remained the nation, even as relations among nations became increasingly necessary and important.

In the context of internationalization, the idea of knowledge, research and action for development was paramount. As part of this complex and variegated set-up, many people from developing countries studied economics, development and applied science in universities in Europe and the United States and were hired by governmental and non-governmental organizations in their home countries, trying to apply the organizational "blueprints" defined in the North. The expansion of universities and systems of higher education in the different regions of the world has been staggering, with the explicit purpose of contributing to development and the construction of modern nations, following the patterns and models of universities in the North (Sörlin and Vessuri, 2007). Thus also began a flow of talents that has been called "brain-drain" and more recently "international circulation of talents", by which the developing world made a reverse transfer to the developed world of its best scientists, raised and schooled in the developing countries (Johnson and Regets, 1998; Smith and Favell, 2006; Boeri et al., 2012).

From 1946 through the early 1990s these actors were shaped by two main factors: the Cold War and the political and ideological rivalry between Western capitalism and Eastern communism; and, a corollary to this, the paradigm of economic development and modernization, perceived by Western powers as the sole path to progress for the decolonized Third World (itself a key battleground of the Cold War). But as early as the 1950s, it was clear that the post-war reconfiguration of world power brought few benefits to the former colonies. In 1964 the G-77 movement of non-aligned (with either the Soviets or the Americans) countries was founded to confront neocolonialism in development aid, to demand respect for sovereignty in decision-making, and to denounce unfair international trade arrangements and the lack of democracy in UN agencies. Yet this was also arguably the high point of each of these concerns.

Three decades later, for instance, the institutional landscape related to development had changed its nature, often abandoning even the ideational commitment to former goals. Instead, programs and agencies were increasingly constrained by an ideological context attacking the role of the state and favoring private-sector, for-profit approaches. The case of a UN agency like the World Health Organization (WHO) is exemplary. By the 1980s, WHO had ceased to be at the heart of international health activities, as stipulated in its 1946 Constitution (Birn, 2014). Less than half of WHO's budget came from annual dues subjected to "democratic" World Health Assembly decisions. Donors, who included a variety of private entities in addition to member countries, increasingly shifted WHO's budget away from dues-funded activities to *a priori* assignment of funds to particular programs and approaches. In this period, the World Bank—exerting pressure under the banner of health care services and efficiency reforms and privatization—had a far larger health budget than WHO, and many bilateral agencies simply bypassed WHO in their international health activities.

This process of institutional hollowing out has continued to date. Presently almost 80 percent of WHO's budget is earmarked, whereby donors designate how their "voluntary" contributions are to be spent (WHO, 2011). Since the 1990s the WHO hobbled along on public–private partnerships (Nitsan 2012), which particularly the Rockefeller Foundation had helped to innovate in order to fund its vaccine initiatives (Muraskin, quoted in Birn, 2014). Public–private partnerships have provided business interests, such as pharmaceutical corporations, with a major, arguably unjustified, role in international public health policymaking.

Moreover, as these events were unfolding, international health, in which the basic unit remained the nation, was renamed "global health", with the integration of many formerly national institutions in one global setting. The role of international philanthropy, i.e. the private charitable funding by a handful of Global North-based and individually owned foundations, was thereby greatly inflated as against supposedly public international institutions.

The globalized economy of the present is often presented as if it no longer made sense to think of national teams of labor and capital. We witness an effective erasure of national boundaries for economic purposes in organizations such as the International Monetary Fund and the World Bank, as they abandon internationalization and promote globalization, contrary to the interests of their member nations, and to the intent of their charter (Daly, 1999). As part of this, despite the fact that the increase of transparency is a *topos*, or basic concept, in international UN organizations is the increase of transparency, skepticism reigns about the possibility of "communicating" to citizens about subjects of great technical and political complexity (Abeles, 2011). Hence, the "globalization" of a "global health" agenda that is being pushed hard by powerful transnational corporations, in fact turns out to be unfettered individualism for such corporations on a global scale, governed by the ideal of absolute advantage, an unexamined ideal as such.

The evolution of philanthrocapitalism

Despite an uncertain position in the popular and political imagination, the philanthropic foundations of the early 20th century in the U.S. perceived themselves as custodians of a better world, using the fortunes amassed by entrepreneurs of industrial capitalism to create a program of social progress (Brooks, 2015). They "saw their mission as not simply to heal the sick or repair the effects of conflict, but to enhance society's ability to solve fundamental scientific and social problems" (Fleishman, 2009). However, the foundations were often accused of using personal interests to interfere unduly in public affairs, acting as "*Don Quixotes in limousines*" (Whitaker, 1974, quoted by Brooks, 2015), frequently contributing, directly or indirectly, to enhance the donors' business and investment interests, many of them linked to industries that were highly exploitative and damaging to the environment.

Models of corporate philanthropy have been shown to see social responsibility as a sort of add-on (Kleine, 2014). Business models have proliferated in the development field. Companies operate "normally" and in pursuit of profit, and once the profits have been generated, a percentage of the gains is then reinvested in charitable causes, for example, in the communities where the Northern consumers live or indeed in poverty-reducing projects in the Global South.

The Rockefeller and Gates Foundations are two remarkable examples of the nature of philanthropy in the contemporary world and their role in accompanying, supporting and/or confronting the nation-states to which they belong. Both have focused their actions on generating and applying new knowledge. The former appeared when the international field of science assistance for development in the first half of the 20th century was still in gestation; the latter in a very different set-up of neoliberal globalization and fading hegemony of the U.S.

On the one hand, the Rockefeller Foundation (RF) sought to establish scientific cooperation with developing countries as a legitimate sphere for (inter) governmental action, creating, largely from scratch, the principles, practices, and key institutions of international development in fields like health (Fosdick, 1952). On the other, the Gates Foundation has challenged the leadership and capacity of public multilateral agencies, pushing ahead an overlapping global development governance arrangement with a huge role allotted for the private sector (Richter, 2003).

The RF was probably the major influence upon international health's 20th-century agenda, approaches, and actions. The League of Nations' Health Organization, founded after World War I, was partially modeled on the RF's International Health Division (IHD), active since the early days of the RF in 1913, and shared many of its values, experts, and know-how in disease control, institution-building, and educational and research work, even as it challenged the RF's narrow, medicalized understandings of health. With the creation of the WHO in 1948, the IHD was subsumed into the larger RF in 1951, discontinuing its overseas work.

The RF's efforts, however, went well beyond health, stabilizing colonies and emerging nation-states by helping them meet the social demands of their populations, encouraging the transfer and internationalization of scientific, bureaucratic, and cultural values, stimulating economic development and growth, expanding consumer markets, and preparing vast regions for foreign investment, increased productivity, and incorporation into the expanding system of global capitalism.

The RF's international program sought to generate goodwill and promised social advancement in place of gunboat diplomacy and colonial repression (Berman, 1983). It helped build the U.S.'s "international health as foreign policy" proficiency. When in the mid-1930s Germany started to use medical aid to befriend Mexico, Brazil, and other countries in Latin America as it sought allies and essential resources, including oil, rubber, and minerals—and these countries began to play off the Anglo-American-German rivalry—the RF redoubled its public health efforts in the region. This heightened RF involvement, requested by the U.S. State Department, and reflected in the activity of the Office of Inter-American Affairs (OIAA) headed by Nelson A. Rockefeller, who held the position of the "Coordinator of Inter-American Affairs", was instrumental in persuading Latin Americans to side with the Allies (Cramer and Prutsch, 2006; Price, 2008).

The new business philanthropy

Philanthropic and business interests have long been involved in international health, but it was not until the 1990s that public–private partnerships (PPPs) were formalized as a central element of global health. Following the policy of privatizing public goods put forth by the World Bank and IMF, PPPs consciously drew on profit-making principles as a driver of policies, product development, and other activities, further weakening the WHO and any semblance of democratic global health governance.

The Global Fund was established in 2002 as a PPP organization between governments, civil society, the private sector and people affected by AIDS, tuberculosis and malaria, being formally designed to accelerate the end of those diseases as epidemics. However, it turned out to serve, among other things, to weaken an important transnational movement for intellectual property (IP) reform that had emerged in the late 1990s to address the gross profiteering of pharmaceutical companies that impeded access to HIV/AIDS drugs in low- and middle-income countries, particularly in Africa. For example, a case filed by the AIDS Law Project (a human rights advocacy organization) in South Africa in 2002 against excessive pricing by foreign pharmaceutical companies found a sympathetic ear with the country's Competition Tribunal. Settling out of court, the companies agreed to issue voluntary generic licenses for AIDS drugs, an outcome that inspired activists in other countries to follow suit (Singh, 2007).

The Global Fund, like many PPPs, offered "business opportunities"—lucrative contracts—as a prime feature of its work. This illustrates how global health is being captured by business interests in a way that was not even part of the original RF strategy; by contrast, this saw international health to be in the public, not the profiteering, domain, even if ultimately benefiting the private sector. PPPs promote profit-making at the front end of global health work, as opposed to strategic public health activities (for example, against yellow fever by RF in the first quarter of the 20th century) that benefited capitalist interests indirectly, once the public health work was carried out.

The current infusion of profit-making in philanthropic ventures has reached entirely new dimensions. The Bill and Melinda Gates Foundation (BMGF) efforts appear to be emblematic of an overall trend towards for-profit style management, leadership training, and goal-setting in global development and health, as well as the privatizing of public activities. PPPs have been among the key levers of BMGF influence through a global health funding and operations modality enabled by the massive entry of private capital into the health and development arena at the end of the Cold War. Today the BMGF is by far the largest philanthropic organization involved in global health. Its primary aim in this area is "harnessing advances in science and technology to reduce health inequities" (BMGF website) through the innovation and application of health technologies, encompassing both treatment (via diagnostic tools and drug development partnerships) and prevention (through, for example, vaccines and microbicides).

Like the RF before it the Gates Foundation's influence and dominance over the global health and development agenda stems from multiple factors: the magnitude of its donations; its ability to mobilize resources quickly and allocate substantial sums to large or innovative efforts; the renown of its patron; its technology-driven and cost-effective emphases; as well as the clout and leverage it garners from the extraordinary range of organizations that it partners with or funds. Echoing the RF, the BMGF follows a technically oriented approach—with programs designed to achieve positive evaluations through narrowly defined goals—and adheres to a business model that emphasizes short-term achievements.

The BMGF appeared in 2000 at a time when overall spending for global health was stagnant, and when suspicion by political and economic elites (and, via hegemonic media, by voters in many countries) of public and overseas development assistance was at a near all-time high. Many low- and middle-income countries were floundering under the multiple burdens of HIV/AIDS, re-emerging infectious diseases, and soaring chronic ailments, compounded by decades of World Bank and IMF-imposed social expenditure cuts. Thus, despite the manifold shortcomings of an approach that is focused on technology (e.g. vaccines that do not require refrigeration in infrastructure-poor tropical climates were one key targeted technology that failed to materialize) and drugs, as well as a disease-by-disease approach (polio, tuberculosis, malaria), the BMGF has stuck with its ambitious goals of eradicating four diseases, including polio, by 2030. This model prevails at present, abetted by the BMGF's prime influence at formal global health decision-making bodies. This, despite the critics' argument that this approach is failing to deliver within the timescales originally envisaged a group of innovation initiatives funded by the Gates Foundation and various governments that were intended to solve key global health and development problems.

In recent years the BMGF has been accused of investing its endowment in profiteering pharmaceutical companies and polluting industries—including ExxonMobil (whose forerunner was founded by John D. Rockefeller) and Chevron, which have been linked to environmental and health crises in the Niger Delta and other oil-rich regions (Piller et al., 2007)—as well as in "private corporations that stand to gain from the Foundation's philanthropic support of particular global health initiatives" (People's Health Movement, 2008).

For instance, the BMGF's involvement in the Alliance for a Green Revolution in Africa (AGRA), like its global health efforts, illustrates the profound contradiction between the aims of philanthropy (or philanthrocapitalism) and the needs of poor populations (Morvaridi, 2012). AGRA, like the RF's Green Revolution programs in the 20th century, focuses on technological and market models for increased agricultural output. This emphasis comes at the expense of equitable, democratic, and sustainable approaches based on securing land rights for small producers (all the more pressing in a context of large-scale foreign land grabs in countries facing dire hunger and malnutrition problems) and supporting local and regional food distribution networks (Jarosz, 2012). In addition to profound concerns about AGRA's role in the research and promotion of genetically modified organisms (GMOs) and the development of privately patented seeds, local analysts have also linked AGRA to the fostering of private ownership and corporate control of Africa's genetic wealth without the sharing of credit or benefits with the cultivators (Thompson, 2012).[1]

The importance of public scrutiny is growing as other donors, including the Canadian and South African governments, are adopting the Grand Challenges approach, originally launched by the BMGF in 2004 to accelerate the pace of research (Sharma 2015). The Grand Challenges in Global Health initiative aimed to catalyze scientific and technological innovation to achieve major breakthroughs in global health. In 2014 a consortium of partners including Brazil, Canada, India, Norway, South Africa, the United Kingdom and the United States decided to fund a new phase of Grand Challenge initiatives, around three main actions: infant health, gender inequality and new scientific and technical interventions for global health. The BMGF is central to this effort.[2]

Philanthropists, past and present, have typically rationalized their actions as necessary to address "market failures" (Payton and Moody, 2008). Of course, (global) public health, like many other social goods and services, by definition resides in the realm of market failure because it is externalized from the costs of doing business in bilateral transactions. The need for philanthropy to become more like the for-profit capital markets is a common theme among the new philanthropists, especially those who have made their fortune in finance (*The Economist*, 2006). Whether their promotion of capitalist approaches as superior to the public sector in regulating and delivering services is correct or not does not seem substantiated. In the global health arena of more recent decades, the argument that the public sector is incapable of addressing societal needs has contemptuously disregarded the full-fledged assault on public spending and infrastructure on the part of international financial institutions' conditionalities and structural adjustment programs in the 1980s and 1990s, not to mention the wave of predatory private bank lending, unfair trade practices, and hegemonic leverage over the WTO by powerful countries (Stiglitz, 2007).

Tapping knowledge globally: the new markets for policies

Business relationships as much as international civil society, now online, and academia all afford channels for the international mobility of generic ideas and means for the penetration of particular forms of knowledge and kinds of relations within the state and society. Business philanthropy acts as intermediary between national and international policies. National governments, especially those of small and fragile states, experience a reduction in their capacity of driving the educational and science systems. A proliferation of policy networks nationally and globally made up of "operationally autonomous" but "structurally coupled" organizations blurs the boundaries between state, economy and civil society.

Since the 1970s there has been an explosive growth of "policy intermediation" institutions (such as think tanks, policy networks and centers, reform advocates and consultants), the modus operandi of which is defined in terms of the generation, circulation and implantation of potentially agenda-shifting ideas, models and strategies. A basic ingredient of development assistance today can be broadly described as the "importation" of "innovative policies developed elsewhere" by the national elites, and the imposition of policies by multilateral agencies, and/or processes of structural convergence. It is part of a broader set of processes that include new modes of philanthropy and assistance for scientific development and education, the market processes of capital growth and expansion, and the search by business of new opportunities for profit.

New social actors, hybrid social subjects who are spatially mobile, ethically malleable, and able to speak the languages of public, private and philanthropic value are part of a global service class increasingly but not necessarily disconnected from national identities and loyalties (Vessuri,

2010; Ball, 2010). As at different times in the past, cosmopolitized resistance to this particular model is also present among the existing intellectual diasporas from Southern countries. As members of a "specialists elite", experts linked to powerful transnational agencies and groups—the World Bank, the WTO and the OECD in particular—disseminate new forms of policy and expertise in policies, ready to take the opportunities of reform and modernization of the public sectors in countries all over the world. They have played an important role in packing, selling and implementing *New Public Management* techniques, as state agencies contemplating institutional change or strengthening often enlist the services of expert consultants to clarify options—and recommend courses of action (Larbi, 1999).

The literature on the social studies of science emphasizes that the generation of knowledge takes place in different localities and under particular circumstances (Livingstone, 2003). The situated character of knowledge has been particularly demanding for developing countries in their need to dominate the conditions of science implementation locally (Waast and Mouton, 2007). In the 1990s globalization processes developed in parallel with substantial changes in the global framework of knowledge production. The central features with regard to cooperation started to change from being framed as *assistance* to particular countries to *joint work* in research programs (shared labs) and exchanges of teachers and students connected in networks within broader supra-national programs (Finholt and Olson, 1997).

The modalities of research internationalization that led to new forms of collaboration in North America and the European Union fostered the creation of international research networks (Castells, 1996, 2006; Cantwell and Piscitello, 1999), and a new wave of internationalization of higher education (Altbach and Knight, 2007; Mollis, 2006). In the new institutional set-up, think tanks together with consultants and educational firms, deliver policy assistance (for a potential profit), developing local policy infrastructures, instilling the discourses of prevalent Western policy directly or as spillovers in the local policy systems. They often have specific and effective points of entry in the political systems, nested as they are in networks of relationships. Their authority and legitimacy are not natural but are cultivated through management practices and intellectual activity. The "aura" of intellectual authority and independence may be misleading for ideas are often harnessed to political and economic interests (Ball, 2012).

Non-governmental organizations and actors have growing significance in all the functions of governance, from the establishment of objectives and norms to the selection of the means, the regulation of the operations and the verification of results. This is particularly relevant for science, which is internally governed by its own members—the scientists—and externally through its interactions with the society in which it is immersed (European Commission, 2009). The multiplication of supra-national organizations and multinational corporations in the funding of research has contributed to redefining the space of scientific-technical research, removing it from the previously dominant paradigm of *national science*. The expansion and acceleration of global interconnectivity has significant socioeconomic and ideational implications that serve to reconfigure the international system, fostering in part the emergence of new economic spaces incongruent with existing political frontiers (Matthews, 1997).

The current descriptive narrative of knowledge shows it as a network with multiple nodes and connexions, and as a dynamic system very different from the notion common a few decades ago as a basic or lineal structure of disciplinary rhetoric. The metaphor of unity, together with the values of universality and certainty, has been largely replaced by metaphors of plurality and relationality in a complex world. The values of control, dominance and expertise are currently being redefined as values of dialogue, interaction and negotiation (Rip, 2010; Ravetz, 2012). It is not clear yet whether this is to be considered a good, bad, neutral or ambivalent and complex change.

Conclusion

Crucially since the early 20th century the foundations saw themselves as distinct from charities: a "scientific philanthropy", as it was sometimes referred to, was to develop society according to its own rationale and to encourage others to do the same as a means of social salvation (Sealander, 2003). More recently new ideas are being advanced, for example Hacker Philanthropy, proposed by billionaire entrepreneur Sean Parker; and Effective Altruism, championed by philosopher Peter Singer (http://philanthrocapitalism.net, 2015). The first refers to focusing philanthropy on finding solutions that work; the second refers to focusing philanthropy where it can have the greatest impact. Clearly, there is some overlap between the two ideas, both of which go to the heart of what philanthrocapitalism is about.

Philanthropic foundations have been and continue to be significant transnational actors "because of their direct and indirect influence on other actors in world politics" (Bell, 1991). An understanding of how transnational philanthropy works in the interstices of state–private networks, both as quasi-market and quasi-state, is critical in understanding how it is related to geopolitical projects. The collaboration between state and private agencies increased through joint-supported institutes and researches. But whereas in the past, profit-making in connection with the public sphere was denounced for being self-serving and a violation of the principle of separation of public and private interests that should be avoided as problematic and unethical, today it is viewed by private capital—and rationalized by a disquietingly quiet public—as a desirable outcome that ought to be encouraged.

As the world globalizes and becomes more integrated, more opportunities emerge for collective action. There is a whole series of global public goods, such as world peace, global health, the protection of environment, and global knowledge. If the global community does not provide them collectively, it is likely that they will be insufficient. While the existence of an adequate balance between private and public sectors continues to be unsolved, the provision of some system for funding public goods is obviously required. The contemporary large philanthropic foundations concentrate an important portion of the wealth of the world that might be devoted to global public goods. In their rhetoric business philanthropies are devoted to them, and in fact they could set in motion huge resources, spread more advanced technology and increase human wellbeing in an exponential way.

However, the tenet that such business models can solve social problems and are superior to redistributive, collectively deliberate policies and actions employed by elected governments remains unconvincing.

Acknowledgements

I wish to thank the DesiguALdades.Net and the IAI-SPK in Berlin that through a fellowship gave me the time and peace of mind to write the bulk of this paper.

Notes

1　In this regard, AGRA differs from the earlier RF-sponsored efforts, which kept hybridized seeds in the public domain, given that this was before gene patenting was legalized in 1980 (Fitzgerald, 1990).

2　For this and further information on partners see (www.gatesfoundation.org/Media-Center/Press-Releases/2014/10/Gates-Foundation-Grand-Challenges-Breakthrough-Science).

References

Abeles, M. 2011. *Des anthropologues à l'OMC. Scènes de la gouvernance mondiale.* Paris: CNRS Editions.

Altbach, P. and J. Knight. 2007. "The Internationalization of Higher Education: Motivations and Realities". *Journal of Studies in Higher Education*, 11: 290–305.

Arnove, R.F. (ed.). 1982. *Philanthropy and Cultural Imperialism. The Foundations at Home and Abroad.* Bloomington: Indiana University Press.

Ball, S. J. 2012. *Global Education Inc. New Policy Networks and the Neo-Liberal Imaginary.* Routledge.

Ball, S. J. 2010. "Is there a global middle-class? The beginnings of a cosmopolitan sociology of education: a review". *Journal of Comparative Education*, 69: 135–59.

Bell, P. 1991. "The Ford Foundation as transnational actor". *International Organization*, 25: 465–478.

Bennett, B. and J. Hodge (eds.). 2011. "Science and Empire". *Knowledge and Networks of Science across the British Empire, 1800–1940.* Palgrave Macmillan.

Berman, E.H. 1983. *The Influence of the Carnegie, Ford, and Rockefeller Foundations on American Foreign Policy: The Ideology of Philanthropy.* Albany: State University of New York Press.

Birn, A-E. 2014. "Philanthrocapitalism, past and present: The Rockefeller Foundation, the Gates Foundation, and the setting(s) of the international/global health agenda". *Hypothesis*, 12(1): e8, doi:10.5779/hypothesis.v12i1.229.

Birn, A-E. 2005. "Gates's grandest challenge: transcending technology as public health ideology'. *Lancet*, 366: 514–519. http://dx.doi.org/10.1016/S0140-6736(05)66479-3.

Boeri, T. H., Brücker, F. Docquier, and H. Rapoport (eds). 2012. *Brain Drain and Brain Gain: The Global Competition to Attract High-Skilled Migrants*, Oxford University Press.

Boomgaard, P. (ed.). 2013. *Empire and Science in the Making: Dutch Colonial Scholarship in Comparative Global Perspective, 1760–1830.* Palgrave Macmillan.

Brooks, Ch. 2015. "'The ignorance of the uneducated': Ford Foundation philanthropy, the IIE, and the geographies of educational exchange". *Journal of Historical Geography*, 48: 36–46.

Cantwell, J. and L. Piscitello. 1999 "The Emergence of Corporate International Networks for the Accumulation of Dispersed Technological Competences". MIR *Management International Review*, 39(11): 123–147.

Castells, M. 1996. *The Rise of the Network Society.* Oxford: Blackwell Publishing Ltd.

Castells, M. 2006. *La sociedad red: una visión global.* Madrid: Alianza Elditorial.

Cooper, F. and R. Packard. 2005. "The history and politics of development knowledge". In: Edelman, M. and A. Haugerud (eds.) *The Anthropology of Development and Globalization: From Classical Political Economy to Contemporary Neoliberalism.* Oxford: Blackwell.

Cramer, G. and U. Prutsch. 2006. "Nelson A. Rockefeller's Office of Inter-American Affairs (1940–1946) and Record Group 229". *Hispanic American Historical Review*, 86(4):785–806.

Daly, H.E. 1999. "Globalization versus internationalization: some implications". *Ecological Economics*, 31: 31–377.

The Economist. 2006. "The birth of philanthrocapitalism: The leading new philanthropists see themselves as social investors". *The Economist*, February 23.

European Commission 2009. *Global Governance of Science.* Report to the Science, Economy and Society Directorate, Directorate-General for Research. European Commission, Brussels: EUR 23616 EN.

Finholt, T.A. and G.M. Olson. 1997. "From laboratories to collaboratories: A new organizational form for scientific collaboration". *Psychological Science*, 8: 28–36.

Fitzgerald, D. 1990. *The Business of Breeding: Hybrid Corn in Illinois 1890–1940.* Cornell University Press. Ithaca and London.

Fleishman, J. L. 2009. *The Foundation, a Great American Secret: How Private Wealth is Changing the World.* New York.

Fosdick, R.B. 1952. *The Story of the Rockefeller Foundation.* New Brunswick, NJ: Transaction.

Jarosz, L. 2012. "Growing inequality: agricultural revolutions and the political ecology of rural development". *International Journal of Agricultural Sustainability*, 10(2): 192–199. http://dx.doi.org/10.1080/14735903.2011.600605.

Johnson, J. and M. Regets. 1998. "International mobility of scientists and engineers to the United States: brain drain or brain circulation", National Science Foundation (NSF 98–316), Washington: NSF.

Kleine, D. 2014. "Corporate social responsibility and development". In: V. Desai and R.B. Potter (eds.), *The Companion to Development Studies.* Routledge: London and New York.

Larbi, G.A. 1999. *The New Public Management Approach and Crisis States* (vol. Discussion Paper No. 112). United Nations Research Institute for Social Development: Geneva.

Livingstone, D. 2003. *Putting Science in its Place: Geographies of Scientific Knowledge*. University of Chicago Press: Chicago and London.

MacLeod, R. 1996. "Reading the discourse of colonial science". *Les Sciences Coloniales: Figures et institutions*. Vol. 2 (general editor Roland Waast), ORSTOM-UNESCO: Paris.

Matthews, J. T. 1997. "Power shift". *Foreign Affairs*, 76(1): 50–66.

Mollis, M. 2006. Geopolíticas del saber: biografías recientes de las universidades latinoamericanas. Vessuri, H. (comp.) *Universidad e Investigación Científica. Convergencias y Tensiones*. UNESCO-CLACSO: Buenos Aires: 85–101.

Morvaridi B. 2012. "Capitalist philanthropy and hegemonic partnerships". *Third World Quarterly*. 33(7): 1191–1210. http://dx.doi.org/10.1080/01436597.2012.691827.

Muraskin W. 2010. "The Rockefeller Foundation's Health Sciences Division: 1977–2002: an overview of a quarter century of fighting the infectious diseases of the developing world". Unpublished manuscript.

Nitsan C. 2012. *The World Health Organization between North and South*. Ithaca: Cornell University Press.

Palmer, S. 2010. *Launching Global Health: The Caribbean Odyssey of the Rockefeller Foundation*. Ann Arbor: University of Michigan Press. Available from: www.hypothesisjournal.com/?p=2503#22.

Payton, R.L. and Moody, M.P. 2008. *Understanding Philanthropy: Its Meaning and Mission*. Indiana University Press: Bloomington.

People's Health Movement, GEGA. 2008. "Global health watch 2: an alternative world health report". *Global Health Watch*. London: Zed Books. Available from: www.ghwatch.org/ghw2.

Piller, C., Sanders, E., and Dixon, R. 2007. "Dark cloud over good works of Gates Foundation". *Los Angeles Times* [Online]. January 7. Available from: www.latimes.com/news/la-na-gatesx07jan07,0,2533850.story.

Price, D. 2008. *Anthropological Intelligence: The Deployment and Neglect of American Anthropology in the Second World War*. Duke University Press: Durham and London.

Pyenson, L. 1985. *Cultural Imperialism and Exact Sciences*. Peter Lang Publishers: New York.

Ragouet, P., T, Shinn and R. Waast. 1997. "South for the South/Science for the North. The Great Divide? ORSTOM versus CNRS". In: T. Shinn, J. Spaapen and V. Krishna (editors) *Science and Technology in a Developing World*, Kluwer Academic Publishers: Dordrecht: 179–209.

Ravetz, J.K. 2012. "Paradoxes and the future of safety in the global knowledge economy". *Safety Paradoxes KB Future Studies 03\Z 1*. http://citeseerx.ist.psu.edu/viewdoc/summary?doi=10.1.1.618.422.

Richter, J. 2003. *"We the People" or "We the Corporations"? Critical Reflections on UN-Business "Partnerships"*. Geneva: IBFAN/GIFA.

Rip, A. 2010. "Processes of entanglement". In: M. Akrich, Y. Barthe, F. Muniesa et P. Mustar (eds.), *Débordements. Mélanges offerts à Michel Callon*. Transvalor – Presses des Mines: Paris: 381–392.

Sealander, J. 2003. "Curing evils at their source: the arrival of scientific giving". In: L.J. Friedman, M.D McGarvie (eds), *Charity, Philanthropy, and Civility in American History*, Cambridge: 217–239.

Sharma, J. 2015. "Gates Foundation reviews funding focus after criticism". *ScidevNet*, London.

Singh, J.A., M. Govender and E. Mills. 2007. "Do human rights matter to health?" *Lancet*, 370: 521–526. http://dx.doi.org/10.1016/S0140-6736(07)61236-7.

Smith, M. P. and A. Favell. 2006. *The Human Face of Global Mobility: International Highly Skilled Migration in Europe, North America and the Asia-Pacific*. Transaction Publishers: New Brunswick, N.J.

Sörlin, S. and H. Vessuri 2007. *Knowledge Society vs. Knowledge Economy: Knowledge, Power, and Politics*. Palgrave, New York.

Stiglitz, J. 2007. *Making Globalization Work*. W.W. Norton and Co.: New York.

Thompson, C.B. 2012. "Alliance for a green revolution in Africa (AGRA): advancing the theft of African genetic wealth". *Review of African Political Economy*, 39(133): 500–511.

Vessuri, H. 2010. "The current internationalization of the social sciences in Latin America: Old wine in new barrels?" M. Kuhn and D. Weidemann (eds.) *Internationalization of the Social Sciences. Asia – Latin America – Middle East – Africa – Eurasia* [Transcript] Science Studies, New Brunswick & London.

Waast, R. and J. Mouton, 2007. (eds.) *National Research Systems: A Global Overview of Current Trends*. Paris: UNESCO Forum.

Whitaker, B. 1974. *The Foundations: An Anatomy of Philanthropy and Society*, London: Eyre Methuen.

WHO (World Health Organization) 2011. "Proposed Programme Budget 2010–2011". World Health Organization Avm: http://apps.who.int/gb/e/e_amtsp3.html.

31

TRAVELING IMAGINARIES

The "practice turn" in innovation policy and the global circulation of innovation models

Sebastian Pfotenhauer and Sheila Jasanoff

Introduction

In December 2011, the then-mayor of New York City, Michael Bloomberg, announced that Cornell University and Israel's Technion had jointly won a bid to build a new Institute of Technology on Manhattan's Roosevelt Island. The announcement and the preceding bidding process drew a lot of attention from media, politics, and academia alike: Bloomberg was heralded for his "bold vision" that promised to finally dissolve the city's longstanding stigma of offering an anemic, second-rate innovation environment. Cornell Tech was seen as a "game changer" that could "help dreamers and entrepreneurs from around the world come to New York and help us become the world's leading city for technological innovation" (*Cornell Chronicle*, 2011) and "positioning New York for 21st-century global supremacy" in the wake of the financial crisis (Bellafante, 2011). Seemingly overnight, the project attracted private donations on the order of half a billion dollars, adding to the precious land grant of prime New York real estate and a pledged total investment of $2 billion by the city and the state.

As with any flagship development initiative, Cornell Tech stirred controversy. Public reactions included insinuations of legacy-building by the mayor, concern about the implications for New York's other premier institutions such as NYU and Columbia, the socially questionable repurposing of what up to this point was a hospital island, and protests against Technion's involvement by pro-Palestine advocacy groups. Yet, overall, the level of public contestation was relatively modest for an initiative that involved a major land grant to a private university with an endowment of more than five billion dollars and shutting down hospitals in an era of public fiscal scarcity and Occupy Wall Street. In particular, no one seemed to question the two most basic premises of the initiative: first, that New York City needed to step up its innovation game, and, second, that importing an Institute of Technology to the heart of the city with the help of outside expert partners was a sound strategy. While the competition aroused much speculation, virtually no public debate ensued as to whether New York's competitive strengths really required a new university or an innovation hub; whether New York stood a chance competing with established innovation regions such as Silicon Valley or the Boston area; or whether innovation capacity could indeed be obtained from a plug-in institution serviced by two universities whose principal activities and interests lay elsewhere.[1]

The creation of Cornell Tech speaks to a curious two-fold shift towards regionalism in the imagination of innovation. On the one hand, innovation has become a key concern of policy-

416

making at the regional and city level, guiding investments and shaping communal self-imagination in ever more pervasive ways (Pfotenhauer et al., forthcoming). Hardly a week passes without a regional or city government announcing an "innovation strategy" or an institution (re-)branding itself as a driver of innovation. Likewise, innovation research is increasingly focusing on regions and cities (Cooke et al., 2009; Braczyk et al., 2004; Marceau, 2008). On the other hand, our imagination of innovation today is fundamentally linked to certain regions and institutions that seem to have transcended their own particularity, such as the doublets of Route 128/MIT, Silicon Valley/Stanford, or Israel/Technion. *Being* an innovative region or institution, it seems, is equivalent to *being like* one of these places, and competitiveness concerns and ambitions for development are increasingly articulated vis-à-vis them. As a result, it has become common practice for policy-makers and institutional leaders to look to these supposed innovation leaders for "best practices" to be distilled and emulated at home. What, in the case of New York City, might twenty years ago have been dismissed as a futile, indeed hubristic, attempt at "catching-up" in the style of an ambitious Middle Eastern nation today counts as plausible policy strategy for even highly developed regions. It is against this background that Mayor Bloomberg's initiative suggested to New Yorkers: we know that innovation is the key to the future of our city. We also know what innovation success looks like. With Cornell and Technion as trusted partners at our side, we will give New York its "Silicon Island" (*The New Yorker*, 2012).

In this chapter, we aim to interrogate this two-fold re-localization of the global political economy of science and innovation – the almost automatic re-imagination of regions as future innovation hubs on the one hand, and the re-imagination of innovation around the practices of a few select places on the other. We argue that the creation of Cornell Tech and the like speaks to a broader "practice turn" in innovation policy that requires a different kind of theorization than currently available in mainstream innovation theory. This mainstream theory continues to explain and enact innovation in terms of universal models, thus failing to account for how much our notion of what constitutes an innovation *model* has become interwoven with notions of *place* and *practice* (as observed in the circulation of "best-practice models" such as the "MIT model," the "Silicon Valley model," or "Responsible Innovation").

A more productive way of understanding models in contemporary innovation discourse is to see them as *Traveling Imaginaries of Innovation*. With this term, we elaborate on the concept of sociotechnical imaginaries by adding a dimension of global circulation to capture how innovation policy simultaneously mobilizes *local* understandings of what constitutes a desirable sociotechnical future and a set of transnational practices that legitimize innovation as a *global* policy imperative. What bridges this seemingly self-contradictory duality is the interpretive flexibility of traveling imaginaries. Using a brief comparative analysis of three implementations of the "MIT model" in the United Kingdom (UK), Portugal, and Singapore, we demonstrate that societies envision fundamentally different things under the label innovation even when making reference to, and implementing, the supposedly same model. At the same time, actors draw upon a globally certified vocabulary and forms of expertise to articulate local visions, mobilize local resources, and justify local policy changes. Identifying these multiple layers of practice allows us to explain how the same innovation model – and the notion of "innovation" it encodes – are locally co-produced along with a specific diagnosis of a societal need and a complementary vision of the required remedy, leading to utterly different configurations of the imported model (Pfotenhauer and Jasanoff, forthcoming). In contrast, the prevalent "universalist" approach to innovation, which presupposes a single underlying model, identical systems components, and shared rationales about development, leaves key variations in the rationalization, design, implementation, and performance of regional innovation policy unexplained.

The "practice turn" in innovation policy

Innovation has become an imperative for pulling societies out of perceived economic and social doldrums around the globe. As a policy objective, innovation has attained the status of a go-to answer – a *panacea*, so to speak – that carries the promise of solving socioeconomic woes regardless of their nature or history (Pfotenhauer and Jasanoff, forthcoming). It has become virtually impossible to talk about economic development or social progress in terms that do not invoke, explicitly or implicitly, the necessity of innovation. In fact, it seems as if all governmental functions *must* increasingly turn to innovation in order to appear legitimate, economically defensible, and modern: from education and research to immigration, labor market regulation, and taxation, all the way to environmental regulation and risk governance.

Alongside this rise to prominence, something has shifted in the way we think about innovation. For a long time, the phenomenon of innovation was the sole prerogative of academics trying to explain technological change, economic growth, and social progress. Standard innovation theory held that innovation could be captured through abstract models that reflect general understandings of what innovation *is*, what it is *for*, and how it ought to be implemented. The literature on innovation is replete with such theoretical models – from the linear (pipeline) model, to push–pull or chain-link models, to today's innovation systems and triple helix models (Godin, 2006; Godin and Lane, 2013). These models share a belief that the universal mechanics of innovation can be distilled, packaged, and transferred to different settings. In this view, what differs across settings (and often prevents a specific innovation model from working) is the "context" of innovation – not innovation itself – which explains why some regions lag behind others. As a result, innovation scholarship tends to evaluate innovative regions against an implicit presumption of organizational "completeness," consisting of an ideal set of components, actors, conditions, and functions that need to be arranged in slightly different yet ultimately parallel ways to stimulate innovation (Pfotenhauer and Jasanoff, forthcoming).

In contrast to these analytic roots and their commitment to universal theory, innovation discourse today is increasingly dominated by a plurality of practitioners – policy-makers, institutional leaders, tech transfer managers, and a whole new profession of consultants – all of whom are tasked with *doing innovation* across a multitude of settings, rather than simply explaining or theorizing it. This "doing innovation" may include activities as diverse as managing university incubators in Lisbon, re-envisioning urban mobility in Ulaanbaatar, funneling oil revenues through a sovereign wealth fund in Alberta, merging a headphone company and a computer manufacturer in the United States, or undertaking biodiversity sampling in the Amazon.

While the notion of innovation seems effortlessly to encompass this cacophony of activities, traditional theories and models are less accommodating. Those charged with implementing innovation increasingly find it hard to make sense of the terms and components of the supposedly universal models in the contexts in which they are envisioned to be useful. Moreover, accuracy in emulating certain models has proven a poor predictor of success. Yet, policy-makers and institutional managers try to orient themselves by looking to the practices of presumed innovation leaders, whether determined by explicit measurement or mere reputation. Indeed, the aura of the "MIT" and "Silicon Valley" models has grown brighter as policy desiderata throughout the world, giving rise, respectively, to such emulations as the "Karlsruhe Institute of Technology" (Germany), "Masdar Institute of Science and Technology" (Abu Dhabi), and "Skolkovo Institute of Technology" (Russia), or the "Silicon Fen" (UK), "Silicon Wadi" (Israel), and "Silicon Plateau" (India). Both "Cornell Tech" and "Silicon Island" fall squarely within this pattern. Here, "innovation models" are no longer understood as an analytic abstraction, simplification, or metaphor – such as "linear model," "innovation systems," or "triple helix" – but as "modeled after the successful practice of a real-world institution or region" – a role model rather than a theoretical model. In contrast, abstract theoretical models have remained largely within specialist discourses and have not entered public and broader policy imagination in similarly pervasive ways.

This turn to "models of practice" marks a fundamental reconceptualization of innovation's real and imagined landscape. Defined by the practice of a real place rather than by theory, it links the notion of an "ideal model" to a process of comparative benchmarking, thus reframing the purpose and mechanics of innovation around an aspirational goal of similitude. Indeed, much of the recent innovation literature has been concerned with pinning down "best practice models" – including Silicon Valley and MIT – and turning them into standardized toolkits and how-to guides. In this new paradigm, knowledge of the inner workings of Silicon Valley or MIT has become a desirable form of innovation expertise in and of itself, with resulting pressures to codify tacit knowledge in ways that lend themselves to circulation. This authorization of MIT and Silicon Valley as models is reminiscent of Thomas Gieryn's "truth-spots" as spaces that derive their authority from being both field-sites for the empirical observation of local reality (in this case: the inner workings of innovation) and sites of controlled experimentation that can lead to the extension of the local into universal scientific truth (Gieryn 2006). In contrast, best practice models of innovation derive their authority, and their ability to circulate, from the efforts of translocal communities of practice to instrumentalize perceived success stories and to apply them to other contexts.

We call this three-fold shift in our understanding of innovation (1) as the go-to answer for policy challenges and a touchstone for governmental legitimacy; (2) subject to standardization in response to increasing pluralism; and (3) conceived in terms of competitive benchmarking and implemented through "best practice transfer" – the *practice turn* in innovation policy. It is indicative of, and reinforced by, a broader trend in innovation policy towards comparative benchmarking, where policy-makers habitually look to experts for pre-packaged plug-in solutions that promise a quick fix for complex policy problems. As an analytic lens, it is consistent with repeated efforts in STS toward theorizing practice (Schatzki et al., 2001). In particular, it is consistent with practice theorists' call for qualitatively different kinds of analysis at the meso-scale, taking into account collective phenomena such as shared goals or mutual monitoring, while not resorting to explaining them as residuals of macro-structures at the individual scale.

Three best practice models

Best practice models of innovation, the bread and butter of innovation policy after the "practice turn", are plentiful. However, several stand out in terms of promise and prominence (Table 31.1).

First, the MIT model is an *institutional* best practice model. In common usage, it is taken to mean that excellent technical universities in conjunction with supportive ecosystems are a master key to technology commercialization and regional development. MIT is a product of the American land grant college tradition that introduced an economic mission to the academic ivory tower. Famed for its achievements in basic and applied science as well as its economic impact, MIT's success is often traced back to its key role in the development of innovative Second World War military technology, which set the stage for a long and successful history of capturing government contract research, establishing close ties to industry, and producing entrepreneurs in an assembly-line fashion. MIT's "impact of innovation" has been documented in regular publications by the Kauffman Foundation, BankBoston, and MIT itself, which find,

Table 31.1 Three widely circulated "best-practice" models of innovation

Model of Practice	MIT model	Silicon Valley model	Responsible Innovation model
Unit of analysis	Institutional	Regional	Community (innovators + recipients/users)
Imagined key to innovation	Excellent technical universities in supportive ecosystems	Mix of excellent academic institutions, high-tech industries, venture capital, close networks of highly skilled individuals with entrepreneurial mindset, self-organized in decentralized cluster	Consulting with citizens on major questions of sociotechnical change to achieve acceptance and improve innovation
Origin	Cambridge, MA	Northern California	European Union
Uptake	E.g., 'KIT' (Germany), 'Masdar Institute of Science and Technology' (Abu Dhabi), 'SkolTech' (Russia), 'Cornell Tech' (USA)	E.g., 'Silicon Fen' (UK), 'Silicon Wadi' (Israel), 'Silicon Plateau' (India), 'Silicon Island' (USA)	E.g., Horizon 2020 'Science with and for Society' (EC), standardized RRI tools, proliferating public engagement and open innovation practices

for example, that there are "over 30,000 active companies founded by living MIT alumni, employing 4.6 million people and generating annual world revenues of nearly $2 trillion. This group of companies, if its own nation, would be the 10th-largest economy in the world" (Roberts et al., 2015). In the innovation policy literature, MIT is frequently cited as living proof of the central role of universities in innovation and their emergence as heavyweight economic actors that increasingly engage in the creation of proprietary knowledge and research commercialization through spin-offs or licensing. The "MIT model" has repeatedly been the target of scholarly attempts to abstract MIT's institutional practice into a theoretical model, most notably in the "entrepreneurial university" (Etzkowitz, 2002) and "triple helix" models, in which innovation occurs at the intersection of universities, industry, and government (Etzkowitz and Leydesdorff, 2000).

A second, arguably even more prominent best practice is the **Silicon Valley model**. Silicon Valley signals that the key to innovation success is located at the *regional* level, which is usually understood to include a mix of excellent academic institutions, technology industries, venture capital, close networks of highly skilled individuals, and a risk-taking mentality that together drive an abundance of start-ups and multinational companies. The success of the Silicon Valley region has been tied to its capacity to repeatedly re-invent itself, from an economically lagging agricultural area to an eager government contractor in the post-Second World War era, a center of semi-conductor and electronics manufacturing in the 1970s and 1980s, to the dot-com boom and rise of Internet giants of today. The "valley" metaphor emphasizes physical proximity between mutually synergistic actors and organizations – high "concentrations of skill and technology" paired with a nimble, "decentralized process of experimentation and learning," in the words of Saxenian's (1996) classic *Regional Advantage*. Academic scholarship on Silicon Valley has spawned a rich literature on regional innovation systems, clusters, and ecosystems, and has been at the forefront of a relatively recent turn to the meso-scale of city-regions. Silicon Valley is often cited as evidence for a blatantly unequal, "spiky" geography of innovation, where a few highly innovative and economically prosperous regions dominate the global innovation landscape. Moreover, the Valley's success is frequently associated with the stereotypical tech-entrepreneur and a particular set of social characteristics such as openness to change and failure, a welcoming attitude towards risk and disruption, and an outsized ambition to "change the world," "improve the life of a billion people," or bring about "singularity"-type game-changers – frequently paired with a certain disregard for established social orders, equality concerns, and government regulation. Silicon Valley, too, has been the target of scholarly attempts at codifcation and practice transfer (Bania et al., 1993; Bresnahan and Gambardella, 2004; Casper, 2007)

A third and relatively recent best-practice model of innovation is that of Responsible Innovation. Responsible Innovation is aimed at the *community* of innovators and innovation recipients such as affected publics and users, who are in turn envisioned as part of the creation and dissemination processes of emerging technologies. The model thus shares some common ground with open innovation approaches, although it is usually less firm-centered. It is commonly interpreted to imply that researchers, governments and firms should consult with citizens on major questions of sociotechnical change for reasons of both social acceptance and efficient development. Responsible Innovation owes some of its prominence to the political presumption holding that modern publics, if properly consulted and managed through a suite of "technologies of democracy," will not challenge policy elites' judgments concerning the benefits of innovation. It ties into recurring patterns of perceived crises regarding the risks and failures of new technologies around the world – including the BSE crisis to the GMO debacle in Europe. Responsible Innovation builds on earlier and related concepts such as the public understanding of science, public engagement, anticipatory governance, and open innovation. Hence, it is not tied to one specific region of origin. Yet, it has emerged and been circulated most prominently as a governance framework for research and innovation in the European Union (as witnessed for example by the Horizon 2020 funding programs), with increasing spillovers into North America and Asia. Responsible Innovation is arguably the least formalized model, yet the desire for standardized toolkits and practices is growing, contributing to a flourishing body of literature (RRI Tools, 2015; Stilgoe et al., 2013). In the following section, we analyze the circulation of one of the three models – the "MIT model" – to three different sites. Additional detail can be found in more comprehensive descriptions of the cases (Pfotenhauer et al., 2016; Pfotenhauer and Jasanoff, forthcoming).

The circulation of the MIT model to three countries

United Kingdom

In November 1999, the Cambridge–MIT Institute (CMI) was launched to create "an anglicized version of the 'MIT approach' and all that has delivered in terms of economic dynamism to Boston and the regional economy of New England" (CMI, 2008). CMI was conceived by Gordon Brown as a much-needed rejuvenation for an ailing economy and university system, implemented through a targeted injection of innovation practices directly into the very heart of the British university system. An innovative Cambridge would reassert the UK in the world against the background of ever-rising fears about the decline in British economic leadership and vitality in the wake of de-industrialization, which Brown linked to the "historically weak commercial awareness" of universities, despite the "high quality of academic science in the UK" (DTI, 2001).

CMI was framed as a symmetric "joint venture" between universities of equal standing – an "Institute" rather than a program or partnership, capable of "bringing together two of the world's great universities to build on the complementary strengths of each" (CMI, 2005). Yet, CMI was met with utter skepticism (and at times outright indignation) at Cambridge. According to one MIT faculty member, MIT's first emissaries to Cambridge ("non-Brits with an engineering background [who] could not be less Cambridgey") prompted comments such as: "Who does MIT think it is, parachuting in and telling the University of Cambridge [what to do]?" For many, the working assumption was that Cambridge already excelled in everything it did. Excelling in *innovation*, however, was generally not perceived as a matter of necessity for the standing of the university and rather encountered concern about the impurity of commercialization-driven research.

Consequently, efforts to transplant concrete MIT practices proved challenging. For example, Cambridge refused to touch its doctoral programs to implement an industrially linked PhD, and struggled institutionally to accommodate interdisciplinary master's programs bridging science, management, and policy. Research at CMI was mainly based on what already existed at Cambridge. At a time when higher education and research funding underwent dramatic cuts, many Cambridge faculty viewed CMI as a "sort of a golden pot of money [...] with no commitment. They didn't care about whether CMI did well or poorly, whether the government was right or wrong, ... [or] the importance of a 6-year relationship with MIT," one Cambridge faculty remembers. In the end, the "MIT model" was viewed as a kind of institutional add-on that would neither substantially interfere with already existing activities nor fundamentally alter the way in which the university operated, thus arguably under-delivering on its promise in the eyes of many. Hence, Gordon Brown's vision of transforming the UK by injecting MIT practices into one of Britain's most iconic universities collided with the political necessity of a co-equal partnership and the self-images of two institutions with different understandings of their academic mission.

Portugal

While Portugal's dignified university system stands up to historical comparison with the UK, its modern university landscape was shaped by a half-century of dictatorship until 1974, when a leftist revolution ushered in a fledgling democracy, a wave of nationalization, the loss of the colonies, and a massive brain drain by former elites. This experience of disruption continues to shape the country to the present day. Universities after 1974 primarily underwent a push for social and institutional equality, effectively inhibiting the emergence of strong national research universities and an entrepreneurial orientation (Heitor and Horta, 2011). The post-revolutionary years contributed to a Portuguese image and self-imagination as a "peripheral," "catching-up" country (Aiginger, 2004; Lains, 2003), which was closely tied to narratives of loss, self-inflicted backwardness (Pfotenhauer and Jasanoff, forthcoming).

In early 2006, the Portuguese government launched the MIT Portugal Program (MPP) to "leverage MIT's experience in [science, technology, and higher education] to strengthen the country's knowledge base through an investment in human capital and institution building" (Pfotenhauer et al., 2013). The main figure behind the initiative, Secretary of State Manuel Heitor, was a prolific innovation policy scholar who argued for the key role of universities in the knowledge economy and the imperative for Portugal to participate in international knowledge networks and risk bold institutional change (Conceição et al., 2003; Conceição and Heitor, 2005).[2] The "MIT model" was thus not framed as a minimally invasive intervention as in the UK; rather, it was a conscious break with inherited structures and constraints in the name of "catching up," as Portugal turned to external assistance to make up for the self-inflicted fractures of the past. In contrast to Cambridge, Portugal embraced incomparably more drastic interventions: for example, MPP introduced seven American-style graduate programs – four PhDs with integrated master's and three professional master's programs – all taught in English and with an unprecedented curricular focus on innovation. Portuguese junior faculty were encouraged to visit MIT and audit MIT classes on innovation to adapt them for a Portuguese context (for example, more than twenty Portuguese faculty audited MIT's popular "innovation teams" course, in which students develop business plans for emerging biotech research in cooperation with company partners). At the same time, MPP was leveraged to jump-start entire new research fields drawing on expertise at MIT, including stem cell research.

Portugal's history also explains why the MIT model was envisaged in a less elitist fashion than in the UK. In line with the enduring post-revolution tradition of egalitarianism, rather than affirming the leadership of a single elite institution, MPP included a consortium of seven Portuguese universities. This structure was also intended to create "distributed critical mass" across several universities, recognizing that no single institution was on a par with MIT or Cambridge. Here, the MIT model acted as a kind of "glue," as one Portuguese senior government official put it, to incentivize Portuguese universities to work together through the opportunity to jointly work with MIT.

Singapore

The history of the "MIT model" in Singapore is long and multi-layered. The first major agreement between Singapore and MIT, the Singapore–MIT Alliance (SMA), was launched in 1999, primarily as a long-distance educational collaboration to "develop talented human capital for Singapore's industries, universities, and research establishments" and to "attract and retain the very best engineering and life sciences graduate students and researchers from across Asia" (SMA, 2005). Here, the key to the "MIT model" was understood to be research-intensive graduate programs with a strongly applied orientation and interdisciplinary curricula, which set SMA apart from traditional engineering approaches and departmental structures at Singapore's public universities. With the 2003 renewal of the program, Singapore also seized the opportunity to move away from classical engineering areas such as computer science, micro- and nanosystems, and manufacturing, and turn to the life sciences, which were seen as the most promising innovative industry in the 21st century (Chuan Poh, 2010). This shift mirrored parallel trends at MIT and Route 128 at that time and was part of a broader transition in Singapore's self-image from "intelligent island to biopolis" (Clancey, 2012).

In 2006, MIT and Singapore launched the Singapore MIT Alliance for Research and Technology (SMART) – which changed the focus of the "MIT model" from education to research. SMART aimed to attract MIT scientists to work in Singapore for extended periods on Singaporean research priorities. In the words of a senior administrator, Singapore could not afford "to wait until it's grown [a domestic research talent pool] before we can do significant research." At the same time, SMART adopted MIT's institutional best practices of technology transfer by establishing an Innovation Centre modeled after MIT's Deshpande Center.

In 2010, MIT and Singapore signed yet another agreement to jointly establish the new Singapore University of Technology and Design (SUTD), with ambitions "no less" than MIT itself to "create a new type of technologically grounded leader" that has the "the passion to literally change the world" (SUTD, 2012). SUTD was born out of the fear that the key factor hampering innovation was a lack of creativity, not engineering capability (Remaking Singapore

Committee, 2003), and that Singapore needed to transition "from efficiency-driven growth to innovation-driven growth" (Tan and Phang, 2005). To achieve this, the government decided to break decisively with the established Singaporean research and education landscape and build "something different from the existing institutions," according to Singapore's Prime Minister Lee Hsien Loong – for which it curiously turned *again* to the "MIT model" (even though MIT had helped existing structures in the past). SUTD reflects many of the latest trends at MIT, including a focus on design, creativity, and other educational "best practices" developed by MIT-internal task forces (Pfotenhauer, forthcoming).

SMA, SMART, and SUTD represent an even more elusive, constantly changing "MIT model" – yet one that at each point remains closely tied to the Singaporean imagination of what innovation is and which perceived deficits it ought to address. This repeated adaptation befits a young and decidedly modernist country that has narrated its inception as a "tabula rasa" (Lim, 2004) and defined its national identity and policies through extreme outward orientation, vigilance, and responsiveness (Choon, 2004). The repeated renewal of linkages to MIT further resonates with the decades-long concern for economic and geopolitical sovereignty and the pursuit of cohesive identity outside its own multi-ethnic and turbulent history through extreme outward orientation and constant adaptation. The "MIT model" arguably retains a particularly firm grip on Singapore's imagination of progress due to a sizable group of MIT alumni among Singaporian leadership, including current Prime Minister Tony Tan, S.M. '64.

Imaginaries of innovation

The brief case studies above reveal how three innovation initiatives in three countries envisioned fundamentally different things – different challenges, different solutions, different organizational models – when trying to foster innovation with the help of the same model – the "MIT model." Given this lack of a common definition, how should we make sense of the model's manifest appeal to a common innovation identity and its thriving circulation around the globe? How can we reconcile the appeal to a universal "best practice" despite the evident divergences in perceived local needs?

One productive theoretical inroad emanates from Benedict Anderson's (1983) work, which explains cohesion in identity within nation-states through the social and material construction of "imagined communities."[3] These communities are "imagined" because it is impossible for one member to meet, let alone meaningfully connect to, all other members; yet, a common identity develops because of shared reference points, symbols, experiences, and materially mediated patterns of collective life. As Anderson implied, technologies of communication play a key role in enabling this cohesion: in particular, the printing press and the power of print capitalism put everyone literally "on the same page" with regard to events that should concern a society and may affect its well-being, thus creating a sense of synchronized time and shared experience.

Accepting Anderson's focus on shared imaginations as a point of departure, we accord technology a more plastic and creative role in the projection of collective societal futures. Modern societies, as Jasanoff and Kim (2015) have argued, steer and develop themselves in important part through "sociotechnical imaginaries," defined as "collectively held, institutionally stabilized, and publicly performed visions of desirable futures" that are "attainable through, and supportive of, advances in science and technology". Innovation after the practice turn mobilizes sociotechnical imaginaries in what we might call *imaginaries of innovation*, on two levels: first, the "MIT model" both sustains and is sustained by a transnational community of policy-makers for whom the model acts as a common reference point in places as geographically dispersed as the

UK, Portugal, and Singapore. This community is professionally committed to a range of social practices associated with the MIT model – from the imperative of identifying "best practices" to shared processes of appraisal, circulation of standard packages (Fujimura, 1992) and re-organization of institutional structures according to the model, communication with the same cadre of innovation experts, relative benchmarking vis-à-vis MIT, etc. In this logic, *to become an innovative institution or region* is to compete within frames of reference set by innovation leaders such as the United States, and, by extension, to accept MIT as a shared reference point. Those not able to recreate MITs and the like on their own soil are de facto not competing in innovation as collectively imagined.

Second, however, the far-ranging reorganization of society and its institutions in the name of innovation necessarily interacts with communal scales of socio-cultural cohesion and meaning-making – i.e., those underwritten by shared histories, political commitments, and practices of governance. As a result, globally traveling imaginaries such as the "MIT model" remain pegged to situated imaginations at the nation-state level, but also (as illustrated in Jasanoff and Kim, 2015) in regions, institutions or user communities. CMI, for instance, was informed by a felt need in the UK for successful translation of science into industry to retain global economic leadership. It was envisioned as a targeted, local injection of innovation capability, built upon an elitist sense that this national crisis could and should be addressed through one of the country's preeminent academic institutions, which (perhaps understandably) did not feel the pressure to change. CMI tried to implement the "MIT model" by adding specific innovation activities to existing Cambridge structures, with minimal disruption to the overall system. MPP, by contrast, was born out of Portugal's social and institutional heritage of decolonization, post-dictatorship shock, and subsequent self-image as a "delayed," "catching-up" country, which in the national consciousness was ascribed to self-inflicted internal causes. Portugal's historical experience called both for a less elitist, more societally consensual, multi-institutional approach, as well as a more decisive import of foreign practices to break with existing institutional traditions. The "MIT model" was envisioned as an external aid to overcome this self-inflicted lag and catch up with other countries whose development Portugal had once helped spark. Finally, Singapore's SMA, SMART, and SUTD represent a sociotechnical imaginary of maintaining economic, geopolitical, and cultural sovereignty, and strong outward orientation in science and technology. Implemented through multiple generations of partnerships, the "MIT model" was envisioned in Singapore as a functionally distinct set of enhancement activities – graduate education in traditional engineering and later bio-engineering, research and tech-transfer, creativity and design in undergraduate education – implemented in a sequenced fashion that not only mirrored parallel shifts in governmental priorities but also reflected Singapore's decades-long concern to remain relevant within global networks of circulation.

The above case studies suggest that these two layers of imagination – the global community of innovation policy-makers and practitioners who imagine practices that travel, and the imagined local community of socio-political meaning-making in which practices stick – co-exist at each location in their own locally specific configurations. They may endure side by side or even collide (as in Cambridge's rejection of the "MIT model" as imagined by Gordon Brown); support one another (Portugal's mobilization of the "MIT model" as part of a catching-up with modernization); or co-evolve with one other (Singapore's repeated adoption of various "MIT models" over time). The juxtaposition of two layers of imagination explains why "best practice models" can be mobilized as epistemic and political resources for defining an institution or region as part of a local *and* a global community of innovation, thus blurring distinct semiotic frames of reference. *Imaginaries of innovation* thus also allow us to understand heterogeneity in innovation practice against the presumed universality of innovation theory, by tracing how practices change when they travel while at the same time acknowledging innovation's global reference points, circulations, and entanglements.[4] The comparative cases show how *traveling imaginaries* are inflected by local understandings of the kinds of futures that seem worth aspiring to, the legitimate mechanisms for attaining them, and the arguments in favor of innovation that seem plausible.

Admittedly, this brief analysis raises more questions than it answers. For one, it challenges us to study in a more comprehensive fashion how and where different innovation imaginaries travel, how they are locally interpreted, and how innovation itself is co-produced with other imaginaries at various sites. It is conceivable that the three traveling imaginaries identified in this chapter (i.e., Silicon Valley, MIT, Responsible Innovation) could be actively "pitched" against one another in some places while converging in others, providing added clues as to why some models stick while others "fail." It is also tempting to ask how the circulation of these models feeds back into the redefinition of each model at its site of origin. MIT's close ties to Singapore, and educational and research experiences over decades of partnerships, have had considerable impact on MIT's own self-imagination and strategic orientation.[5] Finally, the rise of innovation to policy prominence prompts us to ask what social and political functions the concept of innovation, and its standardized forms of practice, are playing in broader discursive and political arenas (Pfotenhauer et al., forthcoming). Here, questions as to which societal deficits and solutions are articulated, or elided, through innovation discourse could provide a fruitful way forward.

Acknowledgements

This work was supported by the NSF Science of Science and Innovation Policy (SciSIP) Program under Collaborative Grant No. 1262263 'Technology, Collaboration, Learning: Modeling Complex International Innovation Partnerships' (Sebastian Pfotenhauer) and the NSF Science, Technology and Society (STS) Program under Grant No. 1457011 'Traveling Imaginaries of Innovation' (Sheila Jasanoff).

Notes

1 Cornell University's main campus, including its engineering school and the bulk of basic research facilities, are located in the small university town of Ithaca, New York, but Weill Cornell Medicine, the university's medical school, is located in midtown Manhattan.
2 Heitor was also an official external examiner of Cambridge–MIT.
3 Elsewhere (Pfotenhauer, forthcoming), Pfotenhauer has suggested that "best practices" can be understood as "boundary objects" that are, to use Star AND Griesemer's (1989) definition, "both plastic enough to adapt to local needs and constraints of the several parties employing them, yet robust enough to maintain a common identity across sites." Yet, while the concept of boundary objects explains how diverse initiatives can effectively be perceived as part of the same model, emphasizing that "consensus is not necessary for cooperation nor for the successful conduct of work," it is less suited to tackle questions of circulation, standardization of practice, or broader stabilizations as part of durable political culture and the institutional superstructures, which are the focus of this chapter.
4 This self-conscious and partly instrumental identity-building through innovation initiatives adopts a different approach to *imaginaries* than the unexpected, quasi-accidental synchronization of society through the printing press presented by Anderson. Our approach necessitates a more thorough weaving-together of social and technical aspects in explaining how the nation-state (or an innovative region) mobilizes, and is being reconfigured by, innovation as a political resource. As an analytic lens, sociotechnical imaginaries are particularly helpful in calling attention to large-scale national science and technology initiatives as key sites of contemporary state-making and societal reconfiguration, and vice versa.
5 More research is underway to detail these initial findings.

References

Aiginger, K., 2004. "The bumpy road of convergence: The catching up experience in Portugal, Spain and Greece". *Estud. Econ. Apl.* 22(3), 451–473.

Anderson, B.R., 1983. *Imagined communities: Reflections on the Origin and Spread of Nationalism.* Verso, London.

Bania, N., Eberts, R.W. and Fogarty, M.S., 1993. "Universities and the Startup of new companies: can we generalize from Route 128 and Silicon Valley?" *Rev. Econ. Stat.* 75, 761. doi:10.2307/2110037.

Bellafante, G., 2011. "New York as a Tech hot spot: is it just a sci-fi dream?" *The New York Times,* 18 November [Online]. Available at: www.nytimes.com/2011/11/20/nyregion/new-york-as-a-tech-hot-spot-is-it-just-a-sci-fi-dream.html.

Braczyk, H.-J., Cooke, P. and Heidenreich, M. (Eds.), 2004. *Regional Innovation Systems: The Role of Governances in a Globalized World,* 2nd ed. Routledge.

Bresnahan, T. and Gambardella, A., 2004. *Building High-Tech Clusters: Silicon Valley and Beyond.* Cambridge University Press, Cambridge; New York.

Casper, S., 2007. "Creating Silicon Valley in Europe: Public policy towards new technology industries". (OUP Catalogue). Oxford University Press.

Choon, B.K., 2004. "Narrating imagination", in: Choon, B.K., Pakir, A., Kiong, T.C. (eds.), *Imagining Singapore.* Eastern Universities Press, Singapore.

Chuan Poh, L., 2010. "Singapore betting on biomedical sciences". *Issues in Science and Technology,* 26 (3).

Clancey, G., 2012. "Intelligent Island to Biopolis: smart minds, sick bodies and millennial turns in Singapore". *Science, Technology and Society,* 17(1), 13–35. doi:10.1177/097172181101700102.

CMI, 2008. *Accelerating Innovation by Crossing Boundaries: The Cambridge MIT Institute 2000–2006.*

CMI, 2005. "Cambridge MIT Institute Annual Report".

Conceição, P. and Heitor, M., 2005. *Innovation for All? Learning from the Portuguese Path to Technical Change and the Dynamics of Innovation.* Praeger, Santa Barbara, CA.

Conceição, P., Heitor, M. and Veloso, F., 2003. "Infrastructures, incentives, and institutions: Fostering distributed knowledge bases for the learning society". *Technol. Forecast. Soc. Change* 70, 583–617. doi:10.1016/S0040-1625(03)00046-5.

Cooke, P., Laurentis, C.D., Todtling, F., and Trippl, M., 2009. *Regional Knowledge Economies: Markets, Clusters and Innovation.* Edward Elgar Publishing.

Cornell Chronicle, 2011. "'Game-changing' tech campus goes to Cornell, Technion", www.news.cornell.edu/stories/2011/12/nyc-chooses-cornell-technion-build-tech-campus (accessed 5.3.15).

DTI, 2001. *UK Innovation Performance: Strengths, Weaknesses, Opportunities, Threats and Main Problems.* UK Department of Trade and Industry.

Etzkowitz, H., 2002. *MIT and the Rise of Entrepreneurial Science.* Routledge, New York.

Etzkowitz, H. and Leydesdorff, L., 2000. "The dynamics of innovation: from National Systems and 'Mode 2' to a Triple Helix of university–industry–government relations". *Res. Policy* 29, 109–123. doi:10.1016/S0048-7333(99)00055-4.

Fujimura, J.H., 1992. "Crafting Science: standardized packages, boundary objects, and translation", in: Pickering, A. (Ed.), *Science as Practice and Culture.* University of Chicago Press, pp. 168–211.

Godin, B., 2006. "The Linear model of innovation: the historical construction of an analytical framework". *Sci. Technol. Hum. Values* 31, 639–667. doi:10.1177/0162243906291865.

Godin, B. and Lane, J.P., 2013. "Pushes and Pulls hi(S)tory of the Demand pull model of innovation". *Sci. Technol. Hum. Values* 38, 621–654. doi:10.1177/0162243912473163.

Heitor, M. and Horta, H., 2011. "Science and technology in Portugal: From late awakening to the challenge of knowledge-integrated communities", in: Neave, G., Amaral, A. (Eds.), *Higher Education in Portuga,l 1974–2009.* Springer Netherlands, Dordrecht, pp. 179–226.

Jasanoff, S. and Kim, S.-H. (Eds.), 2015. *Dreamscapes of Modernity: Sociotechnical Imaginaries and the Fabrication of Power.* University of Chicago Press, Chicago; London.

Lains, P., 2003. "Catching up to the European core: Portuguese economic growth, 1910–1990". *Explor. Econ. Hist.* 40, 369–386.

Lim, W.S.W., 2004. *Architecture, Art, Identity in Singapore: Is There Life After Tabula Rasa?* Singapore: Asian Urban Lab.

Marceau, J., 2008. "Introduction: Innovation in the city and innovative cities." Innovation Management, Policy and Practice, 10, 136–145. doi:10.5172/impp.453.10.2-3.136.

Pfotenhauer, S.M., Juhl, J. and Aarden, E., forthcoming. "A solution looking for a problem? Interrogating the 'Deficit Model' of Innovation."

Pfotenhauer, S.M., forthcoming. "Understanding 'Best-practice transfer' in innovation: expertise, legitimacy, and identity in the globalizing MIT model", in: Wisnioski, M., Hintz, E., Stettler (eds.), *Can Innovators Be Made?*

Pfotenhauer, S.M., Jacobs, J.S., Pertuze, J.A., Newman, D.J., Roos, D.T., 2013. "Seeding Change through international university partnerships: the MIT-Portugal Program as a Driver of internationalization, networking, and innovation". *High. Educ. Policy* 26, 217–242. doi:10.1057/hep.2012.28.

Pfotenhauer, S.M. and Jasanoff, S., forthcoming. "Panacea or Diagnosis? Imaginaries of Innovation and the 'MIT model' in Three Political Cultures". *Social Studies of Science.*

Pfotenhauer, S.M., Wood, D., Roos, D., and Newman, D., 2016. "Architecting complex international science, technology, and innovation partnerships (CISTIPs): a study of four global MIT collaborations". *Technol. Forecast. Soc. Change* 104, 38–56. doi:doi:10.1016/j.techfore.2015.12.006.

Remaking Singapore Committee, 2003. "Changing Mindsets, deepening relationships: the report of the remaking Singapore committee" (chaired by Vivian Balakrishnan). Singapore: The Committee.

Roberts, E.B., Murray, F. and Kim, J.D., 2015. *Entrepreneurship and Innovation at MIT: Continuing Global Growth and Impact.* Martin Trust Center for MIT Entrepreneurship.

RRI Tools, 2015. "Fostering Responsible research & innovation" www.rri-tools.eu/ (accessed 3.5.16).

Saxenian, A., 1996. *Regional Advantage: Culture and Competition in Silicon Valley and Route 128.* Harvard University Press.

Schatzki, T.R., Knorr Cetina, K., and Savigny, E. von (eds.), 2001. *The Practice Turn in Contemporary Theory.* Routledge.

SMA, 2005., "SMA Homepage – Prospective Students (CPE)", http://web.mit.edu/sma/students/programmes/cpe.htm (accessed 2.24.14).

Star, S.L., Griesemer, J.R., 1989. "Institutional Ecology, 'translations' and boundary objects: amateurs and professionals in Berkeley's Museum of Vertebrate Zoology, 1907–39". *Soc. Stud. Sci.* 19, 387–420. doi:10.1177/030631289019003001.

Stilgoe, J., Owen, R., and Macnaghten, P., 2013. "Developing a framework for responsible innovation". *Res. Policy* 42, 1568–1580. doi:10.1016/j.respol.2013.05.008.

SUTD, 2012. "SUTD President's message", www.sutd.edu.sg/presidents_message.aspx (accessed 3.2.15).

Tan, K.-S. and Phang, S.-Y., 2005. *From Efficiency-Driven to Innovation-Driven Economic Growth: Perspectives from Singapore.* World Bank Publications.

The New Yorker, 2012. "Silicon Island". *The New Yorker.* www.newyorker.com/culture/culture-desk/silicon-island (accessed 5.3.15).

32

WHAT IS SCIENCE CRITIQUE? LESSIG, LATOUR

Philip Mirowski

This handbook makes the case for the need for Science and Technology Studies (STS) to address and analyze problems of political economy. But just as science operates in a world of political and economic forces, so too does STS. The aim of this chapter is to consider some of the ways that the field of STS has itself been shaped by the larger political program of neoliberalism. Consequently, I would like to examine two important theorists of the role of critique in the study of science: Larry Lessig and Bruno Latour. I recognize that Lessig is not often portrayed as participating in the conversation within science studies; however, it is a little-appreciated fact that both were heavily influenced by neoliberal political thought, a fact which makes them more instructive to compare and contrast.

The main reason to meditate on this duo is that they each, in different ways, attempt to respond to the challenge that, if one accepts some version of a social constructivist approach to the generation of scientific knowledge, then what should be the implications for political action in the rough and tumble world of power and money? Now, many contemporary political activists from Noam Chomsky to Naomi Klein feel that they can sidestep this problem simply by treating contemporary natural sciences as occupying a special status, subject to a dispensation wherein challenge and critique is not an option. For them, everything is simply as prosaic as they insist things seem. They claim to deploy 'good science' to defeat their political enemies, although such victories do seem few and far between. Such science reification may seem potent for many political activists, but is not a serious option for science studies; however diverse in traditions, the field nevertheless tends to be united in a self-image of vanguard critique of science and scientists.

The utter failure of using 'good science' as a club to beat your opponents within an era when science itself has become an adjunct of money and power—for instance, in the widespread use of supposed anti-denialism to gag the anti-GMO movement,[1] or appeals to scientific open-mindedness on the part of the geoengineering crowd[2]—would seem to signal that the time has arrived to revisit a few landmark theorists of science critique.

Thus, the question of the relationship of science critique to political activity is one of the most persistently nagging problems of the modern era. It may help to frame the question by looking at a few embodied responses to the problem.

Larry Lessig

Because Lawrence Lessig lives in a rarified world of Supreme Court litigation and TED talks, almost no one in science studies apparently takes him seriously as a reference point, at least when it comes to the questions of science critique and political activism. I would suggest the time has come to rethink that, since in many ways he might be considered an exemplar of a certain model of living in the world of constructivist science and antagonistic politics. Perhaps the reason most of his fans overlook the constructivist side of his knowledge politics is that his commitments in this regard were broached well before he got famous, soon after he took his first job at the University of Chicago Law School.[3] Furthermore, almost all his lauded contributions actually make extensive reference to the history (and to a lesser extent, sociology) of science, because he has been obsessed with the way controversies over knowledge become baked into political practice.

Larry Lessig is a Harvard Law School Professor who initially became famous for his book *Code and Other Laws of Cyberspace* (1999). While not often cited in science studies circles, this book retailed an idea that had been commonplace in science studies back in that era, namely that seemingly neutral technological artifacts could embody and enforce certain political projects, often without the citizen user being aware that they were being subjected to discipline and regimentation behind their backs, so to speak. In *Code*, Lessig plays upon the technical and legal definitions of code in an attempt to collapse the distinction between the design and implementation of computer programs that facilitate communication—and as a result *define* it—and the regulatory role that law has traditionally played. He argued therefore that computer code needs to be subject to the same kind of scrutiny, accessibility, and malleability that one might initially hope is characteristic of our system of laws. Mostly, things have trended in the opposite direction in the interim, which adds piquancy to his saga, since he has had to come to terms with how and whether to carry on political activism when one is on the losing side.

Code was a champion of constructivist studies of technology, perhaps even *avant la lettre*. "Code is never found, it is only ever made, and only ever made by us" (2006, p.6). There he posited the difference between a first generation Internet, forged by noncommercial academics, and a second stage in the 1990s, largely engineered by commercial interests; he warned of a third generation starting to be imposed by an alliance between government and commerce, which would reverse the earlier open architecture. Here he sounded like a more subdued but better dressed Trevor Pinch: "all of us must learn at least enough to see that technology is plastic" (2006, p.32). Even at this early stage, he was conflicted about the role of money and corporate power in this constructivist project: "When commercial interests determine architecture, they create a kind of private law." But then he immediately backtracked: "I am not against private enterprise; my strong presumption in most cases is to let the market produce…" (2006, p.77). Significantly, in light of our comparison of Lessig to Latour, his attempt to extricate himself from this bind was to appeal to some vaguely defined notion of 'power': "the architecture of cyberspace is power in this sense; how it could be different. Politics is about how we decide, how that power is exercised, and by whom" (p.78).

Lessig, perhaps more than a raft of other commentators on the cosmic significance of the Internet, did seem to capture the zeitgeist back then. He deftly managed to combine the staid demeanor of the law professor with the rebellious stance of the hacker, primarily because he tended (at that stage) to locate the nexus of conflict of code as law with computer code at the point of copyright in particular, and intellectual property more broadly.[4] He presented himself as a champion of 'Free Culture' and amateur artist mashups in the early 2000s, reinforced with just enough in the way of case law to maintain his street cred. Whereas others were concerned with furtive attempts to 'steal' music and movies online, he was inclined to justify the Wild West atmosphere of the Web back then as a noble actualization of knowledge and creativity. He was hip enough to realize that the old 'liberal' prescription that, "if you see an injustice then just pass a new law" might appear a little misguided when the very character of law was being upended by technology and disparaged by rebellious artists; but in the end, true to form, he capitulated to that very same logic by helping establish the Creative Commons Foundation, and to institute the Creative Commons license, sometimes known as 'copyleft'. He even issued a revised version of *Code* under the open license, making it available for free over the Internet.[5] Lessig often paid as much attention to format as to content; he was also one of the first to turn the staid academic PowerPoint lecture into a marvel of audiovisual wizardry, realizing that political speech is a form of *performance*. As Osnos writes, "His style is so widely imitated—his TED talks have drawn millions of views—that it's become known as 'the Lessig method.' The man who made *An Inconvenient Truth*, about Al Gore's efforts to draw attention to climate change, describes Lessig's typical presentation as a 'preacher's sermon with an audiovisual team behind it'."

One of the qualities that made him a cultural rock star is that his audience on the Left immediately warmed to him as one of their own— that is, someone who shared their nominal 'liberal' convictions; but the lights and mashups and pizzazz tended to distract from his actual politics. Those of neoliberal inclinations or experience would fairly quickly detect that the man who clerked for Richard Posner (Mont Pelèrin Society member) at the Seventh Circuit Court of Appeals and for Antonin Scalia (AEI, Federalist Society) on the Supreme Court was anything but a stereotypical academic socialist. His early matriculation at the Chicago Law School was worn on his sleeve, for those who understood something about modern politics. While not stridently consistent, his basic orientation has been expressed repeatedly in interviews:

> His father was an ardent Republican, wary of government regulation, and Lessig became a devout member of the National Teen Age Republicans. ... He later ran the campaign of a candidate for the state senate, and lost, halting his budding career in Republican politics. He said, "I was a libertarian. I still think I'm a libertarian; it's just that I understand the conditions in which liberty can flourish. It's liberty where you have the infrastructures of society that make it possible, and one of the elements is a certain commitment to equality. I vote like a Democrat now." To libertarians, Lessig makes a related case against the influence of big money. Americans are deprived of liberty today because, he says, "the government is dependent on the few and not on the many."
>
> *(Osnos, 2014)*

In the manner so beloved by Americans, he displays the insouciant tendency to run together fundamentally incompatible political positions—libertarian, neoliberal, egalitarian—in part because he believes it is his quest to somehow transcend tired dichotomies of Left and Right.[6] It should be noted that this pretense to tinker with and transcend handed-down notions of political categories is characteristic of both thinkers dealt with in this paper. The standard continuum of political action with their preset functional personae and faux-spatial symmetries would naturally seem fetters to those bent upon rethinking science critique.

Sometime in the mid-2000s, Lessig lost confidence that his pursuit of the technicalities of intellectual property in cyberspace were actually addressing the really big injustices in the real world, or even getting at the root problems of power as deployed through knowledge. More to the point, he began to realize that he had to theorize why it was he so often lost previous battles over narrow legal issues that he had believed were simple and straightforward, in particular, in the context of disputes over science critique:

> In one of the handful of opportunities I had to watch Gore deliver his global warming keynote, I recognized a link in the problem that he was describing and the work that I have been doing during this past decade. After talking about the basic inability of our political system to reckon the truth about global warming, Gore observed that this was really just part of a much bigger problem. That the real problem here was (what I will call a "corruption" of) the political process. That our government can't understand basic facts when strong interests have an interest in its misunderstanding. This is a thought I've often had in the debates I've been a part of, especially with respect to IP.[7]

What he had come to realize was that science/technology critique plus the sorts of political engagement one would expect of a Harvard Law Professor—pleading cases before the court, giving talks and building institutions like the Creative Commons License—were not remotely sufficient when it came to seriously plotting political strategy to win; one should not simply rest satisfied with the noble gesture. One had to begin to understand the structural causes that guaranteed that his opponents would prevail, and that included the structural causes behind the very nature of technological knowledge itself.

Lessig thus has come to exemplify what I consider one of the main contemporary political responses to the problems thrown up by intimations of failure of science critique. He has opted to locate the fundamental failure of major institutions as a matter of *corruption* of the institutions in question. This may have grown out of an attempt to draft him personally to run for Congress, which he decided was a futile path after giving it some consideration. Initially, Lessig seemed to believe that Internet technology could serve as an effective counterweight to political corruption, for instance by setting up a dedicated Wiki to encourage people to report instances of corrupt Congressional behavior. But just as he was getting started, the *Citizens United v. Federal Election Commission* decision was handed down by the Supreme Court in 2010, accepting that campaign contributions were a somewhat modulated form of political speech, and striking down limits on corporate contributions. It brought home to Lessig that raw power was reconfiguring the very meaning of knowledge. From thenceforth, his activist inclinations resulted in increasingly quixotic projects to supposedly root out the corrupt elements from the US Congress, combined with an intellectual project to explain how he might believe that money was the root of this corruption.

It should be made abundantly clear that the neoliberal icons that mentored Lessig would never allow that money could be a corrupting influence: not on people, not on governments, and certainly not on knowledge and technology. His most recent book *Republic, Lost* as well as his 2014 Berlin Family Lectures are attempts to somehow square the circle of remaining a neoliberal fellow traveler and simultaneously preaching hellfire concerning the pervasive corruption of American politics. The most famous of these attempts was launched as a counterintuitive experiment: the Mayday PAC, launched in 2012, a political action committee (PAC) that would spend millions of dollars in 2014 in an attempt to elect congressional candidates who are intent on passing campaign-finance reform—and to defeat those who are not. It was a super PAC designated to drive other PACs into extinction. Stephen Colbert had done something similar on Comedy Central, but Lessig did not approach it as a pedagogic stunt, but rather a serious expression of one of his core beliefs—it would take serious money to defeat serious money, he insisted. He tapped the hipster crowd by setting up a Kickstarter campaign for small donations. He himself spent substantial time hitting up large donors, and adopted the motto 'Embrace the irony'.

In a bracing lesson for postmodern irony, the Mayday PAC turned out a crashing failure in 2014. Almost none of the candidates supported were elected.[8] The question that was hard to avoid after the debacle was how much of this was bad luck, and how much of it should be attributed to some fundamental flaws in the political theory that undergirded the Lessig crusade. Not unexpectedly, a believer in the fundamental plasticity of technology was inclined to propound that political and Internet technologies could be readily adapted to support his position: "You've got Uber, which is the picture of innovation that gets stopped by all these local rent-seekers who have their taxi medallions. That is the dynamic we've got to change." Mayday, he said, "was a game-changing bet. This is what Silicon Valley loves".[9] However, it should be pointed out that Uber does not itself exist to root out evil corruption, unless, of course, one is a diehard believer in neoliberalism. Rather, it exists to undermine worker protections by using temp labor to undercut existing wage and price guarantees, plus have a few venture capitalists get rich off the process of destruction. Weirdly, Lessig's own crusade became the furthest thing from 'creative destruction' one might imagine. Lessig's embrace of 'corruption' as the central problem of modern politics more or less dictates that the modality of 'reform' involves tinkering with existing rules and technologies to get at the pockets of decay and malfeasance that are their nominal target, while avoiding considerations of overall market functioning and structures. Most likely, it would end up as an utterly futile appeal to an empty shell of 'morality'.

This brings us to the recent Berlin Family Lectures of 2014, where Lessig engages in an extended bout of science critique that warrants being brought to the attention of many in the science studies community. Lessig candidly admits in Lecture 1 that copyright—the very topic that made him famous in his early career—doesn't really matter much in the larger scheme of things. Whereas the first lecture proceeds to reiterate much of his previous concern over Congressional corruption, the other three lectures deal more explicitly with the corruption of knowledge, and in particular, a critique of Big Pharma and modern psychiatry. Lecture 2 starts with the interesting admission that, "I am a relativist about institutional corruption." He attempts to clarify that he is not particularly interested in moral failure on the part of individual actors, but rather, "influence, within an economy of influence, that weakens the effectiveness of an institution, especially by weakening public trust in that institution." Skating somewhat close to tautology, Lessig then defines corruption as these forms of influence diverting the operation of the institution away from its (stated or inherent) purposes. Although this sequence of definitions studiously avoids all mention of money, every single example in his lectures explicitly considers money as the instrumentality through which an institution is corrupted.

A better grasp of Lessig's notions of corruption may be obtained from surveying his examples scattered throughout the lectures. In Lecture 2, on the financial sector, he considers that Moody's and the other ratings agencies had become corrupted through the introduction of the business model where issuers of mortgage derivatives paid the ratings agencies to rate the quality of their instruments. Lessig explicitly says that the purpose of those institutions was to provide objective truth, and it was that purpose which had been undermined and corrupted in the run-up to the global economic crisis. Significantly, he blames this change on the government in general and the SEC, which he claims sought to outsource their own regulatory activities to the ratings agencies. In this particular instance, he seems not to notice that the precept that money can corrupt knowledge might be *the* major contradiction situated at the heart of the neoliberal project, something he covers up by endorsing the neoliberal talking point that the causes of the crisis all lay in government activities. I will simply remind the audience that the first commandment of the neoliberal thought collective is that markets constitute the greatest information processor known to mankind, and never mislead participants about the truth.[10] A better example of this contradiction comes in Lecture 4, dedicated to corruption in academia, when he relates a story derived from the work of historians of science Robert Whittaker and Lisa Cosgrove.[11]

There Lessig relates the story of the American Psychiatric Association, which sought to displace an earlier Freudian theoretical stance with what would be perceived as a 'more scientific' therapeutic regimen associated with the infamous *Diagnostic and Statistical Manual of Mental Disorders [DSM]*.[12] Basically, Lessig suggests the profession of psychiatrists came to depend very heavily upon drug companies to fund their attempts to stabilize diagnostic definitions in the *DSM*, and by so doing, ended up inventing all manner of dubious illnesses so that drug regimens would be defined as their remedy, and consequently, such that insurance companies would recognize those diseases and reimburse patients and psychiatrists for the drug prescriptions. Lessig accuses the APA of corruption, given that 'free money' led to dereliction of duty in learning about the truth when it came to human mental illness. In his opinion, public loss of trust in psychiatry is justified, insofar as the profession has lost sight of its true aim, which is bringing to light the truth about mental illness, whether it benefits the profession or not.

The problem, here as elsewhere in Lessig's work, is that the diagnostic of 'corruption' actually diverts attention from the multiple structures of power at play in any high-stakes project of the stabilization of knowledge. While the relevance of insurance companies and Big Pharma to the *DSM* should not be denied, Lessig flinches at the notion that one might equally be obliged to look into the state of play of neuroscience at the relevant junctures, and changing notions of disease that were feeding into the dynamic. In the Q&A after the lecture, Lessig openly speculates (with nothing in the way of proof or evidence) that this form of corruption of diagnosis is more of a problem in the human sciences, and that the natural sciences do not encounter similar problems in the stabilization of knowledge. Strangely for one so concerned to be identified as constructivist, he simply rules out the possibility that ongoing changes in the structure of science funding might begin to shift the attention, content and validation procedures across the gamut of science itself. In other words, it is too easy to posit truth as the unwavering consensus goal of an institution, without consideration of how the institutional purpose becomes revised as the target entity itself undergoes revision.

One must acknowledge that Lessig does not wish to indict specific persons in the history of the institutions that he condemns; his is not the politics of scapegoats. He is an advocate of the position that people are not generally evil when corrupt; they are just weak of will and perception when it comes to their ability to see and resist corruption. It is not so much that Lessig buys into the stock American image of flawed institutions staffed with moral and epistemic angels; rather, he favors the Chicago version of so-called 'behavioral economics', where humans are portrayed as flawed thinkers when compared to some neoclassical notion of complete rationality. One might suspect that such pervasive human cognitive biases might present some problems for any simple notion of an external 'truth', but Lessig rapidly passes that by, in favor of citing cognitive weakness as the supposed reason why the actors internal to the institution will not bring about their own reforms from within. In a very Chicago move, it is the political task of people like Lessig (and fellow lawyer Cass Sunstein) to 'nudge' the actors back toward the straight and narrow. Reputedly, no one is coerced, because Lessig and his followers are just restoring their political subjects back to the path they supposedly had chosen all along. Rather conveniently, the Schmittian definition of politics predicated on the friend/enemy distinction is banished from all consideration.

Perhaps the most important aspect of Lessig's thought for people in the social studies of science is the content and character of his proposed remedies and nudges. Here in Lecture 5 he sets out an important precept: from his perspective, policies that induce 'transparency' concerning conflicts of interest will do little or nothing to mitigate corruption. Lessig posits that awareness of conflicts, which in his examples mostly refer to money payments, will have no impact if the actors involved have no idea what to do about their predicament. Here Lessig the constructivist re-emerges, with suggestions that disclosures may alter the social relationships of the persons involved, and not necessarily is a good way. Knowing who holds the purse strings will not remedy cognitive biases infecting various audiences, such as flagging attention by the public as to who pays for what, lack of contextual background for non-specialists, easy manipulation of public through framing of rhetorical techniques, the existence of virtual threats and emoluments, the moral license problem,[13] and more.

Lessig argues counter-intuitively that induced ignorance may actually offset conflicts of interest more effectively than full disclosure.[14] In particular, he argues that if choice of experts in pronouncing on policies were fully 'blinded' in the sense that competing parties were equally uncertain who would be chosen to pronounce upon the truth (perhaps by some randomized process), or precisely how it would be validated, then the credibility and legitimacy of the outcome would be substantially greater than in a pure adversarial system. Note well, Lessig does not seek to devolve expertise to some independent public agency; experts are still paid by the parties, pay to play is still the coin of the realm, and knowledge is still fully commercialized. Lessig nods toward the work of one of his Safra Center colleagues, Marc Rodwin, who has laid out the case for a similar scheme for pharmaceutical clinical trials.[15] Rodwin rejects older statist schemes of independence, such as the NIH or academics paid by the government enjoined to directly conduct independent clinical trials. Instead, he proposes a more neoliberal response: short of totally randomly assigning for-profit Contract Research Organizations (CROs) to individual drug firms to conduct trials, reformers could instead develop a separate regulatory structure which would dictate which CRO could perform which clinical trial, with research protocols also dictated by some outside agency. Rodwin is especially enthusiastic about the imposition of some percentage cap on the amount of trials any single CRO might do for Pharma firms. Presumably, diversity in clientele would tend to encourage greater independence and desire to foster a truth less tied to the purse strings of those calling the tune.

Although Lessig and his colleagues never got around to closely considering the quality of science actually published in the professional journal literature, it seems there exists a parallel reform movement that reasons along much the same lines. While acknowledging that many indicators of the medical literature suggest the quality of reports are degenerating—rising rates of retraction, rampant ghost authorship, the gross exaggerations of statistical significance, and so on—some activists have proposed similar piecemeal reforms reminiscent of the Lessig crusade. Perhaps the best exemplar of this tendency is John Ioannidis at the Stanford University Medical School. In the past, Ioannidis had argued that the preferred counter to the corruption of research is the implementation of a few statistical and research protocols, such as the randomization and blinding discussed by Lessig and Rodwin, the regular application of meta-analysis, and the imposition of what he considers to be 'correct' statistical algorithms. In this previous incarnation, he appeared the rather conventional champion of intensified technical protocols—in layman's terms, more baroque data massaging—to automatically guarantee truth. However, more recently, Ioannidis shows signs of realizing his anti-corruption campaign might require something a bit stronger in the way of social engineering than simple statistical technocracy (Ioannidis, 2014). Figure 32.1 enumerates some of his proposed reforms.

- Large-scale collaborative research.
- Adoption of replication culture.
- Registration (of studies, protocols, analysis codes, datasets, raw data and results).
- Sharing (of data, protocols, materials, software and other tools).
- Reproducibility practices.
- Containment of conflicted sponsors and authors.
- More appropriate statistical methods.
- Standardization of definitions and analyses.
- More stringent thresholds for claiming discoveries or 'successes'.
- Improvement of study design standards.
- Improvements in peer review, reporting and dissemination of research.
- Better training of scientific workforce in methods and statistical literacy.

Figure 32.1 Some research practices that may help increase the proportion of true research findings
Source: Ioannidis (2014)

On the face of it, many of these rather generic 'reforms' sound reasonable, until one starts to delve into the fine structure of details of what it means to counter the 'corruption' of the scientific process. For instance, large-scale collaboration in the modern setting often cashes out as the de-skilling and fine division of labor prosecuted through proprietary Internet platforms, often sold to the unwary as 'Science 2.0'. Under these auspices, intellectual property is far easier to control, and therefore, results are more easily skewed to the interest of the funders.[16] Or consider the supposed content of a 'replication culture'. It is a watchword of science studies that airtight replications are almost impossible to perform, because the decision as to what it means for an experimental set-up to be 'the same' is itself a passel of auxiliary hypotheses with near-infinite flexibility; and in any event, all the rewards and penalties of replication behavior are such that the incentives are arrayed against a replicator, as opposed to someone claiming to extend and amend the results.[17] The attempt to mandate registration of all clinical trials on the government website clinicaltrials.gov is pretty widely conceded to have been a failure, at least within the medical literature.[18] In a world of science riddled with Materials Transfer Agreements, the very notion of 'sharing' has been encumbered with all manner of contractual revisions, and thus deformed beyond recognition.[19] The very structure of peer review has been undergoing profound re-engineering in the last decade, much of it rejigged to capture profit from labor that had been performed for free prior to the spread of social media and the movement of journals online. None of these changes seem to have been instituted with the express goal of 'making scientific research more true'; mostly, they are driven instead by a quest to render it more profitable.

Of course, Ioannidis is vaguely aware of this, although one wonders about Lessig. Ioannidis concludes his article:

> The fine-tuning of existing policies and more disruptive and radical interventions should be considered, but neither presence nor absence of revolutionary intent should be taken as reliable surrogate for actual impact. There are many different scenarios for the evolution of biomedical research and scientific investigation in general, each more or less compatible with seeking truthfulness and human well-being.
>
> *(Ioannidis, 2014, p.5)*

Ioannidis does understand that an imperious injunction to banish all possible conflicts of interest would render published scientific research bland and uninteresting; but the sleeping policeman where he stumbles is located more or less in the same place as Lessig: 'truth' for them seems to exist peacefully inviolate outside all these structures that exist to unearth and validate it. The relationship of social structures to knowledge is many-to-one for both of them, rather than many-to-many. Some institutional structures may seem corrupt from their dual vantage point, but supposedly the definition and content of truth remains impervious to both the rapscallion and the overweening hubris of the crusading reformer. Both Lessig and Ioannidis cannot be bothered to separate out the True and the Useful from the Profitable, because that would necessarily involve consideration of the neoliberal construct of the market as the ideal processor of all human knowledge, more powerful than any individual scientist or intellectual. Perhaps the misbegotten character of our institutions is not simply chalked up to 'corruption', but rather, an integral part of the business plan. Maybe some market processes exist to make people more ignorant; indeed, that is the major insight of the literature on agnotology.[20] This recognition, in turn, would carry Lessig and Ioannidis far outside their normal comfort zones, the boundaries of which are constituted by the belief that only more money can counter the putative ill-effects of old money. As Lessig says, we are enjoined to embrace the irony.

Bruno Latour

I want to explore the possibility that, although most science studies authors are pretty oblivious to Larry Lessig and his writings, their unexamined everyday default political beliefs probably come fairly near to those exemplified by Lessig. By stark contrast, the 'theorist' they most frequently explicitly cite in the introductions to their papers, Bruno Latour, does not at first blush represent or otherwise stand as iconic proxy for many of their political predispositions, if only because a vanishing minority of science studies writers appear to possess a firm grasp on what it is that is particularly 'political' about Latour's voluminous writings.

It would seem on the face of it that it should not be such a stretch to understand more or less what the *appellation* 'Chateau Latour' on the label means, given that Latour the lecturer is all over YouTube, and maintains a lively website.[21] It is a daunting task to attempt to keep up with all his 'projects', art installations, feuilletons, web MOOCs, media appearances, and so forth; he relishes his 'translation' across the contemporary disciplines. But the downside of someone as prolific an author as Latour is that he has changed his tune quite a bit over time, without either openly acknowledging that fact, or even giving signposts as to how his key terms have changed their meaning. There is a phenomenon that he has been conventionally associated with called 'actor-network theory'; but with his usual genial humor he repudiated both the term and the project decades ago. In a 1999 workshop called 'Actor Network and After', Bruno Latour was noted to say that there are four things wrong with actor-network theory: 'actor', 'network', 'theory' and the hyphen.[22] This joke seems not to have dented his popularity much, probably because there was so little of substance in ANT in the first place; no one but the meanest hobgoblins of consistency have been sorry to see it go. In his most recent and abstract philosophical treatise, ANT-style networks are downgraded to merely one of fourteen separate modes of existence—a very deft way to repudiate some inconvenient earlier doctrines.

Furthermore, the science studies community has persisted in feting him for their own; but the fact of the matter is that since his early books *Laboratory Life* and *The Pasteurization of France* (1988), there has been no longer any science to speak of in any of his voluminous writings. After a quarter-century, one might have thought someone in STS might have noticed. While repeatedly pontificating about the abstract character of science and its social surround, Latour evidently no longer pays any attention to how science is actually prosecuted on the ground in this, or any other era. From time to time, he may give a shout out to certain historians of science or STS scholars; but it never gets much beyond name-dropping. In this, he resembles a certain style of professional philosopher, which is no accident, as we shall explore below.

Latour often lectures (and writes) as though he were giving a TED talk, but somehow absent the usual *son et lumière* effects, which is quite an accomplishment.[23] He claims to address scholars in the humanities and social sciences, which is just as well, since most natural scientists don't even accord him the time of day. Many nonscientists are drawn to the man because he has the air of someone on some sort of reformist crusade; but perhaps the most important thing about the comparison of Latour to a figure like Lessig is that there is no evidence of any political activism whatsoever in his numerous public appearances. In the last few years, one must acknowledge that Latour has taken to speaking with some fervor concerning global warming and against 'economics'; but whether this has any palpable scientific or political consequences is something we shall explore below.

There is no (humanly!) concise way to summarize Latour's oeuvre, and in any event, there has grown up around it a secondary literature which attempts to distill and bottle him for the uninitiated.[24] I shall undoubtedly not do this literature justice by simply suggesting that Latour first gained fame by pointing out, quite correctly, that much of modern culture is based upon the presupposition that nature and society are thoroughly separate entities; but, in practice, they were so entangled that the distinction amounted to little of consequence. Latour was of course not the first to insist upon this point, but he was certainly the most entertaining author to drive the notion home to a broad audience, especially in his *Science in Action*. Neoliberals like Friedrich Hayek were also playing around with connectionist metaphors for human action while Latour was still in short pants. Hence there was little novel in the components that eventually went into the (dare I say it) 'construction' of Latour's constructivist crusade; what mattered was how those elements were recombined, reoriented and played out in the nascent field of science studies. Quoting Latour, "Society is constructed, but not socially constructed" (1999, p.198).

Latour so frequently operates on the meta level of the philosopher in his published writings that one must repair to his more pedagogic contexts, such as his MOOC on 'Scientific Humanism,' to observe just what kind of doctrines he would nominally support concerning social thought. Figure 32.2 is taken from that source, and reveals someone of rather conventional Comtist ambitions, leavened with a heavy dose of technological determinism embodied in an idiosyncratic stage theory. Auguste Comte, like Bruno Latour, was famous for insisting that philosophy of science could not be separated from political philosophy. Indeed, Latour's career even seems to follow the rough trajectory of Comte: In the *Course*, Comte said that science was transformed into philosophy; in the *System*, philosophy was transformed into religion. This may become important later, when we enquire into the sorts of political activity he supports in practice.

Latour's opponents were characterized by him not as standard Realists, but in a presumptuous ploy, as the 'Moderns', at least from 1993 onwards.[25] Who it may transpire that belongs in his category 'Modern' has turned out to be extremely vague, but this is because Latour has never really been interested in history. What has become clearer in numerous repetitions of this point over two decades was that the targets in his sights were those who lived by the credo that critique had real consequences. In any number of repetitive diagrams consisting of circles, boxes and arrows, Latour preached that science critique—and, later, religious critique and political critique—were ineffectual because they purportedly undermined themselves. In *Modern Cult* Latour retails this theme as if from the viewpoint of a Western anthropologist: When Moderns encounter the alien Other, they disparage the beliefs of the Others that their human-made fetishes possess divine powers. The Moderns think they know that it is Nature that produces

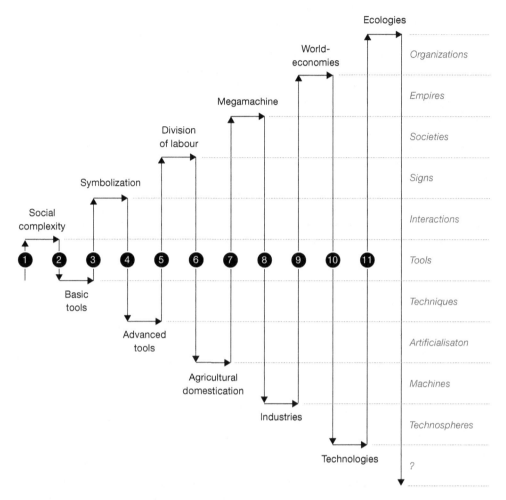

Figure 32.2 Latour's Comtean schema of social differentiation

the mystical effects instead, and by revealing this through critique, they bequeath true power to the Human Other. But then, says Latour, the critique of the Moderns turns upon itself; supposedly objective causes determine the newly freed individual humans, reducing them to mere pawns of metaphysical forces beyond their control. So much for the liberationist promise of critique. Really, says Latour, the Moderns have all along been no different from the Other. Critique operates through dualisms, deceit and sleight of hand; the Moderns delude themselves and the Others with their own fetishes of nature and society. The right way to think about things, hints Latour, is to embrace the status of the Other: the ontology of reality should be considered a flat horizon—or, if you prefer, an arbitrary topology of assemblages and networks defined by local interests—which is equally constructed and pre-existent from the perspectives of other actants. They do it; we do it; success or failure comes in the resultant trials of strength. Critique is the disease; constructivism of this idiosyncratic vintage is the supposed cure.

Since social constructivism was a hot topic in STS in the 1980s and early 1990s, Latour was often lumped together back then with other more purist constructivists, such as David Bloor,

Simon Schaffer and Harry Collins; but some early *contretemps* suggested he did not share their English empiricist tendencies nor their constructivist interpretations. Indeed, what his erstwhile fellow travelers had noted was a penchant for using economistic and/or Hobbesian metaphors when attempting to describe what he insisted was going on in lab life. There were hints that the way forward was to treat humans and non-humans on the same plane of contest and struggle; but most people back then wrote this off as Francophone friskiness, a mere *façon de parler*, not knowing to what extent they were expected to take it seriously. In the meantime, Latour gathered around himself a small band of followers at the Paris Ecole de Mines and was observed to be propounding that they were acolytes of a new 'theory', the afore-mentioned actor-network theory. Perhaps the first lieutenant was Michel Callon, but numerous other platoon leaders were John Law, Vincent Lepinay, Noortje Marres, and Fabien Muniesa.

In my opinion, this was the juncture wherein Latour abandoned any semblance of work in science studies as most others had known it, and became an unapologetic academic philosopher. More strikingly, he became the most armchair sort of philosopher, namely the sort that propounded grand theses about ontology and the nature of the Real. In France, the established philosophers would not deign to usher him into their midst, but in a pattern frequently repeated in the late 20th century, some Americans became besotted with a garbled version of 'French theory',[26] which otherwise fueled his popularity. For instance, Latour visited at the Sociology Department at UCSD in the mid-1980s, which by most accounts eventually did not go well from the viewpoints of faculty. Many people have told me that Latour has always been more popular in the Anglophone world than in Paris, although it is difficult to pin this down with plausible evidence. In any event, starting with *We Have Never Been Modern* (1993), he embarked on his trademark habit of denouncing 'the Moderns', the 'postmodernists', 'sociologists', 'critique', dualism, and a whole host of other categories with distressingly intangible referents. More pertinent to present concerns, Latour kept mentioning 'politics' in oblique ways, but drew back at the precipice of actually saying anything intelligible about political life. In particular, in *Never been Modern* he cites 1989 as 'The Year of Miracles' which he equates with the Fall of the Wall and the return of the repressed breakdown of limitless nature (no explicit discussion of global warming yet, mind you) (1993, pp.8–9); he compares the failure of socialism with ecological obscurantism, although he cannot be bothered to explain of what either consisted, only to prescribe that the way out of the 'dual debacles' is to pretend as though nothing has ever really changed. This might seem a sour prescription for lassitude, but Latour simply denies this: "To notice that we have never been modern and only minor divisions separate us from other collectives does not mean that I am reactionary ... Seen as networks, however, the modern world, like revolutions, permits scarcely anything more than small extensions of practices, slight accelerations in the circulation of knowledge, a tiny extension of societies, miniscule increases in the number of actors, small modifications of old beliefs" (1993, pp.47–48). This political quietism, which could have been propounded just as easily by Karl Popper decades before, starts out as a tiny seed in the 1990s, but grows and grows over time to blossom in much of Latour's later work.

Rather than to try and make sense of Latour's ontological project,[27] I will be concerned here to trace out the changing rationale of his frequent mentions of politics in his later incarnations. This issue seems to have begun to bother some other writers in science studies, and I am lucky to have their commentaries to hand so that I can make what might seem a few rather bald generalizations, in pursuit of my comparative tropes.[28]

The place to start is to acknowledge that, if one's maintained hypothesis was that ontology is really flat, undifferentiated and pretty uniform in ways I have suggested, then you will have serious problems getting most notions of politics off the ground. The artifactual and the divine, the immanent and the transcendent, the scientific and the hermeneutic: they all melt into an undifferentiated mush. If this ontology is thought to remain pretty constant over time, then, moreover, robust concepts of change will be even fewer and farther between than they had been in the heyday of structuralism.[29] But, furthermore, if your brief really means to suggest that 'critique' in the usual sense has been ineffectual and self-defeating, based upon old discredited notions of 'fact' and 'value' that are holdovers from the Modernist period, then the pilot light of much political mobilization has been snuffed at the outset. One of the more careful commentators on Latour's oeuvre seeks to square this circle by suggesting Latour *has no political aspirations*:

> Latour is as resolutely non-modern in his politics as in everything else. He does not aspire to rebuild the world in the shape of some particular idea of how things ought to be built (as the Left generally wishes) … Revolutionary aspirations in politics tend to go hand in hand with philosophical idealisms … which hold that truth is directly accessible to rational procedure. Latour is deeply committed to the notion that actors always outrun our conceptions of them.
>
> *(Harman, 2014, p.31).*[30]

While this might seem to square with the dearth of direct evidence of Latour engaging in political activities, it still rings false, especially given his increasingly alarmist articles concerning global warming as we approach the present, not to mention the palpable fact that he cannot cease and desist banging the table over and over again about how we must understand science and politics in precisely the manner that he does. Furthermore, I doubt if most STS scholars would understand their appropriation of his work as an open invitation to give up once and for all on the sum total of their own personal political aspirations. There must be something a bit more complicated going on here.

I believe the key to Latour's 'political turn' can be found in the period of strife known as the 'Science Wars' of the 1990s. This set of disputes, now fading in memory, consisted of a number of scientists attacking what they considered to be garbled illegitimate commentary on science on the part of postmodernists, literary folk and science studies scholars; we can pass the details by here.[31] However, Latour himself came in for a vicious onslaught by Alan Sokal and Jean Bricmont in their *Fashionable Nonsense* (1998). Whether deserved or not, it clearly stung; Latour was made to feel the Hobbesian war of all against all in a manner that got a bit deeper under the skin than the polite academic disquisitions he had truck with prior to that juncture. At roughly the same time, the general press had begun to uncover various techniques of public manipulation of knowledge on the part of neoliberal think tanks, in cases such as weapons of mass destruction in the run-up to the Iraq war, the notorious 'tobacco strategy', and the first waves of pushback towards the science of global warming. Journalists began to put the two together: the doctrines of constructivism and the deployal of doubt on the part of the science critics was deemed by Bricmont and others as very similar to the techniques of doubt and deconstruction practiced by the think tanks and Republican operatives like Frank Luntz. In a travesty of events, some journalists accused STS of having *taught* the New Right these techniques of obstruction and obfuscation.

It was this swirling sirocco of bad news that prompted Latour to pen his notorious screed, "Why Has Critique Run out of Steam?" As he wrote:

> Do you see why I am worried? I myself have spent some time in the past trying to show the 'lack of scientific certainty' inherent in the construction of facts. I too made

it a 'primary issue'. But I did not exactly aim at fooling the public by obscuring the certainty of a closed argument—or did I? After all, I have been accused of just that sin. Still, I'd like to believe that, on the contrary, I intended to *emancipate* the public from prematurely naturalized objective facts ... Why does it burn my tongue to say that global warming is a fact whether you like it or not? Why can't I simply say the argument is closed for good? Should I reassure myself by simply saying that bad guys can use any weapon at hand, naturalized facts when it suits them and social construction when it suits them? ... Or should we rather bring the sword of criticism to criticism itself and do a bit of soul-searching here: what were we really after when we were so intent on showing the social construction of scientific facts?

(2004a, p.227)

Of course, Latour had no intention of indulging in anything resembling a *mea culpa*.[32] It wasn't his fault, he pleaded; it was the fault of those Moderns, of those deluded sociologists, and finally, of 'critique' itself. "What if explanations resorting automatically to power, society, discourse had outlived their usefulness?" (2004a, p.229). Here the Latourist gives away an impetuous resort to an ungrounded concept of 'usefulness', since it would appear to those still encumbered by the lumbering yoke of the Modernist settlement that these techniques were indeed apparently useful, at least in a political sense, to the think tanks, the ExxonMobils, the George Bushes of the world. As expected, we are treated to some circles and arrows in Latour's talk that insist that critique based on dualisms must undo itself. Indeed, the bizarre practice of attributing will and intentionality and cognition to featureless faceless monads while somehow pronouncing upon winners and losers as if from a great height separated from the battle leads to a brace of assertions lacking all referent and grounding:

> [C]ritique was useless against objects of some solidity...But critique is also useless when it begins to use the results of one science uncritically, be it sociology itself, or economics, or postimperialism, to account for the behavior of people...Objects are much too strong to be treated as fetishes and much too weak to be treated as indisputable causal explanations of some unconscious action... [Latour denounces] the pride of academia, the crème de la crème, who go on ceaselessly transforming the whole rest of the world into naïve believers, into fetishists, into hapless victims of domination, while at the same time turning them into the mere superficial consequences of powerful hidden causalities coming from infrastructures whose makeup is never interrogated?
>
> *(2004a, pp.242–243)*

I am aware *tu quoque* is an inferior form of critique; but I am not the first to suggest that Latour has learned an important lesson from the New Right: always accuse your opponent of what you yourself are guilty of doing; and furthermore, try to be quick off the mark to get the accusation in before your opponent twigs. Impudence wins the day, however unjust it may seem. This is only the beginning of Latour's appreciation of Machiavelli. In the above quote, one is moved to retort: *whose critique proved useless?* Wasn't it in fact the critique of Latour and his cadres in science studies? And who precisely had been using economics uncritically in the early book *Laboratory Life*? And what academic precisely dealt in 'powerful hidden causalities' like the so-called Modernist settlement whose makeup is never interrogated, because it never came within hailing distance of any historical or empirical phenomena? If this seems a bit harsh, let me quote the more measured version by Keir Martin:

For all that Latour attempts to set out his differences with structuralism, there is a sense in which this aspect of his theory marks a continuation of an earlier form of antihumanism ... Although Latour abhors the 'social' as a contextualizing device, the modernist settlement comes to act as such a contextual explanation, a structure by another name, a *langue* determining the *parole* of minds trapped in a vat ... For all that Latour says we emerge in interaction with the nonhuman world, he has recourse to an ideological structure to explain why we apparently constantly manage to convince ourselves otherwise.

(2014, pp. 13–14)

It appears that what Latour advocates in this circumloquacious fashion is a type of politics that banishes science critique. Almost anyone who comes into contact with Latour's extensive web presence tends to notice this. In his MOOC on 'Scientific Humanities', one of the first issues to arise with the students was to try and understand Latour's use of the term 'political'. Students would bring up tense divisive issues, and avuncular Bruno would turn them into anodyne translations, associations, plasmas, and worse. Or, consider when the anthropologist Kim Fortun decided to survey Latour's AIME project (An Enquiry into Modes of Existence),[33] and compare it to the way that similar issues in chemistry were dealt with on the website of the American Chemistry Council, an industry trade and lobbyist association.

To some extent, Latour and the AIME project replay the resolute positivity of the ACC, disavowing bad actors, conflicts of interest, and an array of externalities produced by the ontologies they characterize. The antagonism of the agora is discounted, as are its covert action and backroom deals. Much work to create and defend particular truths (about toxics, for example) is carried out not in the open assemblies Latour counts on, but in corporate labs and strategy rooms, which link too easily to regulatory science panels, which end up licensing hazards... The AIME project aspires to provide a 'middle ground' for working through and with different ontologies, in the building of a common world. But the structure it has built for this rules out so many kinds of entanglements that links to late industrialism are minimal at best.

(Fortun, 2014, pp. 320–321)

What is perhaps most incongruous about this Latourist program is the extent it goes out of its way to indict everything that a normal person thinks constitutes politics in science, consequently only to replace science critique with the most bland account of science that can be found in contemporary culture. As is his wont, when not denouncing 'The Moderns', his whipping boy is the sociologists:

[C]ritical sociology has too often substituted an invisible, unmovable and homogeneous world of power for itself... I reproach critical sociology for having confused society and the collective. Its mistake wasn't that it appeared political or confused science with politics, but it gave a definition of both science and politics that could only fail... It does not require enormous skill or political acumen to realize that if you have to fight against a force that is invisible, untraceable, ubiquitous and total, you will be powerless and roundly defeated... To put it bluntly, if there is a society, *then no politics is possible*.

(Latour, 2005, p. 250)

So, from Latour's perspective, what sort of politics is possible? In his entire MOOC, Latour conducts a discussion with precisely one natural scientist, the neuroscientist Andrew Tobin. The only practical prescription to arise out of that interview is Latour's praise for patient organizations; namely, sufferers and their families who organize around a single issue disease identity, in order to supposedly help guide medical research. The impression given of democratic participation in the setting of the scientific agenda therein entirely ignores one of the most important facts about contemporary patient organizations, namely that most patient organizations are either astroturfed or captured by Big Pharma, for the purpose of the promotion of particular novel commercial therapies over older therapies.[34] The patient lobbies are used to achieve political goals of the drug companies that might be more difficult to attain if pursued directly through normal regulatory channels. Hence, the track record of patient groups in guiding and funding research is nowhere near as impressive as Latour makes out, and the upshot of Latour's position is to passively accept the status quo ante.

But more germane, given that Latour has given a number of talks on Gaia, the 'Anthropocene', and global warming (2013a, 2014a, 2014b), people may have gleaned a misleading impression that he has enlisted on the side of the environmentalists and those who want drastic political action to curb carbon emissions; but nothing could be further from the truth. One must penetrate below the surface froth of these public talks to arrive at the *actual political implications* growing out of all the palaver behind cosmograms, giving a voice to carbon, a state of war with Gaia, and all the rest. There is a hint of it in one of the lectures—"No wonder that climatoskeptics are denying the reliability of all those 'facts' they now put in scare quotes. In a way they are right" (2014b, p.2) – but the actual content is only spelled out in some interviews, and in Latour's actual political affiliations.

One of the most revealing is an interview from November 2014 with Verdeseo, a Chilean think tank whose self-professed goal has been to "think green politics away from the idealism of those environmentalists enamored with a rigid idea of nature". Alongside the usual denunciations of the 'Moderns', one finds the following admissions:

> Activism is localized everywhere in very interesting issues, from slow food to carbon, and so on. And everybody, so to speak, sort of absorbs from this activism. But the work, which still should be done, is to say this is not an ecological crisis, it is a mutation. … I think there is no way to get back to environmentalism, environmentalism is the past … So, what I did in *"Politics of Nature"* was to analyze the disconnect between massive and very important and interesting activism and the generally poor intellectual work done on what it is in the end to absorb the end of nature, the end of naturalism … Everybody is post-environmentalist, to use a term of the Breakthrough Institute (from which I'm a member, even though I disagree with their position all the time). In practice everyone has become post-environmentalist.[35]

As usual with Latour, we don't get anything more specific than that, but we can then repair to the website of the Breakthrough Institute, where we find Latour's face and name prominently represented, to find out more about the content of this 'post-environmentalism'.[36] What we discover there is a think tank that has made its name by attacking environmentalists for over a decade now: Breakthrough founders Ted Nordhaus and Michael Shellenberger made their first big splash with an essay preaching the 'Death of Environmentalism' back in 2004. The infamous Roger Pilke Jr is one of their more prominent members. In 2010, the Breakthrough Institute, along with the Brookings Institution and the neoliberal American Enterprise Institute, published the report *Post-Partisan Power*, which called for increased federal investment in innovation in order to make cheaper so-called 'clean energy'. This nicely captured its default rhetoric of somehow transcending Left and Right, in the usual myth of apolitical politics so beloved by the patrons of such research. These days Breakthrough is known for propounding the doctrine that governments really don't need to do much more about global warming than encourage speedup of technological change, which is guaranteed to save us. The irony of Latour's comrades preaching the most vapid sort of technological determinism curdles when one finds that the technologies that Breakthrough thinks holds the most promise are nuclear power, fracking, and various geoengineering schemes such as carbon capture, while simultaneously attacking programs to develop renewable energy sources like wind and solar.[37] Although Latour in his interview leaves room for plausible deniability, I think it especially noteworthy that the very group he has chosen to ally with is precisely the one attacking the Left he so frequently disparages, in the name of bland comfortable status quo.

Serendipitously, I stumbled across a critique of the Breakthrough Institute on the website of Larry Lessig's Safra Center for Ethics at Harvard, which described the secret to Breakthrough's success as "hippy-punching your way to fame and fortune".[38] The source explaining this felicitous phrase went on as follows:

> Predictably, the attacks aimed at green groups drew outrage from their targets. Just as predictably, the outrage was used as evidence that [Breakthrough] are brave truth-tellers, renegades, the "bad boys of environmentalism." I don't know if [Breakthrough] planned it that way, but the strategy turned out to be pure media gold.
>
> If [Breakthrough] had come forward with nothing but a positive agenda for the future of clean energy, they likely would have been politely ignored by the mainstream media just like dozens of earnest green agenda-bearers before them. (Grist's bookshelves sag under their weight.) But [Breakthrough] capitalized on an insight that had been ignored by their forebears: nothing, but nothing, draws media interest like liberals bashing liberals. They enjoy conservatives punching hippies. They dig centrists punching hippies. But they looove ex-hippies punching hippies. A pair of greenies bravely exposing the corruption and dumbassery of all the other greenies? Crack rock.

Here we begin to gain insight into Latour's affiliation with Breakthrough, because 'hippy-punching' is a wonderful shorthand for Latour's own approach to politics. Since Latour finds the bulk of his audience amongst academic humanists, he often speaks in soothing tones as if he shares much of their social and political orientations—even though he patently doesn't believe in humanity, society, or as we have seen, their politics. For this reason, he comes across, as Harman says, a "politically elusive figure" (2014, p.109). But then Latour proceeds to thrill them by hippie-punching some phalanx of 'sociologists' or science studies scholars for believing in the boring old Left doctrines—maybe disparaging environmentalism, or by insisting "there is no such thing as an economy" (2004b, p.135), or suggesting "the liberal State is opposed to the *liberated* State, a state freed of all forms of naturalization" (2004b, p.206), or intoning "Even though we have to continue fighting those who are in denial, I propose that we let them alone for a moment" (2014b, p.4)—and proposes we should then instead do nothing! Those silly people with their theories of economy and society are just masochistic losers:

> [T]hose who call themselves the Left and even the radical Left are simultaneously sure of failing and sure of being right—yes being right in the sense of conniving happily

with the Right in letting capitalism be even more systematic than it is. Like science, politics opens possibilities… If you have failed, it's not capitalism you should revolutionize but rather your ways of thinking. If you keep failing and don't change it does not mean you are facing an invincible monster, it means you like, you enjoy, you love to be *defeated* by a monster.

(2014c, p.9)

Here the two-faced character of the Latourist persona again surfaces. He is chiding the science critics for being stupid and naïve and defeatist: it is a war of all against all out there, don't they get it? Provoked, they retort: But how about you, Monsieur Latour? Where do you stand in the war? Incongruously, Latour then presents himself as situated somewhere above the fray, basically indifferent as to whether it is even possible to triumph, to improve on the situation, or falling into the trap of acting in a conventionally political manner. Latour hates losers and cannot imagine himself a loser. This explains, I think, the one obvious common denominator throughout Latour's career, the insistence that inert things possess the same agency as humans. As Harman sagely observes, Latour "tends to call on nonhuman things for assistance whenever he seems to be most in danger of advocating a free-for-all for human power struggles" (2014, p.163). Is it starting to get a little too obvious that this is just engaging in yet another round of hippy-punching? Has the war against his peers engaging in science critique begun to belie his jovial demeanor? Does his deference to power border on the unseemly in someone who loudly denounces power? Then just call a halt, bring those Things back on stage, and start extolling the Parliament of Things and *Dingpolitik*. Send in the clones!

This, in turn, raises an interesting question: Is Latour really as self-contradictory as he appears, or is there a deeper dynamic boosting his popularity? It has occurred to more than one person that many component parts of Latour's 'politics' resemble nothing better than a muddy version of the dominant political ideology of our day, namely, neoliberalism. The resemblance begins with Mrs. Thatcher preaching that "There is no such thing as Society", a common refrain of Latour as well. The absence of a nature/society divide was characteristic of the later Hayek, long before it became the catchphrase of Latour. Indeed, Hayek's doctrines of 'spontaneous order' and 'complexity' are trademark enthusiasms of the Latourist canon. Harman points out "there is no 'macro level' for Latour, just larger and smaller micro level" (2014, p.119); this hostility to the ontology of macro structures is equally canonical for the Austrian variant of neoliberalism. Hayek was loudest in the neoliberal vanguard of those who argued that no human being could possess sufficient knowledge to adequately plan and organize society; Harman summarizes Latour as believing "knowledge claims are a terrible basis for politics" (2014, p.119). Although Hayek derided something he called 'constructivism' in his day, modern commentators on neoliberalism have argued that 'constructivism' is one of the best ways to describe their cherished political doctrines.[39] Hayek's hostility to intellectuals was legendary, because he said they were all in the grip of a pernicious *Weltanschauung*; we have already commented on Latour's disparagement of the 'Moderns' and their supposed mindset. Perhaps the one thing which initially seems to set Latour apart from the neoliberals is his persistent habit of denouncing 'the economists'; however, some familiarity with the history of neoliberalism reveals that the Mont Pelèrin Society has been divided into two factions—one, the Chicago School, which upheld neoclassical theory as the gospel of the neoliberal movement; and the other, the Austrian variant, which rejected neoclassical economics as having any validity whatsoever. Both have been reconciled with neoliberal practice.

As in the other cases we have unearthed in this chapter, the strongest impression one gets from reading Latour on capitalism is the sheer quietism he preaches along that front. This is taken from his most explicit talk on economics in his archive:

> The mere invocation of capitalism renders me speechless ... It might be best to abandon the concept entirely. You remember Hamlet's expression in Marx's *18ᵗʰ Brumaire*: 'Well done old mole!' What sort of mole would dig down enough to subvert in the end not capitalism but some of the affects generated by this odd way to read history and to give an expression to our passions and indignations? Is there an alternative? It appears the solution will not come from dialectics with capitalists 'digging their own grave' but from the first nature. It is ironic to think that so much saliva has been spent to save higher values from the risk of commodification when the question should rather have been to bring this whole enterprise down to earth ... To be radical a 'radical critique of an unfair, destructive and unsustainable system should abstain from falling into the trap of fighting a system.
>
> *(2014c, pp. 9–10)*

I don't think any subset of this is unexpected: the hostility to Marxism, the waving aside of the issue of the commercialization of science, the denial that there is anything ontologically lawlike about the economy, the injunction that political mobilization to attack the economic system is pointless. These are all rather bog-standard neoliberal ideas. What is more important is his stated insistence that he wants to push back against "the feeling of helplessness that is associated with any discussion of economics", while obviously himself promulgating his own version of passivity and quietism.

This advocacy of the transformation of the humanist rebel into the passive cog in the modern political economy of technoscience is the one thing which best qualifies Latour to be considered a fellow traveler of the neoliberals, at minimum. That is why I cannot agree with those, such as Harman, who vehemently deny the possibility: "Latour is by no means a free-market 'neoliberal', the lazy person's polemical term of choice in early 21st century political thought" (Harman, 2014, p.115). People in science studies need to get up to speed when it comes to theories of modern political economy, at least sufficiently to appreciate that neoliberalism is not at all equivalent to libertarianism, or other caricatures of 'free-market' thought. It is explicitly a constructivist doctrine, which preaches that the state must be co-opted to produce the regime of 'freedom' that the neoliberals equate with a smoothly functioning marketplace of ideas.

To summarize: Latour believes politics consists of struggle without any hope of a transcendent court of appeal, which is why he is so attracted to figures like Hobbes, Walter Lippmann and Carl Schmitt. He explicitly eschews any appeal to Truth to ground politics, growing out of a conviction that constructivism dictates that truth is the outcome of struggle, but exhibits no special epistemic regularities or ontological stability. Because the portrait is one of unceasing agonistic strife, there is no program of reform, no conception of superior political institutional structures, no exemplar of political virtue to be found in his work. Science may be roiled with dispute and dissention from time to time, but the public just has to learn to roll with it. Most of all, there is nothing but ill-concealed contempt for those who strive to undertake science critique.[40] The upshot of this Latourist project is that what exists in the way of science organization and scientific research is just fine the way it is.

Notes

1 See Tim Wise, "The War on GM Food Critics" at www.nakedcapitalism.com/2015/02/war-genetically-modified-food-critics.html; and www.counterpunch.org/2015/02/27/monsanto-wants-to-know-why-people-doubt-science/.

2 See Stilgoe (2015).

3 See especially Lessig (1995).

4 One can observe this in his role as observer in the movie *The Internet's Own Boy: The Story of Aaron Schwartz*.

5 See Lessig (2006). Subsequent quotes in this paragraph come from Osnos (2014).

6 One observes this in his recent book (Lessig, 2011), but more significantly in his 2014 Berlin lectures at Chicago: https://berlinfamilylectures.uchicago.edu/page/video-gallery.

7 Lessig blog, June 2007 at: www.lessig.org/2007/06/required-reading-the-next-10-y-1/.

8 The actual number elected was two out of eight supported by Mayday PAC. Some Monday-morning quarterbacking suggested that the money might have been irrelevant in those cases.

9 Osnos (2014).

10 Mirowski (2013), chapter 2.

11 See Whittaker and Cosgrove (2015).

12 For further consideration of the most recent *DSM V*, see Hacking (2013).

13 Here disclosure increases the bad behavior on the perpetrator, while making the bamboozled believe that they are wise to cooperate with the perpetrator. See Loewenstein et al. (2012).

14 Extolling the virtues of ignorance is an especially poignant neoliberal theme. See Mirowski (2013).

15 See Rodwin (2015).

16 See Mirowski, "Science 2.0" presentation to CPERI, York University, 2014.

17 See Mirowski (2004) and Collins (1992).

18 See Fisher et al. (2014); Viergever et al. (2014).

19 See Mirowski (2011), pp.152–181.

20 See Fernandez-Pinto (2015).

21 Consult www.bruno-latour.fr; for some YouTube lectures, www.youtube.com/watch?v=8i-ZKfShovs; the MOOC is at: www.france-universite-numerique-mooc.fr/courses/SciencesPo/.

22 See Law and Hassard (1999).

23 This has been rectified in the recent SciencesPo introductory course: www.france-universite-numerique-mooc.fr/courses/SciencesPo/05004S02/Trimestre_1_2015/courseware/748395737cb343f1a2e43716e755e65f/5fb9a9b6559b41f3908bf340611ec394/.

24 See, for instance, Harman (2009); McGee (2014).

25 It has occurred to me that Latour in effect reverses Comte's 'three stages', preaching a retrogression from the 'positive' to the 'theological' state.

26 A story entertainingly recounted in Cusset (2008).

27 Which as materialized as his recent (2013b).

28 Perhaps the best of these is Harman (2014), although more critical sources would include Hekman (2009); Martin (2014).

29 Even Harman, who is cheerfully styles himself an acolyte of Latour, admits this in Latour et al. (2011), p.37.

30 In a future work, I will explore the thesis that the work of Michel Foucault has similar political aspirations in this respect.

31 See, however, the response of one of the targets: www.cardiff.ac.uk/socsi/contactsandpeople/harrycollins/science-wars.html.

32 "In spite of my tone, I am not trying to reverse course, to become reactionary, to regret what I have done, to swear that I will never be a constructivist anymore" (Latour, 2004a, p.231).

33 See www.modesofexistence.org/; and Latour (2013b).

34 See Columbo et al. (2012); Rose (2013).

35 All quotes in this paragraph from https://enverdeseo.wordpress.com/2015/01/19/bruno-latour-modernity-is-politically-a-dangerous-goal/. More information on Verdeseo can be found at: http://verdeseo.cl/verdeseo-in-english/.

36 See www.thebreakthrough.org/.

37 See, for instance, Klein (2014), p.57.

38 The Safra critique by Paul Thacker is at: http://ethics.harvard.edu/blog/breakthrough-institutes-inconvenient-history-al-gore. It in turn cites the source of the following quote, David Roberts's "Why I've avoided commenting on Nisbet's 'Climate Shift' report".

39 See Mirowski (2013).
40 One finds this stance in the work of many recent historians of science, even those who do not endorse Latour. On this, see Turnbull (2016).

References

Boland, Tom. 2013. "Critique is a thing of this world: Towards a genealogy of critique," *History of the Human Sciences*, (27):108–123.

Brown, Mark. 2015. "Politicizing science: conceptions of politics in STS," *Social Studies of Science*, (45):3–30.

Callon, Michel. 2009. "Civilizing Markets: carbon trading between in vitro and in vivo experiments," *Accounting, Organizations and Society*, (34):535–548.

Collins, Harry. 1992. *Changing Order: Replication and Induction*. Thousand Oaks: Sage.

Columbo, Cinzia, Paola Mosconi, Walter Villani, and Silvio Garattini. 2012. "Patient organizations' funding from pharmaceutical companies: Is disclosure clear, complete and accessible to the public?" *PLoS One*, 7(5): e34974. doi:10.1371/journal.pone.0034974.

Cusset, Fancois. 2008. *French Theory: How Foucault Derrida Etc Transformed Intellectual Life in the US*. Minneapolis: University of Minnesota Press.

Dumit, Joseph. 2014. *Drugs for Life*. Durham: Duke University Press. Edmond J. Safra Center for Ethics, Harvard University, http://ethics.harvard.edu/.

Fernandez Pinto, Manuela. 2015. "Tensions in agnotology: Normativity in the studies of commercially-driven ignorance." *Social Studies of Science*, 45(2).

Fisher, Jill, Marci Cottingham and Corey Kalbaugh. 2015. "Peering into the pharmaceutical pipeline," *Social Science & Medicine*, (131):322–330.

Folkers, Andreas. 2015. "Daring the truth: Foucault, Parrhesia and the genealogy of critique," *Theory, Culture and Society*, 33(1).

Fortun, Kim. 2014. "From Latour to late industrialism," *HAU: Journal of Ethnographic Theory*, (4):309–329.

Hacking, Ian. 2013. "Lost in the forest," *London Review of Books*, 8 August, 35(15).

Harman, Graham. 2009. *The Prince of Networks*. Melbourne: repress.

Harman, Graham. 2014. *Bruno Latour: Reassembling the Political*. London: Pluto.

Hekman, Susan. 2009. "We have never been postmodern: Latour, Foucault and the material of knowledge," *Contemporary Political Theory*, (8):435–454.

Ioannidis, John. 2014. "How to make more public research true," *PLoS Medicine*, October (11:10): e1001747.

Jensen, Caspar. 2004. "A nonhumanist disposition: on performativity, practical ontology, and intervention," *Configurations*, (12):229–261.

Kitcher, Philip. 1993. *The Advancement of Science*. New York: Oxford University Press.

Kitcher, Philip. 2001. *Science, Truth and Democracy*. New York: Oxford University Press.

Kitcher, Philip. 2011. *Science in a Democratic Society*. Amherst: Prometheus.

Klein, Naomi. 2014. *This Changes Everything*. New York: Simon & Schuster.

Latour, Bruno. 1993. *We have never been Modern*. Cambridge: Harvard University Press.

Latour, Bruno. 1999. *Pandora's Hope*. Cambridge: Harvard University Press.

Latour, Bruno. 2004a. "Why has critique run out of steam?" *Critical Inquiry*, (30):225–248.

Latour, Bruno. 2004b. *Politics of Nature*. Cambridge: Harvard University Press.

Latour, Bruno. 2005. *Reassembling the Social*. Oxford: Oxford University Press.

Latour, Bruno. 2010. *On the Modern Cult of the Factish Gods*. Durham: Duke University Press.

Latour, Bruno. 2013a. "Telling friends from foes in the time of the Anthropocene," Lecture, "Thinking the Anthropocene," EHESS, Paris, 14-15 November, 2013.

Latour, Bruno. 2013b. *An Inquiry into Modes of Existence*. Cambridge: Harvard University Press.

Latour, Bruno. 2014a. "War and peace in an age of ecological conflicts," Paris: Sciences Po working paper.

Latour, Bruno. 2014b. "Agency at the time of the Anthropocene," *New Literary History*, (45):1–18.

Latour, Bruno. 2014c. "On some of the affects of capitalism," Lecture to Royal Academy of Copenhagen, 26 February.

Latour, Bruno. 2015a. "Your idol is my icon," *Die Zeit*, 5 Feb.

Latour, Bruno. 2015b. "Modernity is politically a dangerous goal," at: https://enverdeseo.wordpress.com/2015/01/19/bruno-latour-modernity-is-politically-a-dangerous-goal/.

Latour, Bruno, Harman, Graham and Peter Erdelyi. 2011. *The Prince and the Wolf*. Winchester: Zero Books.

Law, John and John Hassard. (eds.) 1999. *Actor Network Theory and After*. Oxford and Keele: Blackwell and the Sociological Review.

Lessig, Lawrence. 1995. "The Regulation of social meaning," *University of Chicago Law Review*, (62):943.

Lessig, Lawrence. 2006. *Code Version 2.0* New York: Basic at: http://codev2.cc/download+remix/Lessig-Codev2.pdf.

Lessig, Lawrence. 2011. *Republic, Lost*. New York: Twelve.

Lessig, Lawrence. 2014. "Institutional corruption," Berlin Family Lectures, University of Chicago, at: https://berlinfamilylectures.uchicago.edu/page/video-gallery.

Loewenstein, George, Sah, Sunita and Cain, Daylian. 2012. "The unintended consequences of conflict of interest disclosure," *Journal of the American Medical Association* (307):669–670.

MacKenzie, Donald, Muniesa, Fabien, et al., eds. 2008. *Do Economists Make Markets?* Princeton: Princeton University Press.

Martin, Keir. 2014. "Knot-work not networks, or anti-anti-antifetishism and the ANTipolitics machine," *HAU: Journal of Ethnographic Theory*, 4(3).

McGee, Kyle. 2014. *Bruno Latour: The Normativity of Networks*. London: Routledge.

Mirowski, Philip. 2004. *Effortless Economy of Science?* Durham: Duke University Press.

Mirowski, Philip. 2011. *ScienceMart: Privatizing American Science*. Cambridge: Harvard University Press.

Mirowski, Philip. 2013. *Never Let a Serious Crisis go to Waste*. New York: Verso.

Morozov, Evgeny. 2014. *To Save Everything, Click Here*. New York: Public Affairs.

Osnos, Evan. 2014. "Embrace the irony," *The New Yorker*, Oct. 13.

Rodwin, Marc. 2015. "Independent drug testing to ensure safety," *Journal of Health Care Law and Policy*, 18(1).

Rose, Susannah. 2013. "Patient advocacy organizations: institutional conflicts of interest, trust, and trustworthiness," *Journal of Law Medical Ethics*. 41(3):680–687

Sokal, Alan and Bricmont, Jean. 1998. *Fashionable Nonsense*. London: Picador.

Stilgoe, Jack. 2015. "Experiment earth", forthcoming in Von Schomberg (ed.) *Handbook of Responsible Research and Innovation*, Cheltenham: Edward Elgar Publishing.

Turnbull, Thomas. 2016. "I need a hero: reaffiming critical diagnoses of science–society relations," *Science as Culture*, 1–6.

Viergever, Roderick; Ghassan Karam, Andreas Reis, Davina Ghersi. 2014. "The quality of registration of clinical trials: still a problem," *PLoS Medicine*, 9(1):e84727.

Whittaker, Robert and Cosgrove, Lisa. 2015. *Psychiatry Under the Influence*. New York: Palgrave Macmillan.

INDEX

Locators in **bold** refer to tables; those in *italic* to figures

451

Printed in the United States
by Baker & Taylor Publisher Services